CAMBRIDGE CLASSICAL TEXTS
AND COMMENTARIES

41

OCTAVIA

OCTAVIA

A PLAY ATTRIBUTED TO SENECA

EDITED WITH INTRODUCTION
AND COMMENTARY

BY

ROLANDO FERRI

Associate Professor of Latin, Università di Pisa

CAMBRIDGE UNIVERSITY PRESS
Cambridge, New York, Melbourne, Madrid, Cape Town, Singapore, São Paulo, Delhi

Cambridge University Press
The Edinburgh Building, Cambridge CB2 8RU, UK

Published in the United States of America by Cambridge University Press, New York

www.cambridge.org
Information on this title: www.cambridge.org/9780521117722

First published 2003
Reprinted 2005
This digitally printed version 2009

A catalogue record for this publication is available from the British Library

Library of Congress Cataloguing in Publication data
Octavia (Praetexta)
Octavia / PS.-Seneca; edited with introduction and commentary
by Rolando Ferri.
p. cm. – (Cambridge classical texts and commentaries; v. 41)
Roman tragedy previously attributed to Seneca but probably written by an
imitator at a later date.
Commentary originally presented as author's thesis (perfezionamento) –
Scuola Normale Superiore, Pisa.
Includes bibliographical references and index.
ISBN 0 521 82326 9 (hardback)
1. Octavia, consort of Nero, Emperor of Rome, ca. 42-62 – Drama.
2. Rome – History – Nero, 54-68 – Drama. I. Seneca, Lucius Annaeus,
ca. 4 BC-ca. AD 65 II. Ferri, Rolando. III. Title. IV. Series.
PA6664.Z5 2003 872′.01 – dc21 2003048474

ISBN 978-0-521-82326-5 hardback
ISBN 978-0-521-11772-2 paperback

A LAURA E GIULIO

CONTENTS

PREFACE

This book originated as a Tesi di Perfezionamento of the Scuola Normale Superiore, Pisa, where it was examined in July 1998. Most of the work, however, was done during my earlier tenure of the Momigliano Fellowship in the Arts at University College London (1993–96), and during my subsequent residence in the same city until October 1998. The rest of the book was completed during my successive academic postings at Cremona (Università di Pavia) and at Pisa. The final version was delivered to the Press in the summer of 2002.

Of the many debts of gratitude I have contracted in the course of writing this book, the first I wish to acknowledge is to the electors to the Momigliano Fellowship in the Arts, endowed by Anna Laura and Giulio Lepschy in memory of Laura's father, Arnaldo Momigliano. It is to Laura and Giulio that I dedicate this book, for their friendship and inspiring intellectual support over the years. I do not think the book would have existed without them.

Of other London friends, Helen Gregory has put me in the greatest debt, helping me to revise the English of sizeable portions of both Introduction and Commentary, as well as discussing and disagreeing with me on many points of substance and detail. The Italian Department at UCL provided a congenial and inspiring place for work and research, even for a classicist, as did the Institute of Classical Studies and its splendid library. The then Scuola (now Facoltà) di Paleografia of the Università di Pavia helped me financially in various ways, especially in contributing towards the cost of acquiring MS microfilms.

I also wish to thank the Series Editors, above all Michael Reeve, Richard Tarrant, and Jonathan Powell for including the volume among the *Cambridge Classical Texts and Commentaries*. Anyone who knows these scholars knows what it means to receive their advice. I thank them for their patience, their intelligent suggestions, and for all they have taught me. Gian Biagio Conte and Elaine Fantham read different semi-final drafts and gave me great encouragement and the benefit of their critical insight along the way. In the commentary, the initials of all these scholars identify some of the more specific proposals they have advanced. Of people I have never met, but who have been with me on my desk these several years, I have to thank Otto Zwierlein. I have taken issue sometimes with what he argues about *Octavia*, but I have learned most of what I know about Senecan tragedy from his edition and his *Kommentar* (Mainz, 1986).

The Cambridge staff who saw the book through the press, and particularly Muriel Hall, Alison Powell and Michael Sharp, deserve praise for dealing so efficiently and helpfully with a difficult typescript.

Finally, I wish to thank my parents for their support, and my wife, Barbara, for accompanying some critical moments with her understanding and intelligence.

INTRODUCTION

1. *OCTAVIA* AND ITS GENRE

Octavia is the only complete Latin drama of historical subject which has come down to us. The title of the play given by the MSS is simply *Octavia*, but the drama is often referred to in modern secondary literature as *Octavia praetexta*, a practice which should be abandoned.[1]

The title heroine, *Claudia Octauia*, was the daughter of the emperor Claudius and of Valeria Messalina. Born in 40, she became Nero's wife in 53,[2] reportedly after being adopted into an unknown family to avoid rumours of incest within the imperial family. In legends of this period, her name always appears without the patronymic *Claudia*.[3] The name *Octauia*, however, was hardly that of an adoptive *gens*. Rather than a *gentilicium*, it must have been an inherited *cognomen* of the imperial family; like her older sister's name, *Antonia*, it was probably given to stress the link with a previous generation of Julio-Claudian women.

The play dramatizes the events of three days in June 62 (a chronological fiction: see next section), culminating in Nero's divorce from Octavia, his subsequent marriage to Poppaea, and, lastly, Octavia's deportation to Pandateria.

[1] The normal way of quoting dramatic titles is, e.g., *Accius (in) Bruto* or *Aeneadis*. Titles in the form (proper noun) + *tragoedia, comoedia, fabula*, in either order, are found: cf. Plin. *Nat.* 18.65 *Sophocles poeta in fabula Triptolemo* (other instances of this appositive use in titles are given in *TLL* vi.1, s.v. *fabula*, 33.67–9; 34.3–6, also with a genitive); Don. *GL* Keil iv 375.24–5 *sunt . . . sono masculina, intellectu feminina, ut Eunuchus comoedia, Orestes tragoedia.* On the forms of Latin comic and tragic titles in the ancient sources, mainly grammatical, cf. Jocelyn, *Ennius*, 58–63.

[2] Cf. Brassloff in *RE* iii.2 (1899), s.v. Claudius, 428, coll. 2893–98; *PIR*² C 1110.

[3] In inscriptions and coin legends, her name seems to appear simply as *Octauia* (so, for instance, in *Acta fratrum Arualium*, Henzen (Berlin, 1874), 67.16; 71.41; 77.26). There are only three exceptions, one inscription (*IGRR* 4.969) and two coin legends (cf. *Roman Provincial Coinage* (London, 1992), 1033 (Crete); 2341 (Methymna)).

Very little is known of *fabulae praetextae*, or *praetextatae*, the historical 'dramas in purple-bordered toga' performed under the Republic.[4] They may have been anything from simple historical pageants, celebrating a triumph, to full-scale dramatizations of significant historical episodes along the lines of Greek tragedy. Ancient critics did not recognize significant differences between *praetextae* and *cothurnatae*, dramas in Greek dress dealing with mythological characters. At any rate, the influence of Greek tragedy, alongside that of Seneca, is very important in *Octavia*, and, as far as can be seen, more significant than that of early Roman drama.[5]

In Republican *praetextae* the celebration of important military and political events, and even of eminent aristocratic individuals, seems to have been prominent.[6] The genre remained productive in the first century of the Empire, but topicality and the reference to contemporary events is unlikely to have been so direct as in early *praetextae*. To judge from some of the extant titles, celebration of Republican heroism played a central part (Maternus wrote a *Cato* and a *Domitius*; Pomponius Secundus an *Aeneas*), sometimes in an anti-imperial key. This element may partly account for the progressive disappearance of *praetextae* from the stage.[7] Political caution, a propensity for themes increasingly irrelevant to popular audiences at large, and a long-term process of 'gentrification' of literature at Rome[8] made *praetextae* more

[4] On *praetextae* in general cf. R. Helm, *praetexta*, in *RE* 22.2 (1954), 1569–75; for an exhaustive collection of the *testimonia* cf. Klotz, 358.

[5] The genre of *Octavia* has often been discussed, especially as regards its kinship to the Republican *praetextae*: for a survey of the relevant bibliography cf. Schmidt (1985), 1425; Manuwald (2001), 95, n. 86. A recent monographic issue of *Symbolae Osloenses* hosts a debate on *praetextae* in the imperial age: cf. *SO* 73 (2002), 5–105; see also *infra*, 61–2.

[6] On the occasions for performance of Republican *praetextae* and on subsequent restagings of some of them cf. H. I. Flower, *CQ* n.s. 45 (1995), 175.

[7] For a discussion of the staging–recitation debate specifically with reference to *praetextae* cf. the *SO* issue cited in n. 5, *passim*.

[8] See *infra*, chapter 5, n. 137.

suitable for recitation in the auditoria of a few aristocratic patrons than for onstage performance before large theatre audiences.

2. THE HISTORICAL BACKGROUND OF *OCTAVIA*

The narrative of Tacitus concerning Octavia in *Ann.* 14.59–64, which is the most complete account of the events covered by the *praetexta*, is compressed and elliptical, and reconstruction of the incidents leading to Octavia's divorce and subsequent execution is accordingly difficult.

According to Tacitus, Nero finally resolved to get rid of Octavia and to marry Poppaea after disposing of Sulla and Plautus (14.59 *posito metu nuptias Poppaeae . . . maturare parat Octauiamque coniugem amoliri*). After a first attempt to suborn a charge of adultery failed, the reason adduced to justify divorce was Octavia's inability to produce an heir (14.60 *exturbat Octauiam, sterilem dictitans; exim Poppaeae coniungitur*). Octavia was at first not removed from Rome, receiving Burrus' house and Plautus' estate in compensation. Tacitus does not relate any specific charge to account for her subsequent banishment to Campania (*mouetur . . . primo ciuilis discidii specie . . . mox in Campaniam pulsa est*): perhaps none was on record, if the princess had been whisked away unobtrusively. There was at first discontent among the Roman people at the treatment meted out to Octavia; then rejoicing, as if Nero had given in and recalled her (text uncertain). Under pressure from Poppaea, Nero decided to eliminate Octavia. A plot was set up against her, and Anicetus, fleet commander at Misenum, was bribed into confessing to adultery with her. Deportation to Pandateria and, shortly afterwards, execution ended the story.

The account of the same events given by Suetonius (*Nero*, 35.2) is even more summary: (*Octauiam*) *dimisit ut sterilem, sed improbante diuortium populo . . . etiam relegauit, denique occidit sub crimine adulteriorum.* Suetonius omits the temporary banishment to Campania, as do Dio's epitomizers (*Hist. Rom.* 62.13.1 Boiss.; but the story may have been just as succinct in Dio himself). Suetonius (*Nero*, 35.3) also states that eleven days elapsed between Octavia's divorce and Poppaea's marriage (*Poppaeam duodecimo die post diuortium Octauiae in matrimonium acceptam*). The chronology of the events in the play is compressed for reasons of dramatic effectiveness. In fact, while in *Oct.* 437 Nero orders the elimination of Plautus and Sulla on the day preceding the marriage, we deduce from Tacitus that Nero set about the divorce only after receiving confirmation of the two opponents' deaths: as many as thirty days probably elapsed after Nero issued the order and before news of its execution reached him.[9] In the play, on the other hand, the divorce takes place on the same day as the marriage (666).

Clearly, succession was a crucial concern for Nero, and peace and stability required a legitimate heir. If Octavia was really incapable of producing one, divorce was inevitable, and Nero, legally, did not need a pretext. Divorce in similar circumstances was a prerogative of all husbands in Rome.[10] Yet a divorced princess of royal birth, alive and in distress, was too great a temptation for anyone aiming at removing Nero. This point is made explicit by Poppaea in Tac. *Ann.* 14.61, for the benefit of readers not fully alive to the level of violence and political calculation involved in the whole affair: Nero conceivably did not need to be reminded. It has been argued persuasively that the demonstration in favour of Octavia was much more threatening than suggested by our sources and that indeed there were grounds for Nero to fear a general insurrection, masterminded by the Claudian faction.[11]

9 Plautus was in exile in Asia Minor, and the average time of a journey from Rome can be calculated as between ten and fifteen days (cf. L. Casson, *Ships and Seamanship in the Ancient World*, Princeton, 1971, 281–99).

10 Cf. S. Treggiari, *Roman Marriage* (Oxford, 1991), 436–8. *exturbat*, in *Ann.* 14.60, is a *t.t.* for divorce; the expulsion from the husband's house was one of the sanctions of separation. Domitian probably divorced his wife under circumstances similar to Octavia's case in 84: evidence and secondary literature in Griffin, *CAH*^{2} xi (2000), 61, n. 294.

11 Cf. E. Meise, *Untersuchungen zur Geschichte der Julisch-Claudischen Dynastie* (München, 1969), 173.

The charges of adultery subsequently set up against Octavia appear, in this light, as a natural course of events in the context of the ruthless dynastic infighting of Julio-Claudian Rome.[12] If the elimination of Octavia was part of a long-term scheme, divorce was equally necessary as a preliminary step, because charges of adultery could not be brought against a married woman: a husband had to divorce his wife first, then formally accuse her.[13] Under the Julian law, the punishment for adultery was relegation to the islands; in Octavia's case, there was the aggravation that the crime could be presented as a conspiracy against the life of the emperor.[14]

The extant sources are clearly biased against Nero, and fail to give an objective analysis of the political stakes involved in the affair. While Octavia may well have been an innocent victim, the account of her story given by the tragedian is entirely in keeping with, indeed dependent on, the fiercely anti-Neronian stance taken by the historiographical *vulgata*, a fact which has a considerable bearing on the question of the date of the work.

3. THE DATE OF THE PLAY

The case for an early dating

Few scholars at present grant serious consideration to the thesis that Seneca himself wrote *Octavia*, perhaps as an attack on Nero. Even leaving aside all questions of language and style (see *infra*, p. 31), the prophecies of 618 ff. speak in favour of a date later than

[12] Very probably, Claudius' marriage to Agrippina had been eminently political, a pacificatory move aiming at reuniting the two feuding branches of the royal house. The choice of Nero as his successor was probably made in this spirit, as an attempt to ensure the allegiance of the army to the descendants of Germanicus and Augustus.

[13] Cf. Treggiari, *Roman Marriage* 286: in Ulpian's words, 'as long as a marriage lasts, a woman cannot be accused of adultery'. After the divorce, the husband could set up the suit within sixty days.

[14] In general, an adultery in the emperor's household was a graver matter: cf. Woodman-Martin ad Tac. *Ann.* 3.24.3 (Cambridge, 1996).

68.[15] Giancotti's argument[16] that 'astrologers had prophesied to Nero the end in his life-time' fails to see that the story is a blatant fabrication *post eventum*. What astrologer would have gone and told Nero that he would die an outlaw and a fugitive?

A case has been made more recently for relatively early composition. P. Kragelund[17] has proposed that the play was written to celebrate Galba's triumph in 68.[18] Kragelund's main argument

[15] The attribution to Seneca was questioned as early as Petrarch (*Fam.* 24.5.17) and Salutati (*Ep.* 3.8 Novati, 1.152 *nonne Neronis exitus . . . plane, prout accidit, recitatur? que premoriens Seneca nec uidit nec . . . potuit diuinare*). Petrarch's letter (1348) blames Seneca for leaving a scathing portrayal of his former pupil after pandering to his vicious inclinations; yet from the charge of composing *Octavia* Seneca could be exonerated if the rumour were true that 'another Seneca' had composed this, as some passages of the play seem to suggest (*Octauie . . . locus aliquis hanc suspitionem recipit, Fam.* 24.5.17); cf. R. Sabbadini, *Le scoperte dei codici latini e greci ne' secoli XIV e XV* (Florence, 1905–1914), 2.178. Elsewhere, Petrarch expressed some amazement at the words of 'Seneca' in 377 ff., which seemed to him to forecast the future end of the philosopher too truly (cf. Martellotti, *IMU* 15 (1972), 153–4). Salutati's doubts pivoted mainly on 618–31, where Nero's death is foretold, but considerations of style and literary convention also played a part (cf. Martellotti, 161). For views analogous to Salutati's, or influenced by his judgement, in the margins of several MSS cf. Kragelund (1982), 72–3; Tarrant, *Agam.*, Introd. 37. The author of the marginalia in BL Harl. 2484 (who, however, predates Salutati), for instance, notes at 620–1: *describit mortem Neronis futuram et ex hoc tu potes scire quod Seneca non composuit hoc opus quia Nero necauit Senecam ut dicit Boetius de consolatione et alii.* The question of the authenticity of *Octavia* overlaps with that of the identity of that elusive *Doppelgänger* of Seneca, 'the tragedian', who was believed (since late antiquity: cf. Sid. Apoll. *Carm.* 9.230–4) to be different from the philosopher, probably on account of an equivocal passage in Martial 1.61.7–8, where the 'two Senecas' in question are the rhetor and the philosopher. Older editors discussing the problem conjure up the ghost of Marcus Annaeus Seneca, the supposed son of the philosopher, to whom some ascribe the, in their view, less successful dramas of the corpus. Also of interest is the *Vita Senecae* of Gasparino Barzizza (1411), in L. Panizza, *Traditio* 33 (1977), 297–358, esp. p. 348 for Gasparino's position on the authorship of the tragedies. An extract from Petrus Crinitus' *De poetis Latinis* (1505) is enclosed in Avantius' preface, which seems to give *Octavia* to the 'alter Seneca'. The *Ad lectores* of Farnabius has a useful survey of positions held by sixteenth- and seventeenth-century critics.

[16] Giancotti (1954), 23.

[17] Kragelund (1982), *passim*; (1988), 492–508.

[18] Emphasis on the necessity for peace (279–81) and the condemnation of cruelty (982) may well reveal the attitude of a witness to the events of 68–69.

consists of a supposed parallelism between Galba's 'republican' slogans and the alleged populism of the play.[19] Yet Galba's recognition of the authority of *Senatus populusque* is widely paralleled in early imperial history. Vespasian initially followed very much the same guidelines, and so did Nerva and Trajan.[20] In addition, the lines in which the Chorus summons itself to rebel against the *princeps* display little Republicanism: the rebels only want to restore the Claudian princess to her legitimate share in the government.[21] There is nothing triumphalistic about the play, and the final lament over the fickleness of the *uulgus* (877–7· *o funestus multis populi | dirusque fauor*) seems to dispel any impression that the people could be considered a political body, and could describe Galba's end as aptly as Octavia's. The *praetexta* is remarkably vague and non-committal on all constitutional issues regarding the position of the *princeps*. Nothing can be gleaned from supposed references to constitutional debates. No traces of the so-called Senatorial opposition under Vespasian can be detected. The language in which political issues are discussed applies to situations which range through the whole of the first century. In the words of its first choral ode, *Octavia* proclaims allegiance to the legitimate branch of the Claudians – a harmless proclamation which would in fact fit well with the Flavian emperors' attitude towards Claudius.

T. D. Barnes[22] has also argued for a very early date (Galba's reign), maintaining that the author of *Octavia* was familiar with the political events of 62 at first hand. He claims to recognize in

[19] Cf. *Oct.* 676–82 *ubi Romani uis est populi . . . ?*

[20] Legends with *Libertas* were coined under several rulers (Octavian VINDEX LIBERTATIS: *RIC* I², 79, 476; Claudius (?): LIBERTAS AVGVSTI: *RIC* I², 128, 97; Vespasian: LIBERTAS PVBLICA, LIBERTAS RESTITVTA: *RIC* I² 271, 69; 272, 80; Nerva: LIBERTAS AB IMP. NERVA RESTITVTA (*CIL* VI.472); for Trajan cf. P. L. Strack, *Untersuchungen* I.176–7. For other revivals of *Libertas* and related ideas in post-Neronian coinage of various date cf. Kragelund (1998), 152 n. 2.

[21] Cf. *Oct.* 789–90 *reddere penates Claudiae diui parant | torosque fratris, debitam partem imperi.*

[22] *MH* 39 (1982), 215–17.

the play a sympathetic attitude towards Messalina which would reveal a somewhat different approach to the history of the Julio-Claudians, one which precedes the establishment of the official historical *vulgata*.[23] Yet the only sympathetic remarks made about Messalina in the play are uttered by her daughter,[24] and no pre-vulgata tradition need be presupposed behind them. They are simply adapted to the point of view of a bereaved daughter. On the other hand, Nero's references to Messalina already attest the diffusion of the tradition depicting her as driven by an insatiable lust.[25]

Barnes also drew attention to the play's failure to mention Otho as Poppaea's husband at *Oct.* 731, which is taken as an argument in favour of a Galban dating. Under Galba, Otho was an influential figure, and caution would have recommended passing over in silence his past acquaintance with the Neronian court. After the fall of Nero, however, there were two competing versions in circulation of Otho's relations with Poppaea. One, attested in Suetonius, Plutarch, Cassius Dio and Tacitus, and commonly claimed for Pliny's historical work, represented Otho's marriage to Poppaea as a fiction contrived by Nero to cover his encounters with Poppaea while still officially married to Octavia.[26] But no such sham-marriage is mentioned in the later version represented by Tac. *Ann.* 13.45, wherein Nero came to know of Poppaea only through Otho's incautious praise of her beauty. The divergence between the two conflicting versions followed by Tacitus in his two successive works has been tentatively explained by the hypothesis that, while working on the *Annales*,

[23] A view shared by Meise (1969), 175.

[24] *Oct.* 259–60 *furore miserae dura genetricis meae, | quae nupta demens nupsit . . .* ; 266–7 *cecidit infelix parens | heu nostra ferro.*

[25] 536 *incesta genetrix detrahit generi fidem.* On doubts raised against Claudius' paternity on account of the notorious conduct of Messalina cf. Juv. *Sat.* 6.115–32, 10.329–45; Suet. *Nero* 7 (*Nero*) *Britannicum . . . ut subditiuum apud patrem arguere conatus est.*

[26] Suet. *Otho* 3 *Poppaeam Sabinam . . . nuptiarum specie recepit*; Plut. *Galba* 19.2; Cass. Dio *Hist. Rom.* 61.11.2; Tac. *Hist.* 1.13 *Poppaeam Sabinam, principale scortum, ut apud conscium libidinum deposuerat* (sc. *Nero*) *donec Octauiam uxorem amoliretur.*

Tacitus finally had the opportunity to consult Cluvius's history, probably published in the intervening time.[27] If the author of *Octavia* was following the same source as Suetonius, Plutarch and the *Historiae*, there is no compelling reason why Otho should have been mentioned as Poppaea's husband.

Barnes's other argument concerns Tigellinus' failure to turn up in a play on Nero's atrocities, which he again ascribes to chronological reasons: Tigellinus was protected by Vinius, and so it would have been dangerous for the author of *Octavia* to blacken him in his play. Tacitus actually only goes so far as to say that Tigellinus was not executed, as many would have wished, owing to Vinius' protection, which is a long way from stating that Tigellinus was still powerful enough to silence and to intimidate his accusers.[28]

The subject matter of *Octavia* and the lost histories of the Flavian age

There is nothing in the play incontrovertibly suggesting that the author had witnessed the events himself. We have no means of establishing with absolute precision the date of the tragedy, say, through a fortunate anachronism or a transparent allusion, but consideration of the play's structure strongly suggests that it was composed by someone who worked from written sources. This clarifies the dating in so far as it establishes a *terminus post quem*, that is the publication of the historical books of Pliny, Cluvius and Fabius.

The tradition about Nero must have been to a large extent the creation of the annalists writing in the Flavian age: political

[27] A. Gercke (1896), 197; A. Momigliano *RAL* 8 (1932), 293–300; Syme, *Tacitus* 1.290; G. B. Townend, *Hermes* 88 (1960), 98–120; id. *Hermes* 89 (1961), 227–48. Fabius Rusticus must have published his work after the year 84 perhaps in response to Pliny's, which had been published posthumously, after 79.

[28] Cf. Tac. *Hist.* 1.72; in Plut. *Galba* 17.4 Tigellinus, though publicly disgraced, appears to scorn the public condemnation thanks to Vinius' protection; *Otho* 2.1, however, tells a different story, describing Tigellinus' fears throughout the reign of Galba.

assassinations were committed under Augustus too, even within the imperial family, and Vespasian probably gave his consent to the killing of the six-year-old son of Vitellius after his victory.[29] Yet no one regards these emperors as monsters, owing to a benevolent and idealizing historical tradition. Otho's and Vitellius' efforts to assert themselves as Nero's legitimate successors suggest that the legend of Nero the monster had not gained currency widely by 69. On the contrary, Nero's memory was an important political instrument in the immediate aftermath of Galba's fall. Nero appears still to have been popular in the year of the Four Emperors. Otho was acclaimed by his troops as *Nero Otho* (cf. Tac. *Hist.* 1.78); he used this name in his *diplomata* (Plut. *Otho*, 3.2; Suet. *Otho*, 7.1;[30] Cass. Dio *Hist. Rom.* 64.6), re-erected the statues of Poppaea and set about enlarging the *Domus aurea*; Vitellius offered propitiatory sacrifices to the shade of Nero (Tac. *Hist.* 2.95; Suet. *Vit.* 11; Eutrop. 7.18).[31] The unfavourable tradition seems to have established itself only with the advent of the Flavian dynasty, presumably following the publication of such influential historical accounts as Pliny the Elder's and Fabius'.[32] We may imagine that in 68–69 much of what happened in the household of the *princeps* was still shrouded in obscurity.

In *Octavia* the tradition associated with Nero's atrocities has already taken its final form: Nero figures there as the matricide, the murderer of Claudius, Britannicus and Octavia, the incendiary of Rome, the defiler of the gods. Since these assassinations appear to have taken place, it was perhaps inevitable that Nero should be portrayed as a monster. The fact remains

[29] Tac. *Hist.* 4.80.

[30] *Ab infima plebe appellatus Nero, nullum indicium recusantis dedit, immo ut quidam tradiderunt, etiam diplomatibus primisque epistulis suis . . . Neronis cognomen adiecit.*

[31] Cf. B. W. Henderson, *The Life and Principate of the Emperor Nero* (London, 1903), 418–19; M. T. Griffin, *Nero. The end of a dynasty* (London, 1984).

[32] Perhaps the earliest attestation of the legend of Nero in the form of a list of Nero's crimes (the murders of Britannicus, Octavia, Agrippina) is found in Jos. *Bell. Iud.* 2.250–1 Niese (II. xiii, 1–2), published around 75. The story is presented as 'well known to all'. On the existence of favourable sources cf. Griffin, *Nero*, 235–7; Jos. *Bell. Iud.* 4.9.2; Paus. 7.17.3; 9.27.4.

that Vespasian's two immediate predecessors had thought it necessary to stress continuity with Nero's regime. This suggests that Nero was still popular in some sectors of Roman society, and not many modern historians are prepared to accept at face value the story that Nero set ablaze the whole city of Rome, or that he endorsed a policy of programmatic impiety. This is significant, because the author of *Octavia* appears to have endorsed the stories about Nero's cruelty unreservedly, perhaps also in order to exculpate Seneca (see *infra*).

In support of the hypothesis that the playwright relied on preexistent historical accounts there is the assumption that even a contemporary witness would have found it difficult to write a historical play solely on the score of a personal mixture of rumours and vague recollections, unless he had been closely involved in the events (still a possibility, at this stage). In addition, the agreement of the story as told in *Octavia* with the consensus of the historical tradition is overall too complete to allow for an independent genesis. A certain lack of strict relevance to the dramatic plot can be observed in the accumulation of details of historical, or pseudo-historical, information. I believe that not only the endemic interest of ancient historians in prodigies, but even the narrative rhythm of a sequence of 'chapters' in a book on the Neronian principate, can be recognized in *Octavia.*

First of all, the succession, interpretation and connection of historical events in the *praetexta* coincide in full with the historical tradition as we can reconstruct it from Tacitus and Cassius Dio. Significantly, this includes events which, though important from a historian's perspective, did not need to have a place in a plot concentrating on the last days of Octavia; the tragedy none the less records them in the sequence in which they seem to have figured in the historiography.[33]

The execution of Sulla and Plautus is perhaps the most striking of these elements. Recorded by Tacitus in *Ann.* 14.57–9

[33] The parallelism between *Oct.* and Tacitus on this point was already remarked by Helm (1934), 326.

immediately before the Octavia chapters begin (cf. *Ann.* 14.59.4 *posito metu nuptias Poppaeae ob eius modi terrores dilatas maturare parat Octauiamque coniugem amoliri*), the episode marks the first appearance of Nero in the *praetexta* (*Oct.* 437–8 NER. *perage imperata, mitte qui Plauti mihi | Sullaeque caesi referat abscisum caput*) and precedes his resolve finally to get rid of Octavia in order to marry the by now pregnant Poppaea (590–2). Tacitus' narrative stresses how political considerations (namely the fear of an upheaval masterminded by his opponents) forced Nero to take steps to divorce Octavia only after news of his two rivals' deaths had reached him,[34] which invalidates the chronology of *Octavia*, where Nero is made to order their execution on the day before the new marriage.[35] Of course, dramatic necessities forced the author to compress and misrepresent actual chronology and there is thus no need to accuse him of ignorance of the material constraints of ancient seafaring. But why the straining of the chronology when the event had thematically so little point? No messenger is brought on to describe the death of the opponents in the play, nor does Nero carry around their severed heads. No lack of credibility would have resulted from the author's passing over the two executions in silence. Indeed, a likely possibility is that the *ignotus* only mentioned them because the two executions and the divorce of Octavia were linked by his source and thus these events followed one another in two successive 'chapters', very much as in Tacitus.

34 Plautus and Sulla had their heads severed and brought to Nero (Tac. *Ann.* 14.57.6 *relatum caput eius*; 14.59.4 *caput interfecti relatum*).

35 In fact, at least two months may have elapsed between the execution of Plautus and the death of Octavia, in view of the twenty days it would have taken just for the dispatch to reach Asia Minor from Rome and come back; thereafter, eleven days passed between Nero's divorce and his remarrying Poppaea, and Octavia was not immediately disposed of by Nero. It could be surmised that the execution of the two personages was a climactic event in the historical account of Nero's reign in the work of one of the Flavian historians (although Miriam Griffin, *Seneca*, 426, argues that Tacitus was probably original in so greatly stressing the year 62 as the turning-point).

At 227–48 Octavia prays to Jove that Nero be annihilated by a thunderbolt: she herself saw a comet portending ruin to humankind (a comet related to have been sighted in 60); why does Jove's thunder fail to bring down that monster? (a possible allusion to the story of the lightning said to have struck Nero's dining-table: see ad 246–8). The impious ruler of the world drives the gods away from their temples (usually taken to signify either the spoliation of temples[36] or the destruction of the shrine consecrated by Agrippina to Claudius on the Caelian).[37] It is no coincidence, again, that reference to these events occurs within so few lines in *Octavia* and that they are dealt with in the same chapter in Tacitus.[38] Why did the author of the *praetexta* choose to spell out all these portents if not because he found them conveniently assembled in a single chapter of his source? Written sources are bound to be recognized here, especially since the reliability of much of this material is debatable. A kind of misconceived *effet de réel*, perhaps, but also an effect akin to what a reader of, say, Valerius Flaccus can often experience, when a detail of the story of the Argonauts emerges which can only be understood through Apollonius' version: yet Valerius does not seem to have envisaged such awareness as an intended part of a reader's decoding of his poem. These details appear to be intertextual residues jutting out of the receiving text.

[36] But the financial strictures which prompted Nero to such extreme measures only occurred after Octavia's death, in 64: cf. Tac. *Ann.* 15.45 *inque eam praedam etiam dii cessere, spoliatis in urbe templis.* The allusion is perhaps to the demolition of a temple consecrated to the cult of Claudius (attested in Suet. *Vesp.* 9). Modern interpreters tend to dismiss this information: what advantage could Nero have hoped to derive from a deconsecration of Claudius? Denying his divinity was politically counterproductive, and it is in fact unconfirmed by our evidence (cf. Griffin, *CAH*[2] xi (2000), 19, n. 62; M. P. Charlesworth, *JRS* 27 (1937), 57).

[37] Cass. Dio-Xiph. *Hist. Rom.* 61.16.5 wrongly attributes this portent to the previous year: see ad 245–6.

[38] Cf. *Oct.* 231–2. *uidimus caelo iubar | ardens cometen pandere infaustam facem* = Tac. *Ann.* 14.22.1 *inter quae et sidus cometes effulsit*; and *Oct.* 245–6 *pro summe genitor, tela cur frustra iacis | inuicta totiens temere regali manu?* = Tac. *Ann.* 14.22.4 *ictae dapes* (sc. *fulmine*) *mensaque disiecta*, all pertaining to the year 60, i.e. two years before the date of the action of the play.

At 107 the heroine prays to be spared an unspeakable *crimen* (*absit crimen a fatis meis*): what she means cannot be the threat, made explicit at 174, to kill the tyrant (see ad loc.). Octavia must have in mind the accusation of adultery with a freedman,[39] yet the further developments of the tragedy disregard this charge. This continuous series of veiled allusions is only justified by the presence of a historical subtext, which gets the better of the tragic plot, and sometimes disrupts it. This lack of cohesion is an outcome of the very method of writing adopted by the author, who fits in all information relating to the characters involved.

The unspecified *monumenta* of Acte hinted at in 193–7 are not on record in extant historical accounts of this period, and the passage is among those most frequently adduced to assert the playwright's first-hand knowledge of events, alongside the tears of Agrippina at Britannicus' funeral (170).[40] F. Ladek aroused a wave of excitement (in 1891!) when he called attention to *CIL* XI 1414, CE]RERI SACRVM / [CLAVDIA] AVG. LIB. ACTE, possibly the personage in question. These words are inscribed on a fragment of granite, 0.52 high, 1.77 long, probably an epistyle, now in the Cimitero Monumentale in Pisa,[41] thought to have come in medieval times from the region of Olbia, where the rich *liberta* was the owner of large estates. At any rate the identification of *CIL* XI 1414 with the *monumenta* of 196 presents a number of problems: is Ceres the most appropriate goddess to turn to for assistance in matters of love? Is Acte likely to have sought such publicity, on such a grand scale (if the inscription was part of a temple), for her private dealings with the emperor? More to the point, what prevents us from ascribing the story to a historian rather than to the poet himself? Indeed, the cryptic, allusive character of this remark can equally well be explained either

[39] Cf. Tac. *Ann.* 14.60 *destinaturque reus cognomento Eucaerus*; 62–3 (Anicetus).

[40] Concerning Agrippina's tears, reference should perhaps be made to Tacitus' allusion to her despair when she realized that Britannicus had been her last resource against an increasingly intolerant son (cf. *Ann.* 13.16.18).

[41] 35A est. (= parete esterna) in E. Cristiani–P. Arias–E. Gabba, *Il Camposanto monumentale di Pisa. Le antichità* (Pisa, 1977), 77 (with photograph).

as an innuendo for the court cognoscenti or as a reference to written accounts well known at the time. Pliny, to mention one possible candidate, is known to have used epigraphic evidence when other sources were deficient or not available (Suet. *Cal.* 8 *Plinius Secundus . . . addit etiam pro argumento aras ibi ostendi inscriptas* OB AGRIPPINAE PVERPERIVM).

At 831, the idea of setting Rome on fire comes to Nero's mind as a retaliation for the popular riots in favour of Octavia, two years in advance of the actual events of 64. Even if Nero had really been responsible for the fire, this long-term *vendetta* is a clear invention: the poet of *Octavia* is obviously trying to encompass within the short temporal span of the play all the salient crimes of Nero's rule. This again I interpret as a clear sign that the author was composing from written sources, and collecting in his portrayal of Nero all that was best known and, as it were, *typical* about Nero: Nero had to be *recognizable* as the legendary emperor that everybody had read about.

In a fully-fledged account of Nero's tragic reign, the matricide of Agrippina could not fail to figure (cf. *Oct.* 310–376). Yet one might question whether this was a necessary ingredient in a tragedy concentrating on Octavia. Of the heroine herself the author knew remarkably little. One's suspicion is that Octavia takes centre stage in a number of grand scenes drawing on established theatrical tradition: the initial monody, the Nutrix-heroine scene, the *exodus* imitating Sophocles' *Antigone*. If we remove this literary patina, very little is left about Octavia which we did not know from Tacitus. This lack of specific interest in the pallid protagonist of the *praetexta* may very well reflect the outlook of the play's sources, obviously focusing on Nero and leaving Octavia's story necessarily in the background.

These elements suggest the method of a poet composing from written sources: overwhelmed by the bulk of information at his disposal he struggles to fit it all into a dramatic frame without destroying the psychological plausibility of the characters, although at times at the expense of clarity and internal consistency. This heavy dependence on written accounts, with the result that many details are not turned into dramatic action, is excusable: unless the *auctor Octauiae* was one of the political protagonists of the Neronian court, he would have found it impossible to have first-hand, independent knowledge of the inside story of imperial intrigues.

Octavia and the Flavians

The necessity of postulating recourse to written accounts shifts the date of the play to the middle Flavian period, when the histories of Pliny and Fabius at least became available.[42] The Flavians' need for legitimation has been seen as providing an apt background for a play eliciting pity for the doomed family of Claudius.[43] Vespasian and his elder son paid tribute to the memory of Claudius;[44] Titus had been a member of Britannicus'

42 On the identity of the source cf. the literature cited at n. 27. The absence of Otho, as we have seen, may point to any of the Flavian historians. The rumour about Nero's role in the Great Fire of Rome was widespread. It must have been in Pliny (cf. *Nat.* 17.1.5; cf. also Suet. *Nero*, 38; Cass. Dio *Hist. Rom.* 62.16–17), but G. Townend, *Hermes* 88 (1960), 111 makes a strong case for Cluvius as the main source hostile to Nero. Interest in portents might have been a feature of Pliny's history, but we have no reason to believe that Cluvius and Fabius did not share this trait; Pliny may have shown respect for Claudius' memory, the official Flavian line, but the play is not lacking in criticism of Nero's adoptive father. Of the three historians, Fabius Rusticus is said to have been the most favourable towards Seneca, a possible link with the *ignotus*. The verbal parallel with Josephus (cf. ad 335–7) used to be taken as pointing to Cluvius. But there are diverging opinions regarding the identity of Josephus' source in *Ant.* 19–20: cf. D. Timpe, *Historia* 9 (1960), 474–503.

43 Cf. Herington, *CHCL* 2.530; Zwierlein, *KK*, 445; Griffin, *Nero*, chap. vii. Kragelund (1998), 152–73 reviews the evidence for rehabilitation of Octavia, as well as of other members of the imperial family executed by Nero, under Galba (documented in Cass. Dio *Hist. Rom.* 64.3.4c Boiss. = Zonaras 11.13, and indirectly suggested by a fragment in the Mausoleum of Augustus, in which the letters OC[are seen as referring to a memorial set up for an imperial Octavia).

44 The evidence, literary and epigraphical, is discussed by M. Griffin, *The Flavians*, in *CAH*² xi (2000), 19–23; earlier discussions include M. P. Charlesworth, *JRS* 27 (1937); A. Ferrill, *CJ* 60 (1965), 267–9; J. Gagé, *REA* 54 (1952), 290–315 (esp. 313). G. Alföldi argues (on *CIL* vi. 8.2 (1996), n. 40452,

retinue, perhaps a friend, in his early years,[45] and H. Mattingly once argued that coins bearing the image of Britannicus were struck during Titus' reign.[46] The new dynasty seems to have sought to create an atmosphere of legitimacy by presenting itself as the successor of the good rulers among the Julio-Claudians. One can imagine that this created the context in which the doomed lives of the last of the unfortunate Claudians were to become the subject of a drama.

This state of things, however, need not have changed radically under Domitian, when Statius and Martial still felt free to talk disparagingly of Nero.[47] An important element in this discussion is the possible acquaintance of the *Octavia* poet with Statius' *Siluae*, a consideration which, if accepted, shifts the *terminus post* to the 90s.

Statius' *Siluae*

What I consider to be the most significant points of contact with Statius are concentrated in two *cantica* in which the same items of the stock-in-trade mythological vocabulary are deployed, namely the motif of the numerous transformations of Jupiter in his amorous dalliances.

Near the end of the long first act, Octavia's *Nutrix*, who has undertaken to console her charge for Nero's estrangement, draws a parallel between Octavia and none other than Juno, on the basis of the sufferings undergone by both in their unfortunate predicament of betrayed wives. Did Juno – sings the old servant – not

a fragment of a statue of Agrippina offered by one of her freedmen) that Agrippina's memory was rehabilitated under Vespasian, on the strength of the number of dedications to Agrippina datable to Vespasian's reign.

45 Suet. *Titus*, 2 *educatus in aula cum Britannico simul . . . erant autem adeo familiares, ut de potione qua Britannicus hausta periit Titus quoque iuxta cubans gustasse credatur . . . quorum omnium mox memor statuam ei auream in Palatio posuit et alteram ex ebore equestrem, quae circensi pompa hodieque praefertur, dedicauit prosecutusque est.* The story may or may not be true, but it well attests the Flavians' need for legitimation.

46 *NC* 5th series, 10 (1930), 330–2; *contra* cf. J. Babelon, in *Hommages à L. Herrmann* (Brussels, 1960), 127.

47 Cf. Griffin, *CAH*² xi (2000), 61.

endure a lot as hard as Octavia's, every time her husband turned himself into an earthly being and took the shape now of a swan, now of a bull, and even of raindrops, in pursuance of his illicit love affairs? Yet Juno has become, through patient stifling of her feelings, sole queen over a now pacified husband (201–18):

passa est similes ipsa dolores
  regina deum,
cum se formas uertit in omnes
dominus caeli diuumque pater
et modo pennas sumpsit oloris,
modo Sidonii cornua tauri,
aureus idem fluxit in imbri
. . .
uicit sapiens tamen obsequium
coniugis altae pressusque dolor:
sola Tonantem tenet aetherio
secura toro maxima Iuno
nec mortali captus forma
deserit altam Iuppiter aulam.

Attention was first drawn to this passage by Rudolf Helm.[48] Helm compared it to a passage in Statius' poem celebrating the marriage of Arruntius Stella and Violentilla, *Silu.* 1.2, where Venus herself, at last persuaded by Cupid to grant Stella a reward for his enduring love, sings the praises of Violentilla, whose beauty could catch many a divine eye. Had Apollo seen her wandering through the fields of Thessaly, Daphne would have roamed secure; Ariadne would long have continued to lament her lot, had Dionysus caught a glimpse of Violentilla on the couch deserted by Theseus on the shore of Naxos. Jupiter would have donned again all his animal guises to seduce her, had not Juno herself with insistent complaints elicited from the goddess the promise to leave her husband alone from now on (*Silu.* 1.2.130–6):

[48] Helm (1934), 283–347, esp. 343.

hanc si Thessalicos uidisses, Phoebe, per agros
erraret secura Daphne. si in litore Naxi
Theseum iuxta foret haec conspecta cubile,
Gnosida desertam profugus liquisset et Euhan.
quod nisi me longis placasset Iuno querellis
falsus huic pennas et cornua sumeret aethrae
rector, in hanc uero cecidisset Iuppiter auro.

According to Helm, the parallelism between the two poems is borne out by both a thematic and a linguistic correspondence in the description of Jupiter's traditional metamorphoses (the swan, the bull, and the golden rain), and he compared in particular *Oct.* 204–6 *dominus caeli . . . modo pennas sumpsit oloris | modo Sidonii cornua tauri* and *Silu.* 1.2.135–6 *pennas et cornua sumeret aethrae | rector*. This claim was however impugned by Hosius,[49] and, more recently, by Junge, with the argument that both poets in fact draw on a repertoire of mythological commonplaces.[50]

A more original element in the Nurse's *canticum* is the statement that Juno's *obsequium* has at last won back Jupiter's heart, so that her husband no longer descends on earth to pursue illicit love affairs. One would be hard pushed to identify a mythological episode in which Juno fits the picture drawn by the old woman of a long-suffering, submissive wife, resigned to accepting whatever marital misfortunes fate has cast upon her, but achieving in the end a complete victory over her rivals. Even in the famous story told in Book 14 of the *Iliad*, where Hera bolsters her husband's desire by putting on a magic girdle, the actual encounter of Zeus and Hera (*Il.* 14.300–51) cannot be the notional episode presupposed by the words of the Nutrix *sapiens . . . obsequium . . . pressusque dolor*. Throughout the book, Hera is neither submissive nor patient, nor does she make any notable display of affliction, while her husband launches into a comparison, flattering in his view, between Hera and his previous flames. Even her seduction is not performed as an act of restoration to her conjugal rights,

[49] K. Hosius, *Gnomon*, 13 (1937), 135. [50] Junge (1999), 281, n. 904.

but has the sole purpose of luring Zeus away from the battlefield while Poseidon fights for the Achaeans.

In later literature, Juno is still aggrieved by her husband's conduct. She has to 'digest' or 'repress' her anger in Cat. *Carm.* 68.138–9 (*saepe etiam Iuno, maxima caelicolum, | coniugis in culpa flagrantem concoquit iram*), where she provides an example for Catullus' resolve to tolerate Lesbia's occasional infidelities. She has an unfaithful husband in Martial's epigram celebrating the marriage of Stella (Mart. *Epigr.* 6.21.8 *tam frugi Iuno uellet habere uirum*). Hera makes a scene with her husband over the recent rape of Ganymede in Lucian *Deor. Dial.* 8(5), 2.

I would like to suggest that the precedent we are looking for is literary, and the lines of the *Nutrix* are best understood if we situate them in the context of Hellenistic and Roman love poetry and its appropriation of myth.

One of the hyperbolic compliments devised in erotic poetry for a poet's beloved, "s/he is so beautiful that a god would descend on earth to woo her/him", may appear in the variant form 'Zeus is no longer the insatiable lover he used to be, unless he comes down now from heaven and takes the young boy from me.' In *AP* 12.20 (Julius Leonides, active at the court of Nero),[51] the list of transformations of Zeus is capped by such a typically epigrammatic conclusion:

ὁ Ζεὺς Αἰθιόπων πάλι τέρπεται εἰλαπίναισιν
ἢ χρυσὸς Δανάης εἴρπυσεν εἰς θαλάμους·
θαῦμα γὰρ εἰ Περίανδρον ἰδὼν οὐχ ἥρπασε γαίης
τὸν καλόν· ἦ φιλόπαις οὐκέτι νῦν ὁ θεός.

The motif of multiple metamorphosis is deployed here to provide a foil against which the poet measures the intensity of his passion, and evaluates his case in a humorous mood.[52] The gap between mythical times and the present is bridged by the poet,

[51] Cf. D. L. Page, *FGE*, 503, 539.
[52] Cf. e.g. *AP*. 5.64 (Ganymede, Leda); 5.125 (Danae, Europe, Leda); 9.48 (Leda, Europe, Antiope, Danae); 12.20, given in full *infra*; in Latin cf. Ov. *Am.* 1.10.8 and 3.12.33–4.

who sets himself on a plane with Jupiter and compares their respective lots, if only to say, jokingly, that his predicament is much the simpler, 'let others turn into bulls or swans melodious on the shore. Such tricks shall be reserved for Zeus; I shall give Corinna her twopence, and make no use of wings' (*AP* 5.125, Bassus, transl. Gow-Page).[53]

As Hellenistic (Greek and Roman) love poetry appropriates mythology, the protagonists of myth become infused with the attitudes and feelings of the love poet himself. The traditional stories of myth are given a new lease of life, as gods and heroes live on as poetic characters and the poets foist on them their own sentiments and reactions, and treat them as equals or even rivals in their quest for love.[54]

This is the cultural frame within which Stat. *Silu.* 1.2.130–6 must be interpreted, even if the laudatory motif 'she is so beautiful I fear a god may take her from me' is now given an original twist for the sake of epigrammatic originality: Jupiter would love Violentilla under no matter what animal disguise (such is her beauty), if only Venus had not given in to Juno's repeated complaints. Statius' vignette verges on comedy because the poet focuses this time not on Zeus' adventures, present or past, but on the pre-emptive reaction of his wife. Even now, Jupiter would have lost no time in carrying off Violentilla, but Juno has been quick to take action to stop this happening. I suggest Statius' querulous but successful Juno is the source of the patient and in the long run victorious Juno of *Oct.* 217–18, a suggestion which is reinforced by, and in its turn adds force to, the thematic and linguistic correspondences already highlighted by Helm.

The echoes of Statius are concentrated in the ornamental and descriptive sections of the play. One of these passages is the joyous song at 762 ff., perhaps a chorus of soldiers stationed

[53] *The Greek Anthology. The Garland of Philip* (Cambridge, 1968), I, 176–7.

[54] Cf. *AP* 12.70 (Meleager), where Zeus answers the prayers of the supplicating lover with (4) οἶδα παθὼν ἐλεεῖν.

outside the royal apartments. In striking contrast to the mounting anger of the people of Rome, ready to storm the imperial palace, this chorus sings in celebration of the newly married Poppaea's beauty. From their tone of exultation, we may surmise, they are still under the effect of the revels and toasts following the marriage ceremony. They are unaware of the turn events are taking, and their song is undimmed by any sense of impending disaster, providing a fitting example of 'tragic irony' (762–75).

si uera loquax fama Tonantis
furta et gratos narrat amores
(quem modo Ledae pressisse sinum
tectum plumis pennisque ferunt,
modo per fluctus raptam Europen
taurum tergo portasse trucem),
quae regit et nunc deseret astra,
petet amplexus, Poppaea, tuos,
quos et Ledae praeferre potest,
et tibi, quondam cui miranti
fuluo, Danae, fluxit in auro.
formam Sparte iactet alumnae
licet, et Phrygius praemia pastor,
uincet uultus haec Tyndaridos

In this song, the beauty of Poppaea is set off against a number of proverbial beauties of myth, in typical priamel form.[55] Again a catalogue of divine transformations provides the apt background for courtly praise: if it is true that Jupiter took the shape of earthly beings and inferior creatures to make love to Leda, Europe, and Danae, now is the time to expect the miracle to happen, since Poppaea's beauty far outstrips that of all those heroines. He may well prefer her to Leda and Danae; Helen too, whose shapely features are deservedly the pride of native Sparta, will have to bow down to this new paragon of beauty (773–5):

[55] The priamel is often used in praises of the poet's woman: cf. ad 545; 775.

formam Sparte iactet alumnae
licet, et Phrygius praemia pastor,
uincet uultus haec Tyndaridos

The motif that a given nation or city takes pride in having given birth to a legendary hero, an eloquent poet, a famous triumphator is common in ancient poetry.[56] The beauty of one's 'nursling', however, is a less common reason for pride in Latin literature, and in the form *licet . . . iactet*, 'no matter how much such and such takes pride in . . .', the range of possible models becomes narrower. It is not found either in Vergil[57] or in Ovid, next to Seneca the two most frequent names in the apparatus of *loci paralleli* assembled by *Octavia* commentators. The closest parallels seem to me to come again from the *Siluae*.

In Stat. *Silu.* 1.2.262–5 nature is exhorted to rejoice at the glory of the bride with the words:

nitidum consurgat ad aethera tellus
Eubois et pulchra tumeat Sebethos alumna,
nec sibi sulpureis Lucrinae Naides antris
nec Pompeiani placeant magis otia Sarni

where one may notice, at 263, the occurrence of the word *alumna* in connection with the names of Violentilla's birthplace (*tellus Eubois*, Parthenope), and of the river Sebethos, prouder of their 'nursling' than the Naiads of Lake Lucrinus and sleep-inducing Sarnus are of themselves.

This mode of expression is in fact characteristic of Statius, and a similar priamel occurs in *Silu.* 1.3.27–8, where the sequestered calm of Manilius Vopiscus' riverside villa is praised against the background of stormy Hellespontine shores: *Sestiacos nunc fama sinus pelagusque natatum | iactet.* In similar terms, in *Silu.* 3.4.13–19,

[56] On which cf. E. Fraenkel, *Horace* (Oxford, 1957), 304–5; M. Citroni (ed.), *Martialis Epigrammaton liber* I (Florence, 1975), ad 1.61; id. *Spect.* 1.2.

[57] For *alumnus* indicating the child of a given country that has brought glory to it cf. Verg. *Aen.* 6.876–7 *nec Romula quondam | ullo se tantum tellus iactabit alumno* (more parallels in *TLL* i. s.v. *alumnus*, 1796.52–83; s.v. *alumna*, 1798.17–26).

Pergamum, the birth-place of Domitian's favourite Flavius Earinus, is contrasted with Ida, no matter how much the latter takes pride in Ganymede: *illa* (sc. Mount Ida) *licet sacrae placeat sibi nube rapinae . . . at tu* (sc. Pergamum) *grata deis pulchroque insignis alumno* . . . Again, as in 1.2.263, the parallelism extends here to *alumnus*, a frequently met word in Statius, who is apt to replace proper names with allusive periphrases often exerting considerable demands on a reader's classical schooling.[58]

Another possible echo of *Silu.* 1.2 occurs in the apostrophe to Danae in 771–2: she too must yield to the superior charms of Poppaea, though once Jupiter fell on her in the shape of golden rain.

et tibi quondam cui miranti,
fuluo, Danae, fluxit in auro

Danae is caught in a pose rendered familiar by a long iconographic tradition, as she stares in amazement (*miranti*) at the golden rain falling into her lap. A comparable scene can be found in Stat. *Silu.* 1.2.207–8, where a beautiful Naiad, Arethusa, reacts with the same rapture (*miratur*) to the embrace of an unseen lover coming to her in the shape of a water current:

miratur dulcia Nais
oscula nec credit pelago uenisse maritum

So far, the most important finds have concentrated our attention on Statius' celebratory piece for Stella, *Silu.* 1.2. Indeed, what may have smoothed the way leading from the *Siluae* to the *praetexta* is the poem's theme, the description of a grandiose marriage in Rome, which provided a source of inspiration for the narrative of Poppaea's marriage in *Oct.* 693–709.

[58] Note that, in Statius, periphrases formed by *alumnus/a* and the genitive are more or less esoteric *griphoi* at the service of poetic erudition (cf. e.g. 1.4.21 *aut mitem Tegeae Dircesue hortabor alumnum*; 1.5.22 *Herculei praedatrix cedat alumni*), whereas in *Oct.* 773 the enigma *formam Sparte iactet alumnae* is easily decipherable.

Statius gave his poem an original twist by talking of the marriage, not, following the tradition of nuptial poetry, in synchrony with the event, but in retrospect, in the form of a sequence of flashbacks. In *Octavia*, similarly, the description of the ill-fated marriage in which the drama culminates is pronounced by Poppaea's *Nutrix* at dawn, after the first night of the marriage. The memory of the happy day just passed serves to comfort the distraught Poppaea, anguish-stricken by a nightmare which has caused her to leave her chamber in panic.

Statius' epithalamium begins with the ceremony at its culminating point: the bride is led by Venus, who acts as *paranympha*, the woman in charge of the bridal couch. It is she who burns the ritual offerings on the altars (*Silu.* 1.2.11–13 *ipsa manu nuptam genetrix Aeneia duxit . . . ipsa toros et sacra parat*). The house of the groom is crowded with the magistrates and the common people, all enraptured by the beauty of the new bride (*Silu.* 1.2.47–8 *feruent agmine postes | atriaque et multa pulsantur limina uirga*; 233–7 *omnis honos, cuncti ueniunt ad limina fasces . . . felices utrosque uocant sed in agmine plures | inuidere uiro*). Statius goes on to inquire into the causes of this event. He traces it back to a scene in Venus' residence, where Amor makes a plea in favour of Stella, whose love-suit has aroused even the ruthless god's pity. Venus declares herself aware of Violentilla' charms, and promises to surrender her to Stella.

A great nuptial procession in the midst of an excited crowd of onlookers is also at the centre of the Nurse's narrative in *Octavia*. The old woman dwells first on the reaction aroused by the sight of Poppaea (as her pupil takes her place on the *genialis lectus* at the end of the *deductio*, 698–700), with an adjective whose hyperbolical tones have a parallel in the astonishment and incredulity of Stella as described by Statius,[59] and then goes on to describe various other crucial episodes of the marriage ceremony: the sacrifice and a public procession (perhaps the formal *deductio*, with Nero standing at the side of

[59] Cf. ad 699–700.

Poppaea), the universal acclamation emphasizing the sense of occasion.[60]

The dispersion of Statian reminiscences in several different passages of the *praetexta* makes a chronological dependence of the latter on the former more likely. This was to be expected, as Statius is unlikely to have sought inspiration from the work of a rhetorically second-rate and undistinguished poet. The marriage commemorated by Statius is to be dated to 89–90 by means of Mart. 6.21, which celebrates the same event in more jocular terms.

Possibly the author of *Octavia* had come to know Statius' poem while it was still being circulated prior to publication in the *Siluae* as a homage to the couple. While Statius repeatedly echoes Senecan tragedy in his *Thebaid*,[61] a link between this poet and the survivors of the Annaei is also proved by Statius' poem composed for Polla Argentaria (*Siluae* 2.7), Lucan's widow. Had the poet of *Octavia* some personal attachment to that circle, where the survivors of the exterminated clan of the Annaei gathered? On first impression there could have been nothing further apart than the jejune *Octavia*, and Statius' mannerist eloquence, yet the two poets seem to have come into contact. Perhaps the meeting ground was Polla's literary salon. The author of *Octavia* may have been an old pupil of Seneca, a survivor left with little to rejoice at by the advent of the Flavian dynasty, who had found a haven in the house of the last surviving grand ladies of that circle, and set about composing *Octavia* hoping to ingratiate himself with his protectress.

Quintilian's negative criticism of Seneca's style is often used as a possible chronological *terminus ante quem* for dating the play, on the basis of an alleged reaction against the so-called 'Senecanism' of the previous age.[62] By Domitian's time, literary

[60] I have discussed other possible echoes of Statius *ad* 8; 149–50; 219; 532; 695–6; 706–8.

[61] Cf. Zwierlein, *Prolegomena*, 239; P. Venini, *RFIC* 95 (1967), 418–27.

[62] Cf. Tac. *Ann.* 13.3 with Furneaux's note; Quint. *Inst.* 10.1.125–131; Fronto 155 N; Gell. *Noct. Att.* 12.2.

taste had changed, it is claimed. Seneca, who used to be in great favour, and the sole author in the hands of Roman youth, had by then lost his appeal. If *Octavia* is post-Statian, we may have to correct this view. The fashion may not have changed uniformly, or perhaps a core of Seneca's admirers simply resisted till the end of the first century. Seneca's fame may not have suffered so greatly from the censures of Quintilian, and of even more fierce detractors, such as the archaizing writers of the following century. Moreover, stylistic considerations need not have weighed much in this poet's choice of a model. The 'apologetic' undercurrent noticeable in the play suggests that the tragedy was composed as a response to posthumous criticisms addressed to Seneca, although not necessarily by someone who had known him in person.

A militant tragedy?

Given a date in the 90s, we could speculate that the play was written under Domitian, and one of the author's intentions may have been that of suggesting a parallel between the old and the new Nero. According to Cass. Dio *Hist. Rom.* 67.3.1 Domitian repudiated his wife Domitia on a charge of adultery, although he later took her back.[63] *Praetextae*, and tragedies in general, were often intended to encourage their audiences to draw parallels with contemporary topics, sometimes at considerable risk to the tragedian's neck, and often made political statements.[64] This, at any rate, was how Maternus wanted his *Cato* and his imminent *Thyestes* to be received. Yet allusion to contemporary individuals

[63] This appears to be a recurrent story pattern of imperial Rome; cf. Cassius Dio, *Hist. Rom.* 59.23, where a somewhat similar story is told of Gaius' first wife, in connection with whose repudiation some upheaval erupted in Rome.

[64] The tragedian Scaurus was put to death by Tiberius for allegedly insulting the *princeps* in his *Atreus* (cf. Tac. *Ann.* 6.29.5; Cass. Dio *Hist. Rom.* 58.24). In Suet. *Dom.* 10.4 Domitian is said to have had Helvidius Priscus junior executed (probably in 93) on the pretext that allusions to Domitian's divorce from his wife were contained in his interlude *Paris and Oenone*: cf. Griffin, *CAH*[2] xi (2000), 67 and n. 328.

and to specific events does not seem to feature prominently in the play, although generally an antityrannical, constitutional atmosphere can be recognized.

Perhaps more interestingly, a distinct parallel can be traced between the way in which Tacitus portrays senatorial behaviour during the years of Domitian's rule[65] and the words with which the *chorus Romanorum* of the *praetexta* describe their subservience to Nero and what amounted to a betrayal of the Claudian house.

Curiatius Maternus, one of the protagonists of Tacitus' *Dialogus*, and possibly the σοφιστής executed under Domitian 'for declaiming against tyranny' (Cass. Dio-Xiph. *Hist. Rom.* 67.12.5), wrote *praetextae* under Nero and in the early Flavian period. A possible candidate for the authorship of *Octavia*, Ritter thought in 1843, but the nature of the evidence does not allow more than wishful thinking on the subject.

The *Vita Persii* designated Annaeus Cornutus as a *tragicus . . . sectae stoicae*, and confusion between *Annaeus Seneca* and *Annaeus Cornutus* would neatly account for the false attribution of *Octavia* in the corpus, but the line of the *Vita* has long been put in doubt either as a gloss or as containing a corruption (of *grammaticus*), and at any rate Cornutus was probably no longer alive under Domitian.[66]

A persistence of interest in the Neronian period is attested up to the reign of Trajan: Pliny the Younger speaks of one Fannius who died leaving an unfinished work on eminent men

65 Cf. Tac. *Agr.* 2.3 *memoriam quoque ipsam cum uoce perdidissemus, si tam in nostra potestate esset obliuisci quam tacere*; 3.2 *pauci et, ut* <*ita*> *dixerim, non modo aliorum sed etiam nostri superstites sumus*; 45.1 *mox nostrae duxere Heluidium in carcerem manus.* See ad 288 ff. *nos quoque nostri sumus immemores.*

66 It has been suggested that the sentence referred originally to Seneca, mentioned shortly after: cf. M. Hertz, *De Scaevo Memore poeta tragico commentariolum* (Breslau, 1869), 5, n. 4. Equally speculative was Delrius's suggestion that the hypothetic *Annaeus* who fathered *Octavia* should be identified with *Annius* (or *Annaeus*) *Florus*, whom he thought to be related to the *Annaei* on the basis of the *gentilicium*. One of the putative three individuals into whom this character has disintegrated in modern times can be ascribed to the Domitianic age, the author of the incomplete dialogue on Vergil, but not much can be said with certainty about him.

killed or relegated under Nero.[67] Juvenal's satires, with their frequent allusions to the many legends flourishing around the Julio-Claudians, show them to be still a topic of interest in his time; Seneca too does not fail to be mentioned in Juvenal, where he is opposed to Nero as good to evil. In its reminiscences of the Julio-Claudians, *Octavia* may be as bookish as Juvenal's allusions.

No direct argument can be adduced against the possibility of the play being much later than the events it represents, although numerous considerations make this hypothesis less attractive, such as the conspicuous absence of any recognizable influence of Tacitus' works, the poet's accuracy in his handling of titles and even the minutiae of Claudian etiquette, or the 'modernist' imitation of Senecan tragedy and prose, in an age which was soon to revive the authors of early Latin.

The case for a much later date has been examined by Nordmeyer. One of his main points is that the author of *Octavia* shows himself an informed contemporary in his use of the titles of the imperial house.[68] *Diuus Claudius* completely disappears

[67] Cf. Plin. *Epist.* 5.5.3; on *exitus*-literature cf. F. Marx, *Philologus* 92 (1937), 83–103.

[68] Nordmeyer (1892), 286, drew attention to the accurate use of *Augusta*, only with reference to Agrippina. Compare, by contrast, *meretrix Augusta* of Messalina in Juv. *Sat.* 6.118, with Courtney's note (and of course coin legends in the Greek East). A similarly inaccurate use of this title can be identified in Cass. Dio-Xiph., *Hist. Rom.* 62.13 ἐν δὲ τῇ Ῥώμῃ ὁ Νέρων Ὀκταβίαν τὴν Αὔγουσταν ἀπεπέμψατο. The last dated occurrence of *Diuus Claudius* in a private inscription (except sparse instances in legal literature, where survival of the title says nothing with regard to the actual survival of the cult in everyday life) is the epitaph of Crescens the charioteer, commemorating victories obtained in the circus games that were held on Claudius' birthday: *post* AD 124, *ILS* 5285, discussed by Mommsen, *Ephem. Epigr.* 4.82. The last record of the *natalis diui Claudii* on 1 August in an extant official calendar is in the Feriale Duranum (dated *c.* AD 223–227), which was not known to Nordmeyer and Charlesworth. Cf. R. O. Fink-A. S. Hoey-W. F. Snyder, 'The Feriale Duranum' *YCS* 7 (1940), 183–4. The entry in the Dura-Europos calendar proves Nordmeyer and Charlesworth (*JRS*, 27 (1937), 59) to have been wrong when they both independently suggested that the name of Claudius was ousted by that of Pertinax, whose *natalis* recurred on the same day: in the Feriale Duranum both emperors' names figure on that date.

only after the beginning of the third century (though it already went out of common use after the end of the first), alongside the cult of that emperor in the official calendars of the Empire.[69] Even so, the accuracy of the anonymous poet in his use of titles could be explained on a purely antiquarian basis, rather than by appealing to contemporary cult. Having access to well-informed sources, the author would naturally be aware of the divine status of Claudius and consequently apply the appellative *diuus* to him. A foil for the playwright's accuracy is provided by the crass ignorance of, or perhaps disregard for, historical truth exhibited by the epistolary exchange of Paul and Seneca, a fourth-century fabrication where, in a rather cavalier manner, late Roman and Neronian freely meet.[70]

There is nothing in the *praetexta* showing influence from Tacitus,[71] and *Octavia* transmits evidence which Tacitus seems to have overlooked.[72] Tacitus' characterization of Octavia is rather different from the sketch we have in the play. In the *Annales* Octavia is a passive figure of quiet endurance, singularly unappealing to a dramatist's imagination.[73] Notice however that the *ignotus'* use of Flavian historiography is not a conclusive argument on its own to date the play before Tacitus: Cassius Dio, writing in the third century, certainly had access to those historians, and he seems to have used their works more than those of Tacitus.

69 As Charlesworth, *JRS* 27 (1937), 57–60, unaware of Nordmeyer's arguments (1892), 293–308, also showed.

70 Cf. A. D. Momigliano, *Note sulla leggenda del Cristianesimo di Seneca*, in *Contributo alla storia degli studi classici* (Roma, 1955), 13–32, esp. 16–17 on the language of the *Correspondence*.

71 See Ladek (1891), *passim*. I have tried to show that Tacitus knew *Octavia* and made use of it in *Ann.* 14.63–4 in *HSCPh* 98 (1998), 339–56.

72 Tacitus knows, or says, nothing of: (1) Acte's *monumenta* (*Oct.* 196) (2) Poppaea's pregnancy as a decisive reason for Nero to hasten the divorce (591); (3) the tears of Agrippina on Britannicus' pyre (170–2); (4) the removal of Agrippina's *tituli* (611).

73 Cf. Tac. *Ann.* 13.16 *adfectus abscondere didicerat.*

4. *OCTAVIA* AND THE SENECAN CORPUS

The language and style of the play

How *Octavia* came to be included in the corpus is a topic of speculation. Seneca's appearance in the play, the pervasive adaptation of Senecan material, the documentary evidence provided by the play on Seneca's relationship with Nero, are the most obvious elements which at some time prompted an ancient editor to include *Octavia* in the Senecan corpus. The likeliest scenario is that the play was attributed to Seneca by some late-antique editor with an antiquarian penchant.[74] I am inclined to doubt whether the play was written as an intentional fake. *Octavia* was composed with the implicit aim of exculpating Seneca, who is portrayed as an advocate of 'constitutional' monarchy and as an innocent adviser of the *princeps*, powerless to restrain the autocrat's fury (see *infra*, 70–5).

Of the different arguments on the basis of which Senecan authorship of the play can be disproved, language and style are perhaps the most conclusive. The *praetexta* stands out in the corpus of Senecan tragedy as a very peculiar literary artifact. Senecan tragedy is a significant representative of a highly rhetorical style, modelled *in primis* in the Ovidian mould. But the author of *Octavia* shows very little awareness of the dominant *elegantiae* in fashion, and lives on the margins of the literary field.[75] Even if the author may have been influenced by the Flavian critique of Seneca, especially adverse to the philosopher's abundance of sharply pointed *sententiae*, the impeded and difficult flow of the style of *Octavia* seems to tell a different story.

One important indicator of individual linguistic idiosyncrasies is the different use of particles, adverbs and conjunctions, which

[74] Tarrant argued for a very late inclusion (early thirteenth century); cf. *Agam.* Introd., 59–60. MacGregor, *Philologus* 122 (1978), 103 also favours a late date. Zwierlein, *Prolegomena*, 43, dates the inclusion to the sixth century.

[75] Cf. Richter (1862), 3 'omnino . . . in hac fabula desideramus exuberantem illam . . . orationis abundantiam.'

I regard as a less conspicuous and therefore less controllable factor in composition. Richter[76] was the first to draw attention to the repeated occurrence of *mox* for *deinde* (at 45, 166, 409, 418, 688, 831, 938, 956), a sense which occurs only once in the other tragedies of the corpus (in this I henceforth include, except when explicitly stated otherwise, *H.O.*).[77]

I also consider significant the extensive postponement of prepositions and conjunctions in the play. Trajection of particles and a somewhat mannerist use of the enclitic *-que*[78] are the most common devices used to get round the problems of metrical composition, especially that of managing a short syllable for the third element. In comparison with the easy flow of the iambic verse in Seneca, the contortions of the word-order and the frequently strained hyperbata occurring in *Octavia* contribute to the picture of a poet with much poorer compositional skills.[79] These elements should not be taken as relevant to the absolute dating of the play. Most differences from Seneca in this area appear to reflect different levels of stylistic elaboration rather than a chronologically more evolved state of the language: *Octavia* exhibits an even more artificial Latin than Seneca.

et is postponed after one word at 256, 329, 387, 478, 516b; after two at 418; after three at 688. Postponement of this conjunction is common in Seneca as well, but only after one word.

atque is postponed after one word at 110, 165, 244, 474, 561; postponement of *atque* occurs only once in the corpus (*Agam.* 418, though *tantis* might be interpreted as an *apo koinou*; *Thy.* 912 in ***E***). Trajection of *atque* is elsewhere rare in poetry (only three cases in *TLL* ii, s.v., 1050.6–9).

-que is attached to the second word from the sentence beginning in 153, 361, 363 (see ad loc.), with no parallels in Senecan tragedy.

76 Other arguments adduced by Richter are inconclusive, such as the absence of adjectives in *-ficus*, of *retro*, the relative infrequency of *at*; the occurrence of *confestim* (439) and *ut ne* (870), neither ever found in Seneca.

77 *Hf.* 458; cf. ad 166.

78 For which, however, there were precedents in Seneca as well; cf. ad 544.

79 Helm (1934), 318.

nec is postponed after one word at 511, 573, 783, 823, 836; after three at 609, after four at 402.

nam is always postponed (108, 714, 718). *nam* is never postponed in the corpus and rarely elsewhere: once in Hor. *Carm.* 4.14.9 (cf. Norden, Verg. *Aen.* 6, p. 394).

namque is postponed at 9 (never elsewhere in the corpus, where the word occurs 7 times): cf. Zwierlein, *KK* ad *Oct.* 9.

aut is postponed after two words at 421 (*TLL* ii, s.v., 1565.18–21: only in Ovid and post-Ovidian poetry; in the corpus cf. *Hf.* 212).[80]

Figures on *cum* are given ad 732.

Another linguistic indicator of non-Senecan authorship is the presence of exclamatory phrases not found in the authentic plays. *ei* (*mihi*) is a common exclamatory particle shunned by Seneca. Not so by his imitators (*Oct.* 150 and in *H.O.* several times; cf. Leo, *Obs.* 68–9). *eheu*, on the other hand, which had a more conspicuous archaic flavour, is never found in *Octavia*.[81] There are no notable morphological deviations from Senecan practice.

Billerbeck (1988) 172–3 has shown that *Octavia* does not diverge significantly from Senecan tragedy in its range of vocabulary. In fact adherence and divergence of lexical items cannot be considered a conclusive criterion in the question of attribution. As pointed out by Zwierlein,[82] the length of the individual tragedies of the corpus is too modest to make them statistically significant for lexical searches: the number of terms in each tragedy

[80] The classic study on postponement of particles is the *Anhang* IIIB.3 in Norden's commentary on Verg. *Aen.* 6 (1957⁴, 402–4); but much useful material, including evidence from post-Ovidian poetry, can be found in J. Marouzeau, *L'ordre des mots* (Paris, 1949), 3.67–120; *LHS* 2.398–9; Maurach, *EP*, 94 and n. 75; P. E. Knox, *Ovid's Metamorphoses and the Tradition of Augustan Poetry* (Cambridge, 1986), 88–90. The prevailing interpretation of this phenomenon is that poets affect postponement in imitation of a practice of Hellenistic poetry. In Latin this practice affects elegiac and satiric poetry more than epic. V. Tandoi (*Scritti*, 2.710) regards this as a particularly prominent phenomenon in poets imitating Ovid.

[81] Only *heu me* (*Oct.* 31, 169) is Senecan (*Troad.* 476, 681; *Phae.* 898, 997, 1173; *H.O.* 1761).

[82] (1992), 504, n. 10, with figures.

unparalleled in the rest of the corpus is higher than the number of *hapax legomena* in *Octavia* within Senecan tragedy, yet this does not raise concerns about the authorship of any of them. The list of *Octavia* words not present in Senecan tragedy would still be compatible with Senecan authorship. Indeed, one conclusion emerging from Billerbeck's list regards the poet's effort to resemble Senecan tragedy as far as possible.[83] When he endeavours to reach out beyond that scope, he looks for inspiration from the Augustan poets, mainly Vergil and Ovid.

Octavia shares with Senecan tragedy the selective vocabulary of the Augustan poets,[84] to which we can trace the vast majority of the idioms and phrases present in both Seneca and *Octavia*.[85] More markedly than Senecan tragedy, however, *Octavia* refrains from verbal coinages and in general also from obsolete or archaic words; compound words are in general avoided.[86] Verbal imitations from Senecan tragedy are mostly notable in line-endings (see *infra*). It is, however, at the level of style and sentence

[83] Words not attested in Senecan tragedy ([*] = occurring in *H.O.*; I have underlined words for which no precedents in Augustan poetry can be found): *adimo, adolescentia, audacia, augustus, breui*[*], *caelestis*[*], *caenum, clementia, cometa, commendo, comprobo, confestim, confirmo, consecro, cratis, dementia, destruit, discidium, effigies*[*], *ei mihi*[*], *enitor, excubo, falso* (adv.), *firmus, flammeum, foedo, illucesco*[*], *impietas, inrumpo, insitiuus, insociabilis, intermitto, iuste, luxuria, monumentum, naufragium*[*], *no, obsequium, ominor, praecipio, praefectus, praepotens, princeps, proauus*[*], *probitas, procreo, proueho, recolo, reticeo, satelles, senatus, senesco, singuli, solor, spondeo*[*], *studium, stulte, udus.*

[84] Only 5% of Senecan diction is not found in the works of either Vergil, Ovid or Horace (Billerbeck, 1–2), and even then, the 'unauthorized' words are often new formations, mainly nominal compounds, rather than vulgarisms, colloquialisms, and prosaic words (Billerbeck, 35). In this, Seneca follows a trend already well established in Roman poetry, esp. in Horace (e.g. *Carm.* 2.14.9–11 *(unda) scilicet omnibus . . . enauiganda*), but also in Vergil and Ovid (cf. Kenney, *Style*, 125, 149, on Ov. *Met.* 2.605 *indeuitato . . . telo*).

[85] Some typically poetical phrases of *Oct.* are not found in the Senecan corpus, e.g. *litare* + double accusative; *parce* + infinitive as a periphrastic alternative for the negative imperative; *inuideo* + infinitive; *ualeo* + infinitive; *cesso* + infinitive.

[86] *Oct.* lacks for instance adjectives in *-ficus, -ger, -fer*, which can frequently be found in Senecan tragedy (see Billerbeck, 38–42). For the use of long adjectives at line-end see ad 541; 870.

construction that the peculiar position occupied by *Octavia* within the Senecan corpus becomes especially clear. In addition, *Octavia* exhibits numerous cases of repeated expressions, which acquire the status of fillers or near-formulae, betraying a poet less at ease in composition.

One feature conspicuously absent is that pattern of pleonastic descriptions and participial constructions which contributes so much to the impression of baroque artificiality experienced by readers of Senecan tragedy. Octavia's first song (1–8) is clearly reminiscent of Sen. *Hf.* 125–151, but a close reading of the two passages (set out below) shows that the poet of *Octavia* does not take from Seneca more than an initial cue.

Iam uaga caelo sidera fulgens
Aurora fugat.
surgit Titan radiante coma
mundoque diem reddit clarum.
Age, tot tantis onerata malis
repete assuetos iam tibi questus
atque aequoreas uince Alcyonas,
uince et uolucres Pandionias.

Oct. 1–8

Iam rara micant sidera prono
languida mundo, nox uicta uagos
contrahit ignes luce renata,
cogit nitidum Phosphoros agmen;
signum celsi glaciale poli
septem stellis Arcados ursae
lucem uerso temone uocat.
iam caeruleis euectus aquis
Titan summa prospicit Oeta;
iam Cadmeis incluta Bacchis
aspersa die dumeta rubent
Phoebique fugit reditura soror.
[. . .]
pendet summo stridula ramo
pinnasque nouo tradere soli
gestit querulos inter nidos
Thracia paelex,
turbaque circa confusa sonat
murmure mixto testata diem.

Hf. 125–151

The Senecan passage combines linguistic sophistication (abundance of descriptive ablatives, fondness for expanded noun groups: cf. *signum celsi glaciale poli | septem stellis Arcados ursae*) and attention to detail, exploiting all possibilities of the traditional rhetoric of sunrise. His dawn is a mosaic of vignettes sketched in the 'idyllic' style (Bootes gathering his stars; Procne sitting among her young ones). The comparison is instructive in bringing to light the different poetical agendas of the two writers. Admittedly, the relaxed, descriptive pace of the first choral ode in *Hf.* fits in rather awkwardly with the drama of Megara and Amphitryon as sketched at the beginning of the play, whereas the less elaborate, almost offhand description of the new day in Octavia's initial lament might be taken to reveal a keener interest in characterization and dramatic relevance.

Overall, the poet of *Octavia* plays down the style of Senecan tragedy, gravitating toward unspecific, generically 'poetic' words and phrases, frequently repeated: euphemisms for death like *exstinctus, scelere interemptus, ademptus, raptus, ereptus*; threadbare metaphors like *flagrare odio, incendere ira pectus, exstinguere sanguine, pignora* for children, and common metonymies like *thalamus* for marriage (but not "wife" as in Seneca), *ignes* for *faces, uultus* for *oculi, penates* for *domus.* Other common literary idioms found in the play are *post fata, gradum ecferre / inferre, poenas dare.*

These and other similar idioms occur frequently in Senecan tragedy as well. What is striking in *Octavia* is the absence of *variatio*: the same idioms are repeated two or more times across the play, which gives an idea of the limited range of literary solutions available to this poet. The originally Vergilian *post fata* (*Aen.* 4.20 *miseri post fata Sychaei*), to give just one example, occurs four times (96, 112, 289, 529): clearly, it has simply become a formula for 'after the death of', without the poignancy of its original source. One cannot escape the feeling that the frequency of such high-flown, typically poetic expressions, just as high as in Seneca, or even higher, is a feeble attempt to compensate for the author's comparative weakness in the composition of more elaborate syntactical units.

The phrase *parentis* . . . + a form of possessive pronoun, for instance, occurs four times (*p.* . . . *tui* 137; *p.* . . . *tuae* 271; *p.* . . . *suae* 416; *p.* . . . *sui* 481) in the same metrical position, to accommodate a convenient short syllable for the *elementum breve* of the last metron; *thalamis tuis*, with little variations, occurs six times at line-end (131, 252, 755 *thalamis meis*, 120 *in thalamos meos*, 690 *[coniugis] thalamis tui*, 718 *thalamos meos*).[87] Formularity, whatever its possible extent in early drama, was clearly avoided by Seneca: the constant repetition of the same syntagms at line-end in *Octavia* would have met with, one imagines, a condescending reception by the sophisticated audience of the recitation hall.

Periodic construction, in Seneca, is simple and made up of neat syntactic blocks, short and incisive.[88] In this respect, Senecan tragedy develops a tendency long established in Latin poetry, whereby the long chains of subordinate sentences so typical of prose discourse are replaced by appositive word-groups or by ablatival constructions. *Octavia* lacks the clipped style and the pointed *sententiae* of its model: the flow of the argument is hampered by longer, unbalanced and tortuous sentences, sprouting from one another without an apparent plan (111–14). Relative clauses, the most common type of subordinates in *Octavia*, are made to follow one another, as in a rambling sequence with no concentration.[89] *Octavia* links successive phrases making them depend asyndetically on the same connective (cf. 38–40 *cuius imperio fuit | subiectus orbis, paruit liber diu | Oceanus et recepit inuitus rates*; 41–4 *en qui Britannis primus imposuit iugum, | ignota tantis classibus texit freta | interque gentes barbaras tutus fuit | et saeua maria;* 45–7 *mox illa nati* (sc. *occidit*), *cuius extinctus iacet | frater uenenis, maeret infelix soror | eademque coniunx . . .*). Another transitional, high-falutin formula of which this poet is fond is *atque idem/eadem*: it is found

[87] For repetition of similar expressions cf. 26 (*modo cui totus paruit orbis*), 39; 45 (*mox illa nati*), 166; 10, 167; 86, 222; 89, 240; 105, 950; 24, 594; 32, 150; 282, 535; 54, 784 (*sed . . . uires capit*); 79, 958 (*mittit ad umbras*); 84–5, 177; 11, 650 (*causa malorum*); 124, 270 (*renouare luctus*); 17, 722 (*sparsa cruore*); 49, 132 (*odio . . . flagrat*); 370, 733, 752 (*ensem condere*); 375, 629–30 (*animam reddere*); 243, 521 (*hausit cruorem*); 96, 112, 289, 529 (*post fata*: in Sen. only twice, *Agam.* 38; *Troad.* 654); 250, 412[bis] (*premere iugo*); 264, 608, 830 (*sanguine extinguere* i.e. *iram, odia, faces*); 275, 670 (*totiens iactata*); 279, 938 (*pignora pacis*); 272, 304 (*poenas dedit*); 330, 906 (*spes est nulla salutis*); 331, 902 (*uicta malis*); 286, 357; 363, 605 (*ingens geminat . . . nefas*); 372, 643, 824 (*qui/quae tale[m] tulit*); 109, 124 (*miserae mihi*). Cf. Helm (1934), 321.

[88] See ad 34, 108, 599.

[89] See ad 45–7, 126–8; 908.

in Vergil and Ovid, but in *Octavia* this formula, repeatedly deployed, produces an impression of uninventive rhetoric.[90] I give as an example of the author's flat construction of his sentences the long period at *Oct.* 108–14

> poena nam grauior nece est
> uidere tumidos et truces miserae mihi
> uultus tyranni, iungere atque hosti oscula,
> timere nutus, [*sc.* Neronis] cuius obsequium meus
> haud ferre posset fata post fratris dolor
> scelere interempti, cuius imperium tenet
> et sorte gaudet auctor infandae necis.

Compare, for contrast, Stat. *Theb.* 3.409–13, which gives an apt idea of how it was possible to turn even potentially unwieldy constructions into a sophisticated bravura piece:

> cui turba profundi
> Nereos et rapidis adcurrunt passibus Horae
> frenaque et auratae textum sublime coronae
> deripiunt, laxant calidis umentia loris
> pectora.

Observe in particular how in the Statius passage the syntactical dependence on the initial *cui* is obliterated by the elaborate description of the Sun, as the Horae assist him in taking off his robes (trappings, coronet) and unharnessing his chariot.

Such constructions tend, instead, to be found outside the corpus of canonical Latin poets, wary of repetition and fastidiously addicted to rhetorical polish. I will give as a parallel a funerary epigram (first cent. AD), *CE* Buech. 1119.3–5, where a similar sequence of interchained relative clauses is found:

> fatum miserabile cernis:
> Parcae nam impubem quem rapuere mihi
> maeret cara soror quae fratrem luget ademptum.

[90] See ad 45–7; 164–5.

In this epigram, the heavy-going sense-structure is generated by the juxtaposition of ready-made half-lines, and the parallel is telling in suggesting the literary status of *Octavia*.[91] Like a lapidary poet, he has a mind full of remembered verse, but is ill at ease with the tools of those who had made them. Almost paradoxically, the comparatively modest figure cut by *Octavia* under the profile of stylistic elaboration makes *Octavia* all the more interesting as a representative of the context of Silver Latin literary production.

Relative position of adjectives and nouns

In iambics, the number of lines filled by two nouns and two adjectives is not high. I have counted 52 cases, compared with 114 in *Oed.* and 95 in *Agam.* The two favourite types in Augustan literature are *abAB* and *abBA*, of which there are in *Oct.* respectively 4 and 5 occurrences, to compare with *Hf.* 33/15; *Oed.* 22/11; *Agam.* 25/12; *Med.* 9/5; *Phoe.* 9/6; *Thy.* 5/12. Even considering that the length of these plays varies considerably, the difference between *Octavia* and Senecan tragedy is significant.

Fitch[92] made a significant contribution towards the relative dating of Seneca's plays. He observed that the incidence of sense-pauses within iambic lines significantly increases from *Agam.* to *Thyestes.* There is now widespread agreement that *Thyestes* and *Phoenissae* are the latest plays. The figures relating to the combination of nouns and adjectives within metrical units can be brought into line with Fitch's data. As was perhaps to be expected, the ratio of Golden and Silver lines decreases in plays where the frequency of syntactical breaks at mid-line is highest, that is in the allegedly 'late' plays.

[91] For more parallels of this use of relative pronouns cf. Rosén, *Latine loqui*, 167 (on the so-called continuative-expanding relative clauses in Plautus); on accumulation of relative connectives in late or vulgar authors cf. *LHS* 2.821; G. Schepss, *ALL* 3 (1886), 323.

[92] *AJPh* 102 (1981) 289–307. Fitch is right, to my mind, to consider sense-pauses as a determining factor.

Octavia exhibits contrasting features in this respect. The frequency of Golden/Silver patterns is low (the nearest figures in Seneca come from *Phoe.* and *Thy.*), yet under the heading 'sense-pauses at mid-line' *Octavia* ranges with Seneca's 'early' dramas, where figures for lines in which traditional noun-adjective patterns occur are highest. In *Oct.*, out of 297 sense-pauses (including speaker-changes), I have counted 91 pauses within the line. This (*c.* 31%) ranges the *praetexta* along with Seneca's 'early' period (*Agam.*, *Oed.*, *Troad.*). I interpret this as one of the marked features pointing to the play's less elaborate stylistic and literary composition.

The relative rarity of the more elaborate patterns of verbal composition in *Octavia* is not due to a recognizable intention to approach a more colloquial level of speech, as Flinck argued (why should *praetextae* be more realistic than mythological tragedies?). In addition, the high number of end-stopped lines in the *praetexta* and consequent rarity of *enjambement* compares with that of the 'early' plays of Seneca, where indeed Golden and Silver lines occur in the highest numbers.

Often, however, these adjectives are banal, *tantus, tristis, noster, dirus, miser.* Helm[93] provides interesting figures on word-usage, contrasting *Octavia* with the rest of the corpus: cf., for instance, the use of *tristis* in *Oct.* (21 out of a total of 61 in the other tragedies including *H.O.*); *diu* (16:43);[94] *saeuus* (34:111); *dirus* (23:71).

Metrics and prosody

The iambic trimeter of *Octavia* is modelled on the same pattern as Seneca's, who in his turn adhered to what is thought to have become the standard practice of the imperial age. The deviations of *Octavia* from Senecan precedent are at most sporadic, although our understanding of imperial metrical practice is considerably

[93] (1934), 314.

[94] Especially common at line-end: cf. *Oct.* 39, 190, 194, 429, 479, 515, 523, 540, 663, 669, 798, 846, 940*, 956.

weakened by the loss of comparative evidence (Augustan drama). In the few cases in which a given metrical usage of *Octavia* has no parallels in Seneca, the possibility exists that the *ignotus* is following the lead of earlier dramatic models, Augustan, if not archaic.[95]

Porson's law often falls into abeyance, in Seneca, because of the concomitant (and stronger) 'rule' of replacing the third *indifferens* with a *longum*. Consequently, the sequence ⏑/ – ⏑ ⏓ (/ = word-end), permitted in Greek tragedy, is generally speaking impossible in Seneca. Final cretics are freely admitted if coalescing with the preceding word or if preceded by a monosyllable.[96] More rarely, a consonant-initial word of cretic quantity at line-end can be preceded by a spondaic word (e.g. *nato sospite*), a sequence which must have been felt disruptive to rhythm. A line-ending of the type *uoces amoue* is even more rare.[97]

[95] The principal points of difference between the tragic senarius and the Hellenizing trimeter adopted by Seneca (and in Augustan tragedy) are: the introduction of an obligatory short in the third and seventh element; the prevalence of disyllabic line-endings, usually preceded by a spondee- or molossus-shaped word; greater regularity in the system of caesurae; restraint in the deployment of synaloephe; avoidance of specific types, such the coalescing of a long syllable into a short element: cf. Soubiran, (1966) 568, 610; (1984b) 86; and especially before caesura: Soubiran (1987), 113. Within this context, certain elements of Senecan drama stand out as recognizable hints at early drama, such as the deployment of longer compounds at line-end: Soubiran (1964), 457, n. 1.

[96] In Greek tragedy, exceptions to Porson's Law are attested with monosyllabic prepositives (e.g. articles), elided, trochee-shaped non-lexicals, or spondee-shaped non-lexicals (cf. Devine-Stephens *PGS*, 309–18 for figures and examples), but these linguistic distinctions may not have been operating in Roman versification, which is the outcome of a crystallization of Greek practice. In post-Classical Greek drama, infringements of Porson's Law can also be observed in the *Exagōgē*: cf. B. Snell, *Glotta* 44 (1966), 25–32 (elided lexicals before the final cretic).

[97] Vowel-initial final words of cretic quantity not in synaloephe with the preceding (non monosyllabic) word occur in the authentic plays only ten times (Strzelecki (1938), 19, e.g. *Hf.* 397 *agedum efferatas rabida uoces amoue*), twice in *H.O.* This, incidentally, suggests that 173 could be retained in the form transmitted by *recc. flamma feruens abstulit*, correcting *A*'s unmetrical *feruens flamma abstulit*. See ad loc.

Octavia stands alone in the corpus in not exhibiting the type *nato sospite*. The only certain infraction is 393 *genus impium*, which does violate Porson's law also in the laxer form valid for Seneca, since the final creticus is neither preceded by a monosyllable nor in synaloephe. This is the only line in the corpus, alongside three others from *H.O.* (406, 757, 1847) where a fifth-foot anapaest is 'broken', i.e. the resolved element is separated from the arsis.[98] The metrical type *nato sospite* also fails to emerge in *H.O.*, which is in line with Senecan practice in its treatment of Porson's law.

In other respects, the metrical practice of *Octavia* is more restrictive and rigid than Seneca's – a feature which can perhaps be brought into line with the poet's more self-conscious approach to composition. *Octavia* has no cases of first-element synaloephe, as e.g. *Agam.* 274 *quae Europam.*[99] The initial sequence ∪ / ∪ – (e.g. *Phae.* 726 *fer opem*; 948 *fer abominandam*) is only found once (*Oct.* 844 *sed adesse*); there are no monosyllabic line-endings of the type *Phae.* 713 *et hic* | *contactus ensis* . . . Synaloephe of a long element in a short vowel is also avoided.

Like Seneca, the author of *Octavia* constructs his lines with two main caesurae, after the fifth element and after the seventh. Either caesura (but not both) can be replaced by diaeresis after the fourth or the eighth element. Caesurae are, however, occasionally obscured by the occurrence of synaloephe (although never with syntactical break), on which the praxis of *Oct.* appears less strict than Seneca's own.[100]

[98] Cf. Schmidt (1860), 53; Strzelecki (1938), 83.

[99] Cf. Schmidt (1860), 19–20, Richter (1862), 4; Zwierlein (1977), 165. *Agamemnon* is usually placed among the 'early' plays. Richter also noted that the sequence of first epitrites (∪ – – –) as well as words of five syllables (∪ – ∪∪ –) before the final iamb (e.g. *superbifica manu*), frequent in the Senecan corpus, is not found in *Octavia*. See Richter 18 n. 3 on *Oct.* 632: in Seneca, words scanned as ∪∪ – or ∪∪∪ – receive the metrical *ictus* invariably on the first and last syllables (e.g. *cíneribús*).

[100] For specific discussion of problems relating to the absence or irregularity of incisions in *Oct.* within the corpus see ad 446, 447, 457; 482, 564. Fifth-foot caesura is marked by a conjunction (*ne, cum*) in 146, 467; but these cases are not especially significant. Seneca allows prepositions to stand before penthemimeres. This has no parallels in *Oct.*

The only prosodical peculiarity is the occurrence (in 273) of *modo* scanned with a long final *o*. *Octavia* does not share Seneca's (apparently) late preference for short final *-os*, or at least sides with his more conservative early plays.[101] Final *-o* in *Octavia* (I do not take into account the final *anceps*) is long on thirteen occasions, and shortened only on three. Observe also that *modo* is very rarely long, in any genres (instances given *ad* 273).[102]

Anapaest colometry

In *Octavia* the majority of the deviations from Senecan practice appear to occur in the composition of anapaests. The following phenomena are not strictly speaking unparalleled in Seneca, but the number of occurrences in *Octavia* alone is often greater than their total in the entire corpus (cf. also Zwierlein, *Prolegomena*, 193–4).

1. hiatus in the middle of a sentence[103]
2. *brevis in longo*, except at period-end[104]
3. hiatus and *brevis in longo*[105]
4. holospondaic anapaests (eight instances, against a total of ten in the remaining plays)

[101] Cf. Fitch (1981) 289–307 on the different treatment of final *-o* in Seneca's early and late plays.

[102] At the *elementum indifferens*: 144, 199 *cupido*; 177 *obsequendo*; 254 *quaeso*; 397, 424 *uirgo*; 405 *ultro*; 432 *libido*; 531 *occuparo*; 725 *subito*; 844 *cerno*; occupying the *longum* (not lengthened *positione*) or providing the arsis in anapaests: 216, 219, 283 *Iuno*; 273 *modo*; 274 *falso*; 296 *uirgo*; 299 *libido*; 532 *fundaro*; 548 *perpetuo*; 658 *ero*; 683 *imago*; 807 *cupido*; 907 *cerno*; occupying the *breve* or, in anapaests, the second short syllable of an anapaestic thesis or resolved arsis: 425 *cupido*; 205, 206, 764, 766 *modo*.

[103] *Oct.* 16, 21, 206, 362, 374, 686, 778, 897, 936.

[104] *Oct.* 26, 28, 62, 67, 93*, 204, 297, 306, 319, 658(*-o*), 768, 776, 890, 899, 926 (text uncertain), 955, 964, 978.

[105] *Octavia* 17, 335, 936, 975. Leo, *Obs.* 98: the simultaneous occurrence of hiatus and *syll. anc.* in anapaests is only paralleled in *Agam.* 79, 646, 652 (a play now dated to Seneca's early period). Hiatus or *syll. anc.* at the end of a line occurs 10 times in *H.O.*; 31 times in *Oct.* and 11 in *Agam.*

5. the sequence of dactyl and anapaest, only found in *Oct.* (twice) and *H.O.* 185, 196, 1884, 1888 (see my note ad 646)[106]
6. laxer attitude towards synaloephe/apheresis[107]

Following the lead of Leo's *Obs.* 98 ff., editors have opted for dimeters as the main unit of Senecan *cantica*, adhering to MS colometry whenever possible, with *brevis in longo* and hiatus as guiding criteria for the colometric arrangement. The so-called *Kongruenzgesetz*, i.e. the tendency to compose sentences no longer than two metra, based on an observation of the ancient grammarians (Marius Victorinus, *GLK* VI.77.2), is also referred to, although sense-units more often than not extend over three and four (and more: cf. Zwierlein, *Prolegomena*, 190–5) rather than two metra, and across clearly demarcated metrical boundaries, and this 'rule' cannot be regarded as a decisive criterion.[108]

A dissonant voice had been raised by L. Mueller,[109] contending that, unlike those of Greek drama, anapaestic metra in the corpus are composed as independent metrical units (= lines). He was led to this conclusion by the numerous cases of hiatus and *brevis in longo* within the dimeters of the transmitted MS colometry. While this objection can be thought of as largely overruled

[106] Anapaests across three words: *Thy.* 827, 965; *H.O.* 173, 186, 191.

[107] Mantke (1957–8), 115 calculated the proportion of synaloephe in anapaests, which in *Octavia* is much higher than in the rest of the corpus (36: 377 *vs.* 82: 1293). Richter would emend lines in *Oct.* where synaloephe occurs in the last element (9 *grauior namque his fortuna tua est*), but this strict approach has not met with acceptance: see also Mueller, *DRM*, 297. Synaloephe in anapaests or other lyrical lines is found at (cf. Richter, 1862, 20) *Oed.* 739, 993 (*an.*); *Agam.* 684 (*an.*); *H.O.* 1888 (*an.*); *Thy.* 802 (*an.*); 342, 350 (*glyc.*); *Med.* 355 (*an.*); *Troad.* 857 (*hend. sapph.*).

[108] For the principles governing anapaest colometry in modern editions cf. Tarrant, *Agam.* App. 369–70; Zwierlein, *Prolegomena*, 182–3, attempted to make a case for trimeters as a possible unit of colometry in the anapaests of the corpus. In *Oct.*, however, two sequences like 898–9 *quatiunt altas saepe procellae | aut euertit fortuna domos* and 899–900 *quo me trahitis quodue tyrannus | aut exilium regina iubet?* show the limitations of the *Kongruenzgesetz*, because sense-units extend over clearly distinct lines, marked off by, respectively, hiatus (*procellae/aut*), and *syll. anc.* (*tyrannus*).

[109] Esp. *DRM*, 104. Independently, the same contention had been advanced by Richter (1862) 20; so also F. Münscher, *Hermes* 54 (1919), 11.

by a readjustment of the inherited colometry, for instance with the insertion of monometers at period-end, the strict observance of diaeresis across first and second metron, as well as the avoidance of resolution in the fourth element of each metron, makes Mueller's thesis deserving of closer scrutiny.

Mueller's emendation of *Oct.* 779 *aut quid pectore portat anhelo*, to *a. q. portat pectore a.*, has been generally accepted, and is confirmed by the consistent avoidance of resolution of the second arsis throughout the corpus, yet this is unobjectionable, albeit rare, in Greek drama,[110] and is also attested in early Roman tragedy,[111] to say nothing of Plautus, where it is commonplace.

This places Seneca in a distinct position in the tradition of dramatic versification, but is not a strong enough argument for rejecting arrangement by dimeters. The practice of writing continuous 'runs' of marching anapaests as dimeters in drama was ancient and well established,[112] and is therefore quite acceptable for Seneca as well. The possibility exists that Seneca and his imitator(s), although interpreting anapaests as sequences of dimeters, followed stricter metrical principles, and treated them to some extent as if they had been in fact monometers.

One possible consequence of this is that *brevis in longo* can no longer be used as a decisive criterion for demarcating successive dimeters: why should a diaeresis after the first metron prohibit resolution of the second arsis if not because the concomitant pause was perceived as protracting the final element? We either allow the resolved *pec(tore)* to stand in 779, or renounce the belief that *brevis in longo* is permitted only at the end of a dimeter (hiatus is treated by Greek poets as a somewhat different and more extreme phenomenon).[113] In *Octavia* this might hold the key to such disputed MS colometric arrangements as 890–1 *plura referre*

110 Cf. West, *GM*, 95; M. C. Martinelli, *Gli strumenti del poeta* (Bologna, 1995), 159–60.

111 Cf. Enn. *Trag.* 87 Joc. *o pater o patria o Priami domus*, with note ad loc. Later, Laeuius 7 Courtn. *corpore pectoreque undique obeso ac*, if anapaestic, also exhibits a dactylic second foot.

112 Cf. M. L. West, *BICS* 24 (1977), 89–94.

113 Cf. C. Questa, *Introduzione alla metrica di Plauto* (Bologna, 1967), 146–9.

prohibet praesens | exempla dolor, where Zwierlein divides after *referre*, which cannot be lengthened by *muta cum liquida* (see ad loc.), and even proposes, as an alternative, to write *referri*.

If there is a pause at the end of the first metron, as the constant observance of diaeresis / caesura seems to suggest, as well as the absence of resolution of the second arsis, the widely held opinion that the occurrence of *brevis in longo / syll. anc.* should be used as a marker for line-end is weakened, because this effect is produced by the selfsame cause (recitation pause) which prohibits resolution, namely the indifference of the corresponding element. Hiatus and sense-pause become our only two guiding criteria in establishing the colometry of Senecan anapaestic lyrics.

The alternative interpretation is that Latin dramatists of the imperial age were under the influence of some metrical theorist who had observed the comparative rarity of fourth element resolutions in Greek drama, and had raised this to the status of a rule. The separation of the no-resolution rule from *brevis in longo* at the diaeresis would be yet another instance of the rigidity with which Greek metra are adapted to Latin versification. Horace, in his adaptations of Sapphic and Alcaic metra, shows parallel inconsistencies in the treatment of cola which were not separate lines in his models (hiatus in Hor. *Carm.* 1.12.7; 1.2.47 (*sapph.*), before the final adonius).

Composition and imitation

Our perception of the relationship between the plays of the corpus and the *praetexta* is certainly affected by the loss of Roman tragedy, although it is difficult to determine to what extent. The recurrence of identical or near-identical line-endings in *Octavia* and in the other plays of the corpus (cf. APPENDIX A) suggests a very close link, but the question arises whether these similarities might not go back to established dramatic versification, which we cannot trace any more.[114] Other Roman dramatists

[114] For a more detailed discussion of the place of *Oct.* in the Roman dramatic tradition see 'Tradition and Imitation in Pseudo-Seneca *Octauia*', *Prudentia*

had adopted the Greek trimeter before Seneca, and we might reasonably assume that the poet of *Octavia* turned to them as well for inspiration. The disyllabic line-ending, which, following a Senecan trend, has become almost a rule in *Octavia* (as a sequence of two final words – –/ ∪ – or as ∪ ∪ – –/ ∪ – or as – ∪∪ –/ ∪ –), was certainly typical of Augustan tragedy as well.[115] Thus the impression of formulaic composition presented here and there by *Octavia* might be diminished by a comparison with the tragedies of the Augustan poets, had any survived.

One cannot escape the suspicion that there is nothing intrinsically specific in the similarity between line-endings like *mente horreo* (in *Oct.* 436) and *mente horrui* (*Agam.* 226); *perpetuo manent* (*Oct.* 548 = *Med.* 196); 409 *quod sequi cursu feras* | *auderet acres* and *Phae.* 110 *consequi cursu feras*; *Oct.* 388 *sortis alternae uices* (233 *noctis alterna uice*) and *Phae.* 411 *cuius relucet mundus alterna uice*; *Oct.* 422 *aut petit praedae imminens* and *Oed.* 95 *iam praedae imminens*; *Oct.* 195 *nempe praelatam sibi* and *H.O.* 304 *capta praelata est mihi*. Some of these resemblances are probably coincidental, ready-made *clausulae* helping out in iambic composition, as is the case for epic formulae. *Claudiae gentis decus* (*Oct.* 534) and *gentis Actaeae decus* (*Phae.* 900) suggest an intertextual link; yet *decus* with reference to a person is extremely common in poetry, and a very similar clausula occurs in Mart. *Epigr.* 9.1.8 *Flauiae decus gentis* (*ia. scaz.*). Tradition, rather than direct derivation, might similarly account for the coincidence between *Oct.* 441 *remedium clementia est* and *Oed.* 515 *remedium ignorantia est*: cf. *CRF inc.* 88 R^2 *iniuriarum remedium est obliuio*; Publ. Syr. *Sent.* 96 (106) R^2 *cuiuis dolori remedium est patientia.* The description of the mob overturning Poppaea's statues 797–8 *membra per partes trahunt* | *diducta laqueis* may well imitate Sen. *Thy.* 60–1 *membra per partes eant* | *discerpta*, with the same type of *enjambement* involving a participle; but the iambic *Troiae Halosis* in Petr. *Sat.* 89.1.50 (a description of the sea-snakes

35 (2003 – a monographic issue devoted to the play), where I have stressed more emphatically the role played by Senecan vis-à-vis Republican tragedy, in all technical and stylistic aspects of verse composition.

[115] Soubiran (1987), 113.

dragging their, or Laocoon's, limbs) exhibits a similar line-end pattern *membraque ad terram trahunt.*

This does not amount to denying the strong schooling the author of *Octavia* has received from Seneca. There are echoes which reveal an unmistakable imitative purpose, and in one instance *Octavia* comes close to resembling the technique of cento-like composition: cf. *Oct.* 233–4 *qua plaustra tardus . . . regit Bootes frigore Arctoo rigens*, conflating *Med.* 314–15 *flectit . . . Arctica tardus plaustra Bootes* and *Med.* 683 *frigore Arctoo rigens.*

Alongside that of Senecan tragedy, the influence of Vergil and Ovid is predictably significant, especially but not only in the anapaestic sections (see APPENDIX B). In particular, adaptations of Ovid's elegiac poetry are favoured by the similar metrical layout of iambic and pentametric clausulae, typically containing disyllabic line-endings:[116] cf. *Oct.* 694 *Caesari iuncta es tuo* and Ov. *Pont.* 2.8.4 *Caesaribus Liuia iuncta suis*; in anapaests cf. *Oct.* 769 *petet amplexus, Poppaea, tuos* and Ov. *Her.* 16.268 *dum petit amplexus, Deianira, tuos.*[117]

The two examples also show how in both Ovid's elegiacs and Senecan tragedy a great number of disyllabic line-endings are provided by personal pronouns and possessives. The poet of *Octavia* continues this trend, indeed, takes it to excess, a fact which is rightly held to be a key indicator of his imperfect versificatory expertise. The percentage of personal pronouns and possessives at line-end in *Oct.* is 22.5%, whereas that of the other tragedies in the corpus ranges between 4.8% (*Phae.*) and 13.2 (*H.O.*).[118]

In Ovid's elegiacs, however, metrical constriction cannot be regarded as the sole factor accounting for the predominance of this layout, and possessive pronouns occur at the end of a line

[116] On disyllabic line-endings in Ovid's elegiacs cf. B. Axelson, in *Ovidiana* (Paris, 1958), 121–35. Cf. also Lindsay, ad Plaut. *Capt.*, 360.

[117] This pattern is, however, found elsewhere in the corpus: cf. *H.O.* 583 (*an.*) *flemus casus, Oenei, tuos.* See also ad 83. A similar arrangement can be found in Scaev. Mem. *Inc.* 1–2 R² *scindimus atras veteri planctu, | Cissaei, genas.*

[118] A phenomenon discussed also by Helm (1934), 317; Flinck (1919), 44. Figures in Hahlbrock (1968) 191.

mainly in order to be separated from the noun to which they refer.[119] The poet of *Octavia* recognizably uses possessives as a convenient line-filling, often without separating them from their nouns: cf. 107 *a fatis meis*, 120, 131, 415, 138, 139, 171, 261, 252, 253, 466, 600, 612, 644, 730, 752, 755, 855. The type-ending *a fatis meis* (3%, 18: 598 trimeters in *Oct.*) is not wholly alien to the versification of Senecan tragedy either, but the ratio is different. *Thy.*, for instance, gives a percentage of the type-ending *aduentu tuo* (*Thy.* 55) of 0.9% (8: 820 trimeters).[120]

It is in the anapaestic passages, mainly narrative in content, that the influence of dactylic poetry is most conspicuous. This *modus operandi* was perhaps under the influence of the derivationist approach: cf. e.g., Mar. Vict. *GLK* VI.122.28–31 *anapaestica metra per epiplocen . . . ex heroo originem trahunt . . . nam si hexametro uersui . . . primam detrahas syllabam, erit anapaesticus catalecticus.* Vergilian and Ovidian final adonii are frequently found. Cf. 971 *Pandatariae litora terrae*, clearly adapting Verg. *Aen.* 7.10 *Circaeae . . . litora terrae.* Some of these final adonii may have been common property in Latin: a glance at Mastandrea's *Concordances*[121] shows, for instance, that the line-ending *litora terrae* occurs several other times in Latin poetry; 367 *pectora ferro* was already in Ps.-Liv. Andronicus; and the similarity between the following dimeters and several *clausulae* in hexametric poetry appears coincidental: 26 *paruit orbis*; 279 *pignora pacis*;[122] 333 *munere reddis*;[123] 980 *barbara tellus*. In other cases, however, a context in Ovid or Vergil can be traced: cf. 203 *uertit in omnes* (= Verg. *Georg.* 4.411); 364 *fata parentis* (= Ov. *Met.* 7.346); 340 *f/muneris auctor* (= Ov. *Met.* 10.199); 375 *uulnera reddit* (= Ov. *Fast.* 5.469); 914 *tristis Erinys* (= Ov. *Met.* 1.241).

119 Cf. Axelson, 134, adducing Ov. *Ars* 3.196 *quaeque bibant undas, Myse Caice, tuas* (where *bibant* and *tuas* are metrical equivalents, but the possessive went to occupy the line-ending to be separated from *undas*).

120 *Thy.* 55, 103, 247, 281, 464, 710, 977, 1030.

121 P. Mastandrea, *De fine uersus* . . . (Hildesheim, 1993).

122 Also in Sil. *Pun.* 10.494; 13.68, but not of children.

123 *Culex*, 414 *funeris officium uitae pro munere reddit.*

One suspects that the poet's timidity in independent recreation of his models would have given rise to censure in the literary circles of declamatory poetry. Literary imitation was not regarded as a flawed practice, but sharp criticism could easily be triggered by too literal a borrowing. Imitation was regarded as an art of subtle adaptation. By the standards of its putative age, *Octavia* would often have failed the test.[124]

Does the *praetexta* aim at imitating Seneca's own style? Senecan tragedy was a constant referent for the author of the play, but he was not trying to write a forgery or pseudepigraphon.[125] In *Phoenissae* we possess a likely example of a Senecan *non-finito*; *Octavia* bears no resemblance to it. The lack of the regular extensive pattern of descriptive ablatives and appositive constructions so characteristic of Seneca's own poetic style, the number of repetitions of fixed phrases, the often meagre use of adjectives make it incredible, in my judgement, that the play's attribution to Seneca should still find acceptance. *Octavia* does indeed imitate Senecan tragedy, but seems to shrink persistently from that recognizable marking, declamatory rhetoric. I believe that this is a feature of the author's comparative weakness in composition rather than the result of a conscious reaction against Seneca's style.

Octavia and *Hercules Oetaeus*

Between *Octavia* and *H.O.* there are a number of parallels so close that imitation is certain beyond coincidence. Zwierlein, who

[124] Cf. esp. Sen. *Suas.* 2.17; 3.7; J. Fairweather, *The Elder Seneca* (Cambridge, 1976), 311–16; S. F. Bonner, *Roman Declamation* (Liverpool, 1949), esp. 144.

[125] A distinct set of questions relates to whether an ancient reader was susceptible of believing Senecan authorship of *Octavia*. Obviously someone must have done so at some point. Yet a specific expertise of ancient literary criticism was attention to questions of authorship. For ancient tragedy cf. A. Körte, ΧΑΡΑΚΤΗΡ, *Hermes* 64 (1929), 69–86; W. Ritchie, *The authenticity of the Rhesus of Euripides* (Cambridge, 1964), 13 ff. discussing the hypothesis, where the spuriousness of the play is suspected on the basis of its 'rather more Sophoclean *character*'.

maintains the priority of *Octavia*, dates *H.O.* to the age of Juvenal (*KK* 319–28). His argument is based on (1) the identification of a number of linguistic features which, in his view, might even be compatible with a late-antique dating; (2) a number of imitations of Silius and Statius allegedly recognizable in *H.O.*

In the absence of a detailed linguistic study of *H.O.* it is best to limit discussion to essentials. My feeling is that Zwierlein has overstated the case about the presence of late Latin linguistic features in *H.O.* For instance in *H.O.* 1884 *nondum Phoebe nascente genus*, Zwierlein claims to see the sign of an incipient confusion between present and past participles, a late development.[126] In fact, the intention of stressing aspect, rather than tense, may sometimes cause an author to use a present participle when a perfect or a subordinate clause might be expected. *nondum Phoebe nascente genus*, with reference to the Arcadians, προσέληνοι, may be explained as an attempt to describe the astronomical 'birth', that is her monthly cycle ('when the moon was not yet waxing and waning in her monthly course'). *H.O.* 1865 *cui concepto lux una perit*, playing up the antithesis between Hercules' long-protracted conception and the day's concomitant 'demise', is similarly seen by Zwierlein as a case of late-Latin tense confusion (= *cui concipiendo* for Zwierlein). This is a passage which needs, in my view, further study, although the use of participles in the place of deverbatives (the type of *ab Vrbe condita*) might perhaps account for this admittedly odd phrase.[127]

The gerundive construction develops in some late Latin instances a sense close to a periphrastic 'to be likely to': cf. e.g. Matt. 17.22 *filius hominis tradendus est* ('will be handed over'); Acts 28.6 *at illi existimabant eum in tumorem conuertendum et subito casurum et mori*).[128] This is however a far cry from *H.O.* 984–5 *si uera pietas, Hylle, quaerenda est tibi, | iam perime matrem*, where *quaerenda* cannot

[126] K. Rossberg, *ALL* 4 (1887), 49–50, for instance Cor. *Iohan.* 8.635 *extemplo turbatae acies pereunte tyranno*; Drac. *De deo* 1.661–2 *et cinis exstinctus gelida moriente fauilla | tollitur alta petens*; *LHS* 2.386; P. Stotz, *HLSM* 4.318.

[127] *LHS* 2.393, e.g. Plaut. *Epid.* 144 *ante solem occasum*.

[128] Ph. Thielmann, *ALL* 2 (1885), 76.

be explained as a mere future or present passive, as Zwierlein has suggested. *si* introduces a rhetorical condition: killing his mother is, in Deianeira's view, the only viable option for Hyllus: 'if indeed you must strive for true *pietas* (which you must) . . .'

Zwierlein regards *H.O.* 1938–9 *uadis ad umbras . . . ad quas semper mansurus eris* as an example of a late Latin periphrastic future. Yet the use of future forms as auxiliary is amply paralleled throughout all stages of Latin, with sixteen instances in Senecan prose and even four cases in Augustan poetry.[129]

Other linguistic features can indeed be regarded as anomalies within the rather selective grammar of classical Latin poetry, but do not allow conclusions about chronology. The vocative *deus*, at 561, is not found in Augustan poetry, but occurs in *Priap.* 42.2 (first century AD) and Scrib. Larg. 84 (a contemporary of the emperor Claudius).[130] The occurrence of *obiter* at 1049 *Centauros obiter ferens* and in Juv. 3.241 and 6.481 also proves nothing as regards chronology. The word is prosaic, perhaps a colloquialism,[131] but its presence in Juvenal does not imply that the adverb had gained admittance in the *Dichtersprache* of the Hadrianic age.[132]

Some of the alleged imitations from Silius are interesting, none entirely beyond coincidence.[133] Be that as it may, the *H.O.* would

[129] Cf. N-W III.3, 162–3. [130] Cf. Löfstedt, *Syntactica*, 1.92.

[131] It is found in Sen. *Ira*, 3.1.3; Petr. *Sat.* 34.5; 38.3, Plin. *Nat. saepe.*

[132] Charisius attests it for Laberius as well (*Gramm.* 271.10 Barwick). The reported *zetema* ascribed to *Diuus Hadrianus* (in the same passage), debating *an* (*sc.* '*obiter*') *Latinum sit*, does not concern linguistic legitimacy, but stylistic appropriateness. This is also clarified by Hadrianus' subsequent remark about Augustus, who is excused for using it, as a *non pereruditus homo* who had learned it *ex usu potius quam lectione.* One is reminded of the lines parodying Verg. *Buc.* 3.1 *quoium pecus anne Latinum?*, where the question at issue is about linguistic standards and registers, not idiom, a matter of synchrony rather than diachrony.

[133] Cf. *H.O.* 836 *fluctisona quaerit litora* = Sil. *Pun.* 12.355 *insula fluctisono circumuallata profundo*: the adjective is not attested elsewhere in Latin; *H.O.* 1047 *(auditis uaga cantibus) ales deficiens cadit* = Sil. *Pun.* 14.595 *fluxit deficiens penna labente uolucris* (but cf. Lucr. *D.R.N.* 6.743–4 *remigii oblitae pennarum vela remittunt | praecipitesque cadunt); H.O.* 1059–60 *serpens latebras fugit | tunc oblita ueneni* = Sil.

still belong to a time before the turn of the century. One finds it difficult to believe that the poet of *H.O.* would want to imitate *Octavia*, a tragedy on a subject which had no bearing upon his own and one which was endowed with no particular stylistic qualities to commend it to his attention. Imitation of *Octavia* is especially hard to believe if we consider that the author of *H.O.* has a much better command of Senecan style, and indeed I do not think that the case against Senecan authorship has been proved conclusively. To the poet of *Octavia*, on the other hand, the *H.O.* must have appeared as Senecan.

The following are the most conspicuous points of contact.

H.O. 225–6 *quid regna tui clara parentis* | *proauosque tuos respicis amens?*	*Oct.* 665–6 *sed quid patrios saepe penates* | *respicis?*
339 *meo iugales sanguine extinguam faces*	264 *raptasque thalamis sanguine extinxit faces*
478 *quid istud est quod esse secretum petis?*	691 *quidue secretum petis?*
909 *cur tuas damnas manus?*	863 *cur meam damnas fidem?*
1940 *quid me tenentem regna siderei poli*	396 *tenente regna Saturno poli*
1005–6 **A** *quid me flagranti dira persequeris face,* | *Megaera? poenas poscit Alcides? dabo*	617–18 *poscit auctorem necis.* | *iam parce, dabitur.*

Priority on the basis of internal argument is difficult to establish, but *Oct.* 691 and 617–18 make a good case for the imitation to have proceeded from *H.O.* to *Octavia*.

Oct. 691 *quidue secretum petis* is pronounced by the *Nutrix* at the beginning of the new act. But the word *secretum* is confusing. Poppaea is indeed doing the very opposite, leaving her bedchamber (690) in order to come out into a more public space. In the corresponding passage in *H.O.* 478 *quid istud est quod esse*

Pun. 3.301–2 *ad quorum cantus serpens oblita ueneni* (sc. *iacuit*). A convincing case for the independence and priority of the *Oetaeus* vis-à-vis Silius has been made by R. Nisbet, *Collected Papers* (Oxford, 1995), 209–10.

secretum petis, the *Nutrix* refers to a secret in which Deianeira is asking for her complicity.

Agrippina's ghost at *Oct.* 617–18 suddenly turns to address the dead Claudius, whose spirit demands vengeance. In *H.O.* Deianeira is being pursued by her remorse, in the form of a fury demanding vengeance for the dead Hercules. As documented ad 617–18, the scene has close parallels in *Phoe.* 39–40 *genitor uocat: | sequor sequor, iam parce*, spoken by Oedipus haunted by a vision of Laius' shade; *Med.* 958–67, esp. 964–5 *frater est, poenas petit. | dabimus, sed omnes*, where Medea believes herself to be pursued by the ghost of her brother. The passage in *Octavia* is more likely to be derivative, because the scene, ultimately going back to Aeschylus' Orestes, is a graphic representation of a guilty conscience tormented by remorse, and fits a living person who will in the end commit suicide (Deianeira) more than the ghost of Agrippina, insistently tormented by Claudius for the murders committed by her son, Nero.[134]

5. STRUCTURE AND DRAMATIC TECHNIQUE OF *OCTAVIA*

The cultural setting in which *Octavia* must be placed is that of the flourishing production of dramas for recitation in Roman literary circles. Abundant evidence for the popularity of tragedy in

[134] Parallel passages also suggesting a link between the two tragedies, with line numbers for *Oct.* shown in bold: *H.O.* 115 *non puppis lacerae fragmina conligit*: **Oct. 323–4** *alii lacerae puppis tabulis | haerent nudi*; 292 and 1691: **760**; 417 *non ut aequetur Ioui*: **500–1** *Ioui | aequatus*; 602 *rara fides*: **844** *rara quem pietas*; 717 *thalamisque maerens intuli gressum meis*: **73** *cesset thalamis inferre gradus*; 937 *et umbra tristis coniugem excipiam meum*: **170** *et tristis umbra*; 1023 *superosque testor*: **963** *testor superos*; 1065 *tristes Erebi deos*: **964–5** *Tartara testor | Erebique deas* (*Oed.* 410; *Hf.* 611); 1103 *mundo cum ueniet dies* and 1132 *pereat hic mundo dies*: **392–3** *tunc adest mundo dies | supremus ille*; 1507 *parce iam lacrimis*: **646** *parcite lacrimis*; 1707 *diem pande* and 1711 *pande tunc Stygios lacus*: **135** *Stygios sinus . . . pande*; 1805–6 *utinam meis uisceribus Alcides foret | exsectus infans*: **636–7** *utinam . . . saeuae nostra lacerassent ferae | uiscera;* 199: **914** (= *Agam.* 670 ff.); 437 *At Ioue creatum:: nempe et Alcmena satum*: **195** *iam metuit eadem:: nempe praelatam sibi*. Cf. Nordmeyer (1892), 286.

these circles comes from Pliny, Juvenal and Martial.[135] Whether any of these dramas were in fact composed for regular theatre performance is doubtful, and a multiplicity of factors have been thought to account for this: the lack of state patronage, the corruption of popular taste, a snobbish reluctance, on the part of the elite, to produce elaborate dramas in the style of fifth-century Athenian tragedy and expose them to the whimsical reaction of the uneducated. From Hor. *Epist.* 2.1.180–216 we can deduce a general disdain for theatre as an artistic medium in which sight and word combine to produce meaning – which comes at the end of a long intellectual tradition stretching back as far as Aristotle[136] – and the passage is significantly concluded with an appeal to Augustus to become a sponsor of poetry written with readers, not spectators, in mind. Performance is seen there as an excuse for indulging the tasteless inclinations of the populace.[137]

In the absence of direct proof for either medium, the context in which we can place the tragedies of this age is perhaps best conjured up when we leaf through the Elder Seneca's collection of declamatory extracts, the *Controuersiae* and the *Suasoriae.* The

[135] Collected in Schanz-Hosius, *Geschichte der römischen Literatur. 2. Teil: Die Römische Literatur in der Zeit der Monarchie bis auf Hadrian* (München, 1935[4]), 292–6; 821–6.

[136] Cf. Arist. *Poet.* chapt. 6 (50b). A similar disgust for performance as opposed to *Buchdrama* as voiced by a possible contemporary of *Oct.* is in Dio, *Or.* 7.119–22; 11.9; 32.41, 61, 100.

[137] For a good collection of the evidence relating to drama and spectacle in the Roman Empire cf. E. Csapo–W. J. Slater, *The Context of Ancient Drama* (Ann Arbor, 1995), 310–30; R. E. Fantham, *Roman Literary Culture* (Baltimore and London, 1996), 145–52; S. M. Goldberg, *TAPA* 126 (1996), 265–86. A sensible survey of the *recitatio* vs. performance debate can be found in J. G. Fitch, in G. W. Harrison (ed.), *Seneca in Performance* (London, 2000), 1–12, although he somewhat overstates the case for performance, even of selected climactic scenes. It is only partially true that the words spoken by the characters on stage, in such scenes as *Thy.* 1004–5 and *Med.* 935–77, are insufficient to visualize the action on stage: this action can be assumed to be well-known, and at any rate, as Fitch himself observes, a reciter could have supplemented his words with expressive gesture or even prefaced his recitation with a short description of what was to happen.

third *suasoria*, for example, 'Agamemnon deliberates whether he should sacrifice Iphigenia', could easily be read as a workshop on the composition of tragic monologues, delivered by a succession of declaimers who speak in character, *ethicōs*, donning theatrical personas often taken from myth.[138]

The only extant dramas of this time are the tragedies of the Senecan corpus, to which *Octavia*, as we have seen, bears a strong resemblance in several respects. It is only to a lesser extent, however, that the poet of *Octavia* imitates Seneca's dramatic technique.

The majority of the peculiar features of the Senecan *Rezitationsdrama* (such as the pre-eminence of ecphrasis over action; the suspension of dramatic time during choral odes[139] and asides, the disappearance even of major characters, who fall into silence in conformity with the three-actor rule;[140] the sudden emergence

[138] Argentarius' words at *Suas.* 3.2 strike a very Senecan chord: *iterum in malum familiae nostrae fatale reuoluimur: propter adulteram fratris liberi pereunt*, to be compared with the words of the Fury at *Thy.* 23–45, stressing the recurrence of the same crimes in the house of Tantalus, only under different names. Cf. Leo, *Obs.* 147–159 on the recurrence of *ut solet, semper, non semel* in the corpus of Senecan tragedy and its parallels in the *controuersiae* and the *suasoriae*. Scenes of a drama in the Senecan mould could easily be culled, for instance, from *Contr.* 7.1–3 (Blandus) and from the fragments transmitted in Quint. *Inst.* 9.2.42 (= fr. 1 Winterbottom) *in controuersia cuius summa est quod pater filium et nouercam inducente altero filio in adulterio deprensos occidit: 'duc, sequor, accipe hanc senilem manum et quocumque uis imprime' et post paulo 'aspice, inquit, quod diu non credidisti. ego uero non uideo, nox oboritur et crassa caligo'* (cf. Sen. *Phoe.* 90–5; 171–4, esp. *ades atque inertem dexteram introrsus preme magisque merge*): a good presentation of the material in N. T. Pratt, *Seneca's Drama* (Chapel Hill–London, 1983), 141–9. For a survey of the evidence relating to performance of tragedy in the imperial age, both in the form of recitation and as pantomime, see H. A. Kelly, *Ideas and Forms of Tragedy from Aristotle to the Middle Ages* (Cambridge, 1993), esp. 16–23.

[139] E.g. at *Hf.* 524–591.

[140] E.g. Megara after *Hf.* 500; Theseus after *Hf.* 829; Clytemnestra after *Agam.* 588. The lack of concern shown in imperial tragedy for the supposed presence on stage of characters when they cease to speak is perhaps one of the strongest elements indicating that the author did not try to produce the play, but had in mind an imaginary stage, where the physical presence of an actor was no hindrance to the others.

of new ones without announcement,[141] as if they gushed forth from a character's conscience, and without an intervening lapse of time) are absent from *Octavia*,[142] but we have no reason to think that the context of production was different from that of Senecan tragedy.

Octavia has a considerable number of secondary characters (two prefects, two Nurses, Seneca, Agrippina), and some of these would perhaps have been difficult to identify on their first appearance for a theatrical audience, because the action is not continuous, and the classical pattern of entrance and exit announcement by an omnipresent chorus is no longer available. Octavia, when she first appears (1–33), fails to identify herself in a clear manner, up to 28, when mention is made of the Britanni, nor does the *Nutrix* (at 34) identify herself up to 72 *uox . . . tristis alumnae.* Similarly, Seneca (377) and Agrippina (593) fail to introduce themselves directly, although the mention of exile in Corsica (382) and the words *Poppaea nato iuncta* (596) provide information. But the relative lack of explicit introductions in

141 Contact is thus made into a psychological circumstance, as if the new character suddenly emerging from the dark, usually an adviser, were a figure of the conscience of the soliloquizing actor: cf. *Agam.* 125; *Oed.* 81; *Thy.* 23; 204; *Phae.* 129.

142 The formula of *Rezitationsdrama*, as we know it from Seneca, exploits, in many ways, the clash between the conventions of drama and the conventions of narrative poetry. Once the label *Rezitationsdrama* ceases to be associated with a kind of debased quality, its features can be recognized, at least in part, as innovative and concerned with creating new effects. The recitation drama does away with the need to reconcile dramatic and narrative time, and the need to adhere to the many artificial conventions this involved in Greek drama. Hence leaps in time; successive scenes can represent simultaneous events; choral odes are used to enhance the suspense of a passage; monologues and asides give voice to the silent thoughts of the characters. Time becomes a psychological function, expanding as the point of view of a given character comes into focus. A scene *described* may also be *seen* immediately after, from different viewpoints. One may think of cinematographic montage, when two immediately successive scenes presuppose a time lapse (cf. the time overlap at *Phoe.* 427 ff., where Jocasta is first seen by the messenger from atop the walls, then, with a leap back in time, speaks in the first person).

Octavia should not be taken as evidence against theatrical production. An audience, however superficially informed, would know what to expect.

Even in Greek tragedy, not all characters speaking at the beginning of a play name themselves, until a second character entering addresses them.[143] Modern theatrical practice, where the names of the characters are often disclosed later in the play, shows the early naming of characters to be more a question of convention than intrinsic necessity. We might surmise that the author of *Octavia* shunned explicit self-announcement patterns out of a dislike for the flavour of artificiality attached to them. Senecan tragedy, too, varies greatly in this respect.[144]

Masks and, above all, dress, if the play was acted, might have yielded clues to assist in the identification of characters. In the Poppaea–*Nutrix* scene at 690 ff., however, a theatrical audience might have been mystified by the entrance of two characters who on first impression might be mistaken for the couple Octavia–*Nutrix* seen early in the play. It would be anachronistic to suppose that the resemblance between the two heroines was in fact intentional on the part of the author.[145]

[143] This is especially noticeable in Sophocles, where the drama steps *in medias res;* cf. *Trach. Phil.;* also *infra*, ad 1–20.

[144] Cf. *Med.* 8–9 *quosque Medeae magis | fas est precari*; *Thy.* 180 *iratus Atreus*; *Hf.* 1 *soror Tonantis.* There are, however, exceptions, such as Amphitryon (*Hf.* 205), Talthybius (*Troad.* 164). In *Troad.* 204 Pyrrhus and Agamemnon, too, appear on stage unannounced and without the dramatic device of naming themselves, or each other, on entrance. Cf. also *Phae.* 1 ff. The same is true of Seneca's Nurses: cf. *Med.* 150 (*alumna* 158); *Agam.* 125 ff. (the Nurse is not identified at all throughout). Oedipus' only self-identification is giving Polybus' name (12).

[145] The convention adopted by Zwierlein in his *OCT* (*Prolegomena*, 249–57; following the extreme solution of Leo, *Obs.* 82–8, sceptical about the origin and merits of the scene-headings of our Seneca MSS; similarly in Leo, *PF* 15, n. 1 on the corruptions suffered by scene titles in the text of Plautus) of writing at the head of each scene only the names of the individual characters when they first speak, relegating the fuller MS *nota* to the apparatus, is often misleading, because it gives the impression that the first words pronounced by each character successively speaking coincide with his/her first appearance on 'stage'. MS scene-headings are deserving of promotion into the

Two main concerns in the play oppose successful dramatization. One is a preoccupation with painstaking, almost over-detailed description of the narrative background in the words of the characters, which happens at the expense of psychological study. When there is a debate between two characters, as between Octavia and her Nurse, this is not so much to illustrate a conflict of opposing principles and personalities, as in the *agōn* of Greek drama, but to give an account, in a long over-drawn coda to the prologue proper, of the state of affairs in 62 (death of Messalina, of Claudius, of Britannicus, love-suit of Acte and Poppaea, suicide of Silanus, portents announcing the evil of the times, spoliation of the temples). In Nero's tirade on the civil wars, his argument is soon lost sight of, as is characterization itself.

A further element countering dramatic construction in *Octavia* is literary imitation. The difficulty in tracing the movements of Octavia in the first three scenes of the play may fall under this

text, because they reproduce ancient editorial practice, at least for dramatic texts, as shown by the MSS of comedy, where scene-headings 'photograph' the cast present in each scene, and their successive entrances and exits, although even there we can only hope to recapture an ancient scholar's reconstruction of stage events (cf. Duckworth, *NRC*, 98). One significant case is 690, where clearly Poppaea is first 'seen' on stage before she speaks (her dumbstruck silence is part of the effect envisaged by the playwright: see ad loc.), and the MS heading *nutrix. poppea* should accordingly be preserved. At 877 Octavia may be thought of as either present or absent depending on whether we write, with most MSS, *chorus. Octauia* at the beginning of the scene, or, with Zwierlein, *chorus* (and I think that the former is correct). Clearly, in these two instances, Leo's scepticism makes us miss part of the scene's dramatic impact. The practice of the *A* MSS of Seneca is however partly discredited, for *Octavia*, by their habit of adding scene-headings even in the absence of any action on stage, to mark a change in the delivery of the actors, for instance before *Oct.* 100 and 201. More generally, on the compendiary, resumptive character of the headings in both branches, especially if compared with the relative accuracy of those in the comic authors cf. Leo, *Obs.* 87 ('ita enim in universum res instituta est ut personae scaenis inscribantur non quae ab initio re vera compareant, sed etiam quae personis iam quantumvis conlocutis accessurae sint, ut binas scaenas singuli indices complectantur'). There are, however, counter-examples (cf. *Thy.* 404, 491, where a new heading signals Atreus' entrance; *Agam.* 208, 226).

heading: the result of insufficient visualization by a dramatist more concerned with putting together and almost juxtaposing famous 'typical' scenes of Greek tragedy.[146] The play begins with the protagonist setting out her grievances to the rising sun, after one more sleepless night spent in mourning. This is the *mise-en-scène* of Soph. *Electra*, 77 ff. Octavia does not announce her withdrawal to the palace, but the next we hear is the *Nutrix* delivering a formal prologue, until Octavia is again heard lamenting from inside (57). This is an adaptation of the beginning of Eur. *Medea*.[147] There was no compelling reason for Octavia to re-enter the palace after delivering her monody, nor is any such reason produced. The author wanted to make the most of another Euripidean scene, that of the *Nutrix* describing her mistress' misery while the latter weeps and broods on vengeance inside. The scene is thus overladen with famous theatrical models, which has the effect of making movement on 'stage' somewhat overdone.

Further evidence of a certain lack of theatrical visualization seems to emerge in the scene at 690, where, on an empty stage, Poppaea rushes in, terror-stricken. But we only 'see' this entrance in the words with which her *Nutrix* addresses her; Poppaea remains silent for about thirty lines. The *Nutrix*, taking only superficial notice of her pupil's distraction, embarks on a lengthy and long-winded description of the marriage ceremony held the previous day,[148] which undermines the dramatic tension of the passage. One would be hard put to it to devise stage directions for

[146] A warning already issued in Arist. *Poet.* chap. 17 (55a).

[147] See notes ad 1–20; 47–50; 55–6; 57.

[148] A passage imitating Sen. *Med.* 380–430, where the new act is initiated by a rushing entrance of Medea followed by her *Nutrix*. We only 'see' the scene through the latter's words (380 *alumna, celerem quo rapis tectis pedem?*). Medea herself begins her monologue only at 397, but before she speaks, her anger against Jason is described by the *Nutrix*. The scene may be imagined to take place with the Nurse addressing the 'audience' at one end of the stage while, at the other, Medea seethes with anger and silently contemplates her revenge. The lines uttered by the *Nutrix* provide, however, an apt introduction for Medea's own soliloquy which follows, well expressing Medea's isolation and incapacity to heed advice.

the actor impersonating Poppaea, with the *Nutrix* holding forth on the pomp and glory of the ceremony. Moreover, Poppaea scarcely needs to be told all these facts, since she was there.

Octavia is not a drama in the Aristotelian sense, where the plot progresses as a result of an interaction between the various characters involved.[149] The play is simply a three-day chronicle in which the successive developments of the action take place outside the dramatic frame. Several separate *tableaux* succeed one another, in the course of which the characters comment on what has happened off-stage. There is no clash of personalities from which the action on stage takes its momentum. True, there are indications that the playwright intended to make Octavia into a Greek heroine, an Antigone or Electra, bent on bringing ruin upon her own head, and there is a build up of expectation that the two leading roles will be made to meet, but this is an unrealized motif, and the expectation of a decisive encounter remains unfulfilled.[150] In the end the catastrophic event is provided by the popular insurrection, which happens independently of Octavia's knowledge and involvement.

This fragmentation of the action is also determined by the subject-matter and by the necessity of adhering to historical 'truth', and it may have been a feature of other historical dramas in Rome (although Aesch. *Pers.* proves that different courses were available).[151] *Octavia* also disrupts the Greek fifth-century tragic convention whereby playing time and time of the story coincide, and time lapses are independent of choral interludes, possibly a post-classical feature.[152]

[149] Cf. Arist. *Poet.* chap. 10 (52a).

[150] Cf. ad 48, 174, 540, playing up the motif of Octavia's anger.

[151] This is quite distinct from disintegration of the action as a characteristic hypothetically attached to post-classical tragedy, a development for which the loss of importance suffered by the chorus and the increased weight of virtuosic solo-parts are commonly blamed. Cf. B. Gentili, *Theatrical Performances in the Ancient World* (Amsterdam, 1979), 15–62.

[152] This disregard for established convention might be explained by an editorial feature of post-classical tragedy, the lack of choral connecting parts in the existing books containing tragedy. In a famous post-classical example,

Like a Greek tragedian, the poet of *Octavia* focuses on the emotional, private, psychological side of the events, or on the highly-strung conflict between disaster-bound personalities. In the words of O. Taplin, 'the stuff of [Greek] tragedy is the individual response to such events [battles, riots, miracles, natural disasters] . . . ; it is the life-sized actions of this personal dimension that are the dramatist's concern.'[153]

How much action could we have expected to find in Roman *praetextae?* One would tend to imagine Roman historical dramas more in the line of Shakespeare's *Coriolanus* than of Aeschylus' *Persians.* In a genre glorifying the military exploits of either mythical or historical commanders, Roman spectators can be supposed to have cherished on-stage swashbuckling. A battle, then a triumph make up the early Augustan *praetexta* performance alluded to by Horace, if that is indeed a *praetexta.*[154]

Octavia displays the restraint characteristic of Greek drama in handling onstage action. In fact, there is almost no action to speak of: no onstage scuffles, no fighting, no pageantry, not even eavesdropping, plotting, looking around.[155] Even the toing and froing of Republican tragedy, with characters emerging from the palace in reaction to cries and other noises they have heard, is absent in *Octavia.* A series of protracted dialogue scenes, first

Medea starts off by addressing a group of Corinthian women whose song has been recorded in the papyrus only by the usual shorthand, χοροῦ (l. 5). Cf. *PLit Lond.* 77; cf. also *PHib* 4; *PHib* 174 (where a lyric solo part follows the indication χοροῦ = Snell, *TrGF* 60**F1h?, fr. 1, col. 2.11). Sutton (1983), 27–31, has argued that the rapid 'cutting' of *Octavia* after 593 was influenced by mime.

153 O. Taplin, *Greek Tragedy in Action* (London, 1978), 161.

154 Cf. Hor. *Epist.* 2.1.189–93 *quattuor aut pluris aulaea premuntur in horas, | dum fugiunt equitum turmae peditumque cateruae; | mox trahitur manibus regum fortuna retortis, | esseda festinant, pilenta, petorrita, naues, | captiuum portatur ebur, captiua Corinthus.* Livy (5.21.9), speaking of the capture of Veii, describes the Roman tradition whereby the Romans made a surprise attack digging tunnels into the citadel as a legend more appropriate for the stage (*haec ad ostentationem scenae gaudentis miraculis aptiora quam ad fidem*). On action in historical dramas cf. Manuwald (2001), 72–3, n. 48, who surveys various contrasting opinions.

155 For these details of stage business, mainly found in post-classical drama, cf. Tarrant (1978), 213–63, esp. 246–50.

between Octavia and her Nurse, then between Seneca and Nero, expatiate at great lengths on the background of prior events. The sequel of the play is taken up by the portrayal of the conflicting emotions of the three leading female roles: Agrippina, Octavia, Poppaea. It is from their contrasting viewpoints that we catch a glimpse of the marriage, in the words of, in turn, an indignant Agrippina casting her curse upon it, a resigned Octavia leaving her chambers amidst the despair of her retinue, and, lastly, of the Nurse, attempting to calm the fears dawning on a newly-married Poppaea. Even the catastrophic event, the popular uprising, is mainly seen in its aftermath, namely the deportation of Octavia. More than as the result of insufficient dramatic skill, I view this restraint as a statement, perhaps an intentional distancing from mime and other forms of more popular entertainment, in which action got the upper hand over eloquent verbiage.

Many scenes in the play cannot easily be reconciled with the notional setting 'outside' of ancient drama, nor is much made of the divide between on- and offstage so typical of fifth-century tragedy, with most of the violence being committed inside the palace, although still within the hearing of the other characters. Some effort to set the initial scenes involving Octavia and her Nurse is made in the first act, where an exterior scenery is conjured up also by the intertextual link with Sophocles' *Electra*. The setting is similarly suspended in a vacuum in the final acts of the tragedy, where the guards' song and all subsequent scenes up to 877 would be more realistically placed inside the imperial residence, rather than in the open.

As in Seneca, an act is introduced by a monologue, which expands into a dialogue, in the Euripidean fashion,[156] on the arrival of a second speaking character ('acts' I, II, VI). When the soliloquizing character who has begun the act is joined by a second actor, the poet of *Octavia* relies upon traditional conventions for contact and entrance announcement. Accordingly, there are no soliloquizing entrance monologues with other characters 'on

[156] Cf. Leo, *Monolog*, 92–3.

stage', a striking post-classical feature of Senecan drama.[157] The dialogue successively develops from long *rheseis* to *stichomythia* and *antilabē*, but this succession is less linear in the dialogue between Nero and Seneca. A character is never left alone on stage to pronounce an act-closing monologue. *Octavia* goes beyond Senecan tragedy in its avoidance of scenes in which more than two actors speak.

The choruses featured in the *praetexta* go on and off stage as in Seneca (indeed as in Republican drama: cf. ad 646), without clear indications of their reasons for coming and going. The choruses in *Octavia*, unlike those of Seneca, do not convey philosophical reflections, but often take part in the action. Interaction with the actors is, however, restricted to the *nuntius* scene at 776 ff. and to the final *kommos. Octavia* is also the sole play in the corpus in which the chorus on one occasion justifies its entrance on stage (they have heard news (of the impending divorce): a commonplace for entrances in Greek fifth-century dramatic practice).[158] The active role taken up by the chorus at 669 ff. is also without parallels in Senecan tragedy. The *kommos* at 899 ff., where the taking away of Octavia is attended and lamented by a chorus, although without parallels in Seneca, is a clear reminiscence of Soph. *Ant.* 806 ff. (as shown in detail *infra*, ad 924). The anapaestic duet Octavia-*Nutrix* at 75–100 also has no straightforward precedent in Seneca.

Less surprising is the importance assumed by monodies, in the form of anapaestic parts 'sung' by the main heroine (1–33; 646–68; 899–923)[159] and even – more strikingly – by her *Nutrix* (201–21). Monodies of lamenting heroines are a not infrequent

[157] On this feature of post-classical drama in Seneca cf. Zwierlein, *Rezitationsdramen*, 69.

[158] ad 273.

[159] The delivery of anapaests in Greek tragedy is clarified by dialectal and metrical elements, and a clear distinction is always maintained between 'recited' and 'sung' (cf. West. *GM*, 121–2). In Seneca, a clue is provided by a passage in Sen. *Thy.* 918–19 *iam cantus ciet | festasque uoces*, with reference to the anapaests of Thyestes. Of lesser significance cf. *Apocol.* 12. 3 *ingenti enim μεγάλωι χορικῶι nenia cantabatur [anapaestis]*.

feature of fifth-century Athenian tragedy, especially in connection with *parodoi*;[160] and monodic scraps have emerged from papyrus fragments, for instance the lament of (?)Hecuba in *TrGF* adesp. 644. Anapaestic monodies in non-initial contexts, however, (i.e. not in connection with a *parodos*-like or introductory choral song) occur in Sen. *Troad.* 705; *Thy.* 920; *H.O.* 1863; 1944.

The influence of fifth-century tragedy accounts for some of the individual features of *Octavia* within the Senecan corpus. Other elements, however, point to the conventions of post-classical theatre. Tarrant (1978), 238 n. 113, has adduced Plautine parallels for the manner in which the presence of Octavia is noticed and signalled by her *Nutrix* at 72–4.[161] This is a case in which the author of *Octavia* exhibits the traditional artificial conventions of contact between characters, whereas Seneca seems to have dismissed this pattern. I give a similar evaluation of the introduction of the *persona protatica* at 435–7, also not paralleled in Seneca. In these cases, the overemphasizing of a 'stagecraft' veneer may be trying to make up for the recitation context, and, more generally, the *ignotus* may have been too diffident to follow Seneca in his disregard for the traditional techniques of dramatic 'naturalism'.

The tragedies of Seneca are structured following a pattern which assigns to choral songs the function of separating different phases of the action:[162] four choral songs moralizing upon the circumstances of the previous *epeisodion* conclude all acts except the last.[163] This is usually interpreted as an application of the 'five-act law' first found in Hor. *Ars* 189–90, but possibly formulated earlier. In comedy, five acts or *merē* are attested for Menander and, for Terence, by the evidence of Donatus. In the

[160] *Octavia* 1–33 is, however, clearly inspired by Soph. *El.* 86–120 even if no *parodos* follows. On monody in Greek tragedy cf. the useful review in M. Di Marco, *La tragedia greca* (Roma, 2000), 272–5.

[161] *uox en nostras perculit aures | tristis alumnae; | cesset thalamis inferre gradus | tarda senectus?*

[162] The classic discussion of the problems of act-division in ancient drama is Taplin, *Stagecraft*, 49–60.

[163] With the sole exception of *Oed.* which counts five choral songs. Cf. Tarrant (1978), 219.

Latin plays, however, where there was no chorus, a different rule is stated by the ancient commentators, whereby the occurrence of an empty stage, an anomalous feature in classical Greek drama, is assumed as the major criterion for act-division.[164]

There is only one long choral ode in *Octavia* (273–376),[165] but I believe that the poet assigned an act-dividing function of some sort to all, no matter how brief, choral odes delivered when no one else is on stage (the ode at 877 ff. evolves into the final act of the play, as Octavia appears under guard, possibly after 892, with the chorus exceptionally remaining on the stage for the final exchange). However, division into acts following the 'act-dividing odes' principle cannot be maintained consistently, because the major break in the action after 592 is not marked by any such song. Taplin's method of counting act-dividing odes, with this necessary corrective, yields seven units.[166] The greater

[164] Cf. Don. ad Ter. *Andr. praef.* II.3 Wessn. *animaduertendum ubi et quando scaena uacua sit ab omnibus personis ita ut in ea chorus uel tibicen obaudiri possint; quod cum uiderimus ibi actum esse finitum debemus agnoscere.* Ancient commentators on Roman comedy, while trying to subdivide plays into acts, were often at a loss as to where to draw a line between episodes, their main criterion (empty stage) often not allowing as many as five act-divisions. In fact, the empty stage rule was often disregarded by necessity, as was the case for the break between acts II and III in *Andria* (cf. Don. ad Ter. *Andr. praef.* III.6 *illud nos commouere non debet, quod in horum actuum distinctione uidentur de proscaenio non discessisse personae quaedam, sed tenere debemus ideo Terentium uicinitatis mentionem fecisse in principio, ut modico receptu et adesse et abesse personam intellegamus.* The evidence of the ancient commentators on Terence is discussed by W. Beare, *The Roman Stage*, London, 1964³, 186–208. For the existence of some common ground between comedy and tragedy in Roman theoretical discussions of drama, and the role of Varro in dividing Roman comedy into five acts, cf. Leo, *PF*, 224–34. Ribbeck, *RT* 641–2, discusses the evidence relating to the hypothetical three-acts structure of early Roman tragedy, pre-dating Varro.

[165] Cf. Tarrant (1978), 220, n. 34. Münscher (1922), 138, rejects the attempt to apply a five-act structure to *Octavia*, favouring a threefold division which corresponds to the three days of the action. He cites as a parallel Ps.-Lucian's *Tragodopodagra*. He also notes a structural parallel between *H.O.* and *Oct.*, in that both tragedies are concluded by a section in which shorter choral interludes alternate with speaking parts.

[166] In Athenian tragedy, seven units (including the prologue) are found at least in Soph. *Ant.*; Eur. *Med., Herc., Ba., Hel.* For a recent discussion of the

integration of choral parts into the action of the drama also raises the question of whether songs should be considered to end or to begin an act (cf. *infra*, on 669 *en illuxit*): a clear-cut answer does not emerge from a thematic analysis of the odes.[167]

The structure of Octavia

I.

1–33 Octavia's initial monody
34–56 prologue proper recited by the Nurse
57–71 a brief lament of Octavia, inside the palace
72–99 exchange in anapaests Octavia-Nurse
100–272 dialogue Octavia-Nurse
273–376 chorus

II.

377–436 monologue of Seneca
437–439 Nero-Prefect
440–592 Seneca-Nero

problems of act-division in Greek tragedy cf. V. Di Benedetto–E. Medda, *La tragedia sulla scena* (Torino, 1997), 168–71. In the late historical drama about the Goths which can be reconstructed from the list of stage costumes and paraphernalia found in *PBerl* 13927 the action may have been distributed in seven units: cf. I. Cazzaniga, *SCO* 7 (1958), 7–17.

[167] Act divisions in Seneca make their first appearance in Trevet's commentary, and early printed editions follow suit. Trevet divides *Oct.* into five acts, but does not remark on the difficulty presented by the absence of a chorus as a marker of textual divisions. His act beginnings are placed where one would have expected (at 377, 593, 780), with the exception of the fifth, at 845, where neither the empty stage criterion nor that of the act-dividing ode are satisfied. On Trevet's terminology referring to acts (*actus*) and scenes (*carmina, partes*) cf. Junge (1999), 136–42. For MSS exhibiting traces of act divisions cf. C. Questa, *Parerga plautina* (Urbino, 1985), 69, on *Vat. Lat.* 1647 (dated: 1391), and R. Scarcia, *RCCM* 4 (1962), 235, on *Vat. Lat.* 2899, containing Senecan excerpts, where the citation of *Oct.* 625–31 is preceded by *Seneca actu III*; also on *actus* in xv cent. Seneca MSS in Leyden cf. J. P. Gumbert, in C. Leonardi–B. Munk Olsen (eds.), *The Classical Tradition in the Middle Ages and the Renaissance* (Spoleto, 1995), 31. Act divisions in these MSS are probably influenced by Trevet's commentary, which exerted a vast influence on the Italian tradition (cf. MacGregor, *TAPA* , 102 (1971), 347).

III. (day 2)
593–645 the ghost of Agrippina
646–668 departure of Octavia
669–689 chorus

IV. (day 3)
690–761 dialogue Poppaea-Nurse
762–779 chorus

V.
780–805 dialogue Messenger-chorus
806–819 chorus

VI.
820–845 Nero alone
846–876 Nero-Prefect

VII.
877–898 chorus moralizing on the inconstancy of *uulgus*
899–923 Octavia's lament, as she is taken away by Nero's soldiers
924–957 chorus' reaction
958–971 Octavia again
972–982 choral tailpiece

I. The first act is articulated in four scenes (Octavia's initial monody, 1–33; a prologue pronounced by the Nurse, 34–56; an exchange in anapaests between Octavia and the Nurse, 57–99; a dialogue 100–272, interrupted by the anapaests of the Nurse (201–21) and concluded by a choral ode, vaguely imitating a classical *parodos*, 273–376.

II. The second act is divided into two scenes, Seneca's monologue, 376–436, and a Seneca-Nero dialogue, 437–592. Although no choral ode follows, the critics are unanimous in establishing an act division at 592, where the first day ends.[168]

III. The appearance of Agrippina's ghost, 593–645, signals the dawn of a new day. The lack of a choral ode marks a break

[168] With the exception of Mette (1964), 192, n. 1.

from dramatic tradition, but there seems little alternative to assuming a major division here. This act shows how even the empty stage rule cannot be relied upon consistently as a criterion for act-division: after Agrippina's departure, Octavia pronounces a brief lament, then leaves; the chorus pronouncing 669–89 may perhaps be imagined as present throughout. 689 marks the end of the third act. 593–689 represents the second day of the action, the day of the marriage, preceded by Octavia's expulsion from the palace in the early hours of the same day. From 682–4, however, we gather that statues of Poppaea have already been erected (before the marriage?). It is also surprising that the revolt should begin on day two and be reported to Nero only on the following day (804–5). Should 669 *en illuxit*... be taken as marking the beginning of the third day? But the lines pronounced by the chorus at 669–89 correspond to Octavia's song, and comment on what has just happened before rather than introduce a new act. What is more, the scene between Poppaea and her Nurse imitates *Med.* 380, which marks the beginning of the third act. The three-day view is on the whole the more reasonable, but the tragedian does not seem to have brought all elements into line with it.

IV. The fourth act is entirely occupied by the dialogue between Poppaea and her Nurse, with the narrative of Poppaea's dream. This is followed at 762 by a choral ode celebrating Poppaea's beauty (762–79) which is performed by, possibly, a group of guards.

V. The exchange between the messenger and chorus (780–805) forms an independent act (like *Oed.* 915–79, responding to 914, *ede quid portes noui*). The act-dividing ode is sung by the same chorus, deprecating the riots and foretelling ruin for the rebels (806–19).

VI. The next act begins at 820 with Nero's monologue, followed at 846–76 by a dialogue with the prefect.

VII. The choral ode at 877–98, moralizing on the inconstancy of popular support, quickly evolves into the long anapaestic exit scene, a lyric exchange between the chorus and Octavia, who is being led away by Nero's guards.

6. THE POLITICS OF *OCTAVIA*

Some modern critics have read the tragedies of the Senecan corpus as anti-tyrannical statements in disguise.[169] This hypothesis is probably too extreme, but *Octavia* may be the earliest witness in the history of political and libertarian interpretations of Senecan tragedy. When Nero repeats the thundering *sententiae* of Seneca's mythological tyrants,[170] the point is probably made that all those fictional characters were aliases of Nero, as if the tyrant had taken off their masks at last.

Seneca's *De clementia* also is reinterpreted by the author of *Octavia* as a courageous entreaty to Nero to act forbearingly, to behave according to clemency. In reality the pamphlet was to all effects a propagandistic work, promoting the view that an enlightened monarch held sway over the Empire, giving

[169] See T. Birt, *NJA* 27 (1911), 336–64; O. Herzog, *RhM* 77 (1928), 51–104; R. G. M. Nisbet (1995), 293–311. Peiper (1870), 23 proposed a reading of Senecan tragedy which persistently emphasizes supposed references to the crimes of the Julio-Claudians. *Phae.* 555–6 (*a fratre frater, dextera gnati parens | cecidit, maritus coniugis ferro iacet*) is interpreted as a series of allusions to Nero's rise to power. In modern times, this anti-tyrannical reading was already in the writings of Sicco Polenton (cf. id. *Scriptores illustres latinae linguae*, ed. B. L. Ullman (Rome, 1928), 116–9). Earlier, Mussato's *Eccerinis* is already an implicit statement of the same: see I. Opelt, 'Eccerinis, das tyrannendrama des Albertino Mussato', *Annali della Fac. di lett. e Filos. dell' univ. di Napoli* 30 (1987–8), 330–76. On Neostoicism and the interpretation of Senecan tragedy in Early Modern Europe see R. G. Mayer, *JWCI* 57 (1994), 151–74.

[170] Cf. *Oct.* 453–4 = *Troad.* 333–6; *Oct.* 471 = *Oed.* 702. Not only does Nero imitate *sententiae* spoken by Pyrrhus or Atreus; the exchange between the tyrant and the philosopher in 437 ff. is modelled on the typical Senecan scene in which an evil tyrant and his foil confront each other, and the well-intentioned counsellor attempts to restrain the tyrant's fury (e.g. *Thy.* 204–19, where the *satelles* initially expresses concern for public opinion (204–5) and humanity, which have no place in Atreus' moral world). This too might well have induced a contemporary reader to believe that Seneca had been representing himself in those unheeded mentors who turn up again and again in an attempt to restrain their rulers, like Creon in *Oed.* 511–29; 668–709, Jocasta in *Phoe.* 651–64, Agamemnon (against Pyrrhus) in *Troad.* 327–36, and the *satelles* in *Thy.* 204–19.

heed to advice, and surrounding himself with wise men as his counsellors.[171]

The details of the personal relationship between the philosopher and the emperor must have been consigned to oblivion after the death of both: so much of it was probably secret business and high political intrigue. In the historical accounts circulating about the time when *Octavia* was composed, there must have been contrasting versions of Seneca's involvement in the political disaster of the last Julio-Claudians,[172] but a generally malevolent account of the philosopher's political career had gained currency, as Cassius Dio's *Roman History* proves.[173] The poet of *Octavia* must have been reacting against this negative estimate when he made up a wholly idealized version of his Seneca.

In Tacitus, Seneca is an old *politico*, a dissimulator superior to the man he has to serve,[174] a cunning minister to whom an irresolute Nero has recourse in some highly dramatic and momentous circumstances of his early reign.

The portrayal of Seneca in *Octavia* is apologetic, indeed, revisionistic. Seneca's hand in the murder of Britannicus, and to

[171] For another recent discussion of the relationship between *De clementia* and *Oct.* see G. Manuwald, 'Der Fürstenspiegel in Senecas *De clementia* und in der *Octavia*', *MH* 59 (2002), 107–26.

[172] Seneca had been involved in political intrigue since Caligula's time. On Seneca's entanglements with the political circle gathered round Caligula's scheming sisters and during Claudius' early years cf. Z. Stewart, *AJPh* 74 (1953), 70–85, with the criticism of Griffin, *Seneca*, 47–54.

[173] Cf. Cass. Dio *Hist. Rom.* 61.20.3 (Seneca encourages Nero's histrionic exhibitions); 61.12.1 (urges Nero to murder his mother). On the negative estimate of Seneca in Cassius Dio cf. Griffin, *Seneca*, 428. From Tacitus we gather that Fabius, a historian Quintilian recommended as one of the best of his age, was favourable to Seneca, but it is impossible to determine what role he played among the *auctores* of *Oct.*

[174] Cf. Tac. *Ann.* 14.7, with the stark contrast between the cool and phlegmatic behaviour of Seneca and the panic of Nero; *Ann.* 13.5, for Seneca's prompt reaction in preventing Agrippina from sitting on the throne next to Nero when the envoys from Armenia are received; even in the episode (*Ann.* 14.54) in which Seneca begs to be discharged from office, Seneca emerges as a consummate courtier, a master in the crafts of dissimulation and hypocrisy that best serve one under a tyranny.

some extent of Agrippina, is left unmentioned. Indeed, it is striking to find Seneca so eagerly loyal to Claudius' memory (587 *merita . . . diui patris*), even convinced of his divine status. He is a good old man, abstemious and temperate, who does not shrink from speaking the truth even in the face of danger, who tries to warn his one-time pupil from going too far in his disregard for humanity, endeavours to curb his inclination towards vice and anger, and loses no occasion to spell out the good principles by which a ruler should always abide (cf. 472–6). Seneca speaks his true, however idealized, self throughout, as good counsellors are wont to do in tragedy.

Yet this Seneca never misses a chance to speak in quotation. There is virtually nothing about him which the specialist finds new or not elsewhere documented and which the non-specialist might feel to be 'authentic'. Much as we like the fantasy of the *ignotus* as one of the last faithful disciples of the old philosopher, we are forced to wonder why he made his Seneca so bookish.[175]

Octavia sets up its own agenda in its treatment of political themes, and betrays different concerns from those that can be discerned in Senecan tragedy.

A good start is provided by the dialogue between Atreus and his *satelles* in *Thy.* 204–19, which bears some resemblance to the Seneca-Nero scene in *Octavia* in that the *satelles* initially expresses concern for public opinion (204–5) and humanity, opposes the tyrant and presents the people as potentially adverse to his plans and possibly ready to threaten his domination. But the objections voiced by the *satelles* are only there to provide a cue for Atreus, an excuse to give a display of his amoral *Realpolitik* and ruthless political paradoxes, his Machiavellian pursuit of power as an art, and the attendant is quick to give in to Atreus and to help him carry out his scheme.

Seneca, on the contrary, stands up to Nero in his defence of Octavia, and tirelessly upholds the ideal of the good king against the values of despotism. Indeed, Seneca's confrontation

[175] Cf. ad 382, 385–7, 485; 460; 487–9, 504.

with Nero gives the author an opportunity to present a sanitized version of Seneca's views on government, as set out in *De clementia*.

In *De clementia* the emperor is shown towering over immense multitudes that could not but suffer self-destruction if their moderator were removed.[176] In *Octavia* the emphasis has noticeably been shifted.[177] The cosmic gaze over the unruly multitudes has become the usual Roman scenario of popular acclamation. Whereas in *De clementia* Seneca was insinuating the idea of divine election, Nero's election in *Octavia*, though it retains marks of divine favour, has been ratified by the sanction of the traditional Roman orders.

Another passage of *Clem.* paid lip service to the Roman Republican tenet that the emperor, as a magistrate, is a faithful executor of the existing laws: cf. 1.1.4

sic me custodio tamquam legibus, quas ex situ ac tenebris in lucem euocaui, rationem redditurus sim.

These are the Laws with a capital letter, not a precise political institution, or the body politic. There follows an even more significant section:

hodie diis immortalibus, si a me rationem repetant, adnumerare genus humanum paratus sum.

Nero is only accountable to the Gods and to such superhuman entities as the Laws, and significantly, the community over which he presides and with respect to which he plays the role of a god on earth is not one of social classes and governing bodies, but a confused restless multitude for which the most apt parallel are the bees and other animal societies, mentioned explicitly by Seneca later on.

The poet of *Octavia* takes a different line. A tendency to bridle the powers of the *princeps* is apparent throughout. A crucial

[176] Cf. *Clem.* 1.1.2; 1.3.5: the emperor stands as reason stands to the chaotic forces of the universe, as the principle regulating the fragile harmony of things.

[177] Cf. ad 485–90.

passage is the quick repartee at 459–61, culminating in Seneca's words at 460, *quae consensus efficiat rata*, which introduce the idea of a limit to the prerogatives of the *princeps*. Yet *consensus* as a political notion failed to figure in Seneca's *Clem.*, which completely ignored all constitutional issues involving limitation of the powers of the *princeps*. In Seneca *consensus* was treated as a universal and innate concept, not as a political idea.[178] How far an emperor should be bound by the existing laws must have been a controversial issue in the political debate in the aftermath of Nero's fall. Although in practice the prerogatives of the emperor were not subject to a limit or control, in the first century AD 'good' emperors paid formal respects to the Laws and to the traditional institutions. The emperor is always presented as the supreme magistrate.[179]

The poet of *Octavia* is aware of the existence of a debate concerning the prerogatives and the limits of the emperor, though he fails to give a technical answer to the question of the limitations of the emperor's prerogatives, as, after all, does every other source we possess.[180]

Another point must be mentioned. The author of *Octavia* has no intention of making Seneca into a heroic figure. Seneca does

[178] ad 460.

[179] Compare the following passage in Pliny's panegyric addressing Trajan, *Pan.* 65.1 *in rostris quoque simili religione ipse te legibus subiecisti, legibus, Caesar, quas nemo principi scripsit. sed tu nihil amplius uis tibi licere quam nobis . . . quod ego nunc primum audio, nunc primum disco: non est princeps super leges, sed leges super principem.* Similarly, the *Lex de imperio Vespasiani*, by specifying the cases in which the *princeps* is exempted from certain laws of his predecessors, reinforces the idea that the *princeps* is not always above the law, and that there are laws from which he is not exempted (*ILS* 6.244, ll. 28–32).

[180] It is difficult for us to determine how far the poet of *Oct.* was influenced by the political action of the so-called Stoic opposition. We know next to nothing of the programme of Helvidius Priscus, who is commonly considered the chief exponent of the 'Republican' opposition under Vespasian. It can be presumed that he fought for the Senate to enjoy an equal share in the administration of the state, but most of what we know of his political programme depends on the polemical representation of his conduct given by Eprius Marcellus in Tac. *Hist.* 4.8 *suadere etiam Prisco ne supra principem scanderet, ne Vespasianum . . . praeceptis coerceret.*

not upstage Nero: his role is still that of a counsellor, a mentor figure resigned to withdrawing when he is dismissed (589–90) rather than a staunch opponent who maintains his stand for the good cause at the cost of his life. This is significant, because it places the author at some distance from the fashion for martyrdom which seems to have become current at the time of Pliny the Younger, although this should not necessarily be construed as a chronological element. The Seneca who here confronts Nero has not yet become the Stoic martyr; compare, by contrast, the sketch of the encounter between Helvidius Priscus and the emperor Vespasian in Epict. *Diss.* 1.2.19–21 Schenkl.[181] There was a tradition of heroic philosophers opposing the tyrant even in the face of death, which had been appropriated by the so-called Senatorial opposition. A handy list occurs in Phil. *Vita Apoll.* 7.1–4 (and then also in Clem. *Strom.* 1.15; 4.8.56). Up to a point, this tradition overlaps and blurs with the stories of the so-called martyrs of freedom, or pagan martyrs, and with the tradition of the *exitus inlustrium uirorum*, which became popular in the age of Nerva and Trajan.

7. TEXTUAL TRANSMISSION AND EDITORIAL HISTORY

Comparison of the two families of MSS in which the corpus of Senecan tragedy has been transmitted shows that they go back to two widely diverging recensions (known as *E* and *A*), circulating separately perhaps as early as the fifth century, with *A* commonly assumed to be the product of extensive interpolation. These two editions, however, must ultimately have descended from the same archetype, the necessity of which is shown by the presence of numerous common errors and lacunae.[182] The

[181] Cf. H. A. Musurillo, ed., *The Acts of the Pagan Martyrs* (Oxford, 1954), 236–42. See also C. G. Starr, Jr. *CPh* 44 (1949), 26–7.

[182] Tarrant, *Agam., Introd.* 53; Zwierlein, *Prolegomena*, 9–10. Tarrant's *Introduction* and Zwierlein's *Prolegomena* are also the most extensive treatments of the MS tradition of Senecan tragedy.

possibility cannot be excluded that the archetype in turn had inherited from one or more Senecan autographs a number of authorial alternative readings in the form of supralinear variants and marginalia, which would account for part at least of the observed variety of readings.

This complex picture is considerably simplified in *Octavia* by the absence of the play in *E* and, as far as the evidence goes, in the strand of textual transmission this manuscript represents. The two sub-families into which *A* must be further divided do not exhibit a picture of comparable textual variety. A better understanding of *A* and its ramifications has therefore proved particularly crucial for *Octavia*. Yet progress in the *recensio* of *A* dates only from the early years of the twentieth century: editions up to Richter's Teubner of 1902, for all their merits, are little different, in their knowledge and evaluation of *A* MSS, from their early modern predecessors, which had drawn only on descendants of the mainly Italian, and interpolated, β-family.

The identification of a less debased, northern European group of MSS virtually exempt from contamination (made up of a handful of MSS, *PTCSV*, and later *G* for *Octavia* alone), rested on the test of significant lacunae, devised by Hoffa–Düring, and put to good use by Stuart.[183] The principle was based on the observation that some of the MSS, in fact the earliest in date, exhibited gaps which later MSS had filled, possibly by consulting a different MS source. The purest *A* MSS can be further subdivided into two families (β = *CSV* and δ = *GPT*).[184] The division of the two branches is not much earlier than its earliest extant representatives, as proved by the number of trivial errors shared in *GPC*, and corrected by later MSS (such as, in

[183] The three crucial lacunae whose presence suggests absence of contamination with the *E*-family are *Hf.* 125–61; *Oed.* 430–71; *Med.* 1009–27 (cf. MacGregor (1985) 1224; id. (1978), 90–1 on the presence of 36 diagnostic lacunae preserved in *PTCSV*). *P* shows a few coincidences in error with *E*, but Woesler (1965) 24–42 made a good case for taking this to represent an archetypal stage, corrected by β (which he calls γ).

[184] A list of the most significant separative errors in Zwierlein, *Prolegomena*, 53–5.

Oct. only, 46 *ueneris*, 166 *tuo quoque*, 252 *thalamis meis*, 534 *generato diuo*, 694 *iuncta est tuo*). This proves, as Herington argued, that the archetype of *A* does not lie very far back in time.[185]

The recovery of δ has healed the text of *Octavia* at significant points, clearing the ground of obvious conjecture of *recc.*, and yielding a more genuine text in a significant, if modest, number of instances, if only to confirm successful conjecture or to add force to what had hitherto appeared to enjoy only insecure support in the tradition (cf. ad 36 *subito*, 89, 254 *uiolenti*, 388 *sortis*, 489 *spiritu*, 689 *feri*, 882 *Gracchos*). The crucial question of when the play was included in the corpus cannot be answered with any certainty.[186] The likeliest scenario for the inclusion of *Octavia* is the fourth to fifth century divide, when new editions in codex

[185] Herington (1958), 375–7. Rouse (1971) 117 n. 6 lists the following cases of agreement of one or more of *recc.* against *GPCS* in the text of *Oct.* (the first reading is the accepted one; *O* = *Oratorianus*, Naples, Bibl. Gerolamini CF. 4.5, saec. xiv ex.): 19 lux *OeKQ*: nox *GPCS* 46 uenenis e^2 *(in ras.)KQ*: ueneris *GPCS* 87 fera quam *Oe*: fera que *PCK*: fera *G*: fera qu(a)e S^1 Q^1 105 grata *OeKQ*: grate *GPCS* 166 tu quoque *OeKQ*: tuo quoque *GPCS* 181 expectat e^2*KQ*: -tet *O*: -tas *GPCS* e^1 252 tuis $MQ^2 e^2$ *Ox*: meis *GPC* 360 credent *Oe*: credunt *GPCSKQ* 379 grauius OK^1: grauis *GPCSe* 399 terra *GPCSKQ*: terras *O* 413 uulnere *GPCSe*: uomere OG^1 *(mg.) KQ* 463 opprimar *e*: opprimamur OKQ^1: opprimatur *GPCS* 534 generata *V*Σ: -o *GPC* 694 es Σ: est *GPC* 798 diducta *PGCSe*: deducta $KQ^{1\text{-}2}$ 805 iussa *Oe, om. sp. rel. S, om.* $PGCKQ^1$ 883 quos *Oe*: quod *PGC*: qui SKQ^1.

[186] The hypothesis that *Octavia* was included in the corpus as late as the twelfth century was advanced on the basis of its presence in *G* (a miscellaneous compilation whose contents include Isidorus' *Etymologiae*, various items of Senecan prose, including spurious works, *Octavia*, and excerpts from the other tragedies: full description in Herington (1958), 375–7) and, conversely, of its absence from the fairly large selection from the tragedies present in Leiden, University Library 191B, suggesting that perhaps *Octavia* circulated separately (cf. Tarrant, *Agam.* p. 60; MacGregor (1978), 103–4). MacGregor's argument that *G* should ultimately be envisaged as the MS from which *Octavia* entered the corpus (104–5) cannot be accepted: his suggestion that the order of *Oct.* 677b ff. in *GT* is the original order of *A*, indeed the correct order, is unacceptable. Other facts do not square, for example the presence of the 26-line gap in *P* after 173 (while *GT* have nothing), hardly reconcilable with *P*'s stemmatic position as a *descriptus* in MacGregor's hypothesis. Cf. Zwierlein (1979), 163. MacGregor (103–4) has also argued that two separate textual traditions are represented in *A* for the

form were being prepared; eagerness to recover pieces of the waning classical age was at its highest, but the means of ascertaining authorship were subjective. Unfortunately, no help is provided for *Octavia*[187] by study of the authors who are used to

corpus and *Octavia*. This cannot be solidly proved solely from a comparison of textual errors present in *Oct.* and in any tragedy of the corpus. True, the agreement of δ and β (= *A*) in *Oct.* yields the correct text, or at least a text not clearly corrupt, more often than it does in the rest of the tragedies, where *E* is available (according to MacGregor, the *A* error rate in *Phae.* is 14 %, with 180 corruptions peculiar to *A*, out of a total of 1280 lines). On this hypothesis, the lower percentage of errors present in *Oct.* would show that there are fewer intermediate copies between its archetype and extant MSS. *PGC* exhibit a faulty text at 19, 34, 41 (*ora tanais, iugo*), 46, 49, 52, 82, 87, 105, 114, 134, 141, 149, 152, 159, 166, 173, 175, 181, 195, 198, 232, 233, 234, 237, 240, 249, 252, 262, 290, 316, 349, 360, 377, 379, 387, 391, 392, 410, 412, 420, 449, 458, 461, 463, 463, 487, 489, 500, 503, 516, 533, 534, 541, 559, 566, 572, 577, 591, 602, 617, 631, 640, 654 (*saeue, cogor*), 661, 685, 688, 691, 694, 696 (*et culpa senece, uictum*) 701, 731, 732, 740, 742, 747, 760, 761, 762, 764, 765, 772, 779, 780, 786, 792 (*hic, furor*), 795 (*ara, era*), 800, 803, 805, 811, 821, 823, 827, 850 (*metus, impio*), 858, 859, 862, 870, 872, 883, 887, 895, 898, 901, 903, 915* (*redderet, edon*), 926, 958, 971, 973, 979, adding up to a total of 119 errors (with 140 as the expected number at the 14% rate of *Phae.*). Such statistics should be treated with caution: the comparatively simpler, less flamboyant style of *Oct.* was less susceptible of either misinterpretation or interpolation. However, one of the most characteristic features of *A* in the other tragedies, the interpolation of synonyms, sometimes unmetrical (cf. Zwierlein, *Prolegomena*, 42–3), seems largely absent in *Oct.* (however hard this may be to trace).

187 Only *Phoe.*, *H.O.* and *Oct.* are absent from the quotations of late-antique grammarians and scholiasts, whose interests seem to concentrate mainly on choral parts (a list of the relevant passages in Leonhardt, *DS* 144; De Nonno, *Le citazioni dei grammatici*, 624 n. 86, in G. Cavallo, P. Fedeli, A. Giardina *Lo spazio letterario di Roma antica* (Roma-Salerno 1990) vol. III *La ricezione del testo*). The earliest recognizable imitation of *H.O.* (607) is in Theodulf of Orléans (ix cent.; *MGH* Poetae 1.375: cf. Trillitzsch (1978), 125). Boethius does seem to have known Senecan tragedy, and he regards Seneca as a role model in having suffered persecution at the hands of his former pupil (*Cons.* 3.5.10–2; cf. also 2.m.6 on Nero), yet none of the alleged imitations of *Oct.* adduced by Peiper, in the *Index locorum quos Boethius ex Senecae tragoediis transtulit* (in his edition of Boethius' *Cons.* (Leipzig, 1871), 228–33), and, in his wake, by Woesler (1965), 107, is beyond coincidence. Suggested parallels include *Cons.* 1.1.3 *et ueris elegi fletibus ora rigant* = *Oct.* 328–9 *laceratque comas | rigat et maestis fletibus ora*; *Cons.* 2.2.4 *caelo sidera fulgent* = *Oct.* 1–2 *caelo sidera fulgens | Aurora fugat*; *Cons.* 4.4.8 *iniustas acies et fera bella mouent* = *Oct.* 806

establish the division of the two branches, such as Claudian, whose imitations point to errors, or interpolated versions, characteristic of one or the other *recensio*.[188]

Collation of the tragedies for which *E* is available has shown that *P* contains errors in common with *E*, to be explained more as archetypal corruptions than as a result of contamination. This shows that β had corrected some of the easiest blunders. At a somewhat later stage, in the course of the fourteenth century, with interest in Senecan tragedy on the rise, and with copies multiplying, a group of MSS from the dawn of Humanism, most notably *KQeOx*, had corrected, often quite subtly, most of the blunders of *A*.[189] In the editorial history of *Octavia* there has not been a momentous leap forward comparable in scale to Gronovius' discovery of *E* (the famous *Etruscus*) for the other tragedies. The progress in emendation that the first printed

quid fera frustra bella mouetis. In *Cons.* 4.5.3 *cur legat tardus plaustra Bootes, legat* was corrected into *regat* on the basis of *Oct.* 232–3 *qua plaustra tardus . . . regit Bootes*. *Contra* cf. Zwierlein, *Senecas Hercules*, 46; (1979), 166. The only parallel which seems to have some bearing on the question is *Cons.* 4.5.3, but even here Sen. *Med.* 314–15 *flectitque senex | Attica tardus plaustra Bootes* might alone be sufficient as a reference. On another possible echo of *Oct.* in Boethius cf. ad 385–7. The earliest indirect witness of the existence of *Oct.* is Vincent of Beauvais (xiii cent.), in *Speculum historiale* 9.113 *idem* (sc. *Seneca*) *in Octavia: luxuria pestis blanda. uictrix orbis immensas opes auaris manibus ut perdat rapit* (= 427, 433–4), which is coeval with our earliest MSS of *A*.

188 Cf. Zwierlein, *Prolegomena*, 30–5. To his considerations (disputed by Billerbeck, *Hf.*, *Introduction*) must be added those of D. Markus-G. Schwender (*ZPE* 114, (1997), 73–80), who have published a fourth-century fragment of Sen. *Med.* on parchment from Egypt, which, in the editors' view, contains conjunctive errors with the *A*- family (their readings, however, are not easy to verify on the included reproduction).

189 It is methodologically unsound to postulate an Italian representative of the *A* family, independent of our earlier MSS, as an ancestor of such fourteenth-century MSS as *KQeOx*, as proposed by Giardina (1965), 64. The readings on which Giardina has based his conclusions are all right readings, more likely the product of conjectural activity. All corrections were well within the reach of even modestly competent medieval editors: cf. Rouse (1971), 117–18. The history of the popularity of Senecan tragedy at the dawn of Humanism has been treated by several scholars: for a recent account of commentaries preceding and following Trevet's cf. Marchitelli (1999), 36–63 (I); 87–104 (II).

editions made came mostly through advance in classical learning, especially about realia and historical details for which Tacitus is our only other source of information (cf. Maserius' *Crispinus*, Delrius' *Liui*, Lipsius' *Pandataria*),[190] and, later, a more nuanced understanding of metrics fostered by the parallel progress in Greek and early Latin studies.[191]

Zwierlein's Oxford edition of Senecan tragedy (1986; 1994^5) is unlikely to be replaced as the standard edition in the near future. Zwierlein has devoted very careful attention to the MSS, and his critical apparatus is always reliable. His *Kommentar* and *Prolegomena* are the starting point of every serious attempt to re-examine all textual questions. Later editions of *Octavia* have marked no comparable advance in textual or other matters. Chaumartin's altogether more conservative edition with French translation and notes is sometimes helpful; his apparatus seems to be a simple reproduction of Zwierlein's, with a few errors. Liberman's select critical notes are also useful, sometimes very attractive.

Of the MSS that I report in the apparatus criticus I have collated *in situ G, C* and *M*, and I have seen microfilms of the rest, except for *Q* and *Ox*, for which I rely on Zwierlein. The abbreviation *recc.* indicates a reading found in one of the more recent MSS: when this reading is found in at least one MS I have seen, I identify it in the apparatus or in the commentary. Otherwise references to *recc.* derive from previous editors, essentially Giardina and Zwierlein, who are not always more specific. Line-numbers are the same as Zwierlein's, and I have adopted his custom of printing '•' next to some of the monometers he writes as separate

[190] One of the most signal editorial merits of Lipsius is his annotated Tacitus of 1576.

[191] Avantius' Veronese MS appears to have been very close to BL King's 30 (MacGregor's 389). A useful survey of MSS declared to have been used by early editors in Peiper–Richter (1867), xl–xliii; MacGregor (1985), 1179–80. Some of the MSS used by early modern editors have been identified: Lipsius' *Melisseus* has been identified with Holkham Hall 390 by MacGregor; Caietanus' MS, which is the origin of *prouecta* at 316, is BL Harley 2482 (MacGregor (1985), 1202).

lines altering the MS sequence. The printed sources of older conjectures are usually identified, except for Scaliger and Fabricius (which I have found in Scriverius).

In punctuating the text, my aim has been mainly that of clarifying the sense. I have followed Zwierlein and other Senecan editors in writing a capital letter at the beginning of each new character's speech, and I have used capitals also to mark important new turns of an argument, as a substitute for paragraphs, which I do not use. As a rule, I do not write commas before conjunctions such as *et, nec, atque*, except when the sense would be unclear, for example because of a particularly unusual instance of postponement.

My text differs from Zwierlein's in the following cases.

Zwierlein, OCT (1991[3])	This edition
18 *nox*	*lux*
49 *quem spreta*	*secreta*
50 *ardens mariti mutua flagrat face*	*ardet maritus, mutua flagrant face*
133 *poscit*	*captat*
141 *fratris*	*fratre*
153 *capaxque scelerum*	*scelerum capaxque*
173 *saeuiens flamma abstulit*	*flamma feruens abstulit*
197 *falsa*	*fassa*
232 *infaustam*	*infestam*
262 *illos*	*illi*
290 *omnem suadente metu*	*aeuo suadente metum*
294 *expulerunt*	*expulerant*
295, 301–3, 300, 296–9, 304–	I have retained the MS order
354 *quamuis*	*quam uix*
388 *noctis alternas uices*	*sortis alternae vices.*
407 Lacuna after *mitis*	No lacuna
412 Lacuna after *crate*	Lacuna after *uolucres, crate* expunged
413 *uomere*	*uulnere*
Lacuna after 414	No lacuna
415 *interior*	*interius*
503 *tum*	*tunc*
516 Lacuna after *Philippi*	†*hausit*

522 *non*	*nunc*
577 *furor*	*fauor*
677 *diros*	*claros*
735 *ossa*	*ora*
747 *inter*	*intra*
761 *maneat ut p. status*	†*maneat ut p. metus*
789 *diri*	*Diui*
811 *laesi*	*laeso*
827 *en*	*at*
Lacuna after 848	No lacuna
868[a] *mulier* to the Prefect	868 to Nero
889 *suae*	*sui*
908 *hac est*	*haec est*
952 *et caelum*	*in caelum*

TEXT

INCERTI AVCTORIS OCTAVIA

SIGLA

conspectus siglorum

G = *Exoniensis,* Bibl. Capit. 3549B, saec. xiii (alt. quart.)		
P = *Parisinus Latinus* 8260, saec. xiii (alt. quart.)	}	= δ
T = *Parisinus Latinus* 8031, saec. xv^{in}		
C = *Cantabrigiensis* C.C.C. 406, saec. xiii^{in}		
S = *Scorialensis,* T III 11, saec. xiii^{ex}	}	= β
V = *Vaticanus Latinus* 2829, saec. xiii^{ex}		
F = *Parisinus Latinus* 11855, saec. xiv (prim. quart.)		
M = *Ambrosianus* D 276 inf., saec. xiv	}	= Σ
N = *Vaticanus Latinus* 1769, saec. xiv		

e libris recentioribus saepius adhibentur

K = *Cameracensis,* Bibl. mun. B 555 (513), c. an. 1300
Q = *Casinensis* 392 P, saec. xiv^{in}
e = *Etonensis* 110, saec. xiv^{med}
Ox = *Oxoniensis* Canon. Class. Lat. 93, c. an. 1400

A = consensus codicum *δβ*
δ = consensus codicum *GPT*
β = consensus codicum *CSV*
Σ = consensus codicum *FMN*

INCERTI AVCTORIS OCTAVIA

OCTAVIA

Iam uaga caelo sidera fulgens
  Aurora fugat.
surgit Titan radiante coma
mundoque diem reddit clarum.
Age, tot tantis onerata malis
repete assuetos iam tibi questus
atque aequoreas uince Alcyonas,
uince et uolucres Pandionias:
grauior namque his fortuna tua est.
Semper genetrix deflenda mihi,
prima meorum causa malorum,
tristes questus natae exaudi,
si quis remanet sensus in umbris.
utinam ante manu grandaeua sua
mea rupisset stamina Clotho,
tua quam maerens uulnera uidi,
oraque foedo sparsa cruore!
O lux semper funesta mihi!
tempore ab illo lux est tenebris
  inuisa magis.
tulimus saeuae iussa nouercae,
hostilem animum uultusque truces;
illa, illa meis tristis Erinys
thalamis Stygios praetulit ignes
teque extinxit, miserande pater,
modo cui totus paruit orbis
  ultra Oceanum
cuique Britanni terga dedere

lucii annei senece agamenon explicit (feliciter *CSV*). incipit octauia eiusdem *PTCSV*: incipit octauia senece *G*: marci lucii annei senece hercules (oetheus *N*) explicit. incipit octauia *MN*   1–33 *dimetri in A praeter monometros* 6^{b} (i.t.q.), 20, 27, 30   18 nox *Helm*   19 lux *Σ*: nox *A*   es *Bothe*

ducibus nostris ante ignoti
  iurisque sui:
coniugis, heu me, pater insidiis
oppresse iaces seruitque domus
cum prole tua capta tyranno.

NVTRIX

Fulgore primo captus et fragili bono
fallacis aulae quisquis attonitus stupet,
subito latentis ecce Fortunae impetu
modo praepotentem cernat euersam domum
stirpemque Claudi, cuius imperio fuit
subiectus orbis, paruit liber diu
Oceanus et recepit inuitus rates.
En qui Britannis primus imposuit iugum,
ignota tantis classibus texit freta
interque gentes barbaras tutus fuit
et saeua maria, coniugis scelere occidit;
mox illa nati, cuius extinctus iacet
frater uenenis, maeret infelix soror
eademque coniunx nec graues luctus ualet
ira coacta tegere: crudelis uiri
secreta refugit semper atque odio pari
ardet maritus, mutua flagrant face.
animum dolentis nostra solatur fides
pietasque frustra; uincit immitis dolor
consilia nostra nec regi mentis potest
generosus ardor, sed malis uires capit.
Heu quam nefandum prospicit noster timor
scelus: quod utinam numen auertat deum.

34 fragili *recc.*: fac- *A* 36 subito *δC*: sub uno *C(mg.) SV* 41 Britannis *Scaliger*: ora tanais *A* iugum *recc.*: -o *A* 46 uenenis *ΣKQe*[2] *(in ras.)*: -ris *A* 49 secreta *recc.*: quem s. *A*: quem spreta *Baehrens* 50 ardet maritus (ardent mariti *Peiper*), mutua flagrant face *Gronovius*: ardens mariti m. flagrat f. *A* 52 uincit *Buecheler*: mittit *A*

OCTAVIA. NVTRIX

OC. O mea nullis aequanda malis
  fortuna, licet
repetam luctus, Electra, tuos!
tibi maerenti caesum licuit
  flere parentem,
scelus ulcisci uindice fratre,
tua quem pietas hosti rapuit
  texitque fides:
me crudeli sorte parentes
raptos prohibet lugere timor
fratrisque necem deflere uetat,
in quo fuerat spes una mihi
totque malorum breue solamen.
nunc in luctus seruata meos
magni resto nominis umbra.
NV. Vox en nostras perculit aures
  tristis alumnae:
cesset thalamis inferre gradus
  tarda senectus?
OC. Excipe nostras lacrimas, nutrix,
testis nostri fida doloris.
NV. Quis te tantis soluet curis,
  miseranda, dies?
OC. Qui me Stygias mittet ad umbras.
NV. Omina quaeso sint ista procul.
OC. Non uota meos tua nunc casus,
  sed fata regunt.
NV. Dabit afflictae meliora deus
  tempora mitis;
tu modo blando uince obsequio
  placata uirum.

57–99 *dimetri in A praeter* 58, 61, 64, 75^{a} (e. n.), 76^{b} (f. d.), 78, 82, 87^{b} (c. t.) *monometros*   63 quem *Tβ*: quam *GP*   82 fata *recc.*: uota *A*   83 dabit *δ*: –s *β*

OC. Vincam saeuos ante leones
tigresque truces,
fera quam saeui corda tyranni.
odit genitos sanguine claro,
spernit superos hominesque simul,
nec fortunam capit ipse suam,
quam dedit illi per scelus ingens
infanda parens.
Licet ingratum dirae pudeat
munere matris
hoc imperium cepisse, licet
tantum munus morte rependat:
feret hunc titulum post fata tamen
femina longo semper in aeuo.
NV. Animi retine uerba furentis,
temere emissam comprime uocem.

OC. Toleranda quamuis patiar, haud
umquam queant
nisi morte tristi nostra finiri mala.
genetrice caesa, per scelus rapto patre,
orbata fratre, miseriis luctu obruta,
maerore pressa, coniugi inuisa ac meae
subiecta famulae, luce non grata fruor,
trepidante semper corde non mortis metu
sed sceleris: absit crimen a fatis meis,
mori iuuabit. poena nam grauior nece est
uidere tumidos et truces miserae mihi
uultus tyranni, iungere atque hosti oscula,
timere nutus, cuius obsequium meus
haud ferre posset fata post fratris dolor
scelere interempti, cuius imperium tenet
et sorte gaudet auctor infandae necis.

87 quam *SΣ*: que *PTCV*: *om. G* 89 superos hominesque δ (superbos h. *P*): superbos humilesque β *ante* 100 octauia. nutrix *A* 100 quaeuis *Lipsius* 105 grata *Σ*: -e *A* 112 fata post fratris *PTSV*: fratris p. f. *GC* 114 sorte *Lipsius*: morte *A*

Quam saepe tristis umbra germani meis
offertur oculis, membra cum soluit quies
et fessa fletu lumina oppressit sopor!
modo facibus atris armat infirmas manus
oculosque et ora fratris infestus petit,
modo trepidus idem refugit in thalamos meos:
persequitur hostis atque inhaerenti mihi
uiolentus ensem per latus nostrum rapit.
tunc tremor et ingens excutit somnos pauor
renouatque luctus et metus miserae mihi.
Adice his superbam paelicem nostrae domus
spoliis nitentem, cuius in munus suam
Stygiae parentem natus imposuit rati,
quam, dira post naufragia, superato mari,
ferro interemit saeuior pelagi fretis.
quae spes salutis, post nefas tantum, mihi?
inimica uictrix imminet thalamis meis
odioque nostri flagrat et pretium stupri
iustae maritum coniugis captat caput.
Emergere umbris et fer auxilium tuae
natae inuocanti, genitor, aut Stygios sinus
tellure rupta pande, quo praeceps ferar.
NV. Frustra parentis inuocas manes tui,
miseranda, frustra, nulla cui prolis suae
manet inter umbras cura, qui nato suo
praeferre potuit sanguine alieno satum
genitamque fratre coniugem captus sibi
toris nefandis flebili iunxit face.
Hinc orta series facinorum, caedes doli
regni cupido, sanguinis diri sitis.
mactata soceri concidit thalamis gener

121 in haerentem *Ageno*: inhaerentem . . . *Reeve, etiam* ense *pro* -em *corr. in seq. uersu* 122 nostrum *A*: strictum *Helm* 133 captat *A*: poscit *Gronouius* 134 emergere umbris *Heinsius*: emerge ab umbris *Gronovius*: emerge tenebris *Withof*: emergere undis *A* 140 preferre *β*: perf- *δ* 141 gnatamque *Heinsius* fratre *Gronouius*: fratris *A* pactus *Peiper* 144 diri *A*: clari *Buecheler*

uictima, tuis ne fieret hymenaeis potens.
pro facinus ingens! feminae est munus datus
Silanus et cruore foedauit suo
patrios penates, criminis ficti reus.
intrauit hostis, ei mihi, captam domum
dolis nouercae, principis factus gener
idemque natus, iuuenis infandi ingeni,
scelerum capaxque, dira cui genetrix facem
accendit et te iunxit inuitam metu
tantoque uictrix facta successu ferox
ausa imminere est orbis imperio sacri.
Quis tot referre facinorum formas potest
et spes nefandas feminae et blandos dolos
regnum petentis per gradus scelerum omnium?
tunc sancta Pietas extulit trepidos gradus
uacuamque Erinys saeua funesto pede
intrauit aulam, polluit Stygia face
sacros penates, iura naturae furens
fasque omne rupit. miscuit coniunx uiro
uenena saeua, cecidit atque eadem sui
mox scelere nati. Tu quoque extinctus iaces,
deflende nobis semper, infelix puer,
modo sidus orbis, columen Augustae domus,
Britannice, heu me, nunc leuis tantum cinis
et tristis umbra, saeua cui lacrimas dedit
etiam nouerca, cum rogis artus tuos
dedit cremandos, membraque et uultus deo
similes uolanti flamma feruens abstulit.
OC. Extinguat et me, ne manu nostra cadat!
NV. Natura uires non dedit tantas tibi.

146 fieret *Gβ*: fient PT^{ac} 149 ficti *Lipsius*: facti *A*: factus *recc.* 152 infandi *recc.*: nef- *A* ingenii *A* 153 scelerum capaxque *L. Mueller*: capaxque scelerum *Ascensius*: scelerumque c. *A* 157 quis *β*: qui *δ* 159 gradus *recc.*: -um *A* 166 tu *Σ*: tuo *A* 172 dedi *Buecheler* 173 flamma feruens abstulit *recc. (N)*: f. fl. a. *A*: saeuiens fl. a. *Baehrens* *post 173 spatium XXVI uersuum rel. PK, XXX uersuum CS (spatium non intermiserunt GTV)* 175 uires non *recc.*: n. u. *A*

OC. Dolor ira maeror miseriae luctus dabunt.
NV. Vince obsequendo potius immitem uirum.
OC. Vt fratrem ademptum scelere restituat mihi?
NV. Incolumis ut sis ipsa, labentem ut domum
genitoris olim subole restituas tua.
OC. Expectat aliam principis subolem domus;
me dira miseri fata germani trahunt.
NV. Confirmet animum ciuium tantus fauor.
OC. Solatur iste nostra, non releuat mala.
NV. Vis magna populi est. OC. Principis
  maior tamen.
NV. Respiciet ipse coniugem. OC. Paelex uetat.
NV. Inuisa cunctis nempe. OC. Sed cara est uiro.
NV. Nondum uxor est. OC. Iam fiet, et genetrix simul.
NV. Iuuenilis ardor impetu primo furit,
languescit idem facile nec durat diu
in Venere turpi, ceu leuis flammae uapor:
amor perennis coniugis castae manet.
uiolare prima quae toros ausa est tuos
animumque domini famula possedit diu,
iam metuit eadem . . . OC. Nempe praelatam sibi
NV. Subiecta et humilis, atque monumenta exstruit
quibus timorem fassa testatur suum.
et hanc leuis fallaxque destituet deus
uolucer Cupido: sit licet forma eminens,
opibus superba, gaudium capiet breue.
    Passa est similes ipsa dolores
      regina deum,
    cum se formas uertit in omnes
    dominus caeli diuumque pater
    et modo pennas sumpsit oloris,
    modo Sidonii cornua tauri;

181 expectat *recc. (KQ)*: -as *A*   186 uetat δ: *bis* β   195 metuit *C, recc.*: -et *A* *uerba* n. p. s. *post Bothium Octauiae tribuit Ritter; nutrici A*   197 fassa *CFM*: falsa δ*SVN*   198 destituet *recc.*: -it *A*   *ante* 201 nutrix *A*   201–21 *dimetri in A praeter* 202 (r. d.), 221 (u. d.) *monometros*

aureus idem fluxit in imbri;
fulgent caelo sidera Ledae,
patrio residet Bacchus Olympo,
deus Alcides possidet Heben
nec Iunonis iam timet iras,
cuius gener est qui fuit hostis.
uicit sapiens tamen obsequium
coniugis altae pressusque dolor:
sola Tonantem tenet aetherio
secura toro maxima Iuno
nec mortali captus forma
deserit altam Iuppiter aulam.
Tu quoque, terris altera Iuno,
soror Augusti coniunxque, graues
  uince dolores.

OC. Iungentur ante saeua sideribus freta
et ignis undae, Tartaro tristi polus,
lux alma tenebris, roscidae nocti dies,
quam cum scelesti coniugis mente impia
mens nostra, semper fratris extincti memor.
utinam nefandi principis dirum caput
obruere flammis caelitum rector paret,
qui saepe terras fulmine infesto quatit
mentesque nostras ignibus terret sacris
nouisque monstris. uidimus caelo iubar
ardens cometen pandere infestam facem,
qua plaustra tardus noctis alterna uice
regit Bootes, frigore Arctoo rigens.
en ipse diro spiritu saeui ducis
polluitur aether, gentibus clades nouas
minantur astra, quas regit dux impius.
non tam ferum Typhona, neglecto Ioue,

215 aetherio *recc.*: -eo *A* 232 cometen *Zwierlein, Heringtonium secutus*: -em δ: -am β infestam *A*: infaustam *Heinsius* 233 alterna *Heinsius*: aeterna *Auantius*: eterne *A* 234 frigore *recc.*: frigido *A* arct(h)oo β: -eo δ 237 quas *recc.*(*Ox*): que *A* 238 tiphona *A*: tithoea Σ

irata Tellus edidit quondam parens.
haec grauior illo pestis, hic hostis deum
hominumque, templis expulit superos suis
ciuesque patria, spiritum fratri abstulit,
hausit cruorem matris: et lucem uidet
fruiturque uita, noxiam atque animam trahit?
pro! summe genitor, tela cur frustra iacis
inuicta totiens temere regali manu?
in tam nocentem dextra cur cessat tua?
utinam suorum facinorum poenas luat
Nero insitiuus, Domitio genitus patre,
orbis tyrannus, quem premit turpi iugo
morumque uitiis nomen Augustum inquinat.
NV. Indignus ille, fateor, est thalamis tuis,
sed cede fatis atque fortunae tuae,
alumna, quaeso, neue violenti moue
iram mariti. forsitan uindex deus
existet aliquis, laetus et ueniet dies.
OC. Graui deorum nostra iam pridem domus
urgetur ira, prima quam pressit Venus
furore miserae dura genetricis meae,
quae nupta demens nupsit incesta face,
oblita nostri, coniugis legum immemor.
illi soluta crine, succincta anguibus,
ultrix Erinys uenit ad Stygios toros
raptasque thalamis sanguine extinxit faces:
incendit ira principis pectus truci
caedem in nefandam, cecidit infelix parens,
heu, nostra ferro meque perpetuo obruit
extincta luctu, coniugem traxit suum
natumque ad umbras, prodidit lapsam domum.
NV. Renouare luctus parce cum fletu pios,

240 hic *recc.*: hec *A*   249 insitiuus *Lipsius*: insidiuo (nisi diuo GT^{ac})*A*   252 est *δ*: et *β*   tuis *recc. (MOx)*: meis *A*   254 uiolenti *δC*: -am *SVΣ*   259 dira *recc.*(M^2)   261 nostri coniugis *A*: iusti –gii *recc.* (M^2 *in marg.*): nostri coniugii *recc.* (*VKQOx*)   262 illi *Heinsius*: illos *Zwierlein*: illo *A*   269 perdidit *recc.*   270 cum *A*: iam *N*

manes parentis neue sollicita tuae,
graues furoris quae sui poenas dedit.

CHORVS ROMANORVM

Quae fama modo uenit ad aures?
utinam falso credita perdat,
frustra totiens iactata, fidem,
nec noua coniunx nostri thalamos
principis intret teneatque suos
nupta penates Claudia proles,
edat partu pignora pacis,
qua tranquillus gaudeat orbis
seruetque decus Roma aeternum.
Fratris thalamos sortita tenet
  maxima Iuno:
soror Augusti sociata toris
cur a patria pellitur aula?
sancta quid illi prodest pietas
  diuusque pater,
quid uirginitas castusque pudor?
Nos quoque nostri sumus immemores
post fata ducis, cuius stirpem
prodimus aeuo suadente metum.
Vera priorum uirtus quondam
Romana fuit, uerumque genus
Martis in illis sanguisque uiris.
Illi reges hac expulerant
  urbe superbos
ultique tuos sunt bene manes,
uirgo dextra caesa parentis,
ne seruitium paterere graue et

273–376 *dimetri in A*   290 euo *A*: aegro *Richter*: omnem *Delz*   metum *Wilamowitz*: -u *A*   294 expulerant *A*: -unt *recc. (Ox)*   *post* 295 *ordinem mutauit Baehrens, ut fieret* 295, 301–3, 300, 296–9   296–300 *del. put. Richter*

improba ferret praemia uictrix
   dira libido.
Te quoque bellum triste secutum est,
mactata tua, miseranda, manu,
   nata Lucreti,
stuprum saeui passa tyranni.
dedit infandi sceleris poenas
cum Tarquinio Tullia coniunx,
quae per caesi membra parentis
egit saeuos impia currus
laceroque seni uiolenta rogos
   nata negauit.
Haec quoque nati uidere nefas
   saecula magnum,
cum Tyrrhenum rate ferali
princeps captam fraude parentem
   misit in aequor.
Properant placidos linquere portus
   iussi nautae,
resonant remis pulsata freta;
fertur in altum prouecta ratis,
quae resoluto robore labens
pressa dehiscit sorbetque mare.
tollitur ingens clamor ad astra
cum femineo mixtus planctu;
mors ante oculos dira uagatur;
quaerit leti sibi quisque fugam:
alii lacerae puppis tabulis
haerent nudi fluctusque secant,
repetunt alii litora nantes;
multos mergunt fata profundo.
Scindit uestes Augusta suas
   laceratque comas

315 resonant δ: -ent β   316 prouecta *Caietanus*: -fecta *A*   317 quae *A*: cum *M. Müller*

rigat et maestis fletibus ora.
postquam spes est nulla salutis,
ardens ira, iam uicta malis,
'haec' exclamat 'mihi pro tanto
munere reddis praemia, nate?
hac sum, fateor, digna carina,
quae te genui, quae tibi lucem
atque imperium nomenque dedi
  Caesaris amens.
Exsere uultus Acheronte tuos
poenisque meis pascere, coniunx:
ego, causa tuae, miserande, necis
natoque tuo funeris auctor,
en, ut merui, ferar ad manes
inhumata tuos,
obruta saeuis aequoris undis.'
Feriunt fluctus ora loquentis,
ruit in pelagus rursumque salo
  pressa resurgit,
pellit palmis cogente metu
freta, sed cedit fessa labori.
Mansit tacitis in pectoribus
spreta tristi iam morte fides:
multi dominae ferre auxilium
pelago fractis uiribus audent,
bracchia quam uix lenta trahentem
uoce hortantur manibusque leuant.
Quid tibi saeui fugisse maris
  profuit undas?
ferro es nati moritura tui,
cuius facinus uix posteritas,
tarde semper saecula credent.

342 ferar *A*: -or *Heinsius* 345 feriunt *β*: ferunt *δ* 349 freta set *Buecheler:* fata et *A* 354 quam uix *Lipsius*: quamuis *A* 360 credent *Σ*: -unt *A*

Furit ereptam pelagoque dolet
  uiuere matrem
impius, ingens geminatque nefas:
ruit in miserae fata parentis
patiturque moram sceleris nullam.
Missus peragit iussa satelles;
reserat dominae pectora ferro.
Caedis moriens illa ministrum
  rogat infelix
utero dirum condat ut ensem:
'hic est, hic est fodiendus', ait
'ferro, monstrum qui tale tulit'.
  Post hanc uocem
cum supremo mixtam gemitu,
animam tandem per fera tristem
  uulnera reddit.

SENECA

Quid, impotens fortuna, fallaci mihi
blandita uultu, sorte contentum mea
alte extulisti, grauius ut ruerem edita
receptus arce totque prospicerem metus?
Melius latebam procul ab inuidiae malis
remotus inter Corsici rupes maris,
ubi liber animus et sui iuris mihi
semper uacabat studia recolenti mea.
O quam iuuabat, quo nihil maius parens
Natura genuit, operis immensi artifex,
caelum intueri, solis et cursus sacros
mundique motus, sortis alternae uices

377 impotens . . . mihi *Siegmund*: me impotens . . . diu *Heinsius*: me potens . . . mihi *A* 379 grauius *recc.* (*Ox*): grauis *A* 383 mihi *A*: sibi *Gronouius, etiam* pia *pro* mea *scripto in seq. uersu* 387 cursus *recc.*: currus *A* 388 sortis alternas (-ae *scripsi*) u. δ: solis a. u. β: noctis *pro* solis *Gronouius*: 387^{b}–8^{a} solis . . . motus *del. put. Delrius*: 388 *del. Ritter*

orbemque Phoebes, astra quam cingunt uaga
lateque fulgens aetheris magni decus;
qui si senescit, tantus in caecum chaos
casurus iterum, tunc adest mundo dies
supremus ille, qui premat genus impium
caeli ruina, rursus ut stirpem nouam
generet renascens melior, ut quondam tulit
iuuenis, tenente regna Saturno poli.
Tunc illa uirgo, numinis magni dea,
Iustitia, caelo missa, cum sancta Fide
terra regebat mitis humanum genus.
Non bella norant, non tubae fremitus truces,
non arma gentes, cingere assuerant suas
muris nec urbes; peruium cunctis iter,
communis usus omnium rerum fuit;
et ipsa Tellus laeta fecundos sinus
pandebat ultro, tam piis felix parens
et tuta alumnis. Alia sed suboles minus
conspecta mitis. tertium sollers genus
nouas ad artes exstitit, sanctum tamen,
mox inquietum, quod sequi cursu feras
auderet acres, fluctibus tectos graui
extrahere pisces rete, uel calamo leui
decipere uolucres †crate uel calamo aut leui†
tenere laqueo, premere subiectos iugo 412bis
tauros feroces, uulnere immunem prius
sulcare terram; laesa quae fruges suas
interius alte condidit sacro sinu.
Sed in parentis uiscera intrauit suae

389 quam *GT*: que *P*: quem *β* 391 si senescit *Scaliger*: se senescit *GP*: sese nescit *Tβ* 392 tunc *Ritter*: nunc *A* 399 terrae *uel* -is *Bothe* 400 non t. *V recc. (Ox)*: nec t. *A* 407 *post* mitis *lac. Zwierlein* 410 auderet *β*: audent *δ* graui *Gronouius*: -es *A* 412 *uerba quae in A* uolucres *sequuntur corrupta puto, post Leonem, qui a* crate *glossemate iuxta* 411 *posito errorem processisse coni.; totum uersum* 412 *om. P, uerbo* aut *in mg. sup. uersus adscripto*: crate uel <tereti uagas> *Siegmund* 413 uulnere *A*: uomere *G (in mg.) recc.* *post* 414 *excidisse put. Zwierlein uersum huiusmodi* <summisit aegre, quasque habet largas opes> 415 interius *recc.*: -or *A*

deterior aetas; eruit ferrum graue
aurumque, saeuas mox et armauit manus;
partita fines regna constituit, nouas
exstruxit urbes, tecta defendit sua,
aliena telis aut petit praedae imminens.
Neglecta terras fugit et mores feros
hominum, cruenta caede pollutas manus,
Astraea uirgo, siderum magnum decus.
cupido belli creuit atque auri fames
totum per orbem, maximum exortum est malum,
luxuria, pestis blanda, cui uires dedit
roburque longum tempus atque error grauis.
Collecta uitia per tot aetates diu
in nos redundant: saeculo premimur graui,
quo scelera regnant, saeuit impietas furens,
turpi libido Venere dominatur potens;
luxuria uictrix orbis immensas opes
iam pridem auaris manibus, ut perdat, rapit.
Sed ecce gressu fertur attonito Nero
trucique uultu. quid ferat mente horreo.

NERO. PRAEFECTVS. SENECA

NE. Perage imperata, mitte qui Plauti mihi
Sullaeque caesi referat abscisum caput.
PR. Iussa haud morabor, castra confestim petam.
SE. Nihil in propinquos temere constitui decet.
NE. Iusto esse facile est cui uacat pectus metu.
SE. Magnum timoris remedium clementia est.
NE. Extinguere hostem maxima est uirtus ducis.
SE. Seruare ciues maior est patriae patri.
NE. Praecipere mitem conuenit pueris senem.
SE. Regenda magis est feruida adolescentia.
NE. Aetate in hac satis esse consilii reor . . .

420 sua *Buecheler:* suis *A* 423 h. et *recc.*: h. ac *Heinsius* 438 abscissum *recc.* 441 iusto *GCS*: -um *TVΣ*: -e *P* 444 patri *GTCS*: pater *PV* 447 satis *A*: sat *L. Mueller*

SE. Vt facta superi comprobent semper tua.
NE. Stulte uerebor, ipse cum faciam, deos.
SE. Hoc plus uerere, quod licet tantum tibi.
NE. Fortuna nostra cuncta permittit mihi.
SE. Crede obsequenti parcius: leuis est dea.
NE. Inertis est nescire quid liceat sibi.
SE. Id facere laus est quod decet, non quod licet.
NE. Calcat iacentem uulgus. SE. Inuisum opprimit.
NE. Ferrum tuetur principem. SE. Melius fides.
NE. Decet timeri Caesarem. SE. At plus diligi.
NE. Metuant necesse est . . . SE. Quicquid
exprimitur graue est.
NE. Iussisque nostris pareant. SE. Iusta impera.
NE. Statuam ipse. SE. Quae consensus efficiat rata.
NE. Destrictus ensis faciet. SE. Hoc absit nefas.
NE. An patiar ultra sanguinem nostrum peti,
inultus et contemptus ut subito opprimar?
exilia non fregere summotos procul
Plautum atque Sullam, pertinax quorum furor
armat ministros sceleris in caedem meam,
absentium cum maneat etiam ingens fauor
in urbe nostra, qui fouet spes exulum.
tollantur hostes ense suspecti mihi;
inuisa coniunx pereat et carum sibi
fratrem sequatur: quicquid excelsum est cadat.
SE. Pulchrum eminere est inter illustres uiros,
consulere patriae, parcere afflictis, fera
caede abstinere, tempus atque irae dare,
orbi quietem, saeculo pacem suo.
haec summa uirtus, petitur hac caelum uia.
Sic ille patriae primus Augustus parens
complexus astra est, colitur et templis deus.

448 ut β: et δ: ita *Heinsius* 449 ipse *recc.*: esse *A* 450 tibi δ*S (in mg.)*: sibi β 458 metuant *mihi suspectum* 461 destrictus *Raphelengius*: despectus *A*: respectus *G* 462 ultra *A*: -o *recc.* 463 inultus *Raphelengius*: inuictus *A* opprimar Σ: -atur *A* 467 absentium δ: -tum β

Illum tamen Fortuna iactauit diu
terra marique per graues belli uices,
hostes parentis donec oppressit sui;
tibi numen incruenta summisit suum
et dedit habenas imperi facili manu
nutuque terras maria subiecit tuo.
Inuidia tristis, uicta consensu pio,
cessit; senatus equitis accensus fauor;
plebisque uotis atque iudicio patrum
tu pacis auctor, generis humani arbiter
electus, orbem spiritu sacro regis,
patriae parens. quod nomen ut serues petit
suosque ciues Roma commendat tibi.
NE. Munus deorum est, ipsa quod seruit mihi
Roma et senatus, quodque ab inuitis preces
humilesque uoces exprimit nostri metus.
seruare ciues principi et patriae graues
claro tumentes genere quae dementia est,
cum liceat una uoce suspectos sibi
mori iubere? Brutus in caedem ducis
a quo salutem tulerat armauit manus:
inuictus acie, gentium domitor, Ioui
aequatus altos saepe per honorum gradus
Caesar nefando ciuium scelere occidit.
Quantum cruoris Roma tunc uidit sui,
lacerata totiens! ille qui meruit pia
uirtute caelum, diuus Augustus, uiros
quot interemit nobiles, iuuenes senes,
sparsos per orbem, cum suos mortis metu
fugerent penates et trium ferrum ducum,
tabula notante deditos tristi neci!
exposita rostris capita caesorum patres

483 imperii *A* 484 suo *P* 487 iudicio patrum *Lipsius*: -ium p. est *A* 489 spiritu sacro *Gruterus*: spū sacra *GP*: sap'ie sacra *C*: spe (*uel* sp'e *uel* specie) s. *TSVΣ* 495 seruare *β*: -ire *δ* ciues *δ*: uices *β* 497 tibi *K* 500 gentium domitor *Σ*: d. g. *A* 503 tunc *recc.*: non *A* 506 quos *Σ*

uidere maesti, flere nec licuit suos,
non gemere dira tabe polluto foro,
stillante sanie per putres uultus graui.
Nec finis hic cruoris aut caedis stetit:
pauere uolucres et feras saeuas diu
tristes Philippi, †hausit et Siculum mare
classes uirosque saepe caedentes suos.
concussus orbis uiribus magnis ducum.
superatus acie puppibus Nilum petit
fugae paratis, ipse periturus breui.
hausit cruorem incesta Romani ducis
Aegyptus iterum, nunc leues umbras tegit.
Illic sepultum est impie gestum diu
ciuile bellum. condidit tandem suos
iam fessus enses uictor hebetatos feris
uulneribus et continuit imperium metus.
armis fideque militis tutus fuit,
pietate nati factus eximia deus,
post fata consecratus et templis datus.
Nos quoque manebunt astra, si saeuo prior
ense occuparo quicquid infestum est mihi
dignaque nostram subole fundaro domum.
SE. Implebit aulam stirpe caelesti tuam
generata Diuo, Claudiae gentis decus,
sortita fratris more Iunonis toros.
NE. Incesta genetrix detrahit generi fidem
animusque numquam coniugis iunctus mihi.
SE. Teneris in annis haud satis clara est fides,
pudore uictus cum tegit flammas amor.
NE. Hoc equidem et ipse credidi frustra diu,

512 nec *C*   516 hausit *A*, *quo accepto* ferae saeuae . . . Philippos *Liberman*, *post* Philippi *lac. Zwierlein*, *518[ba] Reeve*, *ut fiat ordo* Philippi, uiribus m. d. | c. orbis, hausit: clausit *M. Müller*: mersit *Gronovius*   517 caedentes *Fabricius*: ced- *A* suis *Baden*   522 non *M. Müller*   526 metus *A*: -u *Auantius*   533 implebit *Q*[2] *recc.*: -uit *A*   534 generata *VΣ*: -o *A*   536 generi *A*: -is *P*

manifesta quamuis pectore insociabili
uultuque signa proderent odium mei.
tandem quod ardens statuit ulcisci dolor
dignamque thalamis coniugem inueni meis
genere atque forma, uicta cui cedet Venus
Iouisque coniunx et ferox armis dea.
SE. Probitas fidesque coniugis, mores pudor
placeant marito; sola perpetuo manent
subiecta nulli mentis atque animi bona;
florem decoris singuli carpunt dies.
NE. Omnes in unam contulit laudes deus
talemque nasci fata uoluerunt mihi.
SE. Recedat a te (temere ne credas) amor.
NE. Quem summouere fulminis dominus nequit,
caeli tyrannum, saeua qui penetrat freta
Ditisque regna, detrahit superos polo?
SE. Volucrem esse Amorem fingit immitem deum
mortalis error, armat et telis manus
arcuque sacras, instruit saeua face
genitumque credit Venere, Vulcano satum.
Vis magna mentis blandus atque animi calor
amor est, iuuenta gignitur, luxu otio
nutritur inter laeta Fortunae bona.
quem si fouere atque alere desistas, cadit
breuique uires perdit extinctus suas.
NE. Hanc esse uitae maximam causam reor,
per quam uoluptas oritur, interitu caret,
cum procreetur semper, humanum genus,
Amore grato, qui truces mulcet feras.
hic mihi iugales praeferat taedas deus
iungatque nostris igne Poppaeam toris.

541 insociabili *recc.*: insac- (insat-) *A* 543 quod *GP*: que *TCV* (que *uel* qui *S*) 545 cedet *A*: -at *TV*: -it *recc.* 546 ferox *Pβ*: -ax *GT* 559 arcuque sacras *Buecheler*: -usque -os *A* 566–9 *Neroni dant recc., Senecae A* 571 igne *A*: ipse *Bothe*

SE. Vix sustinere possit hos thalamos dolor
uidere populi, sancta nec pietas sinat.
NE. Prohibebor unus facere quod cunctis licet?
SE. Maiora populus semper a summo exigit.
NE. Libet experiri uiribus fractus meis
an cedat animis temere conceptus fauor.
SE. Obsequere potius ciuibus placidus tuis.
NE. Male imperatur, cum regit uulgus duces.
SE. Nihil impetrare cum ualet, iuste dolet.
NE. Exprimere ius est, ferre quod nequeunt preces?
SE. Negare durum est. NE. Principem cogi nefas.
SE. Remittat ipse. NE. Fama sed uictum feret.
SE. Leuis atque uana. NE. Sit licet, multos notat.
SE. Excelsa metuit. NE. Non minus carpit tamen.
SE. Facile opprimetur; merita te diui patris
aetasque frangat coniugis, probitas pudor.
NE. Desiste tandem, iam grauis nimium mihi,
instare, liceat facere quod Seneca improbat.
Et ipse populi uota iam pridem moror,
cum portet utero pignus et partem mei:
quin destinamus proximum thalamis diem?

AGRIPPINA

Tellure rupta Tartaro gressum extuli,
Stygiam cruenta praeferens dextra facem
thalamis scelestis: nubat his flammis meo
Poppaea nato iuncta, quas uindex manus
dolorque matris uertet ad tristes rogos.
Manet inter umbras impiae caedis mihi
semper memoria, manibus nostris grauis
adhuc inultis, reddita et meritis meis

572 possit *Q*: -et *A*   573 uidere *A*: fidesque *Heinsius*   577 furor *Auantius*   591 *lacunam possis suspicari uel ante uel post 591, ubi Poppaeae nomen desideratur.*   *ante* 593 mater *CS*: mater Neronis *V*: mater Neronis sc. Agrippina *FM* [A. m. N. *N*]: *notam om., relicto spatio,* δ   596 uictrix *G*   597 uertet β: -at δ   600 est *Buecheler*

funesta merces puppis et pretium imperi
nox illa qua naufragia defleui mea.
comitum necem natique crudelis nefas
deflere uotum fuerat; haud tempus datum est
lacrimis, sed ingens scelere geminauit nefas.
perempta ferro, foeda uulneribus sacros
intra penates spiritum effudi grauem
erepta pelago sanguine extinxi meo
nec odia nati; saeuit in nomen ferus
matris tyrannus, obrui meritum cupit,
simulacra titulos destruit mortis metu
totum per orbem, quem dedit poenam in meam
puero regendum noster infelix amor.
Extinctus umbras agitat infestus meas
flammisque uultus noxios coniunx petit.
instat minatur imputat fatum mihi
tumulumque nati, poscit auctorem necis;
iam parce: dabitur, tempus haud longum peto.
Vltrix Erinys impio dignum parat
letum tyranno, uerbera et turpem fugam
poenasque quis et Tantali uincat sitim,
dirum laborem Sisyphi, Tityi alitem
Ixionisque membra rapientem rotam,
licet exstruat marmoribus atque auro tegat
superbus aulam, limen armatae ducis
seruent cohortes, mittat immensas opes
exhaustus orbis, supplices dextram petant
Parthi cruentam, regna diuitias ferant:
ueniet dies tempusque quo reddat suis
animam nocentem sceleribus, iugulum hostibus
desertus ac destructus et cunctis egens.
Heu quo labor, quo uota ciciderunt mea,

601 imperii *A* 602 nox *recc. (Ox)*: uox *A* 607 intra *β*: inter *δKe* 611 mortis metu *A*, *uix sanum*: matris metu *Buecheler*: *an* nostri metu? 617 nati *Σ*: nasci *A* 626 immensas *β*: uniuersas *δ* 631 ac . . . et *recc.* (ac . . . a *G*): et . . . ac *A*

quo te furor prouexit attonitum tuus
et fata, nate, cedat ut tantis malis
genetricis ira, quae tuo scelere occidit?
utinam, antequam te paruulum in lucem edidi
aluique, saeuae nostra lacerassent ferae
uiscera! sine ullo scelere, sine sensu, innocens,
meus occidisses, iunctus atque haerens mihi
semper quieta cerneres sede inferum
proauos patremque, nominis magni uiros,
quos nunc pudor luctusque perpetuus manet
ex te, nefande, meque quae talem tuli.
Quid tegere cesso Tartaro uultus meos,
nouerca coniunx mater infelix meis?

OCTAVIA. CHORVS

OC. Parcite lacrimis urbis festo
laetoque die,
ne tantus amor nostrique fauor
principis acres suscitet iras
uobisque ego sim causa malorum.
Non hoc primum pectora uulnus
mea senserunt: grauiora tuli.
dabit hic nostris finem curis
uel morte dies.
non ego saeui cernere cogar
coniugis ora,
non inuisos intrare mihi
thalamos famulae.
soror Augusti, non uxor ero;
absint tantum tristes poenae
letique metus –

634 *post* nate *uarie interpunxerunt libri; signum ut uidetur interrogationis posuit P* 640 quieta . . . sede *Heinsius*: -am . . . -em *A* 646–89 *dimetri, praeter* 655 (c. o.), 657 (t. f.) 660 (l. m.), 684 (i. N.) *monometros, in A* 653 dabis *SΣ* 654 saeui *Auantius*: -e *A* cogar *Σ*: -or *A* 655 *om. P*

scelerum diri, miseranda, uiri
potes hoc demens sperare memor?
hos ad thalamos seruata diu
uictima tandem funesta cades.
Sed quid patrios saepe penates
respicis udis confusa genis?
propera tectis efferre gradus,
linque cruentam principis aulam.
CHO. En illuxit suspecta diu
fama totiens iactata dies:
cessit thalamis Claudia diri
  pulsa Neronis,
quos iam uictrix Poppaea tenet,
cessat pietas dum nostra graui
compressa metu segnisque dolor.
Vbi Romani uis est populi,
fregit claros quae saepe duces,
dedit inuictae leges patriae,
fasces dignis ciuibus olim,
iussit bellum pacemque, feras
  gentes domuit,
captos reges carcere clausit?
Grauis en oculis undique nostris
iam Poppaeae fulget imago
  iuncta Neroni!
affligat humo uiolenta manus
similes nimium uultus dominae
ipsamque toris detrahat altis,
petat infestis mox et flammis
telisque feri principis aulam.

661–8 *choro dedit Baehrens* 661 scelerum *recc. (S in mg.)*: socerum *A*: soror o *recc.* 662 hec *VM* 669–89 *rectum ordinem seruauit β*: *ante 669 uu.* 677^{b}–684 *exhibet P*, 677^{b}–684 *et* 687–9 *GT* 685 affligat *recc.*: -fig- *A* humo *Gβ*: -i *P* 688 infestis *Grotius*: infelix *A* 689 feri *δ*: -is *β*

NVTRIX. POPPAEA

NV. Quo trepida gressum coniugis thalamis tui
effers, alumna? quidue secretum petis
turbata uultu? cur genae fletu madent?
certe petitus precibus et uotis dies
nostris refulsit; Caesari iuncta es tuo
taeda iugali, quem tuus cepit decor,
et culta sancte tradidit uinctum tibi
genetrix Amoris, maximum numen, Venus.
O qualis altos, quanta pressisti toros
residens in aula! uidit attonitus tuam
formam senatus, tura cum superis dares
sacrasque grato spargeres aras mero,
uelata summum flammeo tenui caput;
et ipse lateri iunctus atque haerens tuo
sublimis inter ciuium laeta omina
incessit habitu atque ore laetitiam gerens
princeps superbo: talis emersam freto
spumante Peleus coniugem accepit Thetin,
quorum toros celebrasse caelestes ferunt
pelagique numen omne consensu pari.
Quae subita uultus causa mutauit tuos?
quid pallor iste, quid ferant lacrimae doce.
PO. Confusa tristi proximae noctis metu
uisuque, nutrix, mente turbata feror,
defecta sensu. Laeta nam postquam dies
sideribus atris cessit et nocti polus,
inter Neronis uincta complexus mei
somno resoluor nec diu placida frui
quiete licuit. uisa nam thalamos meos
celebrare turba est maesta; resolutis comis
matres Latinae flebiles planctus dabant.

691 quidue *recc.*: quodue *GPCV*: quod ut *SK*: quoue *T*   692 madent *δM*: manant *C*: manent *SV* (d *s.l. V*)   694 es *Σ*: est *A*   696 et culta sancte *Birt*: et culpa senece *A* (senecte *M*)   uinctum *Σ*: uic- *A*   701 sacrasque *Σ*: sacras *A*   708 quorum *δ*: quarum *β*   715 atrae *Peiper*   716 uincta *β*: uic- *δ*: iunc- *recc.*

inter tubarum saepe terribilem sonum
sparsam cruore coniugis genetrix mei
uultu minaci saeua quatiebat facem.
quam dum sequor coacta praesenti metu
diducta subito patuit ingenti mihi
tellus hiatu, lata quo praeceps toros
cerno iugales pariter et miror meos,
in quis resedi fessa. uenientem intuor
comitante turba coniugem quondam meum
natumque: properat petere complexus meos
Crispinus, intermissa libare oscula,
irrupit intra tecta cum trepidus mea
ensemque iugulo condidit saeuum Nero.
tandem quietem magnus excussit timor,
quatit ora et artus horridus nostros tremor
pulsatque pectus, continet uocem timor.
quam nunc fides pietasque produxit tua.
Heu quid minantur inferum manes mihi?
aut quem cruorem coniugis uidi mei?
NV. Quaecumque mentis agitat intentus uigor,
ea per quietem sacer et arcanus refert
ueloxque sensus. coniugem thalamos toros
uidisse te miraris amplexu noui
haerens mariti? sed mouent laeto die
pulsata palmis pectora et fusae comae?
Octauiae discidia planxerunt sacros
intra penates fratris et patrium larem.
fax illa, quam secuta es, Augustae manu
praelata, clarum nomen inuidia tibi
partum ominatur. inferum sedes toros
stabiles futuros spondet aeternae domus.
iugulo quod ensem condidit princeps tuus,

731 Crispinus *Aegidius Maserius apud Ascensium*: pristinus *A* 732 irrupit *SΣ*: -rump- *δCV* tum *Σ* 735 ossa *Buecheler* 736 pulsatque *δ*: pulsat *β* timor *β*: tremor *δ* *(uersum om. P)* 740 intentus *Gronouius*: -fest- *A* 742 toros *recc.*: rogos *A* 744 laeto *δVΣ*: -a *β* 747 intra *Auantius*: inter *A*

bella haud mouebit, pace sed ferrum teget.
Recollige animum, recipe laetitiam, precor;
timore pulso redde te thalamis tuis.
PO. Delubra et aras petere constitui sacras,
caesis litare uictimis numen deum,
ut expientur noctis et somni minae
terrorque in hostes redeat attonitus meos.
Tu uota pro me suscipe et precibus piis
superos adora, †maneat ut praesens metus†.

CHORVS

Si uera loquax fama Tonantis
furta et gratos narrat amores
(quem modo Ledae pressisse sinum
tectum plumis pennisque ferunt,
modo per fluctus raptam Europen
taurum tergo portasse trucem),
quae regit et nunc deseret astra,
petet amplexus, Poppaea, tuos,
quos et Ledae praeferre potest
et tibi, quondam cui miranti
fuluo, Danae, fluxit in auro.
formam Sparte iactet alumnae
licet, et Phrygius praemia pastor,
uincet uultus haec Tyndaridos,
qui mouerunt horrida bella
Phrygiaeque solo regna dedere.
Sed quis gressu ruit attonito
aut quid portat pectore anhelo?

753 mouebit *β*: -is *δ* 760 tu *Gronouius*: et *A* 761 maneat . . . metus *A*: iam abeat . . . m. *Helm*: monuit . . . m. *Gronouius*: status *pro* metus *Buecheler* 762 loquax *recc.*(*S^2e*): -ar *A* 764 quem *recc.*: que *A*: qui *G* 765 ferunt *recc.* -um *A* 766 Europen *SΣ*: -em *A* 772 Danae *Ascensius*: Dane *A* fluxit *A*: fulxit *S*: fulsit *recc.* 779 ecquid *Richter* quid portat pectore anhelo *Ascensius:* pectore q. portat a. *Schmidt*: q. pectore portat a. *A*

NVNTIVS. CHORVS

NVN. Quicumque tectis excubat miles ducis,
defendat aulam, cui furor populi imminet.
Trepidi cohortes ecce praefecti trahunt
praesidia ad urbis, uicta nec cedit metu
concepta rabies temere, sed uires capit.
CHO. Quis iste mentes agitat attonitus furor?
NVN. Octauiae fauore percussa agmina
et efferata per nefas ingens ruunt.
CHO. Quid ausa facere quoue consilio doce.
NVN. Reddere penates Claudiae Diui parant
torosque fratris, debitam partem imperi.
CHO. Quos iam tenet Poppaea concordi fide?
NVN. Hinc urit animos pertinax nimium fauor
et in furorem temere praecipites agit.
Quaecumque claro marmore effigies stetit
aut aere fulgens, ora Poppaeae gerens,
afflicta uulgi manibus et saeuo iacet
euersa ferro; membra per partes trahunt
diducta laqueis, obruunt turpi diu
calcata caeno. uerba conueniunt feris
immixta factis, quae timor reticet meus.
Saepire flammis principis sedem parant,
populi nisi irae coniugem reddat nouam,
reddat penates Claudiae uictus suos.
Vt noscat ipse ciuium motus mea
uoce, haud morabor iussa praefecti exsequi.

CHORVS

Quid fera frustra bella mouetis?
inuicta gerit tela Cupido:

780 excubat miles *Bothe* (m. excubat *Raphelengius*): m. exultat *A* 786 fauore *Grotius*: furore *A* 789 diri *Ritter* 790 imperii *A* 792 hinc *M.Müller*: hic *A* fauor *recc.*: furor *A* 795 aere *Lipsius*: ara *A* ora *Σe*: era *A* 798 deducta *recc.* 800 pudor *Tarrant* reticet *Delrius*: recipit *A* 803 uictus *recc.*(*MNe*): uinc- *PVFOx*: iunc- *A* 805 iussa *Σ*: *om. A (spatium reliquerunt SV)* 806–19 *dimetri in A praeter* 812 (s. u.) *et* 817• (d. u.) *monometros*

flammis uestros obruet ignes
quis extinxit fulmina saepe
captumque Iouem caelo traxit.
Laeso tristes dabitis poenas
  sanguine uestro;
non est patiens, feruidus, irae
  facilisque regi.
Ille ferocem iussit Achillem
  pulsare lyram,
fregit Danaos, fregit Atriden,
regna euertit Priami, claras
  diruit urbes.
Et nunc animus quid ferat horret
uis immitis uiolenta dei.

NERO

O lenta nimium militis nostri manus
et ira patiens post nefas tantum mea,
quod non cruor ciuilis accensas faces
extinguit in nos, caede nec populi madet
funerea Roma, quae uiros tales tulit!
Admissa sed iam morte puniri parum est:
grauiora meruit impium plebis scelus.
At illa, cui me ciuium subicit furor,
suspecta coniunx et soror semper mihi,
tandem dolori spiritum reddat meo
iramque nostram sanguine extinguat suo;
mox tecta flammis concidant urbis meis,
ignes ruinae noxium populum premant
turpisque egestas, saeua cum luctu fames.
exultat ingens saeculi nostri bonis
corrupta turba nec capit clementiam

811 laeso *Bothe*[2]: -i *A* 816 Atriden *Housman*: -em *A* 821 nefas tantum *recc.*: t. n. *A* 822 quod *A*: quid *recc.* 823 madet Σ: madent *G*β (mandent *P*) 827 at *Bothe*: et *A* 834 ingens *uix sanum*: audax *uel aliquid tale scribendum puto*

ingrata nostram ferre nec pacem potest,
sed inquieta rapitur hinc audacia,
hinc temeritate fertur in praeceps sua.
malis domanda est et graui semper iugo
premenda, ne quid simile temptare audeat
contraque sanctos coniugis uultus meae
attollere oculos. fracta per poenas, metu
parere discet principis nutu sui.
Sed adesse cerno rara quem pietas uirum
fidesque castris nota praeposuit meis.

PRAEFECTVS. NERO

PR. Populi furorem caede paucorum, diu
qui restiterunt temere, compressum affero.
NE. Et hoc sat est? sic miles audisti ducem?
compescis? haec uindicta debetur mihi?
PR. Cecidere motus impii ferro duces.
NE. Quid illa turba, petere quae flammis meos
ausa est penates, principi legem dare,
abstrahere nostris coniugem caram toris,
uiolare quantum licuit incesta manu
et uoce dira? debita poena uacat?
PR. Poenam dolor constituet in ciues tuos?
NE. Constituet, aetas nulla quam famae eximat.
PR. Tua temperet nos ira, non noster timor.
NE. Iram expiabit prima quae meruit meam.
PR. Quam poscat ede, nostra ne parcat manus.
NE. Caedem sororis poscit et dirum caput.
PR. Horrore uinctum trepidus astrinxit rigor.
NE. Parere dubitas? PR. Cur meam damnas fidem?

840 audeat *δV*: uid- *β (corr. S² in marg.)* 842 uicta *G* 843 discat *recc.* *post* 848 *aliquid excidisse put. Zwierlein, Leonem secutus* 849 compescis *A*: compressit *Peiper*: compressus? *Buecheler* 850 cecidere *β*: re- *δ* motus *Bernardinus Marmita*: me- *A* impii *recc.*: -o *A* 853 tantam *M* 854 *an* libuit? 858 tua *Buecheler*: qua *A*: quam *recc.* 859 expiabit *Erasmus apud Ascensium*: expectabit *A* (expectabat *P*) 862 uinctum *Σ*: uic- *A*

NE. Quod parcis hosti. PR. Femina hoc
 nomen capit?
NE. Si scelera cepit. PR. Estne qui sontem arguat?
NE. Populi furor. PR. Quis regere dementes ualet?
NE. Qui concitare potuit. PR. Haud quemquam reor.
NE. Mulier, dedit natura cui pronum malo
animum, ad nocendum pectus instruxit dolis.
PR. Sed uim negauit. NE. Vt ne inexpugnabilis
esset, sed aegras frangeret uires timor
uel poena, quae iam sera damnatam premet
diu nocentem. Tolle consilium ac preces
et imperata perage: deuectam rate
procul in remotum litus interimi iube,
tandem ut residat pectoris nostri tumor.

CHORVS. OCTAVIA

CHO. O funestus multis populi
 dirusque fauor,
qui cum flatu uela secundo
ratis impleuit uexitque procul,
languidus idem deserit alto
 saeuoque mari.
Fleuit Gracchos miseranda parens,
perdidit ingens quos plebis amor
 nimiusque fauor,
genere illustres, pietate, fide,
lingua claros, pectore fortes,
 legibus acres.
Te quoque, Liui, simili leto
 fortuna dedit,

864 quid Σ 867 qui *KQ*: quis *A* 870[a] (s. u. n.) *praefecto dedit Peiper*, 868–76 *totum Neroni continuatur in codd.* 872 iam *P*: tam *GTβ* premet *uel* -at *Bothe*[2]: -it *A* 876 timor Σ 877–983 *dimetri in A praeter* 913[b] (t. E.), 957[b] (u. n.) *monometros;* 980–1 (h. i. c. l. n. s.) *trimetrum habent Tβ, dimetrum monometro addito G* (981 n. s. *om. P)* 877 o *β*: *om. δ* 882 grac(c)os *δ* (grecos *G*[ac]): gratos *β* (*in V* c *legitur s. l.*): gnatos Σ *(in mg. V)* 883 quos Σ: quod *A:* qui *S* 887 Liui *Delrius*: leui *δ*: leuis *β*

quem neque fasces texere sui
nec tecta domus –plura referre
prohibet praesens exempla dolor:
modo cui patriam reddere ciues
aulam et fratris uoluere toros,
nunc ad poenam letumque trahi
flentem miseram cernere possunt.
Bene paupertas humili tecto
   contenta latet;
quatiunt altas saepe procellae
aut euertit fortuna domos.
OC. Quo me trahitis quodue tyrannus
aut exilium regina iubet?
sic mihi uitam fracta remittit,
tot iam nostris euicta malis?
sin caede mea cumulare parat
luctus nostros, inuidet etiam
cur in patria mihi saeua mori?
Sed iam spes est nulla salutis:
fratris cerno miseranda ratem;
haec est cuius uecta carina
quondamest genetrix; nunc et thalamis
expulsa soror miseranda uehar.
Nullum Pietas nunc numen habet
   nec sunt superi:
regnat mundo tristis Erinys.
Quis mea digne deflere potest
mala? quae lacrimis nostris questus
   reddere aedon?
cuius pennas utinam miserae
   mihi fata darent!

889 quem β: quam δ suae *Wilamowitz*: tui *recc.* 895 possunt Σ: -it *A*: -is *recc.*(*T*) 898 domos *recc.*: -us *A* 899 quodue *T*β: quidue *GP* 901 sic *Heinsius*: si *A* 903 sin *Gronouius*: si *A* 908 hec est cuius *recc.*: hac e. c. *A*: hac e. eius *Damsté* 909 est *scripsi* 915• reddere *recc.*(*e*): redderet *A*: reddat *N* aedon *Jacobus Bononiensis apud Ascensium*: edon *A*

fugerem luctus ablata meos
penna uolucri procul et coetus
hominum tristes caedemque feram.
sola in uacuo nemore et tenui
  ramo pendens
querulo possem gutture maestum
  fundere murmur.
CHO. Regitur fatis mortale genus
nec sibi quicquam spondere potest
  firmum et stabile
quem per casus uoluit uarios
semper nobis metuenda dies.
Animum firment exempla tuum
iam multa domus quae uestra tulit.
quid saeuior est fortuna tibi?
Tu mihi primum tot natorum
memoranda parens, nata Agrippae,
nurus Augusti, Caesaris uxor,
cuius nomen clarum toto
  fulsit in orbe,
utero totiens enixa graui
pignora pacis, mox exilium,
uerbera, saeuas passa catenas,
funera luctus, tandem letum,
  cruciata diu.
Felix thalamis Liuia Drusi
natisque ferum ruit in facinus
  poenamque suam.
Iulia matris fata secuta est:
post longa tamen tempora ferro
caesa est, quamuis crimine nullo.
Quid non potuit quondam genetrix

925 quicquam *recc.*: quis- *A*   926 stabile et f. *Reeve*   927 quem per *Herington*: per quem *A*: per que *uel* quam *recc.*: *monometrum excidisse put. Richter huiusmodi* f. et stabile<m uitae cursum>; *alii alia*   930 iam *β*: tam *δ*   947 quid *Tβ*: quod *GP*

tua, quae rexit principis aulam,
cara marito partuque potens?
eadem famulo subiecta suo
cecidit diri militis ense.
Quid, cui licuit regnum in caelum
sperare, parens tanta Neronis?
non, funesta uiolata manu
  remigis ante,
mox et ferro lacerata diu,
saeui iacuit uictima nati?
OC. Me quoque tristes mittit ad umbras
ferus et manes ecce tyrannus.
Quid iam frustra miseranda moror?
rapite ad letum quis ius in nos
  Fortuna dedit.
Testor superos– quid agis demens?
parce precari quis inuisa es
numina diuum: Tartara testor
Erebique deas scelerum ultrices
  et te, genitor,
dignum tali morte et poena:
non inuisa est mors ista mihi.
Armate ratem, date uela fretis
uentisque, petat puppis rector
Pandatariae litora terrae.
CHO. Lenes aurae Zephyrique leues,
tectam quondam nube aetheria
qui uexistis raptam saeuae
uirginis aris Iphigeniam,
hanc quoque tristi procul a poena
portate, precor, templa ad Triuiae.
Vrbe est nostra mitior Aulis

952 et caelum *Watt*   954 uiolata *GT*[ac]*SV*Σ: -enta *PC*   957 nati δ*CV*: -o *S*   958 mittit *recc.*: -et *A*   959 ad *M*   967 digna haut tali *Zwierlein*   971 Pandatariae *Lipsius*: tandem Phariae *A*   973 aetheria *recc.*: -ea *A*   977 portate *GT*[ac]: -are *P*β   978 est β: e δ

et Taurorum barbara tellus:
hospitis illic caede litatur
numen superum;
ciuis gaudet Roma cruore.

979 Taurorum *Lipsius*: mau- *A*   982 ciuis *C*: cuius *δSV* Lucii annei senece octauia explicit feliciter (fel. *om. PT*). Incipit hercules etheus eiusdem *A*: Explicit Octauia Senece. Incipiunt quedam sumpta de tragediis Senece *G*: marci lucii annei octauia explicit *Σ*

COMMENTARY

1 Numerous Greek and Latin tragedies begin at dawn, a phenomenon whose most likely explanation seems to be that performances at the festivals began very early in the morning (Pickard-Cambridge, *DF*, 68–9). This convention is consistently reproduced by Senecan tragedy, where only *Phoe.* and *H.O.* contain no indication of the supposed time of the action at the start. In *Octavia*, whose action spans three successive days, this sunrise has even less significance than usual and only maintains a long-established literary convention, besides signposting the tragic character of the piece. The playwright also wished to reproduce Electra's song in Soph. *El.* 86–120, where the heroine pours out her grievances to the elements after yet another sleepless night spent in mourning (cf. 86–91 ὦ φάος ἁγνόν | ... ὥς μοι | πολλὰς μὲν θρηνῶν ᾠδὰς | ... ᾔσθου | ... ὁπόταν δνοφερὰ νὺξ ὑπολειφθῇ see *infra*). The parallel was investigated in full by Ladek (1909), but attention had already been drawn to *Electra* by Delrius (*Syntagma*, iii. 521–4, ad 8, 30, 58, 77 in his line numbering). The parallel carries the implication that Octavia, like her Greek counterpart, can find no comfort in the quiet of the night, so great is the bereavement consequent upon the destruction of her whole family.

The two first speeches of the play, delivered respectively by Octavia and by the *Nutrix*, were censured as repetitious by Peiper (1863, and again in his 1867 edition); he transposed the monody of Octavia after the Nurse's speech (34–56), also in order to eliminate an initial *canticum*. There are no cogent reasons for this alteration of the transmitted order, even if dislocations involving anapaestic sections are fairly common in the Senecan corpus: something of this kind appears to have occurred in *K*, where 34–56 follow 71, and the same hand which penned the body of the text annotates in the margin of 34 *hic deficit actus*. Shorter lines – anapaestic, and half-lines in *antilabē* – were copied in multiple columns to save space, which often generated transpositions: cf. Zwierlein, *KK* ad *Hf.* 146; (1979), 176 n. 3; a similar corruption has occurred in *Oct.*, at 669 ff. (in *GT*).

The song of the distraught Octavia creates an emotionally charged, typically tragic atmosphere, in which tension is at its peak from the very start, while the subsequent iambic passage supplements the background information in the plainer style suited to the expository prologue. There is, however, a great amount of thematic overlapping between this song and the following iambics of the *Nutrix*. A comparable impression of repetition is sometimes aroused by the succession of sung and spoken parts in Greek tragedy (cf. ad 100), a feature which is probably enhanced by the loss of the music and, in *Oct.*, by the lack of the distinctive linguistic and stylistic features characteristic of sung parts in Greek drama.

Expository prologues spoken by a character in dire straits or, alternatively, in the grip of fierce passion are common in Euripides and in Seneca (cf. Leo, *Monolog*, 90–1), yet formal parallels for pre-prologic anapaestic monodies similar to Octavia's are difficult to adduce. This results partially from the Greek audience's expectations of some information from the very first lines of a play. Eur. 114–15 N², a monody sung by a distressed Andromeda, are said by the scholium to Arist. *Thesm.* 1065–68 to be part of the beginning of the prologue (τοῦ προλόγου . . . εἰσβολήν), but this initial position is often disputed: cf. W. Ritchie, *The Authenticity of the Rhesus* (Cambridge, 1964), 101–4; R. Klimer-Winter, *Andromedatragödien* (Stuttgart, 1993). On the other hand, the dialogic anapaestic beginning in Eur. *I.A.* 1–48 (Agamemnon and the old servant) may safely be regarded as the text read by Alexandrian scholars. More generally, beginnings *in mediis rebus*, with a delayed or disguised prologue, are already common in fifth-century drama and in New comedy, where various devices help to avoid the artificial explanatory prologue: cf. Don. ad *Ter. Phorm. praef.* 1.11 Wessner: *nam officium prologi ante actionem quidem rei semper est, uerumtamen et post principium fabulae inducitur, ut apud Plautum . . . et apud ceteros magnae auctoritatis ueteres poetas.* On postponed prologues in Aristophanes and Menander cf. Gomme–Sandbach, 20–1. Musically accompanied openings are also attested for Roman comedy: cf. Plaut. *Cist., Epid., Pers., Stich.* In fifth-century tragedy a monody can introduce the parodos, though both songs regularly follow the prologue (Aesch. *Prom.*; Soph. *El.*; Eur. *Troad., Hec., Andr., El., Hel., Ion, I.T., Hyps.*). In *Octavia* a choral ode with parodos-like features occurs at 273, after the long exchange, partly sung, between Octavia and her Nurse, with the latter virtually taking over the consolatory function normally assigned to the chorus. In Greek tragedy, more than one scene may occasionally precede the *parodos* (in Eur. *Phoe.* the Chorus does not enter until 202). On tragic monodies, cf. W. Barner in Jens, *Bauformen*, 277–320, esp. 308–12, discussing the function and position of monodies in the structure of extant Greek dramas. In Seneca, the only other anapaestic *exordium* is *Phae.* 1–84, describing preparations for Hippolytus' hunt. While this points to similarity in technique, the *Phaedra* passage is not imitated here.

A tentative reconstruction of the stagecraft of act 1 (= lines 1–272) must take into account the interplay of dramatic models conjured up in the tragedy. As night lifts its veil, Octavia comes out of the palace, to declare her misfortunes to the Sun. She then withdraws into her apartments, while her Nurse emerges to pronounce a formal prologue. Octavia's following lament (57–71) comes from inside, as the Nurse's reaction (73–4) makes clear. The Nurse then makes herself go in and bring comfort to her pupil, but Octavia probably comes out before the other can complete her movement.

It is in theory possible to see Octavia's first monody (1–34) as delivered inside her residence: so Ballaira, who asserts that the first scene shows the interior of

Octavia's chamber; also Leo, *Monolog*, 93; Kragelund (1999), 243–5. Zwierlein, *Rezitationsdramen*, 44 n. 10 maintains that at 75 ff. Octavia is coming out of the palace. Herington (1977), 278, casts doubt on Ballaira's hypothesis, although his own claim that indoor scenes are unheard of in ancient theatre is hardly sustainable. Even in fifth-century Greek tragedy, the line between indoors and outdoors is often uncertain, and the illusion is often created that a scene is taking place indoors (cf. Di Benedetto ad Eur. *Or.* 147, 170; A. M. Dale, 'Interior Scenes and Illusion in Greek Drama', in *Collected Papers* (Cambridge, 1969), 259–71; V. Di Benedetto, *Studi Della Corte* (Urbino, 1989), 1.121–39). In Senecan tragedy, some scenes are explicitly set in interiors: cf. *Thy.* 920–69, sung by Thyestes from the dining-hall (cf. *Thy.* 902–3; 908). Indoor scenes are also common in Latin comedy, and Tarrant (1978), 238 n. 113 adduced the precedent of Plaut. *Stichus* 58–88 in support of this interpretation. After a *canticum* (partly anapaestic, 1–57) sung by the two sisters, who are pining for their husbands, long absent from home, Antipho leaves his house declaring the intention to visit his daughters. The two women, however, carry on their dialogue without apparently taking any notice of him until 88 *certo enim mihi paternae uocis sonitus auris accidit.*

The heroine's description of the sunrise (1–3) and her subsequent address to *lux semper funesta* are more effective if she is thought to be 'outside' – unless we assume that she is speaking from a window (cf. T. P. Wiseman, 'The principal thing' (Sherborne 2001), 10–11; Liv. 1.41.4 *ex superiore parte aedium per fenestras in Nouam uiam uersas . . . populum Tanaquil adloquitur*), or from the high *fastigia* of the palace (cf. Sen. *Phae.* 1154 *quae uox ab altis flebilis tectis sonat*). But this is not a default assumption in ancient drama; it would need to be signalled by the dramatic situation. It is more reasonable to assume that Octavia comes out to greet nature and to set her own grief against the background of nature reviving for the toils of the day. This is also more in keeping with the allusion to Sophocles' *Electra*. The first appearance of Octavia in the play sets the emotional tone. No pragmatic consideration explains Octavia's coming out of the palace, and it can be assumed that she has only emerged to vent her despair. Sophocles' Electra, on the other hand, is allowed to express her mourning more freely outside, because Aegisthus is out of town. Octavia's Nurse, likewise, seems to have come out only in order to express her despair for the house of Octavia. By this time, however, Octavia must have withdrawn into her chambers, because the Nurse declares that she heard Octavia's subsequent lament as a cry from inside (72–4 *uox en nostras perculit aures | tristis alumnae; | cesset thalamis inferre gradus | tarda senectus?*). Tragic parallels for these movements of Octavia can be adduced from Eur. *I.T.* 1–66; *Phoe.* 1–87. In the former, Iphigenia comes out of Diana's temple to recite the prologue, only to go back inside the temple immediately after speaking (65–6), then to reappear and perform an *amoibaion* with the chorus (123). The movements of Jocasta in Eur. *Phoe.* are less explicit, but she is certainly not present during the following *teichoskopia*. The Nurse's failure to take any notice of Octavia could be explained within post-classical theatrical conventions, whereby characters simultaneously present on stage speak in succession without any contact for a while: cf. Plaut. *Rud.* 185–257, a scene possibly echoing tragedy, where the shipwrecked Palaestra sings of her misfortunes, while Ampelisca does the same at the other end of the stage, but the two characters seem to take no notice of each other for some time. At last they hear each other and engage in a *canticum*. The Nurse's reaction on finally hearing Octavia's laments, however, carries the implication that the new voice is heard from within, as she persuades herself to go inside and try to console her mistress.

Octavia returns on stage and a 'lyrical' exchange between the two takes place. This has no parallels in either Sophocles' or Euripides' *Electra*. In the former, after Orestes's arrival, a brief cry is heard from inside the palace (77) and the two men leave in order to dedicate ritual honours to the tomb of Agamemnon. This is followed by Electra's song *apo tēs skenēs*, in recitative anapaests with some lyrical features, and, in turn, by the parodos in the form of a *kommos*. It is this very monody which the introductory first scene of *Octavia* on the whole imitates until the expository prologue delivered by the Nurse. The long lament from within may be an imitation of Eur. *Med.*, especially in connection with the Nurse's final words (see note ad 55–6), foreboding impending ruin for her obstinate mistress. The combination of several different famous tragic models is unsurprising, in a play so predominantly based on imitation. The 'stagecraft' of the prologue is also discussed by F. Stoessl in *RE* s.v. *Prolog*, xxiii. 2.2429, who cites Euripides' *Medea* as a parallel for the cries from within.

The audience of the imperial recitation halls may be assumed to have been sufficiently well acquainted with mythical and historical plots to make it unnecessary for the prologue to provide much preliminary information. Moreover, it is conceivable that the *praefatio*, read by the author, would have provided the audience with the essentials of the plot and the identity of the *personae* involved.

No clues are provided to the identification of the speakers until 38, when the name *Claudius* is mentioned by the Nurse (though the address to her dead *pater* at 25 ff. may be thought sufficient to identify Octavia). But the absence of a formal introduction has no implications for the performability of the *praetexta*, since even in Greek tragedy characters do not always identify themselves explicitly at the beginning of a play and cases such as Eur. *Andr.* 5 or *Or.* 23 coexist with more indirect, though equally informative, forms of introduction: cf. Soph. *Trach.* 6–7 (which identifies Deianeira as the speaker). Senecan characters tend to give their name during their entrance monologue: cf. *Med.* 8–9 *quosque Medeae magis | fas est precari*; *Thy.* 180; *Hf.* 1; *Troad.* 36. Later entrances are handled differently, and it happens not infrequently that a character appears with no announcement and no formal introduction, as is the case with Talthybius (*Troad.* 164), Pyrrhus and Agamemnon (*Troad.* 203). This is paralleled in *Oct.* by the entrances of Seneca (377) and Agrippina (ad 593). On the self-presentation of characters in Senecan drama cf. Leo, *Obs.* 76. According to Cicero (*Ac.* 2.20) eager theatre-goers could identify a given scene from the first few measures of the accompanying tune: *primo inflatu tibicinis Antiopam esse aiunt aut Andromacham.*

The *Nutrix* identifies herself indirectly only at 72 *uox . . . tristis alumnae*, that is after the end of the prologue. But the same can be observed of other nurses in Seneca (cf. *Med.* 150 (the speaking character addresses Medea as *alumna* at 158); *Agam.* 125) and is in keeping with the presentation of social inferiors in Greek tragedy, whereby nurses and maids do not introduce themselves explicitly: cf. Eur. *Andr.* 56, where the first word uttered by Andromache's devoted *therapaina* is δέσποινα; *Med.* 6–7; *I.A.* 3; Soph. *Trach.* 49.

1–2 Iam uaga caelo sidera fulgens | Aurora fugat Descriptions of dawn are used by Seneca for decorative effects in most plays, and this beginning probably imitates (as has been observed since Delrius) the first lines of the chorus of *Hf.* 125–7 *iam rara micant sidera prono | languida mundo, nox uicta uagos | contrahit ignes luce renata*; cf. also Acc. *Inc. Trag.* 675–6 R² *iamque Auroram rutilare procul | cerno.* By comparison with the other plays in the corpus, however, this astronomical introduction is an apt illustration of the author's comparatively poor literary abilities.

'Now doth flushing dawn drive the wandering stars from heaven' (Miller); *caelo* is *apo koinou*, although its position suggests that it would be more natural to take it as a qualification of *uaga . . . sidera*: cf. e.g. Verg. *Aen.* 3.204 *erramus pelago*; Sen. *Phae.* 167 *non uagi campis Getae* ('ablativus viae' or 'ablativus prosecutivus': cf. Hillen, *Dichtersprache*, 152 n. 1). *Fugo* can be construed with or without a preposition, with an ablative indicating 'removal from', as usual in Augustan and post-Augustan poetry (*LHS* 2.131–2), although I have not been able to trace parallels for *fugat caelo* in the tragedies (cf. *Phae.* 867 *e vita fugat* or *Hf.* 640 *ex oculis fuga*). *sidera* is the common word for both 'stars', too far to be seen to move by the human eye, and 'planets', commonly confused with stars in poetry: cf. Verg. *Aen.* 9.21 *palantisque polo stellas.*

For *sidera fulgens Aurora fugat* cf. Ov. *Met.* 2.144 *fulget tenebris Aurora fugatis*, *ibid.* 15.665 *postera sidereos Aurora fugauerat ignes*; *Fast.* 4.390 *et dederat Phoebo stella fugata locum*; on the military imagery of sunrise descriptions cf. Fitch, ad *Hf.* 126. *surgens* of some early editions cannot be right before 3 *surgit Titan radiante coma.*

3 surgit Titan radiante coma *radiante coma* does not occur in this form anywhere else in Latin poetry (*radiate Titan* in *Phae.* 678, *H.O.* 1518; *Troad.* 1035 *radiante uillo*; *H.O.* 1239 *radiante . . . fronte*). With reference to *coma, crines, radio* seems to occur only in Stat. *Theb.* 1.28–9 *tuis alte radiantem crinibus arcum | imprimat* (sc. *Phoebus*); Claud. *Carm. min.* 30.4 *solitam . . . rubro radiare mari . . . comam* (sc. *Serenae*). The expression illustrates a type of sociative or descriptive ablative ('there rises the Sun with radiant mane'), a periphrastic construction which in Latin makes up for the lack or insufficient assimilation of the compound nominals so characteristic of Greek poetic language: cf. Kroll, *Studien*, 266–7; Leumann, *KS*, 150–2; e.g. Verg. *Aen.* 7.30 *fluuio Tiberinus amoeno* (*radiante coma* = λαμπραυγής or χρυσοκόμης).

5 age, tot tantis onerata malis The MSS unanimously preserve the lines as a series of dimeters until line 6. However, no modern editor accepts the hiatus that would thus result between 4 *reddit clarum* and *age tot tantis*. Zwierlein writes *Aurora fugat* as a monometer followed by dimeters, which separates off *clarum* and *age*. Older editors took offence at the asyndetic *tot tantis . . . malis*, but the correction *tot tantisque* (Gruterus) is unacceptable for metrical reasons (synaloephe across the diaeresis has no parallels in the corpus). Curiously enough, precise parallels for the asyndeton *tot tantis* are lacking (always *tot tantisque*: see e.g. Caes. *BC* 1.85.6 *tot tantasque classis*; Acc. *Scaen.* 175 R[2] *te propter tot tantasque habemus vastitatis funerum*; Cic. *Pro Lege Man.* 96 *qui a diis mortalibus tot et tantas res tacitus auderet optare*; Ov. *Met.* 2.96 *eque tot ac tantis . . . malis*; Sen. *Cons. Pol.* 15.3 *tot tantosque luctus*; *ibid.* 12.1 *ad haec tot et tanta quae consolantur*), but this is probably coincidental, and it seems impossible to postulate a grammatical restriction against this nexus alone, especially in view of the frequency of asyndetic tricola (Ter. *Eun.* 1047 *quae* (sc. *Fortuna) tot res tantas tam opportune . . . conclusit*; Cic. *Dom.* 76 *tot tantis tam onoratis iudiciis comprobatum*; also with *qui-* forms in exclamations, in Enn. *Trag.* 339–40 Joc.; cf. H. Sjögren, *De particulis copulatiuis apud Plautum et Terentium quaestiones selectae* (Upsaliae, 1900), 57) or when the grammatical function of the two elements is different: cf. Plaut. *Poen.* 310 *uerba tot tam suauia*; Sen. *Contr.* 1.2.8 *inter tot tanto maiora scelera*; Liv. 25.24.13 (with Weissenborn-Müller ad loc.) *tot tam opulenti tyranni.*

The lack of connectives is intended to be emotional, and similar emphatic geminations are characteristic of tragic or para-tragic lamentation (cf. Eur. *Hec.* 199–201 οἵαν οἵαν αὖ σοι λώβαν | . . . ὦρσέν τις δαίμων, Ter. *Phorm.* 903 *heus quanta quanta haec mea paupertas est*). Sluiter drew attention to 698, exhibiting a comparable asyndetic sequence *o qualis altos quanta pressisti toros*: see ad loc.

The metaphoric 'the weight of my griefs' in *onerata* combines Soph. *El.* 119–20 ἄγειν οὐκέτι σωκῶ | λύπης ἀντίρροπον ἄχθος, in Electra's monody (for the recurrence of the same metaphorical field in tragedy cf. Eur. *Hec.* 103; *I.T.* 710 ὦ πόλλ' ἐνεγκὼν τῶν ἐμῶν ἄχθη κακῶν), with the language of Verg. *Aen.* 4.549 *his germana malis oneras.*

5–6 age . . . repete assuetos iam tibi questus Cf. Eur. *El.* 125–6 ἴθι, | τὸν αὐτὸν ἔγειρε γόον, | ἄναγε πολύδακρυν ἁδονάν. *Repete* seems to translate ἄναγε, although the Greek word specifically describes the raising of the voice. τὸν αὐτὸν ἔγειρε γόον, however, indicates a refrain, not 'the same as always', as in the Latin. Seneca's Hecuba, *Troad.* 96, invites the Trojan captives to revive their old laments, *iterum luctus redeant ueteres*, that is the lamentations for

Hector's death. For the topos that lamentation has been made one's preserve by habit, in tragedy, cf. Eur. *Andr.* 91–3 οἷσπερ ἐγκείμεσθ' ἀεὶ | θρήνοισι καὶ γόοισι καὶ δακρύμασιν | πρὸς αἰθέρ' ἐκτενοῦμεν.

assuetos has here a passive sense (cf. *Troad.* 1069 *assueta Priamo*; *Thy.* 952 *lacrimas . . . assuetas*), while the active meaning occurs in *Troad.* 152 *adsuetas ad sceptra manus.* On similar oscillations between an active and passive meaning in derivatives of *suesco* cf. Austin ad Verg. *Aen.* 2.520, *desueta . . . arma*; Norden, ad Verg. *Aen.* 6.832. *assuetos* is scanned as a trisyllable, as always in dactylic poetry and in Senecan tragedy.

7–8 atque aequoreas uince Alcyonas, | uince et uolucres Pandionias *uince* sc. *lamentis tuis*; cf. *Troad.* 97 *solitum flendi uincite morem*; *H.O.* 554 (sc. *amor Herculis*) *uincat exempla omnia.* Exhortation to vie with the querulous songs of nightingales and halcyons is a common motif (cf. Eur. *I.T.* 1094–5 ἐγώ σοι παραβάλλομαι | θρήνους 'I compare my laments with yours'; Aesch. *Agam.* 1140–48; Soph. *El.* 106; Sen. *Agam.* 664–92). The song of these birds of tragic fame salutes the new day in many scenes of sunrise: cf. Sen. *Hf.* 146–52 *pendet summo stridula ramo | pinnasque nouo tradere soli | gestit . . . Thracia paelex.* Conventional catalogues of mythical mourners often include Niobe as well (cf. Prop. 3.10.9–10 *Alcyonum . . . Ityn*), and this passage is only a pale imitation of the larger Senecan sequences (cf. *Agam.* 670–92). The nightingale reappears at the end of the play (915).

The epithet *Pandionius* has no clear precedents in Greek, with only one instance of Πανδιόνιος, for 'Athenian', in an epigram quoted in Paus. 4.1.8; the swallow, however is called Πανδιονίς in Hes. *Op.* 568; Sapph. 135 V; *A.P.* 9.70. The patronymic is much more frequent in Latin, where, however, in reference to Procne and Philomela, *Pandionius* occurs only in *Culex* 251 *iam Pandionias, miserandas prole puellas* and Stat. *Theb.* 8.616 *sic Pandioniae . . . uolucres*: on the possibility that the *ignotus* knew Statius see Introduction, 17–27. Cf. however also the anonymous *Laus Pisonis* 77, *Pandionis ales.* The word *uolucris* is specified by a patronymic also in Ov. *Met.* 12.581 *uolucrem Phaethontida*; *Med. fac.* 33 *uolucris Iunonia.*

A long epithet occupying the whole second half-line in an anapaestic system occurs at *Troad.* 153, *Agamemnonios*; *Agam.* 340; *H.O.* 187 *Phaetontiadum*; in Greek, e.g. Eur. *Troad.* 139, *Ion* 86.

9 grauior namque his fortuna tua est The use of explanatory particles in self-address after an exhortation to lament (as if Octavia were to persuade herself to outdo Procne's lament) is particularly high-flown: γάρ is commonly so used in Greek tragedy, especially after exclamations of sorrow: cf. e.g. Soph. *Ai.* 432–3 νῦν γὰρ πάρεστι καὶ δὶς αἰάζειν ἐμοὶ | καὶ τρίς· τοιούτοις γὰρ κακοῖς ἐντυγχάνω, *El.* 788 οἴμοι τάλαινα· νῦν γὰρ οἰμῶξαι πάρα . . ., Eur. *Troad.* 106; 793; *Hel.* 857; *Alc.* 217–8; in Early Latin drama, *ita* occurs as a plainer stylistic equivalent. On the use of *namque* and καὶ γάρ to introduce a mythical example strengthening the validity of advice or exhortation cf. Fraenkel, *Horace*, 185–6. There are no precedents for this pattern in the Senecan corpus.

Comparatio compendiaria occurs also *infra* ad 58, 172, 770; elsewhere cf. Luc. *Bell. Ciu.* 7.100–1 *mortemque suorum | permiscere suis*; 7.144 *si liceat superis hominum conferre labores*; Val. Fl. *Arg.* 2.226 *notaque sonat uox coniuge maior*; in Greek, cf. Eur. *I.T.U* 1094–5, quoted ad 7–8, 'I compare my laments with you'. On this brachylogic construction in general cf. *LHS* 2.826.

Richter (1862), 4, wanted to emend the line in *namque his grauior*, but synaloephe in the arsis of both second and fourth foot is not unparalleled in the play (cf. e.g. 297). Mueller *DRM*, 296–7, lists several examples of synaloephe in the last element of various meters devoid of synapheia, as anapaests are in the Senecan corpus.

On *namque* postponed, cf. Introd. p. 33.

10 semper genetrix deflenda mihi Messalina's death in 48 marked the beginning of Octavia's misfortunes. A similar motif is found in the lament of another Electra at Eur. *Or.* 195–207: Clytemnestra has been the origin of all trouble for Electra. Later on Octavia completely forgets her mother, who is recalled only once again in a similar context at 269. This address to the dead Messalina should not be interpreted as a sign that the play predates the historical *vulgata*, generally unfavourable to Messalina. Rather, it is in keeping with the casting of Octavia into the tragic mould, the innocent victim of a curse which has deep roots in her family.

11 prima meorum causa malorum Cf. Verg. *Aen.* 4.169–70 *ille dies primus leti primusque malorum | causa mihi*; 11.361 *caput horum et causa malorum*; Val. Fl. *Arg.* 7.37 *tu prima malorum causa mihi*; also Hom. *Il.* 22.16; and common elsewhere. *causa malorum* at line-end also at 650.

The rhyming jingle *-orum -orum* is not uncommon in Latin poetry: cf. Verg. *Aen.* 11.361 *horum . . . malorum*; 3.549 *uelatarum . . . antemnarum* (although in these examples the first word is always in synaloephe); Ov. *Her.* 19.127 *at tibi flammarum memori, Neptune, tuarum*; *Met.* 5.265 *siluarum lucos circumspicit antiquarum*; 5.305 *stolidarum turba sororum*; 5.320 *magnorum facta deorum*; 5.360 *curruque atrorum uectus equorum*. In addition, homoeoteleuta are a very common feature of anapaestic lines in *Octavia* and in Senecan tragedy. They may be intended as a mimetic reproduction of the long and dragging sounds of lament. Cf. also 5 *tantis . . . malis*, 57 *nullis . . . malis*, 75 *nostras lacrimas*, 77 *tantis . . . curis*, 79 *Stygias . . . umbras*; in Senecan tragedy cf. e.g. *Troad.* 69, 104; *Agam.* 665–5*; 669, 672. From the fragments of imperial tragedy cf. Pomp. Sec. *Inc. fab.* 5–6 R² *Rhoeteis procul a terris | Priamique aras damnare pias*; Scaev. Mem. *Inc. fab.* 1–2 R² *scindimus atras ueteri planctu, | Cissaei, genas*. The rhyming *-orum/-orum* in 11 is in keeping with this proliferation of patterns of sound in anapaests, and is certainly intentional. More generally on homoeoteleuta and rhymes in

Greek and Latin drama cf. *LHS* 2.705–6; *OCD*³ 194–5; Norden, *AK*, 832–41; Jocelyn ad Enn. *Trag.* 92–4; Peiper, *Suppl.* (1870), 9.

12 tristes questus natae exaudi As no request for either deliverance or revenge follows, the prayer is somewhat surprising: to what end is Messalina simply to listen to her daughter's laments? *preces* would have been the expected complement of the formula: cf. Ov. *Met.* 13.855–6 *precesque | supplicis exaudi*; Sen. *Phae.* 636 *tacitae mentis exaudi preces*. An initial prayer to a dead parent is also found in Aesch. *Choe.* 4–5.

This is the only instance in the anapaests of the Senecan corpus of a diphthong as the first element in synaloephe (Mantke, *Eos* 49 (1957–78), 117–18).

13 si quis remanet sensus in umbris Cf. *Cons. Liv.* 469 *si quid modo sentit in umbra*; Ov. *Pont.* 2.2.98 *si quid habet sensus umbra diserta*, with Galasso's note (other parallels are given by Hosius ad loc.). In Greek tragedy cf. Bond ad Eur. *Herc.* 490; Tandoi, *Scritti* 2.773–4 (esp. Cic. *Fam.* 4.5.6 *si qui etiam inferis sensus est*).

14–16 ante . . . tua quam maerens uulnera uidi Cf. Aesch. *Agam.* 1537, where the chorus bewail the death of Agamemnon and express the wish that they had never lived to see their master slaughtered by his wife. Cf. also Ap. Rh. *Arg.* 3.798.

As the event described by *uidi* is presented as one which would not have happened, if the wish expressed by the antecedent *utinam* had been fulfilled, the indicative may sound odd. It is however regularly used after *antequam*: cf. Char. *GLK* 1.228, quoting Aen. *Verg.* 4.27 *ante, pudor, quam te uiolo aut tua iura resoluo*; in the Senecan corpus cf. *Thy.* 201 *antequam se firmat aut uires parat* and also *infra* 636–7 *utinam, antequam te parvulum in luce edidi . . . lacerassent ferae*. This (unreal) desiderative clause with *ante . . . quam* is rather unwieldy, and it would be difficult to find syntactic parallels; paratactic structures seem to be more common: cf. e.g. Cic. *Ad Att.* 3.8.4 *utinam iam ante vidisses neque totum animum tuum maerori mecum simul dedisses*; in Greek cf. Eur. *Andr.* 1189–93; Soph. *Ai.* 1192. Parallels for hypotaxis come only from archaic Latin: Plaut. *Capt.* 537 *utinam te di prius perderent quam periisti a patria tua*; *Rud.* 494–5 *utinam te prius quam ego oculis uidissem meis | malo cruciatu in Sicilia perbiteres* (= *perisses*).

uidi may also have been prompted by recollection of such intense scenes of *evidentia* as Enn. *Scaen.* 91 R² *uidi uidere quod me passa aegerrume*; cf. also Sen. *Agam.* 656–7 *uidi, uidi senis in iugulo | telum* . . . (with Tarrant's note); *H.O.* 207–7• *uidi, uidi miseranda mei | fata parentis*; *Hf.* 245 *ante ora uidi nostra (. . .) gnatos (. . .) cadere*; Ov. *Her.* 2.49.

17 oraque foedo sparsa cruore Only with a certain degree of exaggeration can the dying Messalina be described in these terms, her face bathed in blood as if she had been bludgeoned to death in a fierce combat. Messalina committed suicide and, even if the fatal blow was, as Tacitus says, struck by a tribune, she need not have been disfigured. Death by any means can be envisaged as a disfigurement in itself, but the poet here gets somewhat carried away by an epic visualization of the scene, casting Messalina in the posture of a blood-stained Hector (cf. Verg. *Aen.* 2.277–8 *squalentem barbam et concretos sanguine crines | uulneraque illa gerens*) or a mutilated Deiphobus (6.494–7, esp. 495–6 *lacerum crudeliter ora, | ora manusque ambas*).

This high-flown use of *spargo*, especially with reference to parts of the body spattered with blood (one's own or one's victims') is common in Senecan tragedy: cf. *Hf.* 1217 *cruore corpus impio sparsum*; *Med.* 709 *sparsus cruore Caucasus Promethei*; *Oct.* 722 *sparsam cruore . . . facem*; Acc. *Scaen.* 23 R² *cui manus materno sordet sparsa sanguine*; cf. *OLD* s.v. 8; Junge (1999) 241. On poetic plurals (esp. words like *ora, pectora, uulnera*) see Austin ad Verg. *Aen.* 4.673; Kroll, *Studien*, 258; Leumann, *KS* 145.

The occurrence of hiatus and *brevis in longo* strongly marks the end of a section.

18–20 o lux semper funesta mihi! | tempore ab illo lux est tenebris | invisa magis Despite its apparent simplicity, the passage is textually problematic. *PCS* read *o lux* at 18 and *nox est* at 19 (*o nox* in *G*):

o lux semper funesta mihi
tempore ab illo nox est tenebris
inuisa magis

Some *recentiores* (for instance *KQeO*) emended *nox* at 19 to *lux*. Thus emended, the passage is comprehensible, if somewhat abrupt and unconvincing, especially in the transition from second-person address (*o lux*) to comment (*lux est*). Helm (*SBDA* 16.1 (1934), 287, n. 1) was the first to propose *nox* at 18, which on first impression lends Octavia's words a greater and more dramatic impact, especially after the vivid evocation of Messalina's enforced suicide (cf. 17). In the interpretation of Zwierlein, who prints *nox* in his text: 'O Nacht [in der dies (sc. Messalina's execution) geschah], für alle Folgezeit mir verderblich! Seit jenem Augenblick ist mir das (Lebens)licht verhaβter als die Finsternis, denn ich muβte nunmehr die Tyrannei der Agrippina ertragen . . .' *nox* was also favoured by Herington (*CQ* n.s. 11 (1961), 20 n. 6), who adduced a comparison with Soph. *El.* 201–4 ὦ πασᾶν κείνα πλέον ἁμέρα | ἐλθοῦσ' ἐχθίστα δή μοι· | ὦ νύξ, ὦ δείπνων ἀρρήτων | ἔκπαγλ' ἄχθη, containing a reference to the evening feast during which Agamemnon and his retinue were slain (cf. Hom. *Od.* 11.405–26, whereas in the version followed in Aesch. *Agam.* 1107–29 the king is murdered in his bath, which was taken before the meal). For other references to disastrous nights cf. Eur. *Troad.* 204 ἔρροι νὺξ αὕτα καὶ δαίμων, *Hec.* 914; Ov. *Her.* 2.59–60 *quae fuit ante illam, mallem suprema fuisset, | nox mihi*; Tac. *Ann.* 1.58.2 *testis illa nox, mihi utinam potius nouissima.* Addresses to the (present) night are found in Eur. *El.* 54 (Electra calls upon the night to witness her misery, 'pouring her laments to the sky'); *Or.* 174, *Hec.* 68, fr. 114 N²; cf. Jocelyn, *Ennius* p. 254. There are, however, difficulties with an address to *nox*, and on balance

I prefer to retain the transmitted *lux*. Zwierlein's attempt to deduce from the presence of *nox* at 19, where it is nonsensical, that the word originally stood one line above, at 18, in the ***A***-text, is not the most straightforward explanation for the origin of the corruption. In fact, the easy assimilation *nox tenebris* (from *lux tenebris*) springs first to mind as a likelier cause of error.

The parallel from Soph. *El.* is tempting, but *hamera* in the Greek text might be taken to support *lux* equally strongly. It is also surprising for Octavia to expatiate so little on the conceit that her mother was forced to commit suicide at night, a night which was to be forever wretched. In fact, the only extant account of Messalina's final hours (Tac. *Ann.* 11.30) is not explicit about the time at which the events occurred, and, in pointed contrast to the circumstances of Agrippina's death in *Ann.* 13, does not make much of a supposedly nocturnal scenario. Nightfall is only presented as imminent. The episode probably happened in mid-October, not later than the 15th (see Furneaux ad loc.). At the time when Claudius took *tempestiuas epulas*, thus earlier than the *hora nona*, at which it was customary to start the evening meal (roughly 3p.m.: cf. Marquardt, *Privatleben* 298–9), the fate of Messalina still hung in the balance; then the fear of Claudius' indecisiveness, as night approached and nostalgic feelings for his wife might arise (*propinqua nox . . . timebatur*), prompted his freedmen to action, and they disposed of Messalina as quickly as possible. News of her death was brought to Claudius, while he was still having his protracted dinner, and was received with the somnolent and lethargic behaviour often attributed to this emperor by his historians.

Tacitus' witness, then, does little to support *nox*. Those who accept *lux* as the text of both 18 and 19 have two alternatives: either (1) interpreting the first *lux* as a reference to the day of Messalina's death (as in Verg. *Aen.* 5.49–50 *dies . . . quem semper acerbum . . . habebo*) and the second line as a general reflection on the hideousness of light; or (2) interpreting 18 as an invocation to daylight, the day now rising, which is contextually the preferable explanation. Indeed an invocation to the light of the new day would effectively pick up the somewhat underelaborated initial sunrise description (cf. *supra*, 1–4), and has a parallel in the (also prologic) invocation of Electra's song in Soph. *El.* 86 ὦ φάος ἁγνόν . . . ; *ibid.* 103–6 ἀλλ' οὐ μὲν δὴ | λήξω θρήνων στυγερῶν τε γόων, | ἔστ' ἂν παμφεγγεῖς ἄστρων | ῥιπάς, λεύσσω δὲ τόδ' ἦμαρ. *semper* takes up, on this interpretation, a slightly different meaning, not 'for all time to come', but 'again and again', i.e. on every new occurrence of the phenomenon; this makes no difficulty in Latin: see *OLD* s.v. 2. An address to the light of the rising day fits well within the dramatic pattern whereby distressed heroes and heroines invoke the elements (the night, the sun, the sky) to be the witnesses of their misery. One objection that could meet this proposal is that *tempore ab illo* seems to contain an allusion to a specific event. This event, however, need not be found only in the preceding line, and *tempore ab illo* could pick up 16–17, describing the horrified reaction of the child Octavia at the sight of her mother's corpse. Fuchs (*WS* Beih. 8 (1977), 73) tied *tempore ab illo* to the preceding invocation: this makes no significant difference for the sense, but is rhetorically inept, leaving the second colon too bare.

The main weakness of the proposed interpretation lies in the flatness of having the comment *tempore ab illo lux est tenebris | inuisa magis* follow the invocation to *lux*. Bothe attempted to meet this objection by conjecturing *es*:

o lux, semper funesta mihi!
tempore ab illo,
lux, es tenebris inuisa magis

Sense and palaeographical plausibility would be satisfied (ESTTENEBRIS < ESTENEBRIS), and vocatives are easily overlooked by copyists. The attending word-order, however, is somewhat problematic; *es* usually takes second position in a colon, finding a host in the preceding word (a vocative must be considered an interruption of the sentence and provokes a pause: cf. E. Fraenkel *KB* (Rome, 1964), 100, 104). Exceptions are usually motivated by emphasis ('truly, you are . . .'). On *esse* in sentence initial position cf. J. N. Adams, *Wackernagel's Law and the placement of the copula* esse *in classical Latin* (Cambridge, 1994), 69–70. In the corpus of Senecan tragedy I have found only two cases of *es* at the beginning of both a new line and a new syntactical unit (never elsewhere *within the line* and beginning a new colon) and they seem identifiable as emphatic: Sen. *Hf.* 413 *es rege coniunx digna*; *H.O.* 1980 *es numen, et te mundus aeternum tenet.* The copula occupies the initial position in cases of special emphasis (cf. *Hf.* 523 *est est sonitus Herculei gradus*). The pattern (vocative) + *es* + predicate is occasionally found: cf. Plaut. *Rud.* 527 *edepol, Neptune, es balineator frigidus* (comic examples in Marouzeau, *L'ordre des mots*, II.11–13). But why introduce a less acceptable word-order in a case where no emphasis is placed on the copula, and, above all, when *es* was not necessary to the sense? What prevented the author from writing *o lux tenebris inuisa magis*? The phrasing, moreover, is too fussy and over-detailed: what point have the two vocatives, *lux . . . lux*?

The hideousness of daylight is a standard formula expressing mourning: for those bereft of their beloved, life is odious ('the sight of the sky, the very sojourn among the living has now become loathsome to me'). Cf. Sen. *Cons. Marc.* 3.3 *inuisa haerebis in luce* (like Augustus' sister Octavia, mourning her son Marcellus); Eur. *Hec.* 167–8 οὐκέτι μοι βίος | ἀγαστὸς ἐν φάει, *Alc.* 868 οὔτε γὰρ αὐγὰς χαίρω προσορῶν, Ar. *Thesm.* 1052–3 οὐ γὰρ ἔτ' ἀθανάταν φλόγα λεύσσειν | ἐστὶν ἐμοὶ φίλον (Andromeda). For Octavia every new light is hateful ever since she has had to endure the cruelty of her *nouerca.*

19 tempore ab illo Cf. Ov. *Her.* 12.7–8 *quicquid ab illo | produxi uitam tempore poena fuit.*

21–22 tulimus saeuae iussa nouercae, | hostilem animum uultusque truces This account of Octavia's sufferings in the household now lorded over by her step-mother Agrippina, an imperious, domineering woman in all sources, is psychologically credible; there may also be an element of literary elaboration, imitating the complaints of Electra in Soph. *El.* 288–92 (τοιάδ' ἐξονειδίζει κακά κτλ.); cf. also Verg. *Aen.* 3.326–7 (Andromache speaking) *stirpis Achilleae fastus iuuenemque superbum* | ... *tulimus*. Note how Vergil prefers to co-ordinate even components which are not logically co-ordinate, whereas the word-arrangement here tends to be plainer. The logical transition between this and the preceding line is left somewhat unclear: *tempore ab illo tulimus.*

Octavia's speech switches from second to first person (*tua fortuna, malorum meorum*) and then from singular to plural (*tulimus*). The oscillation between first person singular and plural forms is more common than that from self-address (*tuus*) to first person (*meus, noster*). See e.g. Soph. *El.* 115–19 τείσασθε πατρὸς | φόνον ἡμέτερου, | καί μοι τὸν ἐμὸν πέμψατ' ἀδελφόν, Eur. *Ion* 108, *Med.* 314–5, *Troad.* 98, *El.* 112, *Hec.* 736–8; Barrett ad Eur. *Hipp.* 349; Bond ad Eur. *Herc.* 858; *KG* 1.83. In Latin cf. Prop. 2.8.17–20; Cat. *Carm.* 8.1–5. In Seneca cf. *Med.* 398–9 *imitare amorem. regias egone ut faces* | *inulta patiar?* 411–14 *non . . . uis ignium . . . possit inhibere impetum* | *irasque nostras: sternam et euertam omnia*; Töchterle ad Sen. *Oed.* 31.

23–24 illa, illa meis tristis Erinys | thalamis Stygios praetulit ignes The divinities expected to administer their blessing over a fortunate union are Juno and Hymenaeus, but this exchange of roles, with a malevolent deity replacing a benevolent one, is a long-established poetical commonplace (Erinys also presides over Messalina's marriage in 262–4 *illi . . . ultrix Erinys uenit . . .*). Amata performs a similarly ominous function when she celebrates the marriage of her daughter with Turnus in the frenzy sent to her by Allecto, Verg. *Aen.* 7.341–98 (397–8 *ipsa . . . natae Turnique canit hymenaeos*). Octavia's exasperated cry of despair, with the emphatic *geminatio* of the deictic (cf. Wills, *Repetition*, 79 for stylistic parallels in Senecan tragedy, e.g. *Troad.* 721 *ille ille ferox . . . dixit*), is modelled on Ov. *Her.* 6.45 *tristis Erinys* | *praetulit infaustas sanguinolenta faces* (as first seen by Gronovius); cf. also Sen. *Oed.* 644 *et mecum Erinyn pronubam thalami traham*; *Med.* 13–14. The idea that ill-omened *nuptiae* are celebrated by the presence of the Furies is a common motif: the Fury becomes a personification not so much of revenge but of ill-fortune and mishap. The motif is recurrent in funerary epigrams, usually for immature deaths, cf. *AP* 7.188; *infra*, ad 596; elsewhere Ov. *Met.* 10.5; Prop. 4.3.13–14 *quae mihi deductae fax omen praetulit,* | *illa traxit ab euerso lumina nigra rogo*; Tac. *Ann.* 14.30 *in modum Furiarum, ueste ferali, crinibus deiectis faces praeferebant.* Further materials in Bömer ad Ov. *Met.* 6.430; Heinsius ad Ov. *Her.* 2.117. The custom to which reference is made is mainly Greek: in the Greek marriage ceremony the bride's mother raised the nuptial torches.

Octavia refers to her stepmother as a living Erinys. This extensional meaning of the word is already present in Greek tragedy, where the word is a virtual synonym of δαίμων, ἀλάστωρ, and indicates a person sent by the gods to persecute or punish a guilty party (cf. *LSJ* s.v., II; e.g. Aesch. *Agam.* 1500; Soph. *El.* 1080; Eur. *Med.* 1260; Garvie ad Aesch. *Choe.* 652). This usage is also common in Latin: Helen is called an *Erinys* in the famous episode of *Aen.* 2.573; Val. Fl. *Arg.* 8.396. For living people compared with Furies see also Enn. *Scaen.* 56 R[2] (= 49 Joc.); Cic. *Fam.* 1.9.15 *illa furia qui . . . impunitatem . . . est assecutus*; Liv. 21.10.11 *hunc iuuenem . . . furiam facemque huius belli*; Stat. *Theb.* 7.477.

The accumulation of words ending in *–s* is probably expressive of distressful or painful memories: *sigmatismus* was a rhetorical figure to which ancient literary theory and practice were most attentive: for examples cf. Marouzeau, *Styl.* 28; Conte ad Luc. *Bell. Ciu.* 6.151.

26–28 modo cui totus paruit orbis | ultra Oceanum | cuique Britanni terga dedere The author intends to represent Claudius as the omnipotent king of the earth, thus making his subsequent death all the more poignant and exemplary. The passage seems (see also *infra* ad 534), to echo the parodic *naenia* for Claudius in Sen. *Apocol.* 12.2.13–14 *ille Britannos ultra noti | litora ponti* (sc. *subiecit*). On the strength of that parallel, Buecheler (1872), 474 (followed by Richter), transposed 27 after 28:

modo cui totus paruit orbis
cuique Britanni 28[a]
ultra Oceanum terga dedere

'to whom the Britons, (who live) beyond the Ocean, turned their backs'. Buecheler's suspicions were raised by *totus . . . orbis ultra Oceanum*, and his proposal receives some support from 38–9 *cuius imperio fuit | subiectus orbis, paruit liber diu | Oceanus. totus orbis* seems much more effective if it is taken on its own (cf. Verg. *Aen.* 4.231; Hor. *Epist.* 2.1.154; Ov. *Fast.* 1.85, of Augustus' empire). On the encomiastic topic 'you have brought the entire world under the yoke' in Augustan literature see W. Theiler, *Untersuchungen zur antiken Literatur* (Berlin, 1970), 404–5. The English Channel is sometimes viewed as part of the Ocean, and, from this Continental standpoint, the Britons obviously live beyond the Ocean (Hor. *Carm.* 4.14.41 *beluosus qui remotis | obstrepit Oceanus Britannis*). The hiatus resulting from Buecheler's correction (*cuique Britanni | ultra*) does not pose a problem: the author of *Oct.* is more tolerant of hiatus and final short syllables between dimeters: see Introd. p. 43. Hiatus in the middle of a sentence occurs at 16, 21, 206, 362, 374, 686, 778, 897, 936.

Sometimes, however, the conquest of the British islands was celebrated as the acquisition by the Roman empire of a new *orbis*: Serv. ad Verg. Buc. 1.66 *(Britannia) a poetis alter orbis terrarum dicitur*; Jos. *Bell. Iud.* 2.363 ὑπὲρ ὠκεανὸν ἑτέραν ἐζήτησαν οἰκουμένην καὶ μέχρι τῶν ἀνιστορήτων πρότερον Βρεττανῶν διήνεγκαν τὰ ὅπλα; Philo, *Legatio ad Gaium*, 10 [the Roman Empire includes] τήν τε ἐντὸς ὠκεανοῦ καὶ ὑπερωκεάνιον [sc. *oikoumenēn*]; *AL* 423.5 R *at nunc Oceanus geminos interluit orbes. alius orbis terrarum* occurs in *Cons. Liu.* 457; Ov. *Trist.* 3.12.51; Luc. *Bell. Ciu.* 7.223; Mart. 7.8.2 (on this see V. Tandoi *SIFC* n.s. 34.2 (1963), 143 n. 2); *TLL*, ix.2, s.v. 918.15–46.

The presence (as in *orbis*) of a short element, lengthened at line-end (*brevis in longo*), does not necessarily entail a syntactical break. In fact 297–8 shows that this metrical feature is not incompatible with syntactical continuity: *graue et | improba*. Zwierlein (*Prolegomena* 192) suggested writing a comma after *orbis*, with *cuique* as an instance of postponement:

. . . paruit orbis,
ultra Oceanum cuique Britanni

Postponement of particles and relative pronouns is extremely common in *Oct.* (eight occurrences of postponed relative pronouns: at 868 *cui* is postponed by two words: *dedit natura cui pronum malo*), but a double postponement is without parallels in *Oct.* There is only one case of similar postponement in the Senecan corpus (*Phoe.* 459–60 *sollicita cui nunc mater alterna prece | verba admovebo*?). Of other authors cf. Prop. 2.32.14 *flumina sopito quaeque Marone cadunt. orbis ultra Oceanum* is sufficiently well attested to support the text in its present form. A cycle of poems in *AL* (421–7 R) celebrates Claudius' conquest of Britain. Sen. *Suas.* 1.1 *aiunt fertiles in Oceano iacere terras ultraque Oceanum rursus alia litora, alium nasci orbem.*

I find it impossible to decide whether the relative clause at 26–30 should be tied to the preceding *teque* or to *pater* at 31, although perhaps the sentence is rhetorically more effective if the relative precedes the main clause: cf. Ov. *Pont.* 4.3.43–7 *cuique uiro totus terrarum paruit orbis | . . . ille . . . quo uictrix totiens consule Roma fuit | in caeno Marius iacuit cannaque palustri* (Müller (1911), 125); *Oct.* 892–5 *modo cui patriam reddere ciues | aulam et fratris uoluere toros, | nunc ad poenam letumque trahi | flentem miseram cernere possunt.*

29–30 ducibus nostris ante ignoti | iurisque sui Cf. Luc. *Bell. Ciu.* 6.301–2 *libera regum . . . iurisque sui*; also *infra* 383. *ignoti* means 'untested', 'untried', rather than literally 'unknown'.

32 oppresse iaces The attraction of a predicative into the vocative case is common in Augustan poetry, following Greek stylistic precedent (Löfstedt, *Syntactica* 1.103: cf. Verg. *Aen.* 10.323–7 *tu quoque . . . miserande iaceres*). The like occurs in the corpus also in *H.O.* 4 *secure regna*; *Oed.* 403 *effusam redimite comam*; Stat. *Theb.* 2.103 *secure iaces.* At 166–7 a similar invocation to the dead Britannicus occurs (*tu quoque extinctus iaces, | deflende nobis semper, infelix puer*), although without the vocative attraction, which was impossible in the metrical context.

34 The appearance on the stage of a Nurse describing the sorrows of her mistress is familiar from Eur. *Hipp.* and *Med.* Cf. also Eur. *I.A.* 1100–02 ἐν δακρύοισι δ ' ἡ τάλαινα παῖς ἐμή, | πολλὰς ἱεῖσα μεταβολὰς ὀδυρμάτων, | θάνατον ἀκούσασ ' ὃν πατὴρ βουλεύεται, *Andr.* 802; *Med.* 119–30. Octavia's *Nutrix* lacks distinctive characterization, uttering no statement of personal preferences (compare, by contrast, the *trophos* of Eur. *Med.* 119–20, praising the simple life of the poor); she simply lectures on a piece of threadbare platitude, Fortune's treacherous ways. In Seneca the praise of the simple life is normally sung by the chorus (cf. *Phae.* 1123–40).

The Nurse's speech partly repeats what Octavia had said (esp. on Claudius' end). Thematic overlappings in successive lyrical and iambic sections in Greek tragedy are a common feature: cf. T. v. Wilamowitz, *Die dramatische Technik des Sophocles* (Berlin, 1917), 170 n. 2, with reference to Soph. *El.* 86–327, *Ant.* 891, *Ai.* 284–330, 430–80; *O.T.* 1369. In Greek tragedy, however, the distinction between sung and spoken was formally much more noticeable, and repetition less cumbersome for this reason. In *Oct.* there are no immediately conspicuous markers of 'lyrical' style in the anapaests: word-order and vocabulary are hardly more sophisticated, with the result that a sense of expressive monotony arises.

34 fulgore primo captus *primo* does not set up an opposition between various qualities or degrees of 'brightness', but between the outward appearance of regality, deceptively attractive, and the dangers attending upon it, which are often discovered too late. For this predicative use of *primus* for 'outward, superficial', or 'the first which one encounters' (especially with *fronte, facie*), virtually equivalent to the adverb *primum*, see *OLD*, s.v. 1b, *TLL* x.2, 1348–9 (on the adverbial use of *primus*, mainly in Vergil, e.g. *Aen.* 3.69 *ubi prima fides pelago*; 5.87 *primos . . . quies laxauerat artus*); 1351–2; cf. *infra*, 189 *impetu primo furit*). For the idea cf. Sen. *Troad.* 271–3 *ego esse quicquam sceptra nisi uano putem | fulgore tectum nomen et falso comam | uinclo decentem? H.O.* 617 *plures fulgor concitat aulae*; *Epist.* 21.2 *haec* (sc. *uita*) *fulgore extrinsecus ueniente percussa est.* For this use of *capior* in connection with deceptive or specious spectacles cf. *TLL* iii. s.v. *capio*, 342.31–48.

The same word (*cum prole capta | fulgore captus*) is repeated in two consecutive lines, pronounced by different speakers. The inelegance is worsened by repetition in two different senses, the proper and the metaphorical. Roman poets did not avoid repetition. There are many examples in Vergil and even more in Lucan; cf. e.g. *infra* 435–6 *fertur / ferat*; 734–6 *timor / tremor / timor*; Luc. *Bell. Ciu.* 4.741–2, *collibus / colle*; 5.423–5, 435–6, 438 (*unda*); *Il. Lat.* 107–8 *Olympi . . . Olympo*; *H.O.* 1403–4 *excussit . . . dolor. / dolor iste furor.* See Norden on *Aen.* 6.423, quoting relevant bibliography (other apparent slips in Vergil's *Aen.* 4.413–14; 5.135–6).

Here, however, the style is flawed not simply by repetition but also by the inelegant arrangement of the cola: *quisquis captus fulgore primo et fragili bono fallacis aulae stupet attonitus*. Augustan poets would have rearranged the period into a sequence of more balanced members, e.g. *fulgore quisquis capitur atque aulam stupet* | *fallaxque regnum*. Cf. the syntactic arrangement by parallel cola at Sen. *Troad.* 1–3 *quicumque regno fidit et magna potens* | *dominatur aula nec leues metuit deos* | *animumque rebus credulum laetis dedit*, in which the same thought trails over three lines. Similar reflections on reversals of fortune are typical of both tragedy and historiography; cf. Dio Cassius on Sejanus' fall (*Rom. Hist.* 58.11.1–3).

34–35 fragili bono | fallacis aulae The *aula* is a *fragile bonum* (an instance of the so-called *genetiuus inhaerentiae*), that is one that presents itself under a deceptive appearance, only to precipitate its victims into a spiralling abyss of anguish: cf. *Thy.* 391–2 *stet quicumque uolet potens* | *aulae culmine lubrico* and K-S 1.418–19, under the heading 'appositional genitive'; cf. *infra* 381 *procul ab inuidiae malis*. Outside the Senecan corpus cf. Ov. *Met.* 10.563 *formae(. . .) bono*; 14.684–5 *decoris munus*.

fragili is a deft conjecture, already found in some *recc.*, and confirmed by *Phae.* 773–4 *quis sapiens bono* | *confidat fragili?* (of beauty) in turn imitating possibly Ov. *Ars* 2.113 *forma bonum fragilest* (Hosius); for the figurative use of the adjective as 'impermanent' cf. *TLL* vi.1, s.v. 1228–9; Sall. *Cat.* 1.4 *diuitiarum . . . gloria fluxa atque fragilis est*; Sen. *Troad.* 5–6 *quam fragili loco* | *starent superbi*. The transmitted *facili* can be explained as a majuscule error (FRAGILI/FACILI, majuscule R and A often being confused), as well as a banalization. In *fallacis aulae* a reminiscence of the famous Horatian *nescius* | *aurae fallacis* (*Carm.* 1.5.11–12) can perhaps be recognized. Notice how adjectives and their nouns are not interlaced.

36 subito latentis . . . Fortunae impetu The transmitted *subito* of δ*C* should raise no concerns (cf. *Med.* 343 *subito impulsu*): one wonders why the unmetrical *sub uno* gained such easy acceptance in β. The majority of the conjectures concerning this passage have been brought about by *latens*, which is apparently without parallels as an epithet of *Fortuna*. Richter printed a *crux*, Herrmann conjectured *solito fauentis*; Leo *subito inuolantis*, Damsté *subito labantis*, probably suggested by *Thy.* 33–4 *dubia uiolentae domus* | *fortuna reges inter incertos labet.* Zwierlein, *KK*, offers parallels to illustrate Fortune as 'unpredictable', 'inscrutable': (τὴν τύχην) ἄδηλον αἰτίαν (*SVF* 2.966); ἀίδαλος τύχα (Peek, *GV* 1.1539, 5–6). *subito . . . impetu* conjures up the idea of 'Fortune' who assails man like a warrior waiting for the enemy to lower his guard (as in Verg. *Aen.* 11.763 *hanc Arruns subit et tacitus uestigia lustrat*). A similar turn is found in Cic. *Tusc.* 3.71 (*ia*$_6$ transl. from Soph. 666 N^2) *cum fortuna mutata impetum* | *conuertat.* Ladek (1909, 197 n. 1) drew attention to Sophocles' description of the Erinys ambushing the guilty, in *El.* 488–91 ἥξει . . . ἁ | δεινοῖς κρυπτομένα λόχοις | χαλκόπους Ἐρινύς ('the Erinys which always hides in insidious traps'); similarly

Soph. *Ant.* 1075. Fortune engages the virtuous man in single combat: cf. Sen. *Cons. Pol.* 2.2 *cum bene illud undique circuisses, intellexisti hac parte tantummodo patere ictibus tuis.* Fate cruelly hides behind man's misfortunes (cf. *latens*) in *Carmen de Bell. Act.* 55–6 Courtn. *procul hanc occulta uidebat | Atropos inridens*; Plin. *Nat.* 37.4 *piscis* (sc. *anulum*) *rursus Fortunae insidiantis manu reddidit*; Quint. *Inst.* 6 *prooem.* 8 *illud insidiantis . . . fortunae fuit, ut. . . .*

The present tense of *latentis* may have played a role (alongside the uncertainty about the original reading of *A*, at a time when this tradition was still very imperfectly known) in feeding older scholars' reluctance to accept the paradosis, because the action described by *latentis* is obviously not simultaneous with the sudden assault on Claudius, when the traps of Fortune became apparent ('*Fortune* who was lurking in ambush' or, less plausibly, 'who (always) escapes human comprehension'). A similar concern regarding the tense of *latentis* must have prompted Birt (1915), 112 to conjecture *latentis ante*, unnecessarily. Present participles are sometimes used as equivalents of Greek perfect and aoristic participles, in reference to action which precedes that of the main verb: cf. e.g. Verg. *Aen.* 1.305 *at pius Aeneas per noctem plurima uoluens*; Sall. *Iug.* 35.10 *Maurus secum ipse diu uoluens tandem promisit*; Cat. *Carm.* 64.238–9 *haec mandata prius constanti mente tenentem | Thesea . . . liquere*; K-G 1.200, n. 9; *LHS* 2.387; Kroll, *Glotta*, 15 (1927), 292. For a comparable use of *latens* cf. Amm. 16.12.59 (*cohors uerita*) *ne fraude latenti . . . exciperetur*; *ibidem*, 24.3.14 *sagittariorum . . . impetu latenti temptatus* ('a surprise attack').

37–38 modo praepotentem cernat euersam domum | stirpemque Claudi The Nurse's tirade about the fickleness of Fortune in dealing with royal houses draws on Hecuba's prologic speech at Sen. *Troad.* 1–6, *quicumque regno fidit . . .* (4) *me uideat et te, Troia*, but the commonplace had a vast diffusion: for all-powerful rulers and generals prostrated by a sudden turn of events cf. Skutsch ad Enn. *Ann.* 312; Pac. *Scaen.* 366–75 R^2, esp. 375 *uelut Orestes modo fuit rex, factust mendicus modo*; Liv. 30.30.16–17 *quem modo . . . signa inferentem ac iam prope scandentem moenia Romana uideras, hic cernas . . . ante moenia prope obsessae patriae . . . deprecantem* (Hannibal); Sil. *Pun.* 17.143–5 *ducitur ex alto deiectus culmine regni | qui modo sub pedibus terras et sceptra potensque | litora ad Oceani sub nutu uiderat aequor* (Syphax); Plut. *Aem.* 27; [Sen.] *Epigr.* 45 Prato (= *AL* 437 R) 1–2 *quisquis adhuc nondum fortunae mobile regnum | nec sortem uarias credis habere uices, | aspice Alexandri . . . corpus.* This theme is described as a quintessentially tragic one in Boeth. *Cons.* 2.2 *quid tragoediarum clamor aliud deflet nisi indiscreto ictu fortunam felicia regna uertentem?*

praepotens was metrically intractable for hexametric poetry, and its use is restricted to a few places in early drama (cf. *TRF inc.* 151–2 R^2 *nimirum hic ille est uir talis tantis opibus praepotens. | ubi nunc est secundis rebus adiutrix* <*fortuna*>*?*; Acc. *Praet.* 37 R^2) and in other late authors; it is not found in Senecan tragedy except here. It is however fairly common in prose, and its occurrence here does not seem a notable archaism.

38 Claudi The contracted monosyllabic genitive ending in *-i* of names issuing in *–ius (-ium)*, the only morphological possibility up to the age of Cicero, is the form used by preference in poetry for metrical convenience: cf. also *infra* 152 *ingeni*, 308 *Lucreti*; E. Bednara, *ALL* 14 (1906), 339–41.

38–40 cuius imperio fuit | subiectus orbis, paruit liber diu | Oceanus et recepit inuitus rates The three subordinate clauses depend on the same connective (*cuius*). A tendency to write longer, even unwieldy, periods, with various embedded subordinates, is not uncommon in *Octavia*, and comparable constructions occur at 41–4 *en qui Britannis primus imposuit iugum, | ignota tantis classibus texit freta, | interque . . . et saeua maria*; 45–6 *cuius* (sc. *Neronis*) . . . *iacet frater uenenis, maeret infelix soror | eademque coniunx*; 464–8. The attending monotony of construction was, however, avoided by most classical authors, who had a marked preference for short independent cola. Even if longer periods are occasionally found, individual cola tend to acquire prominence, and the exact syntactical relationships tend to be obliterated. This is the result of a strive for greater expressive immediacy and for rhetorical impact. Cf. Stat. *Theb.* 3.409–13 *cui* (sc. *Soli*) . . . *rapidis adcurrunt passibus Horae | frenaque et auratae textum sublime coronae | deripiunt, laxant calidis umentia loris | pectora*, where the elaborate description and the refinement of the subject matter compensate for the absence of syntactical symmetry (the initial *cui* is soon forgotten). In the third colon, *et recepit inuitus rates*, the connection is zeugmatic, as *cuius imperio* cannot be understood as a dative, nor can *imperium* retain the same sense as before: it must mean 'at Claudius' command'. Cf. also *infra* ad 57.

41 en qui Britannis primus imposuit iugum Scaliger's *Britannis* rightly ousted the MS *ora tanais* (*primus imposuit iugo*, with some *recc.* reading *iugum*), a tentative readjustment of the corrupt *oritannis*, possibly influenced by *Troad.* 9 *septena Tanain ora*. Trevet went to some lengths to justify the paradosis (6.10–13 J) *hoc dicit* (sc. *ora tanais . . . imposuit iugo*), *quia illius maris insulas subiecit, in quod influit Tanays. Cuius ingressum in mare uocat 'ora Tanays'. Non enim legitur quod triumphauerit regiones Scithie, sed tantum Britanniam et Orchades.* 'Tanays' (i.e. the Don) is a river flowing through Scythia, too far away from Britannia to be of much use. What Tanais and Britannia have in common, however, is their position with regard to the North Sea, in which the long river, for Trevet at least, exhausts its course. The North Sea, by the figure synecdoche, may be thought to include Britain as well.

en expresses the speaker's indignation, and provides a convenient transitional formula.

42 ignota tantis classibus texit freta For the hyperbolic *texit freta* and related expressions cf. Verg. *Aen.* 4.582 *latet sub classibus aequor*; Sen. *Suas.*

2.17 *iste qui classibus suis maria subripuit*; Sen. *Agam.* 40–1 *rates* | *Iliaca uelis maria texerunt suis* (Hosius) with Tarrant's note for more references.

43 interque gentes barbaras tutus fuit The paradox that Claudius was safe amongst the barbarians of the North, and was murdered by his wife at his home, has a a parallel in Soph. *El.* 95–7 πατέρα, ὃν κατὰ μὲν βάρβαρον αἶαν | φοίνιος Ἄρης οὐκ ἐξένισεν, | μήτηρ δ' ἡμὴ χὠ κοινολεχὴς | Αἴγισθος... σχίζουσι κάρα (first adduced by Ladek); cf. also Sen. *Agam.* 208–19 *quem non Achilles ense uiolauit fero . . . paras mactare*, 'another example of *Oct.* mentioning briefly a motif treated much more expansively by Seneca' [RJT]. For the thought that disaster may come from a little cause after successfully withstanding greater perils cf. Verg. *Aen.* 2.196–8 *captique dolis . . . quos . . . non anni domuere decem.*

45–47 mox illa nati, cuius extinctus iacet | frater uenenis, maeret infelix soror | eademque coniunx The antecedent of *cuius* is *nati* (i.e. Nero). *eademque coniunx* at 47 makes it impossible to take *cuius* with the following *soror*, with a stronger punctuation after *nati* (*nati. cuius . . . iacet frater . . . maeret infelix soror*): Octavia is 'sister and wife' to Nero alone. Note again the author's propensity for deploying chains of co-ordinate subordinate clauses: cf. *supra*, ad 38–40. The sequence parallels in particular 908–10 *haec est* (sc. *ratis*) *cuius uecta carina* | *quondam genetrix; nunc et thalamis* | *expulsa soror miseranda vehar.* Too many conflicting ideas are compressed in one sentence: Octavia is mourning for her natural brother, Britannicus, poisoned on Nero's orders; *eademque coniunx* adds nothing to this picture of a bereft Octavia, and is only a formula-like coda, intended to link up with the following scenario of conjugal feud. On this poet's tendency to overload his sentences with too many ideas, often not strictly relevant, cf. also ad 557 *uolucrem esse Amorem.*

Some MSS have the spelling *gnati* at 45 (*βK*). The archaic spelling occurs only here in *A* for *Octavia*, but is very common in the other tragedies (cf. Zwierlein's *OCT*, *Orthographica*, 465; Tarrant ad *Agam.* App. p. 367); in this position, however, *gnatus* would produce an unmetrical sequence. *gnatus*-forms are never employed to lengthen a preceding syllable in the corpus, and lack of *productio* is thought to be a vulgarism: cf. Housman, *CP* 3.1136–46; J. W. Beck, *Terentianus Maurus. De syllabis* (Göttingen, 1993), ad 380–3, 856–907.

The adverbial use of *idem* (= *simul*, 'at the same time'; cf. *OLD* s.v. 8; K-S 1.627) in *soror eademque coniunx* is common in poetry, and is also frequently found in the corpus. The poet of *Octavia* also uses *idem* to connect successive sentences: cf. 119–20 *ora fratris infestus petit* (sc. *Britannicus*), | *modo trepidus idem refugit in thalamos meos*; 164–6 *miscuit coniunx uiro* | *uenena saeua, cecidit atque eadem sui* | *mox scelere nati*; 189–90; 194–5; elsewhere. This latter variety is not found in Senecan tragedy, where *idem* is only used to connect two co-ordinated subjects or two appositions to the subject, stressing the paradoxical duplicity of an object or event: cf. *Agam.* 985 *idem sororis gnatus et patris nepos*; *Hf.* 1070–1 *futuri* |

certus et idem pessimus auctor; *Hf.* 1151–2 *quonam abit tegimen meum* | *idemque somno mollis Herculeo torus?*

This construction must have been felt by the poet of *Octavia* as an elegant transitional formula, and both types have numerous poetic parallels. For the appositive use of *idem* cf. Verg. *Aen.* 3.80 *rex idem hominum Phoebique sacerdos*; 10.607 *o germana mihi atque eadem gratissima coniunx*; for *idem* as a connective between successive sentences cf. Ovid *Met.* 14.72 *mox eadem* (sc. *Scylla*) *Teucras fuerat mersura carinas*. Cf. Helm (1934), 319.

Venenis is a poetic plural: cf. also 164–5 *miscuit* . . . *uenena saeua*.

47–50 nec graues luctus ualet | ira coacta tegere: crudelis uiri | secreta refugit semper atque odio pari | ardet maritus, mutua flagrant face The words of the Nurse contain a sketch of the drama's background, almost the *argumentum* of the play, pivoting on Octavia's refusal to compromise with Nero, for whom she expresses an absolute disdain: on this underelaborated motif, which has not been developed into a fully dramatic plot, cf. Introd. p. 61.

The overall sense of the passage is clear, although the precise sense of some phrases is ambiguous. This is one of the cases when syntax alone does not yield a conclusive clue to interpretation, and the reciter's voice would have been needed to disambiguate the passage. The text is transmitted in the manuscripts as follows:

maeret infelix soror
eademque coniunx nec graues luctus ualet
ira coacta tegere crudelis uiri
quem secreta refugit semper atque odio pari
ardens mariti mutua flagrat face

The Nurse describes Octavia's predicament: she hates her husband and is hated by him. '[Octavia] cannot prevail on herself to conceal her grief, but she is overpowered by her anger against her cruel husband: she avoids him and burns with equal hatred . . .' *ira coacta* must mean 'carried away by her anger (against Nero)'. The mention of Octavia's anger is fully justified after reference to the murder of her relatives has been made and, furthermore, anger is appropriate in a tragic heroine. Anger is the main sentiment of Euripides' Medea, in the words of her Nurse (24 ff.). Likewise, Sophocles' Electra admits that she has been led into doing terrible deeds by her wrath: *El.* 221–2 δεινοῖς ἠναγκάσθην, δεινοῖς· | ἔξοιδ', οὐ λάθει μ ' ὀργά, while the benevolent and compassionate women of the chorus try to persuade her to relent; *ibid.* 256 ἀλλ' ἡ βία γὰρ ταῦτ ' ἀναγκάζει με δρᾶν, *O.T.* 523. For *cogo[r]* 'to be forced by the agency of some overpowering, ungovernable passion' cf. *OLD* s.v. 12b.

Helm (1934), 325 n. 1, and Müller (1912), 126, understood *ira* as Nero's (*crudelis uiri*). This involves interpreting the participial *coacta* in a concessive sense ('although repressed (?) by the anger of her cruel husband'), but the resulting ambiguity and compression put excessive strains on the Latin, especially in a negative clause (*nec graues ualet . . . tegere*). *ira coacta* contains a clear explanation of Octavia's inability to stifle her feelings: Octavia cannot restrain herself from making this display of her mourning (*nec . . . luctus ualet . . .*) for the very reason that her anger leads her to do so. The objection that Octavia herself later professes to be prevented from lamenting by fear (65–6 *me crudeli sorte parentes | raptos prohibet lugere timor*) is too logical: Octavia's characterization is made up of different features, sometimes hardly consistent, and 65–6 is outweighed by 176 *dolor ira maeror miseriae luctus dabunt.* Zwierlein (*KK* ad loc.), who follows Helm's interpretation, adduces parallels for concessive participles, none of them really relevant, because in no case does the required concessive meaning produce ambiguity (e.g. *Hf.* 168 *congesto pauper in auro*; *Oed.* 196 *aliturque sitis latice ingesto*; cf., by contrast, Sen. *Phae.* 362–3 *inclusus quoque, | quamuis tegatur, proditur uultu furor*). Zwierlein's further argument that *maeror* and *ira* are irreconcilable is also weak: Liv. 1.59.2, which he cites in support of this view, proves the opposite: *totique ab luctu uersi in iram.*

quem secreta at 49 is unmetrical, and was corrected by *recc.* with the excision of the pronoun. I interpret the sequence as 'Octauia, ira coacta, non ualet luctus tegere: crudelis uiri secreta refugit semper': *crudelis uiri* belongs with the following *secreta*, rather than with *ira* (although the sequence of *ira* with an objective genitive, indicating anger felt for a particular reason or against a particular person, is linguistically unobjectionable: cf. Verg. *Aen.* 4.178 *ira inritata deorum*; Ov. *Met.* 4.235 *stimulataque paelicis ira uulgat adulterium*; *ibid.* 277). Failure to understand this word order prompted the interpolation, in the form of an explanatory gloss, *quem.*

crudelis uiri secreta refugit could either mean 'she flees any occasion of meeting the cruel man in private' or 'she keeps away from the cruel man's apartments' (for the poetic use of *secreta* to indicate the lodgings or abode of a character cf. Verg. *Aen.* 8.463 *Aeneae sedem et secreta petebat*; *ibid.* 6.10; *Georg.* 4.403 *in secreta senis ducam*). I tend to prefer the former interpretation, even if admittedly *secreta* seems out of place in reference to a wife's intimacy with her husband, because secrecy has negative associations, suggesting the caution of an adulterous liaison: cf. Liv. 1.46.3 *secretis alieni uiri adsuefacta*, of Tullia becoming Tarquinius' mistress; Tac. *Ann.* 13.18 *inrepserat per luxum et ambigua secreta*, 'secret meetings'; *Hist.* 4.49 *secreto eorum nemo adfuit* (with no erotic connotations). This is also the view of Ladek (1891, 99) and Herington (*Gnomon*, 55 (1977), 276), adducing as parallels for *crudelis uiti secreta Oed.* 805 *secreta thalami* and *Phae.* 885 *secreta mentis.* The poet is trying to describe the estrangement of the imperial couple using very high-flown and poetic language: hence the resulting obscurity of expression. This manner of expression was probably quite as strained to a Roman reader as it is to us.

secreta could also be interpreted as a feminine nominative, referring to Octavia's aloof behaviour ('she stays apart from him', in a middle sense: cf. Verg. *Aen.* 4.494 *tu secreta pyram . . . erige*), but *refugit* seems to require an object.[1] A further possibility could be to change *crudelis uiri* to *crudeli a uiro*, punctuating *ira coacta tegere, crudeli a uiro secreta refugit.*[2]

Baehrens' (*quem*) *spreta* (*Miscellanea* 1878, 116), accepted by Zwierlein in his text, is only palaeographically attractive, and places emphasis on the wrong element. Octavia does not stay away from Nero because he despises her; it is she, on the contrary, who detests him more than anybody else. In the course of this scene, Octavia is repeatedly exhorted to relent in her hatred against Nero: the Nurse seems never to lose faith that Nero and Octavia may be reconciled (cf. 84–5, 177), and at 540–2 Nero even goes so far as to express the regret that Octavia never succumbed to his affection. Indeed, the whole point of the Nurse is that Octavia's obstinate behaviour will bring mishap upon her. *sancta* (Leo, Richter) is not necessary in the context. In addition, *quem spreta* renders the sentence stilted: *quem* (sc. *crudelem uirum*) . . . *refugit semper atque odio pari* | *ardet mariti.* The pleonastic repetition *uir* | *maritus* would not be problematic in itself (cf. *Phae.* 272–3 *meus iste labor est aggredi iuuenem ferum* | *mentemque saeuam flectere immitis uiri*; *Med.* 662–3 *coniugis fatum redimens Pheraei* | *uxor impendes animam marito*; Ov. *Fast.* 5.157–8 *ne non imitata maritum* | *esset et ex omni parte secuta uirum*), but the relative pronoun makes the sequence less satisfactory (Sen. *Phae.* 272 would be less acceptable in the form of, e.g., *iuuenem ferum, quem meus labor est aggredi et saeuam mentem flectere immitis uiri*).

49–50 odio pari | ardet maritus, mutua flagrant face The transmitted *odio pari . . . mariti* (supposedly 'feeling a hatred which her husband reciprocates'; 'pari odio quam mariti odium in eam' in Ballaira's paraphrase) yields dubious Latin, at least in this linguistic register, because the objective genitive, *mariti*, and the adjective *pari* are mutually exclusive. *odio pari* is a self-contained, reflexive expression, of a type very common in Senecan tragedy (cf. *Phoe.* 384 *sed utrumque quamvis diligam affectu pari*; 461 *in utramque partem ducor affectu pari*), and is usually found with a dual or plural subject, expressing reciprocation: cf. *Phoe.* 391–2 *septena reges bella dispositi parant,* | *animo pari Cadmea progenies subit*; Ov. *Her.* 19.114 *incitat et morsus error uterque pares*; *Trist.* 4.10.6 *cum cecidit fato consul uterque pari*). Several instances of the idiom *pari* + noun as an ablative of quality are given by E. Wölfflin, *ALL* 11 (1896), 203. On the Latin for 'one another' cf. P. Thielmann, *ALL* 7 (1892), 343–88.

[1] Cf. in contrast Ov. *Met.* 2.501 *et cognoscenti similis fuit. ille refugit*; *ibid.* 443 *uisamque uocat. clamata refugit*, where a real running away is described, and the bare verb is intended to emphasize the sequence of input and rapid reaction.

[2] For synaloephe *i/a* in the arsis of the fifth foot cf. *Phoe.* 49 *discede a patre*; *ibid.* 494 *falli a suis*, with Zwierlein, *Prolegomena*, 225 ff. For the palaeographical plausibility of confusion between *s* and *a* in minuscule writing cf. Zwierlein, *KK* Appendix.

The two successive cola *odio pari ardet . . . mutua flagrant face* are in effect redundant, but this kind of abundant expression is well-paralleled: cf. Prop. 1.5.29–30 *pariter . . . socio cogemur amore | alter in alterius mutua flere sinu*; Ov. *Met.* 3.122–3 *exemploque pari furit omnis turba suoque | Marte cadunt subiti per mutua uulnera fratres*; Val. Fl. *Arg.* 1.550–1 *qui gemitus irasque pares et mutua Grais | dona ferat.* The metaphorical field of fire appears to be used interchangeably to evoke both love and hatred, and both *flagro* and *fax* are commonly so used. *mutua . . . face* seems more appropriate in reference to the intensity of reciprocated affection (as in e.g. Hor. *Carm.* 3.9.13 *me torret face mutua*). This is probably what raised Leo's suspicions and prompted him to conjecture *impia* for *mutua*. *fax*, however, is also found in connection with hatred and anger: cf. *OLD* s.v. 5b; *TLL* vi, s.v. 402–3; Cic. *De domo sua* 8.18 *sceleris sui faces*; Val. Fl. *Arg.* 3.664 *non ea fax odiis*; Tac. *Ann.* 14.3.3 *Anicetus . . . mutuis odiis Agrippinae invisus.*

I have chosen to adopt *ardet maritus, mutua flagrant face* of Gronovius, to replace *flagrat* of MSS (with *atque* in line 49 = 'on the other hand'), but Peiper's *ardent mariti*, with the adjectival use of the word (see ad 132–3), is also a possibility, and would account for the corruption. Although *flagrat* is in no way impossible, Gronovius' solution yields a more rhetorically effective text. It makes best sense of the conclusive asyndeton, and provides the typical capping *sententia* in the Senecan style, summarizing the thought expressed in a passage with memorable metaphorical brevity: cf. *Phae.* 415 *amare discat, mutuos ignes ferat, Oed.* 70 *cadunt medentes, morbus auxilium trahit*; *ibid.* 705–6 *qui sceptra duro saeuus imperium regit timet timentes: metus in auctorem redit.* A catalogue of conclusive *sententiae*, of various forms, in the tragedies of Seneca can be found in Canter, 86–99.

52–53 uincit immitis dolor | consilia nostra The transmitted *mittit* is unretainable, and the best solution seems to me Buecheler's *uincit*: *mittit* was influenced by the following *immitis*. Various attempts to defend *mittit* were made by Ladek, Carlsson (1926, 51) and Frassinetti (1973, 1100). There is nothing of use in J. F. Gummere, *CJ* 67 (1971), 59, often adduced in this connection: this meaning of *mitto* is restricted to fixed phraseological formulae, mainly imperative (Cic. *Pro Sestio* 138 *missos faciant honores* or Verg. *Aen.* 1.206 *timores mittite* (for *praetermittite* or *demittite*); 6.85 *mitte hanc de pectore curam*; Hor. *Epist.* 1.5.4 *mitte certamina*; Sen. *Phoe.* 347–8 *mitte uiolentum impetum | doloris*). A sense stronger than 'to abandon, to let go, forbear' (*TLL* viii, s.v. *mitto*, 1177.25–40; *OLD* s.v., 4) is required here. *mitto* for 'to pay no heed to' has an entry in *TLL* s.v. 1177.43 ('neglegit, non curat'), *OLD* s.v. 5, but the instances therein listed mean 'to pass over, disregard, refuse to mention': cf. Plaut. *Asin.* 79 *omnia haec mitto.* Octavia is here at her most tragic, and the description of her stubbornness evokes Eur. *Med.* 27–31 οὔτ' ὄμμ' ἐπαίρουσ' οὔτ' ἀπαλλάσσουσα γῆς | πρόσωπον· ὡς δὲ πέτρος ἢ θαλάσσιος | κλύδων ἀκούει νουθετουμένη φίλων, | ἢν μή ποτε στρέψασα πάλλευκον δέρην | αὐτὴ πρὸς αὑτὴν πατέρ ' ἀποιμώξηι φίλον). Like a true tragic heroine, Octavia vehemently rejects the Nurse's wise advice, because her grief is too strong to suffer counsel. For *uinco*, 'get the better of' cf. *OLD*, s.v. 7–8: Verg. *Aen.* 6.688 *uicit iter durum pietas*; Cic. *Clu.* 15 *uicit pudorem libido, timorem audacia, rationem amentia.* The expected Latin was perhaps *spernit, reicit* (cf. Sen. *Phae.* 582 *uerba sic spernit mea*; *ibid.* 855 *fletusque nostros spernit*, adduced by Zwierlein). Another possible solution is ***frustra, admittit immitis dolor | consilia nulla*** (cf. *Phoe.* 241 *nullas animus admittit preces* and *Troad.* 588 *animosa nullos mater admittit metus*); for examples of synaloephe at the penthemimeres in Seneca cf. *Med.* 220 *praecepsque regno eripuit*; *Phae.* 1004 *tum multa secum effatus* (Zwierlein, *Prolegomena* 214–16; Soubiran (1996), 526–8), but the combination of synaloephe and syntactical break in this metrical position seems objectionable. The only real advantage is the elimination of the double *nostra* (51, 52) and consequently, a better introduction for the generalized statement of the following line: *nec regi mentis potest | generosus ardor.*

53–54 nec regi mentis potest | generosus ardor, sed malis uires capit The metaphorical field of horsemanship with reference to passions and extreme psychological states is commonly found in Senecan tragedy: cf. *Troad.* 279–80 (with Keulen's note) *sed regi frenis nequit | et ira et ardens ensis*; *Med.* 558 *feruidam ut mentem regas*, 592 *nec regi curat.*

For *malis uires capit* cf. *Hf.* 33 *crescit malis*, with Billerbeck's note. The *Nutrix* is hinting at the motif that even women may be led to strong deeds under the drive of passion, a tragic motif fairly common in Latin poetry: see *infra*, ad 176.

55–56 heu quam nefandum prospicit noster timor | scelus: quod utinam numen auertat deum Cf. Eur. *Med.* 37 δέδοικα δ' αὐτὴν μή τι βουλεύσηι νέον, perhaps also Soph. *El.* 374 εἰ μὴ κακὸν μέγιστον εἰς αὐτὴν ἰὸν | ἤκουσα, Sen. *Med.* 395–6 *magnum aliquid instat* . . . *di fallant metum*; *Phae.* 623–4 *summus hoc omen deus | auertat*; *Thy.* 132 *auertat placidum numen et arceat.*

There is some uncertainty about the *scelus* feared by the *Nutrix* in 56. Trevet thought of the threat of Octavia's self-inflicted death. Vürtheim sees the *scelus* as Nero's marriage to Poppaea, while others see a reference to the fear that Octavia could kill her husband in a moment of despair (cf. *infra*, 174). A further possibility is the charge of adultery brought against the princess (to which there is certainly an allusion in Octavia's words at 107 (see ad loc.), *absit crimen a fatis meis*; cf. Tac. *Ann.* 14.63) or, more likely, the elimination of Octavia, which the Nurse envisages as a certain course in view of Octavia's obstinate behaviour.

57 Octavia is now heard from within. The dramatic situation is reminiscent of Eur. *Med.* (esp.) 161–7, where the laments of the distraught Medea are uttered from within the palace and the *trophos* responds from outside, although it cannot be said that there is an exchange. A cry from within also signals the entrance of Electra in Sophocles' play. Cf. also Soph. *Ai.* 331. The anapaestic exchange taking place between the Nurse and Octavia imitates a feature of Euripidean drama (cf. especially the anapaestic *amoibaion* in Eur. *Med.* 96–130;

Hipp. 176–266; *Hec.* 177–96 (not anapaestic)). Duets involving two soloists are rare in extant fifth-century tragedy, where normally a character engages in a lyrical exchange with the chorus (*parodos commatica*: e.g. Eur. *Hel.* 165, *Or.* 140; Soph. *El.* 121–250); elsewhere (as in *Med.*) one of the actors pronounces recited anapaests. There are no parallels in Senecan tragedy for this kind of duet. The words of Diomedes in *GLK* I 491 hinting at similar restrictions in early Roman drama (*in canticis autem una tantum debet esse persona, aut si duae fuerint, ita esse debent ut ex occulto una audiat nec conloquatur, sed secum, si opus fuerit, uerba faciat*: cf. Ribbeck, *RT*, 634) are not borne out by the evidence available for comedy, where duets are common (cf. e.g. Plaut. *Amph.* 551–85). On the possible presence of such duets in early Roman tragedy see Fraenkel, *EP*, 321–32.

The words supposedly pronounced by Octavia from within are rather elaborate, whereas in Greek tragedy this type of utterance is restricted to interjections rather than complete lines (although Eur. *Med.* 161–7 is a complete sentence). Whereas in Greek tragedy a distinction was always made between recited and sung anapaests, no such distinction is perceptible in the anapaests of *Octavia*, at least in the present passage: the sudden change of metre and the mythological subject matter may evoke such a distinction in the anapaests of the *Nutrix* at 201 ff. (see ad loc.).

While it is possible to imagine Octavia as singing the initial anapaestic monologue of a distressed lady (1–33), the present exchange with the Nurse could in no way be imagined as sung, if this were a Greek play, largely because humble characters do not sing in duets (compare the contrast between sung and recited anapaests in the exchange between Phaedra and her Nurse in Eur. *Hipp.* 176–266). ἀμοιβαῖα of this kind are often found in Greek tragedy, where one of the characters sings in lyrical metres, answered by another's iambics, as in Eur. *Andr.* 825–65; *Alc.* 244–79. In Greek tragedy, lyrical exchanges involving two characters alone or with the chorus are found in Eur. *Hel.* 625–99; *Hec.* 173–215; *Andr.* 501–544; *El.* 1177–1237; *Troad.* 595–606. This passage in *Octavia* is the only place in the Senecan corpus where two characters address each other in a metre other than iambics. All other scenes in which a dialogue is carried out in 'lyrical' metres are *kommoi* in which a character leads the rest of the chorus: e.g. *Troades* 67–163 (see Fantham ad loc.). This is interesting in itself, if only to point out the distance which separates the technique of the author of *Octavia* from that of the Senecan corpus, despite his intention of imitating Seneca's prose and poetry.

As always in anapaestic sequences, sentences are shorter than in iambics. This is relevant in *Octavia* because in iambics its author often elaborates convoluted sense-constructions, whereas in anapaests he tries to conclude the sense within each metrical unit. Some scholars argue that the exchange between Octavia and the *Nutrix* also takes place indoors, although there do not seem to be sufficient grounds for this interpretation and the model of Eur. *Medea* is against it. In ancient tragedy and comedy (Eur. *Orestes* and Aesch. *Eum.*) certain scenes are imagined to take place in interior settings.

There is a greater abundance of three-meter units in this section (although the incidence of monometers is not high in absolute terms within the anapaestic sections of the corpus), especially striking in 72–86˙, where the structure of the *amoibaion* (made up of short parts assigned to the two characters involved) renders the arrangement into such units virtually certain (cf. esp. 72–72•, 73–4, 77–8, 81–2, 83–83•; 84–5, 86–86•). It is, however, uncertain to what extent this could be ascribed to the poet's intention to signal a 'change of metre' for this section.

58–59 licet | repetam luctus, Electra, tuos Cf. Ov. *Her.* 19(20).10 *uerba licet repetas quae* . . . and *supra*, 6 *repete* . . . *questus*. The same interlaced word order in anapaests occurs at 769 *amplexus, Poppaea, tuos*: it appears to be typically Ovidian (cf. ad loc.); *Met.* 10.185 *in uultus, Hyacinthe, tuos*. The analogy between the Julio-Claudians and Pelops' stock was well established, perhaps as a declamatory topos. Nero was commonly nicknamed 'the matricide Orestes' and an extension of the analogy to the unfortunate Octavia can also be recognized in Juv. *Sat.* 8.217–19: (Orestes, unlike Nero) *nec | Electrae iugulo se polluit aut Spartani | sanguine coniugii*. The thought corresponds functionally to the prefatory topos 'not even if I had a brazen mouth', but the present tense suggests that this is a statement, rather than the expression of an impossible desire. The line has a metalinguistic ring ('even if I imitate your laments, Electra, my woes are not matched by anyone's', and she is indeed imitating Electra's lament, as found in Sophocles), which is somewhat surprising in a relatively unsophisticated poet such as the writer of *Octavia*. While the dramatic hero or heroine may occasionally compare their misfortunes to those of a previous mythological hero, this is usually done without explicit metaliterary resonances of this kind: cf. Soph. *Ant.* 823–4, relating the precedent of Niobe, imprisoned in a rocky tomb. For the different form taken by allusion to a theatrical precedent in Greek tragedy see P. Burian, in Easterling, *Companion*, 196. References to mythical precursors occur more freely in comedy, where the 'titles' of comedies and tragedies are mentioned without embarrassment: cf. Plaut. *Merc.* 469–70 *Pentheum diripuisse aiunt Bacchas; nugas maximas | fuisse credo, praeut quo pacto ego diuorsus distrahor*; *Bacch.* fr. xv Leo; *Rud.* 86 *non uentus fuit, uerum Alcumena Euripidi*; *Rud.* 508–9 *scelestiorem cenam cenaui tuam | quam quae Thyestae quondam adposita et Tereo*; Fraenkel, *Elementi*, 7–12. One may perhaps surmise that many such references to mythological figures, which simultaneously signify the tragedies written about them, will have been found in Ovid's *Medea*. In Seneca, there are frequent allusions to mythological precedents which are about to be completed or surpassed. This feature is in keeping with the rhetorical and allusive use of *ut solet, ut solitus*, on which Leo remarks (*Obs.* 147): cf. *Hf.* 500 *dest una numero Danais: explebo nefas*; *Thy.* 275–6 *animum Daulis inspira parens |*

sororque; causa est similis. Outside theatre, Horace in *Carm.* 4.9.10–14 gives an example of Pindar's style while talking of him (see N-H, *Odes. Book 1*, xii).

Notice *Electra* with a short final *-a*, already so in Seneca, *Agam.* 924: cf. Richter 1862, 15, quoting Lachmann ad Lucr. *D.R.N.* 6.971, on *Electra, Phaedra, Oechalia,* with short final *-a* in the *Agam.* and in *Phae.* 435, 584, 1155; *H.O.* 423, whereas *Megara* with long final *-a* appears in *H.O.* 203, 1009. Augustan poetry prefers to retain original Greek quantities. Senecan tragedy, however, uses Greek proper nouns in the forms in which they appear in early Roman drama as well, sometimes alternating these with more regular forms (*e.g. Troad.* 533, 925 have *Andromacha* at line-beginning, scanned as – ∪∪∪, but *Troad.* 968 has *Andromache*). On the shortening of the long final *-a* of Greek nouns in Latin see Lindsay, *LL* 210; N-W[3] 1.83–6.

60–62 tibi maerenti caesum licuit | flere parentem, | scelus ulcisci uindice fratre Sophocles' Electra, in fact, complains that not even mourning is permitted to her, οὐδὲ γὰρ κλαῦσαι πάρα | τοσόνδ' ὅσον μοι θυμὸς ἡδονὴν φέρει (285–6) because, on account of her lamentation, she is constantly scolded by Clytaemnestra.

It is characteristic of the play that co-ordinated independent clauses or two cola which depend on the same conjunction or relative are linked to one another asyndetically (see also 679 ff.). In anapaests, these constructions may aim at representing emotion. In Greek tragedy, for instance, asyndeton is a feature of lament, which highlights the clipped, broken delivery of a distraught character (cf. Eur. *Phoe.* 1551–2 πάρα γὰρ στενάχειν τάδ', ἀυτεῖν (with Mastronarde's note; *ibid.* 1574–5), and the effect of a more pathetic delivery may be consciously aimed at by the author. On asyndeta and *pathos* in Greek rhetorical and stylistic theory cf. Ar. *Rhet.* 3.1413b29; Aesch. *Eum.* 144 (with schol. **M**); *De subl.* 19–20; N. O'Sullivan, *Alcidamas, Aristophanes and the Beginnings of Greek Stylistic Theory* (Stuttgart, 1992), 47, 59.

This type of strongly emotional asyndeton is frequent in early Latin poetry (cf. Timpanaro, *NC*, 2–74, who, however, concentrates on sequences of nouns and adjectives). Augustan poetry adopts more restrictive practices, and asyndeta tend to be avoided. Among the few comparable examples in Vergil, not conspicuously emotional, are *Aen.* 8.132; 9.265–6 (cf. Conington's note ad *Aen.* 9.315). Ovid, a poet well known for his abundant use of conjunctions, exhibits few relevant cases (cf. e.g. *Fast.* 6.495–6 *est spatio contracta breui, freta bina repellit, | unaque pulsatur terra duobus aquis*). Lucan is less restrained than either Vergil or Seneca in the tragedies: cf. e.g. *Bell. Ciu.* 3.368; 4.320–33; 4.705–6; 4.776; 9.24–6; 9.547–8. In Senecan tragedy, asyndeta often have an explicative function, marking the pointed conclusion of a period (cf. *Phae.* 127–8 *nulla Minois leui | defuncta amore, iungitur semper nefas*), so that editors print a colon (:) in order to make the asyndetic connection less harsh. Shorter cola linked asyndetically are otherwise frequent in Silver Latin and are indeed a characteristic feature of a pointed style which aims to surprise. For an overall assessment of asyndeton and its diffusion in Latin poetry cf. G. Calboli in *EO* 2.799–803.

63–64 tua quem pietas hosti rapuit | texitque fides In Eur. *El.* 16, 286 the rescue of Orestes is attributed to the Paedagogus; in Soph. *El.* 12–13 the old man tells how he received the child from Electra's hands; while in Sen. *Agam.* 910 ff. Electra consigns Orestes to Strophius.

65–67 me crudeli sorte parentes | raptos prohibet lugere timor | fratrisque necem deflere uetat Fear prevents Octavia from giving vent to unrestrained grief. *timor* is the common subject of *prohibet lugere* and *deflere uetat.* Latin poets, especially after Vergil, resort largely to a stylistic device known as *dicolon abundans*, or 'theme and variation', a special case of hendiadys consisting of two parallel cola partly overlapping in sense (e.g. Verg. *Aen.* 10.270–1 *ardet apex capiti cristisque a uertice flamma | funditur*): cf. *LHS* 2.786–8; Maurach, *EP*, 20–6; W. Görler, in *EV* 2.276. This figure of speech allows the viewing of a process from different standpoints by means of subsequently added cola. For some post-Vergilian examples cf. e.g. Ov. *Fasti* 1.419 *fastus inest pulchris sequiturque superbia formam*; Luc. *Bell. Ciu.* 5.437–8 *cum glacie retinente fretum non impulit Hister | immensumque gelu tegitur mare.* In Seneca cf. *Agam.* 88–9 *sidunt ipso pondere magna | ceditque oneri fortuna suo*; *H.O.* 178–80 *alio nostras fortuna uocat | lacrimas, alias flere ruinas | mea fata iubent.* In Senecan tragedy, however, the expected pattern of parallel constructions is sometimes disrupted by a disinclination for the *Gesetz der wachsenden Glieder.* The three commonest varieties of *dicola abundantia* are the following: (1) each colon has its own subject (e.g. *apex* and *flamma* in the instance from Vergil); (2) there is only one common subject, but it is left unexpressed until the second colon: cf. Ov. *Met.* 5.357 *ne pateat latoque solum retegatur hiatu*; (3) there is one common subject, which is placed in the first colon.

65–66 crudeli sorte parentes | raptos 65–6 show that coincidence of metrical and syntactic cola (*Kongruenzgesetz*: cf. Introd. p. 44) is not always the rule in anapaests, since it would be impossible to establish a colometry by which nouns and their attributive adjectives figured on the same line. Notice also the absence of hyperbaton in the collocation of nouns and adjectives at 65–6 *crudeli sorte parentes raptos*; similarly 34–5 *fragili bono | fallacis aulae*; also ad 136. The comparative rarity of cases of dislocated word-order places *Oct.* in a peculiar position within the dominant trends of Latin poetry. The poet's aspiration to attain a high poetical register is conspicuous (note the balanced arrangement in pairs of nouns and adjectives, the lexical choice), but only successful on the level of vocabulary. On hyperbata in Latin poetry, in general and in historical perspective, cf. *LHS* 2.689–94; Norden, *AK* 1.65–8, *Nachträge*, 7; for a linguistic assessment of this phenomenon cf. Rosén, *Latine loqui*, 27–8; *ibid.* 160–2; Calcante, *passim.* On hyperbata in Greek, where this phenomenon appears to have a firmer linguistic, pragmatic grounding, cf. Devine-Stephens, *DS*.

crudeli sorte . . . raptos echoes the hexametric clausula *crudeli funere raptus* (with many variations): cf. e.g. *CE* 467.4 *sed iniqua sorte maligna rapta*; *CE* 501.2; *CE* 1143.2; *CE* 1336.12; *CE* 1973.1; *CE* 1996.11; *CE* 2246.3.

68 in quo fuerat spes una mihi The exchange between pluperfect and imperfect or perfect tenses is a commonly observed feature of hexametric poetry, usually for metrical convenience: cf. Williams ad Verg. *Aen.* 5.397; *LHS* 2.321; Platnauer, *LEV*, 112.

69 totque malorum breue solamen Cf. Verg. *Aen.* 3.661 *ea sola uoluptas | solamenque mali*; 3.709 *omnis curae casusque leuamen*; Sil. *Pun.* 2.470.

70 nunc in luctus seruata meos Gronovius proposed *meros* ('erat superstite fratre aliquod intervallum luctus, nunc unus et perpetuus est'), but there is no compelling reason to alter the paradosis. Octavia has been spared the doom undergone by the rest of her family only so that she can now drown in her sorrows. The sentence is meant to describe the misery of those who survived, and the good luck of those who died and were spared the sight of what followed (cf. e.g. Sen. *Troad.* 145 *felix Priamus*). The expression is an adaptation of Verg. *Aen.* 11.159 *felix morte tua neque in hunc seruata dolorem* (of Pallas' mother, who did not live to see her son's death in battle); Ov. *Met.* 12.309 *ad Herculeos seruaberis arcus*; Sil. *Pun.* 11.361–2 *seruatus in arma | Scipiadae Poenus*; *infra* 663 *ad hos thalamos seruata diu.*

71 magni resto nominis umbra Cf. Luc. *Bell. Ciu.* 1.135 *stat magni nominis umbra* (with reference to Pompeius, who has outlived his fame). *nomen* in 71 means 'family', of which Octavia sees herself as the last survivor.

72–72' uox en nostras perculit aures | tristis alumnae In ancient theatrical practice, characters appearing in mid-act are announced by the chorus or by some other character already on stage, whose words must have provided some sort of entrance cue. This function is performed here by the Nurse, who has remained silent during Octavia's song at 57–71. Her delay in acknowledging Octavia's presence, regardless of whether the latter's words are thought to be pronounced in- or outdoors, is consistent with post-classical dramatic technique (cf. Tarrant (1978) 231–41, on entrance monologues delivered in isolation). Compare, for instance, the recognition scene of Palaestra and Ampelisca in Plaut. *Rud.* 185ff. where the two women deliver their parts ignoring each other, up to 233–4 PA. *certo uox muliebris auris tetigit meas.* | AM. *mulier est, muliebris uox mi ad auris uenit.* It is striking, in *Oct.* 75 ff., that Octavia addresses the Nurse without any formal acknowledgement. By way of parallels from early Roman drama cf. Enn. *Scaen.* 296 R² *sed sonitus auris meas pedum pulsu increpat*; Acc. *Scaen.* 448–9 R² *timida eliminor | e clamore simul ac nota uox ad auris accidit*; Plaut. *Stich.* 88 *certo enim mihi paternae uocis sonitus auris accidit*; *Trin.* 45 *quoia hic uox prope me sonat*: cf. Leo, *Monolog*, 93. In Seneca an act is often initiated by a monologizing character who is then joined by a foil, or subordinate figure, but the arrival of the second character is mostly sudden and there is no proper entrance announcement (cf. *Phae.* 129 with Mayer's note; *Hf.* 279; *Agam.* 125; *Oed.* 81; *Med.* 150; *Thy.* 204). The author of *Oct.* seems to have been exposed to the influence of other dramatic models beside Seneca.

For *uox . . . perculit (aures, animum)*, cf. *TLL* x.1, s.v. *percello*, 1197.30–5, always suggesting reaction at shocking news. Prosodically, *tristis* could either be nominative or genitive, but the latter interpretation is preferable in my view.

I have discussed the cries from within ad 37. In comparable episodes of classical Greek tragedy, characters mostly pronounce inarticulate laments from inside, before they come out to lament. This is in particular the case for Soph. *El.* 77–9 (El.) ἰώ μοί μοι δύστηνος | (Paed.) καὶ μὴν θυρῶν ἔδοξα προσπόλων τινὸς | ὑποστενούσης ἔνδον αἰσθέσθαι.

The formal plural *nostras . . . aures* is less common for humble characters, but cf. the words of Medea's *Nutrix* at Sen. *Med.* 394 *irae nouimus ueteris notas*; *Phae.* 855 NV. *fletusque nostros spernit.* The Nurse uses the plural also at 55 *noster timor*; 53 *consilia nostra.*

73–74 cesset thalamis inferre gradus | tarda senectus? The Nurse summons herself to go inside, but her intention is anticipated by Octavia. Although the scene is treated in a somewhat elliptical manner as regards the movements of the characters on the notional stage (contact is not formally established, and Octavia addresses the Nurse in a rather abrupt way), the passage appears to pick up a dramatic convention of early Roman drama, where a character announcing his or her intention to leave the stage is often forestalled by another's entrance: cf. Pacuv. *Scaen.* 214 R² *ibo ad eam ut sciscam quid uelit. ualuae sonunt*; Ter. *Heaut.* 410 *cesso pultare ostium uicini?* (where Menedemus comes out of the house before Chremes, the speaker of 410, can knock at his door); Acc. *Scaen.* 302 R² *quid cesso ire ad eam? em praesto est* (where Alcmaeon catches sight of his mother as he is about to go into the house); Plaut. *Poen.* 740–1; *Rud.* 454 *sed quid ego cesso fugere in fanum*; 677 *cesso ego has consolari*, followed by an exchange with the suppliant women (outside the temple). Expressions of this kind are the equivalent of modern stage-directions: '(*X makes to go in, but suddenly halts as he catches sight of Y rushing out*)'. For the opposite view that the exchange between Octavia and her Nurse is set indoors cf. Zwierlein (1966), 44, n. 10.

The construction of *cesso* with an infinitive belongs to elevated diction. In Senecan tragedy it occurs also at *Troad.* 870; *Phoe.* 91; *Agam.* 986 (the first two in a self-address). For the similarity of the phrasing cf. Enn. *Scaen.* 181–2 R² *gradum proferre pedum, | nitere, cessas, o fide?* In *Octauia*, as in the Senecan corpus, items of traditional or archaic vocabulary seem to occur most frequently in the more stereotypical scenes (exits, entrances).

For the more formal use of the abstract *senectus* (for *senex*) in reference to the speaker cf. 674–5 *cessat pietas dum nostra*. For another instance of this use in the Senecan corpus cf. *Phae.* 262–3 *sic te senectus nostra praecipiti sinat | perire leto?* also pronounced by a *Nutrix*. Elsewhere cf. Ov. *Met.* 5.27 *per quem haec non orba senectus*; 10.396 *non est mea pigra senectus* (Myrrha's Nurse); Luc. *Bell. Ciu.* 9.234–5 *iustas sibi nostra senectus | prospiciat flammas*. In Greek cf. Eur. *I.A.* 4 μάλα τοι γῆρας τοὐμὸν ἄυπνον, said by the old servant.

For the construction of *infero* with a bare dative of movement cf. *H.O.* 717 *thalamisque . . . intuli gressum meis*; Stat. *Theb.* 5.240–1 *thalamis . . . paternis inferor*; Luc. *Bell. Ciu.* 10.56–8 *cum se Cleopatra . . . intulit Emathiis . . . tectis*; Lucr. *D.R.N.* 5.976 *sol inferret lumina caelo*; Verg. *Aen.* 10.300 *aruis rates inferre Latinis*. The dative after compound verbs expressing motion is a poeticism: cf. Williams' note ad Verg. *Aen.* 3.34. K-S 2.1.331 records the use as post-classical in prose. *Oct.* has also *efferre gradum* + simple ablative (*tectis* 160; 667). On the simple *ferre gressum* cf. Zwierlein, *KK* 354.

75 excipe nostras lacrimas *excipere lacrimas* is found in Ov. *Am.* 3.9.11 *excipiunt lacrimas sparsi per colla capilli* (cf. also Stat. *Theb.* 5.234–5 *undantemque sinu conlapsa cruorem | excipit*). In *Oct.* the expression is used metaphorically: Octavia is not asking the old Nurse to soak herself in her tears, but to listen to her laments and comfort her. These two figurative senses, 'to listen' and 'to embrace', already have precedents in the Senecan corpus: cf. *Hf.* 361 *uerba . . . excipe*; *Troad.* 799–800 *oscula et fletus, puer, | lacerosque crines excipe*.

76 testis nostri fida doloris The *Nutrix* takes over the consolatory function normally performed by the chorus in the *parodoi* of Greek tragedy: cf. Soph. *El.* 130 ἥκετ' ἐμῶν καμάτων παραμύθιον, Eur. *Or.* 132–3 αἵδ' αὖ πάρεισι τοῖς ἐμοῖς θρηνήμασιν | φίλαι ξυνῳδοί (both passages referring to the arrival of the chorus); Sen. *Troad.* 83 *fidae casus nostri comites* (Hecuba to the chorus); *Med.* 568–9 *tu fida Nutrix, socia maeroris mei | uariique casus*. For the language cf. also Ov. *Trist.* 3.7.2 (*littera*) *sermonis fida ministra mei*. This is one of the relatively few lines in *Octavia* that exhibit an interlaced pattern of words and adjectives.

77–78 quis te tantis soluet curis, | miseranda, dies? Cf. Eur. *Or.* 187–8 CHO. θρόει τίς κακῶν τελευτὰ μένει; EL. θανεῖν θανεῖν, τί δ' ἄλλο; (but Electra's answer refers to Orestes). For *quis* see ad 157.

79 qui me Stygias mittet ad umbras *Mittit/misit ad umbras* is an established formula in hexametric poetry: cf. Ov. 6.676 *dolor Tartareas Pandiona misit ad umbras*; 12.257 *Tartareas . . . mitti ad umbras*; Hom. Lat. 431 *et Strophio genitum Stygias demittit ad umbras*. In *Oct.* cf. 958. The hyperbaton *Stygias . . . ad umbras* is also very common: cf. e.g. Luc. *Bell. Ciu.* 5.667 *et dictator eam Stygias et consul ad umbras*; *H.O.* 1983–4.

81–82 non uota meos tua nunc casus, | sed fata regunt The placement of two possessives in close proximity for effect seems a characteristically elegiac mannerism, and is especially frequent in Ovid: cf. Prop. 4.11.41–2 *neque ulla | labe mea uestros erubuisse focos*; Ov. *Her.* 2.8 *non uenit ante suam nostra querela diem*; 2.87; 4.16 *figat sic animos in mea uota tuos*; 5.5 *quis deus opposuit nostris sua numina uotis?*; 5.146; 6.40 *detegit ingenio uulnera nostra suo*; 15.2 *oculis cognita nostra tuis*; 15.26 *in portus et mea uota suos*; 15.127 *saepe tuos nostra ceruice . . . lacertos*; 16.170 *permanet in uoto mens mea firma suo*; *Met.* 6.281 *satia . . . meo tua pectora luctu*; 12.490–1 *nostro tua corpora ferro | temptemus*; 13.128 *si mea cum uestris ualuissent uota*. In Seneca cf. Sen. *Phoe.* 51–2 *a tuo nostram manum | corpore*; elsewhere Stat. *Silu.* 5.1.20 *mense meo tua Roma*. The interlaced word-order found at 81–2 (*meos tua . . . casus . . . fata*) seems more awkward than the other parallels I have found, where only one pair of noun-possessive is in hyperbaton (e.g. *in portus . . . mea uota suos*).

83–83ˑ dabit afflictae meliora deus | tempora mitis The line echoes Verg. *Aen.* 1.199 *dabit deus|his quoque finem*; cf. also Sen. *Troad.* 872–3 *melior afflictos deus | respicere coepit*. For the indefinite *deus* ('some god'; = Gk. θεός τις), indicating an unspecified deity, either because still unknown or because a generically divine action is meant, cf. *Oct.* 255–6 *forsitan uindex deus | existet aliquis*; Ov. *Her.* 1.23 *sed bene consuluit casto deus aequus amori*; Sen. *Hf.* 385 *sequitur superbos ultor a tergo deus*; *Thy.* 489–90 *respiciet deus | bene cogitata*.

Personal pronouns can sometimes be supplied from adjectives or participles: cf. *Troad.* 440 *uenit afflictae quies* (= *mihi afflictae*); *Phae.* 99 *maior alius incubat maestae dolor*. Elsewhere cf. Luc. *Bell. Ciu.* 5.284–5 *quid uelut ignaros ad quae portenta paremur | spe trahis?*

84–85 tu modo blando uince obsequio | placata uirum *Tu modo* followed by an imperative also in Verg. *Aen.* 2.60, and elsewhere: cf. *TLL* viii. s.v. *modo* 1300.21; *LHS* 2.339. The same entreaty to Octavia to relent is repeated at 177 *uince obsequendo potius immitem uirum*. Garrod, *CQ* 5 (1911), 219, proposed *placaque uirum*, but there is no need to suspect *placata*: the Nurse has already described the couple's mutual hatred at 49–50, and points out that Octavia needs to appease her anger first, if she wants to recapture Nero's affection.

86–88 uincam saeuos ante leones | tigresque truces | fera quam saeui corda tyranni The sense of *uinco* must be metaphorical, 'to conquer', 'to prevail upon': 'I shall sooner tame savage lions and blood-thirsty tigers than win over Nero's savage heart', picking up *uince* said by the *Nutrix* at 84. The use of plurals even with reference to the bodily parts of individuals (e.g. *bracchia, colla, corpora, terga*; here in *saeui corda tyranni*) is a normal poeticism, especially frequent in hexametric poetry with neuters; according to Bednara (*ALL* 14 (1906), 555–6) the use of *corda* with reference to individuals is only found after Vergil, and in Ovid: cf. Verg. *Aen.* 6.49 *rabie fera corda tument*; in Seneca this poetic plural is found only in *Agam.* 713.

89 spernit superos hominesque simul Before it emerged from the recovered δ-branch of *A*, the right reading (for the transmitted *superbos hominesque*) had been divined by Delrius, *Syntagma*, iii.524, surprisingly late, considering the blatant impossibility of the metrical sequence: many corrections found in several *recentiores* (e.g. 34 *fragili*, 82 *fata*, 316 *prouecta*, 379 *grauius*, 449 *ipse*, 500 *gentium domitor*, 617 *tumulumque nati*, 661 *scelerum*, 742 *toros*, 762 *loquax*, 765 *ferunt*, 821 *nefas tantum*) healed far more difficult wounds, some requiring comparatively expert metrical competence. The slip was encouraged by a subconscious echo of Vulg. Ev. sec. Luc. 1.51–2 *dispersit superbos . . . et exaltauit humiles*. The right reading seems to have been also in a Cologne MS used by Commelinus (cf. MacGregor (1985), 1180, 1203).

For the characterization of the evil man as a hater of human and divine law cf. Cic. *Phil.* 2.64 *dis hominibusque hostis*; Liv. 3.57.2 *deorum hominumque contemptor* (of Appius Claudius); Verg. *Aen.* 7.648 *contemptor diuom*; *ibid.* 8.7; Stat. *Theb.* 3.602 (of Capaneus) *superum contemptor*, Sil. *Pun.* 1.58 (of Hannibal). This is, predictably, a standard feature of tyrants: cf. Suet. *Nero*, 32.4; 56; *Vesp.* 9.1; Plin. *Nat.* 7.46 (*Nero*) *toto principatu suo hostem generis humani*. Although the murderer of his mother and of most of his relatives can be naturally referred to as a *hominum divumque contemptor*, the tradition about Nero included various stories in which the emperor figured as impious: see *infra* note ad 240–1 *hic hostis deum | hominumque templis expulit superos suis*.

90 nec fortunam capit ipse suam Nero cannot sustain his own fortune, and is carried away by the illusion of his omnipotence. The line probably imitates Ov. *Met.* 6.609–10 *iram | non capit ipsa suam Procne*; 11.118 *uix spes ipse suas animo capit*; Curt. *Hist. Alex.* 3.12.20 *Alexander ad ultimum magnitudinem eius* (sc. *fortunae suae*) *non cepit*; cf. also Verg. *Aen.* 7.466. The closest Senecan parallel is *Thy.* 496 *uix dolor frenos capit*, but *capio* has a different sense. For this use of *capio* cf. *TLL* iii, s.v., 321.67–8; 329.60–81; cf. also *infra*, 835 *nec capit clementiam*. The point is strangely compressed, and one would have expected Octavia to expatiate on the manifestations of Nero's outrageous behaviour. The relative clause is quite detached from what precedes it.

93–95 licet . . . tantum munus morte rependat The present tense of *rependat* in place of the expected perfect *rependerit* must be due to metrical constraints. Agrippina was murdered in 59. On *rependere* see Bömer ad Ov. *Met.* 2.694; Ov. *Met.* 5.15 *hac uitam seruatae dote rependis?* Stat. *Theb.* 7.50 *haec praemia digna rependi*. The same charge of ingratitude in retribution is employed by Jos. *Ant.* 20.153 Νέρων δὲ τὴν ἀρχὴν οὕτως παραλαβὼν Βρεττανικὸν μὲν ἀδήλως τοῖς πολλοῖς ἀναιρεῖ διὰ φαρμάκων, φανερῶς δ' οὐκ εἰς μακρὰν τὴν μητέρα τὴν ἑαυτοῦ φονεύει, ταύτην ἀμοιβὴν ἀποτίσας αὐτῇ οὐ μόνον τῆς γενέσεως ἀλλὰ καὶ τοῦ ταῖς ἐκείνης μηχαναῖς τὴν Ῥωμαίων ἡγεμονίαν παραλαβεῖν.

96 feret hunc titulum . . . femina *titulus* is frequent in Ovid in this metaphorical sense: cf. Ov. *Met.* 4.645 *et hunc praedae titulum Ioue natus habebit*; 13.372 *hunc titulum meritis pensandum reddite nostris*; *Her.* 2.73; 7.76; 21.176.

96 post fata tamen 'Although Nero has tried to conceal that he owes the empire to his mother, nevertheless a woman will for ever, even after her death, have that glory.' Like other adverbs and particles, *tamen* is frequently postponed in Roman poetry (cf. *LHS* 2.496; Marouzeau, *Ordre*, 3.94–6). In this case, however, its position at line-end is not due to metrical constraints, because *tamen* and *feret* have the same prosody. The final position is probably due to the *apo koinou* construction: *tamen* qualifies both *post fata* and the entire sentence. Cf. Introd. p. 36 on how in *Octavia* a comparatively modest control of the syntactical resources of Latin rhetoric corresponds to an evident penchant for high-flown, eminently 'poetical' formulae, such as *post fata*. Moreover, the author of *Octavia* resorted to strange means to compensate for the generally prosaic word-order of the lines (see Introduction). *post fata* (also at 112, 289, 529) is Augustan: Verg. *Aen.* 4.20 *miseri post fata Sychaei*; Sen. *Troad.* 654; *Agam.* 38. Junge (1999), 230 shows how the expression undergoes a stylistic inflation in Silver Latin, with its frequency increasing from a single Vergilian instance to three in Lucan and four each in Martial and Silius (seventeen examples in *CE*, the vast majority of which are clearly post-Vergilian).

97 longo semper in aeuo Cf. Ov. *Met.* 3.445–5 *ecquem . . . qui sic tabuerit longo meministis in aeuo?*; 10.502 *nomen erile tenet nulloque tacebitur aeuo*; 14.731 *et longo facite ut narremur in aeuo*; *Fast.* 5.377 *floreat ut toto carmen Nasonis in aeuo*. *semper* is pleonastic (cf. the emphatic use of *diu* in the play).

98 animi retine uerba furentis Cf. Sen. *Med.* 381 *resiste et iras comprime ac retine impetum*; *Agam.* 224–5; *H.O.* 275–6 *pectoris sani parum, | alumna, questus comprime et flammas doma*; Soph. *El.* 1011 κατάσχες ὀργήν.

99 temere emissam comprime uocem The metonymical sense of *uox* for *uerba* is well-established (cf. *OLD* s.v., 7): e.g. Verg. *Aen.* 4.621 *hanc uocem extremam cum sanguine fundo*; 6.686–7 *uox excidit ore | 'uenisti tandem'*; Liv. 5.51.7 *uox caelo emissa*; Soph. *El.* 214 φράζου μὴ πόρσω φωνεῖν.

100–173 Octavia (100–36) and the Nurse (137–73) pronounce two long *rhēseis* roughly equivalent in length. In Greek tragedy these *rhēseis* would be an *agōn*, that is, the debate of two characters confronting each other on a disputed issue. In Seneca, even *rhēseis* of great length are sometimes divested of a clear argumentative function: two characters can pronounce long tirades in succession only to expatiate on the mythical background and its implications, often at the expense of dramatic effectiveness: cf. e.g. *Hf.* 205–308, where Amphitryon and Megara, who have sought protection as suppliants at the altar of the gods to escape from Lycus, are at leisure to expatiate on Hercules' labours in two successive unrelated monologues; *Phae.* 435–64. On this feature of Senecan drama cf. Leo, *Monolog*, 92; Zwierlein (1966), 119–24. Similarly, the Nurse's address to Octavia at 137 (*frustra parentis inuocas manes tui*) shows little concern with the immediate needs of their dramatic situation, as she goes on to enumerate and moralize on the events leading to Agrippina's rise and culminating with the death of Britannicus. Apart from 137, everything else the *Nutrix* says might as well be said by Octavia, who, one might add, hardly needed to be reminded of her misfortunes. The Nurse's tirade is mainly an excuse to launch into a catalogue of Julio-Claudian atrocities. In Greek tragedy, change of metre (from lyrics to iambics) does not always signal the entrance of a new character: in particular, a *parodos commatica* is often followed by a scene in iambics with no new entrances: cf. for instance Eur. *Hel.* 252–329; Soph. *El.* 251–327; Aesch. *Cho.* 370.

100–101 toleranda quamuis patiar, haud umquam queant | nisi morte tristi nostra finiri mala Octavia, who has been summoned to restraint by her Nurse, contrasts the abuse of which she is personally a victim, in itself not past endurance, with her deeper affliction when she considers the miserable fate of her relatives, as well as with the prospect, certain, of death as the final act: 'although I suffer mishaps which in themselves are tolerable, my sorrows can never be ended but by death' ('quamuis quae patior ferri possint' in Leo's paraphrase, *Obs.* 385). *toleranda*, in my opinion, indicates possibility rather than obligation: cf. *LHS* 2.370–1. It is true that Octavia, at 57–8, described her lot as miserable and beyond comparison with anyone else's (*o mea nullis aequanda malis fortuna*). Now, however, she wishes to draw a more precise distinction between her individual sufferings and what she suffers on account of her loved ones, murdered by Nero. This has the result of portraying Octavia as an altruistic and generous figure.

I find this interpretation preferable to Baden's 'aerumnas mihi tolerandas quamuis patienter feram', defended by Zwierlein and others, but less appropriate, I think, to the argument. I believe *toleranda* to mean 'ills [that are] tolerable', rather than '[those ills] which it is my fate to endure'. After her burst of indignation against Nero at 86–90, it would be anticlimactic for Octavia to show the acceptance of her state implied by Baden's interpretation, and there has been no hint so far in her words that it is proper for her to submit to the treatment she has undergone. By way of parallel for this use of the gerundive with *patior* cf. Sen. *Troad.* 412 *si flenda patimur* ('if we are the victims of evils that it is enough to mourn by crying only').

More drastically, emendation seemed necessary to Lipsius, who proposed *toleranda quaeuis patiar*, later modified by Gronovius to *toleranda quaeuis paterer*. Lipsius' conjecture (with *patior* meaning 'to bear strongly, courageously') lends Octavia a more confrontational and more 'tragic' attitude, and has the advantage of making Octavia actually answer the Nurse's request to moderate her anger (98 *animi retine uerba furentis*). She starts with a seeming concession to the

Nurse: 'imagine I bear my lot patiently, as you exhort me to: would this make my life any better? My ills surpass endurance, and only death will bring an end to them.' Indeed, Senecan characters often react with indignant rhetoric when they are summoned to restraint (in *Oct.* cf. 177–8 *ut fratrem ademptum . . . restituat mihi?*; 461–2 *an patiar ultra sanguinem nostrum peti . . . ?*; *H.O.* 275–7; *Phoe.* 584–6), but the change of metre, marking the transition from a more emotional to a more expository section, can perhaps account for the less tense tone of Octavia's answer. Tac. *Ann.* 13.16.4 *quamuis modeste ageret* is sometimes adduced in this connection; the passage refers mainly, however, to Octavia's secluded and withdrawn life, away from court intrigue.

For similar expressions cf. Acc. *Scaen.* 91 R² *pertolerarem uitam cladesque exanclarem impetibilis* (with L. Mueller's proposed supplement *quodsi spes restaret ulla in melius mutandi mea*); Ov. *Trist.* 3.2.14 *uix . . . ferenda tulit*; Stat. *Ach.* 2.17 *paruimus, genetrix, quamquam haud toleranda iubebas*. In Greek cf. Aesch. *Cho.* 748 τὰ μὲν γὰρ ἄλλα τλημόνως ἤντλουν κακά.

101 nisi morte tristi nostra finiri mala Cf. Cic. *Tusc.* 1.115, 4 (= Soubiran, p. 278, Traglia, 77, 4, after Eur.) *at qui labores morte finisset grauis*; Verg. *Aen.* 12.880 (*morte*) *possem tantos finire dolores*; Ov. *Met.* 1.661 *nec finire licet tantos mihi morte dolores*; *Trist.* 3.3.96 *finitis gaude tot mihi morte malis*; Sen. *H.O.* 1021 *mors sola portus dabitur aerumnis meis*.

102–105 The period is made up of a sequence of participial constructions, comprising two ablative absolutes (*genetrice caesa, per scelus rapto patre*) and five *participia coniuncta* in asyndetic sequence. Lists of ablative absolutes are a feature of the militaresque style of the *commentarii* (cf. Leeman, *Orationis ratio*, 176, citing Plaut. *Persa* 753–5 *hostibus uictis, ciuibus saluis, re placida, pacibus perfectis . . .* ; *Amph.* 188–9), but there are tragic precedents in which a character enumerates his or her misfortunes in accumulations comparable to 102–5: cf. Soph. *Ant.* 49–57; *El.* 261–5. In Seneca cf. *Phoe.* 510–13 *hostium es factus gener, | patria remotus, hospes alieni laris, | externa consecutus, expulsus tuis, | sine crimine exul*; *Med.* 118–19 *erepto patre, | patria atque regno sedibus solam exteris*; *Agam.* 991–3 *inops egens, inclusa, paedore obruta, | uidua ante thalamos, exul, inuisa omnibus, | aethere negato sero succumbet malis*. *Octavia* 102–5 is closely paralleled by Tac. *Ann.* 14.63, as noticed by most commentators: *huic primum nuptiarum dies loco funeris fuit, deductae in domum in qua nihil nisi luctuosum haberet, erepto per uenenum patre et statim fratre; tum ancilla domina ualidior et Poppaea non nisi in perniciem uxoris nupta, postremo crimen omni exitio grauius*. I have discussed this passage in *HSCPh* 98 (1998), 329–42.

102 genetrice caesa, per scelus rapto patre Cf. Tac. *Ann.* 14.63 *erepto per uenenum patre*; *rapio* is a case of *simplex pro composito*, normal in poetry. The figurative use of *rapio/eripio* in the sense of 'carried off by death' is high-flown and typically poetic: cf. Ov. *Pont.* 1.9.1 *de rapto . . . Celso*; Corn. Sev. fr. 13.3 Courtn. *rapti Ciceronis imago*; Sen. *Phae.* 1199 *rapto . . . gnato*; also *supra*, 65–6 *crudeli sorte parentes raptos*.

For the prepositional construction *per scelus* (= murderously) cf. Verg. *Aen.* 5.793 *per scelus . . . Troianis matribus actis*; Ov. *Her.* 6.10 *per facinus.*

103 miseriis luctu obruta *Asyndeta bimembria* with nouns and adjectives are common in early Latin literature. On this phenomenon generally cf. S. Mariotti, *Lezioni su Ennio* (Urbino, 1991^2), 48; S. Timpanaro, *JRS* 44 (1954), 157; id., *Nuovi contributi di filologia e storia della lingua latina* (Bologna, 1994), 1–74, especially on asyndeta involving pairs of adjectives; *LHS* 2.828–30; K-S 2.2.150; 577. While less frequent in Augustan poetry, this pattern re-emerges in Silver Latin; cf. e.g. Tac. *Hist.* 5.5 *instituta sinistra foeda*; Sen. *Epist.* 84.11 *tumida res est, uana uentosa*; in *Oct.* cf. 506 *iuuenes senes*; 562 *luxu otio*, involving nouns, apparently the more archaic type; see also Goodyear ad Tac. *Ann.* 1.33.2; Axelson, *NSS* 29, 103; H. Lindgren, *Studia Curtiana* (Uppsala, 1935), 25–6; M. Winterbottom, *Problems in Quintilian* (London, 1970), 70. In Senecan tragedy asyndetic pairs are not very frequent, but cf. *Hf.* 1335 *Theseu, latebram quaere longinquam abditam.*

Notice the presumably unintentional paronomastic echo *orbata . . . obruta*; cf. ad 579–80. Acc. *Scaen.* 94 R^2 *miseret miseriarum luctuum orbitudinis.*

For *obrutus* 'overwhelmed','overcome', in the description of psychological states cf. Pac. *Scaen.* 356 R^2 *aerumnis obruta*; Liv. 42.28.12 *obruit animum . . . luctus metusque*; Curt. *Hist. Alex.* 9.9.23; Tac. *Hist.* 3.67. 1; more in *TLL* ix.2 s.v. *obruo*, coll. 153–4.

104 maerore pressa The noun *maeror* ('affliction', 'mourning', connected with *maestus*) is absent from Augustan poetry; it is frequent in both Republican and Senecan drama (alongside a number of other nominal formations in *–or*, such as *paedor, marcor*): *maerore pressa* is found here only; but *pressa* for 'stricken by' some negative emotion is common: cf. e.g. Verg. *Aen.* 3.47 *mentem formidine pressus*; Sen. *Oed.* 798 *quis premat mentem timor.*

104–105 ac meae | subiecta famulae The personage alluded to with *famula* is Poppaea. Some commentators have interpreted this as a reference to Acte, because Nero's mistress appears to be so designated at 194 (*quae . . . animum . . . domini famula possedit diu*). Indeed, Acte is clearly meant in Tac. *Ann.* 14.63.4 *tum ancilla domina ualidior* (given in full ad 102–5), a passage whose close affinity with *Oct.* 102 ff. is beyond doubt, although the question of priority still remains undecided. Acte no longer appears to be influential on Nero in the play (cf. 196). The word *famula* is inappropriate for Poppaea, who was of a very exalted rank, whereas it is apposite enough for a *liberta* (cf. 194; 950, where *famulo* refers to Narcissus). On the other hand, *famula* is certainly used with reference to Poppaea at 657 *intrare thalamos famulae.* In the official language of the early Empire, freeborn citizens could not generally be referred to as the 'slaves' of the emperors and their relatives (cf. ad 367 on the use of *dominus* in addresses to rulers). Some allowance must be made for the literary context; we must not forget that historical circumstances are to a large extent mythologized in the play: later, Poppaea will be called *regina*, another taboo-word in Rome. Tragedy is the domain of fallen kings and queens: in *Octavia* the 'monarchic' vocabulary of the mythological plays is adapted to imperial Rome. Octavia, a historical princess in tragic trappings, may well sneer at a victorious rival with an insulting *famula*. Literary imitation also plays a part, since the antithesis *domina/famula* is a favourite one in Senecan tragedy, as shown by the parallels given ad 194. *famulus* in a derogatory sense is used in Sil. *Pun.* 13.886 of Hannibal's position at the Syrian court, also a hyperbolic deformation (*Assyrio famulus regi*).

107 sed sceleris The syntactical break after the thesis of the second foot has parallels throughout the Senecan corpus, e.g. after the first arsis in *Thy.* 31 *crescat. superbis*; after the first thesis in *H.O.* 907 *sibi, nam furoris.*

107 absit crimen a fatis meis In Tacitus' passage which narrates the end of Octavia (Tac. *Ann.* 14.63.4), the sentence *postremo crimen omni exitio grauius* refers to the charge of adultery brought against Octavia after the divorce. In the imperial household adultery was dealt with as equivalent to treason, and entailed the death penalty: see Introduction p. 5. Indeed, this must be the sense of *crimen* even in 107. Ladek (1909), 192, however, followed by Giancotti (1954), 86, Bruckner (1976), 192–3, n. 306, and Ballaira, ad loc., argued that there is in the play no other mention of this charge and interpreted *crimen* as an allusion to the 'murder' of Nero which Octavia later threatens to commit (cf. 174 *ne manu nostra cadat*), as if Octavia now turned to this thought for a moment, only to reject it in horror. Octavia, however, is no Christian martyr, and one fails to see why killing Nero should be such anathema to her (though admittedly her resolution to act is less strong than Megara's in *Hf.* 499 *dest una numero Danais: explebo nefas*). More importantly, the poet of *Octavia* often alludes to facts of no immediate dramatic relevance. The real story was not easily accommodated to the dramatic plot. This 'centrifugal' nature of *Oct.* is one of the strong indicators that its poet was drawing on historical sources (cf. Introduction 14–15).

The distinction between *scelus* and *crimen* is typically Ovidian: cf. Ov. *Fast.* 1.484 *est aliquid magnis crimen abesse malis*; *Met.* 3.141–2 *at bene si quaeras, Fortunae crimen in illo, | non scelus, inuenies. quod enim scelus error habebat?*; *Trist.* 1.2.98 *a culpa facinus scitis abesse mea*. But *crimen* and *scelus* are here synonymous, indicating the false accusation which Octavia fears she is going to incur.

a factis meis of Fuchs (1977), 74 is untenable, and rests on the misconception that *crimen* must refer to the murder of Nero. *a fatis meis* is a common metonymy: 'from my lot, from what the fates assigned to me as my share'; cf. *CE* 1122.10 *uiuat et a fatis sit procul usque meis.*

108 poena nam grauior nece est . . . *poena est* + infinitive occurs at *Agam.* 233 *non est poena sic nato mori*; *H.O.* 930, but in shorter sentences; Ov. *Trist.* 2.139–40 *nulla quidem sano grauior . . . poena est quam tanto displicuisse* *uiro*. The accumulation of infinitival clauses adds weight to the burden of evil suffered by Octavia, but the unbalanced construction of the sentence is without parallels in Senecan drama, and perhaps in Roman poetry in general: the period develops into an asymmetric conglomerate, made up of subsequent additions which seem to lack plan:

poena nam grauior nece est
(1) *uidere tumidos et truces miserae mihi uultus tyranni*,
(1) *iungere atque hosti oscula*
(1) *timere nutus* [*Neronis*]
(2) *cuius obsequium meus haud ferre posset . . . dolor (ob fratrem)*
(3) *cuius imperium tenet*
(3) *et sorte gaudet . . .*

A similar sequence of asyndetically linked infinitives occurs at 472. In Greek tragedy cf. Eur. *Hec.* 405–8, where the accumulation of infinitives describes the humiliating treatment in store for Hecuba (πεσεῖν πρὸς οὖδας, ἑλκῶσαί τε σὸν | γέροντα χρῶτα πρὸς βίαν ὠθουμένη, | ἀσχημονῆσαί τ' ἐκ νέου βραχίονος | σπασθεῖσα). Seneca rarely writes long sentences; when he does, *isokolia* and parallelism are his foremost concerns; longer Senecan periods aim at creating rhetorical tension (perhaps somewhat to the detriment of emotional impact): cf. *Troad.* 8–14 *ad cuius arma uenit et qui . . . . et qui . . . et quae . . . excisa ferro est*, which is representative of this style. The elaborate periphrases describing Troy's allies are also part of the effect to which such exceptional periods aspire. Norden, *Kommentar*, p. 386 quotes Verg. *Aen.* 10.362–8 as an exceptional case, but even there, where Vergil adopts a more involved style of sense-construction, *variatio* and interlacing create an elegant flow, and the crisis of the Arcadian contingent, as well as Pallas' brave and enterprising leadership, is beautifully portrayed: *at parte ex alia, qua saxa rotantia late | intulerat torrens arbustaque diruta ripis, | Arcadas insuetos acies inferre pedestris | ut uidit Pallas Latio dare terga sequaci, | aspera aquis natura loci dimittere quando | suasit equos, unum quod restat rebus egenis, | nunc prece nunc dictis uirtutem accendit amaris*. In Ov. *Met.* periods tend not to stretch over more than two lines, a technique developed in the composition of elegiacs, where the first hexameter creates a tension resolved by the second.

109–110 uidere tumidos et truces miserae mihi | uultus tyranni Cf. Liv. 2.10.8 *truces minaciter oculos*; Ov. *Met.* 7.111–12 (of the fire-breathing bulls) *uertere truces uenientis ad ora | terribiles uultus*; *Trist.* 5.7.17; Luc. *Bell. Ciu.* 7.291 *faciesque truces oculosque minaces*; Stat. *Theb.* 3.82 *trucis ora tyranni*. The dative *miserae mihi* seems to be dependent on *truces*, although my only parallel (Hor. *Epod.* 5.4) has *uultus in unum me truces*.

111–112 timere nutus cuius obsequium meus | haud ferre posset . . . dolor Whitman ad loc. interprets the genitive as objective; similarly Treggiari, *Roman Marriage*, 240, who illustrates the sense of *obsequium* as a characteristic virtue of married women (cf. *CIL* 5.6040 *cuius* (sc. *uxoris*) . . . *obsequio usus sum*; Apul. *Met.* 10.23.4 *desciuit ab obsequio mariti*); 85 *tu modo blando uince obsequio placata uirum* and 177 *uince obsequendo . . . uirum* may also seem in favour of this interpretation. However, *ferre* ('to bear') suggests *obsequium* to be Nero's, and Pedroli must be right to translate 'di cui non potrei tollerare neppure le carezze'. For *obsequium* with reference to acts of homage paid by a male lover to his mistress cf. Ov. *Met.* 3.292 *peritura . . . amantis obsequio Semele*; *Fast.* 6.485. Octavia, paradoxically, has to depend on her cruel husband's nod, whereas she would detest 'even his homage'. *obsequium* has to be imagined as pronounced with an emphatic delivery: *obsequium . . . haud* = *ne obsequium quidem*. Contrastive emphasis is more often secured for a noun by its initial position in the line: cf. Luc. *Bell. Ciu.* 5.493–4 *ad Caesaris arma iuuentus | naufragio uenisse uolet*; Sen. *Agam.* 496 *miserisque lucis tanta dulcedo est malae*: | *hoc lumen optant* ('even this light they wish'); Ov. *Her.* 15.85–6 *quid mirum si me primae lanuginis aetas | abstulit atque anni quos uir amare potest?*

Notice the sequence of successive relative clauses, usually avoided in poetry: (111–13) *timere nutus cuius obsequium . . . fata post fratris . . . cuius imperium tenet*, for which cf. the similar case *infra* 125, *cuius in munus suam . . . parentem . . . quam . . . ferro interemit*. Outside the Senecan corpus cf. Cic. *Aratea*, 422–3 (*colles*) *quos tenet . . . Chius*, | *Bacchica quam uiridi conuestit tegmine uitis*; id. *Tusc.* 2.24 (translating Aesch. *Prom.*) *luctifica clades nostro infixa est corpori* | *e quo liquatae solis ardore excidunt* | *guttae, quae saxa . . . instillant Caucasi*. Other cases, mainly from Lucretius, are cited in J. Vorlaufen, *Studien über Stellung und Gebrauch des lateinischen Relativsatzes* (Freiburg, 1974).

113–114 cuius imperium tenet|et sorte gaudet auctor infandae necis Literally: 'Whose reign his murderer holds and possesses Britannicus' legitimate share'. The confusion *morte/sorte* is extremely common and Lipsius' emendation yields a decidedly superior text, doing away with the repetitious *morte gaudet auctor . . . necis*. In support of the transmitted *morte*, Korzeniewski (*Gymnasium* 75 (1968), 296) adduced Lucr. *D.R.N.* 3.71 *caedem caede accumulantes, crudeles gaudent in tristi funere fratris*, not, in my judgement, a very cogent parallel. With Lipsius' *imperium tenet et sorte gaudet*, *imperium* and *sors* are semantically close, but this is a more acceptable pleonasm, theme and variation, a type common in Augustan literature. There may be an echo of Verg. *Aen.* 1.138–9 *non illi imperium . . . sed mihi sorte datum*. *sors* means 'possession' by the figure metonymy; the word also drives home the idea that the throne was Britannicus' by right of birth, and that Nero is an usurper, a point made again and again in the play (cf. ad 249). On *gaudeo* indicating the enjoyment of a possession cf. Verg. *Aen.* 4.157 *gaudet equo*, which Serv. Dan. glosses as *possidet equum*. Cf. also Hor. *Epod.* 14.15 *gaude sorte tua*; *Serm.* 2.6.110 *gaudet mutata sorte*.

115–116 quam saepe tristis umbra germani meis | offertur oculis Octavia's dream, which is presented as recurrent, forebodes the heroine's near death. An assassinated younger brother appeared to the title heroine in Pacuvius' *Iliona* (cf. esp. *Scaen.* 197–201 R^2), but no verbal echoes can be detected. The reading *offertur oculis* (= *obuiam uenit*), competing with *affertur* of some *recc.* (in Giardina's apparatus), seems more idiomatic in a description of images 'offering themselves' to a beholder's gaze: cf. Ov. *Fast.* 1.96 *Ianus* . . . *oculis obtulit ora meis*; Curt. *Hist. Alex.* 8.3.5 *si se oculis eius obtulisset.*

118 modo facibus atris armat infirmas manus Gronovius proposed to emend *modo* to *nunc*, but proceleusmatic first feet are not rare in Seneca, always with thesis and arsis divided across two words: cf. Schmidt (1860), 48, for more examples of second element resolution, e.g. *Thy.* 289 *nisi capere.*

For the content of Octavia's vision cf. Verg. *Aen.* 4.472 *armatam facibus matrem et serpentibus atris*; Sen. *Med.* 15 *atram cruentis manibus amplexae facem.*

119 oculosque et ora fratris infestus petit Britannicus attacks his guilty brother like a Fury seeking vengeance (cf. Ov. *Met.* 10.350–1 *quas facibus saeuis oculos atque ora petentes | noxia corda uident*, a passage certainly echoed here; *Her.* 14.10 *tendat in ora faces*; see also *infra*, 615 *flammisque uultus noxios coniunx petit*).

120 modo trepidus idem Notice the sudden transformation of Britannicus, from frightening apparition to terrified child. For this use of *idem* to link two successive phrases cf. Introduction, p. 37. *trepidus* will then be said of Nero in Poppaea's dream (732–3), apparently designating fear.

121 persequitur hostis The lack of a connective particle before *persequitur* emphasizes the contrast between the two verbs (*refugit* . . . *persequitur*) and is intended to represent the quick, convulsive pace of the scene.

121–122 atque inhaerenti mihi | uiolentus ensem per latus nostrum rapit Nero pursues a terrified Britannicus, who seeks shelter in the arms of his older sister. While Octavia tries to protect the boy, folding her arms around him, Nero transfixes Octavia (or both) with his sword. It is uncertain whether Britannicus or Octavia should be understood as the referent of *inhaerenti*, although the latter is probably preferable (so Ballaira and Helm (1934), 288 n.1). On either interpretation, Nero would be thrusting his sword violently through both bodies with a single blow. The sentence-initial position of *inhaerenti* is a retarding device aimed at enhancing the dramatic impact of the final *rapit*: cf. the somewhat similar effect produced by word arrangement in Ov. *Met.* 6.640–1 '*mater*' *clamantem et colla petentem | ense ferit Procne.*

The grim character of this impalement scene is appropriate to Senecan taste: Axelson (in Zwierlein, *KK* ad loc.) appositely quoted *Phoe.* 475–6 *affusa totum corpus amplexu tegam, | tuo cruori per meum fiet uia*; *Agam.* 199–200 *per tuum, si aliter nequit, | latus exigatur ensis et perimat duos.* Outside Senecan drama cf. Ov. *Met.* 6.244 *traiecit utrumque sagitta.*

Despite the plural *nostrum*, I prefer to interpret *per latus nostrum* as only referring to Octavia. *latus* is a common metonymy designating one's own body, especially when wounding and killing are involved: cf. Ov. *Her.* 10.88 *quid uetat et gladios per latus ire meum?* The part of the body which is being struck is best taken with the person at whom the blow is aimed.

The change from singular to plural – from *inhaerenti mihi* (*Octauiae*) to *per latus nostrum* – can be paralleled by 174 *exstinguat et me, ne manu nostra cadat*; 451 *fortuna nostra cuncta permittit mihi*; elsewhere cf. Ov. *Her.* 8.97–8 *obuia prodieram reduci tibi . . . nec facies nobis nota parentis erat*; Val. Fl. *Arg.* 7.520–1 *tanta utinam fiducia nostri | sit mihi.* For the construction (a dative of disadvantage indicating the victim of the blow, and an ablative, or other prepositional expression, for the part of the body where the blow is received) cf. Liv. 1.25.12 *male sustinenti arma gladium superne iugulo defigit.* Expressions of this kind belong to a common 'redundant' type (as in e.g. Verg. *Aen.* 12.537 *olli per galeam fixo stetit hasta cerebro*): cf. ad 267.

The unusual occurrence of *rapio* for 'to thrust' is not enough to warrant emendation. In Vergil and Ovid *rapio* stands for 'to seize eagerly', 'to grab', 'to lay hands quickly' on one's own sword, or 'to extract' one's weapon from the dead enemy's body (cf. Verg. *Aen.* 10.486 *ille rapit telum de uolnere*; 11.651 *nunc ualidam dextra rapit indefessa bipennem*), and *rapio* is not among the expressions used for 'wounding' or 'killing' in Latin epics (one expects *ensem exigere, condere*). In descriptions of single combat or other scenes of violence, I have only found the following parallels, mainly indicating wounds produced by amputation, and none close to *Oct.* 122: cf. Ov. *Met.* 6.616 *(membra) ferro rapiam*; Val. Fl. *Arg.* 4.291 *celeri rapit ora sinistra*; Stat. *Theb.* 7.644–5 *Caeneos . . . ferro . . . Haemon colla rapit*; Sil. *Pun.* 7.704 *ora rapit gladio.* In my view, however, the sense required in this passage ('thrust') may be explained from the metaphorical use of the verb to denote simply an action, usually violent, which is executed rapidly: cf. e.g. Luc. *Bell. Ciu.* 6.14 *rapiendas tendit ad arces* (= *ad celeriter occupandas*); Val. Fl. *Arg.* 3.341 *(uestes) quas rapuit telis.*

If emendation is thought to be necessary, possibilities for replacing *rapit* include *petit* (*inhaerentem . . . ense . . . petit*: cf. Liv. 40.9.5 *ne per meum latus tu petaris*; 23.9.8 *per meum pectus petendus ille tibi transfigendusque est*), *furit*, *ferit*, but some rewriting is always necessary (mainly replacing *inhaerenti* with *inhaerentem* or *in haerentem*: e.g. *inhaerentem mihi . . . ense . . . rapit*, as proposed by MDR, following Ageno).

inhaerere alicui means here 'to embrace'. Occasionally *inhaerere* refers to the younger person seeking refuge in the arms of the older one (e.g. an affectionate daughter in Plin. *Epist.* 5.16.2 *patris ceruicibus inhaerebat*). Of equals, however cf. Curt. *Hist. Alex.* 5.12.8 (*Dareus Artabazum*) *amplectitur perfususque mutuis lacrimis inhaerentem sibi auelli iubet. haerere alicui* also occurs in this sense, often with *in* or a bare ablative indicating the part of the body to which one clings: cf. e.g. Ov.

Met. 1.485 *inque patris blandis haerens ceruice lacertis*. With a dative cf. Val. Fl. *Arg.* 7.122–3 *subitoque parentibus haeret | blandior*.

123 tunc tremor et ingens excutit somnos pauor Verbal parallels include Ov. *Her.* 10.13 *excussere metus somnum*; Sen. *Troad.* 457 *mihi gelidus horror ac tremor somnum excutit*; Verg. *Aen.* 7.458 *somnum rumpit . . . pauor*; Liv. 39.12.5 *pauor tremorque*. For a dicolon expressing fear and the effects of fear cf. Ov. *Met.* 5.632 *occupat obsessos sudor mihi frigidus artus | caeruleaeque cadunt toto de corpore guttae*.

This displaced word arrangement with a common verbal predicate inserted between two co-ordinate subjects is discussed in *LHS* 2.693–4 (e.g. Enn. *Ann.* 163 V. *soli luna obstitit et nox*; Hor. *Carm.* 3.21.18 *uiresque et addis cornua*), where it is considered alongside cases in which a pleonastic pronoun, such as *ille, idem*, is inserted in the second colon: cf. ad 164–5.

The singular *excutit* with two subjects is normal. A verb in the singular is found even when, given several subjects, one of them is plural, the rule being that the last one determines the number of the verb. Cortius has a long note on Luc. *Bell. Ciu.* 1.200, with examples; 5.244–6 *seu maesto classica paulum | intermissa sono claususque et frigidus ensis | expulerat belli furias*.

124 renouatque luctus et metus miserae mihi Bothe proposed the emendation '*renouantque* (sc. *se*)', to avoid the repetitious, in his view, *pauor . . .* (123) *renouat luctus*. In fact, many such tautologies can be found in Latin poetry: this 'reflexive' figure was illustrated by Housman in his note on Luc. *Bell. Ciu.* 1.102 *nec patitur* (sc. *mare*) *conferre fretum*. In the present case, however, a distinction can perhaps be made between *pauor*, designating the sudden fear by which Octavia is seized after her dream, and *metus* as the 'frightening thoughts' she had managed to drive away during her sleep.

The clausula *miserae mihi* is repeated from 109–10, *truces miserae mihi|uultus tyranni*. The author of *Oct.* does not deploy the more affected type *miserae meos*, which is found in Senecan tragedy (cf. e.g. *Phae.* 119–20 *quis meas miserae deus|aut quis iuuare Daedalus flammas queat?*, with Mayer's note; see also *LHS* 2.61) and in Ovid (cf. Heinsius ad Ov. *Her.* 5.45 *nostros uidisti flentis ocellos*), imitating a Greek idiom; although it should be noted that, in *Phae.* 119, *miserae* is a genitive. *miserae mihi* is also frequent in Ovid: cf. *Her.* 3.59 *quod scelus ut pauidas miserae mihi contigit aures*; 3.82 *hic mihi uae miserae concutit ossa metus* (also thematically close); 5.123 *A! nimium miserae uates mihi uera fuisti*; *Met.* 5.626 *quid mihi tunc animi miserae fuit?*

125 adice This common transitional formula occurs also in Sen. *Med.* 277, 471, 527, 783; *Oed.* 811; *H.O.* 364, always with a short first syllable. The compounds of *iacio* (e.g. *adicio, obicio, inicio*) undergo different prosodic treatment according to whether semi-vocalic *i* was still felt as present (and occasionally preserved in writing: *ad-iicio*) or contracted with the following *i*<*a* (cf. Sommer, *Laut- und Formenlehre*, 486; L. Mueller, *DRM*² 290).

126 spoliis nitentem There are no exact parallels for this expression, which describes Poppaea in terms of a victorious epic warrior. This looks like a variation on a more common idiom (e.g. *onustus, superbus spoliis*). *niteo* is more often employed to describe physical brightness of objects, but can also be said of a person who shines for glory, beauty, or virtue (cf. *OLD* s.v., 3b, 3c, 5).

126–127 cuius in munus suam | Stygiae parentem natus imposuit rati The expression stands both metaphorically for 'consigned his mother to Death' and literally for the actual event of the attempted shipwreck: the sabotaged vessel is identified with the barge of Charon, ferrying the dead to Hades. The image of the ship of Hades is current both in Greek and Latin literature: see ad 311 *rate ferali*, where the chorus gives a detailed narrative of the incident.

The assertion that Poppaea was the decisive influence behind Nero's final resolution to murder his mother occurs so crudely only here and in Cass. Dio *Hist. Rom.* 61.12.1 ἡ Σαβίνα ἀνέπεισε τὸν Νέρωνα . . . αὐτὴν διολέσαι. Tac. *Ann.* 14.1 states it only indirectly (*sibi matrimonium . . . incolumi Agrippina haud sperans*): on the question of historical sources referring to Poppaea cf. G. B. Townend, *Hermes* 89 (1961), 245–6.

For *imposuit rati* cf. Sil. *Pun.* 6.371–2 *rati . . . impositus*; Ov. *Met.* 6.511 *imposita . . . carinae*; Hor. *Carm.* 2.3.28 *cumbae*; Luc. *Bell. Ciu.* 5.801.

128–129 quam, dira post naufragia, superato mari, | ferro interemit The logical subject of the ablative absolute is Agrippina, the object of the governing verb *interemit*. For instances of this 'asymmetrical' use of the abl. abs. see *infra* ad 352–3. For *superato mari* cf. Verg. *Aen.* 1.537 *superante salo*.

129 saeuior pelagi fretis For the metaphorical cruelty of the sea in comparisons cf. Bömer ad Ov. *Met.* 14.711 *saeuior illa freto* (of a woman not responding to love; Ov. *Met.* 11.701–2 *crudelior ipso | sit mihi pelago*; *Fast.* 3.580 *asperior quouis aequore*). The expression is re-contextualized in *Octavia* because the poet has just alluded to Agrippina's narrow escape from shipwreck.

131 imminet thalamis meis Quint. *Inst.* 9.3.1, describes the dative after *incumbo* and other compound verbs as a neologism for the prepositional construction *in, ad* + acc. This figurative use of *imminere* for *inhiare*, 'to hover over something' with an evil purpose in mind (also at 156, 422) is widespread in Augustan literature and in Silver Latin; cf. *TLL* vii.1, s.v. 450.52–70; 451.18–38; Ov. *Met.* 1.146 *imminet exitio uir coniugis*; Sen. *Phae.* 490 *regno imminens*; 855 *morti imminet*; *Thy.* 42–3 *immineat uiro | infesta coniunx*.

132 odio . . . nostri On the exchange between personal and possessive pronouns cf. Leo, *Obs.* 64; Axelson, *NSS* 69. Although this phenomenon is frequent in Senecan tragedy (cf. e.g. *H.O.* 954 *ueram tui|agnosce prolem*; 1242 *haec moles mei est*), this is not an innovation of Silver Latin: cf. e.g. Verg. *Aen.* 12.29 *amore tui*; Ov. *Her.* 3.142 *sustinet hoc animae spes tamen una tui*; 5.105 *amore tui*; *Met.* 3.464 *amore mei*. In *Oct.* cf. 542 *proderent odium mei*.

132–133 pretium stupri | iustae maritum coniugis captat caput This line appears in some of the most authoritative modern editions (Leo, Richter, Zwierlein) in the form advocated by Gronovius, who replaced the MS *captat* with his own conjectural *poscit*. This solution is too extreme. Gronovius' note ad loc. suggests that he misunderstood *maritum . . . captat caput* as a double accusative (on the analogy of verbs of requesting, such as *oro, rogo, posco*, a construction for which he could find no parallels with this verb. Gronovius supported *poscit* with Cic. *Ver.* 2.1.7.5 *iste inuentus est qui . . . parentes pretium pro sepultura liberum posceret*; Ov. *Her.* 5.143 *nec pretium stupri gemmas aurumue poposci*; indeed, this usage is well established: cf. *TLL* x.2, s.v. *posco*, 72.1–16, under the head 'poscunt mulieres ab amantibus': cf. Ov. *Met.* 9.411 *donec eum (Alcmaeonem) coniunx fatale poposcerit aurum*; Prop. *Carm.* 3.10(11).31–2 *coniugii obscaeni pretium Romana poposcit | moenia*), but the strength of the parallel is alone insufficient to justify the change (in defence of *captat* cf. already Heinsius, ad Ov. *Her.* 14.19; Carlsson (1926), 52–3). Older scholars who followed Gronovius were also prompted by a dislike for repetition and paronomasia: in Ovid, however cf. *Met.* 1.386 *pauido rogat ore pauetque*; 1.560; further examples of repetition in Ovid are given by E. J. Kenney, *CR* 22 (1972), 41.

maritum is here used as an adjective, though admittedly its combination with *caput* strikes one as rather odd ('the married head of a legitimate wife'). There are numerous parallels in support of the metonymic use of *caput* with reference to a human being, often when his life is under threat: cf. *TLL* iii. s.v. coll. 404–6; of relevance to *Oct.* 133 for the occurrence of a transferred epithet are: Prop. 4.1.52 *longaeuum ad Priami . . . caput*; Sen. *Oed.* 291 *proximum Phoebo caput*, perhaps on the analogy of Greek κάρα. Analogous is the use of *cognatus* with parts of the body: cf. Ov. *Met.* 9.412 *cognatumque latus Phegeius hauserit ensis*; Ov. *Fasti* 3.426 *cognatum . . . tuere caput*; *TLL* iii, s.v., 1480.44–73. On similar cases of enallage in Greek cf. Diggle, *Euripidea: Collected Essays* (Oxford, 1994), 416–20; Bers, *Enallage*, 69).

The adjectival use of *maritus* is attested already in early Latin and is a clear revival, or archaism, in poetry of the Augustan age, where it is usually found in connection with words associated with nuptials and marriage, such as *torus, fax, lectus, sacra, iura* (cf. the related idioms *torus uiduus, caelebs lectus*; cf. *TLL* viii. s.v. 404.16–30); a metonymical combination is found in Ov. *Her.* 16.285 *Venerem temerare maritam*; Sen. *H.O.* 1801 *marita Thebas regna et Ismenon petam*. Once the adjectival meaning of *maritus* is recognized, Gronovius' conjecture becomes much less cogent. *capto* aptly indicates Poppaea's overpowering desire to eliminate her more virtuous, detested rival (cf. Sen. *Dial.* 11.3.5 *hoc sine dubio, impotens fortuna, captasti*; Ov. *Her.* 17.262 *scimus quid captes*; Sen. *Thy.* 2 *ore captantem cibos*). While imitation of Ov. *Her.* 5.143 (cited *supra*) is likely, I also believe that the author of *Octavia* wanted to introduce some distinctive element in his version. Poppaea's hatred for Octavia is represented by a more forceful verb, which emphasizes Poppaea's insatiable greed. Quite apart from all other considerations, it is difficult to see how *poscit* could have been ousted by the relatively rare *captat. captat caput* gives a good example of *annominatio*, a device not unparalleled in *Octavia* and in Senecan tragedy: 260 *nupta demens nupsit* (of Messalina); cf. also Verg. *Aen.* 11.830 *et captum leto posuit caput*, for the same kind of alliterative, falsely etymological word-play; *Agam.* 175 *amore captae captus*; *H.O.* 335 *captiua capiet*; see also Ov. *Her.* 10.34 *uoce uoco.* On this figure of speech see Leo, *KS* 1.131, with early Latin examples (e.g. Enn. *Scaen.* 87 R^2 *uitam euitari*; 395 R^2 *festiuum festinant diem*).

This is also one of the few lines exhibiting the pattern *abAB* (see Introd. p. 39), comparatively rare in this play, often with a clausular function. On this pleonastic mode of expression, whereby the two pairs of adjective and noun are partly synonymous (*iustae maritum coniugis . . . caput*) cf. Sen. *Troad.* 877 *ad sancta lecti iura legitimi petit*; *Agam.* 111 *et sceptra casta uidua tutari fide*; *Phoe.* 626 *dubias Martis incerti uices*; Ov. *Met.* 1.312 *illos longa domant inopi ieiunia uictu*; Soph. *Ant.* 424–5 κενῆς εὐνῆς . . . ὀρφανὸν . . . λέχος, Eur. *I.A.* 164–5; cf. also Hillen, 28 (among others *Oct.* 225, 227); *LHS* 2.794–5.

134 Octavia's tirade (100–36) is rounded off climactically by an invocation to her dead father. The same rhetorical pattern occurs again at 222–51, where a prayer to Jupiter (245–52) marks a rise of indignation. In Senecan tragedy compare the similar conclusion in Amphitryon's speech in *Hf.* 276–8.

134 emergere umbris The transmitted reading *undis* (accepted by Santoro and Barbera) was first changed by N. Heinsius to *umbris*, which seems preferable. *undis* should have some qualification (as in *Stygiis undis*). Compare, in a similar context, *Oct.* 338 (Agrippina invoking the dead Claudius) *exsere uultus Acheronte tuos*; elsewhere cf. *Cons. Liu.* 410 *mergi Stygia nobile lumen aqua.* In addition, the dead do not dwell underneath the waters, except possibly Tantalus at *Hf.* 752 and the Hydra, *ibid.* 781; in *Agam.* 12–13 *nonne uel tristes lacus | incolere satius? lacus incolere* is used metonymically, indicating the whole expanse of Hell. There is some evidence for punishment being administered in the muddy or burning rivers of the Underworld; cf. Arist. *Ran.* 149; Plato, *Phd.* 114; Sen. *Thy.* 1015–19; Sil. *Pun.* 13.833–6 *Tullia . . . ardenti Phlegethonte natat*; Apul. *Met.* 6.17. See Ettig, *Leipziger Studien für classische Philologie* 13 (1891), 306, 381, 385; E. Rohde, *Psyche* (Leipzig, 1907[4]), 313 n.1. This harsher form of retribution seems reserved for worse sinners than Claudius, mostly murderers and parricides, and so is hardly where his daughter would place him.

The confusion between *umbrae* and *undae* occurs frequently, and *undis* here was a natural corruption after *emergere*; *Stygios sinus* in the following line is not enough to make *undis* acceptable. The use of a simple ablative of separation with both compound and simple verbs is mainly restricted to poetic usage: cf. *LHS* 2.103. *umbris* 134 is picked up by *inter umbras* 139. For *umbrae* with no specifications to indicate the Underworld cf. *OLD* s.v. 7b; Verg. *Aen.* 11.831 *uita . . . fugit indignata sub umbras*; Stat. *Silu.* 2.4.33–4 *at non inglorius umbris | mittitur*.

A more difficult question is raised by the presence of the deponent imperative *emergere*. A deponent alternative to *emergo* (*emergor*) is poorly attested in Latin. *Oct.* 706–7 *emersam freto . . . accepit Thetin* is not decisive in support of the imperative *emergere*. Isolated forms of perfect participles (with an active sense) of *emergo* occur elsewhere (cf. Mart. 12.32.6 *furias nocte Ditis emersas putaui*; Tac. *Ann.* 1.65 *Varum paludibus emersum cernere uisus est*; Cic. *Div.* 2.140; Liv. 1.13.5). The existence of perfect participles of active verbs is by no means a rarity (e.g. *iuratus, peragratus, desperatus*, all with active meaning): cf. N-W^2, 3.110 ff.; *LHS* 2.290. Of the three other occurrences of medio-passive *emergi* given in *TLL*, two fall under the heading of impersonal passives (Ter. *Ad.* 302 *tot res repente circumuallant se unde emergi non potest* (Don. ad loc. rests on a misconception: *noue. nam emergo dicitur, non emergor. sed ideo est usus quia sine compositione et mergo et mergor facit*); Paul.-Fest. p.31 Müll. *barathrum . . . unde non emergi potest*: cf. Löfstedt, *Vermischte Studien*, 137; *LHS* 2.418) and only the late *Cod. Iust.* 1.17.2.18 Krueg. appears to be medio-passive: *non desperamus quaedam postea emergi negotia, quae adhuc legum laqueis non sunt innodata*. In the Latin of the *Codex Iustinianus*, the present infinitive is commonly used in cases where classical Latin would have used a future infinitive (cf. Kalb, *Juristenlatein*, 43–4; here *non desperamus* = 'we are convinced'), and the temptation to emend 'postea <*posse*> emergi' should be resisted. However, although present passive infinitives are commonly used in the *Corpus Iuris* (e.g. *promittit seruum dari* for *se daturum esse seruum*), the passive ending of *emergi* remains difficult to account for, unless we assume the existence of a medio-passive voice as in *Oct.* 134. Gronovius' emendation *emerge ab umbris* is problematic because it entails a rare synaloephe with a monosyllable in thesi (see Zwierlein's tables, *Prolegomena*, 213). *emergo* is occasionally used as a reflexive, in prose and poetry,[3] but Lipsius' *emerge te undis* involves the unsatisfactory elision of a long monosyllable in the second arsis.[4] Schmidt (1865), 26 pleaded for Withof's *emerge tenebris* (*Praemetium*, 209, adducing Verg. *Georg.* 3.551 *in lucem Stygiis emissa tenebris*), which is ingenious and palaeographically convincing; that the paradosis has *undis* should not be counted as a decisive objection.

The verb itself (regardless of its voice, active or medio-passive) should not attract suspicion. *emergo* is normal of an *anastasis* (cf. Ov. *Met.* 14.155 *sedibus*

[3] Cf. Sall. *Hist.* 4.28 *ubi se laniata nauigia fundo emergunt*; Ter. *An.* 562. More examples for reflexive *emergo* are listed by Heinsius ad Ov. *Fast.* 3.367: in poetry cf. Man. *Astr.* 5.197–8 *cum iam uicesima Cancro | septimaque ex undis pars sese emergit in astra*; Avien. *descript. terr.* 126–7 *qua lux se rursus Eoa | emergit pelago*. Not used reflexively with human beings.

[4] Only two cases given by Zwierlein, *Prolegomena* 214: *Agam.* 142 *quocumque me ira*; *H.O.* 1385 *non ipse si in me*; only one case of a monosyllable in synaloephe in *Oct.*, 870 *ut ne inexpugnabilis*.

Euboicam Stygiis emergit in urbem) and is supported by the parallel passage in Sen. *Hf.* 279–80 *emerge coniunx atque dispulsas manu* | *abrumpe tenebras* (does this support Withof's conjecture?), where the original *A* reading was the unmetrical *emergere coniunx*.

In *Oct.* 134 I would still like to defend *emergere*. Oscillations from the active to the deponent voice and vice versa are frequent, the latter often as a form of 'hyperurbanismus' (*LHS* 2.292, Löfstedt, *Coniectanea* 1.50). Isolated occurrences of deponential forms for verbs otherwise only attested as active are found. It is perhaps significant that exchanges from one voice to the other are characteristic of early drama, where the process may have been motivated by metrical convenience: cf. Non. Marc. 292 M. on the series *exanclare/ exanclari*; *eliminare/ eliminari*; also Enn. *Scaen.* 101 R² (= 115 Joc. and note ad loc. for *contemplare/ contemplari*). Deponent imperative forms in the first position occur frequently in Seneca: cf. e.g. *Troad.* 964 *elabere anima* (with synaloephe in the first element of a resolved second arsis). *emergere* could be explained as an archaizing form. The existence of a deponent, archaic or archaizing *emergi* receives some support from the attestation of a reflexive *se emergere*, which may run in parallel with the medial voice, perhaps with different stylistic connotations. For instances of the interchangeability, even in classical Latin, of middle and active voice, see A. Ronconi, *Il verbo latino* (Firenze, 1959²), 23–9.

Similar prayers addressed to the dead Agamemnon are found in Aesch. *Cho.* 456 ff.; Soph. *El.* 453–4 αἰτοῦ δὲ προσπίτνουσα γῆθεν εὐμενῆ | ἡμῖν ἀρωγὸν αὐτὸν εἰς ἐχθροὺς μολεῖν.

134–135 tuae | natae inuocanti The relatively low frequency of hyperbaton in the play is a noteworthy feature of word-order (cf. ad 36, 65–6; 257; 771 *tibi . . . cui miranti*), even if the enjambement *tuae* | *natae* may partially account for its absence here. In Augustan poetry, the succession of three words in the same case must have come to be considered stylistically defective; poets make a constant effort to produce interwoven verbal patterns: cf., by contrast, the sequence of three datives (*nato* + poss. pron. + pres. part.) in Ov. *Met.* 4.383–4 *nato date munera uestro,* | *et pater et genetrix, amborum nomen habenti*). Hyperbata of possessives, usually with recognizable factors at work (contrastive emphasis, focus on a given sentence component), are already frequent in Plautus (cf. *LHS* 2.691, citing, among others, Plaut. *Bacch.* 599 *tuo ego istaec igitur dicam illi periculo*; as a counter-example cf. Plaut. *Capt.* 19 *huic gnato suo*, at line-end). A sequence of words in the same case is more frequently found with ablative absolutes: Ov. *Fast.* 5.571 *ille manus tendens hinc stanti milite iusto*. This addiction to, even obsession with, *traiectio* is commonly interpreted as a post-Hellenistic fashion, popularized by the *neoteroi* in Rome. Greek tragedy is less wary of such sequences: cf. e.g. Eur. *I.A.* 534, 536 τοιαῦτα τἀμὰ πήματα; *Hec.* 580–1.

137–138 frustra parentis inuocas manes tui, | miseranda, frustra Cf. *infra*, 271 *manes parentis neue sollicita tuae*; Soph. *El.* 137–9 (given ad 138). On this kind of epanaleptic *geminatio* with inserted words cf. Canter, 157–8, for a list of parallels, e.g. *Phoe.* 176–7 *haeret etiamnunc mihi | ille animus, haeret*; *H.O.* 13 *quid astra, genitor, quid negas?*; Wills, *Repetition*, 121.

138–139 nulla cui prolis suae | manet inter umbras cura Notice the *cumulus* of co-referential relative pronouns in different cases, in asyndetic sequence (*cui . . . qui*): a pathetic feature, often found in hymnology (cf. Norden, *Agnostos Theos*, 168–76, with Latin examples), but here expressing indignation; cf. Ov. *Met.* 2.848–9; 4.605–6; 5.27–8 *nunc sine qui petiit, per quem haec non orba senectus, | ferre.*

Asserting that the dead are oblivious to their loved ones that are still alive appears an impious remark, and it is surprising to find it in the mouth of the *Nutrix*. Soph. *El.* 137–9 ἀλλ' οὔτοι τόν γ' ἐξ 'Αΐδα | παγκοίνου λίμνας πατέρ' ἀν- | στάσεις οὔτε γόοις οὔτε λιταῖσιν may well have been imitated here, but Sophocles' passage illustrates a different topos: it is useless to cry, the dead cannot rise from underground to give help (cf. Eur. *Alc.* 986; fr. 332 N[2]). In Latin cf. Pease ad Verg. *Aen.* 4.34 *id cinerem aut Manes credis curare sepultos?*; Sen. *Troad.* 802–3 *si manes habent | curas priores*; Bömer's note ad Ov. *Met.* 8.488; *CE* 1849.7 *nec te sollicitat saeuissima cura minorum.* There is no orthodox opinion, however, concerning the attachment felt by the deceased for loved ones: cf. Prop. 4.11.74 *haec cura* (i.e. of Cornelia's children) *et cineri spirat inusta meo. cura manet* is used of the bond uniting the dead and the living also in *CE* 966.3 *tum tibi si qua mei fatorum cura manebit.*

Claudius will not – says the *Nutrix* – come to Octavia's help: did he not disinherit his true offspring in his lifetime? The words of the *Nutrix* betray some hostility towards Claudius, which is widespread in the ancient sources. The adoption of Nero, which cut off Britannicus' prospects, is now currently interpreted as a move to secure a peaceful succession by giving in to the pressures of the influential and threatening party of Germanicus, which retained vast influence in the army and the aristocracy (cf. A. Barrett, *Agrippina* (London, 1996), 96, 111–12). This is, however, a modern interpretation, more favourable to Claudius: in Flavian historiography, the notion that Claudius was a powerless puppet in the hands of Agrippina must have been widely regarded as true. Octavia herself makes a display of indignation toward Claudius in her final words (967 *dignum tali morte ac poena*). The ambivalent attitude towards the memory of Claudius (now a beloved father and *Diuus*, now the imbecile ruler) is one of those features of *Octavia* which can be identified as conflicting or contradictory. The combination of historiographical material and literary characterization (especially the portrayal of Octavia as a latter-day Electra pining away over her father) is a major factor accounting for the contradictory features of the play.

141 genitamque fratre This line has given *genita* a separate entry in *OLD*, for 'daughter', but its claim to independent lexical existence is very weak, and Gronovius' *fratre* is preferable to the transmitted *fratris*. The participial *genitus* is not on record as a noun (and therefore governing a genitive) earlier than Ven. Fort. *Carm.* 8.1.12 *Italiae genitum*, except as a variant reading in Ov. *Tr.* 5.5.55 *cum Peliae genitae tot sint, cur nobilis una est*, which most editors do not accept. The error is easily explained as a linguistic interference: *genitus* is commonly treated as a noun in medieval Latin, where it is accordingly followed by the genitive (cf. e.g. *DMLBS*, s.v. 1.f; 2.b). A genitive of origin would be acceptable in Greek with participial forms of γίγνομαι (cf. e.g. Eur. *Or.* 510 ὁ κείνου γενόμενος), but the usual Latin construction is *genitus aliquo parente* (cf. *TLL* s.v. *gigno* col. 1979): e.g. Sen. *Med.* 635. The ablative is also the construction recurrent elsewhere in *Oct.* (cf. 249 *Domitio genitus patre*; 560 *genitumque credit Venere Vulcano satum*) and is more generally the norm (cf. Plin. *Epist.* 8.18.2 *genitam fratre adoptauerat*; Curt. *Hist. Alex.* 6.2.7 *se filio eius genitam*). The genitive may also have originated from a perceived analogy with the use of *natus*, or by interference from the following *coniugem*, of which *fratris* was erroneously interpreted as a specification. Zwierlein's espousal of T. Baden's explanation in defence of *fratris*, namely to understand 'fratris *sanguine*' from 140 (cf. Ov. *Met.* 2.90 *ut nostro genitum te sanguine credas*), strains the Latin too much: the ellipse would be acceptable only within the same syntactical unit, as in Luc. *Bell. Ciu.* 5.17 *indole si dignum Latia, si sanguine prisco* (sc. *dignum*) | *robur inest animis*, where *dignum* governs both *indole . . . Latia* and *sanguine prisco*; other cases in Luc. *Bell. Ciu.* 9.233, with Housman's note; but in our passage *satum* and *genitam* are governed by separate verbs, *praeferre potuit* and *iunxit sibi*.

Heinsius' *gnatamque* (*Adv.* 501) is unpersuasive. After *prolis . . . nato . . . satum*, the poet was obviously desperate for a synonym, and *genitam* satisfies this requirement better than *gnatam*, which was probably not perceived as a different word from *natus*. The same striving for variation is recognizable in the genealogy of *Trag. inc.* 101–3 R^2 *Ioue propagatus est . . . Tantalus,* | *ex Tantalo ortus Pelops, ex Pelope autem satus* | *Atreus*; Ov. *Ibis*, 473–4 *ut sanguine natus eodem* | *quo genita est liquidis quae caret Arctos aquis*). In *Oct.* the archaic spelling *gnatus* is found only once (out of 25 occurrences of *natus/a*), and only in *β* at 45 *mox illa gnati* (*CSVKQ*), where the metrical context makes it questionable (see ad loc.).

satus is a more high-flown word, as in Verg. *Aen.* 6.125 *sate sanguine diuom*. The simple ablative with such expressions as *natus* etc. is of course normal (cf. Löfstedt, *Syntactica* 1.296–7).

141–142 genitam . . . fratre coniugem captus sibi | toris nefandis flebili iunxit face The past participle *captus* with no agent specified has given rise to suspicions. The implicit agent is obviously *amore*, or *illecebris*, but the combination of the cola is very asymmetrical: the passage makes the impression of a string of disjointed fragments rather than a coherent whole. Peiper conjectured *pactus*, which has the advantage of giving a more orderly appearance to the different cola. Liberman has recently revived

Peiper's proposal in modified form, *coniugem pactus sibi, toros nefandos f. iunxit f.* This yields very plausible Latin: *paciscor* for a marriage contract is entirely idiomatic, and there is a close verbal correspondence with Tac. *Ann.* 12.5.1 *pactum inter Claudium et Agrippinam matrimonium*. Liberman compared Man. *Astr.* 5.578–9 *pactusque maritam | ad litus remeat* (Perseus); Stat. *Theb.* 8.554–5 *pactus Agenoream primis Atys ibat ab annis | Ismenen. paciscor*, however, as the parallels adduced by Liberman make clear, stresses the transaction between the bride's parents and the prospective husband; this seems to be an unwanted detail in the passage, where there is no third party trading with Claudius, and it is preferable to stress, with *captus*, the helplessness of the emperor, a puppet in the hands of courtiers and lovers: compare *infra*, at 259–61, the somewhat similar description of Messalina's powerlessness to react against her love frenzy: cf. esp. *furore miserae . . . quae nupta demens nupsit incesta face. captus* conjures up effectively, though admittedly in a very elliptical manner, the diabolical guiles of Agrippina, shortly to be enumerated in more expanded form at 143–61. Liberman's correction also entails too extensive a rewriting of the passage: while the corruption of *pactus* into *captus* is easy to account for, it is not clear why the simple *toros . . . iunxit* should have caused any confusion. Richter (1862) 5 proposed *captus . . . dolis nefandis* (comparing *infra* 150–1 *captam domum | dolis nouercae*), but *doli* occurs also in the following line, 143, *hinc orta series facinorum, caedes, doli.*

On balance, I prefer to retain the text of the *paradosis*: 'Claudius, smitten with love, took his brother's daughter as his wife (*coniugem*), in an accursed marriage, over which shone inauspicious torches.' For the double accusative *genitam . . . coniugem . . . sibi . . . iunxit* cf. Stat. *Ach.* 1.898 *Peleus te nato socerum et Thetis hospita iungunt*; *SHA* 10.14.8 *maiori* (sc. *filio*) *Plautiani filiam uxorem iunxit.*

The passage well exemplifies the contortion of word-order so characteristic of *Octavia*, as well as the poet's plethoric exaggeration in the accumulation of detail. *coniugem . . . sibi . . . iunxit, toris nefandis*, and *flebili . . . face* are virtual equivalents to indicate marriage, by different degrees of metaphorical and metonymic substitution. *iungi facibus* (Ov. *Met.* 7.49 *te face sollemni iunget sibi*; *H.O.* 404 *facibus suis me iungat Eurystheus licet*) and *iungi thalamis* alone would have been sufficient to express the idea of marriage: for more examples of *iungi* followed by an instrumental ablative cf. *TLL* vii.2, s.v. *iungo*, 657–8, *passim*. A combination of both metonymic expressions can be found in *Hf.* 346–7 *iuncta regali face | thalamisque Megara*. In *Oct.* 142 perhaps a difference of grammatical function can be perceived between the the two ablatives: while *toris nefandis* is an instrumental dependent on *iunxit*, *flebili face* could be explained as an 'ablative of attendant circumstances'.

The use of *capio*, especially its passive and participial forms, has some currency in Latin with the figurative meaning of 'conquered by love', even with no specifications: cf. Prop. *Carm.* 3.19.4 *nescitis captae mentis habere modum*; 4.4.88 *capta dabit uestris moribus illa manus*; Ov. *Met.* 4.62 *captis ardebant mentibus ambo*;

Stat. *Ach.* 1.636–8 *dilectae virginis ignem|aequaeuamque facem captus . . . dissimulas.* This idiom is recurrent in *Octavia*: cf. 217 *mortali captus forma*; 694 *quem tuus cepit decor.* For other cases of passive participles set in a vacuum (i.e. with no agent expressed) cf. Ov. *Her.* 10.98 *externos didici laesa timere uiros*; Kroll, *Glotta* 22 (1934), 19.

On the restrictions concerning marriage between relatives in Rome cf. Rossbach, *Untersuchungen über die römische Ehe* (Leipzig, 1853), 442. The union of near relatives was generally regarded as incestuous by the Romans, and restricted to foreign custom (cf. Luc. *Bell. Ciu.* 8.404–5 *iacuere sorores|in regum thalamis*; Tac. *Ann.* 2.3.2 *liberis eius . . . sociatis more externo in matrimonium regnumque*). Such unions are also deplored in Eur. *Andr.* 175; Aesch. *Eum.* 189–90. The description of Claudius' marriage to Agrippina is very close to the account of Agrippina's seduction of Claudius in the historical sources (cf. Tac. *Ann.* 12.3.1 *illecebris pellectus*; Suet. *Claud.* 26 *inlecebris Agrippinae . . . pellectus in amorem*).

The passage illustrates the motif, tragic in origin, of the 'accursed marriage', common in Latin poetry: a good review of this topos can be found in E. Skard, *Sallust und seine Vorgänger* (Oslo, 1956), 59–60; cf. also *infra*, 595 *thalamis scelestis*; Sall. *Cat.* 15.2 *scelestis nuptiis*; Luc. *Bell. Ciu.* 1.112 *diro feralis omine taedas*; Stat. *Theb.* 1.244–5 *superis adiuncta sinistris | conubia.*

144 sanguinis diri sitis *diri* has been variously corrected, and Buecheler's *clari* is the most persuasive proposal, in the light of 88 *odit genitos sanguine claro.* But the enallage is attractive: cf. Stat. *Theb.* 6.350 *diroque imbuti sanguine currus*, where the blood in which the chariots are soaked is that of the defeated contestants in the Pisan races; Luc. *Bell. Ciu.* 1.444 (the victims of human sacrifices). *dira noui facies leti* (Sen. *Oed.* 180) is as possible as *diri . . . leti facies* (Luc. *Bell. Ciu.* 3.652–3). In addition, *dirus* is a common epithet for *sanguis* or *cruor*: cf. *TLL* v, s.v. *dirus*, 1272.50–55.

Thirst for human blood is a feature of Hannibal in Sil. *Pun.* 1.59–60 *penitusque medullis | sanguinis humani flagrat sitis*; Sen. *Phae.* 542–3 *imperii sitis | cruenta.*

145–146 mactata soceri concidit thalamis gener | uictima, tuis ne fieret hymenaeis potens The appositional phrase is intertwined with the noun it refers to (*mactata . . . gener uictima*): the contrast in gender between nouns and apposition is also customary: cf. *infra* 665. For the antithesis *gener | socer* cf. Verg. *Aen.* 7.317 *hac gener atque socer coeant mercede suorum*; Luc. *Bell. Ciu.* 4.802 *et gener et socer bellum concurrere iussi*; cf. also Liv. 1.49.1 *socerum gener sepultura prohibuit*: more in Prato's note ad [Sen.] *Epigr.* 69.11.

Notice the two consecutive metonymies for 'marriage', *thalami* and *hymenaei.* Silanus was only Octavia's betrothed at the time of his suicide, but the prolepsis *gener* is poetical (cf. Verg. *Aen.* 2.344); compare the similar use of *mater* 'de socru futura' in Verg. *Aen.* 12.74.

147 pro facinus ingens The adverbial *pro*, high-flown and common since early Latin, occurs in *Oct.* before an exclamatory phrase, either a vocative

(245 *pro summe genitor*) or a common noun, rather than as an isolated particle (*pro!*) introducing an entire sentence. In the Senecan corpus *pro* before a common noun is found only in *Agam.* 35 *pro nefas* (and then in *H.O.* 219, 770, 965, 1231, 1419, 1803); but *pro facinus* occurs in Senecan prose (cf. *TLL* x.2, 1439.58–72). Outside the corpus cf. Luc. *Bell. Ciu.* 5.57 *pro tristia fata.*

148–149 cruore foedauit suo | patrios penates In the Roman attitude towards suicide (cf. *OCD*[3], s.v., 1452–3), there is nothing which justifies the strong language of this line, in which Silanus' death is presented as a sacrilegious deed, but *cruore foedauit . . . penates* must be reminiscent of Verg. *Aen.* 2.501–2 *Priamum . . . per aras | sanguine foedantem quos ipse sacrauerat ignis*, suggesting perhaps that the impiety reflects on Agrippina and Claudius, who drove Silanus to take his life; cf. also Liv. 3.18.10 *multi exulum caede sua foedauere templum*; Sall. *Hist.* frg. 1.47; Ov. *Met.* 9.182–3 *foedantem peregrino templa cruore | Busirin*; Sen. *Thy.* 61 *patrios polluat sanguis focos.* Tacitus' narrative of the incident on the very day of Agrippina's marriage with Claudius (Tac. *Ann.* 12.8) hints that Silanus' suicide cast its curse upon that event. The phrase is repeated a few lines later, with only slight variations: 162–3 *polluit Stygia face* (sc. *Erinys*) | *sacros penates.* Both passages may ultimately have been inspired by Cat. *Carm.* 64.404 *impia* (sc. *mater*) *non ueritast diuos scelerare penates.* Unlike Pedroli, I see no allusion here to the fact that Silanus was a descendant of Augustus and therefore a relative of Agrippina.

149 criminis ficti reus Silanus was accused of having an incestuous relationship with his sister Iunia Calvina (cf. Tac. *Ann.* 12.3–4; 8; Sen. *Apocol.* 8.2). Lipsius' emendation of the transmitted *facti* seems certain. The idiom recurs in Ov. *Met.* 7.824 *criminis extemplo ficti temerarius index*, where the same mistake occurs in many witnesses; *Fast.* 4.308 *falsi criminis acta rea est. factus*, found in some *recc.* and advocated by Barbera, is clearly inferior (in spite of the recurrence of the idiom *reum facere* cf. *OLD* 3a 'to bring to trial', often with the genitive of the charge) because of 151 *factus gener*, and because the genesis of the corruption would be more obscure.

150 intrauit hostis . . . captam domum A similar expression is repeated *infra*, 161–2 *uacuamque Erinys saeua funesto gradu . . . intrauit aulam*, describing in mythological terms the havoc wrought by Agrippina in the family of Claudius and among the supporters of the deceased emperor. The phrase *intrare domum* is common as a poetic idiom: cf. Prop. 3.12.33 (*Ulixem*) *domos animarum intrasse silentum*; Ov. *Met.* 9.11 *ut soceri domus est intrata petiti* (compare, by way of contrast, Sen. *Contr.* 2.1.6 with the prepositional *ego in domum uestram intrabo*). More specifically, however, *intro* with the accusative of the house in which a given deity has taken its dwelling, importing either good fortune or ruin, is not attested in Augustan poetry, but has parallels in Seneca (cf. *H.O.* 609–11 *tenet auratum limen Erinys . . . intrant fraudes cautique doli*; *Thy.* 251; *Agam.* 285; *Dial.* 12.16.5). In Flavian poetry cf. Sil. *Pun.* 9.288–9 *discordia demens | intrauit caelo*; Mart. *Epigr.*

6.7.2 *atque intrare domos iussa pudicitia est*, Stat. *Silu.* 3.3.85–6 *iamque . . . domum . . . toto intrauit Fortuna gradu*; 4.8.22–3 *piumque* (sc. *Lucina*) | *intrauit repetita larem*; 5.1.145–6 *piumque* | *intrauit uis saeua larem.* In Greek literature, a daemon has moved into the House of the Tantalids in Aesch. *Agam.* 1468–9 δαῖμον, ὃς ἐμπίτνεις δώμασι καὶ διφυί- | οισι Ταντaλίδαισιν (in an invocation to the god who has exacted vengeance on the house of Tantalus); Eur. *Phoe.* 1065–6 ἐπέσυτο τάνδε γαῖαν . . . δαιμόνων τις ἄτα; *Med.* 1259–60 ἔξελ' οἴκων . . . Ερινύν. It is only in Latin poetry that the Furies figure as deities who inspire murder, rather than as the avengers of Greek tragedy. As the examples given above indicate, the non-prepositional construction of *intro* with the accusative may have been felt as a Grecism (cf. R. Mayer, in *ALLP*, 163).

150 ei mihi *mihi* is scanned as an iambic word; cf. Tarrant ad *Agam.*, p. 367. *ei mihi* is common in Augustan poetry (cf. Leo, *Obs.* 68), but found in the Senecan corpus only in *H.O.* 1024, 1172, 1181, 1205, 1402, 1784.

150–151 captam domum | dolis nouercae Cf. Tac. *Ann.* 12.65 *at nouercae insidiis domum omnem conuelli*, with reference to Agrippina.

151–152 principis factus gener | idemque natus Cf. *Phoe.* 510 *hostium es factus gener* in the same metrical position. Cf. also *infra*, 212 *cuius gener est qui fuit hostis*; Ov. *Fast.* 4.46 *et tuus est idem* (i.e. *Epytus*), *Calpete, factus auus.*

152 iuuenis infandi ingeni The unmetrical reading of *A*, *nefandi*, was corrected by *recc.* to *infandi*. The two adjectives are interchangeable in sense (cf. 92 *infanda parens*; 227 *nefandi principis*): cf. Trevet, ad 142, *thoris infandis id est nephandis* (10.13 J). Leonhardt, *DS* 144, has a convenient collection of passages of ancient and medieval grammarians outlining the structure of the iambic trimeter, a verse imperfectly known in several respects until modern times. Its basic structural principle, namely the alternation of iambic and spondaic feet, could be gauged at least from Hor. *Ars* 256–8 *spondeos stabilis in iura paterna recepit* (sc. *iambus*) | *commodus et patiens, non ut de sede secunda* | *cederet aut quarta socialiter*, but Trevet often confuses even this basic principle, through either metrical or prosodical incompetence. A list of false interpretations of Trevet due to faulty metrical knowledge can be found in Junge (1999), 161. On Petrarch's and other humanists' attempts to reproduce the Latin dramatic metres cf. S. Mariotti, *Scritti medievali e umanistici* (Rome, 1994), 149–55.

153 scelerum capaxque Zwierlein prints Ascensius' *capaxque scelerum* (in the *errata*: Ascensius' text actually read *capax scelerumque*), in place of the unmetrical *scelerumque capax* of the paradosis: mistakes due to a faulty prosodical interpretation of the initial syllable (*ca-*) are commonplace: see ad 379 *grauis*. Even Ascensius' solution, however, is not entirely beyond objection. The metrical treatment of short open syllables preceding word-initial *sp-*, *sc-* etc. is not uniform in Latin poetry. The sequence of final open syllable and word-initial impure *s-* is rare, but both *productio* and *correptio* are possible. The short scansion must have been more current: it predominates in early Latin drama and satire. The single instance of short scansion in Vergil coincides with a strong pause (*Aen.* 11.308 *ponite. spes sibi quisque*); other cases, such as Ov. *Met.* 12.438, are textually dubious. Seneca has 22 instances of a short open syllable followed by impure *s*-, 20 of them in metrically indifferent elements (third thesis, e.g. *Troad.* 605 *expleta fata stirpe sublata Hectoris*). Lengthening occurs in *Hf.* 950 and in *Phae.* 1026 (cf. Leo, *Obs.* 203, n. 4). Cf. H. M. Hoenigswald, *TAPA* 80 (1949), 271–80; id., in *Studia Winter* (Berlin-New York-Amsterdam, 1985), 377–83, esp. 381 n. 9. Of the examples of *correptio* listed in Hoenigswald (1949), 278–9 only the following have *-que*: Hor. *Sat.* 1.2.71 *uelatumque stola, mea cum conferbuit ira*, and Prop. 5.17 *consuluitque striges nostro de sanguine, et in me*. It is hard to reach a certain conclusion, but L. Mueller's *scelerum capaxque* (*DRM* 387) should perhaps be considered as a better option: it does away with the metrical problem, and there are two other examples of postponed *–que* in *Octauia*: cf. ad 361, 363. For the phrase *capax scelerum* cf. Sen. *Phoe.* 159; *H.O.* 1419.

155 tantoque uictrix facta successu ferox Cf. Verg. *Aen.* 5.210 *successu . . . acrior ipso*; Ov. *Met.* 8.385; 8.494–5 *ipso | successu tumidus*; Tac. *Hist.* 4.28 *successu rerum ferocior*; *Ann.* 4.12 *ferox scelerum et quia prima prouenerant* (of Seianus, encouraged to plot further machinations by an initial success).

Zwierlein, following Leo, Peiper-Richter, Giardina, places a full stop at 154 and marks a new paragraph at 155. Cases of non-correlative *-que* at the beginning of a new sentence are sometimes found: cf. *LHS* 2.473 (e.g. Liv. 2.33.9 *Corioli oppidum captum; tantumque sua laude obstitit famae consulis Marcius . . .* where *-que* marks the transition to a new sentence; other examples are quoted by Weissenborn-Müller; Sall. *Iug.* 104.4); in poetry see Ov. *Trist.* 2.40–1 *utere more dei nomen habentis idem. | idque facis. –ue* is somewhat similarly used in poetry: cf. Lease, *AJPh* 34 (1910), 270; Ov. *Met.* 1.151; *Pont.* 2.9.73. On the other hand, *tantoque* seems to come as a conclusion capping the preceding dicolon, and I prefer to link *tantoque* . . . to the preceding relative clause. This makes the syntactical connections somewhat less tight, but anacoluthon involving a sequence of co-ordinated clauses loosely dependent on an initial relative pronoun is very common: cf. Norden, ad *Aen.* 6.284; Vahlen, *Opuscula* (Leipzig, 1907), 1.166; e.g. *Aen.* 9.593–4 *cui Remulo cognomen erat, Turnique minorem | germanam nuper thalamo sociatus habebat*; 12.943–4. In *Oct.* cf. *infra* 250–1; 280–1.

156 ausa imminere est orbis imperio sacri Gronovius, whose proposal was revived by Liberman, considered writing *imperio sacro*, which would enhance the gravity of Agrippina's daring, but *sacri* can certainly stand. Imperial Stoicism justifies monarchy as a manifestation of the order governing the universe (see *infra*, ad 489 *electus orbem spiritu sacro regis*), but sacrality suits *orbis* equally well. For *sacer* with reference to nature cf. 415 *sacro sinu* (sc. *terrae*); Ov. *Met.* 1.254 *sacer . . . aether*; Luc. *Bell. Ciu.* 4.191 *sacer orbis amor*. There is no doubt, however, that the *orbis* is holy also because it is next to the word designating the imperial dignity. From the reign of Augustus onwards, *sacer* is normally associated with the imperial house: cf. Ov. *Fast.* 6.810 *o sacra femina digna domo*: Vollmer ad Stat. *Silv.* 1. *praef.* 14; Coleman ad Stat. *Silv.* 4. *praef.* 6; Stat. *Silv.* 5.1.207–8 *mirandaque sacris | imperiis*; V. Ehrenberg – A. H. M. Jones, *Documents illustrating the reigns of Augustus and Tiberius* (Oxford, 1955[2]) 98; 137.

157 quis tot referre facinorum formas potest Cf. Verg. *Aen.* 6.626 *omnis scelerum comprendere formas* (Hosius). Add, for *quis tot*, Verg. *Aen.* 12. 500–3 *quis mihi nunc tot acerba deus, quis carmine caedes | ... expediat.* The hyperbole seems strained here: in fact the problem is not that Agrippina's crimes are too many, but that they are unspeakable. The δ-family has *qui*, but *quis/ qui* are equivalent only as adjectives: cf. Löfstedt, *Syntactica*, 2.84.

159 per gradus scelerum omnium Cf. Oros. *Hist.* 7.10.1 *per omnes scelerum gradus creuit.* A related expression occurs at 501 *altos ... per honorum gradus* (see ad loc.).

164 fasque omne rupit Cf. Sen. *Thy.* 179 *fasque omne ruptum* in the same position within the line.

164–166 miscuit coniunx uiro | uenena saeua, cecidit atque eadem sui | mox scelere nati Claudius allegedly succumbed to a dish of poisonous mushrooms, after a previous attempt to murder him with a potion failed (*miscuit ... uenena* seems to allude to a drink): cf. Tac. *Ann.* 12.6.6; Suet. *Claud.* 44; Cass. Dio *Hist. Rom.* 65.34.

For this use of the pronominal *idem* as a connective, often with an adversative function, cf. *TLL* vii.1, s.v. *idem*, col. 192, 73–84; 193, 1–42; *TLL* ii, s.v. *atque*, 1052.39–47: see also ad 45–7. *idem*, alongside *ipse, is, ille*, is used occasionally to link two co-ordinated clauses, or to ensure cohesion between successive cola, with no clearly recognizable asseverative or oppositive function: cf. Ov. *Met.* 2.381–2 *squalidus interea genitor Phaethontis et expers | ipse sui decoris*; 1.610–11 *coniugis aduentum praesenserat inque nitentem | Inachidos uultus mutauerat ille iuuencam.*

The whole section from 145 onwards (*mactata soceri concidit thalami gener | uictima*) is indebted to Ovid's representation of the Age of Iron (esp. Ov. *Met.* 1.144–7, *non hospes ab hospite tutus, | non socer a genero, fratrum quoque gratia rara est. | imminet exitio uir coniugis, illa mariti; | lurida terribiles miscent aconita nouercae*, a passage also quoted in Sen. *Ben.* 5.16.3; *Ira* 2.9.2. Cf. also Sen. *Phae.* 553–58.

The use of *mox* as a conclusive temporal particle with past tenses (= *tandem, denique*) is normal: cf. Ov. *Met.* 4.612–4 *mox tamen Acrisium. . .tam uiolasse deum quam non agnosse nepotem | paenitet*: for *eadem ... mox* cf. Ov. *Met.* 14.72 *mox eadem* (sc. *Scylla*) *Teucros fuerat mersura carinas*; also Bömer ad *Met.* 1.562. On *mox* cf. H. J. Rose, *CQ* 21 (1929), 57–66; E. J. Kenney, *CQ* 9 (1959), 253. In the Senecan corpus there is only one occurrence of this adverb, in *Hf.* 458.

166 tu quoque extinctus iaces cf. Verg. *Aen.* 10.324–7 *tu quoque ... miserande iaceres*; 6.882; 11.42; Luc. *Bell. Ciu.* 6.132 *iacuere perempti.*

168 modo sidus orbis, columen Augustae domus For the invocation to an individual addressed as the 'pillar of the house' cf. Hor. *Carm.*

2.17.3–4 (with Fraenkel, *Horace*, 217, n. 2); Liv. 1.39.3 *<co>lumen . . . praesidiumque regiae adflictae* (with Ogilvie's note); 6.37.10; Sen. *Hf.* 1251; *Troad.* 124.

For *sidus* in reference to a person cf. Ov. *Pont.* 3.3.2 *o sidus Fabiae, Maxime, gentis*; in Greek cf. Soph. *El.* 66; Eur. *I.T.* 57. Both terms occur in Curt. *Hist. Alex.* 9.6.8 *hoc Macedoniae columen ac sidus*.

Domus Augusta is regularly attested from the earliest days of the Empire in reference to the imperial family (cf. *TLL* ii, s.v. *Augustus*, 1391.5–60: Ov. *Pont.* 2.2.73–4 *natosque nepotum | ceteraque Augustae membra . . . domus*), later to be replaced by *domus diuina* in inscriptions: cf. R. Cagnat, *Cours d'épigraphie latine*, (Paris, 1914[4]), 167.

169–170 nunc leuis tantum cinis | et tristis umbra For the frequent dittology *cinis . . . umbra* cf. Hor. *Carm.* 4.7.16 *puluis et umbra sumus*; Ov. *Met.* 8.496 *uos cinis exiguus gelidaeque . . . umbrae*, with Bömer's note; *CE* 395.3 *exiguus cinis et simulacrum corporis umbra*. It is found also in Soph. *El.* 1159.

170–172 saeua cui lacrimas dedit | etiam nouerca, cum rogis artus tuos | dedit cremandos There is nothing here to suggest the first-hand evidence of an eye-witness, as is often maintained (so Ladek (1891), 101; Junge (1999), 198; Barbera, ad loc.; cf. Introd. p. 30). Extant sources relating the burial of Britannicus (Tac. *Ann.* 13.17; Cass. Dio *Hist. Rom.* 61.7.4; Suet. *Nero* 33.3; Jos. *Ant.* 20.153; *Bell. Iud.* 2.250) contain no comparable details of the faces and emotions of the participants at the funeral service; in fact, Tacitus, Suetonius and Cassius Dio agree in relating that a violent downpour of rain helped to make the ceremony as inconspicuous as possible. The tears shed by the normally callous Agrippina on the occasion could be a rhetorical fabrication, a vivid detail designed to enhance pathos. In Statius' funerary poetry for prematurely deceased *delicati*, a recurrent motif of praise is the hyperbolic 'even a cruel step-mother would have relented in her hatred at the sight of such beauty': cf. Stat. *Silu.* 2.1.48–9 *cui . . . saeuae uellent seruire nouercae*; 5.2.80. On *saeua nouerca* cf. Junge (1999), 231, with parallels; on the topos in ancient Roman literature cf. P. A. Watson, *Ancient Stepmothers* (Leiden, 1995), 92–134. In Tacitus' narrative, Agrippina's perturbation at Nero's elimination of Britannicus has a deeper significance: the Augusta's fears were fuelled by a sense that her own doom was approaching (*Ann.* 13.16 *at Agrippinae is pauor, ea consternatio mentis . . . quippe sibi supremum auxilium ereptum et parricidii exemplum intellegebat*). On *lacrimas dedit* cf. Ov. *Fast.* 5.472 *lacrimas in mea fata dedit*.

Buecheler's *dedi* for the *dedit* of the MSS at 172, spoken by the *Nutrix*, does not seem an improvement. There is nothing strictly speaking unbelievable in this picture of a maternal Agrippina discharging the role of a commiserating relative at the burial of her stepson, and the description of the empress mother personally placing the corpse on the funeral pyre does not need to be taken literally. It is true that in Roman funerary custom a close relative would place the child on the death-bed, and this operation could be carried out by a woman;

Britannicus, however, was a fourteen-year-old youth at the time of his death, and presumably the assistance of some attendants would have been necessary. Some allowance must also be made for literary convention: the prematurely deceased are laid to rest, metaphorically at least, by their close relatives: cf. Verg. *Aen.* 6.308 *impositique rogis iuuenes ante ora parentum*; Ov. *Her.* 15.115–16 *non aliter quam si nati pia mater adempti | portet ad exstructos corpus inane rogos.*

172–173 membraque et uultus deo | similes uolanti The features of children are often likened to Cupid's, especially in funerary inscriptions: cf. Verg. *Aen.* 1.709–10 *mirantur Iulum | flagrantisque* (acc.) *dei uultus*; *CE* 1994.1 *hic* (sc. *puer*) *fuerat similis roseo Cupidine* (sic) [*uultu*; 1061.7 (*puella*) *quae speciem uultus habuitque Cupidinis artus*; 1590.3–4 *Cupidinis os habitumque gerens*; Kaibel, *EG* 153; Suet. *Cal.* 7 *cuius effigiem habitu Cupidinis . . . Liuia dedicauit.* Other parallels and references in S. Eitrem *SO* 11 (1932), 30 n. 1.

Amor, and *Eros* in Greek, are normally designated with antonomastic periphrases such as 'the flying god': for Greek examples of ὁ πτανός, πτερωτός, πτερόεις without a proper name cf. Roscher, *Lexicon*, vii. *Supplem. Epitheta deorum* (Bruchmann) 115; (Canter) 10 (*uolitans, uolucer, ales, aliger, pinniger*, always with *puer, Amor, Cupido*).

The features of the dead are annihilated by the flames in Stat. *Silu.* 3.3.12 *ora rapi flammis*; with *aufero cf.* Ov. *Met.* 9.262–3 *quodcumque fuit populabile flammae | Mulciber abstulerat*; 15.156–7 *corpora siue rogus flamma . . . abstulerit*; Luc. *Bell. Ciu.* 9.784 *quis rogus abstulit ossa?*; close in sense also *H.O.* 915 *immensa pestis coniugis membra abstulit* (other parallels from epigraphic evidence in *TLL* ii, s.v., 1337).

173 flamma feruens abstulit The simple transposition in *recc.* seems to me the best available emendation of the metrically impossible *feruens flamma abstulit* of *A*. Leo, *Obs.* 44 drew attention to *Laur.* 37.11, with Poggio's marginalia, where the correction first occurs. Among the printed editions, *fl. f. a.* is first found in Avantius. Baehrens' *saeuiens* (*Misc.* 117) has been adopted by Zwierlein, to avoid the unelided cretic at line-end. In Senecan tragedy, a final word of cretic quantity almost always begins with a consonant (the type *nato sospite* occurs in *Hf.* 641 *regina, uultum, tuque nato sospite*; 998 *nostris concidant*; *Med.* 562; 684); final vowel-initial cretics normally coalesce with the last syllable of the preceding word; vowel-initial final words of cretic quantity not in synaloephe with the preceding (non-monosyllabic) word occur in the authentic plays only ten times, e.g. *Hf.* 397 *agedum efferatas rabida uoces amoue*, twice in *H.O.* (cf. Strzelecki (1938), 19). In *Octavia*, 49 out of 50 final cretics are vowel-initial, and all except three (237, 393, 468) coalesce with the preceding word. It seems, however, too inflexible to emend on the basis of the varying approach to final cretics in the play and overall in post-classical versification; cf. Introd. p. 41, and nn. 96–7. It is true that failure to understand the comparatively more recherché *saeuiens* might neatly account for the process of corruption, but transpositions producing non-metrical sequences are also among the commonest forms of error in all MS traditions (in *Oct.* cf. e.g. 112 *fata post fratris*] *fratris post fata GC*; 153 *scelerum capaxque*] *scelerumque capax A*; 193 *prima quae toros*] *toros quae prima C*; 246 *totiens temere regali*] *temere regali totiens P*). There are also no close parallels for *saeuio* in participial form in combination with *flamma* (while *saeuus* is commonly so used): cf. however Sen. *Ben.* 6.32.3 *saeuitum est in opera publica ignibus*.

After this line, *βP* mark a lacuna of thirty lines (26 in *P*), whereas no lacuna is marked in *GT*. The sense is impeccable, and one finds it difficult to imagine how to add thirty lines to the long-winded dialogue of this scene, the longest in the play. I adhere to the explanation given by Leo, *Obs.* 45–6; MacGregor (1978), 105. Since the lacuna is found in MSS belonging to both branches of *A*, the error must have occurred before the tradition split. Leo advanced the likely explanation that 174–99 had been copied twice by mistake in the exemplar, and scribes noting this, while refraining from copying an obvious duplicate, scrupulously left a blank. Subsequent scribes and annotators of Seneca were at a loss confronted by this blank space.

174 extinguat et me, ne manu nostra cadat The idea that Octavia could assassinate Nero must have been suggested by Soph. *El.* 955–7; 1019–29, where Electra proclaims a resolution to kill Aegisthus, which her sister Chrysothemis opposes.

175 natura uires non dedit tantas tibi The transmitted *natura non uires dedit tantas tibi*, as first observed by Herington (*Gnomon*, 49 (1977), 278), would produce a sequence without parallels in the Senecan corpus, for the line lacks both expected word breaks, after the fifth or after the seventh element, not to mention the strained word-order *natura non uires dedit* (not in itself without parallels: cf. *LHS* 2.410; Löfstedt, *Syntactica* 2.397). The reading of *A* was already altered in *recc.*, presumably more to make the word order plainer than to introduce the expected metrical incision after the fifth element: knowledge of these metrical notions cannot be taken for granted even for the early humanists. References to penthemimeres in iambics are not numerous in ancient grammarians and metrical writers; I have found only Marius Victorinus, *GLK* vi.79.19–23 *tomas . . . recipit penthemimerem et hephtemimerem . . . e quibus penthemimeres in trimetris satis probatur, quae per binos iambos et semipedem uerba finit*; no mention in Diomedes, *GLK* i.503–4; Seruius, *GLK* iv.457–8; Atil. Fort. *GLK* vi.286–7; Terent. Maur. *GLK* vi.390–7; Plot. Sacerd. *GLK* vi.517–19; Mall. Theod. *GLK* vi.593–4; even Victorinus' chosen example of tragic verse, *Musae Iouem laudate concentu bono*, lacks a penthemimeres.

Alongside the obligatory realization of the third and seventh elements as short, the observance of fifth-element caesura is the main point of difference between Senecan and archaic drama. It is, occasionally, obscured by monosyllabic conjunctions and prepositives in the fifth element, sometimes coalescing with the following syllable: cf. Soubiran (1987), 116 n. 25; Zwierlein, *Prolegomena* 214–15. On lines lacking a penthemimeral caesura in Senecan tragedy cf. Schmidt (1860), 56. In *Phoe.* 403 *perge o parens et concita celerem gradum*, penthemimeres after *et* is obscured by diaeresis after the fourth element. Caesura after the fifth element can be obscured by monosyllables followed by syntactical pause in Plautus: cf. *Men.* 750 *negas nouisse me? negas patrem meum?*; *Persa* 373 *dicat quod quisque uolt*; in Seneca cf. *Phoe.* 213 *auferre cuiquam mors, tibi hoc uita abstulit.*

The powerlessness of women to oppose men is a common predicament of heroines in Greek tragedy: cf. Soph. *El.* 997 γυνὴ μὲν οὐδ' ἀνὴρ ἔφυς, *Ant.* 61–2 γυναῖχ' ὅτι | ἔφυμεν ὡς πρὸς ἄνδρας οὐ μαχουμένα, Eur. *Hec.* 883 καὶ πῶς γυναιξὶν ἀρσένων ἔσται κράτος; in Latin cf. Ov. *Met.* 9.676 *et uires fortuna negat*, with *v.l. natura.*

176 dolor ira maeror miseriae luctus dabunt The passage is one of many in *Octavia* revealing the all-pervasive influence of Ovid, where female heroines are often cast, not always convincingly, in the attitude of would-be combatants, driven by anger or fierce passion, no matter how weak they are: cf. Ov. *Am.* 1.7.66 *quamlibet infirmas adiuuat ira manus* (other parallels are given by McKeown ad loc.); *Her.* 6.140 *quamlibet ignauis ipse dat arma dolor* (text dubious); *Met.* 4.150; 5.32–3; 12.373 *ipse dolor uires animo dabat.*

Ballaira rightly observes that the *cumulus* of nouns is a frequent feature in Seneca: cf. *Phoe.* 34 *semper cruente saeue crudelis ferox*, where it is probably intended to imitate the style of early Roman tragedy: cf. Pac. *Scaen.* 301 R^2 *metus egestas maeror senium*; Acc. *Scaen.* 349 R^2 *persuasit maeror anxitudo error dolor*; *LHS* 2.830–1 (asyndeta with three or more words); Lausberg, *HLR* on *enumeratio*, §§ 669–74.

177 uince obsequendo potius immitem uirum Cf. Soph. *El.* 396, where Chrysothemis urges Electra to give in to the powerful (τοῖς κρατοῦσι . . . εἰκαθεῖν); see also Eur. *Hec.* 404.

178 ut fratrem ademptum scelere restituat mihi? The compounds of *emo* (*adimo, interimo, perimo*), especially in participial form (*ademptum scelere* = 'murderously cut off from life'; also at 112–13 *fratris . . . scelere interempti* possibly in imitation of *Agam.* 925, given *infra*; 606 *perempta ferro*: cf. Junge (1999), 241, remarking that the clause *ademptus scelere* seems not to occur anywhere else) provide a convenient euphemistic periphrasis which is common in poetic Latin (cf. the repeated occurrences of (*frater*) *ademptus* in Cat. *Carm.* 67.20; 68.92; 101.6; Ov. *Her.* 9.166; *Met.* 11.273; *Fast.* 4.852; *CE* 1119.3–4 *Parcae non impubem quem rapuere mihi | maeret cara soror quae fratrem luget ademptum*); Verg. *Aen.* 6.163 *indigna morte peremptum*. Senecan tragedy, however, lacks *ademptus* (*Oed.* 218 *interemptum Laium*; *Agam.* 925 *pater peremptus scelere materno iacet*). As usual in stichomythia and in heated confrontations, the speakers pick up each other's words to drive home a polemical point: cf. 178 *restituat*, 180 *restituas*; 180 *subole*, 181 *subolem.*

182 me dira miseri fata germani trahunt *Fata trahunt/trahebant* has a quasi-formulaic status in the dactylic tradition, with 8 occurrences in Mastandrea (e.g. Ov. *Her.* 12.35 *et me mea fata trahebant*; add the textually dubious *Her.* 6.28 *me quoque fata trahunt*).

183 confirmet animum ciuium tantus fauor The aura of popular favour surrounding Octavia may have a parallel in Soph. *Ant.* 692–3, where Haemon reminds Creon that the city is aggrieved by punishment inflicted on Antigone. Popular support is stated also at 572–3; 578; 673–5.

185 uis magna populi est Cf. Aesch. *Agam.* 938 φήμη γε μέντοι δημόθρους μέγα σθένει (La Penna).

186 respiciet ipse coniugem The Nurse's words contain an echo of Sen. *Agam.* 155–6, with an exchange between Clytemnestra and the *Nutrix*: NV. *at te reflectat coniugi nomen sacrum.* CL. *decem per annos uidua respiciam uirum? respiciet* corresponds here to *reflectat* in Seneca, 'he will have consideration for' (cf. *OLD* s.v. *respicio*, 8a). σκέπτομαι or other verbs of seeing can take up the same sense in Greek: cf. Eur. *Med.* 460; *Andr.* 257; Fraenkel, *EP*, *Addenda*, ad 213 n. 1.

187 inuisa cunctis nempe The only evidence in support of this statement comes from the largely unfavourable portrayal of Poppaea found in our literary sources, and from the information, contained in Tac. *Ann.* 14.61, that the populace, jubilant at the apparent recall of Octavia, overturned all statues of Poppaea.

189 iuuenilis ardor impetu primo furit Cf. Sen. *Troad.* 250 *iuuenile uitium est regere non posse impetum.*

191 ceu leuis flammas uapor This comparative particle, frequent in Augustan poetry and found even in prose after Seneca, occurs only once in the Senecan corpus (*Troad.* 20).

194 animum . . . domini famula possedit diu Antithetical pairs are a favourite device of Latin rhetoric throughout all genres, and *animum . . . domini famula possedit* has parallels in the Senecan corpus at *Agam.* 796 *ne metue dominam famula*; *H.O.* 279 *Iouisque fiet ex famula nurus?*; 354–5 *in famulae locum | regina cecidit*; *Hf.* 430; Luc. *Bell. Ciu.* 2.149. The passage is reminiscent of the *Nutrix*-Deianeira scene in *H.O.*, esp. 351–79 where the Nurse endeavours to persuade Deianeira that Hercules will soon return to her and leave behind Iole, as he has done with all his previous concubines. *possidere animum* is rare in erotic contexts. In *TLL* s.v. *possideo* only Tib. Claud. Don. ad *Aen.* 1.665 (*Amor*) *facilius potuit mentem feminae* (sc. *Didonis*) *possidere.*

195–196 NV. **iam metuit eadem . . .** OC. **nempe praelatam sibi. |** NV. **subiecta et humilis** Change of speaker after *eadem*, with the caustic *nempe* . . . put in Octavia's mouth, was first proposed by Bothe (who gave Octavia 195b–197), and later independently revived by Ritter. The correction is a definite improvement: *nempe* is often used in animated dialogue, when one of the speakers seizes the occasion to make a sarcastic point (corresponding to Engl. 'you mean, to be sure'): cf. *H.O.* 437 *at Ioue creatum:: nempe et Alcmena satum*; *Troad.* 340 *inclusa fluctu::nempe cognati maris*; *Phae.* 244–5 NV. *aderit maritus*: PHAE. *nempe Pirithoi comes?* The line-end *praelatam sibi* resembles *H.O.* 304 *iam displicemus, capta praelata est mihi*. *nempe* is an asseverative particle (*nam* + *pe*) often used ironically in answers. In *H.O.* 363–77 (perhaps echoed here) the *Nutrix* uses it to introduce the list of Hercules' lovers eventually abandoned (e.g. 369 *nempe Thespiades uacant*). *nempe* tends to occur at the beginning of a sentence, but in poetry its position may vary (cf. Luc. *Bell. Ciu.* 8.351; Ov. *Her.* 20.72; *supra*, 187, *inuisa cunctis nempe*, the only other occurrence in *Octavia*).

On the whole, Ritter's correction, adopted by all editors except Giardina, is persuasive. Interruptions *para prosdokian* are found even in Greek tragedy: cf. Eur. *Suppl.* 818; Soph. *Ai.* 875; in Latin cf. the dialogue between Palaestra and Ampelisca at *Rud.* 238 *dic ubi es :: pol ego nunc in malis plurumis*, with Marx' note. *Antilabē* is adopted in Senecan tragedy with a pointed rhetorical purpose. In Seneca, however, when a second speaker cuts in and completes the sentence of his antagonist, the latter does not resume the syntax of his intended sentence: cf. *Agam.* 956 CL. *quis esse credat uirginem . . .* EL. *gnatam tuam?* CL. *modestius cum matre*; *Med.* 171 NV. *Medea . . .* MED. *fiam* NV. *mater es*; *Thy.* 1101. In 194, the *Nutrix* pays no attention to Octavia's reply, and carries on to complete her sentence with the words *subiecta et humilis*. Nero similarly pays no attention to Seneca's interruption at 459, and indeed paying no notice is often confrontational. This would seem to be inappropriate behaviour here, because the older woman is trying to comfort Octavia, by representing in a somewhat overoptimistic way her prospects of remaining Nero's wife. For more examples of polemical interruptions in heated dialogue cf. Seidensticker (1969), 25; 38 n. 85a. More exact parallels can be found in Greek tragedy and in early Roman drama (cf. Ter. *Ad.* 770–2 DE. *tun si meus esses . . .* SY. *dis quidem esses, Demea. | ac tuam rem constabilisses!* DE *exempla omnibus | curarem ut esses*). Various typologies are analysed in Mastronarde, *CD* 53. This instance would go under Mastronarde's category 'maintaining one's argument despite of interruptions by the other speaker' (74). For interruptions of speaker B which do not prevent A from carrying on with the syntax of his own speech cf. Eur. *Hec.* 1277–9; *Ion* 769–70; *Phoe.* 604–10.

With Baehrens' *alta* for *atque* (*Misc. Crit.* 117), the syntax of 196 would be smoother (*subiecta et humilis* (sc. Acte) *alta m. e.*), and the conjecture, although in my view unnecessary, bears witness to the comparatively awkward run of the sentence.

As it is, we must understand *subiecta et humilis* as predicatives belonging with *metuit*: 'metuit Acte, subiecta et humilis facta' preparing for an expected 'mutatum animum Neronis'. The Nurse carries on her own point pretending not to have heard Octavia's completion of her previous phrase.

For *subiecta* 'she has lost her pride' cf. Prop. 1.10.27 *at quo sis humilis magis et subiectus amori*; Cic. *Orat.* 76 *summissus est et humilis* (of Atticism).

196 atque monumenta exstruit Ladek (1891), 24–6 was the first to mention in this connection *CIL* XI.1414 CE]RERI SACRVM / [CLAVDIA] AVG. LIB. ACTE. These words are inscribed on a fragment of granite, 0.52 high, 1.77 long, probably an epistyle, now kept in the Cimitero Monumentale in Pisa (35A est. [= parete esterna] in Cristiani-Arias-Gabba, *Il Camposanto monumentale di Pisa. Le antichità* (Pisa, 1977), 77), and thought to have come in medieval times from the region of Olbia, where the rich *liberta* was the owner of large estates. Ladek drew attention to the role of Ceres as a goddess averse to, as well as protector of, marriage (cf. Serv. Dan. ad *Verg. Aen.* 4.58; other evidence on this double prerogative in L. R. Farnell, *The Cults of the Greek States* (Oxford, 1896–1909), III, 82; Roscher, *Lexicon*, I, s.v. *Ceres*, 864; Plut. *Quaest. Rom.* 22.4.5; Tert. *Cast.* 13.2).

In fact, in view of the great frequency of the name *Acte* for slave and freedwomen, we cannot be sure that the personage of *CIL* should be identified with Nero's mistress (cf. Solin, *Personennamen*, 566–7, including at least two more certain instances of *Acte ex familia Augusti*). The inscription at Pisa only attests a freedwoman's allegiance to Ceres, and although this could be our Acte there is nothing of significance in a rich landowner's worship of Ceres, the most important divinity presiding over the cultivation of crops.

Whatever the exact relevance of *CIL* XI.1414 for our passage, the author of *TLL* viii, s.v. *monumentum* understood the line as referring to a temple (presumably following Ladek (1891), 25; Nordmeyer (1892), 273). Only mythological heroes are known to have erected temples to ingratiate themselves with the gods in a love-suit or simply to thank some deity for favours obtained in that field: cf. W. H. D. Rouse, *Greek Votive Offerings* (Cambridge, 1902), 248–9, referring to Pelops, Theseus, Paris. The most fitting mythological precedent is provided by Phaedra, who is said in Eur. *Hipp.* 31 to have erected a shrine to Aphrodite to win the support of the goddess in her love-suit (ναὸν Κύπριδος ἐγκαθείσατο, with schol. ad 29 Schwartz οὕτως ἦρα ὡς καὶ Ἀφροδίτης ἱερὸν ἱδρύσασθαι ἐν τῆι Ἀττικῆι ἐξιλεουμένη τὸν ἔρωτα, Tzetzes, schol. ad Lyc. *Alex.* 1329, sch. μ 321), as was observed first by Bothe, p. 265.

The real-life Acte, however, is unlikely to have done the same. Scrutiny of epigraphic evidence yields some material on offerings made by women: only recovery of good health and memorials for deceased relatives are on record. Jealousy and adultery, on the other hand, figure rather conspicuously in the *tabellae defixionum*: cf. A. Audollent, *Defixionum tabellae* (Paris, 1904), Index s.v. *amatoriae*, 472. On *anathemata* and other offerings at Rome cf. A. De Marchi, *Il culto privato di Roma antica* (Milano, 1896), 1.251–307, with a detailed catalogue of votive inscriptions. In our literary evidence, a love-stricken and abandoned woman resorts by preference to magic: cf. Theocr. *Id.* 2; Lucian *Hetaer. dial.* 4.4; Eur. *Hipp.* 478–9; [Sen.] *H.O.* 452–63; 523–30. More in J. Gager (ed.), *Curse Tablets and Binding Spells* (Oxford, 1992), 112–5; C. A. Faraone–D. D. Obbink (edd.), *Magikà Hierà. Ancient Greek Magic and Religion* (Oxford, 1991), esp. 215. In the *Anthologia Palatina* one finds epigrams of offerings by maidens, or by the maidens' tutors, to gain favour for their forthcoming marriage: cf. e.g. *AP* 6.281.2–6. Dido, in Verg. *Aen.* 4.56, offers sacrifices to various deities to make them benevolent towards her union with Aeneas, and later, when she loses all hopes, pretends to resort to magic, *ibid.* 478. In Ovid's *Heroides*, women visit temples not to ask the gods to restore their lovers' affection, but only to pray for their safe return (cf. *Her.* 2.17–8; 6.73; 13.112). Men perform similar sacrifices: cf. Hor. *Carm.* 1.19.16 *mactata ueniet lenior hostia*; Tib. 3.5.33.

Is Acte likely to have sought such publicity, on such a grand scale (if the inscription was part of a temple), for her private dealings with the emperor? After all the liaison had been kept hidden, by having her taken care of by Serenus (cf. Tac. *Ann.* 13.12), who obligingly took it upon himself to pass as her lover in public.

The allusive character of this passage looks like an innuendo for the cognoscenti acquainted with some court gossip, but it could also be explained as one of the features of *Octavia* that point to the *ignotus*' drawing on written accounts. We may see in operation here an ancient historian who had a penchant for misconstruing monuments or other epigraphic evidence when other information failed. Cf. Suet. *Cal.* 8 of Caligula's birth-place: *Plinius Secundus in Treueris uico Ambitaruio supra Confluentes; addit etiam pro argumento aras ibi ostendi inscriptas ob Agrippinae puerperium*; Tac. *Hist.* 3.74 *Domitianus aram . . . posuit casus suos in marmore expressam.*

Lastly, Herington (*Gnomon*, 49 (1977), 276) has put forward the suggestion that the monument here being referred to was a thank-offering for Nero's escape from the conspiracy of 65: Ceres, we know from Tac. *Ann.* 15.53.1, presided over the day of the Circensian Games when the conspiracy was unmasked. In that case the monument would have been misconstrued by the poet (the events he narrates took place in 62), if the inscription is to be linked with it at all.

For the phrasing cf. Tac. *Ann.* 11.10.5 *exstructis monumentis quibus opes suas testabatur* (of the Parthian potentate Vardanes).

197 quibus timorem fassa testatur suum I follow Zwierlein (in his first edition and in *KK* ad loc.) and the majority of earlier editors in giving preference to *fassa* over *falsa* (which, however, has better MS support). Octavia's Nurse is trying to reassure her princess and asserts that from Acte's behaviour they can deduce how frightened she is of losing Nero. As Zwierlein argued in *KK*, *fassa testatur* could be explained as an instance of the syntactical pleonastic type *discernens diuidit* (Cat. *Carm.* 64.179, with Kroll's note), well established in

Seneca (e.g. *Phoe.* 78 *uictasque magno robore aerumnas doma; Agam.* 676–7 (*non*) *lugere tuam poterit digne | conquesta domum*); Vahlen, *Opuscula* 1.448; *LHS* 2.797. In the present case, *testatur* seems to refer to the erection of the *monumentum* and *fassa* to what the monument says about Acte's frame of mind, but the two verbs are virtually interchangeable in sense: for *fateor* 'to reveal' by the means of some telling action or gesture cf. *TLL* vi, s.v. 342, e.g. *Pan. Lat.* 2(12).22.5 *ipse ille rex eius* (sc. *Persidos*) . . . *iam fatetur timorem et in his te colit templis in quibus colitur*; for *testor* as 'revealing one's feelings' cf. Ov. *Met.* 2.486 *adsiduoque suos gemitu testata dolores*; Luc. *Bell. Ciu.* 10.16 (*templa*) *antiquas Macetum testantia uires*: Sen. *Dial.* 2.18.1 *palloris insaniam testantis.*

Main verb and participle share the same object, as in Verg. *Aen.* 4.148 *fronde premit crinem fingens*; also common in Greek: cf. Eur. *I.A.* 1566 ἔθηκεν ὀξὺ χειρὶ φάσγανον σπάσας *Andr.* 813 ξίφη καθαρπάζουσιν ἐξαιρούμενοι. In ordinary language, a pronoun picks up the noun in the main clause.

falsa might have been caused by the following *fallax* . . . *destituet.* I find *falsa* difficult to accept without any modifying or limiting element (the semantic field is obviously that of love: cf. Prop. 2.2.2 *me composita pace fefellit amor*; Verg. *Aen.* 4.17 *postquam primus amor deceptam morte fefellit. decipi* is more common than *falli* in inscriptions: cf. *CE* 1950.12 *decepti senes testemur funera natuum*; *CE* 537.5; De Rossi, 1180 *et decepturus me iugulauit amor.* Zwierlein changed his mind in later editions of the corpus, defending *falsa*, with no very cogent parallels.

200 opibus superba Cf. Tac. *Ann.* 13.45 (of Poppaea) *mater eius . . . formam dederat, opes claritudini generis sufficiebant.*

201 A change of metre without a concomitant change of speaker is paralleled in the corpus at *Phae.* 1199–1212; *Med.* 740–849; *H.O.* 1837–1949, *Agam.* 759, *Troad.* 705, where Andromache summons Astyanax out of his hiding-place (but the sequence is introduced by a half-line uttered by Ulixes in iambics). Only in *Troad.* and *H.O.* is the change from iambics to anapaests. All these passages seem to conjure up the impression of song. In Greek tragedy cf. Aesch. *Prom.* 88–127, where Prometheus' monologue shifts from spoken iambics to anapaests and lyric iambics; see M. Griffith, *The Authenticity of Prometheus Bound* (Cambridge, 1977), 23–4, for comparable passages in Greek tragedy, none so peculiar: Eur. *Andr.* 100; *I.A.* 1474; *Rhes.* 894. Monodies in Greek drama tend to be solipsistic, if not always soliloquies (cf. Barner, in Jens, *Bauformen*, 303–8); on the other hand, the consolatory character of 201–21 is strange in a song.

In Greek, monodies tend to be accompanied by a character's exit or entrance; characters of lower social standing cannot sing monodies (with the exception of Eur. *Or.* 1369; on delivery and social status in Greek tragedy see Maas, *KS*, 47–8, on Soph. *Trach.* 886), or long anapaestic sections in the form of monodies (as distinct from *domina-Nutrix* exchanges); one such scene may, however, occur in a fragment from an unknown tragedy of the post-classical age (*TrGF adesp.* 680a; cf. l. 25 δεσπότι).[5] The passage seems to be a messenger scene.

Change of metre in successive sections of the same *canticum* is a recurrent feature of early Latin drama. In Plautus, the transition from a *diuerbium* to a *canticum* tends to mark the beginning of a new scene and the entrance of a new character: cf., however, the shift from iambic tetrameters to cretics in Sosias' soliloquy in Plaut. *Amph.* 203–47. Only switches from (recitative) iambics to trochaics are found to occur in the same scene (cf. Lindsay, Plaut. *Capt.* Introd. 72). For Republican tragedy, instances of a switch from spoken to sung verse or vice versa, or between different sung measures in a *canticum*, are discussed by Jocelyn, *Ennius*, p. 40; cf. Enn. *Scaen.* 75–88 R², a change from cretics to trochaics to anapaestic dimeters; Soubiran, *RPh* 32 (1969), 271.

In the Senecan parallels given above, the change between iambics and anapaests involves *pathos* and an increased emotional tension. This is not the case with the *Nutrix* in *Oct.* 201–21, who is not distraught. The poet of *Octavia* may have felt that the more ornamental and 'artistic' character of the lines (the mythological subject matter) justified a change of metre, from the factual trimeter to the more decorative anapaests. No outstanding metrical or linguistic features appear to characterize the status of these lines as 'song' rather than 'recitative', and rhetorical ornament does not exceed the expected rates for 'Senecan' tragedy.

201 passa est similes ipsa dolores For this consolatory topos in tragedy cf. Soph. *Ant.* 944 (Jebb compares also Hom. *Il.* 5.382); Soph. *El.* 153–4 οὔτοι σοὶ μούναι, | τέκνον, ἄχος ἐφάνη βροτῶν. In Latin cf. Ov. *Fast.* 1.487–92, esp. 491 *passus idem Tydeus et idem Pagasaeus Iason*; *Met.* 15.493–4. Like τλῆναι, *pati* here may have the double sense 'to endure something bravely' and 'to have to suffer'. The appeal to the common lot of misery shared by all human beings is a motif recurrent in consolatory literature, a genre which includes many commatic *parodoi* of Greek tragedy: cf. Di Benedetto–Medda, 259–60; M. G. Ciani, *BIFG Padova*, 2 (1975), 89–129.

There follows a list of mythical figures whose divine origin has been granted recognition through assumption among the stars. The idea that this promotion of Jupiter's illegitimate offspring is a constant sting for Juno seems to derive from Ov. *Met.* 2, as well as Sen. *Hf.* 1 ff.

203 cum se formas uertit in omnes The line is an almost literal adaptation of Verg. *Georg.* 4.411 *formas se uertet in omnis*, but see also Prop. 4.2.47 *formas unus uertebar in omnis*; Ov. *Met.* 12.559 *formas uariatus in omnes*; 14.685 *formasque apte fingetur in omnes*. Jupiter, unlike Proteus in the *Georg.*, took these appearances on different occasions, and an imperfect subjunctive was perhaps to be expected here. Temporal *cum* + perf. indic. is normal (cf. *LHS* 2.621–22),

[5] S. Eitrem-L. Amundsen, *SO* 31 (1955), 1–87.

though not in this context. Cf. Sen. *Phae.* 299–308 *induit formas saepe minores . . . ; candidas ales modo mouit alas . . . fronte nunc torua petulans iuuencus.*

204 dominus caeli diuumque pater In Ov. *Met.* 2.847–8 the phrase *sceptri grauitate relicta | ille pater rectorque deum* communicates the sense of disproportion and impropriety inherent in the act of changing into a bull for love; no such contrast is perceptible here.

205–207 et modo pennas sumpsit oloris, | modo Sidonii cornua tauri; | aureus idem fluxit in imbri This set of mythological exempla is one of a series; others are the lists of proverbial mourners (cf. *supra* ad 6–7) and the great sinners in Hades (cf. Ov. *Met.* 4.457–63). For a collection of other poems with the same list of women loved by Jupiter in different disguises cf. McKeown ad Ov. *Am.* 1.3.21–4. Gross (1911, 328) attached an exaggerated significance to the parallel between this passage and *Aetna*, 89–90 [*poetae canunt quomodo . . .*] *taurus in Europen, in Ledam candidus ales | Iuppiter, ut Danaae pretiosus fluxerit imber*, but the recurrence of this stock motif is not, in my view, very telling.

The sequence *modo . . . modo* is normally applied to repeated actions (the tenses tend to be present or imperfect: cf. *Oct.* 115 *quam saepe . . . modo . . . armat . . . modo . . . refugit*), but the parallel from *Phae.* 299 ff. given ad 203 shows that *modo* can refer also to specific events viewed in a sequence; e.g. Ov. *Met.* 6.123–4 *utque modo accipitris pennas, modo terga leonis | gesserit*. *modo . . . modo* is often employed to describe a series of sudden metamorphoses, as at Hor. *Serm.* 2.3.73; Ov. *Met.* 8.873 (more examples in Wölfflin, *ALL* 2 (1885) 238–9). The present line could have been inspired by Ov. *Ars* 1.323 *et modo se Europen fieri, modo postulat Io* (of Pasiphae). In Greek cf. Soph. *Trach.* 10–12 (where, as here, a sequence of three transformations is being described, though perhaps repeated on different occasions).

207 in imbri For the ablative *imbri* cf. N-W I^3.362–3. For the use of *in* with the ablative meaning 'clad in', 'in the form, guise of' cf. Löfstedt, *Late Latin*, 34–5, esp. Ov. *Met.* 15.670 *in serpente deus praenuntia sibila misit*; Apul. *Met.* 6.29 *quodsi uere Iuppiter mugiuit in boue*; Firm. Mat. *De errore* 12 *quod deus suus in cygno fallit, in tauro rapit, ludit in satyro* (see also the parallels quoted ad 772 *fuluo fluxit in auro*).

208 fulgent caelo sidera Ledae Castor and Pollux, taken up among the stars (cf. *Hf.* 14 *gemini . . . Tyndaridae micant*), are "the constellation (of the two sons) of Leda": the brachylogic *sidera Ledae* imitates Ov. *Am.* 2.11.29 *tum generosa uoces fecundae sidera Ledae*; the same periphrasis occurs also in Phaedr. *Fab.* 4.25(26).9 *gemina Ledae sidera*. The normal idiom is *Arcturi sidera* that is 'the stars forming the constellation of Arcturus', or, metaphorically, *solem Asiae Brutum* (Hor. *Serm.* 1.7.24); Eur. *Hipp.* 1123. Castor and Pollux would normally occur either as *Ledaea sidera* or in similar formulae (cf. the parallels given by Witlox ad [Ov.] *Cons. Liu.* 330; Hor. *Carm.* 1.3.2 *sic fratres Helenae, lucida* *sidera*), but there is of course no question of emendation here. For a similar use of the genitive, indicating parenthood cf. Hor. *Carm.* 3.12.4 *Cythereae puer ales* 'the winged boy of Cytherea'.

212 cuius gener est qui fuit hostis Cf. Ov. *Trist.* 3.5.42 *Iunonis gener est qui prius hostis erat.*

213–14 uicit sapiens tamen obsequium | coniugis altae pressusque dolor *altus* is a common epithet for gods (cf. *TLL* s.v. 1774.60 ff.), signifying either their seat in the skies or their superhuman size, when they manifest themselves in their true form; *alta* of Juno is found in Ovid (cf. *Met.* 3.284–5; *quantusque et qualis ab alta | Iunone excipitur*, 12.505–6). *pressus . . . dolor* echoes perhaps Verg. *Aen.* 1.209 *premit altum corde dolorem* (of Aeneas); cf. also Cat. *Carm.* 68.138–40 *saepe etiam Iuno, maxima caelicolum, | coniugis in culpa flagrantem concoquit* (text uncertain) *iram | noscens omniuoli plurima furta Iouis*, on which commentators remark that the behaviour of Juno is usually thought to have been the opposite.

217–18 nec mortali captus forma | deserit altam Iuppiter aulam I have been unable to find a source for this alleged 'improvement' of Jupiter's behaviour with regard to his philandering. There was a tradition (apparently of Argive origin: cf. Preller-Robert, *GM* I.138; Diod. Sic. *Antiq.* 4.14.4) according to which Alcmene had been the last mortal woman loved by Zeus. In this tradition, however, the patience of Hera had no part, and Zeus's change of attitude was solely due to his scruple that Hercules, born from Alcmene, should be the most powerful of all men generated by his encounter with a mortal. The present line seems to be based rather on an expansion of the motif found in *epithalamia* as a compliment for the bride or the groom, 'she is so beautiful that a god would descend on earth to woo her'. For the significance of this motif in *Octavia*, and the parallel with Stat. *Sil.* 1.2 cf. Introd. p. 19.

The motif, however, is attested elsewhere: cf. *AP* 12.20.4 (Julius Leonidas) ἦ φιλόπαις οὐκέτι νῦν ὁ θεός, 12.65.1 (Meleager) Ζεὺς κεῖνος ἔτ' ἐστίν, Petr. *Sat.* 126.18.2–3 *quid factum est quod tu proiectis, Iuppiter, armis, | inter caelicolas fabula muta iaces?* (with the implication 'no longer descending to earth in pursuit of beautiful women'). In *AP* 12.70.4, Zeus is made to answer to the poet begging him not to take his minion away from him: 'have no fears, οἶδα παθὼν ἐλεεῖν'. Cf. also *RE* Suppl. xv, col. 1312; *infra*, ad 545; 768 *quae regit, et nunc deseret astra*; *Phae.* 294–5 *iubet caelo superos relicto . . . habitare terras.* One might also quote the topos that gods no longer dwell among mortals as they used to: cf. Cat. *Carm.* 64.385–6, with the parallels given by Kroll.

219 terris altera Iuno *terris* is a dative: cf. 910 *regnat mundo Erinys. terris altera Iuno* is similar to Verg. *Aen.* 2.573 *Troiae et patriae communis Erinys.* On *alter* with proper names, see *TLL* s.v., 1735.38–61: here the expression does not mean 'a Juno *rediviva*' (and it differs from *Agam.* 962 *quis iste est alter*

Agamemnon tuus), but a 'Juno-on-earth'. As a title of imperial rulers cf. Mart. *Epigr.* 9.36.2 *alterius, gaudia nota, Iouis* (that is, Domitian); 9.91.6 *me meus in terris Iuppiter ecce tenet.* In the western provinces, this comparison of a Roman ruler or his spouse to an Olympian is restricted to poetic usage (cf. Ov. *Pont.* 3.1.145 *cum tibi contigerit uultum Iunonis adire* (of Livia); *Fast.* 1.649; Stat. *Silu.* 3.4.18 *Iuppiter Ausonius pariter Romanaque Iuno*). The legend IVNO on the reverse of western coins showing the portrait of Roman empresses is found only much later, in the age of the Antonines (cf. P. Strack, *Untersuchungen*, 3.46–7 (of Faustina Augusta, perhaps in her lifetime)). On inscriptions and dedications to *Iuppiter Augustus* (of Octavian) cf. Weinstock, *Diuus Iulius*, 304–5. Later cf. Calp. Sic. *Buc.* 4.142–3 *tu quoque mutata seu Iuppiter ipse figura, | Caesar . . .* (of Nero); Man. *Astr.* 1.916 (uncertain).

In the eastern provinces, the epigraphic evidence is more abundant: cf. *IGRR* 4.249 (from Assos) θεὰν Λειουίαν; also *IG* XII suppl. 50 Σεβαστὰν Ἥραν (perhaps of Livia, found at Lesbos); *IG* IX 2.333 (a stone now lost, said to have been found at Mylae, in Thessaly) where Livia, as Ἰουλία (i.e. after her adoption by Augustus) appears as Ἥρα Σεβαστή. Valeria Messalina appears with the (inaccurate) legend *Augusta* on Roman coins and as Μεσσαλῖνα Σεβαστὴ νέα Ἥρα on Greek ones.

On the identification of Roman rulers and gods cf. also N-H ad Hor. *Carm.* 1.2.43; on later members of the imperial house called after various gods see G. Wissowa, *Religion und Kultus der Römer* (Munich, 1912[2]), 93; A. Fincke, *De appellationibus Caesarum* (Diss., Königsberg, 1867), 15; 25; P. Riewald, 'De imperatorum Romanorum cum certis dis et comparatione et aequatione', *Dissertationes Philologae Halenses* 20.3 (1912), 277 (Roman poetry), 302 (Greek coins and inscriptions); F. Taeger, *Charisma. Studien zur Geschichte des antiken Herrscherkultes* (Stuttgart, 1957), 2.197–8; H. Temporini, *Die Frauen am Hofe Trajans* (Berlin–New York 1970), 71 and n. 51.

The titles collected here refer to the cult of Julian rulers: the author of *Oct.* was presumably imitating Ovid's flattering lines on Livia, rather than reflecting contemporary practice. On divine honours claimed by the Caesars, see also Furneaux's note ad Tac. *Ann.* 15.74.3–4.

220 soror Augusti coniunxque Cf. Verg. *Aen.* 1.46–7 *diuom . . . regina Iouisque | et soror et coniunx*; 10.607 *o germana mihi atque eadem gratissima coniunx*; more parallels in Bömer's notes ad Ov. *Met.* 3.265; *Fast.* 6.17.[6] A panegyric topos was established in Hellenistic times comparing the ruling couple to Zeus and Hera (cf. Theocr. *Id.* 17.130–2 ἐκ θυμοῦ στέργοισα κασίγνητόν τε πόσιν τε. | ὧδε καὶ ἀθανάτων ἱερὸς γάμος ἐξετελέσθη). In Hellenistic Alexandria

[6] Witlox ad [Ov.] *Cons. Liu.* 304 *nec minor es magni coniuge uisa Iouis* suggests that Drusus and Antonia were adoptive siblings, but no trace of such an official adoption by Augustus can be found in the extant evidence.

'sister and wife' seems to have become one of the queens' honorific titles (cf. *OGIS* 60), and in Roman times Ephesian coins (*RPC* 2620) celebrate Claudius' marriage to his niece Agrippina with the legend ΘΕΟΓΑΜΙΑ, presumably recalling the same range of associations. Octavia's Nurse uses the title *soror coniunxque* as a compliment (it also occurs *infra* in Seneca's words at 535), but unions between close relatives were scandalous to the Romans (on similar prohibitions extending to adoptive kinship cf. Rossbach, *Untersuchungen über die römische Ehe* (Leipzig, 1853), 442); Greek parallels are given in M. S. Smith, 'Greek Precedents for Claudius' Actions in AD 48 and Later', *CQ* n.s. 13 (1963), 139–44. In Sen. *Apocol.* 8.2 *quod (Silanus) sororem suam . . . maluit Iunonem uocare* is reported to have been the charge moved against Silanus, Octavia's betrothed, in AD 49. The union of near relatives was generally regarded by the Romans as incestuous and restricted to foreign custom (cf. Luc. *Bell. Ciu.* 8.404–5 *iacuere sorores | in regum thalamis*; Tac. *Ann.* 2.3.2 *liberis eius . . . sociatis more externo in matrimonium regnumque*). The few relationships between close relatives on record in the imperial age are associated with tyrannical behaviour, and may all be later concoctions. According to Cass. Dio-Xiph., *Hist. Rom.* 59.26.5 Gaius called himself (equal to) Jupiter to justify his incestuous relationships with his sisters (cf. also Aur. Vict. *Epit. de Caes.* 3.5 *Iouem ob incestum . . . se asserebat*). Juv. *Sat.* 2.29–30 *qualis erat nuper tragico pollutus adulter | concubitu* echoes the impression produced by Domitian's affair with his niece Julia. Claudius' marriage with Agrippina is similarly criticized in *Oct.* 141–2 *genitamque fratre coniugem captus sibi . . . iunxit*; Tac. *Ann.* 12.2.5. Octavia and Nero, however, were not really related except by adoption, and Octavia was adopted into another family to exorcise this fear: cf. Cass. Dio *Hist. Rom.* 60.33.2 τὴν θυγατέρα ἐς ἕτερόν τι γένος ἐκποιήσας ἵνα μὴ ἀδελφοὺς συνοικίζειν δοκῇ. Later, Marcus Aurelius married his adoptive sister Faustina. Different is Ov. *Met.* 1.351 *o soror o coniunx*, which may allude to Hom. *Il.* 6.429, but it is also a reference to their being akin (children of brothers); see also Bömer's notes ad Ov. *Met.* 3.265; *Fast.* 6.17.

soror Augusti The bare *Augustus* in reference to Claudius and Nero is found in inscriptions (cf. Dessau, *ILS* 1621, 1786, 1838; *AE* 1953, 251) and on coin legends, in the form of *SECVRITAS AVGVSTI, GENIVS AVGVSTI*: cf. J. Vogt, *Alexandrinische Münzen*, 32. Tacitus restricts *Augustus* to Octavian, with *Caesar* as the commonest appellative for Claudius. *Augustus* refers to Nero in Tac. *Ann.* 16.26.2 *immanitatem Augusti etiam bonos sequi* (text uncertain). *Augustus* is infrequently used in reference to Tiberius, who refused this title at Rome, and only used it in official transactions with the various Eastern monarchs (so Cass. Dio *Hist. Rom.* 57.8.1; Suet. *Tib.* 26.4). In the *S.c. de Cn. Pisone patre*, however, Tiberius' *subscriptio* (l. 174) reads *Tiberius Caesar Augustus* (cf. M. Griffin, *JRS* 87 (1997), 257). For the imperial titles assumed by Vespasian, see Dessau, *ILS* 244. *soror Augusti* occurs also at 658; cf. also *infra* ad 934 *nurus Augusti*.

222–225 iungentur ante saeua sideribus freta | . . . quam cum scelesti coniugis mente impia | mens nostra The revulsion that the mere thought of Nero occasions in Octavia is expressed by a list of unnatural phenomena, all less incredible than that she will be reconciled with Nero: for similar *adynata* in Senecan tragedy cf. *Hf.* 372–8; *Phae.* 568–573; *Thy.* 476–82.

For the repetition of two different forms of the same word in the same phrase cf. Ov. *Trist.* 4.7.15 *quadrupedesque homines cum pectore pectora iunctos*. On this type of *polyptoton* with nouns, common with *iungo* and characteristically Ovidian (cf. *TLL* vii, s.v. *iungo*, 658), and frequent in Senecan tragedy, cf. Wills, *Repetition*, 219–20, who stresses the fact that only one example occurs in *Octavia*; Lausberg, *HLR* §§ 646–8.

The phrase *mens iuncta cum mente* to express mutual love is not well paralleled in this exact form (cf. Stat. *Theb.* 2.365 *tantus . . . mentes iunxit amor*; Man. *Astr.* 2.679 *astra . . . mentes quae iungere possunt*) and must be understood as a zeugma with the first colon, where *iungo* occurs in a more common sense. More commonly one finds *mente, animis, amore iunctus*.

230–231 mentesque nostras ignibus terret sacris | nouisque monstris Santoro adduces as a parallel Tac. *Ann.* 14.12, concerned with the prodigies occurring after Agrippina's assassination: *prodigia quoque crebra et irrita incessere . . . quae adeo sine cura deum eueniebat ut multos post annos Nero imperium et scelera continuauerit*, where the same connection of *monstra* and the indifference of the gods occurs. In the play, however, Octavia seems to hope that Jupiter will intervene against Nero. *ignes sacri* designates the lightning, or perhaps the comet alluded to in the next line.

231–232 uidimus caelo iubar | ardens cometen pandere infestam facem This seems to refer to the comet of 60, as we gather from Tac. *Ann.* 14.22.1 (cf. Introd. p. 13) *inter quae sidus cometes effulsit*. This comet is also mentioned in Sen. *N.Q.* 7.17.2 Comets were linked to changes of rule: cf. Val. Fl. *Arg.* 6.608 *fatales ad regna iniusta cometae*; Stat. *Theb.* 1.708 *quae mutent sceptra cometae*.

Heinsius conjectured *infaustam* in the place of *infestam* to avoid repetition with 229 *fulmine infesto*, comparing Ov. *Her.* 6.46 *praetulit infaustas sanguinolenta faces*, but the correction is unnecessary in this poet, not so fastidious about repetition.

Former editors printed *cometam* from β, which would be acceptable as far as the Latin goes. The reading of δ, exhibiting a solecistic third-declension *cometem*, tips the balance in favour of the more correctly transliterated form *cometen* (for Gk. κομήτης), which was first proposed by Herington, *RhM* 101 (1958), 362, n. 12, and later adopted by Zwierlein. There is no compelling linguistic reason in favour of either form, because Latin writers oscillate between morphologically assimilated endings and Greek forms, with a prevalence of the latter in Augustan authors. While *cometem* is certainly wrong, a decision between *cometam* and *cometen* is more a matter of style than linguistic accuracy. In *Octavia* the Greek accusative is preferable. *cometen* is the form chosen by the editors of all the passages in poetry where this word occurs in the same case e.g. Luc. *Bell. Ciu.* 1.529 *mutantem regna cometen*, the only exception apparently being Calp. Sic. *Buc.* 1.78 *placida radiantem luce cometem*. For the other occurrences cf. N-W I[3]. 54; the classic discussion on the endings of Greek words in Latin poetry is Housman, *CP* 2.818–25 on first-declension Greek words.

Alternative periphrastic solutions are sometimes deployed by Latin poets to find a substitute for the Greek technical term: cf. Ov. *Met.* 15.749 *in sidus uertere nouum stellamque comantem*; and, by contrast, Stat. *Theb.* 7.710 *iubar aduersi graue sideris*.

For the appositive structure *iubar ardens cometen* found at 232–3 Zwierlein has aptly compared *Hf.* 6–7 *Arctos . . . sublime . . . sidus*; 14 *hinc clara gemini signa Tyndaridae*; these appositive constructions are very frequently employed in Augustan poetry, often with recourse to contrasting gender and numbers (e.g. pairing neuters with masculines, singular with plural), and are very popular after Vergil: cf. also Maurach, *EP* §§131–2.

The prosaic equivalent of these appositive structures is the expression *stella cometes*, for which see Tac. *Ann.* 14.22.1 *inter quae sidus cometes effulsit*, where *cometes* is said by Furneaux to be adjectival as in *stella cometes* (Iust. 37.2.2; Cass. Dio *Hist. Rom.* 60.35); κομήτης, however, is a first-declension noun; *sidus cometes* and *stella cometes* represent the appositional type *uir propheta* (on which see *LHS* 2.158); cf. *Epigrammata Bobiensia* Speyer, 29.4 *sideribus canibus*.

233–234 qua plaustra tardus . . . regit Bootes, frigore Arctoo rigens The couplet is meant to indicate the region of the sky in which the comet shone, the northern sector where the Bear and the Ploughman appear. The adjective *Arctous* is not found in Latin before Seneca, and no Greek instance predates Seneca in *LSJ*, but its frequency is considerable in Silver Latin: cf. Luc. *Bell. Ciu.* 10.250 *frigore ab Arctoo*. In Seneca, Greek derivatives in *-(i)os* are not uncommon, e.g. *Eoos* at *Agam.* 483, *Hf.* 25, and *Arctous* occurs in *Hf.* 1326 *Arctoum . . . mare*. The transmitted *frigido Arctoo rigens* of *A* was corrected by *recc.* The error arose because *Arctoo* was mistaken for a noun, a function which this rare word sometimes has in medieval sources. *Arctous* was presumably known to medieval writers from Lucan and Statius: cf. *MLW* 904–5, Paul. Diac. *Lang.* 1.1. *arctoo sub axe*; Anon. Astrolab. p. 371, 31 *inter summos arctoum* (noun!) *ambitus*; also in *DMLBS* 1.121.

The *Octavia* poet combines in cento-like fashion Sen. *Med.* 314–5 *non quae* (sc. *sidera*) *sequitur flectitque senex | Attica tardus plaustra Bootes* and *Med.* 682–3 *quasque perpetua niue | Taurus coercet frigore Arctoo rigens* (cf. also *Oed.* 546 *frigore aeterno rigens*). The choice of model appears somewhat infelicitous: in *Med.* 314–15, the words describing Bootes are part of a list describing the absence of astronomical phenomena before the universe was born; in *Octavia* the elaborate periphrasis strikes one as somewhat oversize merely to indicate the sector of the sky where the comet was sighted. Even *frigore Arctoo rigens* is Ovidian (cf. *Pont.* 2.7.72 *frigore perpetuo Sarmatis ora riget*) and Senecan in conception, with its humorous use of mythological imagery (cf. *rigens*, portraying Bootes as a reluctant herdsman, shivering with cold).

This passage in *Octavia* was suggested as a possible source for Boet. *Cons.* 4. *m.*5.3 *cur legat tardus plaustra Bootes*, corrected to *regat* on the basis of 234.

233 noctis alterna uice The MS *eterne* was first plausibly changed to *aeterna* by Avantius, but Heinsius' *alterna* is in my judgement superior: cf. *infra* 388 *sortis alternae uices*; in Senecan tragedy cf. *Thy.* 25, *Agam.* 561, *Phae.* 411 (*noctis decus*) *cuius relucet mundus alterna uice*; it is also common elsewhere; cf. Enn. *Scaen.* 110–1 R[2] *ignotus iuuenum coetus alterna uice* | *inibat alacris Bacchico insultans modo*: cf. Soubiran (1984b), 90. *uices* is often so used in circumlocutions describing the recurrence and regularity of the astronomical phenomena: cf. also *H.O.* 470–1 *uersa uice* | *medius coactis ferueat stellis dies*; *Troad.* 1141 *astra cum repetunt uices*; *Agam.* 53 *noctis aestiuae uices.*

235–236 ipse diro spiritu saeui ducis | polluitur aether Cf. Ov. *Met.* 2.793 (of Invidia) *afflatuque suo populos urbesque domosque* | *polluit*; Ps.-Quint. *Decl. maior.* 12.28 *caelestes auras contaminato spiritu polluimus* (Hosius). Also *Oed.* 36 *caelum nocens fecimus*; Aesch. *Agam.* 1645 (γυνή) χώρας μίασμα καὶ θεῶν ἐγχωρίων, Soph. *O.T.* 353 (of Oedipus).

236–237 gentibus clades nouas | minantur astra, quas regit dux impius Cf. Sil. *Pun.* 1.464 *terris . . . extrema minatur*; Man. *Astr.* 1.893–4 *terris . . . minantur* (sc. *faces*) | *ardentes sine fine rogos*; Juv. *Sat.* 6.569; 14.294.

The relative pronoun *quas* is distant from the words it refers to. On other cases of anomalous sequences of relative clauses cf. K-S 2.286.9; *LHS* 2.692, Cat. *Carm.* 68.68 with Friedrich's note (a dubious instance); Lucr. *D.R.N.* 2.801–2 *pluma columbarum quo pacto in sole uidetur,* | *quae sita ceruices circum collumque coronat*; Ov. *Her.* 4.127–8; 12.45–7 *populos genitura . . .* (47) *qui peterent*; also *infra* 258.

238–239 non tam ferum Typhona . . . | irata Tellus edidit quondam parens Cf. Verg. *Aen.* 4.178–80 *illam Terra parens, ira inritata deorum,* | *extremam . . . progenuit* (of Fama); Luc. *Bell. Ciu.* 4.595 *nec tam iusta fuit terrarum gloria Typhon*. Some manuscripts appear to read what could be interpreted as *Typhoea* (*tythoea* Σ; cf. Gk. acc. Τυφωέα) which, although at first sight *difficilior*, is metrically impossible (the scribes probably interpreted *oea* as diphthong *oe* + short *a*). However, *Typhoea* in synizesis is found in Ov. *Met.* 3.303 *nec quo centimanum deiecerat igne Typhoea* (N-W 1[3].472: the same phenomenon in Verg. *Georg.* 1.279; Sil. *Pun.* 8.540; a trisyllabic dative *Typhoeo* in Verg. *Aen.* 9.716: all occurrences at line-end). In the Ovidian instance, the metrical position of *Typhoea* (at line-end) makes it impossible to determine which vowels are involved in synizesis, but presumably it is *ea*. A scansion *Ty̆phōe̯ă*, with synizesis *ea* is perhaps not impossible, but has no parallels in Latin poetry (only *ia, iu*: cf. Norden, ad Verg. *Aen.* 6.33; *ei, ea* stand for one long syllable: *ibid.* ad 280), and was unnecessary, given that *Typhon* provided a perfectly acceptable alternative. Serv. Dan. ad Verg. *Aen.* 10.272 relates that one of the comets was called Typhon.

238 neglecto Ioue Traditionally, Earth gave birth, in succession, to the Titans, the Giants and Typhoeus either in envy of, or in anger with Zeus; cf. *irata Tellus* 239; cf. Apollod. *Bibl.* 1.6.3, μᾶλλον χολωθεῖσα. We might have expected a reference to the reasons for her anger, and *neglecto Ioue* is somewhat insufficient, since the Earth's purpose was to overthrow Zeus's power over the gods. *neglego* for 'to disregard the will of the gods', 'to fail to show due reverence to the gods' (cf. Cat. *Carm.* 64.134 *neglecto numine diuum* of Theseus' deceptive oaths; Hor. *Carm.* 3.2.29–30 *saepe Diespiter | neglectus incesto addidit integrum*), is of course possible, but a stronger expression was needed here, since Earth is actively rebellious against the rule of the Olympian gods. I do not have a clear solution; *despecto, deiecto* (cf. Stat. *Theb.* 1.321–2 *sedisse superbus | deiecto iam fratre putat*) and *deuicto* are possibilities. The problem is that Earth defeated Jove, or expelled him from the sky, only *after* giving birth to Typhon. In *Oct.* 422 *neglecta terras fugit* refers to Astraea, but there *neglecta* makes more sense, describing the slight received by Astraea. On consideration, however, it is not impossible even that the *ignotus* wrote the text as it stands, since he can be shown quite often to employ ready-made poetic idioms with a certain rigidity (Earth would then be acting as if Jupiter did not exist, as Theseus does in Catullus).

240 haec grauior illo pestis, hic hostis deum Verg. *Aen.* 3.314–15 *nec saeuior ulla | pestis et ira deum Stygiis sese extulit undis*; Verg. *Aen.* 11.792 *haec dira . . . pestis* (of Camilla). *haec* was corrected to *hic* by Buecheler, and his correction was accepted by Leo, but the MS reading is preferable: for the attraction cf. Tac. *Hist.* 2.79 (of Antiochia and Caesarea) *illa Syriae, hoc Iudaeae caput*; in Senecan tragedy cf. *Phae.* 697 *Colchide nouerca maius hoc* (sc. *Phaedra*), *maius malum est*, with Zwierlein's note ad loc.; *Med.* 547–8 *haec* (sc. *liberi*) *causa uitae est, hoc perusti pectoris curis | leuamen. LHS* 2.442.

241 templis expulit superos suis Most interpreters have recognized here a reference to Nero's destruction of Claudius' temple: Suet. *Vesp.* 9 *(refecit) Diui . . . Claudii in Coelio monte . . . a Nerone prope funditus destructum*; Suet. *Claud.* 45 states that the cult of Claudius was abolished by Nero, but this information seems to possess no historical foundation. This would not be crucial, since Octavia is the mouthpiece of a poet who relied heavily on the information provided by the historical *uulgata* on Nero (on the real reasons for the demolition of this temple cf. Nordmeyer (1892), 296). Alternatively, and more probably, the line may contain a hint at the ransacking of temples ordered by Nero for financial reasons, for which the emperor must have been accused of sacrilege (Tac. *Ann.* 15.45 *per Asiam atque Achaiam . . . simulacra numinum abripiebantur*; Suet. *Nero* 32.4 *templis compluribus dona detraxit simulacraque ex auro* *uel argento fabricata conflauit*; *ibid.* 56.1). These spoliations, however, took place in 64, after the Great Fire, two years after the events represented in the play: cf. Griffin, *Nero*, chap. xiii. *expulit* would then be a reference to the removal of the gods' gold or bronze statues, which were melted down. Or is it that impious deeds naturally drive gods away (like the impiety of humankind causing Astraea's flight at 422–4 *neglecta terras fugit . . .*; Juv. *Sat.* 6.19–20; Ov. *Met.* 1.150 *ultima caelestum terras Astraea reliquit*)? The language may owe something to Verg. *Aen.* 2.351–2 *excessere omnes adytis templisque relictis | di* (with Austin's note quoting Sophocles' *Xoanephoroi* and Macr. *Sat.* 3.9.7 for the *euocatio: loca templa sacra urbemque eorum relinquatis*; Tac. *Hist.* 5.13; Liv. 5.21.5).

243 hausit cruorem matris: et lucem uidet For this indignant and ironic use of *et*, co-ordinating two actions or states apparently irreconcilable with one another, see *infra*, ad 848. In the corpus cf. Sen. *Phoe.* 582–3 *tam ferus durum geris | saeuumque in iras pectus? et nondum imperas*; *Med.* 28–30 *spectat . . . et spectatur et curru insidens | per solita puri spatia decurrit poli?*; 135–6 *quam saepe fudi sanguinem. et nullum scelus | irata feci*; Plin. *Epist.* 3.16.9 *cuius in gremio Scribonianus occisus est et uiuis . . .?* The parallels adduced suggest that a question mark is perhaps appropriate for the sense of astonishment conveyed by these statements.

For *hausit cruorem*, compare the similar usage of πίνω in Greek tragedy (Soph. *El.* 785; *Ant.* 532; *Trach.* 1055), where, however, the drinking of the blood refers metaphorically to the action of snake's poison. *haurire cruorem* is an equivalent of *fundere*: cf. *Hf.* 636; Ov. *Met.* 7. 333; Philostr. *Vita Apoll.* 5. 33 (*Neronem*).

244 noxiam atque animam trahit For this expression cf. Ov. *Met.* 10.351 *noxia corda*; Sen. *Thy.* 1016–17 *noxiae . . . animae uagentur* (Junge (1999), 255).

245–246 tela cur frustra iacis | inuicta totiens temere regali manu? The line seems to contain a reference to events recorded by Tac. *Ann.* 14.22 for the year 60 (i.e. two years before the date of the action of the play), when thunder struck Nero's table; Cass. Dio *Hist. Rom.* 61.16.5 attributes this portent to the year 59.

Inuictus is often used in reference to gods: cf. Ov. *Fast.* 5.560 *et probat inuictas summa tenere deas*; 6.650. The sense is not problematic ('why do you hurl in vain your darts, unconquered, so many times at random, with your regal hand?'), but the interrupted, discontinuous pace of the sentence seems inelegant. *regali manu* at line-end is an idle addition, especially after *temere*, and the redundancy *frustra . . . temere* is also suspicious. A comparable pleonasm of adverbs occurs however *infra*, 274–5 *utinam falso credita* (sc. *fama*) *perdat, | frustra totiens iactata, fidem*; 669–70 *en illuxit suspecta diu | fama* (abl.) *totiens iactata dies*, but the quasi-synonymical adverbial forms depend on different participles. Perhaps ***immissa*** should replace *inuicta*.

There is an implied connection between 245–6, which object to Jupiter's casting so many thunderbolts to no purpose, and 247, asserting that Jupiter is not raising his hand against Nero: why does Jupiter waste his thunderbolts on those who do not deserve punishment, while his hand remains idle against one so guilty? The poet seems to draw on Ov. *Pont.* 3.6.27–8 *Iuppiter in multos temeraria fulmina torquet, | qui poenam culpa non meruere pati. temere*, in this case, would mean, 'at random', targeting the innocent as well as the guilty. I owe this point to RJT. Cf. also Bruckner (1976), 158, n. 19.

247 in tam nocentem dextra cur cessat tua? For other indignant appeals to Jupiter to blast the earth with thunderbolts cf. also Ov. *Met.* 2.279–80 *quid o tua fulmina cessant, | summe deum?* (perhaps a source for this passage, considering also the rare *fulmina cessant*, picked up by 247 *dextra cur cessat tua?*); cf. also *Phae.* 680–1 *cur dextra, diuum rector atque hominum, uacat | tua*; *Phoe.* 91–2 *dextra quid cessas iners | exigere poenas?*; *Il. Lat.* 39 *cur o tua dextera cessat?*; Claud. *Rapt. Proserp.* 2.250 *cur non torsisti . . . in nos tela pater?*. Ladek (1909, 195) quoted Soph. *El.* 823 ποῦ ποτε κεραυνοὶ Διός.

249 Nero insitiuus, Domitio genitus patre Lipsius' *insitiuus* replaces the variously corrupt readings found in the paradosis (*insidiuo, nisi diuo*). One should perhaps also mention Scaliger's earlier *genere insitiuo*, which must have set Lipsius on the right track. Scaliger found fault with the sequence of two proper names, *Nero* and *Domitius*, but *Nero* is here a collective designation of the adopting family, the *Claudii*, and should be taken as 'a pretended Nero'. *Insitiuus*, for 'assuming a false identity in a fraudulent manner', is supported by Cic. *Pro Sest.* 101 *cumque insitiuum Gracchum* (sc. *Equitium*) . . . *censu prohibuisset*; cf. also Phaed. *Fab.* 3.3; Sen. *Contr.* 2.1.21; a variant form is *subditiuus*: Plaut. *Amph.* 497 *Amphitruo subditiuos eccum exit foras*; Sen. *Oed.* 802. The abusive *insitus* is paired with *adoptiuus* in Tac. *Ann.* 13.14.3, where Agrippina gives vent to her anger against Nero, *quod insitus et adoptiuus per iniurias matris exerceret* (sc. *imperium*). *Nero* was a *cognomen* of the Claudii Drusi, by this time used both as *praenomen* and as *cognomen*: the emperor Nero was officially designated in inscriptions as *Ti. Claudius Nero Caesar* and *Nero Claudius Caesar Drusus Germanicus*. For an example of *Nero* used as a surname designating the whole family cf. Tac. *Ann.* 1.28.6 *denique pro Neronibus . . . imperium populi Romani capessent?*

Reference to the Domitii, Nero's own original family, is intended to convey a sneer, as the Domitii, and Nero's father, in particular, had a tarnished and infamous record. In similar fashion, *Domitius* is used as an insulting form of address in the episode of the encounter between Britannicus and his adoptive brother: cf. Tac. *Ann.* 12.41.6 *obuii inter se Nero Britannicum nomine, ille Domitium salutauere*; Suet. *Nero* 7 *Britannicum fratrem, quod se post adoptionem Ahenobarbum ex consuetudine salutasset, ut subditiuum apud patrem arguere conatus est*; *ibid.* 41. In Pliny the Elder, the emperor is repeatedly referred to as *Nero Domitius*, a name of hybrid form, probably derogatory: cf. Kragelund (1998), 166 n. 44.

251 nomen Augustum inquinat *Augustus* can be used adjectivally. On *nomen Augustum* for 'the title of emperor' cf. *TLL* ii, s.v. *Augustus*, 1391.5.30, e.g. Ov. *Fast.* 5.567 *Augusto praetextum nomine templum*; Tac. *Ann.* 1.8.1 *in . . . nomen . . . Augustum adsumebatur.*

252 indignus ille . . . est thalamis tuis Cf. Luc. *Bell. Ciu.* 8.95 *O thalamis indigne meis.*

253 sed cede fatis atque fortunae tuae Cf. Verg. *Aen.* 6.95 *tu ne cede fatis, sed contra audentior ito*; Luc. *Bell. Ciu.* 8.575.

255–256 forsitan uindex deus | existet aliquis, laetus et ueniet dies Older commentators (cf. Giancotti 1954, 46–9) recognized here a prophecy *post eventum* of Vindex' uprising in 68. While the wish that an avenger may come in due course to right the wrongs suffered by the innocent has many parallels (Liv. 3.38.2 *nec uindex quisquam existit aut futurus uidetur*; parallels on the prophetic motif 'a day will come' are collected in Junge 1999, 240–1), contemporary readers of the play would have thought easily of Julius Vindex here: cf. the story of the dagger in Tac. *Ann.* 15.74.2 *pugionem . . . sacrauit inscripsitque Ioui Vindici: in praesens haud animaduersum, post arma Iulii Vindicis ad auspicium et praesagium futurae ultionis trahebatur*; Suet. *Nero* 45.2. As Helm acutely notes (1934, 299), Octavia was not to benefit from Vindex' insurrection, and Vindex was not even remotely in sight in 62.

For the expression *uindex deus* cf. Ov. *Met.* 14.750 *deus ultor.*

257–259 graui deorum nostra iam pridem domus | urgetur ira, prima quam pressit Venus | furore miserae dura genetricis meae In answer to the nurse's prayer that a god may bring relief to Octavia from her sufferings, the heroine retorts that her family has long been an object of persecution by the gods, since Venus was moved to indignation by Messalina's erotic frenzy. *Octavia* is the only source in which Messalina is given the standing of a tragic character, but it should not be taken as an indication that the poet wrote before the historical *vulgata* had established itself: this is an instance of that mythologization of history which is apparent throughout the play (on which cf. Schmidt 1985, 1421). For *deorum . . . iam pridem . . . urgetur ira* cf. Verg. *Aen.* 2.647 *iam pridem inuisus diuis.*

On first impression, it is hard to decide whether *furore* should be tied to *pressit* ('for a long time Venus has proved hostile to us through my mother's madness': so also Chaumartin, Liberman) or to *dura* (so Ballaira, 'divenuta crudele per la follia della mia povera madre', Viansino). If the former is true, *dura* has almost the force of an interjection (almost *furore miserae – dura – genetricis meae*), and Venus is presented as the divine agent responsible for Messalina's fall. Venus, by inspiring Messalina with an erotic frenzy, set in motion a process ultimately leading to the ruin of the entire Claudian family. Yet no reason is given to motivate Venus' enmity against the Claudians, and there is a case for understanding *furore . . . dura* 'made harsh to us by my mother's *furor*', which ultimately puts the blame on Messalina. The author may have thought of the story of Phaedra (cf. Ov. *Her.* 4.53–4 *forsitan hunc generis fato reddamus amorem | et Venus e tota gente tributa petat*; Sen. *Phae.* 113 *fatale miserae matris agnosco malum*), where, at least in some versions, the anger of Venus is motivated by the goddess's desire to have satisfaction on Phoebus for revealing her affair with Mars. Even Aphrodite in Eur. *Hipp.* is spurred to action by Hippolytus' refusal to acknowledge the goddess's prerogatives. Like Phaedra in Euripides (cf. *Hipp.* 28, 39 κέντροις ἔρωτος ἡ τάλαιν' ἀπόλλυται, 47–8), Messalina is depicted as a hapless victim (*misera*), a toy of the goddess's whim. On the relationship between guilt and divine vengeance in Greek culture, especially in Greek tragedy, cf. R. Parker, *Miasma* (Oxford, 1983), 235–56.

On Ballaira's interpretation of *furore . . . dura*, Messalina's sexual intemperance raises the goddess's ire and Venus fatally fools her into marrying Silius, whereby she becomes guilty of treason against the emperor. *prima* must be understood as 'first amongst the various gods' who in succession set their hearts on bringing down Claudius and his family. The difficulty in this interpretation is that Messalina incurs Venus' displeasure for an excess of lust, not an obvious offence against the goddess of love. On the contrary, in Enn. *Euhem.* 134–8 Warm., Venus is the inventor of prostitution, *ne sola praeter alias mulieres inpudica et uirorum adpetens uideretur*. In Ov. *Met.* 10.238–40, prostitution is the punishment inflicted upon the Propoetides for refusing to acknowledge Venus' divinity. In fact the goddess's sphere extends to all forms of love, including illegitimate and extra-conjugal, which makes her unlikely to have resented Messalina's intemperance.

For this use of *premo* in conjunction with *ira*, meaning 'to persecute' cf. Ov. *Trist.* 1.5.78 *me Iouis ira premit*; Sen. *H.O.* 441 *caelestis ira quos premit miseros facit.* For *furor* with reference to Messalina cf. Tac. *Ann.* 11.12 *Messalina nouo et furori proximo amore distinebatur.*

Siegmund (1911), 30 defends the reading of some later MSS *dira*, but the jingle *ira . . . miserae dira* is undesirable (despite 661 *diri . . . uiri*; *Troad.* 301–2 *tumide . . . timide*; *Phoe.* 340–1 *petite . . . metite*), and the adjective *dirus* is inappropriate in Octavia's mouth with reference to a goddess.

The sequence of a noun with two adjectives (*miserae . . . genetricis meae*), one a possessive, is uncommon in Augustan poetry, where it is sometimes taken to reveal Ennian reminiscences (cf. Conington, ad Verg. *Georg.* 2.147), but cf. *infra* 266–7 *infelix parens . . . nostra*; 613 *noster infelix amor*; also Ov. *Her.* 4.77 *tuus iste rigor*; 10.101–2 *tua . . . ardua dextera*; *Met.* 8.61 *haec . . . mea moenia*; *Trist.* 1.9.36 *haec mea dicta*. Cortius has a note on nouns with two adjectives ad Luc. *Bell. Ciu.* 2.207–8 *intrepidus tanti sedit securus ab alto | spectator sceleris*. In Seneca cf. *Oed.* 20–1 *diros toros . . . impia incestos face*. In Greek tragedy: cf. Diggle, *Studies on the Text of Euripides* (Oxford, 1981), 48–9; *Euripidea: Collected Essays* (Oxford, 1994) 96–7. *meae* is unnecessary to the sense, and it appears to be a pure filler *metri gratia*.

260 quae nupta demens nupsit incesta face Chains of successive clauses linked by relative pronouns are frequent in *Octavia* and may be taken as an indication of the poet's modest compositional abilities (cf. ad 111–13; 126–8).

For the *annominatio nupta . . . nupsit* cf. Verg. *Aen.* 2.160 *seruataque serues*; Sen. *Agam.* 575 *fracta frangit*, 869 *uicimus uicti*; Petr. *Sat.* 89.55 *peritura Troia perdidit primum deos.* In Eur. *Andr.* 1186 ff. Peleus deplores in similar terms the ruinous *gamos* which has destroyed his house. It has been argued that the alleged marriage of Silius and Messalina was in fact the celebration of a Bacchic rite. The version of Messalina's story accepted here corresponds to Tac. *Ann.* 11.12; 11.31.

261 oblita nostri, coniugis legum immemor The original reading of *A (GPCS), nostri coniugis,* must have appeared absurd on a hasty reading, or with faulty punctuation, and the competing readings found in some *recc.* (*iusti, ueri*: 'fortasse recte' in Giardina's apparatus) yield a superficially preferable sense. The other variant, *coniugii* (*VM*[2] *KQOx*, from *coniugium*), is metrically acceptable only in contracted form (cf. *Agam.* 155 *at te reflectat coniugi nomen sacrum*, and, for the *cumulus, Phoe.* 296 quoted *infra*). *Octavia* has instances of contracted genitives at 483, 601, 790 *imperi*; 152 *ingeni*; 38 *Claudi*; 302 *Lucreti*; the full form *consilii* is required by metre at 447: cf. Flinck (1919), 87. Either form is in itself acceptable, but *coniugis* has better manuscript support. *coniugis legum immemor* would provide one further example of dicolon asyndeticum, as in 103. *Cumuli* of this kind are a common archaizing feature in Senecan tragedy; cf. *Phoe.* 296 *auidis cruoris, imperi, armorum, doli* (imitating a stylistic turn of early Roman tragedy: cf. e.g. Acc. *Scaen.* 94 R[2] *miseret lacrimarum luctuum orbitudinis*; see *supra* ad 176).

262–263 illi . . . ultrix Erinys uenit ad Stygios toros *illo* 'thither', the MS reading, is not wholly unsatisfactory, but has been ousted from the text for a long time (the last edition in which it figures is Peiper's, 1867), not because this adverb is rare in Senecan tragedy (where the ratio *illuc/illo* is 13:3, with the latter form occurring in *Hf.* 864; *Thy.* 637, 712), but because there is no appropriate referent in the preceding lines: Octavia simply says that her foolish mother re-married while still Claudius' wife, oblivious of her children, heedless of husband and laws: no mention has been made of the place where this happened, or of the circumstances, in such a way as to justify the presence of a subsequent 'thither', and the Fury presiding over the wretched ceremony has no obvious place to go to. Perhaps more important, the presence of a second constituent indicating motion at the end of the sentence, 263 *ad Stygios toros*, also militates against *illo.* One way to rescue this pleonastic manner of expression ('thither . . . to the accursed wedding couches') would be to read it as an instance of appositional word-order, with *illo* proleptic of a noun not yet uttered by the speaker. This mode of expression is acceptable in comedy and satire, where it is aptly seen as a feature of the spoken language: the speaker progressively clarifies his thought in the course of his utterance ('thither she came, that is to the accursed marriage': cf. Plaut. *Rud.* 41 *is eam huc Cyrenas leno* *adduxit uirginem*; *Stich.* 185 *ueni illo ad cenam*; further examples in Rosén, *Latine loqui*, 151–57). Yet this is an unlikely trait in the Latin of the Senecan corpus. Colloquial features have some currency in the more high-flown registers of literature, but only as devices intended to enhance the expressiveness or the pathos of a given passage. On this interpretation, *illo, ad Stygios toros* could stand as the written representation of a *crescendo* of indignation, but as the text stands, *illo* is too distant from *ad Stygios toros* to serve this purpose effectively.

illos, in Zwierlein's text, and accepted by Liberman, is intended to be tied to *ad Stygios toros* in the following line: 'to those funereal couches'. The enclosing word-order thus introduced into the text is commonly found in poetry, where an adjective and its substantive are frequently disjoined, with the former at the beginning of the clause or syntactical unit, and the latter at its end. The present appears, however, as a special case: the following observations are intended to test the linguistic plausibility of the hyperbaton *illos . . . ad Stygios toros.*[7]

Hyperbata of closely linked words across even several lines are not unparalleled in the play, especially in the more diffuse style of iambics, and Zwierlein is able to adduce numerous examples of hyperbata in support of his conjecture from the Senecan corpus alone. The three most representative instances from *Octavia* are:

(1) *Oct.* 311–312· *cum Tyrrhenum rate ferali | princeps captam fraude parentem | misit in aequor*

(2) *Oct.* 661–2 *scelerum diri, miseranda, uiri | potes hoc demens sperare memor?*

(3) *Oct.* 703–6 *et ipse lateri iunctus atque haerens tuo | sublimis inter ciuium laeta omina | incessit habitu atque ore laetitiam gerens | princeps superbo*

There appears to have been in Latin no intrinsic grammatical rule exerting restrictions on the order of constituents. Yet a survey of the cases of disjunction in a large corpus of Latin poetry (see APPENDIX C) shows that disjunction of demonstratives is more limited in domain than Zwierlein's *illos . . . ad toros*, and less common when the demonstrative is unemphatic, or in a case other than subject or direct object. This restriction may be related to the nature of these adjectives, which are semantically the least autonomous elements in the class of adjectives.

illos is a semantically less significant element than (2) *scelerum diri . . . uiri.* Hyperbaton creates a suspension of the sense, and the reader or listener must wait for the end of the sentence to grasp its full meaning. In (2), however, the word group *scelerum diri uiri*, even before it is finally attached to the word on

[7] On anastrophe of prepositions cf. *LHS* 2.216–7; examples in Marouzeau, *L'ordre des mots en latin. Volume complémentaire* (Paris, 1953), 67–9; Maurach, *EP*, 93–4; J. H. W. Penney, in *ALLP*, esp. 263–7; T. E. V. Pearce, *CQ* 16 (1966), 140 ff., 298 ff.; J. N. Adams, *PCPhS* n.s. 17 (1971), 1–16; C. M. Calcante, *Lingua e stile* 26 (1991), 539–59; cf. *ALLP*, 16–18; 97–133. For Greek cf. Devine-Stephens, *DS*, 78–81.

which it depends, conveys some information: the reader knows that something is going to be said about a cruel man who has acted criminally; *illos* has no clear referent to be attached to. Only superficially similar to *illos . . . ad toros* is (1), where *Tyrrhenum* remains unconstrued for over one and a half lines until *in aequor* solves the ambiguity. Yet *Tyrrhenum* has a high chance, in Latin, of being a sea-epithet, especially coming next to a word such as *rate*, and thus prepares for what will come later in a more effective way. (3) should perhaps more readily be interpreted as a case of appositional word-order: the sense is not suspended; *ipse* designates a person familiar to both speakers and implicitly present throughout the previous conversation; the nurse's sentence might end at *incessit* with no detriment to the sense.[8]

Hyperbaton, by virtue of the accompanying syntactic suspension, naturally throws the words involved into some relief, and one would expect sentence initial position to be connected with focus or contrastive emphasis, in *illos . . . ad toros*. A survey of the data, however, shows that it is impossible to establish a univocal connection between hyperbaton of demonstratives (whether pre- or post-nominal) and their function as pragmatic constituents (cf. APPENDIX C p. 413). In addition, focus is not what the context requires, because the new element is the presence of the inauspicious and malevolent Fury, casting her curse on the marriage.

On the available evidence, *illos soluta crine succincta anguibus ultrix Erinys uenit ad Stygios toros* is unacceptable even in the highly dislocated word order of classical Latin poetry, not to mention the rarity of the combination of a noun and two adjectives. A Latin audience was obviously prepared to exercise its capacity for interpretive understanding quite considerably while listening to a reciter reading out his poems, and an able performer would help his hearers to make sense of dislocated word-order sequences by an appropriate use of intonation and pausing. But these could not help with such suspended syntactic constructions, and comprehension may be the reason why anastrophe is usually restricted to word-groups of adjacent words.

In the *Octavia* passage the new element, underlined by the rhetorical climax, is provided by mention of the infernal deity presiding over the marriage: 'there came, with dishevelled hair, snake-girt, an avenging Fury'. Positing *illos* in anastrophe makes the sequence rhetorically inept, because the reader's attention is stretched to find the complement for the suspended pronoun, and in a way bridges over the important description of the Fury. In all comparable instances of trajected *illos, hos, nostros, meos* etc. the pronoun is always assigned an important pragmatic relief, because the reader is compelled to project forward

[8] Instances of this pattern are easy to find even in Seneca: cf. *Oed.* 940–1 *quid ipsi quae tuum magna luit | scelus ruina flebili patriae dabis*, where *ipsi* is separated from its noun by seven words inserted; *Med.* 664–7 *ipse qui praedam spoliumque iussit | aureum prima reuehi carina | ustus accenso Pelias aeno | arsit.*

in order to reach the associated element at the end of the sentence. Here the constituent 'to those weddings' is the thema, the known element, and the new element is the arrival of the terrifying Fury. Heinsius' *illi* (*Adversaria*, 504, with no supporting argument), independently revived by Bothe ('malim *illi* . . . id est *illius*'), remains, in my view, by far the preferable emendation. It gives the sentence the required cohesion, while not disrupting the communicative demands of the passage, with its focus on the Fury. Messalina is the thema, the element assumed to be known to the hearers, because Octavia has been speaking of her behaviour: 'to her [as a consequence of her shameful actions] a Fury came, dishevelled, with a girdle of snakes'.

Examples of *uenire* with a dative of person are numerous in Augustan poetry: see G. Landgraf *ALL* viii (1893), esp. 42, 69, 74; on Greek constructions in Latin see R. G. G. Coleman, *TPhS* 1975 (1977), 101–56. For double locative expressions, indicating the person affected by the movement and the place where one arrives cf. Prop. 2.34a.7 *in hospitium Menelao uenit adulter*; 1.14.11 *mihi . . . ueniunt sub tecta*; 4.3.5; Tib. 1.3.65; Ov. *Pont.* 4.6.1; in prose, Cic. *Att.* 8.9.1 *cui libenter me ad pedes abiecissem*. The emphatic initial position of the dative at the beginning of the line is a feature of all these passages (also Verg. *Georg.* 3.565 *illi compositis spirauit crinibus aura*). The author of *Octavia* is therefore imitating a recurrent stylistic construction of classical Latin poetry, often deemed to be a Grecism (cf. e.g. Eur. *Hec.* 448–9 τῶι δουλόσυνος πρὸς οἶ- | κον κτηθεῖσ' ἀφίξομαι;). *illi* is also strengthened by comparison with Ov. *Her.* 21.157, where Cydippe relates the sudden onset of illness on every eve of her marriage ceremony: *ter mihi iam ueniens positas Hymenaeus ad aras* | *fugit*. This parallels exactly *illi . . . ultrix Erinys uenit ad Stygios toros*, and is also very close in the situation described (an ill-omened marriage). A less certain instance of the same construction is in Ov. *Her.* 21.45–6 *et mihi coniugii tempus crudelis ad ipsum* | *Persephone nostras pulsat acerba fores*, which is simply an ethic dative, and should probably be corrected in *ei mihi*. Coming near an anacoluthon is Verg. *Aen.* 1.254–6 *olli subridens . . . libauit oscula natae*. This seems part of a more generally frequent dative of disadvantage, redundant alongside another local specification, as in Verg. *Aen.* 12.537 *olli per galeam fixo stetit hasta cerebro*. *illi* also yields a more dramatic image, with the picture of a dishevelled and snake-girt Fury standing by an unaware Messalina in the bliss of marriage. A similar scene occurs in Sen. *Troad.* 1132–4 *praecedunt faces* | *et pronuba illi Tyndaris maestum caput* | *demissa*. Funereal marriages, presided over by inauspicious gods, are a topos (on which cf. also note ad 23–4: in Latin poetry cf. Ov. *Her.* 2.117–20 *pronuba Tisiphone thalamis ululauit in illis* | *et cecinit maestum deuia carmen auis.* | *adfuit Allecto breuibus torquata colubris,* | *suntque sepulcrali lumina mota face*; Prop. 4.3.13–14 *quae mihi deductae fax omen praetulit, illa* | *traxit ab euerso lumina nigra rogo*).

262 soluta crine The phrase *(re)soluta crinem/comam/capillos* is recurrent in poetic texts with the retained or Greek accusative (a rich collection of instances in G. Landgraf, *ALL* 10 (1898), 209–28, esp. 222: cf. Verg. *Aen.* 11.35 *crinem de more solutae*; Ov. *Fast.* 4.854 *maestas Acca soluta comas*, where it is a sign of mourning). A sequence of past participles with similar descriptive accusatives is in Ov. *Met.* 7.182–3 *uestes induta recinctas, | nuda pedem, nudos umeris infusa capillos*. The accusative *crinem* is of course impossible here, because the final syllable would be lengthened 'by position' before *succincta*, but I have been unable to find parallels for *soluta* (nom.) *crine* (none in *TLL* s.v. 1204.41–53). Apparently the Greek accusative took such a firm hold as to replace the native Latin construction, at least in poetry (cf., however, Stat. *Theb.* 7.336–7 *crine genisque | caerulus*). Since ablative absolutes of the form *resolutis comis / crinibus* are, on the contrary, commonly found, possibly *soluta* could be corrected, with Liberman, to *soluto*, found in some *recc.*, which is metrically equivalent in this position. Atta, *Epigr.* 1 Courtn. has *fusus resoluta crine capillus*, where *crinis* is feminine; Hor. *Carm.* 2.5.23–4 *solutis | crinibus*; Ov. *Fast.* 3.257 *resoluto crine*; Sen. *Hf.* 202 *sed maesta uenit crine soluto*; Luc. *Bell. Ciu.* 2.23; 7.38. On consideration, however, I have decided to retain the transmitted reading: there is no compelling linguistic reason to alter the paradosis, and the parallelism of *succincta* and *soluta* may be intentional.

262 succincta anguibus *succingo* is often used in reference to gowns and garments: cf. Verg. *Aen.* 6.555 *palla succincta cruenta*; Furies are normally represented with snakes in their hair or worn around their arms as bracelets (Ov. *Her.* 2.119 *breuibus torquata colubris*) rather than around the waist as a girdle; cf. however Cat. *Carm.* 64.258 *pars sese tortis serpentibus incingebant*, and Ov. *Met.* 4.483 *tortoque incingitur angue*; perhaps also Enn. *Scaen.* 28 R^2 *caeruleae incinctae igni incedunt*, where Colonna proposed *caeruleo incinctae angui*; in Greek cf. Aesch. *Cho.* 1049–50; other references can be found in Wüst, *RE* Suppl. viii 125.29–53; *LIMC* III.1, s.v. *Erinys*, 841. These parallels seem to prove that *succingo* is not the idiomatic verb for 'girdle' (cf. by contrast *succincta canibus*, of Scylla in Ov. *Met.* 13.732 *illa feris atram canibus succingitur aluum* and Sen. *Med.* 351 *rabidos utero succincta canes*, both referring to the hybrid nature of the monster, uniting in the same body a woman's torso and animalesque limbs underneath). The horrid picture of a dishevelled, snake-girt Fury parallels the witches of Hor. *Sat.* 1.8.23–4 *nigra succinctam uadere palla | Canidiam, pedibus nudis passoque capillo*; Ov. *Met.* 7.182–3 (of Medea).

263 uenit ad . . . toros For *uenire ad toros* meaning 'to attend one's wedding' cf. *infra* 708 *quorum toros celebrasse caelestes ferunt*. The line also recalls 23–4 *illa illa meis tristis Erinys | thalamis Stygios praetulit ignes*. Zwierlein (*KK*, ad loc.) observes that the word *torus* is not used by Seneca to indicate the marriage ceremony, but I doubt if this is very significant, since the passage from 'married state', 'conjugal union' (the usual sense of *tori* in Senecan tragedy) to 'marriage ceremony' is very natural: cf. Ov. *Met.* 7.91 *promisitque torum*; Val. Fl. *Arg.* 5.460 *distulerant . . . bella toros*.

264 raptasque thalamis sanguine extinxit faces Cf. also *infra* 608–9 *sanguine extinxi meo | nec odia nati*; 830. The hyperbole *sanguine exstinguere*, absent in the authentic plays, occurs in the corpus at *H.O.* 339 *meo iugales sanguine extinguam faces*; elsewhere cf. Ov. *Met.* 1.201 *sanguine Caesareo Romanum exstinguere nomen*; 15.778 *(neue) caede sacerdotis flammas exstinguite Vestae*; Petr. *Sat.* 139.4 *numquam finies hunc ignem* (sc. *amoris mei*) *nisi sanguine extinxeris*, which plays upon the obscene double sense of *sanguis*.

265–266 incendit ira principis pectus truci | caedem in nefandam The metaphorical use of *incendo* is common: cf. *TLL* vii, s.v. *incendo*, 869.17–37.

For *in/ad caedem* with verbs of movement cf. *TLL* iii, s.v. *caedes*, 53.1–10. Here the primary notion is final (cf. also 465 *armat . . . in caedem meam*); a fondness for nominal expressions in the place of an expanded subordinate clause is characteristically a Tacitean feature (cf. Tac. *Hist.* 1.43 *in caedem eius ardentis;* 4.50; *Ann.* 15.68 *percunctanti Neroni cur in caedem suam conspirauisset*), but the construction is not rare enough to suggest a connection (cf. e.g. Hor. *Carm.* 1.8.16 (*ne*) *cultus in caedem et Lycias proriperet cateruas*).

266–267 cecidit infelix parens, | heu, nostra ferro Cf. Ov. *Met.* 13.498 *cecidisti et femina ferro*; Val. Fl. *Arg.* 4.122–3 *armis | concidit infelix*.

268–269 coniugem traxit suum | natumque ad umbras On *traho* 'to drag off' to the realms of death cf. Hor. *Serm.* 2.5.109–10 *sed me | imperiosa trahit Proserpina*; *CE* 1950.8 *iam trahor in tenebras*; *CIL* 8.21179.4. See also ad 182 *me dira miseri fata germani trahunt.*

269 prodidit lapsam domum This is an instance of the metaphorical sense of *prodo* for 'to expose to danger', 'to ruin', from which descends the extensional 'to betray' (close in sense are the phrases *porro dare, in praeceps dare*). Messalina could hardly be said to have 'betrayed' her family, which implies her acting on purpose to harm her children (so Miller, Bruckner (1976), 93). The sense must be '(unwittingly) abandoned, exposed to danger': cf. *TLL* x.2, 1624.15–31; Enn. *Ann.* 413 Sk. *non in sperando cupide rem prodere summam*; Ter. *Ad.* 692 *prodidisti et te et illam miseram et gnatum*; Cic. *Verr.* 2.4.39 (*ut Eriphyle*) *pulchritudine eius* (sc. *monilis*) *incensa salutem uiri proderet*; Luc. *Bell. Ciu.* 8.511 *sollicitat nostrum quem nondum prodidit orbem*. In *Oct.* this sense is probably felt as archaic. The variant reading *perdidit*, found in some *recc.*, and advocated by Lipsius and Liberman, is a clear banalization. *lapsam* may suggest that the etymological sense of *prodo* 'to upset', 'to cause something to capsize headlong', is still felt, almost 'impulit ut laberetur' (cf. *OLD*, 'to thrust forward, or out (from inward)': Lucr. *D.R.N.* 6.606–7 *rerumque sequatur prodita summa | funditus*, collapsing inside; Sen. *Oed.* 143–4 (*sonipes dominum*) *prono | prodidit armo. lapsam* takes on a proleptic value (cf. *LHS* 2.414), anticipating what is envisaged as the result of the action expressed by the main verb, on the pattern of *submersas obrue puppes*: cf. *Hf.* 367 *altus sepultas obruet gentes cinis.*

The action of a woman driven by passion is often seen as the incendiary force causing royal houses to collapse (cf. *H.O.* 221 *tibi cuncta domus concidit uni*; 884 *quid domum impulsam trahis?*), and the metaphorical field 'the collapsing house' is widespread: cf. Cic. *Phil.* 2.51 *labentem et prope cadentem rem publicam*; Verg. *Aen.* 12.59 *in te omnis domus inclinata recumbit*; Plin. *Epist.* 7.19.8 *ac mihi domus ipsa nutare conuolsaque sedibus suis ruitura supra uidetur*; other parallels in Langen ad Val. Fl. *Arg.* 4.569.

270 renouare luctus parce cum fletu pios This form of the periphrastic imperative (*parce renouare* for *noli renouare*) does not occur elsewhere in Senecan tragedy but is extremely common in literary Latin (cf. *TLL* x., s.v. *parco*, 1.332.19–56; cf. Verg. *Aen.* 3.41–2 *iam parce sepulto, | parce pias scelerare manus*, where *parce* has a different sense in the two successive cola, 'spare' and 'refrain'), mostly in poetry: see K-S 2.206.

cum fletu seems open to objection, since instances of instrumental *cum* are rarely found and mainly in early Latin (cf. *LHS* 2.259–60; Cat. *Carm.* 98.3–4 *ista cum lingua . . . possis | culos . . . lingere*, with Kroll's note; Acc. *Scaen.* 445 R^2. *cum corona clarum conestat caput*); other parallels from Augustan and Neronian poetry are given in *TLL* iv. s.v. *cum* col. 1369 (e.g. Val. Fl. *Arg.* 6.532 *frontem cum cornibus auxit*).

I had considered at first writing *iam* (already in ***N***): the confusion is easily accountable, and *fletus* for 'laments' is a common metonymy (cf. *supra*, 75); *iam*, like *modo*, is often used with an imperative (cf. *TLL* vii.1, s.v. *iam*, 104.6–75; in the Senecan corpus cf. *H.O.* 1507 *parce iam lacrimis*; 982 *parce iam mater precor*). *parce iam* followed by an infinitive is less easy to parallel (*CE* 1198.11–12 *manes | parcite iam luctu sollicitare meos*, where *iam* means 'at last'; more frequent is *desine*; cf. Ter. *Haut.* 879 *ohe, iam desine deos, uxor, gratulando obtundere*; Prop. 1.15.25–6 *desine iam reuocare tuis periuria uerbis, | Cynthia, et oblitos parce mouere deos*).

We must therefore retain *cum fletu* as an instance of 'accompanying circumstances', 'amidst shedding of tears' (= *renouare luctus et fletus*) as in Cic. *Mur.* 40 *honestissimo ordini cum splendore fructus quoque iucunditatis est restitutus*; Caes. *Bell. Gall.* 1.20.1 *Diuiciacus multis cum lacrimis Caesarem complexus obsecrare coepit*; Verg. *Aen.* 3.176–7 *tendoque supinas | ad caelum cum uoce manus*; 3.598–9 *sese ad litora praeceps | cum fletu precibusque tulit*; 12.952 *uitaque cum gemitu fugit indignata sub umbras*; cf. K-S 2.1.409, 509; *LHS* 2.116; Löfstedt, *Syntactica*, 1.276.

271 manes parentis neue sollicita tuae For the belief that the dead are disturbed by excessive mourning cf. Ov. *Trist.* 3.11.32 *parce precor manes sollicitare meos*; *CE* 965.7–8 *quid lacrumis opus est . . . extinctos cineres sollicitare meos?* *CE* 995b.7–8 *parce . . . fata . . . maerendo sollicitare mea*; *CE* 1198.11–12 *manes | parcite iam luctu sollicitare meos*; *CE* 1212.13–14 *desistat humatam | ulterius lachrumis sollicitasse suis*; *CE* 1468.2 *parce pios Manes sollicitare manu*.

The enclitic *-ue* is used because the previous clause is positive in form, but negative in sense. In fact, *-ue* is common even when the previous clause is positive (cf. Ov. *Met.* 13.747–8 *refer . . . neue tui causam tege . . . doloris*), alongside the more 'regular' alternative *nec* (cf. e.g. Ov. *Fasti* 6.379–80 *tu modo quae desunt fruges superesse putentur | effice nec sedes desere Vesta tuas*).

An imperative marks the end of the scene, as in 588 *desiste tandem*; 761 *superos adora*; 875 *iube*. In the latter two cases, however, the order signals actions which will be carried out elsewhere (the marriage, the supplication to the gods, the deportation of Octavia), whereas it is harder to detect any such implication in the Nurse's advice not to disturb Messalina's ghost. There is no exit to signal the end of the scene. Octavia and the Nurse disappear with no reason, however conventional, being given for their departure. More acceptable traditional motivations for scene-endings are provided at 592 (where preparations for the marriage can be reckoned as the reason for the exit of Nero and Seneca); 645 (Agrippina's ghost departs, overcome by grief); 760 (Poppaea summons her nurse to perform a propitiatory sacrifice). At 876 no reason is given for Nero's disappearance, but the whole scene is problematic, and a change of setting may be assumed: see ad loc. On the other hand, entrances are no better motivated at 377, 646, 690, 762, 820, 877; they are announced or in some way motivated at 72, 273, 435, 593, 778.

273 The chorus comments on the spreading of the rumours concerning Nero's divorce. The song also provides an illustration of popular favour for Octavia, of which the *Nutrix* had spoken at 183. The singers do not identify themselves explicitly, and we can only describe them as citizens who have remained loyal to Claudius and his family. *Thy.* and *Oed.* are the other two plays in the corpus whose odes are explicitly sung by citizens.

A large part of the ode is devoted to a narrative of Agrippina's death, following a constant feature of this play, according to which historical exempla have a function analogous to mythical antecedents in Greek tragedy. Anapaestic sections of purely narrative character are not found in fifth-century tragedy – but cf. the tragic text where the epiphany of the dead Achilles is described to Deidameia (*TrGF adesp.* 680a; Eitrem-Amundsen (1955), 1–87).

The pessimism expressed by the ode with regard to the lot of Octavia contrasts so strongly with the optimism of the *Nutrix* (cf. *supra* 186; 216) as to give the impression that events have progressed or that some time has elapsed between the end of the first act (272) and the beginning of the ode. In Senecan drama, a chorus can relate events which have occurred off-stage after the end of the act immediately preceding, but before the time when the song is performed. This is so in *Thy.* 336–8 *tandem regia nobilis . . . fratrum composuit minas*, where the chorus talks of the news of the apparent reconciliation between the two rival brothers, which must have been made public after 335, the end of the private dialogue between Atreus and his *Satelles*. In Greek tragedy this seems to be only the task of messengers, and in any case only after a convenient, however conventional, time lapse, usually provided by an intervening choral ode.

The chorus forecasts the *catastrophe* of the play, the divorce of Octavia. In Greek tragic poetry, a chorus often anticipates, by way of obscure forebodings, a mishap which will eventually happen: cf. Aesch. *Agam.* 975–82 (fears preceding Agamemnon's death); Soph. *Trach.* 849–50 (premonition of Deianeira's suicide); *Ai.* 635; Eur. *Med.* 1251 (the chorus foretells the slaughter of the children): cf. Di Benedetto–Medda, 273.

273 Quae fama modo uenit ad aures For the wording cf. *Agam.* 397 *felix ad aures nuntius uenit meas*; Ov. *Met.* 5.256 *fama noui fontis nostras peruenit ad aures* (also giving the reason for a journey: *is mihi causa uiae*, 258), with the parallels given by Bömer; *Fasti* 3.361–2 *haec quoque . . . nostras peruenit ad aures* | *fama.*

This is the only passage in the Senecan corpus where the entrance of the chorus comes near to being motivated within the dramatic frame of the story (cf. Zwierlein 1966, 73), and this is done, in my view, by alluding to the commonplace of Greek *parodoi*, whereby choruses profess to have entered on hearing a voice, or rumour. A close parallel for *quae fama* is provided by the *parodos* of Eur. *Hipp.* 130 φάτις ἦλθε δεσποίνας, where the chorus gives as a reason for its arrival on stage the news of Phaedra's illness; cf. also Soph. *O.T.* 151; *Ai.* 143. The chorus has entered because of hearing a κληδών in Eur. *I.T.* 136; *El.* 167; Soph. *O.C.* 133–5 (this dramatic pattern is discussed in L. Battezzato, *Il monologo nel teatro di Euripide* (Pisa, 1995), 84 n. 20). In other Greek instances, choruses come on stage because they have heard a voice, or a lament: cf. Soph. *El.* 122; Eur. *Med.* 131; *Phoe.* 301 (the last three cases suit the Nurse's arrival on stage better, for hearing a voice rather than a rumour or some news). Sutton (1983, 48) is the only other critic who describes the chorus as a parodos, giving Eur. *Hel.* as a parallel: they come to console because they have heard of her sufferings. In fact this consolatory element is not present in *Octavia*, where the chorus does not interact with the protagonist. The chorus has only heard a piece of bad news.

modo retains the original final long *o*, which is by this date an artificial prosody (this is the only case in the Senecan corpus; elsewhere in *Oct.* the word is measured as a pyrrhichius: cf. 205–6). The iambic scansion is found elsewhere predominantly in early dramatic poetry, in Lucretius and once in Cicero's *Aratea* (Lachmann, ad Lucr. *D.R.N.* 2.1135; Lindsay, *ELV*, 36). In Terence, the only instance of an iambic *modo* occurs in a passage in cretics, *An.* 630. It is perhaps no coincidence that the artificial scansion is deployed in an anapaestic passage, where some sort of more apparent deviation from the 'spoken' may have been envisaged.

274–275 utinam falso credita perdat, | frustra totiens iactata, fidem For *iacto* 'to spread around rumours' cf. Liv. 1.46.1 *interdum iactari uoces audiebat*; Tac. *Ann.* 11.18.5 *quae . . . incertum an falso iacta* (from *iacio*).

277–278 teneatque suos | nupta penates Claudia proles *Concordia* is a virtue of the married imperial couple, and this motif is identifiable in the legend *CONCORDIA AVGVSTA* used on the reverse of some Neronian coins (but in a type dated to 64, therefore relating to Nero and Poppaea: cf. *BMCRE* I, clxxiv; E. Sydenham, *The Coinage of Nero* (London, 1920), 116).

279 edat partu pignora pacis Cf. Verg. *Aen.* 7.660 (*quem*) *partu sub luminis edidit oras* (Hosius). The word *pignus* ('pledge'), by extension, may acquire the meaning 'children' because they are presented as the cement of a marriage (cf. Liv. 2.15; Ov. *Met.* 3.134 *pignora cara, nepotes*; 11.543; *Fasti* 3.218; Tac. *Ann.* 12.2 *proxima suis pignora*; a close parallel occurs in the recently found *SC Pisonianum*, l. 139 *tot pignora edita partu felicissumo*). In this sense, the word is often found with the specifying genitive *amoris* (Prop. 4.11.73; Ov. *Fast.* 3.775–6; Sen. *Med.* 1012; *Oed.* 1022; *Troad.* 766; Quint. 6.1.33; Verg. *Aen.* 4.328: more parallels in Junge (1999), 243–4). With *pacis* the closest parallel comes from Verg. *Aen.* 11.363 *pacis solum inuiolabile pignus* referring to Lavinia. The presence of numerous heirs is envisaged as an element of dynastic stability, leading to lasting peace.

280–281 qua tranquillus gaudeat orbis | seruetque decus Roma aeternum The emphasis on dynastic continuity as a guarantee for peace probably goes back to panegyric literature of the Flavian age. In Tac. *Hist.* 2.77 the fact that Vespasian, on his accession, had two grown sons was regarded as a guarantee for stability (cf. also Jos. *Bell. Iud.* 4.596). The civil wars which followed Nero's death had shown that this concern was at least partially justified. The legends *SPES SAECVLI, TEMPORVM FELICITAS* appear on coins to celebrate the birth of a new heir during the Antonine age: cf. Strack, *Untersuchungen*, 3.112–15; on *AETERNITAS IMPERII*, *ibidem*, 1.186; 2.64; Beaujeu, *Rel. Rom.*, I, 420. On the sovereign as a universal pacifier see Momigliano, II, 413; Nock, *Essays* I, 43, n. 81; Stier, *ANRW* II.2 (1975), 3–54.

The great emphasis placed on peace seems to disclose the attitude of a writer active after the civil wars of 68–9. The point, however, should not be pressed too much: nowhere is the horror of civil war as powerfully expressed as in Lucan, who never lived through one. The prayer that Rome's rule (*decus*) may last eternally is common in religious documents of this age: cf. Beaujeu, *Rel. Rom.* 1.141; Henzen, *Acta* 71, *uota nuncupauit . . . Aeternita[ti imperii*; Henzen, 110–111; *CIL* V, *Suppl. Italica*, 1.745. For *decus* in the extensional sense of 'power' cf. *TLL* V, 240.15–38; Tac. *Ann.* 11.16 *hortatur gentile decus magno animo capessere.*

282–285 fratris thalamos sortita tenet | maxima Iuno: | soror Augusti sociata toris | cur a patria pellitur aula? The logic of the argument deployed here is not very conclusive. The chorus recalls the analogy between Octavia and Juno set up by the *Nutrix* at 201–2, although they have not 'heard' her.

By way of parallel for *soror . . . sociata toris*, Hosius quoted Verg. *Aen.* 9.594 *germanam nuper thalamo sociatus habebat.*

286–287 sancta quid illi prodest pietas | diuusque pater, | quid uirginitas castusque pudor? The *quid/nil profuit* motif is usual in funerary poetry: cf. N.–H. ad Hor. *Carm.* 1.28.4; Courtney, ad Porc. Lic. frg. 3 and ad Corn. Sev. 13.8–9; Prop. 4.11.11–12 *quid mihi coniugium Pauli, quid currus auorum | profuit, aut famae pignora tanta meae?* Ov. *Met.* 4.192–3; 6.95–6 *nec profuit Ilion illi | Laomedonue pater*; *Fast.* 5.591–2; *Cons. Liu.* 41 *quid tibi nunc mores prosunt*; Stat. *Silu.* 5.1.154–5 *quid probitas aut casta fides, quid numina prosunt | culta deum?*

The older interpreters remarked that virginity was no virtue in a married woman (Octavia had been married to Nero since 53): 'inepte laudari uidetur uirginitas in maritata' (Raphelengius). While the virgin-motif had an obvious appeal for the tragedian, casting Octavia in the role of a chaste virgin forced to marry a brutish enemy of her house, a more compelling reason for the chorus' praises of Octavia's *uirginitas* can be suspected. The chorus might be stressing Octavia's virginal *pudor* in order to obscure the charge of sterility which historically was the official reason for her dismissal (never openly formulated in the *praetexta*), as if Octavia's failure to produce an heir were in fact her own decision, as a result of her refusal to discharge her conjugal obligations.

288–289 nos quoque nostri sumus immemores | post fata ducis The two competing interpretations of this passage pivot on *nostri*. If pronominal, it must be tied to *immemores*; if adjectival, to *ducis*. The first interpretation seems suggested by the word order. Moreover *ducis* is clear even with no accompanying adjective.

quoque seems out of place after *nos*: no specific instance of cowardice has been mentioned comparable to the one with which the chorus charges itself. Sometimes *quoque* modifies the following, rather than the preceding word (cf. *OLD* s.v. 2c; *LHS* 2.485; D. R. Shackleton Bailey, *Propertiana* (Cambridge, 1956), 175): 'we are forgetful even of ourselves', because they no longer are the courageous subjects they once were, ready to stand up for their ruler. Alternatively, *quoque* may be employed loosely, to stress in a general way a parallelism between the misery of Octavia and that of the chorus.

For *immemor* with a reflexive pronoun cf. Ov. *Met.* 10.171 *immemor ipse sui* (Bömer ad 8.582 with more parallels). Cf. Tac. *Agr.* 3.2 *pauci et, ut <ita> dixerim, non modo aliorum sed etiam nostri superstites sumus.*

For a representation of guilt in enduring the harshness of tyranny cf. Tac. *Agr.* 2.3 *memoriam quoque ipsa cum uoce perdidissemus, si tam in nostra potestate esset obliuisci quam tacere*; 45.1 *mox nostrae duxere Heluidium in carcerem manus*; Ov. *Fast.* 3.578 *nos sumus imbelles.* The members of this chorus speak of themselves as disbanded soldiers, lost after their commander's death: cf. Ov. *Fast.* 6.581–2 *post Tulli funera plebem | confusam placidi morte fuisse ducis.* The oath of allegiance sworn by the army and by the local communities at each emperor's accession to power included their families: cf. the Cypriot oath sworn to Tiberius and published by T. B. Mitford, *JRS* 50 (1960), 75–9, text ll. 12 ff.); cf. also the oath sworn to Gaius' family in Cass. Dio *Hist. Rom.* 59.9.2. For references to other similar oaths of allegiance cf. P. A. Brunt–J. M. Moore, *Res Gestae Diui Augusti* (Oxford, 1967), 67–8.

289 post fata ducis *dux* as well as *imperator* is a well-known imperial title, beginning with Augustus (cf. Syme, *RR*, 294–5; Aug. *Res Gestae* 25.2 *(Italia) me belli . . . ducem depoposcit*; frequent in Horace and Ovid: *Fasti* 2.60 *cauit sacrati prouida cura ducis*; 6.458). We do not associate the figure of Claudius with military activities, but imperial propaganda laid much emphasis on Claudius as *imperator*. Claudius did not assume the *praenomen imperatoris* at the time of his election, but later more than twenty acclamations followed: cf. Momigliano, *Claudius* (Oxford, 1934), 39 n. 1. The title *dux* undergoes a revival with Domitian (cf. Stat. *Silu.* 3.2.104 *Latius . . . ductor*; 4.3.139) and Trajan. Elsewhere in the play *dux* refers to Nero: cf. 848, *alibi*. On *dux* as an imperial title see also J. Béranger, *Recherches sur l'aspect idéologique du Principat* (Basel, 1953), 47–9.

289–290 cuius stirpem | prodimus aeuo suadente metum The passage echoes perhaps Verg. *Aen.* 1.250–2 *nos, tua progenies . . . prodimur.* The MS reading *euo* (= *aeuo*) *suadente metu* yields no sense. *seuo* in *recc.* is unmetrical; the elision of the final *s* (*prodimu' saeuo*), a solution advocated by some older editors, would be without parallels in Senecan tragedy. Even the transposition of *stirpem* (*cuius prodimus | stirpem*, Farnabius) is not a metrically viable option: dactyls are not allowed at line-end (cf. Introd. p. 45). Trevet read *aeuo* as a dative, to be tied to *prodimus*, 'publicamus euo, id est exponimus perpetuo obloquio, dum non defendimus eam', which is preposterous. Along similar lines is Vürtheim's interpretation (followed by Liberman), 'proicimus et sacrificamus . . . cupiditati et libidini nostri aeui', but this seems too difficult to accept in the absence of any supporting parallel.

A very appealing solution is Wilamowitz' *aeuo suadente metum*, presumably referring to the advanced age of the *chorus* (cf. *TLL* vii.2, 1166–7; for *aeuum* indicating old age even with no qualifying adjective, e.g. Ov. *Met.* 8.712 *annis aeuoque soluti*, Stat. *Theb.* 3.384–5 *gelidis et inertibus aeuo | pectoribus*). In some Greek plays the chorus is composed of old people, servants, citizens or fellow-soldiers of the ruler: cf. Soph. *Ant.* (e.g. 681 τῶι χρόνωι κεκλέμμεθα); Eur. *Herc.* 436–441. However, it is odd for this trait of personal characterization to surface only once, here, so briefly. The chorus will later set aside all such scruples (cf. 669). It could also be objected against this interpretation that old age cuts down one's prospects of success in warfare, not one's courage (cf. e.g. Eur. *Herc.* 232–235; 269).

aeuum could also stand for 'the present times', a corrupt age generating cowardice: cf. *TLL* vii.2, s.v., 1167.61–75; *infra* 309–10 *haec quoque nati uidere nefas | saecula magnum*; 430–1 *saeculo premimur graui, | quo scelera regnant*; Tac. *Hist.* 1.49

(Barbera) *sed claritas natalium et metus temporum obtentui ut . . .* (where the terror of the times is viewed as the cause which made the Romans blind to Galba's shortcomings); Tac. *Agr.* 6.3 *gnarus sub Nerone temporum, quibus inertia pro sapientia fuit* (Ballaira); *metus temporum* also in Plin. *Epist.* 5.1.7; 7.19.6; 9.13.3. This latter interpretation would reinforce the connection with the passages from Tac. *Agr.* adduced ad 288, conjuring up memories of Domitianic fear. One would expect *aeuo* to receive some qualification, such as an adjective, *nostro*, or *in hoc*, but I don't count this as a decisive objection.

Zwierlein writes in his text *omnem*, a conjecture proposed by Delz (*MH* 46 (1989), 61) to replace *euo*, but the present tense of *prodimus* speaks against it; the chorus anticipates the imminent end of Octavia, alluded to by the collective *stirpem* (cf. 32–3 *seruitque domus | cum prole tua capta tyranno*, where *proles* designates Octavia, sole survivor of Claudius' family).

Zwierlein defends *suadente metu*, in view of the frequency of *metus suadet* and related expressions, especially in absolute constructions, such as *suadente* (also in Verg. *Aen.* 10.10), *sollicitante, cogente metu* (also *Oct.* 348; cf. *TLL* viii, s.v. *metus* 907.77–84), but the existence of an established phraseology alone is not a decisive reason to alter the paradosis, and on balance it seems preferable to adopt Wilamowitz' proposal, which entails only a minimal change, in either of the two senses explained *supra*.

If conjecture is thought to be necessary, Richter's *aegro* or Gronovius' *acri* would equally well satisfy sense and form.

In Greek tragedy the chorus often confesses its powerlessness to restore justice or to intervene in the action of the drama and bring help to the victims: cf. Aesch. *Agam.* 1650; Soph. *Ai.* 165–6; Eur. *Andr.* 815; *Hec.* 1042; *Herc.* 254 ff.; 268 ff.; *Hipp.* 782; *Med.* 1275.

291–293 uera priorum uirtus quondam | Romana fuit, uerumque genus | Martis in illis sanguisque uiris For the alliterating *uera . . . uerum . . . uiris* cf. Liv. 22.14.11 *uir ac uere Romanus* (Viansino); Flor. 1.7; Luc. *Bell. Ciu.* 2.532 *o uere Romana manus.* For the claim that Rome's military successes vindicate her legendary descent from Mars (*uerum genus Martis . . . sanguisque*) cf. Liv. 1.3.10; Sil. *Pun.* 1.634–5 (*gens*) *quam rite fatentur | Marte satam.*

Historical exempla take the place of the more usual mythical foils deployed in the choral odes of Greek tragedy. The fact that in Aesch. *Pers.* 852–906 the wretched present is compared with the happy triumphs of the past king, Darius, suggests that use of historical exempla was a feature of all historical dramas. The lament for the loss of early Republican virtues is a commonplace of imperial literature, and is to be expected in a *praetexta*. See also ad 676 *ubi Romani uis est populi?*

293–294 in illis . . . uiris. illi This type of repetition with pronouns in different grammatical cases ('adjacency across two lines' in Wills,

Repetition, 397) betrays some lack of polish. It is different from a carefully balanced *polyptoton* (cf. e.g. Verg. *Georg.* 4.215 *ille operum custos, illum admirantur*).

294–303 The text reads in *A* as follows:

illi reges hac expulerant
urbe superbos ultique tuos
sunt bene manes, uirgo dextra
caesa parentis, ne seruitium
paterere graue et improba ferret
praemia uictrix dira libido.
te quoque bellum triste secutum est
mactata tua, miseranda, manu:
nata Lucreti, stuprum saeui
passa tyranni . . .

The transmitted colometry is obviously erroneous. It violates the metre at 298 (no lengthening at the anapaestic diaeresis is admitted elsewhere in the Senecan corpus) and disrupts syntactical unity within the line (*Kongruenzgesetz*). Writing *urbe superbos* and *dira libido* as monometers (Zwierlein) is enough to solve both these problems.

Richter (1862, 4) believed 296–300 (*uirgo dextra caesa parentis . . . te quoque bellum triste secutum est*) to be interpolated. But, as Zwierlein is right to observe, the language shows no signs of interpolation (the use of *caesa* in reference to human beings, for example, is common in *Octavia*; cf. ad 437–8). Richter was worried by the disruption of the chronological order in the sequence, with the mention of Verginia preceding that of Lucretia. This problem has been largely exaggerated, and the same editors who wish to alter the order of the lines to make room for Lucretia before Verginia find no disturbance in the occurrence of Tullia as the last in the series.

The solution adopted by Zwierlein, reviving Baehrens' proposal (1878, 119), is that of moving the apostrophe to Lucretia (301–3) after 295, *ultique tuos sunt bene manes*. Zwierlein attributes the frequency of transpositions in anapaestic passages to the custom of copying shorter cola on multiple columns. Zwierlein also links 300, *te quoque bellum triste secutum est*, to the apostrophe to Verginia (in this order: 295, 301–3, 300, 296–9). This is not an improvement: the Verginia episode led to the abdication of the decemvirs and to the subsequent death of Appius Claudius, but not to war. It is true that the transition from the kings to Verginia is very sudden: one would have expected the heroic establishment of Republican rule to receive a somewhat more expanded treatment, and it comes as a surprise when *ultique . . . manes* ushers in a wholly new episode of Roman history. There is a difficulty here, but not one great enough to make us alter the transmitted order: it is best to ascribe the poor rhetorical elaboration of this sequence of exempla to the inadequacy of the *Octavia* poet.

Farnaby suggested interpreting *reges* as a reference to the decemvirs, whose haughtiness during their second tenure of office is often likened by Livy to the arrogance of kings (cf. e.g. 3.36.5 *decem regum species erat*; 3.45.8; 3.58.5). This is perhaps too extreme. Note, however, that a parallel between the end of the Decemvirate and the expulsion of the Tarquins was already made in Liv. 3.44.1 (*sequitur aliud in urbe nefas, ab libidine ortum, haud minus foedo euentu quam quod per stuprum caedemque Lucretiae urbe regnoque Tarquinios expulerat, ut non finis solum idem decemuiris qui regibus, sed causa etiam eadem imperii amittendi esset*), and the whole passage in *Octavia* draws extensively on Livy's narrative, often recalling it down to the actual words. *ultique tuos sunt bene manes* at 295 echoes Liv. 3.58.11 *manesque Verginiae . . . tandem quieuerunt*; likewise 294–4• *illi reges hac expulerant | urbe superbos* parallels Liv. 3.44.1 *urbe regnoque Tarquinios expulerat*. The plural *superbos* in 294 recalls *Tarquinios* in Livy's passage, and I think the pluperfect *expulerant* also finds a confirmation in Livy (see following note). On the Livian echoes in this passage cf. also R. Degli Innocenti Pierini, in ΠΟΙΚΙΛΜΑ. *Studi in onore di Michele R. Cataudella* (La Spezia, 2001), 349–55.

A comparable catalogue of Roman heroines figures in Silius Italicus' *katabasis* in *Pun.* 13.820–36, where the sequence is Lucretia, Verginia, Cloelia, Tullia.

294 expulerant The reading *expulerunt* of *recc.* was preferred by Richter and Zwierlein, in combination with their suggested transposition of 296–300: the Romans expelled Tarquinius and his family to avenge Lucretia.

Since I believe the transmitted order to be correct, I have less difficulty in accepting the MS *expulerant*, which is also preferable for considerations of stylistic and linguistic register. There are no other instances of perfect verb forms ending in *-erunt* with short *e* in the Senecan tragic corpus, and the occurrence of the less formal ending would be extremely peculiar in a choral section: even *-erunt* with long *-e* is rarely employed in lyrics, where the high-flown *-ere* largely prevails.

On *–erunt* with short *e* in poetry cf. Housman ad Man. *Astr.* 2.877 (only one disputed occurrence in Manilius); R. B. Steele, *AJPh* 32 (1911), 328–32; F. Muller, *Mnemosyne* 56 (1928), 329–88; D. R. Shackleton Bailey, *CQ* 43 (1949), 25; D. W. Pye, *TPhS* 61 (1963), 1–27; N-W 3.190; *LHS* 1.608.

Quite apart from the question of stylistic acceptability of *expulerunt*, a pluperfect expressing anteriority is certainly in place, and *expulerant* sets the background of Republican heroism against which the episode of Verginia takes place. For the combination of a pluperfect describing the narrative background and a perfect or present introducing the new element cf. e.g. Ov. *Met.* 13.408–14 *Ilion ardebat neque adhuc consederat ignis . . . inuidiosa trahunt uictores praemia Grai*; *Fasti* 2.737–8 (*equi*) *pertulerant dominos, regalia protinus illi | tecta petunt.*

296 uirgo dextra caesa parentis Axelson (*UW*, 67) noted that the author of *Oct.* uses *caedo* more frequently than Seneca, who restricted it to animal sacrifice. This last point is however inaccurate: see my note ad 437 with Senecan parallels (*Oed.* 389; *H.O.* 1785). The *uerbum simplex* is perfectly acceptable in poetry: cf. Ov. *Met.* 15.820 *caesique parentis.*

297–299 ne seruitium paterere graue et | improba ferret praemia victrix | dira libido There are numerous examples of *et*, *-que* after a prohibitive or a negative particle (*non, ne*), instead of the expected *neu/neue*, especially in poetry (*LHS* 2.500; 536). In *Oct.* cf. 648–50 *ne tantus amor . . . suscitet iras | uobisque ego sim causa malorum*; in Sen. *Troad.* 775–7 *non arma . . . tractabis . . . sparsasque . . . feras | audax sequeris*; *H.O.* 1139–40 *ne quis Gyges Thessalica iaculetur iuga | et fiat Othrys pondus Encelado leue.* Elsewhere cf. Luc. *Bell. Ciu.* 1.254; 2.354–5; 6.306–10. The conjecture *aut* is therefore unnecessary, and inferior in sense, as the two clauses do not introduce alternatives.

Synaloephe in the arsis of the last anapaestic foot is avoided by Seneca, but it occurs elsewhere in *Oct.* (cf. Mantke 1957–8, 116): 9 *tua est*; 300 *secutum est*: this case is perhaps more difficult because it also produces a suspension of the syntactical sequence. Parallels (both anapaestic) can be found in Acc. *Scaen.* 525–6 R² *Lemnia praesto | litora rara et*; 289 R² *sed iam Amphilocum huc uadere cerno et.* Although sense overlappings across successive lines in anapaests can occasionally be observed, it is more rare to come across cases of suspended syntactical connections as here: in *Oct.* cf. perhaps 904–5 *inuidet etiam | cur . . .* I have not found significant parallels in the Senecan corpus. Even in Greek tragedy, where anapaestic lines are in synapheia, particles and connectives tend to occur at the beginning of a line/foot/syzygy (some exceptions are *Med.* 133–4; 761–2; *I.A.* 119–20; *I.T.* 181–2). The more usual pattern is to insert the conjunction inside the metron. Indeed, the author of *Oct.* makes extensive use of asyndeton in anapaests (cf. ad 60–2), and *et* could easily have been dispensed with. Perhaps the narrative, non-threnodic tone of this passage is accountable for a more generous use of connectives. There is no evidence for lengthening at the diaeresis (except in the dubious fragment of Gracchus, *sonat impulsa regia cardo*, probably corrupt), therefore *paterere graue et* must be at line-end.

seruitium is used because Appius made a claim that Verginia was a slave from his own household (cf. Liv. 3.44.6). Cf. Laevius fr. 8 Courtney (= Gell. *Noct. Att.* 19.7.3, anapaestic dimeters) *corpore pectoreque undique obeso ac | mente . . .* : Courtney ad loc. remarks that synapheia is particularly strong in anapaests; this may have influenced syntax even in *Octavia* where there is no synapheia; id. fr. 18 Courtney, for *aut* at line end. Final position of co-ordinative particles and adverbs is less common in iambics, presumably because of the lack of synapheia. In Seneca cf. *H.O.* 1028–9 *tamen | in matre peccas.* Instances in archaic Roman drama are discussed by Vahlen, *GPhS* 2.581; W. M. Lindsay, *The Captivi of Plautus* (London, 1900), 64. A dubious case is Acc. *Praet.* 26 R² *resupinum in caelo contueri maximum ac*, where the transmitted *ac* is deleted by Ribbeck. On *ac/atque* at line-end cf. *TLL* ii. s.v. *atque*, 1049.56–69. On line-end placement of καί and other conjunctions in Greek iambics cf. West, *GM*, 83–4.

298–299 improba ferret praemia uictrix | dira libido *improbus* is often found in association with sexual desire: cf. Ov. *Fast.* 2.331 *quid non amor improbus audet*. The other usual idiom with *praemia* is *capere*: cf. Ov. *Fast.* 1.678 *ut capiant cultus praemia digna sui*. Perhaps *uictrix dira libido* echoes Liv. 1.58.5 *uelut* (<*ui*> Müller) *uictrix libido*, in the narrative of Lucretia; *libido uictrix* occurs also at Sen. *Thy.* 46.

304 dedit infandi sceleris poenas The link between this last exemplum, Tullia, and Octavia is less clear. The previous heroines, Verginia and Lucretia, provide an illustration of virtuous virginity defiled by a tyrant, and the chorus cites those stories to celebrate *Romana . . . uirtus*, which they now confess to lacking. Tullia is no foil to Octavia, but her inclusion in this catalogue is motivated by her patricide, a prefiguration of Nero's murder of Agrippina, dealt with at some length in 309–376; as to the *poenae* here being alluded to, Livy has no record of punishment meted out to Tullia besides being exiled from Rome with her husband (cf. Liv. 1.59.13 *inter hunc tumultum Tullia domo profugit exsecrantibus quacumque incedebat inuocantibusque parentum furias uiris mulieribusque*). Tullia commits suicide in Zonaras 7.11 μόνης τῆς Τουλλίας, ὡς λόγος, ἑαυτὴν ἀνελούσης.

tulit enim et Romana regia sceleris tragici exemplum is the introductory remark assigned by Livy (1.46.3) to the account of Servius Tullius' end through his daughter's machinations, and the story has been thought to have inspired some early drama (cf. Ogilvie ad Liv. 1.46–48), but Livy is the likeliest immediate source. Other sources are Ov. *Fast.* 6.587–610; Dion. Hal. 4.39.5; Sil. *Pun.* 13.833–36; Cass. Dio (ap. Zonaras 7.9.17).

306–307 quae per caesi membra parentis | egit saeuos impia currus Cf. Liv. 1.48.7 *amens, agitantibus furiis sororis ac uiri, Tullia per patris corpus carpentum egisse fertur, partemque sanguinis ac caedis paternae cruento uehiculo, contaminata ipsa respersaque, tulisse ad penates suos uirique sui*; 1.59.10 *inuecta corpori patris nefando uehiculo filia*. For a description of the same episode cf. also Sil. *Pun.* 13.833–5 *patrios fregit quae curribus artus | et stetit adductis super ora trementia frenis | Tullia*, which is verbally close.

308–308· laceroque seni uiolenta rogos | nata negauit Tullia denies burial to her father only in this passage. Liv. 1.49.1 *socerum gener sepultura prohibuit* ascribes the refusal of a proper burial to Tarquin. Along the same lines Dion. Hal. 4.40.5. Cf. Ogilvie ad loc. for different, less crude, versions.

The word *lacer* meaning 'disfigured, mutilated' is especially common in poetry: cf. Verg. *Aen.* 6.495 *Deiphobum . . . lacerum crudeliter ora*; Ov. *Fasti* 6.744 *Hippolytus lacero corpore raptus erat.*

309 The account of Agrippina's death given in *Octavia* differs from the version of Tacitus' *Annales* in some respects, but many of the divergent details may be poetic inventions of the author of *Octavia*. Tacitus describes the first botched attempt to murder Agrippina in great detail: the chorus' song is less specific, and at the same time more emotional than Tacitus' narrative. Agrippina's melodramatic address to her ungrateful son and dead husband from on board the sinking ship at *Oct.* 327–44 contrasts sharply with Agrippina's cool self-control at Tac. *Ann.* 14.5.7 *Agrippina silens eoque minus adgnita (unum tamen uulnus umero excepit) nando, deinde occursu lenunculorum . . . uillae suae infertur.* The wound received by Agrippina in her shoulder is not mentioned in this ode, but occurs later on, at 954–5 *funesta uiolata manu | remigis* (also in Cass. Dio *Hist. Rom.* 61.13.3 τῶν τε ναυτῶν ταῖς κώπαις ἐπ' αὐτὴν χρωμένων). The timely arrival of some fishermen rescues Agrippina in Tacitus, whereas in *Oct.* a little crowd of servants loyal to Agrippina has gathered on shore (352–5 *multi dominae ferre auxilium . . . audent . . . uoce hortantur manibusque leuant*). In Tacitus, this crowd makes its appearance only after Agrippina has reached her *villa* (*Ann.* 14.8.2 *alii quantum corpus sinebat uadere in mare; quidam manus protendere; questibus, uotis, clamore diuersa rogitantium aut incerta respondentium omnis ora compleri; adfluere ingens multitudo cum luminibus . . .*).

309–310 haec quoque nati uidere nefas | saecula magnum Cf. *Med.* 329–30 *candida nostri saecula patres | uidere procul fraude remota*; Ov. *Met.* 10.307 *quae (regiones) tantum genuere nefas. videre nefas* also in Sen. *Oed.* 444; Stat. *Theb.* 8.451.

311–312 Tyrrhenum . . . misit in aequor Cf. Ov. *Met.* 4.23–4 *Tyrrhenaque mittis in aequor | corpora*; 14.8 *Tyrrhena per aequora lapsus* (*Tyrrhenum . . . aequor* also in Hor. *Carm.* 4.15.3; Verg. *Aen.* 1.67). On the long hyperbaton, *Tyrrhenum . . . in aequor* cf. ad 262. A verb of movement, such as *misit/mittit/prodit/procedit*, followed by *in aequor* at line-end makes up a common clausula in hexametric poetry (with some thirty occurrences in PHI 5.3): cf. e.g. Prop. 3.9.3 *tam uastum mittis in aequor*; Verg. *Aen.* 10.451 *medium procedit in aequor*; 10.693 *uastum quae prodit in aequor.*

311 rate ferali The poetic *ratis* for 'ship' is also specialized in funerary poetry for the 'barge of Charon': cf. *CE* 1186.9; *CE* 1187V.4 *duceris ad Stygiam nunc miseranda ratem*; *CE* 1265.4 *at (= ad) Styga . . . rate funerea . . . comitata fuisse(m)*; *CE* 1537A.6 *et raptam in ferna me posuere ratem.* In *TLL* vi.1, s.v. 487.15–16 *ferali* is tied to *fraude*, but the word order does not commend this view, and *rate ferali* is supported by 127 *Stygiae . . . imposuit rati*; Ps.-Quint. *Decl.* 6.5 *ferali nauicula.*

313–314 properant placidos linquere portus | iussi nautae *iussi*, according to Giancotti (1954, 98) indicates the sailors' connivance in the plot (denied by the historical sources: cf. Tac. *Ann.* 14.5 *plerique ignari etiam conscios impediebant*). More likely, *iussi* is an epic tag: cf. Verg. *Aen.* 7.156 *haud mora, festinant iussi*; also 3.560–1 *eripite, o socii, pariterque insurgite remis*; | *haud minus ac iussi faciunt*; 10.444; Ov. *Met.* 7.257 *diffugiunt iussi*; Sen. *Troad.* 1044–6 *tuba iussi dare uela nautae, | cum simul uentis properante remo | prenderint altum.*

315 resonant remis pulsata freta The variant *resonent* found in β at 315 must have originated as a subordinate clause governed by *iussi*, the subjunctive expressing the actual order imparted to the mariners. *iubeo*, however, is generally construed with the infinitive in classical Latin (Ov. *Met.* 14.437 *rursus inire fretum, rursus dare uela iubemur*). *placidos linquere portus* is the common object of both *properant* and *iussi.*

The sequence of asyndetic sentences describing the movement of the ship is aimed at reproducing a narrative in the epic style; cf. Verg. *Aen.* 4.582–3 *litora deseruere; latet sub classibus aequor; | adnixi torquent spumas et caerula uerrunt.*

316 fertur in altum prouecta ratis On *prouecta*, replacing *profecta* of MSS, Caietanus' note reads 'non est nauium proficisci sed nauigantium. lege ergo prouecta ut habet antiquarius codex quem ego crediderim uel dextra Senecae uel eius tempestate descriptum fuisse'. Yet no MS likely to have passed through the hands of Caietanus (1461–1528) could have suggested, even to him, such remote antiquity, and the conjecture must be ascribed either to him or to whatever *recentiores* came within his reach. Caietanus' MS has been identified as BL Harley 2482 by MacGregor (1985), 1202. *proueho* is normally applied to the movement of ships (cf. Caes. *Bell. Gall.* 4.28.3 *in altum prouectae*; Liv. 30.43.12 *naues prouectas in altum incendi iussit*). For the pleonastic combination *fertur . . . prouecta* cf. Prop. 1.8.14 *cum tibi prouectas auferet unda ratis*; the participle can be translated adverbially: 'with full sail'.

The redundancies in which the lines describing the shipwreck abound aim at reproducing features of epic style: cf. for instance Luc. *Bell. Ciu.* 4.430 *missa ratis prono defertur lapsa profundo.*

317–318 quae resoluto robore labens | pressa dehiscit sorbetque mare Gronovius seems to be the only editor who wrote a full stop after *ratis*, not without reason, because there is no logical connection between the main clause and the relative, and the two sentences must be thought of as independent (an instance of the so-called *coniunctio relativa*). Indeed, the two successive frames showing the ship in full sail and its sudden falling apart and sinking are clearly in contrast. Similar transitions are common in poetry: cf. Ov. *Met.* 8.445–8 *dona deum templis nato uictore ferebat, | cum uidet exstinctos fratres Althaea referri. | quae plangore dato maestis ululatibus urbem | implet.* Michael Müller's *cum* for *quae* in 317 (1912, 7), though in my view unnecessary, is alive to the faulty transition in the narrative: cf. Tac. *Ann.* 14.5 *nec multum erat progressa nauis . . . cum dato signo ruere tectum loci* (Agrippina's cabin); Val. Fl. *Arg.* 1.637–8 *cum protinus alnus | soluitur et uasto puppis mare sorbet hiatu.* Gronovius' punctuation makes the transition smoother.

Tacitus relates that the vessel had been tampered with so that some boards, loosened on purpose, should come apart in mid-sea (Tac. *Ann.* 14.3 *(Anicetus) nauem posse componi docet, cuius pars ipso in mari per artem soluta effunderet ignaram*). Not everything goes according to plan: the ship did not break apart (*ibid.* 14.5 *nec dissolutio nauigii sequebatur*) and its sinking slowly allowed Agrippina to slip gently overboard. The narrative of Cass. Dio-Xiph. *Hist. Rom.* 61.13 (διελύθη . . . ἡ ναῦς) is much too compressed, and *Octavia* does not dwell on the exact details of the event, so that it is impossible to determine what version the author had in mind. *resoluto robore*, however, seems to indicate the dissolution of the ship's frame, when the boards came apart; *labens* describes the collapse of the high structure of the vessel. Tacitus' account is further complicated by the mention of a second device which should have secured Agrippina's death, by crushing the roof of her cabin on board with some weights. There may be a reflection of this detail in 318 *pressa*: the verb is sometimes used in reference to ships sunk by overloading (cf. Tac. *Hist.* 3.77 *nimio ruentium onere pressas mare hausit*; Ov. *Fasti* 4.300 *sedit limoso pressa carina uado*; Sen. *N.Q.* 6.6.2 (Whitman) *sicut in nauigiis quoque euenit ut, si inclinata sunt et abierunt in latus, aquam sorbeant . . . si immodice depressa sunt*). More likely, however, *pressa* refers to the pressure exerted by the water over the sinking ship: cf. Ov. *Met.* 1.291 *pressaeque latent sub gurgite turres*.

The accumulation of subordinate clauses (an ablative absolute and two *participia coniuncta*) is intended to represent the convulsive rapidity of the event, in language and style reminiscent of epic descriptions: cf. Val. Fl. *Arg.* 8.357–8 *fluctu puppis labefacta reuerso | soluitur*; Verg. *Aen.* 11.627–8 *aestu reuoluta resorbens | saxa fugit litusque uado labente relinquit*. A ship falling apart also in Ov. *Met.* 11.514 *iamque labant cunei*. The hyperbolic *sorbetque mare* (acc.) for 'to ship water' is also epic: cf. Val. Fl. *Arg.* 1.638 *uasto puppis mare sorbet hiatu*, and the passage from *N.Q.* 6.6.2 given above.

319–320 tollitur ingens clamor ad astra | cum femineo mixtus planctu The loud outcry raised by a crowd of anonymous onlookers, enhancing the drama of a scene at its peak, is a typical mass reaction in epic poetry, when the combat or the battle takes a dramatic turn: cf. Verg. *Aen.* 4.665–8 *it clamor ad alta | atria . . . lamentis gemituque et femineo ululatu | tecta fremunt, resonat magnis plangoribus aether*; 11.877–8 *e speculis percussae pectora matres | femineum clamorem ad caeli sidera tollunt*; 5.227–8 (the race of the ships). The parallels would suggest the presence of a crowd observing the scene from the shore, rather than the cries of the women on board, Agrippina and her retinue.

The sentence-initial position of *tollitur* is also an epicism, on the pattern *it clamor ad astra. tollitur in caelum clamor* is Ennian, and imitated by Vergil at *Aen.* 11.745; 12.462.

321 mors ante oculos dira uagatur Cf. *Carmen de Bello Actiaco*, 44 Courtn. *(campo) omne uagabatur leti genus*; also Bömer ad Ov. *Met.* 8.507 and 14.202; Verg. *Aen.* 2.369; Ov. *Met.* 11.537–8; Luc. *Bell. Ciu.* 9.763 *mors erat ante oculos*; Tac. *Hist.* 3.28. In Greek cf. Thuc. 3.81.4 πᾶσα ἰδέα . . . θανάτου.

322 quaerit leti sibi quisque fugam This genitive expressing separation with *fuga* is common in poetry, possibly as a Grecism: cf. Verg. *Aen.* 8.251 *fuga . . . pericli*; 9.538–9 *malorum . . . fugam*; 10.154 *libera fati* (with Conington's note). The idiom normally applies to people who can run.

323–324 alii lacerae puppis tabulis | haerent nudi Cf. Ov. *Met.* 11.428 *et laceras nuper tabulas in litore uidi* (other parallels in Bömer ad loc.); 11.559–60 *alii partes et membra carinae | trunca tenent*; *Ibis* 277–8 *lacerae . . . fracta tenentem | membra ratis*; Luc. *Bell. Ciu.* 3.688 *hi ne mergantur tabulis ardentibus haerent.*

The survivors are 'naked' because they have taken off their clothes to be less hampered in their swim away from the sinking ship. Zwierlein rightly defends the text against various conjectures (e.g. Heinsius' *udi*), comparing Sen. *Troad.* 1028 (see following note). W. Baehrens, *PhW* 43 (1923), 671 adduced Cic. *Rosc. Amer.* 147 *tamquam e naufragio nudum*; Sen. *Ben.* 4.37.4 *nudo et naufrago similem.*

324 fluctusque secant *secare fluctus* normally applies to vessels at full speed, or islands floating in the open sea. In reference to swimming, it is used in Ov. *Am.* 3.12.34 (sc. *Iuppiter*) *secat imposita uirgine taurus aquas*. In the context, however, the expression is puzzling. The more vigorous survivors of Agrippina's crew swim ashore to safety (325, *repetunt alii litora nantes*), but *fluctus . . . secant* seems out of place to describe the condition of the other survivors, hanging on to the scattered timbers of the plank. I can propose no correction; the phrase may have come from Sen. *Troad.* 1027–8 *qui secans fluctus rate singulari | nudus in portus cecidit petitos.*

326 multos mergunt fata profundo The line probably echoes Verg. *Aen.* 6.511–12 *me fata . . . his mersere malis*. The simple ablative of the place where one is submerged is common (cf. *TLL*, viii, s.v. *mergo*, 832.8–43, with *aequore, aquis, gurgite, caeno*, etc.).

327–329 scindit uestes Augusta suas | laceratque comas | rigat et maestis fletibus ora The closest parallel for this stereotypical scene of despair is that provided by Alcyone in Ov. *Met.* 11.725–6 *'ille est' exclamat et una | ora comas uestem lacerat.* For *rigat . . . fletibus ora* cf. Ov. *Met.* 11.419 *fletibus ora rigauit*; *Cons. Liu.* 199 *lacrimis . . . rigantibus ora*; Sen. *Oed.* 978. For other scenes of mourning in Latin poetry cf. Bömer ad Ov. *Met.* 2.335; 3.178.

Agrippina is correctly designated with the title bestowed on her by Claudius: cf. Mommsen, *RS*, 2.788; cf. Furneaux's note ad Tac. *Ann.*12.26; on earlier and subsequent princesses who received this honorific title cf. *TLL* ii, s.v. *Augustus*, 1389–90.

330 postquam spes est nulla salutis Cf. Ov. *Trist.* 1.2.33–4 *nec spes est ulla salutis, | dumque loquor uultus obruit unda meos.*

331 ardens ira, iam uicta malis *victa malis* could either be interpreted as 'overcome by grief' or, as seems perhaps more likely in the context, 'exhausted by fatigue'. Agrippina seems initially to give up all efforts to save herself, but afterwards, driven by an instinct of self-preservation (*cogente metu*) begins to swim away from the wreck.

332–333 'haec' exclamat 'mihi pro tanto | munere reddis praemia, nate?' The use of *exclamat* to introduce direct speech, at some dramatic turn in the action, is common in epic poetry: cf. e.g. Verg. *Aen.*

2.535–8 *'at tibi pro scelere' exclamat, 'pro talibus ausis . . . praemia reddant | debita'*; also Ov. *Met.* 11.725–6 (given ad 327–9). For *reddis praemia* cf. Cat. *Carm.* 64.157 *talia qui reddis pro dulci praemia uita.*

335–337 quae te genui, quae tibi lucem | atque imperium nomenque dedi | Caesaris amens The similarities between Agrippina's last words in Josephus, *Ant.* 20.153 (ταύτην ἀμοιβὴν ἀποτίσας αὐτῆι οὐ μόνον τῆς γενέσεως ἀλλὰ καὶ τοῦ . . . τὴν Ῥωμαίων ἡγεμονίαν παραλαβεῖν), and in *Octavia* arguably point to the narrative of the lost Flavian historian, who must have treated the scene with a full array of rhetorical colour. Cf. also Plin. *Pan.* 6.5 *ille tibi imperium dedit.*

338 exsere uultus Acheronte tuos Agrippina puts up a similar show in Tac. *Ann.* 13.14.6 *simul intendere manus, adgerere probra, consecratum Claudium, infernos Silanorum manes inuocare*, on one of the occasions when it became clear to her that the time of her influence on Nero was coming to an end.

The plural *uultus* is a poeticism, common in this sense after the Augustan poets, often meaning 'eyes', though not here (cf. also Sen. *Agam.* 554; Ov. *Met.* 2.271; 13.838 *nitidum caput exsere ponto*). The spirit of Claudius is invited to rise from the underworld (*Acheronte* is used metonymically for the Underworld in general) and see the just retribution meted out to his murderess, with no implication that the dead lie underneath the infernal rivers: cf. ad 134; Sen. *Oed.* 619–20.

339 poenisque meis pascere, coniunx A possible echo of Ov. *Met.* 6.280 *pascere crudelis nostro, Latona, dolore*; 9.176 *'cladibus' exclamat 'Saturnia pascere nostris'.*

340–341 ego, causa tuae, miserande, necis | natoque tuo funeris auctor Cf. Verg. *Aen.* 6.458 *funeris heu tibi causa fui*; Ov. *Met.* 10.198–9 *tu dolor es facinusque meum . . . ego sum tibi funeris auctor.* For *muneris/funeris auctor* and comparable *clausulae* in hexameter poetry cf. Bömer ad Ov. *Met.* 5.657. Agrippina could be said to be responsible for Britannicus' death only indirectly, by having established her son Nero as the emperor.

342–343 en, ut merui, ferar ad manes | inhumata tuos Agrippina laments that her death, harsh in itself and inflicted by a degenerate son upon his mother, is made more cruel by the prospect of her corpse being lost at sea, and never receiving its proper burial. There was a belief that the souls of the unburied were excluded from their resting place in the Underworld (cf. Waszink's note ad Tert. *De an.* 56 [Amsterdam, 1941], p. 565), but exclusion of these souls is not unanimously presented as their eternal lot: Pedroli rightly adduced Serv. *Aen.* 6.325, where it is stated that the spirit of the drowned person could reach the Underworld if certain funerary rituals were performed, even if the body was never found. *inhumata* (presumably to be tied to *ut merui*) envisages a worsening of lot entailed by the absence of a proper burial; Verg. *Aen.* 6.329–30, for example, asserts that the *insepulti* are to remain wandering on the bank of Cocytus for a hundred years before they are allowed to pass over to the other side. In fact, Agrippina is later shown to be in Tartarus next to Claudius, who – she complains – torments her for her crimes (614–17).

W. S. Watt (*HSCPh* 92 (1989), 331–2) has revived Heinsius' *feror* (*Adv.* 504), on the strength of Sil. *Pun.* 2.678–9 *haec* (sc. *arma*) . . . *ad manes, en, ipsa fero.* The parallel from Silius is only superficially relevant (the use of the present *fero* is explained by the two deictic forms, *haec* and *en*), and there is in my view no compelling reason to alter the transmitted version: cf. Verg. *Aen.* 6.374–5 *tu Stygias inhumatus aquas . . . aspicies?* and Cat. *Carm.* 64.153 *neque iniacta tumulabor mortua terra.*

344 obruta saeuis aequoris undis Cf. Ov. *Pont.* 3.6.29 *obruerit cum tot saeuis deus aequoris undis.*

345 feriunt fluctus ora loquentis *ferire*, in reference to waves, normally refers to hitting ships, or the coast: cf. Verg. *Ecl.* 9.43 *feriant . . . litora fluctus*; Luc. *Bell. Ciu.* 8.698; Stat. *Ach.* 1.100 *feriunt uada Thessala plantas* describes the landing of Thetis in Thessaly, when the shoals hit the goddess' feet; cf. also Ov. *Trist.* 1.11.40 *ipsaque caeruleis charta feritur aquis.*

This picture of the drowning Agrippina, whose words are choked in her mouth by the waves, is indebted to the Ovidian narrative of Ceyx, as the drowning man desperately calls his wife's name: cf. Ov. *Met.* 11.256 *admisitque suos in uerba nouissima fluctus*; 11.665–6 *oraque nostra tuum frustra clamantia nomen | implerunt fluctus*; *Trist.* 1.2.14 *ipsa graues spargunt ora loquentis aquae*; *Her.* 18.36; *Pont.* 2.3.40; cf. also Helle's drowning in Val. Fl. *Arg.* 1.291–3.

346–347 ruit in pelagus rursumque salo | pressa resurgit Agrippina first sinks into the water, then re-emerges at the surface. *premere* is a verb often used to describe a drowning (cf. Ov. *Met.* 11.558 *gurgite pressa graui*; Hor. *Carm.* 1.14.10 *iterum pressa . . . malo*; Verg. *Aen.* 1.129 *fluctibus oppressos*). In the context, however, the presence of *rursum* suggests a thrust from underneath.

348–349 pellit palmis cogente metu | freta *A* reads *fata.* I have accepted Buecheler's *freta* in view of the recurrence of *pellere undam/aquam* as a high-flown periphrasis for 'to swim': cf. [Tib.] 3.5.30 *et facilis lenta pellitur unda manu*; Tib. 1.4.12 *pectore pellit aquam*; Man. *Astr.* 2.59 *priua rate pellimus undas*; *pellere fata* on its own would still be bearable (cf. Germ. *Arat.* 304 *munit eos breue lignum, et fata instantia pellit*), but *palmis* tilts the balance in favour of Buecheler's correction.

349 sed cedit fessa labori *et* in *A* was an obvious corruption: *sed* is often spelled as *set* in the MS tradition (as well as in the epigraphic evidence: cf. Lindsay, *LL* 76–7), in particular before a word beginning with a voiceless consonant (assimilation, or sandhi). On the confusion cf. e.g. Courtney, Stat. *Silu.* (Oxford), *praef.* xxix.

350–351 mansit tacitis in pectoribus | spreta tristi iam morte fides *tacitus* is more commonly said of thoughts left unexpressed and contrasting with the actions one is forced to do: cf. Ov. *Met.* 6.203 *tacito uenerantur murmure numen*; Luc. *Bell. Ciu.* 1.247 *tacito mutos uoluunt in pectore questus*. For this reason *tacitis . . . pectoribus* is suspected of being corrupt (Grotius proposed *famulis*, revived by Liberman): the unnamed faithful do, after all, risk their lives while helping Agrippina, but I think there is no decisive reason to propose a change. The local fishermen and servants of Agrippina coming to rescue their mistress are said to act in defiance of Nero. They are not likely to have perceived any danger in helping Agrippina, at this stage, but the poet uses their unspoken faithfulness as a foil to highlight Nero's vicious deed.

352–353 multi dominae ferre auxilium | pelago fractis uiribus audent Rizza ties *pelago fractis uiribus* to *multi*, but surely this must be wrong, since it is Agrippina who is about to succumb to the waves. The logical subject of an ablative absolute tends to coincide with the subject of the main clause, but there are exceptions: cf. K-S 2.1.772 n. 6, quoting Sall. *Iug.* 10.1 *paruum ego te, Iugurtha, amisso patre* (i.e. *postquam patrem amisisti*) *. . . in meum regnum recepi*; cf. also Ov. *Met.* 6.524–5 *et uirginem et unam | ui superat frustra clamato saepe parente*.

354–355 bracchia quam uix lenta trahentem | uoce hortantur manibusque leuant I have chosen to adopt Lipsius' *quam uix* in preference to the MS *quamuis* ('as she drags her arms, though sluggishly, along', Miller). *bracchia quamuis lenta trahentem* places the emphasis on the wrong element: Agrippina's followers do not come to her rescue *despite* her exhaustion. They arrive, in fact, when the action is at its most critical, with Agrippina about to give up. The alternative interpretation would be to read *quamuis* as an adverb (*OLD* 'to any degree you like' = *lentissima bracchia trahentem*, as Ballaira and, presumably, Zwierlein take it). This use has no parallels in Augustan poetry and is usually styled as a colloquialism (Plautus, Catullus; cf. Mart. *Epigr.* 11.104.15 *quamuis Ithaco stertente marito*). Accordingly, *quamuis* was changed by Lipsius (and after him by Heinsius and Baehrens) to *quam uix* (*uix*, not surviving in any of the Romance languages, undergoes constant corruptions in the MSS: cf. Ov. *Met.* 9.684–5 *iamque ferendo | uix erat* (Heinsius) *illa grauem maturo pondere uentrem*, where MSS offer various corrupt readings, such as *uexerat, uiderat, uinxerat*). Lipsius adduced in support of his conjecture Ov. *Her.* 18.161–2 *saepe per adsiduos languent mea bracchia motus | uixque per immensas fessa trahuntur aquas*, which seems convincing; add Ov. *Fast.* 2.354 *membraque de dura uix sua tollit humo*; Sen. *Oed.* 168–9 *uix assiduo bracchia conto | lassata refert*.

Swimming, in Latin poetry, is *bracchia ducere* or *bracchia iactare*: cf. Ov. *Met.* 4.353; 5.596 *excussaque bracchia iacto*; *Her.* 18.158, 196 (avoiding the Greek loan word cf. Sil. *Pun.* 3.457 *nunc ualidis gurges certatim frangitur ulnis*; Ov. *Her.* 18.23 *dare uerbera*).

356–358 quid tibi saeui fugisse maris | profuit undas? | ferro es nati moritura tui The chorus' address to Agrippina, interrupting the narrative, parallels a feature of epic poetry, found as early as Homer: the epic singer exhibits his knowledge of future events by issuing a vain warning to one of his characters, rushing headlong to ruin: cf. R. Heinze, *Vergils epische Technik* (Berlin, 1915), 370–2; Harrison ad Verg. *Aen.* 10.501–5. In Latin, the closest parallels can be found in some Ovidian passages where the poet apostrophizes a character while something is happening: Ov. *Met.* 3.432–3 *credule, quid frustra simulacra fugacia captas? | quod petis est nusquam* (with Bömer for more Ovidian parallels); *Fast.* 2.811 *quid uictor gaudes? haec te uictoria perdet*; Luc. *Bell. Ciu.* 7.590–2 *ne rue per medios nimium temerarius hostis . . . Thessalia periture tua.* On this kind of apostrophe cf. R. Heinze, *Ovids elegische Erzählung*, in *Vom Geist des Römertums* (Darmstadt, 1960), 353. There are no truly similar examples of this technique in Senecan tragedy, mainly, in my view, because Senecan choruses do not deliver narratives of a comparable scale and elaboration. Amphitryon and then the chorus display an emotional involvement which resembles the epic poet's apostrophe in Sen. *Hf.* 1012 *quo misera pergis . . .* ; 1032 *quo te ipse senior, obuium morti ingeris?*, where both are powerless spectators as the mad Hercules slays his family. In *Thy.* 782–4 the messenger, who has related the slaying of Thyestes' sons, addresses Thyestes, while the banquet is taking place off-stage: *in malis unum hoc tuis | bonum est, Thyesta, quod mala ignoras tua. | sed et hoc peribit.*

For the quasi-formulaic *quid profuit*, see ad 286.

There are no parallels for the aphaeresis *ferro es* in anapaestic sequences (cf. Mantke 1957–8, 116). In other metres cf. *H.O.* 446 *ut laesa es*; Ov. *Met.* 5.261 *animo gratissima nostro es*; Verg. *Aen.* 12.142.

359–60 cuius facinus uix posteritas, | tarde semper saecula credent Schroederus' *tarde semper credula, credet* was accepted by Rizza and has been revived by Watt (*MH* 53 (1996), 255); there are however ample parallels for the pleonastic *posteritas . . . saecula*: cf. *H.O.* 1422–4 *quis per annorum uices | totoque in aeuo poterit aerumnas senex | referre tantas?*; *Thy.* 753–4 *o nullo scelus | credibile in aeuo quodque posteritas neget* (Ladek 1891, 63). Outside the Senecan corpus cf. Luc. *Bell. Ciu.* 8.608–9 *qua posteritas in saecula mittet | Septimium fama, scelus hoc quo nomine dicent?* 9.169; Ov. *Met.* 1.502; for the topos cf. Hor. *Epod.* 9.11 *(posteri negabitis)*, with Mankin's note. Moreover, the sense resulting from the emendation is not satisfactory: an incidental comment on the scepticism of *posteritas* as such is off the mark: the line lays emphasis on the enormity of the crime, so great that no future generation will be prepared to believe it could ever be committed. *tarde* stands for 'reluctantly', a sense which seems to cause little difficulty (and *credula* would be no improvement in this respect). If emendation is needed, I would prefer to correct *posteritas* in *nostra aetas* (but this synaloephe in anapaests is undesirable: cf. *infra* ad 361): ***cuius facinus uix nostra aetas*** (sc. *credidit*), ***tarde semper saecula credent*** (taking a cue from Ov. *Pont.* 2.6.27 *quos prior est mirata, sequens mirabitur aetas*; Curt. Ruf. *Hist. Alex.* 9.10.28 *et praesens aetas et posteritas deinde mirata est*). The occurrence of *saecula* without qualifications reinforces the sense of *aeuum* as *aetas* at 290.

361–362 furit ereptam pelagoque dolet | uiuere matrem The most straightforward explanation seems to be *furit (impius) et dolet matrem ereptam pelago uiuere*, assuming postponement of *-que* after the second word, a construction replicated at 363 *impius ingens geminatque nefas*. Postponement of *-que* is frequent in Latin poetry, especially after Ovid, although Senecan tragedy avoids it: cf. Introd. p. 32; Tandoi, *Scritti*, 710; Maurach, *EP* § 128; Platnauer, 91; Leo *KS* 1.64.3; Norden, ad Verg. *Aen.* 6.817–18, and *Anhang* III.B.3. Possibly, however, the poet has intentionally blurred the dividing line between syntactical units, in an attempt to reproduce a Vergilian 'theme and variation' pattern (e.g. Verg. *Aen.* 10.500 *quo nunc Turnus ouat spolio gaudetque potitus*), and the two cola should be understood as a hendiadys, 'furiose dolens quod mater erepta sit a pelago et uiuat': for 'theme and variation' constructions in *Oct.* cf. ad 65–7.

Ritter's *pelago atque* is unlikely to be right: there is only one case in anapaests of synaloephe involving a polysyllable (*Agam.* 684 *pelago audaces*). *erepta pelago* occurs again at 608.

A bare verb at the start of a new period, followed by a conjunction, of the type *furit et*, with subject change, provides a transitional formula very common in epic narratives: cf. Ov. *Met.* 3.83–4 *furit ille et . . . uulnera dat*; 12.478; 13.967–8 *furit ille inritatusque repulsa | prodigiosa petit Titanidos atria Circes*; *Fast.* 4.233–4 *hic furit et credens thalamis procumbere tectum | effugit*; Val. Fl. *Arg.* 2.146; Stat. *Theb.* 7.320; Sil. *Pun.* 5.276 (all with *furit et*). In this instance, the sudden *furit . . .* stresses the manner, rash and furious, of Nero's response to the news of Agrippina's narrow escape.

363 impius, ingens geminatque nefas The name of Nero is euphemistically omitted, as at 604–5 *haud tempus datum est lacrimis, | sed ingens scelere geminauit nefas*. Since no subject has been given for 361–2, *impius* must probably be tied to the preceding lines. After a strong syntactical pause, a new subject may be delayed for effect until the second colon: cf. Ov. *Met.* 8.399–400 *occupat audentem quaque est uia proxima leto | summa ferus* (i.e. the wild boar) *geminos direxit ad inguina dentes*. In this case, 361–3, enclosing a period extending over three separate lines, would exhibit a clear instance of non-coincidence between metrical and syntactical cola in anapaests (a topic I have discussed in Introd. p. 44). More likely, however, *impius* should be taken as an indignant exclamation (*impius!*), with the added emphasis of a line initial placement: cf. Hor. *Carm.* 3.11.30 | *impiae (nam quid potuere maius)* | *impiae* (the Danaids); Verg. *Aen.* 4.496.

The expression *geminare nefas* occurs only here and at 604–5; elsewhere cf. Ov. *Met.* 10.471 *postera nox facinus geminat* (cf. Junge 1999, 234).

364 ruit in miserae fata parentis *in fata ruere* is Ovidian: cf. Ov. *Met.* 6.51 *in sua fata ruit*; 7.346–7 *quid uos in fata parentis | armat?*; Luc. *Bell. Ciu.* 6.298–9 *inque ipsa pauendo | fata ruit*; more parallels in *TLL* vi.1, s.v. *fatum*, 359.44 ff.

365 patiturque moram sceleris nullam For *moram pati* cf. Ov. *Fast.* 2.722 (*Ardea*) *et patitur lentas obsidione moras*; *Met.* 4.350 *uixque moram patitur*; Sen. *Thy.* 769; *Agam.* 131. The negative *nullam* has no particular contrastive emphasis here; normative grammars would recommend the alternative arrangement *nec patitur . . . ullam*, but such infractions are common: cf *LHS* 2.480. Tacitus is fond of such mannerisms; cf. *Ann.* 6.28.6 *nihilque usurpauisse* = *nec quicquam usurpauisse.* Cf. also Nipperdey-Andresen ad *Ann.* 1.38. In poetry, see Bömer ad Ov. *Met.* 5.446; cf. also *ibid.* 5.629 *nullosque* = *neque ullos.*

The metrical sequence *sceleris nullam an.* + *tr.* does not contravene Reeve's Law, as enunciated in Zwierlein, *KK* ad *Troad.* 158, where it is advocated to reject the reading of *A*, *nemoris tutus*, in favour of *E*, *tutis*, at line end, before vowel-initial word in the following line; see also *KK* ad *H.O.* 180 ff.

366 missus peragit iussa satelles The line has an Ovidian ring: cf. Ov. *Met.* 2.119 *iussa deae celeres peragunt* (with Bömer ad *Met.* 7.502); *Fast.* 2.387 *iussa recusantes peragunt lacrimosa ministri*; Sen. *H.O.* 997; Luc. *Bell. Ciu.* 10.468 *missus . . . satelles.*

367 reserat dominae pectora ferro For the poetic plural *pectora* in reference to an individual cf. Verg. *Aen.* 1.355–6 *traiectaque pectora ferro | nudauit* (*Sychaeus*); 9.432 (*ensis*) *candida pectora rumpit. pectora ferro* is relatively common at line end in hexametric poetry (over 15 occurrences in PHI 5.3).

The phrase *reserat . . . pectora ferro* seems to describe Agrippina's assassin delivering the finishing blow (cf. Verg. *Aen.* 10.601 *pectus mucrone recludit*; Ov. *Met.* 1.227 *iugulum mucrone resoluit*; 7.285–6 *stricto Medea recludit | ense senis iugulum*, all marking the culminating point of a killing scene), but she retains sufficient strength to pronounce her rhetorically elaborated last words. Even in Tacitus (*Ann.* 14.8), Agrippina, bludgeoned by the *fustis* of the trierarch, retains enough breath to fling a memorable line in the face of the centurion poised to finish her off: *prior trierarchus fusti caput eius adflixit. iam in mortem centurioni ferrum destringenti protendens uterum 'uentrem feri' exclamauit, multisque uulneribus confecta est.*

resero is not normally used for wounding; the closest parallel is Ov. *Met.* 6.663–4 *si posset reserato pectore diras | egerere inde dapes.*

The appellative *domina* may appear striking. Roman emperors refused the title *dominus* in public address (cf. Suet. *Aug.* 53; Tac. *Ann.* 2.87; Bömer ad Ov. *Fast.* 2.142). Even in inscriptions, *dominus noster* does not appear until the reign of Antoninus Pius, becoming current only in the third century (Mommsen, *RS* 2^3.760). In his correspondence with Trajan, however, Pliny regularly addresses the *princeps* with *domine.* Poetry and the language of official state occasions are often in conflict in matters of court etiquette and in giving titles to members of the ruling family, as can be seen several times in this play (cf. ad 211, 220, 900). In this line, *domina* may perhaps be excused by referring to the relationship between the soldiers and Agrippina. For lower class individuals, such distinctions were probably irrelevant, and the occurrence of *domina* in this context loses its inappropriateness, if we think that the platoon was commanded by one of Claudius' freedmen, for whom Agrippina was still rightfully a *domina. domina* is also used at *Oct.* 352 *multi dominae ferre auxilium*, more pertinently, because it represents the point of view of Agrippina's *familia*.

371–372 'hic est, hic est fodiendus' ait | 'ferro, monstrum qui tale tulit' Extant historical accounts of the incident unanimously record the defiant pose of Agrippina, offering herself to her executioner: Tac. *Ann.* 14.8 *protendens uterum 'uentrem feri' exclamauit*, whereupon the words *monstrum qui tale tulit* are interpolated in the same hand in *Leidensis* BPL.16B. Agrippina's words are moderately unclear without the interpolation, but Tacitus can be credited with a minor obscurity (Tacitus concludes with *haec consensu produntur*); Cass. Dio *Hist. Rom.* 61.13 παῖε ταύτην, Ἀνίκητε, παῖε, ὅτι Νέρωνα ἔτεκεν. The coincidence of detail suggests that Agrippina's death was thus portayed in the original source transmitting the episode. At any rate, grand melodramatic gestures were a commonplace in declamation (cf. Sen. *Contr.* 2.5.7, adduced by M. Winterbottom, *CR* 22 (1976), 188: *caede uentrem ne tyrannicidas pariat*), and there are parallels in Senecan tragedy: cf. Sen. *Phoe.* 447 *hunc petite uentrem*; *Oed.* 1038–9 *hunc dextra hunc pete | uterum capacem, qui uirum et gnatos tulit*; *H.O.* 1678. Agrippina appears to have already received a blow (*reserat . . . pectora*). Either she is asking for a second one to finish her or 367 must be taken as an anticipation of the final result.

For *hic est hic est* cf. Sen. *Troad.* 707 *hic est hic est terror.*

373–376 Zwierlein's colometric arrangement of 373–4

post hanc uocem cum supremo
  mixtam gemitu,

implicitly ties *mixtam* to *uocem* (Agrippina's last words are mixed with her last sighs). Although this is in itself acceptable, the possibility exists that *cum supremo mixtam gemitu* should be taken together with *animam* in the following line,

post hanc uocem
cum supremo mixtam gemitu
animam tandem per fera tristem
  uulnera reddit

given such parallels in epic death-scenes as Verg. *Aen.* 12.952 (= 11.831) *uitaque cum gemitu fugit indignata sub umbras*, imitating Homer, *Il.* 16.857 (= 22.363) ὃν πότμον γοόωσα, wherein the soul escapes from the body with the last sigh of the dying.

This interpretation entails writing *post hanc uocem* as a separate monometer starting a new syntactical unit, which, in Zwierlein's view of anapaestic colometry, whereby monometers imitate clausular paroemiacs in Greek tragedy, would be anomalous.[9] Even Zwierlein, however, does not enforce strictly the principle of using monometers only as clausulae. Fitch (1987, 96) has taken issue with this view, making a case for a more liberal deployment of monometers, mainly according to the criterion of sense-correspondence (Fitch writes 373 as a monometer, though he does not explain how to interpret the following couplet). The position of *tandem* at 375 has little bearing on the question, considering the great frequency of particle dislocations in *Octavia* (cf. ad 96). Indeed, *tandem* often comes extremely late in the sentence in the play (cf. 663–4 *ad hos thalamos seruata diu, | uictima tandem funesta cades*; 827–9 *at illa . . . suspecta coniunx et soror semper mihi, | tandem dolori spiritum reddat meo*). Nor does the hiatus *gemitu | animam* at 374–5 necessarily entail a stronger syntactical pause; other cases where hiatus is not attended by syntactical pause are 16–7 *uidi | oraque*; 362–3 *uiuere matrem | impius*; 778–9 *attonito | aut quid*; *et* in *syllaba anceps* with no syntactical pause at 298.

On the other hand, an escape route of the soul is already provided by *per fera . . . uulnera*, and parallels such as Ov. *Met.* 8.520–1 *grandaeuumque patrem, fratresque piasque sorores | cum gemitu sociamque tori uocat ore supremo* seems to militate in favour of Zwierlein's interpretation. The ancient idea conjured up here is that according to which the soul leaves the body with the blood or through the wound, which is already in Homer (e.g. *Il.* 16.505 ἅμα ψυχήν τε καὶ ἔγχεος ἐξέρυσ' αἰχμήν, Verg. *Aen.* 10.487 *una eademque uia sanguis animusque sequuntur*; Ov. *Met.* 6.253 *cumque anima cruor est effusus in auras*; *Fast.* 5.469 *crudelem animam per uulnera reddas*.

For *mixtus cum* cf. Verg. *Aen.* 9.349–50 *purpuream uomit ille animam et cum sanguine mixta | uina refert moriens*; *Il. Lat.* 365 *purpuream uomit ille animam cum sanguine mixtam*; Ov. *Met.* 4.728–9.

377 Conventionally portrayed as 'outside' the royal palace, Seneca nervously paces up and down, immersed in thoughts foreshadowing his imminent ruin, and reminiscing about his exile in Corsica. Cruelly has Fortune raised him to the lofty citadels of power if it was only in order to bring him down by a more disastrous fall. Happier was he in the days of his exile, in Corsica, where his spirit forever had time to devote itself to its free pursuits, to science, liberation from fear, and astronomy, and contemplation of the ever-revolving

9 In Greek tragedy, editors order anapaestic systems in sequences of dimeters often concluded by catalectic lines (paroemiacs), which always occur at the end of a period. In lyrical anapaests, like *Hec.* 128–9, a basis anapaestica precedes the paroemiacum. But paroemiacs within the course of the period are not found. Even so, this principle is disregarded in Zwierlein's text at *Oct.* 58 *fortuna, licet* (a monometer occurring in the middle of a syntactical unit), and at 362 *uiuere matrem | impius*.

spheres in their harmonious circles. As he indulges in such memories, he lingers over the picture of the flight of the mind, which philosophy has liberated from the shackles of life in the lower realms. But even the wonderful machine of the universe could come to an end. And well it should, to crush the current breed of men, given to lust, and plunder, and impiety.

Seneca expatiates on the corruption of the present times with expressions recognizably taken from his exilic writings. This is done in an attempt to conjure up a sense of authenticity in the portrayal of the philosopher. This Seneca has no straightforward precedent in tragedy, but his tirade may be compared with those of some Greek or Senecan kings moralizing on the dangers posed by an exalted position. Here these reflections are voiced by a proper philosopher, rather than a philosophizing king (in Greek drama cf. Eur. *I.A.* 16–26, paraphrased in Cic. *Tusc.* 3.57). The sense of Seneca's tragic innocence is enhanced by an analogy with the king-philosopher in *Thyestes*, the eponymous hero of Seneca's play who (in an apparent innovation on Accius' precedent) had become a mirror image of the poet-philosopher himself, finally lured back to an imperilled life in power from his exile, but with a burdened conscience, full of obscure premonitions (cf. *Thy.* 405–490, esp. 447 ff. *dum excelsus steti | numquam pauere destiti*). Oedipus' monologue unfolds along the same lines in the initial scene of Seneca's drama (cf. especially 12–14, expressing regret for the wandering years after fleeing from his position in Corinth, *quam bene parentis sceptra Polybi fugeram! | curis solutus, exul, intrepidus uagans . . . in regnum incidi*, where *quam bene . . . fugeram*! corresponds with *melius latebam procul ab inuidiae malis* at 382). Entrance monologues in the Senecan corpus dispense with the fifth-century Greek convention of addressing a god or the monuments of one's native land, and are freely couched as soliloquies.

Seneca, at the imagined time of the action, had not yet fallen out of favour, but the playwright gathers dark clouds on his horizon, presenting the Nero-Seneca confrontation as the prelude to his ultimate downfall. His political career is visualized in comparable terms of dramatic rise and fall in Plin. *Nat.* 14.51.3 *Annaeo Seneca, principe tum eruditorum ac potentia, quae postremo nimia ruit super ipsum.* Seneca is here portrayed as an embodiment of the powerful man who lives in a state of unhappiness and fear, and is envious of the life of simple folk (Eur. *Ion*, 621–5; *Phoe.* 552; more parallels in Tarrant's note, Sen. *Agam.* pp. 183–4; a commonplace for tyrants, who are tormented by fear of attack and by guilt: cf. Plato *Gorg.* 524e; *Resp.* 9.579d–e; Xen. *Hiero, passim*; Tac. *Ann.* 6.6). This state of mind was also effectively depicted in Seneca's own writings, which may have inspired the *ignotus*. Cf. Sen. *Breu. uit.* 4. 1 *potentissimis et in altum sublatis hominibus excidere uoces uidebis quibus otium optent, laudent, omnibus bonis suis praeferant; cupiunt interim ex illo fastigio suo, si tuto liceat, descendere* (of which Seneca himself gave Augustus as an example); *Epist.* 94.73 *ostendat ex constitutione uolgi beatos in illo inuidioso fastigio suo trementis . . . longeque aliam de se opinionem habentis quam ab aliis habetur . . . tunc laudant otium lene et sui iuris . . . tunc demum uideas philosophantis metu et aegrae fortunae sana consilia.* Cf. also Boeth. *Cons.* 3.5. On the risks of the position of *amicus principis* cf. F. Millar, *The Emperor in the Roman World* (London, 1977), 110–13. Seneca's fictional speech in Tac. *Ann.* 14.53–4 also pivots on the theme of *inuidia*, the ill-will of which the philosopher has become a target. *inuidia*, however, is a predictable affliction of characters who have risen from humble origins: cf. Hor. *Serm.* 2.6.47–8. Tacitus' scene has been shown to draw on Seneca's own writings, but there is no immediately apparent link between the episode and *Oct.* 377 ff. Unlike the Seneca of *Ann.* 14, this Seneca speaks his true mind, as good counsellors are wont to do in tragedy (e.g. Creon and Tiresias in Soph. *Oedipus*; Tiresias and Cadmus in Eur. *Bacchae*). On the selectivity and idealization of this portrayal of the philosopher, which cuts out the 'Machiavellian' elements of Seneca's characterization in the historical tradition, cf. Introduction, p. 71. There was also a fictional sub-genre devoted to encounters between a philosopher or holy man and an emperor.

There is a conspicuous break between the choral ode and the beginning of the new scene, which is intended to mark the beginning of a new 'act'. Seneca's entrance is not announced by the chorus, which has no further part in the action. A long monologue signalling the first appearance of a new character is a common feature of both Greek and Senecan tragedy, but in length and general moralizing tone suitable parallels can be adduced only from prologues. This is true also of the subsequent monologue of Agrippina.

Had *Octavia* been Seneca's, there would have been virtually no parallels for a tragic author writing a play including himself as one of the characters, with the sole known exception of L. Cornelius Balbus, who is reported (by Asinius Pollio, who sounds outraged, in a letter to Cicero, *Fam.* 10.32.3) to have produced a play while a quaestor in Spain, celebrating his own mission to L. Lentulus (*ludis praetextam de suo itinere ad L. Lentulum pro consule sollicitandum posuit et quidem, cum ageretur, fleuit memoria rerum gestarum commotus*). In comedy, we have the fragments of Cratinus' *Putine*, which staged the suit brought against the playwright by Comedy, the poet's wife, accusing him of sleeping exclusively with his mistress, the Bottle (cf. *PCG* IV 197, 200 Kassel-Austin). H. I. Flower (*CQ* 45.1 (1995), 177–8) reviews the evidence on which the assumption is based that in Rome political personages could not be celebrated on the stage, virtually a passage of Cic. *De rep.* 4.12.10 (transmitted by Aug. *Ciu.* 2.9) *ueteribus displicuisse Romanis uel laudari quemquam in scaena uiuum hominem uel uituperari.*

377–378 quid, impotens fortuna, fallaci mihi | blandita uultu, sorte contentum mea . . . The MSS read *quid me potens fortuna . . .* Since Gruterus, however, editors have taken offence at the clash of personal pronouns (*me . . . mihi*), of which *me* is superfluous, because it can easily be supplied from the accusative *contentum*, and indeed this resulting surplus of grammatical information is undesirable, in Seneca as well as in *Octavia.* For parallel cases in which a pronominal object (here *me*) is omitted because easily supplied from a co-referential adjective or participle (here *contentum*) cf. *Oct.* 862 *horrore uinctum trepidus astrinxit rigor*, 872, 874 and *Thy.* 1 cited *infra*. See also ad 83–3*. Earlier efforts to emend the line concentrated on *mihi* (so Gruterus, suggesting *nimis*, followed by Bothe). Zwierlein, however, is right to point out that *Octavia* abounds in pronominal line-endings (cf. 383–4, where the same sequence *mihi . . . mea* occurs). More likely to be at fault is the transmitted *me, potens fortuna*. 'Powerful' as an attribute of fortune is in itself plausible, but the suggested emendation *impotens* makes Seneca's address more effective, and is in keeping with the accusatory tone of the monologue. In connection with *fortuna*, *impotens* (= Greek ἀκρατής) occurs in Sen. *Cons. Pol.* 3.5 *hoc sine dubio, impotens fortuna, captasti, ut ostenderes neminem contra te . . . posse defendi*; also with reference to *fortuna* in *Cons. Pol.* 16.2; *Agam.* 247; 593; *Troad.* 981; *H.O.* 715; see A. Borgo, *Lessico morale di Seneca* (Napoli, 1998), 87, citing Curt. Ruf. 3.11.23 *tunc uero impotentis fortunae species conspici potuit*. Siegmund's *impotens . . . mihi* (1911, 15), unaware of Heinsius' *impotens . . . diu* (*Adversaria*, 505), eliminates the odd reduplication of the pronoun. The same mistake occurred in ***A*** at *Thy.* 1 *quis me furor nunc sede ab infausta abstrahit* for *quis inferorum sede ab infausta extrahit* (***E***); also *Troad.* 981–2 *quis tam impotens ac durus et iniquae ferus | sortitor urnae*. In the Senecan corpus alone cf. *Phae.* 185–6 *potensque tota mente dominatur deus; | hic uolucer omni pollet in terra impotens*, which is Heinsius' conjecture for a transmitted, and obviously impossible, *potens* at 186. Zwierlein is also right to object (against retention of *me* before *impotens*) that synaloephe of monosyllables is a feature absent from *Octavia* (with the exception of 870 *ut ne inexpugnabilem*).

Fortune is commonly spoken of as a malevolent deity enticing her prospective victims with a captivating yet deceptive smile. This has a parallel in the words of the *Nutrix* at 34 ff., where fortune is presented in similar terms. On *fallaci mihi blandita uultu* cf. Publ. *Sent.* F2 *fortuna cum blanditur captatum uenit*; Stat. *Silu.* 3.3.157 *blanda diu fortuna*.

377–380 quid . . . sorte contentum mea | alte extulisti, grauius ut ruerem edita | receptus arce? As Bruckner noted (1976, 33), this plaintive address to Fortune is at odds with Seneca's own doctrine, a constant admonition to the wise man to be above fortune's whims. A harangue against fortune is, however, found in Sen. *Cons. Pol.* 3.5, quoted ad 377, where Seneca speaks on behalf of Polybius. Seneca's complaint is paralleled by the prologue of Laberius (113–18 R^2 *Fortuna, . . . si tibi erat libitum, litterarum laudibus | florens cacumen nostrae famae frangere, | cur cum uigebam membris praeuiridantibus . . . non me flexibilem concuruasti ut carperes?* Cf. also Tarrant ad *Agam.* 57–107 (p. 183); *Agam.* 101–1' *quidquid in altum fortuna tulit, | ruitura leuat*; Liv. 30.30.23 *quanto altius elatus erat, eo foedius conruit*.

The punctuation adopted by Giardina, Ballaira and, lastly, Chaumartin, with the question mark after *extulisti* misses the rhetorical point (*interrogatio indignantis*, almost equivalent to 'if you were set on bringing me down so disastrously'): the *ut*-clause is not to be understood as an answer. This complicated sense-structure has parallels at 633–5 *quo te furor prouexit . . . cedat ut tantis malis | genetricis ira . . . ?*, and in Laberius' prologue given above; cf. also Prud. *Peristeph.* 10.206–8 *quid aureorum conditorem temporum | censes colendum, quem fugacem non negas | latuisse furtim dum reformidat malum?* although alternative punctuations have been suggested. Similarly erroneous is *quid? impotens Fortuna* . . . (Liberman); the colloquial *quid?* 'and so?'; 'so what?' is out of place as the first word of an act-beginning monologue.

For *grauius ut ruerem edita | receptus arce* cf. Hor. *Carm.* 2.10.10–1 *celsae grauiore casu | decidunt turres.* Cf. also Liv. 8.31.7 *etenim inuidiam tamquam ignem summa petere*, with Oakley ad loc. *grauis* is the metrically defective form of ***A***. The mistake in the earlier MSS was probably induced by ignorance of the prosody of *grauis.* There was also a long-established tendency to lengthen the tonic element in bisyllabic words, irrespective of its original quantity; this tendency is widespread in medieval Latin, and is already attested in Late and Vulgar Latin (Leonhardt, *DS*, 45, 84, with bibliographical references). The emendation occurs at least in *Ox* and in *Marc. Lat. Cl.* xii 223 (4514) saec.xv.

381 procul ab inuidiae malis For the epexegetic genitive cf. Ov. *Met.* 10.563 *formae(. . .) bono*; 14.684–5 *decoris munus*; cf. also *supra* 34–5 *bono | aulae.* In the same metrical position, Phaedr. *Fab.* 3.8.15 *nequitiae malis.*

382 remotus inter Corsici rupes maris The cliffs are part of the island, rather than of the sea, but this type of *enallage* is common. Seneca has in mind the rocky outline of the island. The adjective *Corsicus* is found in poetry (cf. Man. *Astr.* 4.638–9 *uicinaque Corsica terris | litora Sardiniae*), next to the parallel forms *Corsus* (Ov. *Fast.* 6.194 *Corsis . . . aquis*) and, as a more high-flown equivalent, *Cyrneus.* A sea is often denominated by the nearest land (cf. Hor. *Carm.* 2.12.2 *Siculum mare*). Seneca describes the solitude and wildness of his exile in *Cons. Helu.* 6.5 and in *Epigr.* 2 and 3 Prato.

383–384 ubi liber animus et sui iuris mihi | semper uacabat studia recolenti mea Seneca dwells on the paradox that, at the time of his public disgrace and exile in Corsica, his mind enjoyed an unrestrained freedom, roaming across infinity; for the philosophical commonplace of the flight of the mind cf. R. M. Jones, *CPh* 21 (1926), 116–23. A subtle problem is posed by the interpretation of *animus . . . mihi semper uacabat.* On the likeliest interpretation *mihi* must be understood as the object governed by *uacabat*, meaning '[my] spirit, at last its own lord and free, devoted itself *to me*, as I turned back to my studies'. *vaco*, without a limiting element, may also mean 'to be disengaged from other tasks or occupations, to have leisure'. The extensional meaning 'to be tranquil, clear of afflictions and fears' is also common, but usually requires an ablative. If *uacabat* at *Oct.* 383 means 'was free from other occupations', *mihi* must be understood as a dative of advantage ('where my spirit . . . had ever time to contemplate my favourite themes', Miller, Loeb) or as an ethical dative, a colloquial equivalent of *meus* (cf. e.g. Plaut. *Aul.* 178 *praesagibat mi animus frustra me ire*; *Merc.* 388 *animus mihi dolet*). However, 'devoted itself to me' is the more obvious interpretation of the passage in Latin (probably = *uacabat studiis recolendis meis*), also because the construction of *uaco* with the dative of the person or occupation somebody devotes himself to is extremely common in Seneca. It would come as an anticlimax to say that the mind was free and its own master, if this is to be followed by a verb describing inactivity, while on the other hand 'Seneca' plunges into a turmoil of visionary thoughts.

Whatever the interpretation of *mihi*, the conception of the self which supposedly underpins these words is un-Senecan, or at least a very rough-hewn and approximate representation of Seneca's thought on the subject, because the *animus* is envisaged as a faculty separate from the rest of the subject's personality (cf. the paraphrase of Bernardinus Marmita 'seruiebat uoluntati meae et uirtuti, non alterius libidini ut nunc').

The *animus* is for Seneca the very essence of the individual, of which it constitutes the highest part. The soul is not a function of the self, and it is this precedence of the mind over the body that is stressed throughout in Seneca's prose writings. In the passages devoted to such a mystique of the mind, the individual, now pure spirit, hovers as a flickering light in the ether (cf. e.g. Sen. *Cons. Helu.* 11.6; *Cons. Marc.* 25). The mind finds the universe in itself (cf. e.g. *Epist.* 92.6 *uacat enim animus molestia liber ad inspectum uniuersi nihilque illum auocat a contemplatione naturae*). For Seneca and later Roman Stoics, if not for mainstream Stoicism, the soul is independent of the body, and the truest part of man: cf. Sen. *Ben.* 3.20.1 *corpora obnoxia sunt et adscripta dominis, mens quidem sui iuris, quae adeo libera et uaga est ut ne ab hoc quidem carcere cui inclusa est teneri queat quominus impetu suo utatur et . . . in infinitum comes caelestibus exeat*; *Epist.* 124.12 *liber animus . . . alia subiciens sibi, se nulli*; 65.22; 92.33; 102.22; 114.23; *Clem.* 1.3.5; *Cons. Helu.* 11.6. In general see F. Husner, 'Leib und Seele in der Sprache Senecas' *Philol. Supplementb.* xvii. 3 (Leipzig, 1924), 134–47; A. Bonhöffer, *Epictet und die Stoa* (Stuttgart, 1890), 33–4.

The philosophical incongruity of this line was perceived by Gronovius, who accordingly proposed *sibi uacabat studia recolenti pia*, an emendation which does not seem to have captured the attention of any of his successors. There are strong parallels in support of Gronovius' correction (cf. *Cons. Helu.* 11.7: (the philosopher's mind) *nec exulare umquam potest, liber et deis cognatus . . .* ; 20: <u>*animus omnis occupationis expers operibus suis uacat*</u> *et modo se leuioribus studiis oblectat modo ad considerandam suam uniuersique naturam . . . insurgit*; *N.Q.* 3 *pr.* 2 *sibi totus animus uacet*; *Vit. beat.* 2.2), but the text requires a further adjustment, because *mea* must be altered to *sua* (or *pia*, as he wanted), and the process of corruption becomes more involved, and entails a conscious operation of re-writing on the part of some scribe. It is perhaps best to put up with the philosophical anomaly, yet another sign of the non-Senecan authorship of the play.

384 recolenti *recolo* may stand for 'to resume', 'to go back to', after an intermission caused by adverse circumstances (cf. Cic. *De orat.* 1.2 *neque uero nobis cupientibus atque exoptantibus fructus otii datus est ad eas artes quibus a pueris dediti fuimus celebrandas inter nosque recolendas*; *Pro Archia* 13 *quis mihi iure suscenseat si quantum ceteris ad suas res obeundas . . . tantum mihi egomet ad haec studia recolenda sumpsero?*) or else 'to go over in one's mind' (Cat. *Carm.* 63.45 *pectore Attis sua facta recoluit*; Verg. *Aen.* 6.681 *lustrabat studio recolens*, where Anchises parades his descendants and in his mind anticipates with joy their future glories). The latter seems preferable here, because the former would convey the implication that Seneca had turned away from philosophical speculation for a while before his time in exile, giving in to ambition and other earthly pursuits. There is some warrant for this inference in the sparse information we glean about Seneca's biography from himself and other ancient sources (collected in P. Faider, *Etudes sur Sénèque* (Gand, 1921), 155–86). That he was interested in philosophy from his earliest youth is stated in *Epist.* 49.2, and we know also from the same passage that he later launched into a dashing career in the forum. This success allegedly elicited Gaius' envy, and Seneca narrowly escaped death, thanks to a plea in his favour made by an unnamed courtier, one of Caligula's favourites. This anecdote associating the abstinent philosopher with the world of intrigue and scandalous love affairs of the Julio-Claudian court, as well as his later indictment for adultery with Julia, depicts the image of a wobbly *sapiens* vulnerable to sin and ambition. The poet of *Octavia*, however, is not interested in making that point here. The only contrast seems that set up between the paradoxically happier time of the exile, in which Seneca's mind was constantly engaged in philosophy, and the time at the court of Nero, when these pursuits are no longer possible.

385–387 o quam iuuabat, quo nihil maius parens | Natura genuit, operis immensi artifex, | caelum intueri . . . Cf. Sen. *Epist.* 90.42 *libebat intueri signa ex media caeli parte uergentia* (describing the state of bliss experienced by humankind in its beginnings); *Cons. Helu.* 8.4 *mundus hic, quo nihil neque maius neque ornatius rerum natura genuit*; 8.6 *dum mihi solem lunamque intueri liceat.* Enthusiasm for astronomical research is commonplace, especially in ancient authors influenced by Stoicism. Many parallels are given by Zwierlein, *KK* ad loc., e.g. Man. *Astr.* 1.13–15 *iuuat ire per ipsum aera . . . et aduersos stellarum noscere cursus*; Cic. *Tusc.* 5.69 *quo tandem igitur gaudio adfici necesse est sapientis animum cum his habitantem pernoctantemque curis! ut cum totius mundi motus conuersionesque perspexerit sideraque uiderit innumerabilia caelo inhaerentia cum eius ipsius motu congruere certis infixa sedibus, septem alia suos quaeque tenere cursus multum inter se aut altitudine aut humilitate distantia, quorum uagi motus rata tamen et certa sui cursus spatia definiant – horum nimirum aspectus impulit illos ueteres et admonuit ut plura quaererent.* Also close is Boeth. *Cons.* 1.m.2, where Philosophy sings a lament commiserating with the imprisoned philosopher, whose present state of enforced inactivity strikes a painful contrast with his former eagerness for research: (esp. 6 ff. *hic quondam caelo liber aperto | suetus in aetherios ire meatus | cernebat rosei lumina solis, | uisebat gelidae sidera lunae | et quaecumque uagos stella recursus | exercet uarios flexa per orbes | comprensam numeris uictor habebat*).

For *parens natura* cf. *OLD* s.v. *parens*, 5a; e.g. Ov. *Met.* 1.383, 393; Luc. *Bell. Ciu.* 10.238; Sen. *Phae.* 959; Verg. *Aen.* 4.178; Man. *Astr.* 2.209 *illa parens mundi natura*; Plin. *Nat.* 22.117 *parens illa ac diuina rerum artifex.* On the topos of *natura artifex* cf. Bömer ad Ov. *Met.* 15.218, with parallels.

387 solis et cursus sacros Zwierlein supports with abundant parallels the reading of *recc.*, *cursus*, more in keeping with the philosophical-scientific slant of the passage. Contemplation of the mythological chariots of the Sun adds nothing to the philosopher's joy, which is aroused instead by the recurrence and geometrical perfection of the eternally regulated workings of the universe, and *mundique motus* in the following line supports *recc.* Among the various passages adduced by Zwierlein, *KK* (p. 463) cf. Lucr. *D.R.N.* 5.76–7 *praeterea solis cursus lunaeque meatus | expediam qua ui flectat natura gubernans;* Cic. *Tusc.* 5.69 (see previous note).

388 mundique motus, sortis alternae uices 388 is transmitted in β in the form *mundique motus, solis alternas uices*, and beginning with Delrius the suggestion was made that the words from *solis* to *motus* (= 387^{b}–388^{a}) should be deleted. This is one of those cases where extensive research on the MS tradition of Seneca has made a difference. Delrius and subsequent editors until Giardina either ignored or had no use for the readings of δ, which were made available especially after Stuart's pioneering work, and later with the discovery of *G* by Herington in 1958. The excision of *solis . . . motus* should be seen in this context. δ has also confirmed conjectures at 89, 489, 689, 882 (cf. MacGregor, 1978, 100), and its reading yields an acceptable sense here, with only a minor change (*alternas* into *alternae*). *sortis*, unknown to the older editors and disregarded even by the most recent (Zwierlein, Liberman, Chaumartin), whereas the reading of δ is advocated by Stuart (1912), 20, and MacGregor, 98 n. 17, provides a welcome link between the description of the sun's orbit and that of its twin star, the moon. A progression is envisaged from the general to the more specific, with *caelum* as a generic introduction to the topic, while *mundi motus* highlights the regulated harmonic motion of the celestial vault. It is true that 'the movements of the universe' (*mundi motus*), which is lacking in the parallel from *Cons. Helu.*, tucked in as it is between the 'course of the Sun' and the 'orbits of the moon' (if *orbis* is to be so taken), gives a rather meandering course to the list, but even the authentic Seneca cannot be emended on the basis of strictly 'geometric' considerations of rhetorical composition. Gronovius' *noctis* is an extremely appealing candidate (it introduces the popular motif of synonymical *variatio*), but on consideration, preference should be given to the reading of δ. For *uices* used with reference to 'the daily interchange of night and day' cf. Sen. *Epist.* 102.28 *dies et nox aeris infimi uices sunt. vices* also provides a neat link between the mention of the sun and the moon in the following line (a colon is commonly expanded and clarified by the following one, a type of meandering sequence of thought which is commonplace in Seneca; cf. e.g. *Phae.* 961–2 *(tu) qui sparsa cito sidera mundo | cursusque uagos rapis astrorum*). *sors* is quite normal to designate both the position and the orbit of a star or more generally a position in the skies (cf. Man. *Astr.* 2.703 *ut sociata forent alterna sidera sorte*; 2.804–5 *quae* (sc. *loca*) *nisi perpetuis alterna sorte uolantem* (sc. *orbem*) | *cursibus excipiant*) and is particularly apt in a sequence of nouns varying on the idea of the orbits and courses of heavenly bodies (*cursus, motus, orbem*). *uices* and *sors* are virtually identical in sense, but Latin poetry is awash with such pleonasms (cf. ad 49–50). The two words may also occur in conjunction: cf. Man. *Astr.* 1.110 *quas . . . uices agerent certa sub sorte notauit*; Apul. *Mun.* 26 *custodiam per uices sortium sustinebant*; Lact. *Inst.* 2.9.11 *diem . . . fecit ac noctem quae spatia et orbes temporum perpetuos ac uolubiles quos uocamus annos alterna per uices successione conficiant.*

389 orbemque Phoebes, astra quam cingunt uaga Zwierlein has suggested that *orbem . . . Phoebes* must refer to the moon's orbit, rather than to her disc: both senses are amply paralleled (Zwierlein compares, among others, Tib. 2.4.17–18 *nec refero Solisque uias et qualis ubi orbem | compleuit uersis Luna recurrit equis*) but, if *orbis* meant 'disc', the combination of this word with *Phoebe* (an epithet of the Moon apparently only popularized by Roman poets: cf. *RE* 20.345) would be awkward, combining the mythological visualization whereby the moon is driven by a goddess in anthropomorphic garb and a more literal image of the planet's rounded outline. This consideration, in turn, lends some support to the δ-reading *quam*, against *quem*. The half-line *astra quam cingunt uaga* shifts away from scientific contemplation of the universe, but pays tribute to a long established decorative tradition, whereby the Moon appears in the sky surrounded by a cortège of minor stars among which she shines; cf. Stat. *Silu.* 1.4.36–7 *uaga cingitur astris | Luna*; Petr. *Sat.* 89.1, l.55 *(Phoebe) minora ducens astra*; it is usually deployed in the context of the praises of women's beauty: cf. Hor. *Carm.* 1.12.47 with N-H for parallels (e.g. Sapph. 34; 96.8–9 L-P); Sen. *Phae.* 743 ff.; Stat. *Silu.* 2.6.36.

390 lateque fulgens aetheris magni decus Cf. *Oed.* 250; *Phae.* 410 for *decus* referring to the moon, not to the stars. Here *aetheris magni* must be an epexegetic genitive, since only so can the transition to the following sentence be understandable. If the star-studded celestial vault crumbles, then the world must come to an end.

391–393 qui si senescit, tantus in caecum chaos | casurus iterum, tunc adest mundo dies | supremus ille The MSS offer a text at fault in at least two places: the corruption must have been caused by the complicated syntactical construction of these phrases, with the unexpected *qui si* (picking up *aetheris*) and the enclosed parenthetical *tantus . . . . iterum*. Scaliger's *si senescit* (after Maserius' *qui sic senescit*) justly ousted the untenable MS readings (*se senescit PG* or *sese nescit βT*), but even with Scaliger's correction some further adjustment is necessary. *nunc ades* in the place of MSS *nunc adest* was first proposed by Grotius, who was followed by Gronovius, and later by Leo. Leo extensively rewrote the whole passage:

> qui si senescit, tantus in caecum chaos
> casurus iterum est: nunc ades mundo dies
> supremus ille, qui premas genus impium.

The number of corrections needed in Leo's version does not commend his solutions: the active periphrastic lacks edge, and is especially disturbing if we consider the pointed use which Seneca often makes of predicative future participles in apposition (cf. ad 520; Westman 1961, 94–5); I think that Ritter (who preceded Richter, unjustly credited as the first proposer in all modern editions) was right to write *tunc*. *tunc* is frequently used as a correlative particle in the apodosis of a conditional sentence after *si* (cf. *OLD* s.v. *tum*, 5b; *LHS* 2.659; in Seneca cf. *Ira* 1.11.5 (*imperium*) *tunc in extremo stabat, si Fabius tantum ausus esset quantum ira suadebat*; *Cons. Pol.* 8.1 *si quando te domum receperis, tunc erit tibi metuenda tristitia*). The combination (*si senescit . . .*) *nunc adest*, in the text of the MSS, is not linguistically impossible (it would parallel the use of *ilico, ecce*, common in temporal conditional clauses, with an asseverative function: cf. *LHS* 2.663), but it lends the passage a very colloquial tone, not very apt in this context. Among recent editors, *nunc* is retained by Chaumartin. A close formal and thematic parallel is Sen. *Clem.* 1.4.2 *quos* (sc. *frenos imperii*) *si quando abruperit . . . haec unitas . . . in partes multas dissiliet*; cf. also *Epist.* 95.52 *societas nostra lapidum fornicationi simillima est: quae, casura nisi in uicem obstarent, hoc ipso sustinetur*; *Clem.* 1.3.5 *haec immensa multitudo . . . illius ratione flectitur, pressura se ac fractura uiribus suis, nisi consilio sustineretur*; Ov. *Met.* 2.295–9 *quos* (sc. *polos*) *si uitiauerit ignis, | atria uestra ruent . . . si freta, si terrae pereunt, si regia caeli, | in chaos antiquum confundimur*; Man. *Astr.* 2.804 (cited ad 387–9).

Lines 391 ff. contain a brief description of the Stoic ἐκπύρωσις, also found, in Seneca, in *Epigr.* 1.5–6 Prato *moles pulcherrima caeli | ardebit flammis tota repente suis*, *Cons. Pol.* 1.2 *hoc uniuersum . . . dies aliquis dissipabit et in confusionem ueterem tenebrasque demerget*; *Cons. Marc.* 26.6; *Thy.* 830–83; *H.O.* 1102–17; elsewhere cf. Lucr. *D.R.N.* 5.91–2 (with Bailey's note); Ov. *Met.* 1.256–8; Luc. *Bell. Ciu.* 1.72–4 *sic cum compage soluta | saecula tot mundi suprema coegerit hora, | antiquum repetens iterum chaos*; 7.184. These parallels show that earlier descriptions of ἐκπύρωσις do not single out the collapse of *aether* as the first step of the process of final conflagration: cf., however, Sen. *N.Q.* 3.27.15 *caelo ipso in terram ruente* (adduced by Bruckner), where Seneca describes the prospect of universal deluge.

393–394 qui premat genus impium | caeli ruina The line-ending *genus impium* violates Porson's law, in the laxer form valid for Seneca, since the final creticus is preceded neither by monosyllables nor by synaloephe. In addition, this is the only line in the Senecan corpus, alongside three others from *H.O.* (406, 757, 1847), where a fifth-foot anapaest is 'broken', i.e. the resolved element is separated from the *longum*: cf. Schmidt (1860), 53; Strzelecki (1938), 83. In the authentic tragedies, no cases of split anapaests are found, whereas in *H.O.* this phenomenon occurs several times. Another possible example of this resolution is *Oct.* 447 (see ad loc.). In Plautus, split anapaests in the first and fifth foot are tolerated (cf. Plaut. *Aul.* 47 *quo modo tibi res se habet?*; Ter. *Ad.* 100 *Demea, haec male iudicas*). The main limitations against such resolved feet seem to concern polysyllabic words: split anapaests are admitted when the two short syllables form a bisyllabic word, whereas when one or both short syllables are at the end of a polysyllable split anapaests are avoided (cf. Petersmann ad Plaut. *Stichus* 59, quoting the relevant literature; Soubiran, *Essai*, 197; Lindsay, *ELV*, 90–1).

The expression *caeli ruina* is found in Verg. *Aen.* 1.129, of a storm breaking out, at line end.

394–396 rursus ut stirpem nouam | generet renascens melior, ut quondam tulit | iuuenis The subject of *generet* is conceivably *mundus*, at 392, but the transition is rather artless, after *qui* at 393 picking up *dies*. Chaumartin (p. 129) rightly compares Sen. *N.Q.* 3.29–30, where a renewed human breed comes to life after the flood, to remain innocent for a short while: cf. esp. 3.30.8 *omne ex integro animal generabitur dabiturque terris homo inscius scelerum . . . sed illis quoque innocentia non durabit.*

The myth of the ages in *Octavia* encompasses four generations, as in the account of Ov. *Met.* 1.89–150, to which *Oct.* is deeply indebted. Other versions comprise respectively a succession of five (Hesiod) or three (Aratus) ages. More elliptically, Verg. *Georg.* 1.125–45 concentrates on the innovations introduced by Jupiter and does not provide a clear succession of generations after him. Only two ages are listed in Tib. 1.3.35–50 and in Ov. *Am.* 3.8. The poet of *Oct.* makes no mention of the metals traditionally associated with each new generation. The four ages are marked by, respectively, (1) absence of social structure and wars; (2) a generic loss of innocence (*minus . . . mitis*); (3) agriculture, hunting and fishing; (4) onset of war and mining. The passage from the second to the third is somewhat brief, and a lacuna is often postulated, probably unnecessarily (see ad 407).

396 tenente regna Saturno poli Zwierlein (*KK* 319–28) has maintained that the similarity between this line and *H.O.* 1940–2 (*quid me tenentem regna siderei poli . . . iubes | sentire fatum?*) points to imitation, and that the poet of *H.O.* knew and imitated *Octavia*. For a discussion of the question of priority cf. Introd p. 53. The phrase *regna/sceptra tenente(m)* is relatively frequent in hexametric poetry and elegy, a consideration which makes direct derivation difficult to establish (cf. Prop. 2.32.52 *hic mos Saturno regna tenente fuit*; Ov. *Her.* 4.132 *rustica Saturno regna tenente fuit*; close are also Ov. *Fast.* 2.384 *patruo regna tenente suo*; 2.432 *hoc illo sceptra tenente fuit*; 4.594 *te caeli sceptra tenente*). *regna poli* is not found elsewhere with reference to Saturnus, whose rule is more commonly associated with the idyllic, rustic reign he established after fleeing to Latium (cf. Wissowa, in Roscher, *Lexicon*, s.v. *Saturnus*, col. 434). This element might suggest that *Octavia* is adapting *H.O.*, rather than the reverse.

398 Iustitia, caelo missa, cum sancta Fide *Iustitia* is the Latin equivalent of the goddess Δίκη in Aratus (*Phaen.* 105): her other name, *Astraea*, figures in Ov. *Met.* 1.149–50 *uirgo . . . terras Astraea reliquit* and *infra*, 424 *Astraea uirgo*. She is usually accompanied by another divinity: in Juv. *Sat.* 6.19–20 she is paired with *Pudicitia* (corresponding to Hes. *Op.* 197–200, where the end of the Golden Age is marked by the flight of Aidōs and Nemesis, πρὸς Ὄλυμπον . . . ἴτον προλιπόντ᾽ ἀνθρώπους Αἰδὼς καὶ Νέμεσις; also in Ov. *Met.* 1.129 *fugere pudor uerumque fidesque*). *Iustitia* figures in close association with *Fides* in Hor. *Carm.* 1.24.7; cf. also *Culex* 226–7 *et iure recessit | Iustitia et prior illa Fides*; Petr. *Sat.* 124.

The simple ablative *caelo missa* is paralleled in Liv. 8.9.10 *sicut caelo missus* (of Decius' sacrifice of *deuotio*); Tib. 1.3.90; Min. Fel. 21.7 (the two latter instances in the sense of 'dropped from heaven' of someone suddenly appearing). *mittor* is sometimes used in a medio-passive sense indicating simply the act of arriving somewhere, without the implication of 'being sent on a particular mission'; cf. Verg. *Georg.* 2.385 *Ausonii, Troia gens missa, coloni* (cf. *TLL* viii s.v. *mitto*, 1167.26–30).

399 terra regebat mitis humanum genus Objections have been raised against the bare *terra* of MSS, because the simple ablative is normally restricted to the so-called *ablativus viae* or to fixed expressions ('by land and sea'), such as *terra marique, terra rem gerere* (cf. *OLD* s.v. 1b). Conjectures include Ascensius' *terras* (with comma after *mitis*) and Bothe's *terris* (or *terrae*), understood as a dative of motion (governed by *missa*). Baehrens (1878, 117) conjectured *terras regebat mite et humanum genus*, with *et* postponed. But the linguistic argument against the simple ablative should not be pressed, as Zwierlein and Frassinetti (1973, 1102) are right to argue: the bare ablative is an archaism, found in poetry and rhetorical prose (cf. *LHS* 2.131, 146 see also *infra*, 913 *regnat mundo tristis Erinys*). Lastly, Liberman has revived Schroederus' *terras regebat miteque humanum genus*, but this correction has the disadvantage of introducing an undesirable synaloephe after the seventh element. Liberman gives as a parallel Hor. *Epod.* 5.1–2 *deorum quidquid in caelo regit | terras et humanum genus*. The plural *terras* occurs also *infra*, 422.

The bliss of humankind in the Golden Age had already been described by Seneca in *Phae.* 525–39. Of other treatments of the topos by Latin authors the most relevant are Ov. *Am.* 3.8.35–48; *Met.* 1.89–112.

400–401 non bella norant, non tubae fremitus truces, | non arma gentes The sequence *non bella . . . nec tubae* is found in the older MSS, whereas *recc.* (e.g. *Marc. Lat. Cl.* xii 26 [3906], *Marc. Lat. Cl.* xii 223 [4514]) have *non . . . non.* A concern for strict linguistic correctness possibly prompted the correction, because *neu* was expected after a negative first colon. This is in fact not a very stringent reason, since there are numerous exceptions in classical Latin. More to the point, it is undesirable to have an asymmetric succession *non . . . nec . . . non*; the fourth *nec* is in place because it introduces a different clause. A close parallel is Ov. *Met.* 1.98–9 *non tuba directi, non aeris cornua flexi, | non galeae, non ensis erant*, which confirms the reading of *recc.*; also Tib. 1.3.47–8 *non acies, non ira fuit, non bella nec ensem | inmiti saeuus duxerat arte faber*; 1.10.9 *non arces, non uallus erat.*

401–403 cingere assuerant suas | muris nec urbes . . . communis usus omnium rerum fuit Cf. Ov. *Met.* 1.97 *nondum praecipites cingebant oppida fossae*; Verg. *Buc.* 4.32–3; Ov. *Am.* 3.8.47 *quo tibi turritis incingere moenibus urbes?* Sen. *Phae.* 531–2 *non uasto aggere | crebraque turre cinxerant urbes latus.* For the 'communism' practised by humankind in the Golden Age see also Sen. *Epist.* 90.36–46. The position of *nec* after four words from the beginning of the phrase is remarkable, but does not seem to have prompted emendation.

404–405 et ipsa Tellus laeta fecundos sinus | pandebat ultro The metaphorical field of the earth as mother offering her breast (*fecundos sinus*) to her offspring is often exploited in Golden Age descriptions. The line seems to echo Verg. *Georg.* 1.127–8 *ipsaque Tellus | omnia liberius nullo poscente ferebat*; 2.331 *laxant arua sinus*; Ov. *Am.* 3.8.39–40 *at meliora dabat, curuo sine uomere fruges*; *Met.* 1.101–2 *ipsa quoque . . . per se dabat omnia tellus.*

405–406 tam piis felix parens | et tuta alumnis Liberman argues for *tum*, a trivial MS variant, but preference should be given to the more authoritative reading of *A*, which yields good sense. The history of human progress is viewed from the standpoint of mother earth: an original feature, apparently, in the tradition of Golden Age stories.

406–407 alia sed suboles minus | conspecta mitis *conspecta* (*est*) is little different from *fuit*, although the use of a verb of seeing can perhaps be justified with reference to Earth, from whose viewpoint the process of human evolution is to some extent visualized. *inuenio* and *reperio* are often deployed with the same predicative or copulative value: cf. Ov. *Fast.* 1.650 *sola . . . digna reperta*; *Met.* 14.108–9 *cuius . . . pietas spectata per ignes*; *Her.* 20.102 *magis in natum saeua reperta parens.* Zwierlein cites Colum. 9.2.2 *ne uniuersitas inchoati operis nostri . . . imperfecta conspiceretur.* εὑρίσκω, ἁλίσκομαι are often so used in Greek (cf. e.g. Soph. *Trach.* 411; *Ant.* 46; Eur. *I.A.* 1105).

Richter, followed by Zwierlein, printed a lacuna after *mitis*. Sense and grammar are unobjectionable, but some explanation is expected of the reasons why the second age of Man was less gentle than the first. A comparable abruptness is found in Ov. *Met.* 1.125–7, where the third age lacks specific identifying features except a generic remark on incipient degeneration: *tertia post illam successit aenea proles, | saeuior ingeniis et ad horrida promptior arma, | non scelerata tamen*. The number of the generations is not uniform in the various accounts of the Myth of the Ages. Vergil and Ovid assign the introduction of agriculture to the second, *argentea*, of which it is the most distinctive feature. Hunting fails to figure in Ovid, whereas Vergil envisages it as a positive aspect at *Georg.* 1.139–40. The *Octavia* poet has obviously shifted all these elements to the third age, and in fact it would be difficult to envisage a possible supplement for the hypothetical lacuna.

The ellipsis of the copula is particularly common, in poetry, with the deponent participle *uisus*, and with all past participial forms (cf. T. Winter, *De ellipsi verbi esse* . . . (Marburg, 1885), 33–5: cf. Verg. *Georg.* 1.139–40 *tum laqueis captare feras et fallere uisco | inuentum*; 1.477–8 *simulacra . . . pallentia . . . uisa . . . pecudesque locutae*; 2.350 *iamque reperti*).

407–408 tertium sollers genus | nouas ad artes exstitit, sanctum tamen Cf. Ov. *Met.* 1.127 *non scelerata tamen* (of the third age). For a similar afterthought at line-end cf. Ov. *Met.* 15.83 *nec tamen omnes*; Sen. *Cons. Helu.* 16.1 *concessum est immoderatum in lacrimis ius, non immensum tamen.* A similar turn, however, already occurred in Hes. *Op.* 142 (as noted by B. Gatz, *Weltalter, goldene Zeit und sinnverwandte Vorstellungen* (Hildesheim, 1967), 78, n. 48). Note however that Ovid presented the third generation only as *non scelerata*, which is weaker than *sanctum*.

nouas ad artes is governed by *sollers*, rather than by *exstitit* ('proved himself inventive of new enterprises'). For other instances of *sollers* in reference to the industriousness of primitive men cf. Lucr. *D.R.N.* 5.1356 *sollertius est . . . genus omne uirile*; see also Ov. *Am.* 3.8.45 *contra te sollers, hominum natura, fuisti.*

exstitit, from *exsisto/ exsto*, can be used predicatively, like *conspecta* in the previous line, a sense which is not excluded by the basic meaning of this verb, aptly describing the succession of generations as they come into existence, almost 'springing forth' to life.

409–411 mox inquietum, quod sequi cursu feras | auderet acres, fluctibus tectos graui | extrahere pisces rete The vigour of the third age turns to disquiet and restlessness, psychological qualities which are marked as negative in Senecan writings, where they are contrasted with the *beatitudo* of the *sapiens*: cf. Sen. *Tranq.* 12.3 *inconsultus illis uanusque cursus est . . . quorum* (sc. *uitam*) *non immerito quis inquietam inertiam dixerit. mox* marks a different stage within the same age, rather than the passage to a different generation of men, the fourth, as maintained by Whitman, ad loc., and Bruckner (1976,

26). The description of this age seems to owe something to Soph. *Ant.* 343–52, where the achievements of men are celebrated in subjugating nature and the animals to their needs: κουφονόων τε φῦλον ὀρνίθων ἀμφιβαλὼν ἄγει | καὶ θηρῶν ἀγρίων ἔθνη | πόντου τ ' εἰναλίαν φύσιν | σπείραισι δικτυοκλώστοις (hunting birds, fish, and wild animals, with nets) | περιφραδὴς ἀνήρ (*sollers*), κρατεῖ | δὲ μηχαναῖς ἀγραύλου | θηρὸς ὀρεσσιβάτα λασιαύχενά θ' | ἵππον ὀχμάζεται ἀμφὶ λόφον ζυγῶι | οὔρειόν τ ' ἀκμῆτα ταῦρον. Like the famous Sophoclean stasimon, the description of this age is poised between celebration and blame for the seeds of degeneration which were thus planted by humankind. Animals were under no threat from humans before this generation: for this topos cf. Ov. *Fast.* 6.173–4 *piscis adhuc illi populo sine fraude natabat* | *ostreaque in conchis tuta fuere suis*; *Met.* 15.99 *tunc et aues tutae mouere per aera pennas*.

The subjunctive *auderet* suggests that *quod* introduces a relative-consecutive clause. Relative-consecutive clauses sometimes follow a sequence of one or more adjectives, to which they are linked by a conjunction: cf. Ov. *Met.* 2.54–5 *magna petis . . . et quae nec uiribus istis* | *munera conueniant nec tam puerilibus annis*; 2.763–4 *tristis et ignaui plenissima frigoris et quae* | *igne uacet semper*; Sen. *Cons. Helu.* 11.7 *animus quidem ipse sacer et aeternus est et cui non possit inici manus*.

The ending of 410, *sequi cursu feras*, is similar to Sen. *Phae.* 110 *consequi cursu feras*; cf. also Lucr. *D.R.N.* 5.966–7 *manuum mira freti uirtute pedumque* | *consectabantur siluestria saecla ferarum*.

For *audeo* describing the daring displayed by this near-heroic age in pursuing wild animals on the run, and in subjugating them for the use of agriculture cf. Ov. *Fast.* 5.175–6 *postquam uirtus adoleuit, in apros* | *audet et hirsutas comminus ire leas*, of Hyas).

The MS *graues* was first corrected by Gronovius. His correction makes the sentence more balanced and satisfies the requirements of sense: the nets are heavy because lead was tied to them to press them under water, or, alternatively, because they envelop the fish caught in them so as to make their escape impossible. The mistake was caused by the tendency to create syntactical links between words in the same line.

411–412bis extrahere pisces rete uel calamo leui, | decipere uolucres †crate uel calamo aut leui† | tenere laqueo The text is corrupt in the MS tradition, with most witnesses exhibiting a duplicated *uel calamo aut leui* after *crate*:

extrahere pisces rete uel calamo leui
decipere uolucres crate uel calamo aut leui
tenere laqueo

A sense can be extracted from the paradosis even in its present form (comma after *calamo leui*, then 'to catch birds with baskets, or with rods or to hold them with easy-flowing nooses'), but the identical repeat of *uel calamo leui* cannot be genuine. One explanation of the error is that a scribe mistakenly transcribed *uel calamo leui* twice because a second *uel* followed *crate* in the original text. *aut* was then added at some later stage to give the sequence a semblance of sense. This is the explanation accepted by most editors, and Zwierlein accordingly prints a lacuna after *crate*; various supplements *exempli gratia* have been proposed (for instance Siegmund's *crate* <*uel tereti uagas*>).

A different line is that taken by Leo (*Obs.* 46), followed by Düring (*Materialien* 4.331: 'ortus est error ex varia lectione *crate* ad *rete* adscripta et cum altera parte versus 411 repetita'), who, remarking on the continuous run in which the words are drafted in some MSS, without indication of line-end, suggested that *uel* originated as a critical mark introducing a variant reading into the text, namely *crate*. The words *uel crate uel calamo leui* moved from the margin of 411 to the text of 412, replacing the original text. The decision on where to mark the beginning of the putative lacuna turns on whether or not *cratis* can be seen as a plausible device for bird-catching. Leo's observation is unjustly rejected by Zwierlein and Ballaira, who argue against the possibility of glossing the straighforward *rete* with the more difficult *cratis*. *cratis* is not a word found in connection with hunting activities. A generic word for any kind of wicker-work, it designates a wattle, a grid, or crate or basket or, metaphorically, a cuirass of chainmail. Birds were caught alive by the means of *uimina*, or rods, as described in Petr. *Sat.* 109.7, where these are made of segments successively fitted to reach out to birds perched on the shipmast. This is not a wattle-shaped device to catch birds in mid-air ([*uolucres*] *quas textis harundinibus peritus artifex tetigit. illae uiscatis inligatae uiminibus deferebantur ad manus*). The passage is aptly discussed by F. Capponi, *Latomus* 18 (1959), 724–41 (esp. 739–40): *illigatae uiminibus* is shown to refer to the practice of inserting shorter sticks diagonally and crosswise at one extremity of the long rod, to provide a branch-like space for the birds to perch themselves on. *uimina* occurs also in Prud. *Hamart.* 807, where the fate of the wretched soul is described falling prey to sin like a flock of milk-white doves, lured to descend to the ground by a bait: (804) *haud uelut ac si olim. . . . columbarum nubes descendat in aruum . . . laqueos ubi callidus auceps | praetendit lentoque inleuit uimina uisco . . . gulamque | innectunt auidam tortae retinacula saetae*, where the last three words make clear that the trap is a net of hair-cord, not a *cratis*, and *uimina* refers to shoots (leaves) of grass smeared with sticky bird-lime. Nets were also used in bird-hunting, but they appear to have been of the loose type (cf. *RE* IA.1 s.v. *retia*, coll. 690–1), which is against *cratis*. On the other hand, *cratis* is conceivably appropriate for fishing. Although it never occurs in that connection (cf. *RE* IV.2.1682–85), the words *uimen* and *iuncus* are found in the description of the *nassa*, a fish trap or wheel made of wicker-work (*RE* XVI.2.1793–94) used for catching fish in shoals and shallow waters (cf. [Ov.] *Hal.* 13–14 *auersus crebro uimen sub uerbere caudae | laxans subsequitur*; 15–16 *arto . . . luctantem . . . hunc* (*sc. scarum*) *in uimine*; Plin. *Nat.* 9.132 *capiuntur purpurae paruulis rarisque textu ueluti nassis in alto iactis*; 21.114; 32.116; Cass. *Variae* 11.408 *iunceum carcer*; the device is related to the κύρτη or κύρτος in Greek, which appears to be etymologically connected: [Ov.] *Hal.* 13 ff. closely corresponds to Opp. *Hal.* 4.49 εὖτε γὰρ ἐς κύρτοιο πέσηι λόχον αἴολος ἰχθύς). In medieval Latin the word appears to have been applied to fishery: cf. *DMLBS*, s.v., *crates piscarie sub pontem . . . attachiari non poterant*; as a synonym for *nassa* also in *MLW* II, s.v. col. 1986, 1c. This seems to reinforce the idea that *crate* was a conjectural emendation for the supposedly erroneous *rete*. *crate* may have been written beside the text by someone who was driven by a hypercorrect scruple to emend the ablative *rete*, for *reti* recommended by the grammarians (the two forms alternate in classical Latin: cf. N-W 1.354; so in medieval Latin: cf. P. Stotz, *HLSM*, par. 35.3). The hypercorrect and metrically defective *reti* is the form found in ***C***, in the *editio princeps* and in various other incunabula. These considerations may suggest that *crate* is indeed an emendatory proposal, which in the course of time found its way into the text.

This is the line taken by Fabricius (quoted in Scriverius), and other early editors in his wake, who in fact expunged the words from *crate* to *laqueo* and printed a continuous sequence

extrahere pisces rete uel calamo leui
decipere uolucres, premere subiectos iugo
tauros feroces . . .

while *Marc. Lat. Cl.* xii 26 (=3906) saec. xiv omitted 412 altogether, probably by haplography: *extrahere pisces rete uel calamo leui,* | *tenere laqueo.*

tenere is somewhat inept for the capture of wild animals or birds in a snare: cf. Vergil's *captare*. *decipio*, whose basic meaning is of course 'to deceive', is commonly used in reference both to fish- and bird-hunting (as *fallere* is in the Vergilian passage given below): cf. Ov. *Met.* 3.586–7 *linoque solebat et hamis* | *decipere et calamo salientis ducere pisces*, of which there may be a reminiscence here: cf. *TLL* v, s.v. col. 178, ll. 51–9, e.g. Aus. *Mos.* 244 *nodosis decepta plagis examina* (*piscium*); Mart. 13.68 (*infra*). The Ovidian passage seems to suggest that *calamo leui* refers to fishing rods, but, in the absence of the rest of 412, it is impossible to determine punctuation: *calamus* is also used in reference to reeds smeared with sticky paste or lime, which were used to catch birds (cf. Blümner, 527 n. 3: Ov. *Rem.* 207–8 *alite capta* | *aut lino aut calamis*; Mart. 13.68.1 *galbina decipitur calamis et retibus ales*). *laqueo* refers to a method of catching wild animals and birds with nets. These methods are also referred to in Verg. *Georg.* 1.139–40 *tunc laqueis captare feras et fallere uisco* | *inuentum et magnos canibus circumdare saltus* (quoted in Sen. *Epist.* 90.31, the letter on human progress); Sen. *Phae.* 44–5 *alius rara ceruice graui* | *portare plagas,* | *alius teretes properet laqueos*; cf. Hor. *Epod.* 2.31–6 *aut trudit hinc et hinc multa cane* | *apros in obstantis plagas* | *aut amite leui rara tendit retia . . . pauidumque leporem et aduenam laqueo gruem* | *iucunda captat praemia.*

412bis–413 premere subiectos iugo | tauros feroces Cf. Ov. *Met.* 7.211 *collum pressistis aratro*; *Her.* 12.40 (*ut*) *insolito premeres uomere colla boum*; *Met.* 1.124 *pressique iugo gemuere iuuenci*; 4.25; *Fast.* 3.376; *Trist.* 4.62. The undomesticated ancestors of the tame oxen (*boues, iuuenci*) are naturally enough referred to as *tauri* (cf. also Soph. *Ant.* 351–2 ἵππον ὀχμάζεται ἀμφὶ λόφον ζυγῶι | οὔρειόν τ' ἀκμῆτα ταῦρον and Ov. *Am.* 3.10.13 *prima* (*sc. Ceres*) *iugis tauros supponere colla coegit*; Tib. 1.3.41 *illo non ualidus subiit iuga tempore taurus*; other parallels in Bömer ad Ov. *Met.* 1.124). *ferox*, however, is not idiomatic to indicate that the animals had not been domesticated and roamed freely in the countryside, the usual antonym of *domesticus* being *ferus* (cf. *TLL* s.v. *ferus* . . .). There is a probable reminiscence of *Med.* 241 *tauri ferocis ore flammanti occidet*, referring to Jason's ordeal. In other sources the process of acculturation is linked to the taming of monsters: cf. Aesch. *Prom.* 462 κἄζευξα πρῶτος ἐν ζυγοῖσι κνώδαλα, Aesch. fr. 194 N².

413–14 uulnere immunem prius | sulcare terram Frassinetti (1973, 1103) defends the better-supported reading of ***A*** *uulnere*, against *uomere*, the marginal reading of *G* and of some *recc.* (*KQ* among the most important of them). The transferred use of *immunis* is widespread (cf. *TLL* vii.1, s.v., esp. 506.22 ff., with *sanguine, metu, clade, malis*, with or without preposition), and *laesa* in the following line is also in favour of *uulnere*. Mention of the plough is attractive, but the reading *uomere* is probably to be ascribed to conjecture, and it does not seem intrinsically superior to the paradosis. It was probably prompted by Ov. *Met.* 1.101–2 *ipsa quoque immunis rastroque intacta nec ullis | saucia uomeribus per se dabat omnia tellus*. Cf. also *Met.* 3.11 *(bos) nullum passa iugum curuique immunis aratri*; *Am.* 3.8.39–40 *at meliora dabat curuo sine uomere fruges | pomaque*. The absence of an instrumental ablative with *sulcare* causes no great difficulty.

414–415 laesa quae fruges suas | interius alte condidit sacro sinu As Zwierlein has observed, there are no precedents for the idea that Earth concealed the crops in her womb as a reaction against human agriculture, and this is the only passage in which agriculture is presented as a form of human degeneration (cf. Crusius, in Roscher, *Lexicon*, s.v. *Erysichthon*, col. 1382). Other passages where agriculture is envisaged as a form of violence or oppression inflicted on the soil, not all straightforward, are Ov. *Met.* 2.286–7, where Earth complains *adunci uulnera aratri | rastrorumque fero*; Verg. *Buc.* 4.40 *nec rastros patietur humus*; perhaps Sen. *Phae.* 535–6 *iussa nec dominum pati | iuncto ferebat terra seruitium boue*. Bömer ad Ov. *Met.* 2.286 quotes Soph. *Ant.* 339–40 as a precedent Γᾶν . . . ἀποτρύεται '(humankind) exhausts land'. In other traditional accounts, the onset of agriculture is less traumatic. In Verg. *Georg.* 1.121 ff., agriculture is part of a providential design of Jupiter, whereby mankind should earn its life with toil. In Ov. *Met.* 1.123–4, tilling of the soil marks the second age, but is not presented as a guilty practice. Earth hides deep in its inner recesses only the metals, and in fact a contrast is set up in many sources between the easy accessibility of what is conducive to life and nurture, and the providential removal of the ominous metals: cf. Sen. *Ben.* 7.10.4 *possum de rerum natura queri quod aurum argentumque non interius absconderit?* Plin. *Nat.* 33.2 *imus in uiscera et in sede manium opes quaerimus tamquam parum benigna fertilique qua calcatur . . . quamquam et hoc* (sc. *remedium*) *summa sui parte tribuit, ut fruges, larga facilisque in omnibus quaecumque prosunt*; Ov. *Am.* 3.8.36–8 *omne lucrum tenebris alta premebat humus | aeraque et argentum . . . Manibus admorat.* Zwierlein accordingly suggests introducing a lacuna, submitting that the lost line must have read, e.g. <*summisit aegre quasque habet largas opes*> *interior, alte condidit sacro sinu*: 'mother earth, wounded by the tilling of the soil, began to be sparing of its yield and the riches with which she abounds in her recesses she hid in the depths of her sacred bosom'. Zwierlein's supplement presupposes that it was the third generation which started to raid the depths of the earth. 416 *deterior aetas* shows, however, that metals and riches started to become an object of interest only with the rise of the fourth generation, which is altogether beyond redemption in its rapacity and thirst for blood. Moreover, earth was never keen to release her metals to humankind: the point made so often is that the metals had always been hidden from sight – and would that they always had been left so.

Bothe, 269, felt *interior* and *alte* to be mutually exclusive, proposing to correct the sentence to *frugem suam interius | altam condidit.* The sequence of *interior (interius?)* and *alte* is acceptable. *interior* describes the 'moving away' of the crops, access to which was made more difficult, *alte* refers to the result of this action. Reaching a decision between *interior* in *A* and *interius* in *recc.* is not simple. Adjectives are often found in classical poetry where ordinary language would prefer an adverb (as in e.g. *rauci sonuerunt postes*, for 'the doors creaked raspingly'), whereby the quality of the action being described seems to be transferred to the object which has produced it. Moreover, *interior* and *intimus* belong to the class of adjectives which can be used with a partitive meaning (cf. Sen. *Phae.* 1161–2 *quidquid intimo Tethys sinu | extrema gestat*; *N.Q.* 5.15.3 *in fundum telluris intimae*), referring to only a part of the noun they qualify: cf. *LHS* 2.161; on the use of adjectives for adverbs cf. Löfstedt, *Syntactica*, 1.87–9 (adjectives expressing position or movement: his only classical example, however, is *praeceps* in such locutions as *praeceps dare, trahere*). On balance, however, *interius* seems preferable, although it is not easy to find a psychological explanation for the corruption, since *interior* would have been difficult Latin for all scribes. *-or* and *-us* are easy to confuse in many medieval bookhands.

For *interior* cf. Ov. *Met.* 2.274 (*fontes*) *qui se condiderant in opacae uiscera matris*; 2.277–8 *paulum subsedit et infra, | quam solet esse fuit*; Sen. *N.Q.* 6.20.3 *madefacta tellus . . . altius sedit.*[10]

[10] *Oct.* 415 is wrongly registered in *TLL* iv, s.v. *condo* 148.78 as an instance of *condo* = *repono.*

416–417 sed in parentis uiscera intrauit suae | deterior aetas The passage was possibly inspired by Seneca's own moralizing passage devoted to mining and the extraction of minerals at *N.Q.* 1.17.6 *postquam deterior populus ipsas subit terras effossurus obruenda*, which lacks, however, the imagery of incest. The fourth age, the iron generation, is only mentioned by way of allusion, and not by its metal (cf. Hes. *Op.* 127 γένος πολὺ χειρότερον): it was then that the world learned the arts of war and fighting. cf. Ov. *Met.* 1.137–40 *nec tantum segetes alimentaque debita diues | poscebatur humus, sed itum est in uiscera terrae, | quasque recondiderat Stygiisque admouerat umbris | effodiuntur opes*; Plin. *Nat.* 2.158 *penetramus in uiscera, auri argentique uenas . . . fodientes*; Sen. *Epist.* 94.57; cf. S. Citroni-Marchetti, *Plinio il Vecchio e la tradizione del moralismo romano* (Pisa, 1991), 203.

417–418 eruit ferrum graue | aurumque Cf. Ov. *Am.* 3.8.53 *eruimus terra solidum pro frugibus aurum.*

420–421 tecta defendit sua, | aliena telis aut petit Buecheler's *sua* for MS *suis* (1872, 474) is unavoidable. In addition to healing the text, Buecheler's correction is also superior from a stylistic point of view, introducing the neat antithesis *sua/aliena*. For other similar antithetical pairs cf. Acc. *Scaen.* 169–70 R² *auris uerbis diuitant | alienas, suas ut auro locupletent domos*; Sall. *Cat.* 5.4 *alieni adpetens, sui profusus;* Sen. *Cons. Helu.* 7.4 *alios excidia urbium suarum . . . in aliena spoliatos suis expulerunt.* The corruption must have been caused by a failure to understand the hyperbaton of *aut*; a comparably harsh example of trajection occurs at 401–2, *cingere assuerant suas | muris nec urbes*. Postposition of *aut* after the second word occurs in poetry from Ovid onwards; cf. *TLL* ii, s.v. *aut*, 1565.21–5, e.g. Ov. *Pont.* 3.3.94; Val. Fl. *Arg.* 5.163–4 *aetherias ceu Iuppiter arduus arces | impulerit, imas manus aut Neptunia terras*, and elsewhere; no certain parallels can be found in Senecan tragedy (a dubious case is *Hf.* 454 ***A***). On inversion of particles in the Senecan corpus cf. Zwierlein, *Prolegomena* 231–3; outside the Senecan corpus cf. Marouzeau, *Ordre* 3.85. Previous editors choosing to retain the paradosis have seen this as an illustration of the inconstancy of humankind, torn between benevolence and hostility towards neighbours (*defendit . . . aut petit*), but I find this position impossible to defend.

Liberman has advocated the reading of *M*, *adpetit*, in the place of *aut petit*. This is linguistically inept, since it would indicate a desire or longing for something, rather than the action of obtaining it. With *aut* the two actions, defence of their settlements and attack on other people's, are not represented as mutually exclusive.

petit at 421 is a contracted perfect; for a discussion of other contracted perfect forms in the Senecan corpus cf. Schmidt (1860), 10; Fitch ad *Hf.* 244. In *Octavia* the deployment of contracted forms is always, as far as one can see, compelled by the metre (cf. 38, *Claudi*, 302, *Lucreti*, and 447, *consilii* where the contraction *consili* was impossible).

422–424 neglecta terras fugit et mores feros | hominum, cruenta caede pollutas manus, | Astraea uirgo Such negligence as may consist in the failure to show due reverence (cf. Cat. 64.134 *neglecto numine diuum*) usually is the reason adduced to explain a god's anger. *neglectus* of the slight that gods may suffer from humans also in Hor. *C.S.* 57 *neglecta . . . Virtus*. Astraea was the last deity to leave earth in the account of Ov. *Met.* 1.149–50 *uirgo caede madentes, | ultima caelestum, terras Astraea reliquit* (observe the occurrence of the same plural form, *terras*) and in Verg. *Georg.* 2.473–4 *extrema per illos | Iustitia excedens terris uestigia fecit*; Man. *Astr.* 4.542–3 *rexit saecula prisca | iustitia rursusque eadem labentia fugit.*

Earlier editors up to Giardina prefer the variant *hominum et* of *recc.* (Heinsius suggested *ac cruenta*), but the asymmetric sequence *terras . . . et mores hominum, . . . pollutas manus*, with the last colon in asyndeton, can be paralleled at 547–8 *probitas fidesque coniugis, mores pudor | placeant marito*, 620–4, and 832–3, *ignes ruinae noxium populum premant | turpisque egestas, saeua cum luctu fames*, and there are no compelling reasons to adopt the reading of *recc.*

For *cruenta caede pollutas manus* cf. Sen. *Hf.* 918–19 *manantes . . . manus cruenta caede*; Stat. *Theb.* 12.673–4 *cruentas caede . . . manus*; *Culex* 112 *infandas scelerata manus et caede cruenta.*

426–428 maximum exortum est malum, | luxuria, pestis blanda, cui uires dedit | roburque longum tempus atque error grauis The emphasis on *luxuria* and *auaritia* betrays its Senecan connections: cf. *Epist.* 90.19 *a natura luxuria desciuit quae cotidie se ipsa incitat et tot saeculis crescit et ingenio adiuuat uitia*; 90.38 *inrupit in res optime positas auaritia et dum seducere aliquid cupit atque in suum uertere omnia fecit aliena*; *N.Q.* 1.17.10 *processit . . . in deterius opibus ipsis inuitata luxuria et incrementum ingens uitia ceperunt.* For parallels in Pliny cf. Citroni-Marchetti (cit. *supra* ad 416–17), 201. The meditation on *luxuria*, seen as a slowly spreading plague, which has been strengthened by time and *error*, presumably lack of philosophical enlightenment, closely parallels the description of love as a pest at 561–3 *uis magna mentis, blandus atque animi calor | amor est . . . luxu otio | nutritur.*

429–430 collecta uitia per tot aetates diu | in nos redundant Seneca repeatedly makes the point that the corruption of present times has roots deeper than the present generation: cf. *N.Q.* 5.15.2 *intellexi enim saeculum nostrum non nouis uitiis sed iam inde antiquitus laborare, nec nostra aetate primum auaritiam uenas terrarum . . . quaesisse*; *Epist.* 97.1 *erras . . . si existimas nostri saeculi esse uitium luxuriam . . . et alia quae obiecit suis quisque temporibus.*

The adverb *diu* (in *per tot aetates diu*) is superfluous after *per tot aetates*; the only parallel given in *TLL* for this redundancy is Drac. *Rom.* 2.122 *per saecla diu*; add Caes. *Bell. ciu.* 2.16 *diu longoque spatio.* In Senecan tragedy only *Hf.* 742–3 *longa permensus diu | felicis aeui spatia.* This is one of many cases of the use of synonymic expressions in asyndeton in *Octavia*: cf. ad 142.

430–431 saeculo premimur graui, | quo scelera regnant Cf. Juv. *Sat.* 13.28–30 *nona aetas agitur peioraque saecula ferri | temporibus quorum sceleri non inuenit ipsa | nomen et a nullo posuit natura metallo*; Hor. *Carm.* 3.6.46. The author of the play probably meant this harangue against the evils of the times as an indirect indictment against Nero, from the horrors of whose regime he meant to exculpate Seneca. Retrospectively, this passage presupposes an antityrannical reading, by the *ignotus* and his circles, of *Phae.* 987 *uitioque potens regnat adulter*, traditionally interpreted as an allusion to the Julio-Claudians. The *locus de saeculo* (which is however not always apocalyptic) is a counterpart to the encomiastic praises of the times in panegyric literature: Nero later in the play boasts about the fullness of his time, which the rebellious populace cannot understand. There are several complaints about the decay of morals in comedy, where they are usually voiced by bores or strict fathers, as in Plaut. *Trin.* 291. The three capital evils of this millenary vision are *impietas, libido* and *luxuria.*

431–432 saeuit impietas furens, | turpi libido Venere dominatur potens *impietas furens* imitates Sen. *Hf.* 97 *impietas ferox*, in the same metrical position. Hosius compared Sen. *Phae.* 184–5 *regnat furor | potensque tota mente dominatur deus. Venus* and *libido* are virtual synonyms: this rhetorical figure, whereby expressions virtually synonymous in meaning occur one in subject-function, the other as a genitive or descriptive-modal ablative, is a frequent feature of Roman poetry (e.g. Hor. *Serm.* 1.5.73–4 *uaga . . . dilapso flamma . . . Volcano*), and is especially recurrent in Senecan tragedy: e.g. *Phae.* 465 *et saeua bella Marte sanguineo gerant; Thy.* 700–1 *in ignes uina mutato fluunt | cruenta Baccho.* The ablative is the so-called 'explicative ablative', of the type *fluuio Tiberinus amoeno*, on which cf. Hillen, 29–147.

433–434 luxuria uictrix orbis immensas opes | iam pridem auaris manibus, ut perdat, rapit Cf. Sen. *Thy.* 45–6 *exultet . . . libido uictrix*, in the same metrical position. *luxuria* is said to be *uictrix* (cf. Sen. *N.Q.* 4b.13.11 *luxuria inuictum malum*) because it has produced the irrepressible drive to amass wealth and to plunder under the compulsion of which the Romans have thrown themselves to the conquest of their empire. For this concept in moral and philosophical writings (starting with Plat. *Resp.* 573c, where Lust, Drink, and Madness are the three evils which generate tyranny) cf. Sen. *Helu.* 10.1–6; *Epist.* 89.22; Tac. *Agr.* 30.4 (Calgacus' speech) *raptores orbis*; Petr. *Sat.* 119.5–6 *si qua foret tellus quae fuluum mitteret aurum, | hostis erat*; Luc. *Bell. Ciu.* 10.156–7 *quod luxus . . . toto quaesiuit in orbe*, 10.169 *discit opes Caesar spoliati perdere mundi*; Friedländer, 2.288, n. 1.

The topos is given rhetorical point by the clausula *perdat rapit*, with the intentional clash, enhanced by assonance, of two semantically conflicting verbs, but even this paradoxical antithesis had already been exploited. The Roman conquerors amass riches only to waste them: cf. Sen. *N.Q.* 1. *praef.* 6 *luxuria pecuniam turpiter perdens quam turpius reparet*; *Epist.* 90.38 (*auaritia*) *multa concupiscendo omnia amisit;* cf. also Ov. *Fasti* 1.213 *quaerere ut absumant, absumpta requirere certant.* The juxtaposition of two verbs producing antithetical or paradoxical meanings in clausula is redolent of the Senecan taste for antitheses: cf. e.g. Sen. *Oed.* 209 *incertus animus, scire cum cupiat, timet*; cf. also the paronomastic word-play at *Cons. Helu.* 10.6 *ultimus mentium error est, cum tam exiguum capias, cupere multum.*

immensas is attributive: the world has immense riches, but Roman avarice is set to plunder them all and waste them. Cf. *infra* 626–7 *mittat immensas opes | exhaustus orbis.* More generally on Seneca's attitude towards wealth, as well as the contrasting, often malevolent, picture of the philosopher in the ancient sources, as a prodigiously rich man advocating restraint cf. Griffin, *Seneca*, 286; Kragelund, *CQ* 50 (2000), 504 n. 63.

435 Nero enters accompanied by an officer (identified in the MS *nota* with the word *prefectus*). His entrance occurs at the climax of Seneca's tirade against the evils of the times, *libido auaritia luxuria*, as if to give them their natural embodiment, as neatly encapsulated by Trevet, 22.12 (Junge 1999), *hoc specialiter in Nerone impletum est.* Nero's angry stride and fierce expression forebode terror (435–6). He commands that two of his kin, Plautus and Sulla, be executed and their severed heads be brought to Rome for him to see. Seneca entreats him not to act rashly against members of his family, but Nero silences his preceptor. Now the time has come for the young prince to be his own master. There ensues a long debate about the nature of the principate. Seneca, while pleading Octavia's cause, reminds Nero of the popular favour towards the princess: the people may well overthrow a hated despot. Nero will be best loved if he defends the weak and espouses justice. Nero retorts that force is a kingdom's best advocate.

The portrayal of Nero in the play does not originate in the tradition of mad and extravagant rulers which dominates senatorial historiography (Tacitus, Suetonius and Cassius Dio). It is to be presumed that considerations of literary decorum led to the playwright's resolution to sketch a figure more suited to tragedy, in preference to the grotesque caricature drawn in so much ancient literature. Accordingly, he also eschews all lubricious and scurrilous details found in connection with Nero in the various historical accounts. Nero's characterization is that of a tyrant in the Senecan mould; his utterances throughout the scene have precedents in the mythological dramas, where tyranny is a favourite theme. Especially relevant are those scenes in which the nature of power and the ruler–subject relationship is investigated (cf. esp. *Oed.* 511–29; 699–706; *Thy.* 204–18; *Troad.* 203–352; *Phoen.* 651–64).

Yet this tyrant is more human than his Senecan avatars. Fear is one of his motives, and at one point he even heaves a sigh of regret that Octavia never came around to loving him, despite his trying to believe it (540). Now he has found a spouse who will give the people of Rome the heir they have been longing for. From Poppaea's fertile womb a line of kings will issue. A marriage ceremony is announced to take place on the following day (592).

435–436 sed ecce gressu fertur attonito Nero | trucique uultu There are several descriptive periphrases accompanying the entrance of a new character in Latin drama, and the formulaic *sed ecce*, not found in the early tragedians, alternates in Seneca with *sed en, sed quid* to mark the beginning of the new scene. In *Oct.* cf. also 778 *sed quis gressu ruit attonito*; in Senecan tragedy cf. *Hf.* 329–31 *sed ecce saeuus ac minas uultu gerens | et qualis animo est, talis incessu uenit . . . Lycus*; *Agam.* 388, 586; *Troad.* 999–1000 *sed en citato Pyrrhus accurrit gradu | uultuque toruo*; *Phae.* 989.

Nero's fixed and terrifying stare denotes the tyrant's inhumane attitude: in Greek tragedy cf. the description of the doomed Pentheus in Eur. *Ba.* 212–14 Πενθεὺς πρὸς οἴκους ὅδε διὰ σπουδῆς περᾶι . . . ὡς ἐπτόηται· (= *gressu . . . attonito trucique uultu*) τί ποτ' ἐρεῖ νεώτερον; Eur. *Hec.* 216–17. The enallage *gressu . . . attonito* (the adjective more usually denotes the facial expression, depicting astonishment or the fixity of madness) has an exact parallel in Eur. *Or.* 1505, at line-end, where the running entrance of Orestes, with sword in hand, is described by the chorus as ἐπτοημένωι ποδί; cf. also Soph. fr. 248 R. ἀποπλήκτωι ποδί, with Radt's note for other similar cases of enallage in Greek tragedy. In Senecan tragedy cf. *Med.* 675 *attonito gradu* (at line-end); elsewhere only in Val. Fl. *Arg.* 8.21 *attonito qualis pede prosilit Ino*. In these parallels, *attonito gradu / pede* describes the frenzy of possession or madness. However, Nero's cold-blooded and composed attitude throughout the scene seems to defy this descriptive periphrasis; *attonitus* possibly refers only to a state of suppressed anger, ready to erupt at the least opposition. Only divine possession may be represented as something approaching an incoherent babble in ancient literature: the supposed insanity of tyrants and emperors, in tragedy or historiography, is never manifested in their inability to produce articulate utterances (cf. D. Lanza, *Il tiranno e il suo pubblico* (Torino, 1977), 201–8). On *attonitus* cf. ad 699–700.

436 quid ferat mente horreo Ballaira ties *mente* to *ferat* ('che cosa rivolga nel suo animo'; likewise Trevet, '*quid mente ferat*, id est cupiat'), on the strength of 779 *quid portat pectore anhelo. mente ferre*, however, has no precise parallels for 'he turns over in his mind' (*gero* would have been more idiomatic in this sense: cf. Ov. *Met.* 5.426–7 *inconsolabile uulnus | mente gerit*): cf. Tac. *Hist.* 2.65 (sc. *laetitiam*) *uultu ferens*; Ov. *Am.* 1.2.30 *noua captiua uincula mente feram*, where the sense is 'I shall bear the fetters of love in my captive mind'; Sil. *Pun.* 2.208 *ore ferens iram*. Comparison with *Agam.* 226 *mente horrui* proves that the sense is 'I tremble at the thought'.

437 The introduction of two characters engaged in a dialogue begun off-stage has parallels in fifth-century tragedy: cf. Soph. *Phil.* 1222, where the chorus announces Odysseus and Neoptolemus, who carry on their exchange paying no attention to the chorus observing them; Eur. *Hipp.* 601; *I.A.* 303; Ps.-Eur. *Rhes.* 565. This pattern appears to have been given ample scope in post-classical drama: cf. Taplin, *Stagecraft*, 364; Stevens ad Eur. *Andr.* 146; Page, *GLP* I, 9.13 (Eur. *Alex.*); Frost, *Menander*, 10–11; Handley, on Men. *Dysk.* 223f. In Sen. *Troad.* 203 the angry exchange between Pyrrhus and Agamemnon on Polyxena's doom may be influenced by this practice, but the typically Senecan proclivity for long tirades kills the flavour of anti-artificiality meant to be attached to the technique. Note, however, that the entrance of two characters in mid-dialogue in fifth-century tragedy always involves major figures, and initiates a scene dominated by their exchange. The prefect accompanying Nero in 437, on the other hand, leaves after pronouncing only two lines and never returns to the stage. This technique draws on a partly different tradition of stage-writing, that of the so-called 'protatic' *persona*, attested only in comedy. A character puts in a brief appearance (mainly in initial scenes), in a dialogue with one of the main *personae*, which serves as a credible excuse for sketching the essentials of the plot. The prefect figures here only to provide a cue for the ensuing dialogue. Cf. Ter. *Ad.* 364, where the monologizing Demea catches sight of Syrus, who is talking to the domestic cook, Dromo. The latter is dispatched to his kitchen as soon as Demea steps forward and addresses Syrus; similarly, in Ter. *Hec.* 415–29, Pamphilus interrupts his monologue as he sees Parmeno and Sosia approach. The two are engaged in dialogue, but Sosia is sent into the house when Pamphilus addresses Parmeno; cf. also *Hec.* 767. In Plautus cf. *Merc.* 272, where the scene begins with a dialogue between Lysimachus and his slave, observed by Demipho, who at first remains silent, and the slave, after a brief *numquid amplius?* (280), is quickly dispatched to the master's *uilla*. The comic parallels seem more apt than the Greek tragic ones for elucidating the particular manner of Nero's entrance in mid-dialogue with his prefect. On conversations begun off-stage in Latin comedy cf. Duckworth, *NRC*, 124–6. We encounter here one of those post-classical dramatic features which Tarrant has highlighted in the structure of Senecan drama, though Seneca provides no parallels for this particular type.

The dialogue between Seneca and Nero, turning on matters of state, would be set more appropriately indoors, but such stretches of the imagination are commonly required of ancient viewers. Interior scenes are relatively rare in Greek tragedy and comedy (cf. ad 1–20 with bibliography); scenes taking place on the threshold of the house can be assumed to satisfy the same privacy requirements as indoor scenes, conventionally being beyond the hearing of a third party. The rhetorical patterns of the dialogue follow the traditional succession of regular *stichomythia*, *antilabē*, and longer speeches.

The scene-heading in ***A*** reads *Nero. prefectus. Seneca.* The question whether this personage is to be identified with one of the successors of Afranius Burrus, dead at the time of the events represented in the play, namely Faenius Rufus and Ofonius Tigellinus (*Ann.* 14.51.5), must be answered negatively. While the inept but righteous moral candour of the officer confronting Nero in 846 ff. suggests Faenius Rufus, I believe that no historical figure is intended to be seen in the attendant hastening to carry Nero's orders into effect: for a different view see Kragelund (1988), 498–503. He is a faceless henchman with a fervent zeal for slaughter, and no more than a fleeting projection of his master's cruelty. According to Tacitus, it was at Tigellinus' behest that the two royal relatives were eliminated. In Tacitus's account, however, Nero is an altogether more nuanced character, a weak youth whose soul is the battleground of the diverse and competing influences of Agrippina, Poppaea and Tigellinus. In *Octavia*, a scheming, Iagoesque Tigellinus would have needlessly complicated the tangle of moral responsibilities at work, while also taking away the focus from Nero, who was to be the principal villain. In addition, it would be difficult to find a tragic precedent for the type of the wicked subordinate manipulating his master.

An encounter between Seneca and Nero is famously described in Tac. *Ann.* 14.53–6 (set in 62, before the divorce), in which the philosopher asks to be granted leave from court. The barely 25-year-old Nero, already verging on becoming an autocrat, is represented as a consummate hypocrite, begging for guidance from the older man: *quin, si qua in parte lubricum adulescentiae nostrae declinat, reuocas ornatumque robur subsidio impensius regis?* (to be contrasted with 445 *praecipere mitem conuenit pueris senem*). In Tacitus' version, the narrative of the deaths of Sulla and Plautus (*Ann.* 14.57–9) follows that of Seneca's meeting with Nero, and seems to assume Seneca's loss of influence over Nero (*Ann.* 14.57 *perculso Seneca*). In *Octavia*, however, Seneca is still acting in his capacity as the youth's preceptor. There is no need to suppose ignorance of the actual chronology: the inaccuracy may just reflect the playwright's intention to enhance the dramatic impact of the plot, irrespective of the sequence of the events, by representing a meeting of the two key figures of the story. In addition, Seneca may not have been granted immediate discharge, and may have remained a member of Nero's *consilium*, to save appearances, at least as late as 64, as we gather from *Ann.* 15.23.6 and above all 15.45.5 *Seneca . . . longinqui ruris secessum orauisse.*

M. Griffin (*Seneca*, 426) has put forward the suggestion that Tacitus, in whose account the executions of the two royal personages mark the transition from the first, positive, half of Nero's reign to the darker years that led to the end, was probably original in so greatly stressing the year 62 as the turning point. The agreement of *Octavia* with Tacitus on this point might, however, suggest that this was already a climactic event in the historical account of one of the Flavian historians. On how this adherence to the historical tradition affects the question of sources cf. Introduction, p. 11. On the political ideas expressed by Seneca, which are neither a pedestrian reproduction of *De clementia* nor a vehement harangue against the principate see Introduction, pp. 73–4.

In Tac. *Ann.* 14.59.4 Nero decides to divorce Octavia after Sulla and Plautus have already been murdered and their heads have been shown to him. In *Octavia*, where this sequence of events is presupposed, the two days in which the dramatic action is imagined to take place are too short a time (Cass. Dio *Hist. Rom.* 62.13–14 relates the death of Octavia before mentioning that of Plautus, but this section of Dio's narrative is only extant in the Byzantine epitomes). In real life, at least two months must have elapsed between the execution of Plautus and the death of Octavia, since it is estimated that an average of forty days was necessary for dispatches to be exchanged between Rome and Asia Minor; then a further eleven days would have passed between Nero's divorce and his marrying Poppaea, and Octavia was not immediately disposed of by Nero. Greek tragedy consistently aimed at preserving the illusion that the time of the action and the time of the performance were coextensive, which sometimes led to compression of the stage action. In Aesch. *Agam.*, for example, the time elapsing between Troy's fall and the return of Agamemnon to Argos is covered by some two hundred lines.

437–438 mitte, qui Plauti mihi | Sullaeque caesi referat abscisum caput The tradition was that both Plautus and Sulla had their heads cut off and brought to Nero (Tac. *Ann.* 14.57 *relatum caput eius*; 14.59 *caput interfecti relatum*). The construction of *mittere* with a final relative clause is mainly restricted to prose (cf. *TLL* viii, 1190.44); in poetry cf. Ov. *Met.* 15.643 *quique petant uentis Epidauria litora mittunt*; Verg. *Aen.* 11.81–2 *uinxerat . . . manus quos mitteret umbris | inferias*.

Ballaira considers whether *abscisum* (*abscido*) or the variant reading *abscissum* found in some *recc.* (from *abscindo*) should be given preference. The question is frequently raised by forms of the two verbs, especially past participles, not least because the spelling with double *s* is the norm in orthographic Roman practice after a long vowel or diphthong until the early imperial age: *caussa* is the normal spelling of the word throughout the last century of the Republic and the first of the Empire, and the undifferentiated spelling of *abscindo/abscido* occurs in inscriptions until the Neronian age: cf. J. Fürtner, *ALL* 5 (1888), 520–31; *LHS* 2.181. If the poet is a contemporary of Quintilian, he will have distinguished the two verbs in spelling. The difference in sense between *abscido* and *abscindo* is small: even ancient grammarians occasionally found it difficult to reach a decision between homographs (in the perfect tense, for instance: cf. Don. ad Ter. *Ad.* 559, citing Asper). A parallel problem appears to have been posed by the pair *discido-discindo*, although the former was relatively poorly attested. The more current Latin idiom appears to have been *caput abscidere* (cf. Sen. *Thy.* 1038–9 *abscisa cerno capita et auulsas manus | et rupta fractis cruribus uestigia* ***EAQ***; *abscissa* ***Ke***) but *abscindo* is also found in similar contexts (cf. *Thy.* 1062–3 *membra* *neruosque abscidi | uiuentibus*, where the metre demands the perfect tense of *abscindo*; the sense is 'I cut their limbs to pieces while they were still alive'; Hor. *Sat.* 2.3.303 *caput abscissum manibus cum portat Agaue*, where Pentheus' head has been rent from its torso). The paronomastic variation deployed in Sen. *Med.* 259–60 *caesi senis | discissa membra* (Pelias, dismembered and boiled in the cauldron in order to be rejuvenated) may tilt the balance of probability in favour of *abscindo* (especially considering that the gap between simplex and compositum is the same in both cases, *discido/discindo* being virtually equivalent in sense). I retain *abscisum* because the examples given in *TLL* in which *abscido/abscindo* are not confused seem to posit a distinction, in authors up to Tacitus, between *abscido* 'to sever, cut off' (*manus, capita*) and *abscindo* 'to tear apart, cut to pieces' and 'to practise an incision' (*uenas*).

One additional consideration might be to ask whether assonance (*caesi . . . abscissum*) would have been preferable to repetition for this poet, but the etymological connection may not have been so obvious. In Greek tragedy, in some expressive and emotional contexts, a compound verb is sometimes echoed by its radical: cf. Eur. *Ba.* 1065 κατῆγεν ἦγεν ἦγεν with Dodds' note for more parallels; for a more general discussion cf. R. Renehan, *Studies in Greek Texts* (Göttingen, 1976), 11–27. The reverse order, simplex-compositum, is also common, even with verbs used, as here, in different senses. In Latin cf. Cic. *Verr.* 2.3.155 *caede concide*; Cic. *De orat.* 3.4 *non tibi illa sunt caedenda . . . haec tibi est incidenda* (*v.l. excidenda*) *lingua*.

Axelson (*UW* 67–8) argued that *caesus* for 'slaughtered, slain', a sense the word bears frequently in *Oct.* (it is also common throughout in literary Latin: cf. *TLL* iii. s.v., 60.70 ff.) is only used in Senecan tragedy with reference to animal sacrifice, and, on two occasions, to men slain as animals. This claim, however, seems inaccurate: cf. *Agam.* 932 *timendum caesus Agamemnon docet*; *Thy.* 1058; *Oed.* 389; *H.O.* 1785.

439 iussa haud morabor, castra confestim petam The phrase *iussa haud morari* has epic precedents: cf. Verg. *Aen.* 6.40–1 *nec sacra morantur | iussa uiri* (with Conington, ad Verg. *Aen.* 8.382); Val. Fl. *Arg.* 7.60–1 *haud ipsa morabor | quae petitis*; cf. *infra*, 805. Flavian poets introduce the innovative *cunctari* with internal accusative. *confestim* is not attested in Senecan tragedy, and is rarely found in poetry. *morabor* and *petam* are futures of resolution and self-exhortation; cf. *LHS* 2.310–1; Plaut. *Amph.* 1048 *certumst, intro rumpam in aedis*. The *castra praetoria* are here meant, the barracks of the praetorian guard.

441 iusto esse facile est cui uacat pectus metu Ballaira advocates the *v.l. iustum* found in some *recc.* (and *T*). The older MSS have preserved an idiomatic Latin construction, the double dative, in which the predicate of *esse* is attracted by the logical subject of the impersonal main clause, *facile est (illi)*. Double dative constructions are mostly found with *licet* in early Latin, but the use becomes more widespread in the Augustan age, perhaps under the parallel influence of Greek (cf. K-S 1.680; *LHS* 2.349–50; Löfstedt, *Syntactica*, 2.107–8). There are no other examples in the Senecan corpus. Other poetic examples include Ov. *Met.* 8.406–7 *licet eminus esse | fortibus*; *Trist.* 5.2.6 *infirmo non uacat esse mihi*; Hor. *Serm.* 1.4.39 *dederim quibus esse poetis*; *Epist.* 1.16.61 *da mihi . . . iusto sanctoque uideri*). The 'mixed' construction is also found, though more rarely (Ov. *Her.* 14.4 *est mihi supplicii causa fuisse piam*). Because of its ungrammatical appearance, the double dative construction seems more likely to have been regarded as a howler by medieval scribes, and it is therefore preferable to retain the dative.

On the commonplace that tyrants live in perpetual fear cf. Sen. *Clem.* 1.7.3; 1.8.7; 1.11.4; 1.13.3–4; 1.19.5; 1.26.1; Eur. *Ion* 627–8; *Heraclid.* 996; Sen. *Thy.* 599–606 (also *supra*, ad 377).

442 magnum timoris remedium clementia est The two polysyllabic words at the end impart the line a solemn, sententious tone. This rhythmic pattern is well-established in the dramatic tradition: cf. (with *remedium*) Sen. *Oed.* 515 *iners malorum remedium ignorantia est*; *CRF*, *Inc.* 88 R^2 *iniuriarum remedium est obliuio* (a fragment only known from Sen. *Epist.* 94.28); Publ. Syr. *Sent.* 96 (106) R^2 *cuiuis dolori remedium est patientia*, and (with *clementia*) *ibid.* 357 (288) *metus improbos compescit, non clementia* (a tyrant speaking?); *ibid.* 500 (372) *perpetuo uincit qui utitur clementia.*

444 seruare ciues maior est patriae patri Seneca's words elaborate on the title ordinarily conferred upon the *princeps* by the Senate, accompanied by the oak-crown *ob ciues seruatos* (first granted to Augustus in 27 BC). The formula reappears on the coinage of Vindex and Galba (cf. *BMCRE* I, p. 327, n. 109); subsequently Vespasian was awarded the same title (cf. *BMCRE* II, xlvii). The prime source of this passage is *Clem.* 1.26.5, where a similar line of conduct is advocated for the *princeps: nullum ornamentum . . . dignius . . . quam illa corona ob ciues seruatos.* There is no literary evidence of this title having been bestowed upon Nero, but an oak-wreath appears on the reverse of Neronian coins (cf. Griffin, *Seneca*, 115–16), which, together with the legend EX SC, is interpreted as a proof that such honour was indeed awarded to Nero.

patris in the place of *patri* was perhaps expected in response to (*uirtus*) *ducis* in the previous line, but the dative is unobjectionable.

446 regenda magis est feruida adolescentia The line exhibits a cluster of metrical phenomena which are rarely found together. The occurrence of a monosyllabic word at the fifth-foot caesura, even after a resolved fourth element, is fairly common in Latin dramatic verse: in Seneca cf. *Phae.* 483 *non alia magis est libera et uitio carens;* Soubiran, *Essai*, 133–4. Synaloephe after the hephthemimeres (as in *feruida adolescentia*) can occur when the second word is a monosyllabic prefix, apparently felt as distinct from its radical: cf. *infra*, 541 *pectore insociabili*, 870 *ut ne inexpugnabilis*; Hahlbrock (1968), 183. This type of synaloephe is rare in the Senecan corpus (cf., however, Sen. *Phoe.* 133, 165).

Resolution of the eighth element is also unusual (but cf. *Phoe.* 117), and the concomitant occurrence of synaloephe and resolution in this position, involving a word extending over two metrical feet, is unique in the Senecan corpus: cf. Zwierlein, *Proleg.* 230. A partial parallel is *Oct.* 140, where synaloephe is found between the seventh and the eighth, resolved, element, *sanguine alieno satum.*

adul-/adolescentia is not found in Senecan tragedy. There are, however, exact parallels in early drama: Plaut. *Trin.* 301 *ab ineunte adulescentia* | (tr_7); Ter. *Ad.* 152 *sperabam iam deferuisse adulescentiam* | (ia_6); cf. also *AL* 809. 4 (= *Phaedri App.* 12.4) *feruidam adulescentiam.* The spelling *adol-* is found alongside the more common *adulescentia,* but no stylistic connotations can be attached to either form (cf. *LHS* 1.84; Sommer, 108: *adolescentia* would be a 'recomposition' from *adolesco* (cf. *suboles, indoles* from the same stem), rather than *adulescens*).

447 aetate in hac satis esse consilii reor . . . The uncontracted form *consilii* is required by the metre: an iambic fifth foot is only admitted with quadrisyllabic words in Senecan tragedy. The construction is *reor in hac aetate* (i.e. *mihi, in me*) *esse satis consilii,* not *reor (me), hoc aetatis, satis consilii* (gen. qualitatis) *esse.* An idiom noun + *nullius consili* exists (cf. Ter. *An.* 608 *tam iners, tam nulli consili sum*; Cic. *Ad Quint. fr.* 1.2.15 *adulescens nullius consili*), but I have not found an exact precedent for *ego sum satis consilii,* and *satis* is obviously the subject of the infinitive clause. Nero's words seem to echo Ov. *Met.* 6.40 *consilii satis est in me mihi* (Arachne); cf. also Sen. *N.Q.* 2.42.1 *ad suum concilium <acciri> a Ioue deos, quasi in ipso parum consilii sit.* Nero gives an illustration of impious behaviour in his disregard for every divine and human power, for which Ovid's Arachne provided an apt precedent. The word *consilium* is ambiguous in Latin, meaning both 'advice' and 'common sense', 'wisdom in giving advice': significantly, the same double meaning is found here: cf. the admonitory words of Pallas, Ov. *Met.* 6.29–31 *seris uenit usus ab annis,* | *consilium ne sperne meum. tibi fama petatur* | *inter mortales faciendae maxima lanae* with the several lines pronounced by Seneca.

hac means *mea:* on the use of deictic pronouns to indicate possession, which is especially recurrent in dramatic poetry because of its expressive, gestural, force, cf. *LHS* 2.180; Hor. *Carm.* 3.10.19–20 *non hoc* (i.e. *meum*) *semper erit . . . patiens latus*; Sen. *Phoe.* 142–3 *effundere hanc cum morte luctantem diu* | *animam.* The unmarked position of demonstratives in Latin seems to be pre-nominal (see *LHS.* 2.407–8) and the unusual word order *aetate in hac* has few parallels in Senecan tragedy (only *Troad.* 1071 *turre in hac*; *Med.* 249 *terra hac* (uncertain); *Agam.* 977 *sanguine hoc dextram ablue*).

L. Mueller (*DRM,* 165) proposed to emend *satis* to *sat,* to remove the split anapaest in the third foot. A decided reluctance to resolve third-foot theses can be observed in Senecan tragedy, and resolution at this point only occurs in words equalling a third paeon (⏑⏑–⏑: *latuisse*) with no synaloephe, because this would weaken one of the main caesuras in the line: Schmidt (1860), 52; Strzelecki (1938), 78. In early Latin *sat/satis* may have been combinatory variants, with *sat* restricted to pre-consonantal position, but this distinction was inoperative by the time of Plautus (cf. Lindsay, *ELV*, 215–16), and in Seneca's practice the two forms can be considered fully interchangeable. Neither *satis* nor *sat* is ever found in this metrical position (third thesis / fifth element) in Senecan tragedy. *sat* (13 occurrences, only as *sat* + *esse, es, est*) always occupies the even theses.[11] It is not found in indifferent elements, and it seems to be the form to which Seneca resorts under metrical compulsion. *satis*, on the other hand, figures in a variety of expressions, either in the idiom *satis esse, sum, est*, or with adjectives (*satis efficaces*), verbs (*satis passae sumus*) and with a partitive in *Troad.* 286–7 *satis | poenarum*. Its metrical position is subject to less evident restrictions: in fact, *satis* is employed to fill the first foot and all the three even feet.[12] It is also found as a pyrrhic in resolved elements.[13] This survey shows that *sat* would be just as peculiar here as *satis*. The argument that *sat/satis esse* in this metrical position (fifth element) would weaken the caesura is inadequate for explaining its absence, since the pattern 'fourth-foot diaeresis + hephthemimeres' is commonly found in the Senecan corpus, but it is likely that the concurrence of the two metrical irregularities (a split anapaest and a word-combination which weakened the penthemimeres) was what made this metrical arrangement unsuitable for Seneca.[14] Strzelecki defended *satis* arguing that *satis esse* may be considered a single word for (prosodic) metrical purposes. This observation is in general confirmed by the occurrence of the word-group *sat/satis est* in metrical positions where word-break would not be admitted (for instance *H.O.* 1122, where *sat est* occupies the final ⏑⏓ of a glyconic: cf. L. Mueller, *DRM*, 466). *Med.* 126 *ferrum exigatur. hoc meis satis est malis?* provides a further example of split anapaest in the fifth foot, with *satis*. Even in Greek tragedy, split anapaests are tolerated if the pyrrhic-shaped word is followed by a postpositive, such as ἐστίν (cf. Devine-Stephens, *PGS* 316). The further consideration that *esse* has existential value (= *inest*) in this context does not refute Strzelecki's argument, because the verb's semantic value has no influence on its prosodic weight. Observe in addition that the metrics of *Octavia* frequently depart from the strictness of Senecan practice, and Ovid's echo may have played a part. Split anapaests in the third foot in iambics are documented in early Latin drama and in Phaedrus, but are rare in tragedy: cf. Enn. *Scaen.* 202 R² *Acherontem obibo ubi mortis thesauri obiacent*; Ter. *Heaut.* 34

[11] 2th: 2x; 4th: 4x; 6th: 7x. [12] i: 2x; ii: 5x; iv: 8x; vi: 6x.

[13] 2ar: 4x; 3ar: 1x (*Agam.* 970); 1th: 1x; 5th: 5x

[14] In the fragments of early Roman tragedy, Acc. *Scaen.* 247 R² ⏓–⏑ *neque sat fingi neque dici potest* would seem to support L. Mueller's emendation of *Oct.* 447, because *sati(s)/sati'/sate* was metrically admissible (Lindsay, *ELV* 127–8). In Acc. *Scaen.* 87 R² ⏓ *si satis recte aut uera ratione augurem* (ia_6), *satis rec-* could be analyzed as a split anapaest, but the anomaly could be excused by the closeness of the two words (*satis* specifying *recte*).

alias nouas, nisi finem maledictis facit; *An.* 59; cf. Strzelecki, (1938),79–80; Soubiran, *Essai* 130–2. A comparable metrical *hapax* in *Oct.* is 393 *genus impium* (see ad loc.) with *genus im-* providing a split anapaest in the fifth foot.

448 ut facta superi comprobent semper tua The interpretation of *ut* in this line has been regarded as problematic. It was questioned by N. Heinsius, *Adversaria* 507, who proposed *ita.* Pedroli suggests a concessive interpretation = *dummodo* (likewise, Thomann translates 'sofern die Götter immer deine Taten billigen'). Others (Santoro, Ballaira, Bruckner, Liberman, Chaumartin) interpret it as an equivalent of *utinam*, a sense in which *ut* is found in poetry (cf. Verg. *Aen.* 10.631–2 *quod ut o potius formidine falsa* | *ludar*; K-S 1.183; *LHS* 2.331). This solution yields feeble sense: the gods, from Seneca's point of view, are already scarcely approving of Nero's deeds. In the cut and thrust of a tense argument Seneca should be deliberately completing and twisting Nero's answer in a fashion contrary to the one intended by Nero and giving a pointed conclusion to his sentence. *ut* can only be understood in connection with *satis* (cf. e.g. Sen. *Troad.* 682–3 *ut Vlixem domes,* | *uel umbra satis es*; Pac. *Scaen.* 304/305 R^2 *quamquam aetas senet, satis habeam uirium ut te ara arceam.* On this interpretation, 447 should be printed with an ellipsis: 'I have enough sense, by now . . . (e.g. *to think for myself*)' 'to act in a way of which the gods should always approve', or 'my age makes me responsible enough – to be accountable for your deeds to the gods'. As usual in stichomythia, the sense of verbal duelling is conveyed by the two interlocutors' cutting in on one another and leaving one another scarcely any time to complete their sentences. This pattern is recurrent: in *Octavia* cf. 195, 458. Another such stylistic expedient for suggesting animation and rapidity of dialogue is synaloephe at change of speaker (*infra* ad 459).

449 stulte uerebor, ipse cum faciam, deos 'I shall be a fool to be afraid of them, since I am the one who creates them', implying that the gods do not really exist. Nero's riposte is likely to contain a pun: Nero not only deified his adoptive father, but also helped him on his way. In Suet. *Nero* 33.1 Nero is said to have uttered a similar ironic comment: *boletos . . . quasi deorum cibum conlaudare . . . solitus*, with an allusion to the poisoning (also in Cass. Dio *Hist. Rom.* 60.35.4). On a different level cf. the jocular words pronounced by Vespasian on his death-bed, *vae, puto, deus fio.* Seneca's reply fails to take any notice of Nero's sarcastic joke: the author of *Octavia*, as I have argued (Introd. p. 72) deliberately obliterates all involvement of Seneca in Nero's schemes, including the *Apocolocyntosis.*

The line is transmitted in ***A*** in the form *esse cum faciam deos*, which yields dubious Latin: the causative construction of *facio* + infinitive is a vulgarism, though occasionally found in poetry (Ovid), especially in combination with *esse* + an adjective (cf. P. Thielmann, *ALL* 3 (1886), 182–3), with only two cases in Sen. trag., *H.O.* 433–4, 1499–500, with passive infinitives. The correction *ipse* is found in *recc.* 'To create a god' is the simple *facere deum*: cf. Man. *Astr.* 4.934 *iam* *facit ipse* (sc. humankind) *deos mittitque ad sidera numen*. Even with the punctuation proposed by Kurfess (*BPhW* 47 (1927), 570), *stulte uerebor esse, cum faciam, deos*, which gives *uereri* a sense this verb normally bears only when followed by *ne* and the subjunctive, *esse* is superfluous, and introduces an infelicitous shift of emphasis, on *esse* rather than *deos*, rounding off Nero's line.

450 hoc plus uerere, quod licet tantum tibi The sense is 'All the more should you have reverence for them, because they bestowed upon you so much power.' Nero is reminded to pay due honour to the gods, by observing moral behaviour. A similar piece of advice is imparted by the wise man Apollonius to Vespasian at the latter's proclamation in Alexandria: cf. Philostr. *Vita Apoll.* 5.36 (I, p. 196 Kays.) τὸ ἐξεῖναί σοι πᾶν ὅτι βούλει δέδιθι· σωφρονέστερον γὰρ αὐτῶι χρήσῃι . . . θεοὺς θεράπευε.

452 crede obsequenti parcius: leuis est dea The heated exchange between the two characters adapts to the line-by-line standard format of antilabe in Greek tragedy, giving rise to a series of proverbial or epigrammatic *sententiae*. cf. Publ. Syr. *Sent.* 295 (253) R^2 *leuis est Fortuna: cito reposcit quod dedit. parcius* is a real comparative, but in poetry adverbial forms in *-ius* are normally preferred to the ones in *-e*.

453 inertis est nescire quid liceat sibi Nero's answer has a parallel in the saying ascribed to this emperor in Suet. *Ner.* 37.3 *negauit quemquam principum scisse quid sibi liceret.* At the same time, this play with words is a feature of the tyrant in other literary texts: cf. Sen. *Agam.* 271–2 *id esse regni maximum pignus putant* | *si quidquid aliis non licet solis licet* (with the Greek precedents adduced by Tarrant); *Clem.* 1.11.2 *quantum sibi in ciues suos liceat.*

454 id facere laus est quod decet, non quod licet The dittology *quod decet . . . quod licet* draws on the paronomastic opposition of *licet* and *libet*. Examples are given in Otto, 193; cf. [Cic.] *Rhet. Her.* 4.25.34; Sen. *Troad.* 336 *minimum decet libere cui multum licet*; *SHA Ant. Car.* 10.2 *si licet, libet; an nescis te . . . leges dare, non accipere?*; Claud. *IV cons. Hon.* 267–8 *nec tibi quid liceat sed quid fecisse decebit* | *occurrat.*

455 NE. **calcat iacentem uulgus.** SE. **inuisum opprimit** Bruckner (1976), 49 (with reference to Phaedr. *Fab.* 1.21 and Otto, 64), presents Nero's statement as a proverbial utterance. Nero defends his aggressive policy by asserting that the people, in their cowardice, are likely to trample on an irresolute ruler: only force wielded strongly gains a ruler obedience. The image underlying Nero's words is that of the Homeric warrior who has conquered his opponent in a duel and crushes his body in triumph: cf. Hom. Lat. 402 *morientum calcat aceruos*; in a metaphorical context, stigmatizing cowardly behaviour cf. Ov. *Ibis* 29 *calcasti qui me, uiolente, iacentem*; *Pont.* 4.3.27–8 *insultare iacenti* | *te mihi*; *Trist.* 2.571; 5.8.10, where *iacens* bears the meaning of *prostratus, afflictus*, because Ovid has been convicted and sent into exile; Juv. 10.86 *dum iacet in ripa calcemus Caesaris hostem*; Macr. *Saturn.* 1.11.9.

In the present passage, however, *iacens* stands rather for 'inactive' or 'indecisive', as in Claud. *Rapt. Proserp.* 1.96–8 *an forte iacentes | ignauosque putas quod non Cyclopia tela | stringimus?* (so also Trevet, '*iacentem*, id est torpentem'). Has Nero heard rumours regarding a projected insurrection against his imminent union with Poppaea? (cf. *supra* 273–90). Seneca mentions the popular support for Octavia later on at 572–3.

457 NE. **decet timeri Caesarem.** SE. **at plus diligi** The occurrence of synaloephe between two words pronounced by successive speakers prompted Leo to excise the line (*Hermes* 10 (1876), 439; *Obs.* 58–9). Synaloephe at change of speaker occurs once more in the Senecan corpus (*Agam.* 794 *credis uidere te Ilium?:: et Priamum simul*, which the author of *Oct.* seems to have in mind here). The only other instance, *H.O.* 892, *uitam relinques miseram?:: ut Alciden sequar* (***E***), is however indefensible in this form, violating as it does two norms: Seneca does not allow change of speaker: (a) after the third arsis nor (b) after a resolved element: cf. Strzelecki (1938), 9. All modern editors accept Gronovius' correction DE *miseram, ut Alciden sequar.* These norms are probably not to be taken as strict (after all in Greek drama and in Plautus, synaloephe at change of speaker was normal: cf. Gratwick, ad Plaut. *Men.*, p. 253; West, *GM* 84), and both are violated in *Agam.* 970 (where no synaloephe is involved) *iustae parenti satis:: at iratae parum.* Examples of synaloephe with syntactical pause (but no change of speaker) are given in Zwierlein, *KK* ad *Phae.* 1229.

For the content cf. Cicero's warning to Antonius in *Phil.* 1.33–4 *illud magis uereor ne . . . gloriosum putes plus te unum posse quam omnis et metui a ciuibus tuis quam diligi malis* (a passage where Cicero, shortly afterwards, quotes Accius' Atreus (14.34): *quod uidemus etiam in fabula illi ipsi qui 'oderint dum metuant' dixerit perniciosum fuisse*).

458–459 NE. **metuant necesse est . . .** SE. **quicquid exprimitur graue est.** | NE. **iussisque nostris pareant** Seneca's *exprimitur* ('what is extorted') refers to compulsion or unwilling action, implying that Nero has advocated such coercion in his half-line. But *metuant necesse est* only suggests 'they must fear me', and does not evoke the image of people forced to do something they would not otherwise do. *exprimere* occurs again at 494 *humiles . . . uoces exprimit nostri metus*, and 581 *exprimere ius est, ferre quod nequeunt preces?*; elsewhere cf. Plin. *Pan.* 2.2 *uoces illae quas metus exprimebat*; Sen. *Oed.* 529; *Clem.* 1.1.7 *omnibus . . . nunc ciuibus tuis . . . haec confessio exprimitur esse felices.* Nero has made no requests to the people of Rome. An appeal to some positive action answering *at plus diligi*, would make the conflict between the people's inclinations and their enforced behaviour emerge more clearly. Should we read ***laudent, probent*** or ***ferant***? Cf. Tiberius' word-play at Suet. *Tib.* 59, *oderint dum probent*; Sen. *Clem.* 1.13.4 *adprobare imperia sua ciuibus cupiens*; Sen. *Thy.* 205–7 *maximum hoc regni bonum est, | quod facta domini cogitur populus sui | tam ferre quam laudare.* ***faueant, ament*** seem also strong candidates, the latter best explaining the error as a polar mistake or an interpolation. Perhaps *metuant* was suggested by the preceding *decet timeri Caesarem.* Various possibilities were put forward by Seneca himself in *Ira* 1.20.4, where Seneca, meditating on that famous epiphonema, propounds various possible alternatives: *dum pareant . . . dum probent . . . dum metuant.*

The enclitic *-que* at 459 implies that Nero takes no account of Seneca's interruption: 'they must fear me . . . :: all that is imposed is hateful :: . . . and obey our orders'. A comparable instance in which a speaker completes a sentence disregarding his interlocutor's interruption in *antilabē* has been discussed ad 198.

459–460 SE. **iusta impera.** NE. **statuam ipse.** SE. **quae consensus efficiat rata** A question of constitutional limitations on the prerogatives of the *princeps* seems to be raised by Seneca's riposte, with *consensus* as a form of control. This might, in theory, be important for placing the *praetexta* in its historical context, but the appeal to *consensus* as the legitimating basis for power is too general to afford any chronological clues. The line provides an example, however, of how the playwright gives Seneca's ideas on the principate a new, possibly more senatorial, spin: *Clem.* ignores all constitutional issues involving limitations on the powers of the *princeps*, and, in Seneca, *consensus* is treated as a universal and innate concept, not as a political idea. Cf. *Clem.* 1.3.4; *Const.* 4.1; *Ben.* 5.4.3. F. Weidauer, *Der Prinzipat in Senecas Schrift de Clementia* (diss. Marburg, 1950), 44; A. Pittet, *MH* 12 (1955), 43–5.

It is sometimes asserted that the Flavian age saw a resurgence of Republican ideals brought back to life by the so-called Stoic opposition, fighting for the Senate to enjoy an equal share in the administration of the state: cf. J. Malitz, *Hermes* 113 (1985), 231–46; P. Desideri, *Dione di Prusa* (Firenze, 1978), 27–32. *consensus*, however, the key word in this context, has no intrinsic Republican connotations, and *consensus efficiat rata* does not necessarily imply senatorial endorsing of the *princeps'* decisions. In our literary evidence, *consensus* is associated with the plebiscitary acclamation of a ruler; Hosius cited Liv. 1.6 *secuta ex omni multitudine consentiens uox ratum nomen imperiumque regi effecit.* Under Augustus, *consensus* became a slogan emphasising the popular foundations of the new regime: cf. Aug. *Res Gestae* 35; Suet. *Aug.* 58.2 *senatus te consentiens cum populo Romano consalutat patriae patrem*; Plin. *Pan.* 10.2 *ad hoc audiebas senatus populique consensum, non unius Neruae iudicium illud, illa electio fuit*; Premerstein (1937), 61, 64, n. 5 on coin legends reading CONSENSVS SENATVS EQVESTRIS ORDINIS POPVLIQVE ROMANI; H. U. Instinski, *Hermes* 75 (1940), 265–78; C. Wirszubski, *Libertas as a Political Idea at Rome* (Cambridge, 1950), 130. On *consensus* in association with legislation passed by the senate and by some local authorities cf. Instinsky, 268. In epigraphic evidence, *consensus* is mentioned to describe the unanimous agreement of the body politic, even of a small community, even in as small a matter as the erection of an honorary statue or an inscription. The only reference to 'parliamentary' proceedings is found in Tacitus, where *consensus* is a unanimous assent (not necessarily a vote) in the Senate. Cf. *Ann.* 13.26; 14.49. The advice to place oneself under the laws figures in other 'mirrors for princes', advocating a rhetorical obeisance to the laws: cf. Seneca, *Clem.* 1.1.4; Philostr. *Vita Apoll.* 5.36 ὁ νόμος καί σου ἀρχέτω; Introd. pp. 73–4. This playwright does not share the political extremism of Vespasian's opponents, and his Seneca has nothing of the martyrs popular in the memorial literature of Pliny's age (on which cf. F. Marx, *Philologus*, 92 (1937), 83–103; A. Ronconi, *SIFC* n.s. 17 (1940), 3–32; see also ad 377).

An influence on Seneca's stance may have been exerted by Greek tragedy, with Nero being identified with the vicious tyrant and Seneca with one of his virtuous antagonists. Ruthless rulers tend to encounter more stubborn and more articulate opposition in Greek than in Senecan tragedy: cf. in Soph. *O.T.* 628–9 the words with which Creon reacts to Oedipus' impositions, suggesting that his subjects may disobey bad orders; CR. εἰ δὲ ξυνίῃς μηδέν; OED. ἀρκτέον γ' ὅμως. | CR. οὔτοι κακῶς γ' ἄρχοντος. Cf. also *Ant.* 666–7 where Creon asserts his prerogative of imposing 'right and its opposite': ἀλλ' ὃν πόλις στήσειε, τοῦδε χρὴ κλύειν | καὶ σμικρὰ καὶ δίκαια καὶ τἀναντία.

efficiat in 460 is picked up by the simple *faciet* in the following line – a common pattern of repetition often with altered meaning, on which cf. also ad 178; 579–80; 849.

461 destrictus ensis faciet *destrictus*, in place of the MSS' *despectus*, which yields no acceptable sense ('scorned' or 'seen from above'), was first proposed by Raphelengius (it was later revived by E. Löfstedt, 'Coniectanea', *Eranos* 11 (1911), 245, unaware of his predecessors). It is supported by comparison with *Hf.* 344 *strictus tuetur ensis*; Hor. *Carm.* 3.1.17–18 *destrictus ensis cui super impia | ceruice pendet*; Sen. *Clem.* 1.1.2 *haec tot milia gladiorum quae pax mea comprimit, ad nutum meum stringentur.* Other corrections proposed (like Buecheler's *respectus*, later discovered in ***G***) do not commend themselves on grounds of sense. *destrictus* means 'held in hand', with the implication that the sword is about to be used against somebody, but this implication may not have been obvious to scribes; or else the corruption may have been purely mechanical.

This threat appears to have been put into effect on the occasion of Thrasea's trial, when soldiers in civilian dress surrounded the Curia to intimidate the senators on the final day of proceedings against Thrasea; cf. Tac. *Ann.* 16.27 *aditum senatus globus togatorum insederat non occultis gladiis*; 16.29 *nouus et altior pauor manus et tela militum cernentibus.*

462 an patiar ultra sanguinem nostrum peti The animated exchange drifts towards a different topic as Nero justifies his intention to use force with the argument that his own life is under threat from his political opponents. According to Tacitus, the case against Sulla had been prepared carefully at the time of the divorce. He had been accused of plotting against

Nero's life: cf. Tac. *Ann.* 13.47, for an account of the ambush at the Pons Muluius, allegedly planned by Sulla.

If Nero is here referring to an event which has, or is alleged to have, happened, Leo's emendation *ultro* (*Obs.* 62) appears less compelling. *ultro* (*OLD* 6a 'with reference to unprovoked military action') is also the reading of various *recc.* as well as the more Senecan solution: cf. *Oed.* 963–4 (*oculi*) *intenti manum* | *ultro insecuntur, uulneri occurrunt suo.* If accepted, it should be linked with *peti*, 'without my doing anything to motivate such attempts against my life', as in *Thy.* 202 *petatur ultro ne quiescentem petat*; Verg. *Aen.* 10.312–13 *ultro* | *Aenean petit* (of a warrior daring to attack Aeneas first). Yet *ultra* seems beyond suspicion, and can be linked to either *patiar* ('should I endure any longer') or *peti*, but preferably to the former, adding weight to Nero's indignation. Against Leo, notice also that *ultro* needs a subject whose determination to act it reinforces, and there is no emphatic subject in *sanguinem . . . peti* (cf. by way of contrast *Agam.* 945–6 *opperiar meos* | *hostes et ultro uulneri opponam caput*). Nero is not waiting for his enemies to take the initiative: he is stating his inability to tolerate their attacks any longer (with the implication that there have been some already). *ultra* is common in such indignant contexts (cf. e.g. *Phoe.* 140 *quid perdis ultra uerba?*; *Oed.* 860; Liv. 5.48.5 *neque ferri ultra fames poterat*; 10.28.12 *quid ultra moror familiare fatum?*). In its wording, this line resembles Sen. *Clem.* 1.9.4 *quid ergo, ego percussorem meum securum ambulare patiar me sollicito?*; *Med.* 398–9 *regias egone ut faces* | *inulta patiar?*

463 inultus et contemptus ut subito opprimar? The antithetical pair offered by the paradosis cannot be accepted (*inuictus et contemptus* are mutually exclusive), despite attempts to explain the sequence as 'scorned despite my invincibility'. *inultus*, which was suggested by Raphelengius, is certainly right, and is often found in conjunction with *patior*: cf. Stat. *Theb.* 11.269–71 *neque te ulterius . . . patiemur inulti*; Ov. *Met.* 8.279–80 *non impune feremus,* | *quaeque inhonoratae, non et dicemur inultae*; Liv. 4.28.4 *praebituri . . . uos telis hostium estis indefensi, inulti?* Nero adopts the heroic ethos: he cannot allow himself to become the laughing-stock of his triumphant enemies: cf. *Hf.* 1187 *ut inultus ego sim?*

464 exilia non fregere summotos procul The metaphorical use of *frango* ('to bend', 'to crush') is common in poetry: cf. Verg. *Aen.* 2.13 *fracti bello*; 7.594 *frangimur . . . fatis*; cf. also *infra*, 575, 677.

465–466 pertinax quorum furor | armat ministros sceleris in caedem meam On *minister* followed by a genitive defining the quality of the action being carried out cf. 368 (a close parallel is Ov. *Am.* 1.7.27 *caedis scelerumque ministrae*). *furor* is later repeatedly used to describe the 'folly' of the populace rising against Nero in defence of Octavia. The word is also commonly deployed to describe any attempt to subvert the established regime, without implying actual madness (cf. Cic. *Cat.* 1.1 *quam diu etiam furor iste tuus nos eludet?*): cf. *TLL* vi. s.v. *furor*, 1630–1. Here *furor* is the stubborn opposition put up by the two pretenders, at least according to Nero's interested opinion.

467–468 absentium cum maneat etiam ingens fauor | in urbe nostra, qui fouet spes exulum The succession, at 465–8, of a relative (*quorum furor*), a temporal (*cum maneat*) and a further relative clause (*qui fouet*), is anomalous by the standards of Senecan tragedy. For other instances of complicated sentence construction in this play cf. ad 38–40; 45–7; 108.

A parallel for Nero's fears is provided by Creon in Soph. *Ant.* 289–92, who complains that the men of Thebes have been murmuring against him.

etiam stands for *etiamnunc* (cf. *TLL* v, s.v. *etiam*, 928.69 ff.). For *spes fouere* cf. *TLL* vi.1 s.v., 1223.39–53; Liv. 22.53.4 *nequiquam eos perditam spem fouere*, Tac. *Hist.* 3.62 *caput eius . . . ostentatum ne quam ultra spem fouerent.*

470–471 inuisa coniunx pereat et carum sibi | fratrem sequatur: quicquid excelsum est cadat The same sarcastic use of *sequi* for 'to follow in death' occurs in Sen. *Agam.* 1003, which is clearly echoed here: *trahite* (sc. *Cassandram*), *ut sequatur coniugem ereptum mihi* (cf. also ad 944): *sibi* is used to add emphasis, and also to mark a distance between Nero's and Octavia's attitudes to Britannicus. Nero's final generalizing statement, *quicquid excelsum est cadat*, subsumes the two categories of enemies previously named. It is pointless to find a further referent for *quidquid excelsum*, following Herzog-Hauser and Ballaira, who imagine that Nero is preparing a general onslaught on the upper class. For the topos of tyrants having to ensure impunity by disposing of the most eminent citizens cf. Liv. 1.54 (with Ogilvie's note); Ov. *Fast.* 2.685–706; in Senecan tragedy cf. *Oed.* 702 *omne quod dubium est cadat*, which seems to be echoed here. The topos has a Greek origin, and is first found in Herod. *Hist.* 5.92. It also occurs in Philostr. *Vita Apoll.* 5.36 (1, p. 196 Kays.).

For *excelsus* as 'raised by fortune to perilous heights' cf. Tarrant's note ad Sen. *Agam.* 59, with several parallels; Liv. 2.9.3 *nihil excelsum, nihil quod supra cetera emineat in ciuitatibus fore.*

With reference to persons, the use of the neuter pronoun *quidquid* seems to convey a nuance of contempt or disparagement; cf. *infra* 531 *ense occuparo quidquid infestum est mihi.* In Senecan tragedy this manner of reference appears to be rare: only *Oed.* 834 *tuto mouetur quidquid extremo in loco est*; *Agam.* 101. Nero sees his opponents as mere physical obstacles he will eliminate. Bruckner (1976), 59, draws attention to a possible parallel in Sen. *Clem.* 1.10.1 *quidquid floris erat in ciuitate*, in which Augustus is praised for winning, through his clement policy, the universal favour of Rome's nobility.

472–475 pulchrum eminere est inter illustres uiros, | consulere patriae, parcere afflictis, fera | caede abstinere, tempus atque irae dare, | orbi quietem, saeculo pacem suo The language of these lines is heavily indebted to Seneca's *De clementia* although the concept of the ideal king herein expressed reflects ideas widespread in the political philosophy of the early Empire, tinged with Stoicism; cf. M. Rostovtzeff, *Social and Economic History of the Roman Empire* (Oxford, 1957[2]), 120 on the ideal king of Dio Chrysostom (esp. *Orat.* 1 and 3): he will behave like a father and a benefactor, selected by divine providence, loved by his subjects and surrounded by 'friends' (senators?), who ought to have a share in government.

Seneca's plea for a just and enlightened government is conveyed by a sequence of five infinitives, lending his recommendations the tone of a monotonous ramble. A similar list of regal duties is found in Sen. *Med.* 222–5 *hoc reges habent | magnificum et ingens . . . prodesse miseris, supplices fido lare | protegere*, and in *Phoe.* 292–3 (*tu . . . potes*) *inhibere iuuenes, ciuibus pacem dare, | patriae quietem, foederi laeso fidem*, which seems echoed here (especially in the final tricolon governed by *dare*); *Clem.* 1.26.5 *felicitas illa multis salutem dare et ad uitam ab ipsa morte reuocare et mereri clementia ciuicam*. In similar terms Cicero praises Caesar's display of clemency towards Marcellus in *Pro Marc.* 8 *animum uincere, iracundiam cohibere, uicto temperare, aduersarium nobilitate ingenio uirtute praestantem non modo extollere iacentem . . . simillimum deo iudico.*

473 parcere afflictis *parcere* bears here the sense of 'act forbearingly towards, show consideration for' (not, as is more common, 'spare' as in e.g. Verg. *Aen.* 6.853 *parcere subiectis et debellare superbos*); cf. Juv. 14.215 *parcendum est teneris*. The dittology *consulere et parcere* occurs in Acc. *Scaen.* 137 R² *me par est tibi consulere et parcere. parcere afflictis*, in the context, invites comparison with the famous passage in Vergil given above, but it is more likely that *afflicti*, which may also be used for *uicti, superati* (cf. Liv. 7.20.5 *populum Romanum . . . felicissimum bello sibi desumerent hostem, cuius adflicti amicitiam petissent?*) should be understood as indicating social status (cf. *TLL* i. s.v. *afflictus*, 1237). The ideal ruler should be a beneficent father, and accordingly bring relief to the poverty-stricken: cf. Sen. *Clem.* 2.6.2 (the ruler) *succurret alienis lacrimis . . . dabit manum naufrago, exuli hospitium*; Muson. Ruf. (p. 32 Hense) δεῖ μὲν γὰρ δήπου δύνασθαι τὸν βασιλέα σώιζειν ἀνθρώπους καὶ εὐεργετεῖν, Philostr. *Vita Apoll.* 5.36 πλούτωι δ' ἂν ἄριστα βασιλέων χρῶιο τοῖς μὲν δεομένοις ἐπαρκῶν, τοῖς δὲ πολλὰ κεκτημένοις παρέχων ἀσφαλῆ τὸν πλοῦτον, Phaedr. *Fab.* 1.2.27 *afflictis ut succurrat* (the frogs asking Jupiter to give them a new king).

475 saeculo pacem suo The word *saeculum* indicates by hyperbole, in the language of imperial writers, the period of an emperor's reign: cf. Plin. *Pan.* 30.5 *saeculo tuo*; 46.7 *tuo in saeculo*; also *infra*, 834 *saeculi nostri bonis*; Sen. *Clem.* 1.13.5 tale saeculum.

suus is used with reference to an impersonal subject, for 'one's own'. The same use can be observed at 497–8 *cum liceat una uoce suspectos sibi | mori iubere*, at which Gronovius took offence, suggesting *tibi* (*cui* for *cum*: Bothe). The impersonal use of third person reflexive pronouns is entirely idiomatic in Latin; cf. Sen. *Phoe.* 493–4 *quotiens necesse est fallere aut falli a suis, | patiare potius ipse quam facias scelus.*

476 petitur hac caelum uia Cf. Cic. *De rep.* 6.16 *ea uita uia est in caelum*; Verg. *Aen.* 9.641–2 *sic itur ad astra, | dis genite ac geniture deos.* Imperial deification is justified by the Stoic tenet that the benefactors of humanity are received into heaven; cf. also Man. *Astr.* 1.755.

477–478 sic ille patriae primus Augustus parens | complexus astra est *primus* refers to *ille . . . Augustus* (Ballaira) rather than *parens*, since already Cicero and Julius Caesar had been publicly acclaimed as *patriae parens* before Augustus (cf. S. Weinstock, *Diuus Iulius*, Oxford, 1971, 201–5). The title existed in two forms, *p. parens* and *p. pater*: see Premerstein (1937), 168, for the different shades of meaning conjured up by the two forms (with *pater* as the more 'imperial' word, because it derives from the relation established between Roman patrons and their clients). In *Oct.*, however, the two forms appear to be used interchangeably (cf. 444, 490).

complecti has here the high-flown metaphorical sense of *occupare, sibi uindicare*; it occurs in conjunction with a word meaning the heavenly vault in Man. *Astr.* 1.150 *ignis . . . summa . . . complexus stellantis culmina caeli* and in *CE* 743.4 *aeternas sedes meruit complecti priorum*; cf. also Vell. 2.108.2 *certum imperium uimque regiam complexus animo*. The line implies the justification of imperial apotheosis through the deified emperor's *benefacta*, a kind of Euhemerism which is found in Hor. *Epist.* 2.1.6 *post ingentia facta deorum in templa recepti* (with Brink's note); Sen. *Clem.* 1.10.3 *deum esse* (sc. *ob clementiam*) *non tamquam iussi credimus*, and in Plin. *Paneg.* 35.4. Griffin (*Seneca*, 219 n. 8), illustrates the precedents for the idea in Cicero's writings.

This line provides an example of a sentence in which aphaeresis of *est* occurs but *scriptio continua* is less acceptable (*parumst*, but not *astrast*), because *astra* and *est* belong to different syntactic constituents: cf. Schmidt (1860), 19. Lachmann (ad Lucr. *D.R.N.* 1.993) defended forms like *laesa figura tuast*, where *tua* and *est* are not part of the same syntactic constituent (i.e. *laesa est figura tua*). There is evidence that this orthography reaches well into late antiquity, but modern editorial practice restricts it to early Latin texts. *est* tends to be found in aphaeresis with nouns or adjectives to which it is linked by the sense: cf. 458 *graue est*; 604 *datum est*; 825 *parum est*. For a modern discussion of the question cf. E. J. Kenney, *CQ* n.s. 36 (1986), 542 proposing the spelling *formosast* with prodelided *(e)st* in Ov. *Rem.* 187. This orthography is supported by some good ancient evidence (Vergil's earliest MSS adopt it).

478 colitur et templis deus Ov. *Met.* 15.818 (of Caesar) *ut deus accedat caelo templisque colatur*; Tac. *Ann.* 1.10.6 *cum se templis . . . coli uellet*. *templis coli* is more readily interpreted as an instrumental, than a locatival ablative.

481 hostes parentis donec oppressit sui Revenge on Caesar's assassins was the official reason for the civil war culminating in the battle of Philippi: cf. Aug. *Res Gest.* 1.2, *qui parentem meum necauerunt eos . . . uici* (Ballaira). The same verbal and rhythmic pattern, a trisyllabic verbal compound + possessive, is repeated at line-end in 481 *oppressit sui*, 482 *summisit suum*, 484 *subiecit tuo*.

482 tibi numen incruenta summisit suum The subject of this sentence can only be *Fortuna* from 479–81 *illum* (sc. *Augustum*) *tamen Fortuna iactauit diu* . . . : cf. Sen. *Epist.* 84.13 *si conscendere hunc uerticem libet, cui se fortuna summisit* . . .), but the sequence is not without ambiguity. In Tac. *Ann.* 13.4, Nero, in his accession speech, speaks of his peaceful ascent to power, in implied contrast to that of Augustus: *neque iuuentam armis ciuilibus aut domesticis discordiis imbutam*. The absence of caesura after the fifth element is remarkable, but the 'hidden' diaeresis after the fourth element compensating for it is a frequent feature in Senecan tragedy: cf. Zwierlein, *Prolegomena*, 229: e.g. *Phoe.* 482 *dum frater exarmatur, armatus mane.*

483 et dedit habenas imperi facili manu Nero was granted an easy ascent to power thanks to fortune's benevolence. For *habenae* as the 'reins of the Empire' cf. *TLL* vi.3, s.v., 2394.4–33, most notably Ov. *Pont.* 2.5.75 (with Galasso ad loc. for more parallels) *succedatque suis orbis moderator habenis*; Verg. *Aen.* 7.600; Ov. *Met.* 15.481. *facili manu* is also in Apul. *Met.* 8.5.31, but cf. Sen. *Apocol.* 4.2 *Lachesis . . . fecit illud plena manu* (also with reference to Nero), with the parallels provided by Eden ad loc.; *Cons. Pol.* 9.7–8 (*frater tuus fortunam*) *stantem adhuc . . . et munera plena manu congerentem reliquit*; *Phae.* 979 *fortuna . . . sparsit . . . manu munera caeca.*

484 nutuque terras maria subiecit tuo The terms describing the jurisdiction of the Roman *princeps* over the different realms of the world suggest a parallel with the superhuman power of the gods. The motif that the Roman ruler enjoys god-like cosmic powers is well attested in panegyrical literature, from Hellenistic times: on the subject see A. D. Momigliano, *JRS* 32 (1942), 64 n. 45. In Latin literature cf. Cic. *Rosc. Am.* 131 *Iuppiter Optimus Maximus, cuius nutu et arbitrio caelum terra mariaque reguntur*; Plin. *Pan.* 4.4 *cuius dicione nutuque maria terrae pax bella regerentur*; Juv. *Sat.* 4.83 *maria ac terras populosque regenti* (i.e. Domitian).

485–486 Inuidia tristis, uicta consensu pio, | cessit; senatus equitis accensus fauor 'Grim hatred, overcome by loyal consent, has withdrawn.' An alternative interpretation is put forward by Liberman, who, reviving a view of Delrius, ties *senatus* to *inuidia* ('à l'animosité chagrine du sénat succéda . . . la piété du consensus'); also in *TLL*, vii, s.v., 724.54:

inuidia tristis, uicta consensu pio,
cessit senatus; equitis accensus fauor

On this interpretation, envy, opposing the smooth transition of power into Nero's hands, is attributed to the senators. This is unacceptable, because it would lend to Seneca's tirade an anti-senatorial slant which is, at this stage, unmotivated, and unlikely to be well received in the putative political context for which *Octavia* was composed. The word-order resulting from this punctuation, *inuidia . . . senatus*, would also be odd in Latin. It is better to interpret the sequence *senatus, equitis* as an asyndetic dicolon. *Inuidia* is no one's in particular, a malignant deity, relishing civic discord, like *Phthonos* in Greek. Consent of all social orders defeats *Inuidia*, which personifies the natural hostility directed against kings and in general against people of exalted rank (cf. ad 381; Lucr. *D.R.N.* 5.1125–6 *e summo . . . deicit ictos | inuidia interdum contemptim in Tartara taetra*). In Verg. *Georg.* 3.37–8 the defeat of *Inuidia* is a key scene in the pediment of the temple erected by the poet to honour the triumphant Caesar, *Inuidia infelix Furias . . . metuet*, where political discontent is presented as a product of superhuman forces, to be banished from the new world order established by the victorious emperor (cf. 486, *cessit*). There is no obvious need to refer *Inuidia* specifically to Nero's invidious situation as an adoptive heir (so Ballaira, joining ranks with Trevet, whose interpretation is 'aliqui inuidebant et tristabantur quod repulso Britannico . . . Nero . . . succedere debebat in imperium').

On *consensus* as a slogan of early imperial politics cf. ad 459–60; for the propagandistic motif describing the unanimous agreement of all social orders cf. Aug. *Res. Gest.* 6.24 *senatus et equester ordo populusque Romanus uniuersus appellauit me patrem patriae*; Ov. *Fast.* 2.127–8 *sancte pater patriae, tibi plebs, tibi curia nomen | hoc dedit, hoc dedimus nos tibi nomen, eques*; Plin. *Pan.* 10.2 *audiebas senatus populique consensum*; Claud. *Cons. Stil.* 3.48–50 *omnis in hoc uno uariis discordia cessit | ordinibus: laetatur eques plauditque senator | uotaque patricio certant plebeia fauori* (Hosius), which may imitate this passage. Claudian's possible knowledge of Senecan tragedy and the importance of his imitations for the history of Seneca's transmission are assessed in Zwierlein, *Prolegomena*, 30–5.

487–489 plebisque uotis atque iudicio patrum | tu pacis auctor, generis humani arbiter | electus The MSS read *p. u. atque iudicium patrum est*, which was first emended by Lipsius, on account of the syntactical *non sequitur* of having *atque iudicium* after the ablative *uotis*. The only attempt to make sense of the transmitted version known to me is Trevet's, who made *plebisque* a genitive dependent on *fauor*: 'fauebant tibi uoto suo tam equites quam plebei', with a comma after *uotis*.

A further problem is posed by *electus*. I take the phrase to fulfil the function of a relative clause ('you, who, in fulfilment of the people's vows and by express recognition of the senate, are the author of peace and appointed arbiter of mankind, you rule over the world with your divine breath'). It is unclear, however, from whom or what Nero's authority over mankind descends. In the passage of *Clem.* which appears to be echoed here, election assumes clearly supernatural connotations: the emperor is the representative of the gods on earth, and no reference is made to consent as a form of ratification of his power: cf. *Clem.* 1.1.2 *egone ex omnibus mortalibus placui electusque sum qui in terris deorum uice fungerer? ego uitae necisque gentibus arbiter?*; Griffin, *Seneca*, 148 n. 2. The adjective *electus* is not a word of univocal connotation, and different shades of meaning can be attached to it in different contexts: it is used with reference to divine election in Plin. *Pan.* 1 *ab Ioue ipso coram ac palam repertus, electus est* (6.1 *imperator et parens generis humani*), whereas in Tac. *Ann.* 1.7.10 *ut uocatus electusque potius a re publica uideretur* the word designates the semblance of popular endorsement to which Tiberius aspires. In *Octavia*, however, the 'calling' of Nero becomes a mixture of divine and human: the presence of *iudicio* introduces a moderating element on the divine election of *Clem.* Cf. Introd., pp. 73–4.

The transposition of 488 and 489 (first proposed by Frassinetti and accepted by Liberman)

> plebisque uotis atque iudicio patrum
> electus orbem spiritu sacro regis, 489
> tu pacis auctor, generis humani arbiter, 488
> patriae parens

is intended to bring *electus* in closer conjunction with *uotis atque iudicio*, making the elevation of Nero the outcome of political action, but the change is unnecessary. The sense is that Nero's proclamation has been recognized by the people of Rome as the fulfilment of their prayers, mainly for peace, and the senate grant Nero the same trust.

On *arbiter* as a designation of Roman emperors (in addition to *Clem.*1.1.2 cited above) cf. Ov. *Trist.* 5.2.47 *arbiter imperii*; Stat. *Silu.* 4.3.83 *maximus arbiter*; Tac. *Ann.* 2.73 *solus arbiter rerum.* On the use of epithets of Greek origin in reference to Roman emperors cf. S. R. F. Price, *JHS* 104 (1984), 79–95; D. S. Levene, *PCPhS* 43 (1997), 66–103.

489 orbem spiritu sacro regis The paradosis is divided between different abbreviations: *spū* (= *spiritu*), the reading of δ (***GP***) is preferable to the unclear *sap'ie sacra* or *sp'e*, *specie sacra* found in β. *spiritu* is supported by *Clem.* 1.3.5 *haec inmensa multitudo, unius animae circumdata, illius spiritu regitur*, first adduced by Gruterus in this connection. The notion that the *princeps* rules the empire like the mind, or spirit, governing the body is common in other early imperial texts: cf. Tac. *Ann.* 1.12.3 *unum esse rei publicae corpus atque unius animo regendum*; Flor. 2.14.6 *quod* (sc. *imperii corpus*) *haud dubie numquam coire et consentire potuisset, nisi unius praesidis nutu quasi anima et mente regeretur.* On *sacer* in association with the imperial household, mainly in poetry, cf. ad 156, *orbis imperio sacri.*

490 patriae parens Nero, on his accession, refused the title of *pater patriae*, offered to him by the Senate, on grounds of his youth, but numismatic evidence (coin legends) shows him as having eventually borne the title (Griffin, *Seneca*, 120, n. 8). All emperors seem to have made a point of refusing the title at first, only to accept it later on, as Nero did. See Durry's note ad Plin. *Pan.* 21.2; Ov. *Fast.* 2.127, quoted ad 485–6.

496 quae dementia est A similar line-end is found at 442 *clementia est.* For *quae dementia est* cf. Ov. *Met.* 13.225 *quae uos dementia . . . concitat . . . captam* *dimittere Troiam*; variant forms are found in Verg. *Buc.* 2.69; *Aen.* 5.465; 9.601 (*cepit, egit*).

498–499 Brutus in caedem ducis | a quo salutem tulerat armauit manus This example of questionable moral behaviour seems to draw on Sen. *Ben.* 2.20.1 *disputari de M. Bruto solet, an debuerit accipere ab diuo Iulio uitam, cum occidendum eum iudicaret.*

500–501 Ioui | aequatus altos saepe per honorum gradus The transmitted *saepe* seemed ineffective to Buecheler, who conjectured *ipse*, but there is no compelling reason to alter the paradosis. 'He [who] was made equal to Jupiter so many times' may indeed seem inept, because the status of equal to the gods would suggest permanence, but the poet of *Octavia* often uses *saepe*, like *diu*, in a pleonastic and superfluous manner.

Building up on Heinsius' *alto paene* (*Aduersaria*, 507), Zwierlein adds the suggestion that *alto* could be read in place of *altos. altus* as an epithet of Jupiter occurs at Ov. *Met.* 15.866; *Fast.* 6.188; Val. Fl. *Arg.* 2.305, and elsewhere, but *altos* must be retained in view of the fact that Caesar's honours were not those attached to the ordinary *cursus honorum. per honorum gradus* would be insufficient to make Caesar's case stand out as an exceptional one, since this periphrasis designates the ordinary progression of the Roman magistrate: Cic. *Cat.* 1.28 (*populus Romanus*) *te . . . ad summum imperium per omnes honorum gradus extulit*; Val. Max. *Mem.* 8.5.1, and elsewhere. The *honores* being referred to at 501 are not Republican magistracies, but the exceptional privileges awarded to Caesar in his last years. For another source using *honor* with reference to Caesar in a non-technical sense cf. Cic. *Phil.* 2.110 *quem is honorem maiorem consecutus erat quam ut haberet puluinar, simulacrum, fastigium, flaminem?* Suet. *Iul.* 76.1 *ampliora etiam humano fastigio decerni sibi passus est, sedem auream in curia . . . templa, aras, simulacra iuxta deos, puluinar, flaminem, lupercos, appellationem mensis a suo nomine*; see S. Weinstock, *Diuus Iulius*, 281–305.

For *Ioui aequatus* cf. *H.O.* 417 *non ut aequetur Ioui*; Plin. *Pan.* 35.4 (*Titus*) *numinibus aequatus est*; Sil. *Pun.* 4.810; 11.494.

503 quantum cruoris Roma tunc uidit sui Zwierlein (*KK* ad loc.) defends the transmitted *quantum . . . non*, the meaning of which would be 'how small was the portion of her blood which Rome did not see'. This construction, however, is unattested in Latin, where 'how small/how little' is *quantulum*, or *quotus* (the form predominating in Senecan tragedy); cf. e.g., *Hf.* 383 *pars quota ex isto mea est.* Rhetorical interrogative and exclamatory sentences containing a negative adverb are commonly introduced by *quis, quid* (cf. e.g. *quae non uicit mala Hercules?* 'what monsters did Hercules fail to defeat?', a construction discussed in Löfstedt, *Synt.* 2.398; Housman, *CP* 1083, 1211–13: cf. *Oct.* 947 *quid non potuit?* Sen. *Agam.* 77–8 *quas non arces scelus alternum | dedit in praeceps?* Hor. *Carm.* 2.1.29–30 *quis non Latino sanguine pinguior | campus?* 34–5 *quod mare Dauniae | non decolorauere caedes?*; 3.6.45; Ov. *Am.* 2.17.30.

Emendation is necessary, and modern editors adopt Leo's *tum*. It is far from certain, however, that *tum* should be printed here in preference to its more emphatic alternative, *tunc*, whose presence in several *recc.* is probably to be ascribed to conjecture. The gradual dominance of *tunc* over *tum* in classical Latin has been assessed as a vulgarism, but *tunc* is far too often done away with by editors of classical texts. For a defence of *tunc* in Lucan cf. P. Flobert, *Traits de latin parlé dans l'Epopée*, in L. Callebat (ed.), *Latin vulgaire, Latin tardif IV* (Hildesheim, 1998), 487–8; see also J. Svennung, *Untersuchungen zu Palladius* (Lund, 1935), 407–418; *LHS* 2.519–20. Vergil seems to avoid *tunc* decidedly: according to Svennung's tables Vergil has *c.*300 cases of *tum*, against 8 cases of *tunc* before a vowel, required by the metre, and 6 dubious cases before a consonant. In Seneca's prose, *tunc* predominates over *tum*, and the ratio approaches parity even in the tragedies. In the tragedies, 30 cases of *tum* occur, against 32 of *tunc*, 21 of them before a consonant and only 11 before a vowel. Apart from the disputed *tum* at 503, only *tunc* is found in *Oct.* (*tunc* in 123 *tunc tremor*; 160 *tunc sancta pietas*; 392 *tunc adest*, 397 *tunc illa*). For all its artificiality, the Latin of Senecan tragedy need not be the same as Vergil's. For example, Senecan tragedy (including *Oct.*) exhibits only two instances of the high-flown *neque* against 241 instances of the more colloquial *nec*, whereas *neque* is still frequently used in Vergil (Löfstedt, *Synt.* 1.338; the proportion of *neque/nec* in Vergil is 109:466). The poet of *Oct.* uses *atque* in pre-consonantal position more often than Seneca (6 out of a total of 23 occurrences of the word, against a ratio 18:100 in the other tragedies of the corpus; cf. Axelson, *UW* 82–3; Junge, 265–7), but in Vergil avoidance of pre-consonantal *atque* is even more marked, yielding a percentage of 11% (47:413). On the exchange *tum/tunc* in the corpus cf. Zwierlein (1980), 186 n. 19.

For this personification of Rome cf. Ov. *Pont.* 2.1.58 *Roma uidebit*; 4.9.66 *Roma uidet*. Compassion for fellow-citizens hardly seems to suit Nero, who steps out of character to launch into a pathetic description of civil war massacres. In thought, this line seems reminiscent of Luc. *Bell. Ciu.* 2.140–1 *quod exiguum restabat sanguinis urbi | hausit* (of Sulla), where the city of Rome is similarly assimilated to a human being.

504–505 ille qui meruit pia | uirtute caelum, diuus Augustus *ille* is often confused with *ipse* in the MS tradition. But *ille* is supported by 477 *sic ille patriae primus Augustus parens*. The idea that conflicting views could be entertained of Augustus' career derives from Sen. *Clem.* 1.11.1, where two different sides of Augustus are opposed as a foil against which Nero's *clementia* is set off: *fuerit moderatus et clemens, nempe post mare Actiacum Romano cruore infectum, nempe post fractas in Sicilia classes et suas et alienas, nempe post Perusinas aras et proscriptiones* (cf. Griffin, *Seneca*, 212 n. 2). Cf. also Tac. *Ann.* 1.9–10. Augustus' role in the civil war is cast in an unfavourable light by Juv. *Sat.* 8.241–3.

The following description of civil war is probably indebted to Livy's lost account of the proscriptions; but the general atmosphere of this passage also owes much to Lucan's account (in Book 2) of the earlier proscriptions during the war between Marius and Sulla, especially with its insistence on gory details and on the prohibition of showing true feelings, even grief for a son's death.

505–507 uiros | quot interemit nobiles, iuuenes senes, | sparsos per orbem *sparsos per orbem* hints at the fact that the victims of the proscriptions were stalked by their assassins as far as the most remote of hiding places: cf. Flor. 2.16 (4.6) 4 *exitus foedi truces miserabiles toto terrarum orbe fugientium*. In fact, most of the killings occurred in Italy, and those who reached the provinces managed to be pardoned later. *spargo* is frequently found in the corpus, where it often accompanies a gory picture of dismembered bodies, 'scattered' by an act of violence. The verb is used here, in a graphic sense, of fugitives: cf. Luc. *Bell. Ciu.* 8.203. The clausula is probably reminiscent of Verg. *Aen.* 1.602 *magnum quae sparsa per orbem*.

The reading *quos* found in some *recc.* is prima facie plausible, since *qui* is sometimes used in exclamatory sentences: Ter. *Heaut.* 363 *quae* (rel. pron.) *solet quos spernere!*, but here *quot* is preferable in sense, because the emphasis is on number rather than quality. *nobilis*, here qualifying *uiros*, can be used on its own as a single noun, for 'aristocrat' (cf. *OLD* s.v. 5c, Juv. 7.91 *tu nobilium magna atria curas?*), but the poet of *Oct.* may have felt this to be a prosaic usage. In Seneca cf. *Ira* 3.2.4 *nobiles consectatus uiros*, against *Clem.* 1.9.10 *agmen nobilium non inania nomina praeferentium*.

509 tabula notante deditos tristi neci The word *tabula* (the board on which the names of outlawed citizens were made public) applies to the proscription list also in Sen. *Suas.* 6.7; 7.1; Flor. 2.9 (3.21.25); Mart. 5.69.2. The use of *dedo* with *neci* is common after Verg. *Georg.* 4.90; *neci deditus*, however, is found only here and in *Troad.* 651–2 *poteris nefandae deditum mater neci | uidere?*

510–511 exposita rostris capita caesorum patres | uidere maesti The spectacle offered by the terrible display of severed heads and of mutilated, unrecognizable corpses and the relatives' grief at the sight of the mangled bodies of their kin are recurrent clichés in the description of civil war horrors: cf. Cornelius Severus fr. 13.1–2 Courtney *oraque magnanimum spirantia paene uirorum | in rostris iacuere suis*; Luc. *Bell. Ciu.* 2.166–8; 7.305. *patres* is here, literally 'fathers', rather than senators. Cf. Flor. 2.16 (4.6) 5 *Romae capita caesorum proponere in rostris iam usitatum erat. uerum sic quoque ciuitas lacrimas tenere non potuit*; Sen. *Suas.* 6.17 *caput . . . inter duas manus in rostris positum . . .*; *uix attollentes prae lacrimis oculos humentes intueri truncata membra ciues poterant*. The agreement of Florus and Seneca Rhetor in relating the horrors perpetrated during this period of civic unrest suggests that the poet of *Octavia* was using

Livy (cf. Bruckner (1976), 78). For other instances of the bare participle *caesus* for 'the people slain' cf. *TLL* iii s.v. *caedo*, 62.9–15 (e.g. Luc. *Bell. Ciu.* 6.626).

511–513 flere nec licuit suos, | non gemere dira tabe polluto foro, | stillante sanie per putres uultus graui Sen. *Suas.* 6.17 commemorates the public display of sorrow at Cicero's corpse in the Forum. The passage in Seneca is, in fact, an excerpt from Livy–another indication that the poet of *Octavia* is using his account of the proscriptions (see previous note). Cf. also Luc. *Bell. Ciu.* 2.166–73 *cum iam tabe fluunt . . . miserorum dextra parentum colligit. tabes* (a metrically convenient substitute for *tabum*) and *sanies* often occur together, with no difference in sense: cf. Enn. *Scaen.* 310 R[2] *saxa spargens tabo sanie et sanguine atro*; Verg. *Aen.* 3.625; 8.487 *sanie taboque fluentis.*

514 nec finis hic cruoris aut caedis stetit *hic* must be linked with *stetit*: 'nor did this event mark the end of bloodshed and slaughter': cf. *OLD*, s.v. *sto*, 10b 'to come to a halt', quoting *Thy.* 744 *hactenus si stat nefas*; Tac. *Hist.* 4.45 *nec finem iniuriae hic stetisse*, with a comparable pleonasm; Man. *Astr.* 1.914 *necdum finis erat* (in a passage which recounts the civil war).

515–516 pauere uolucres et feras saeuas diu | tristes Philippi The concept that a place 'feeds' wild animals with the flesh of unburied corpses is not found elsewhere in this exact form (*pasco* indicates in such contexts that a place 'generates' wild animals), but cf. Ov. *Ars* 3.35–6 *uolucres Ariadna marinas | pauit*; Luc. *Bell. Ciu.* 4.809–10 *Libycas . . . pascit aues . . . Curio*; Sen. *Hf.* 1208–9 *feras | uolucresque pascens Caucasi abruptum latus* (alluding to Prometheus' punishment); *Troad.* 567 *peremptus pascis Idaeas aues*; *Phoe.* 255–7 *pabulum misit feris | auibusque saeuis quas Cithaeron . . . cruore saepe regio tinctas alit.*

In Roman poetry of the Augustan age, the concept is often exploited that the same location, as if by a fatal coincidence, was twice the epicentre of civil war massacres. *diu*, like *iterum*, stresses the doomed compulsion to civil strife and marks the deployement (underelaborated in the play) of the topos (cf. e.g. Verg. *Georg.* 1.489–92 *concurrere . . . Romanas acies iterum uidere Philippi . . . bis sanguine nostro Emathiam . . . pinguescere*; Ov. *Met.* 15.824 *Emathiaque iterum madefient caede Philippi*); also *infra* 521–2 *hausit . . . Aegyptus iterum.* This chimes in with the Senecan tendency to stress literary and mythological precedents, as observed by Leo, *Obs.* 149–52 (*saepe, iterum, semper* as a means to allude to mythical precedents: cf. *Phoe.* 255–7 given above). In fact Philippi and Pharsalus are distinct locations of, respectively, Macedonia and Thessaly.

516–517 tristes Philippi, †hausit et Siculum mare | classes uirosque saepe caedentes suos I prefer to print a *crux* in the text, although Zwierlein's marks of lacuna are equally acceptable. Sense and expression are not such as to suggest a gap (*hausit . . . mare* is a frequent phrase: Liv. 33.41.7 *multae ita haustae mari*; Sen. *Agam.* 414 *quis fare nostras hauserit casus rates*, 500; *Cons. Helu.* 7.3 *quasdam gentes . . . mare hausit*; Tac. *Hist.* 3.77), but the hiatus *Philippi, hausit* (defended amongst others by Ackermann, Ballaira, and Barbera) is very unsatisfactory in the iambic trimeters of the Senecan corpus, which consistently avoid hiatus. A certain conclusion cannot be reached because after all *Octavia* is not Senecan, but it would be odd if the *ignotus* had deviated from Senecan practice in such a conspicuous feature as hiatus.[15] Of the conjectures hitherto proposed to heal the passage, Müller's *clausit* is very appealing, alongside Gronovius' *mersit.* Liberman suggested correcting the passage into *pauere uolucres et ferae saeuae diu tristes Philippos* ('birds and wild animals used Philippi as a feeding ground') to mend the following hiatus. His correction is ingenious, and the implied sense of *pauere* (= *depauere*) can be paralleled (cf. *TLL* s.v., 597–8, e.g. Tib. 2.5.25 *pascebant herbosa Palatia uaccae*), but the correction seems to place the emphasis on the wrong element and the parallels given in the previous note suggest that the topos occurs in the form 'a given place (*Cithaeron, Caucasus*) provided food for wild animals' as a result of slaughter or carnage. Moreover, scribes are unlikely to have altered a sequence verb-subject-object into the less straightforward verb-object-subject. MDR has suggested transposing 518[b] *uiribus magnis ducum* after *Philippi,* to be followed by 518[a]–516[b] *concussus orbis, hausit et Siculum mare,* which is attractive.

The more emotional *saepe caedentes suos* is superior to *saepe cedentes suis* of Baden, better for the retreating of armies in pitched battles than for naval fights (cf. Verg. *Aen.* 11.729 *inter caedes cedentiaque agmina*).

The use of the bare possessive *sui* for 'their compatriots, comrades' is normal in descriptions of military actions: cf. Caes. *B. Afr.* 40.2 *suos caedi a tergo sentit*; Luc. *Bell. Ciu.* 4.245–9 *quae modo complexu fouerunt pectora caedunt . . . dum feriunt, odere suos.*

518 concussus orbis uiribus magnis ducum Somewhat paradoxically, Nero 'steals' a line from his poetic rival, Lucan (*Bell. Ciu.* 1.5 *certatum*

[15] Ackermann's defence of hiatus in the Senecan corpus (*De Senecae Hercule Oetaeo* (diss., Marburg, 1905), 32) places undue reliance on the evidence of ***E*** in all cases where the two branches disagree and ***A*** presents a perfectly acceptable version. In *Hf.* 1284 ***E***'s hiatus *pauidamque matrem* is an overliteral correction (cf. Fitch, ad loc.) and is clearly inferior to ***A***'s *pauidasque matres.* In *Thy.* 302 editors are divided between accepting ***E***'s version *prece commouebo* (involving hiatus) and printing a *lacuna,* or choosing the unparalleled *praecommouebunt* of ***A***, which is persuasively preferred by Tarrant on the analogy of Ovidian neologisms with *prae-*. In *Thy.* 1021 *fugere superi.* ATR: *accipe hos potius libens* was convincingly emended to *iam accipe* by B. Schmidt. ***A***, however, presents an interpolated version *recipe hosce citius. liberis tandem tuis,* which seems to show a tendency to get rid of hiatus in ***A***. The hiatus before exclamatory *o* in *H.O.* 1201 *sortis carerem. o ferae, uictae ferae* (Avantius has *pro*; ***A*** reads *o ferae, uictae o ferae*) may resist emendation, esp. if the claim that *H.O.* is apocryphal receives better substantiation in the future. Hiatus before *o* is well attested in other literary genres (cf. Cat. *Carm.* 3.16; Prop. *Carm.* 2.15.1; Ov. *Met.* 14.832). On the whole, *Thy.* 1021 (hiatus at the change of speaker) and *H.O.* 1201, though both dubious, have a better claim to be genuine than *Philippi hausit* in *Oct.* 516, despite the presence of a caesura and interpunction. Hiatus at the caesura is unacceptable even in the much freer practice of early dramatists (cf. Lindsay, *ELV,* 231; Soubiran, *Essai,* 125).

totis concussi uiribus orbis). I think the echo from Lucan is certain, but the idea that the civil wars were a universal conflagration and that the world (nearly) imploded is commonplace: cf. *AL* 409.5–6 R. (one of the epigrams ascribed to Seneca) *tempore . . . quo uersis uiribus orbis | incubuit belli tota ruina tibi* (Siegmund); Man. *Astr.* 1.912 *imperiumque suis conflixit uiribus ipsum*. Notice the ellipsis of the copula in the second colon, as at 536–7; 600. Flor. 2.14 (4. 3), 8 *ciuilibus . . . bellis omne imperii corpus agitatum est.*

519 superatus acie puppibus Nilum petit The poet of *Octavia* often repeats similar syntactic and rhythmic patterns in the same verse position, which gives the play the appearance of a somewhat naïve and 'primitive' poem: cf. *supra* 500 *inuictus acie*, which was explained by *Caesar* at 502.

Present and past participles can be used with a substantival function, especially in the nominative: cf. *LHS* 2.156; N.-H. ad Hor. *Carm.* 2.16.2: *Carm.* 3.20.16–17 *aquosa | raptus ab Ida*. Such omissions of substantives are motivated by many compositional reasons, often occurring together, such as euphemism, the desire to replace mythological names with poetic *griphoi* (cf. Sen. *Agam.* 19–21, where Tantalus is named only as *exustus siti . . . poenas daturus*), the comparative difficulty of introducing some proper names in verse, and the wish to avoid nominal formations, which are felt as eminently prosaic (cf. Luc. *Bell. Ciu.* 6.293 *non sic Hennaeis habitans in uallibus horret*, where *habitans* replaces the common *habitator*; J. N. Adams, *Glotta*, 51 (1973), 116–36). In this case, a reluctance to name the disgraced Antonius may have played a part. The participle also stresses the anguish of defeat very effectively, and contributes to the rapid evocation of the Actium campaign.

520 ipse periturus breui Future participles often occupy a shorter appositive colon at the end of a longer sentence in Senecan tragedy, in pointed contrast to the preceding clause. Often the future participle conveys a shift of perspective, highlighting the difference between a character's expectations and a disappointing outcome: cf. *Agam.* 42–3 *deuicto Ilio | adest – daturus coniugi iugulum suae*; *Agam.* 623–4 *restitit annis | Troia bis quinis, unius noctis | peritura furto*; *Ira* 3.12.5. . . . *iussit, sua manu ipse caesurus*. This stylistic device (not limited to Seneca and to his followers: cf. Verg. *Aen.* 11.741 *moriturus et ipse*) is favoured by Seneca because of his love for expressive brevity and greater concision, and the poet of *Octavia* follows suit, perhaps to impart a Senecan ring to his narrative: cf. Westman (1961), 121–125, Junge (1999), 267 (who draw attention to the rarity, though by no means the uniqueness, in Seneca, of the inclusion of an appositive pronominal element (*ipse*, 391 *tantus*) alongside the participle in these clauses).

521–522 hausit cruorem incesta Romani ducis | Aegyptus iterum The same rhetorical compulsion to be a theatre of never-ending bloodshed exemplified by Philippi at 515–16 is also attributed to Egypt, described as unchaste on account of Cleopatra's notorious sexual promiscuity, and perhaps also with reference to the custom of inter-marrying in the royal house: cf. Prop. 3.10(11).39 *incesti meretrix regina Canopi*; Luc. *Bell. Ciu.* 10.69 (of Cleopatra); Ov. *Met.* 15.826–7 *Romanique ducis coniunx Aegyptia taedae | non bene fisa cadet.* The land of Egypt 'drank' the blood of the Roman commanders also in Sen. Rh. *Suas.* 6.6 *Romanorum sanguinem hausit Aegyptus.*

522 nunc leues umbras tegit M. Müller's *non* (1911), 132, replaces the MS *nunc* in Zwierlein's text. *non* plays out a paradox exploited by several writers elaborating the contrast between human glory and the little corner where even great heroes are laid to rest: cf. *AL* 438.4 *nempe manet magnos paruula terra duces* (= [Sen.] *Epigr.* 46.4 Prato); *AL* 437.4 *abscondit tantum putris harena uirum* (Tandoi, *Scritti*, 2.827–8). Zwierlein has also drawn attention to the similar litotes at *Hf.* 230 *taurumque, centum non leuem populis metum.* However, I suspect this to be yet another case in which modern conjectures end up by improving on the author, and comparison with *Oct.* 169–70 *nunc leuis tantum cinis | et tristis umbra* renders this conjecture less compelling, in view also of the recurrence of *nunc* in epigram and otherwise funereal compositions, to add a pathetic, emotional note emphasizing the contrast between past and present: cf. Verg. *Aen.* 6.362 *nunc me fluctus habet*; *CE* 1111.7–8 *gratus eram populo . . . nunc sum defleti parua fauilla rogi*; 1310.4 *nunc tumulus cineres ossaque lecta tegit*; 1600 *qui quondam ad superos Mossius . . . nunc tenuis anima*; *alibi.* To *nunc* it might be objected also that Pompey's bones had been translated to Rome and buried by Cornelia (cf. Plut. *Pomp.* 80.5) well before the Neronian age, but every writer expatiating on Pompey's fate ignores this detail (Tandoi, *Scritti*, 2.832).

The line-ending *umbras tegit* is also formulaic in funerary epigram, with *umbra* referring to the remains of a deceased person: cf. *CE* 53.2 *umbram tegit*; 428.7; 1110.4; 1868.1. Hadrian, on a visit to Egypt, restored the monument which had been erected on the spot where the body of Pompey was said to have been found (cf. *SHA Hadr.* 14.4; App. *Bell. Ciu.* 2.362; Cass. Dio *Hist. Rom.* 69.11.1).

523–524 illic sepultum est impie gestum diu | ciuile bellum The metaphorical use of *sepelio* with *bellum* for 'to bring to completion' is well-established in Latin: cf. Cic. *De imp. Cn. Pomp.* 31 *bellum . . . sublatum ac sepultum*; Vell. 2.90.1 *sepultis . . . bellis ciuilibus*, and the newly found *Senatusconsultum de Pisone patre*, l.47 *omnibus ciuilis belli sepultis malis.* More parallels for the image are given by Housman ad Luc. *Bell. Ciu.* 8.529 (esp. Hor. *Epod.* 9.23–6 *bello . . . sepulcrum condidit*); Housman ad Man. *Astr.* 2.879.

524–526 condidit tandem suos | iam fessus enses uictor hebetatos feris | uulneribus These lines play up the (Senecan as well as Lucanean) concept that war came to an end because the warring parties were exhausted (*fessus, hebetatos*); the fight was hampered more by the blunting of overworked swords than by the horror such a sight should have aroused, an idea which has a parallel in Luc. *Bell. Ciu.* 6.186–7 *hebes et crasso non asper sanguine mucro | non facit ensis opus.*

526–527 continuit imperium metus. | armis fideque militis tutus fuit Avantius's *metu* is often preferred to the MS *metus*, but 736 *continet uocem timor* supports the transmitted version (cf. also *Oed.* 704 *regna custodit metus* (Zwierlein); *Troad.* 258 *uiolenta nemo imperia continuit diu*). Both versions are plausible: in support of *metu* cf. Val. Max. 9.11 ext. 4 *habenas Romani imperii quas princeps . . . salutari dextera continet* and Tac. *Ann.* 15.1 *non . . . ignauia magna imperia contineri.*

The passage contains a perceptive historical analysis, since the imperial power was rooted in control of the armies. Awareness that control over the military was an essential requisite for Roman emperors must have gained recognition from an early date. This view is already stated in Herod Agrippa's speech to Claudius in Jos. *Ant.* 19.241; R. Syme, *Tacitus*, 1.129. Nero's accession speech to the Senate (cf. Tac. *Ann.* 13.4 *de auctoritate patrum et consensu militum praefatus*) seems to have expressed a view that agrees with what is attributed to him here. The author of the play appropriates a more 'realistic' and cruder view of the political state of affairs than Seneca had done in *Clem.*

529 et templis datus This use of *do* with the dative (for *trado, prodo, obicio* cf. *TLL* s.v. *do*, 1695) is more commonly found in negative contexts (followed by *neci, tumulo, fato* and similar expressions). Juv. 12.119 has *dabit hanc altaribus*, which refers to the sacrifice of Iphigenia.

530 nos quoque manebunt astra Cf. Man. *Astr.* 4.551–2 *illum . . . caeli post terras iura manebunt*, referring to the deification of Augustus or, perhaps, Tiberius. The construction of *maneo* with the accusative is frequently used by Augustan poets. In this play, it occurs again at 642 *quos . . . pudor . . . manet.*

530–531 saeuo . . . ense occuparo The verb *occupo*, 'to forestall' (cf. *OLD* s.v. 11b) is mainly found in epic descriptions of armed combat, from which this metaphor is taken: cf. Verg. *Aen.* 9.768–70 *tendentem contra . . . gladio . . . occupat*; *Thy.* 716 *quem tamen ferro occupat*; Pac. *Scaen.* 148 R^2 *qui te, nisi illum tu occupas, leto dabit.*

The use of syncopated forms is common in *Oct.* (cf. 532, 637 *lacerassent*, 708 *celebrasse*). This is not a marked colloquialism, and, in adopting these forms, the poet is in line with common poetical standards of the Augustan age. Quint. *Inst.* 1.6.17–21 asserts that the full pronunciation was regarded as an affected drawl in his time.

532 dignaque nostram subole fundaro domum The final *-o* retains the original long quantity. Nero takes up the features of the upstart, as the tyrant was in Greek, who has insinuated himself into a royal house through court intrigue: cf. *Hf.* 345–7 *una sed nostras potest | fundare uires iuncta regali face | thalamisque Megara.*

The line echoes perhaps Stat. *Silu.* 4.7.29–30 *alma | prole fundasti uacuos penates* (as already pointed out by Helm (1934), 343). In *TLL* vi.1., s.v. *fundo*, col. 1562, 21–6 only these two passages and Plin. *Epist.* 4.21.3 *unus ex tribus liberis domum . . . pluribus adminiculis paulo ante fundatam desolatus fulcit ac sustinet*; Apul. *Met.* 7. 6 (*femina*) *decimo partus stipendio uiri familiam fundauerat.*

533 implebit aulam stirpe caelesti tuam *impleo* is used in similarly hyperbolic tones also in Luc. *Bell. Ciu.* 2.331–3 *alios fecunda penates* | *impletura datur, geminas et sanguine matris* | *permixtura domos*; Mart. 1.84.4 *domumque et agros implet equitibus uernis*; Prud. *Psych. praef.* 68 *haerede . . . implere domum*. Nero's future offspring is called *caelestis* because it will form a long line of imperial *diui*. The motif deployed here, that a ruler will give birth to a breed of gods, is recurrent in imperial panegyric literature: cf. Verg. *Aen.* 6.789; 9.642; Stat. *Silu.* 1.1.74 *magnorum proles genitorque deorum*; Sil. *Pun.* 3.625 *o nate deum diuosque dature*; Man. *Astr.* 1.799–800 *descendit caelo caelumque replebit* | *quod reget Augustus*; *CIL*.III.710: cf. L. Berlinger, *Beiträge zur inoffiziellen Titulatur der römischen Kaiser* (diss., Breslau, 1935), 92–3. Seneca's reassurance that a line of demigods will issue from Nero and Octavia presupposes the acceptance of hereditary succession, but it is hard to infer from this detail any certain conclusion about the date of the play. In Pliny's *Panegyricus* adoption is already the recommended method of imperial election, and Syme has argued that Tacitus, in his attention to adoption in *Hist.*, reflects the concerns of his own time (*Tacitus*, 1.150–6). On the other hand, Seneca's hereditary argument is in keeping with his attempt to persuade Nero not to divorce his lawful, and Claudian, wife. Later treatises on kingship betray their post-second-century origins by espousing the hereditary principle, while always trying to represent it as the one whereby the best candidates are always chosen: cf. Philostr. *Vita Apoll.* 5.36 (p. 197 Kays.): Vespasian must spur his children to be virtuous, if they are to succeed him . . . ἵνα μὴ κληρονομίαν ἡγῶνται τὴν ἀρχήν, ἀλλ' ἀρετῆς ἆθλα.

534 generata Diuo, Claudiae gentis decus Cf. *Phae.* 900 *gentis Actaeae decus* in the same metrical position. For *generata Diuo* cf. Verg. *Aen.* 6.792 *diui genus*; Val. Fl. *Arg.* 4.438 *diuis geniti*. Notice the repetition of words from the same stem in 534 and 536: *generata, gentis, genetrix, generi.*

536–537 incesta genetrix detrahit generi fidem | animusque numquam coniugis iunctus mihi Nero's grievances against Octavia include an accusation hinting at Messalina's notorious sexual licence, casting doubts on Octavia's claim to be considered Claudius' legitimate daughter: cf. Introd. p. 8; Suet. *Nero* 7 (*Nero*) *Britannicum . . . ut subditiuum apud patrem arguere conatus est.* Nero's second complaint regards Octavia's aloofness (described as a worrying factor by a friendly source, the Nurse, at 48–56).

The ellipsis of the copula with compound verbal forms, in the second element of a dicolon (*animus . . . iunctus* sc. *est*), is a rather common phenomenon: cf. T. Winter, *De ellipsi verbi esse . . .* (diss., Marburg, 1907), 33–5; see also ad 600): cf. Luc. *Bell. Ciu.* 7.572–3 *pondere lapsi* | *pectoris arma sonant confractique ensibus enses*; Stat. *Theb.* 2.65–6 *gemuit . . . et cunctatus* (sc. *est*); 2.174–5 *ora tenent uisique inter sese ordine fandi* | *cedere.*

538–539 teneris in annis haud satis clara est fides, | pudore uictus cum tegit flammas amor Leo (prompted by T. Mommsen) printed *clarus ferest*, finding fault with the repetition of *fides* at line-end at 536 and 538, where it is, however, employed in a different sense ('loyalty', 'attachment') from 536. *fere* is rare in the tragic corpus (only four occurrences: *Troad.* 438, 1143; *H.O.* 407, 452; cf. Flinck (1919), 98) and its presence here would be redundant, after *haud satis*. *fides* should be retained, as a variation of *animus . . . iunctus* in the previous line (*fides* is the bond uniting two lovers or two partners into a married couple: cf. *TLL* vi.1 s.v. 679.82–4, 680.1–12; *infra*, 547). Seneca warns that a husband should seek *probitas fidesque . . . mores pudor* as the qualities that recommend a good wife. Line 538 may echo *Thy.* 317–18 *tacita tam rudibus fides | non est in annis* (Hosius).

Seneca seems to imply that Octavia's lack of affection for Nero is only a false impression: her tender age makes her conceal her feelings. The idea that love is a sentiment the open expression of which ill becomes young women is implied by Aesch. *Agam.* 856–8, where Clytemnestra says that, with time, she has learned how to overcome her timidity and can now speak of her love for her husband in the presence of the elders of Argos. The sentiments Seneca appears to ascribe to Octavia are comparable to the emotions of Lavinia in Verg. *Aen.* 12.70.

The metaphorical field of the 'blaze of love' was popularized in Latin by Ovid's poems. For *tegit flammas* cf. Ov. *Met.* 3.490 *tecto paulatim carpitur igni*; 4.64 *tectus magis aestuat ignis*, with Bömer ad loc. These passages were imitated in turn by Sen. *Phae.* 362–3 *torretur aestu tacito et, inclusus quoque, | quamuis tegatur, proditur uultu furor*, where the love-smitten Phaedra is described.

The sense borne by *satis* in the present line (*haud . . . satis* 'never . . . quite, entirely, fairly': cf. *OLD* s.v. B9b) is common and colloquial, when a speaker intends to moderate an assertion he has made. Predictably, it is not the sense in which the word is commonly encountered in Senecan tragedy, where I can only adduce *Oed.* 841–2 *nec notus satis | nec rursus iste uultus ignotus mihi*; in the Senecan corpus, *satis* is 'enough', mainly in combination with paradoxical and indignant expressions. No excess of evil, passion, or punishment is ever enough for Seneca's characters (cf. e.g. *Thy.* 252–3 *non satis magno meum | ardet fauore pectus*).

The passage as a whole deviates from mainstream Senecan tragic ethos as well as style, and even Nero is lent a fine nuance, as he voices a regret that his spouse has never relented in her hatred for him. This is seemingly in defiance of Eliot's famous criticism of Senecan characterization, that 'his characters have only one voice, and speak at the top of it'. This attempt to endow Nero with some psychological depth of character has no parallel in the extant sources. Tacitus presents Nero as hostile to Octavia from the very beginning (cf. *Ann.* 13.12.2). At the same time the portrait of Nero in the play is less nuanced than in Tacitus, where the emperor is assailed by remorse for his matricide (14.10.5).

540 hoc equidem et ipse credidi frustra diu *equidem* is often joined to a first person pronoun in Latin, reinforcing the speaker's assertion ('for my part').

541–542 manifesta quamuis pectore insociabili | uultuque signa proderent odium mei In a manner characteristic of this poet, different ideas are compressed in a stilted sequence (likewise *infra*, at 557): 'although unmistakable signs (proceeding) from her expression and her heart – which will suffer no reconciliation – revealed her hatred for me'. The phrasing of the line may owe something to Ov. *Trist.* 3.5.19–20 *multaque praeterea manifesti signa fauoris | pectoribus teneo* (where however *pectoribus* does not belong with *signa*); Sen. *Agam.* 389 *manifesta properat signa laetitiae ferens.*

pectus is mentioned as the seat of the intelligence and the affections, and, commonly, as the place from which the voice, sighs etc. emerge. The dittology *pectore . . . uultuque* is chosen to signify both the outward and the inner being of Octavia, for whom hatred of her monstrous husband has become irrepressible. She is unable to sustain even the look of the husband she abhors. For other passages describing emotions reflected in the face, sometimes in spite of a person's intention to conceal his or her feelings, cf. Cat. *Carm.* 64.194 *frons . . . praeportat pectoris iras*; Sall. *Iug.* 113.3 *uoltu et oculis pariter atque animo uarius: quae scilicet tacente ipso occulta pectoris patefecisse*; Tac. *Agr.* 43.3 *speciem . . . doloris animo uultuque prae se tulit*; in the Senecan corpus cf. *Med.* 446 *fert odia prae se, totus in uultu est dolor*; *H.O.* 247–9. For *prodo* indicating an unintentional 'betraying' of one's sentiments through one's expression cf. Ov. *Met.* 2.447 *quam difficile est crimen non prodere uultu*; Sen. *Phae.* 363 *quamuis tegatur, proditur uultu furor*; Hor. *Sat.* 2.5.104 *gaudia prodentem uultum celare*; *TLL* x.2, 1623.4–37.

The word *insociabilis* normally refers to individuals ('aloof', if not 'hostile': cf. Tac. *Ann.* 4.12.4 *anum . . . insociabilem nurui efficiebat*; 15.68.2 (*Vestinum*) *praecipitem et insociabilem credebant*); elsewhere it is found in reference to savages and barbaric tribes. Seneca has *sociabilis* in *Epist.* 95.52 *haec* (sc. *natura*) *nobis amorem indidit mutuum et sociabiles fecit* (on human progress).

The long compound *insociabilis*, though not a coinage of the poet, has no precedents in poetry. Longer words at line-end of the type *quadrupedantum* in Vergil's epic are regarded as Ennian borrowings (cf. Norden, *Kommentar*, 437–41). They appear in fact to have been a common feature of early Latin drama (cf. Soubiran, (1964), 429–69; id. *Essai*, 372–4). Long compound verbs at the end of a line contributed to solemnity, and they have a long tradition in dramatic poetry: cf. Plaut. *Capt.* 402 (tr_7) *inter nos fuisse ingenio haud discordabili*; Acc. *Scaen.* 270 R^2 *tyranni saeuum ingenium et exsecrabile*; Cic. *Tusc.* 2.22 (= *Soph.* 1.42 Soub.) *haec interemit tortu multiplicabili | draconem. insociabilis* is a word which has no traceable archaic precedents, but acquires antiquarian connotations through its metrical treatment. See also *infra*, ad 870 *ut ne inexpugnabilis | esset.* On compound forms in *–bilis* cf. M. Del Carmen Arias Abellán, *Glotta* 69 (1991), 124–36. The mutual hatred felt by the two partners has also been described, in equally contorted Latin, at 49–50.

542 odium mei Cf. *Hf.* 382 *odium tui*; *H.O.* 52 *odio tuae.*

543 tandem quod ardens statuit ulcisci dolor An incensed Nero asserts his resolution to satisfy his pride, wounded (*dolor*) by Octavia's rejection: his third-person, indirect language belongs to the high-flown register of royal and tyrannical pronouncements (cf. *infra*, ad 829; elsewhere cf. Stat. *Theb.* 3.393 *nobis dolor haud rationis egebit*). Cf. Ov. *Met.* 13.546 *ulcisci statuit* (of Hecuba).

Bruckner (1976), 94, interprets 543 as a reference to the threat posed by Octavia: on this interpretation, *ardens dolor* must be understood as Octavia's poorly suppressed hatred, which, Nero fears, the princess has finally resolved to satisfy (*ulcisci*, to be linked with *quod* = *odium mei*), presumably by an act of violence against Nero. Yet the idea would be strangely underdeveloped, and Nero has shown no awareness so far of any threats posed by the mere survival of Octavia (the charges at 462 ff. are directed against Plautus and Sulla). This becomes an issue only after the rebellion has set Nero on his guard, even if then wounded pride weighs more than political calculation among his motives. Bruckner's interpretation is weak also on account of the meaning of *ulcisci*, which is 'to exact retribution' for, 'to avenge', a wrong one has received; *ulcisci odium, iram* does not appear to be attested in the meaning of 'to take satisfaction against, punish' (someone else).

544 dignamque thalamis coniugem inueni meis Having in his mind already disposed of Octavia, Nero very quickly turns his thoughts to her successor, but the conclusion 'and (almost 'after all') I have found a worthy bride for my bedchamber' seems somewhat anticlimactic, and almost strikes a comic note, after the preceding relative clause has cast an ominous light on Octavia's future, whatever punctuation we choose to interpose between 543 and 544 (Zwierlein writes a dash, to mark the gap in sense between the two clauses). *–que* implies co-ordination, but 544 can neither be linked with *quamuis* at 541 nor with *tandem quod.* Loose co-ordination occurs frequently with *–que*, a convenient connective because it provides a handy short syllable in the third element. Anomalous *–que* sequences occur elsewhere: cf. *Phae.* 989–90 *sed quid citato nuntius portat gradu | rigatque maestis lugubrem uultum genis*, which raised Leo's suspicions (he proposed *properat* for *portat*), but the transmitted text was aptly defended by Housman, *CP* 3.1079, adducing in defence Man. *Astr.* 4.694–5 *Italia . . . quam rerum maxima Roma | imposuit terris caeloque adiungitur ipsa*; Sil. *Pun.* 14.117 *quantos Arethusa tumores | concipiat perstetque suas non pandere portas*, where a break occurs after the initial relative clause; cf. ad 156 (*-que* at the beginning of a new sentence) 779 (*aut*). *Oed.* 977 *inuenta thalamis digna nox tandem meis* may be echoed here.

545 uicta cui cedet Venus The future *cedet* is found in the oldest MSS of ***A***, for *cedat* or *cedit* in *recc.* Zwierlein defends the future with reference to the comparable sequence of future tenses found at *Oct.* 768; 775 *uincet uultus haec Tyndaridos. cedet* should be retained: a hubristic element is appropriate to the characterization of the lover, for whom the charms of his mistress are preferable to those of the loftiest deities, and a jokingly blasphemous element is often present in such comparisons: cf. Sen. *Med.* 83–6 *cedent Aesonio duci | proles fulminis improbi . . . nec non qui tripodas mouet*; Prop. 2.2.13 *cedite iam diuae quas pastor uiderat olim.* Elsewhere, the hackneyed comparison with the three goddesses is couched in the form of an unreal past conditional clause: cf. Ov. *Her.* 16.139–40 *si tu uenisses pariter certamen in illud, | in dubio Veneris palma futura fuit*; Petr. *Sat.* 138.6 *quid contra hanc Helene, quid Venus posset? ipse Paris . . . si hanc in comparatione uidisset . . . et Helenen huic donasset et deas.* See also ad 775.

546 ferox armis dea *ferox* is a standard epithet for Minerva in Latin, though the nexus *ferox armis* is found nowhere else in reference to her (for the simple *ferox* cf. Sil. *Pun.* 9.457; Stat. *Theb.* 9.637; *Achill.* 1.825; Mart. 14.179; Drac. *Rom.* 2.29 *uirgo ferox sexu*; Ov. *Met.* 2.773 *formaque armisque decoram*). Other common epithets with *arma* are *armipotens* and *armigera.*

547–548 probitas fidesque coniugis, mores pudor | placeant marito Cf. Ov. *Trist.* 5.5.45 *nata pudicitia est, mores probitasque fidesque.*

There is an imbalance in the flow of the sentence, in which two terms linked by *-que* (*probitas fidesque*) are followed by a further dicolon without any connective particle (*mores pudor*). This asymmetric construction is not an isolated phenomenon in the play and parallels can be traced in other Latin poets: see ad 832–3, where the asymmetry is even greater.

548 sola perpetuo manent The same line-end at Sen. *Med.* 196 *iniqua numquam regna perpetuo manent.*

549 subiecta nulli mentis atque animi bona On *nulli* = *nulli rei* cf. K-S 1.624 (quoting Ov. *Met.* 1.17 *nulli sua forma manebat*); Bömer ad Ov. *Met.* 2.202. The independence and superiority of the mind over the body is constantly asserted in Seneca's philosophical writings, on which this passage draws: cf. e.g. Sen. *Epist.* 124.12 *liber animus . . . alia subiciens sibi, se nulli*; 92.33 *nec se* (sc. *animus*) *illi* (sc. *corpori*) *cui impositus est subicit*; cf. also ad 382. *mens atque animus*, in this context, are entirely synonymous. Seneca's plea in favour of the soul's attainments, as the sole possessions of an individual not exposed to outward influences, is easily paralleled in the philosophical writings: cf. e.g. *Const. sap.* 5.4; 8.2; *Ben.* 5.13.1 *sunt animi bona, sunt corporis, sunt fortunae.* The opposition *mens/corpus* is a commonplace: cf. Sall. *Cat.* 1.4 *diuitiarum et formae gloria fluxa atque fragilis est, uirtus clara aeternaque habetur.* For *bona animi* cf. Stat. *Silu.* 3.5.63 *formaeque bonis animique meretur.*

550 florem decoris singuli carpunt dies *carpo* combines in this line the two senses, literal and metaphorical, in which it is normally found: 'to pluck' (as in *carpe diem*) and 'to wear away': cf. Ov. *Ars* 2.113–14 *forma bonum fragile est quantumque accedit ad annos | fit minor et spatio carpitur ipsa suo* (Delrius); Sen. *Phae.* 761–76; *Epist.* 26.4 *carpimur, singuli dies aliquid subtrahunt uiribus* (Bruckner (1976), 97). The epexegetic genitive *flos decoris* (suggesting by way of an abbreviated metaphor that beauty is a flower) seems to figure only in this passage, whereas similar expressions (*flos aetatis, iuuentutis, aeui*) frequently occur.

551–552 omnes in unam contulit laudes deus | talemque nasci fata uoluerunt mihi That the gods had a share in the miraculous making of a lover's mistress is a topos of erotic poetry, in which wooing always plays a prominent role. Poppaea embodies the typical *puella* of elegiac poetry, said to have been blessed by the immortal gods with many accomplishments: cf. Prop. 2.3.25–30 (which seems to be directly echoed here) *haec tibi contulerunt caelestia munera diui . . . non, non humani partus sunt talia dona . . . gloria Romanis una es tu nata puellis. | Romana accumbes prima puella Ioui.* On this topos cf. G. Lieberg, *Puella diuina* (Amsterdam, 1962), 264–75. Cf. also Ov. *Pont.* 3.1.117–18 *quae Veneris formam, mores Iunonis habendo, | sola est caelesti digna reperta toro.*

For *confero* as 'to bestow upon/assemble in (one individual)' cf. Plin. *Pan.* 23.5 *ut in unius salutem conlata omnium uota*; Cic. *Rep.* 2.2 *cuncta ingenia conlata in unum.*

553 recedat a te (temere ne credas) amor As Seneca sees his former pupil stray farther and farther from his precepts, he utters a desperate exhortation to steer away from the sirens of passion: Nero is not to commit himself blindly (*temere ne credas*) to love (for this sense of *credo* cf. Verg. *Buc.* 2.17 *nimium ne crede colori*, 'do not set too much store by your beauty'). Parentheses are difficult to delimit, owing to the lack of a codified punctuation system in antiquity, except when a syntactical construction is left suspended as here, where *amor*, the third person subject required by *recedat*, only occurs at line-end. In normal speech, a parenthetic expression serves to introduce caution, to moderate the force of an assertive statement, or to ask for renewed attention: cf. *Phae.* 330–1 *sacer est ignis (credite laesis) | nimiumque potens*; Ov. *Met.* 2.571 *diuitibusque procis (ne me contemne) petebar.* The occurrence of two imperative sentences conveys here a sense of urgency and anxiety in the speaker. By way of parallel for the combination of two intertwined imperative expressions cf. Verg. *Aen.* 12.146 *disce tuum (ne me incuses) Iuturna, dolorem.* The MS reading yields very good sense, and there is no need, in my view, to alter the paradosis. Proposals include *ni credas* (Müller 1911, 133) and *ni cedas* (Stuart 1911, 40): these were prompted by the comparative difficulty posed by the absolute *credas* without an object. The latter is however easily supplied by the context, suggesting *amori*. For a comparable brachylogy in enclosed parentheses cf. Ov. *Rem.* 719 *omnia* (i.e. the letters of his mistress) *pone feros (pones inuitus) in ignes.* I see no improvement in accepting Bothe's *recedet* (Vürtheim, Liberman: 'Ne te fie pas aveuglément à l'amour: il te quittera'): Seneca reacts to Nero's first admission of love for Poppaea with surprise and alarm, sentiments which are expressed more effectively by the imperative.

For the topos that Love is fed by indolence cf. Ov. *Rem.* 161; 746.

554–556 quem summouere fulminis dominus nequit, | caeli tyrannum, saeua qui penetrat freta | Ditisque regna, detrahit superos polo? Nero's answer draws on a popular argument of unrepentant lovers: 'who will resist love, if not even the gods are exempt from it?': cf. Eur. 431 N[2] (*Hipp. Cal.*); *Hipp.* 453–5 (where such stories as tell of love suits of gods and mortals are attributed to the songs of the poets); Sen. *Phae.* 184–96 (with Mayer's note); Soph. *Phae.* 684.4 Radt καὶ τόνδ' ἀπείργειν οὐδ' ὁ παγκρατὴς σθένει (other parallels are given by W. S. Barrett, *Euripides: Hippolytus* (Oxford, 1964), 36 n. 1; Leo, *Obs.* 176). The motif that a lover's conduct is excused by the precedent set by the gods is also found in Hellenistic epigram: cf. Page, *FHE* p. 312 (*AP* 5.100, esp. 3–4), with parallels. Much material on these topoi is collected by B. Snell, *Scenes from Greek Drama* (Berkeley, 1964), 38, 125.

The power of Venus and of Cupid extends over all three realms of the universe, sky, earth, and sea: cf. Eur. *Hipp.* 447–8 φοιτᾷι δ' ἀν' αἰθέρ', ἔστι δ' ἐν θαλασσίωι | κλύδωνι Κύπρις, Ov. *Met.* 5.369–70 *tu superos ipsumque Iouem, tu numina ponti | uicta domas, ipsumque regit qui numina ponti*; Ps.-Quint. *Decl. Mai.* 15.8 = 283.22 *(furor) qui, si credimus, numina quoque detracta sideribus misit in terras* (Bruckner (1976), 98, who also (102–8) offers an extensive comparative analysis of this passage and of *Phae.* 184–96). No MS has *tyrannus*, surprisingly, which would have been easy to assimilate to the preceding *dominus*. But the accusative is obviously right here.

557–558 uolucrem esse Amorem fingit immitem deum | mortalis error 'It is our human ignorance that imagines winged Love to be a cruel god.' The passage imitates Sen. *Phae.* 195–203, conflating and compressing the many topics of the Nurse's lecture to Phaedra, mainly the negation of the divinity of Love and the satire on the traditional representation of Eros as a winged youth accoutred with bow, arrows and burning torches: *deum esse amorem turpis et uitio fauens | finxit libido, quoque liberior foret | titulum furori numinis falsi addidit. | natum per omnis scilicet terras uagum | Erycina mittit, ille per caelum uolans | proterua tenera tela molitur manu | regnumque tantum minimus e superis habet. | uana ista demens animus asciuit sibi, | Venerisque numen finxit atque arcus dei* (where Axelson proposed *uolucrisque* for *Venerisque*: the epithet occurs with reference to the same god only here and in Ov. *Met.* 9.482). As observed by Junge (1999, 279) the imitator is here at his clumsiest: it is not clear whether Seneca intends to deny only that Love is a god with wings, or that he is a cruel god, or a cruel god with wings. The passage is an interesting giveaway of the poet's limited skills in the technical aspects of verse composition.

'Seneca' seems to use some restraint here, perhaps unwilling to risk describing Nero's belief in the divinity of Cupid as a form of *dementia*. The critique of the established belief in the traditional divine imagery is more appropriately received from Seneca's lips than from those of the Nutrix in *Phaedra*. That passage had in turn looked back to the precedent of Euripides, in whose plays a number of characters repeatedly utter rationalistic remarks against the established tradition: cf. W. Nestle, *Euripides. Der Dichter der griechischen Aufklärung* (Stuttgart, 1901), 87 ff. In Eur. *I.T.* 389–90, for instance, Iphigenia criticizes the legend of Tantalus: it was the cannibalistic Thracians who projected their own sin onto the gods, which parallels *mortalis error*; in Eur. *Troad.* 988–9 Hecuba accuses Helen of having hypostasized her own lust into the goddess Aphrodite, as all humans are wont to project their follies onto the gods: ὁ σὸς δ' ἰδών νιν νοῦς ἐποιήθη Κύπρις· | τὰ μῶρα γὰρ πάντ' ἐστὶν Ἀφροδίτη βροτοῖς.

The anthropomorphic representation of the god of Love as a winged youth armed with bow and arrows and a burning torch is humorously targeted in the monologues of unhappy young lovers of Middle Comedy: cf. Eubulus, fr. 41 Hunter (Cambridge, 1983), τίς ἦν ὁ γράψας πρῶτος . . . Ἔρωθ' ὑπόπτερον; | ὡς οὐδὲν ᾔδει . . . ἔστιν γὰρ οὔτε κοῦφος οὔτε ῥάιδιος | ἀπαλλαγῆναι τῶι φέροντι τὴν νόσον, Alexis, fr. 20; 245; Prop. 2.12). In these comic fragments, however, we find no critique of the anthropomorphic representation as such, but only in so far as it lends itself to a more self-pitying representation of a lover's plight. An apter parallel is provided by a passage in *Metiochos and Parthenope* (P.Berol. 7927 col. II, ll. 39–46; S. A. Stephens-J. J. Winkler, *Ancient Greek Novels. The Fragments* (Princeton, 1995), 84), where the protagonist is engrossed in some dispute about the true nature of Love, and counters his antagonists by denying the traditional attributes of the child-god: βωμολόχοι μέν, εἶπεν . . . ἀρχαίαις μυθολογίαις ἐπακολουθοῦσι ὥς ἐστιν ὁ Ἔρως Ἀφροδίτης υἱὸς κομιδῆι νέος ἔχων πτερὰ καὶ τῶι νώτωι παρηρτημένον τόξον καὶ τῆι χειρὶ κρατῶν λαμπάδα. Metiochos rejects the traditional iconography of Love in order to assert a psychological analysis of affection, envisaging love, in philosophical terms, as 'a movement of the mind' (κίνημα διανοίας, l.61). This points to philosophical precedents on which both the poet of *Octavia* and the author of the Hellenistic romance have drawn.

In Seneca's extant prose writings we never encounter comparable discussions of the nature of Love. On the other hand, polemic against superstition as a potentially immoral set of beliefs is constant in Seneca's prose writings: cf. *Vit. beat.* 26.6; *Breu.* 16.5 *inde etiam poetarum furor fabulis humanos errores alentium . . . quid aliud est uitia nostra incendere quam auctores illis inscribere deos et dare morbo exemplo diuinitatis excusatam licentiam?* (on Seneca's position against poetical mythology cf. Dingel (1974), 20–5). It is possible that the definition of Love as a *blandus animi calor* was found in Seneca's own (lost) treatise *De matrimonio*, of which we have excerpts in Jerome (cf. esp. fr. 81–2 Haase = 25 Vottero, where Love is defined as a form of *insania*). In Plut. *Amat.*, 756A one of the speakers makes light of the views of those who declare Love to be a god, proposing a purely materialistic interpretation of passion (ἡδέως ἂν ἀκούσαιμι πρὸς τί βλέψαντες ἀπεφήναντο τὸν Ἔρωτα θεὸν οἱ πρῶτοι τοῦτο λέξαντες). From Quintilian, *Inst.* 2.4.26, we gather that in school exercises pupils were asked to discuss the question *quid ita crederetur Cupido puer atque uolucer et sagittis ac face ornatus*. The iconography of the child-god is widespread, and well attested from the early Hellenistic age.

558–559 armat et telis manus | arcuque sacras, instruit saeua face Buecheler's correction of the transmitted *arcusque sacros instruit saeua face* is necessary: the bow and the torches of Love are distinct weapons in the imagery of Cupid. Buecheler had been preceded by Heinsius, with *arcuque sacro et* (*Adversaria*, 503). Buecheler's emendation is preferable because it establishes the usual type of *apo koinou* pattern of interlaced word-order which is commented on ad 698, an elegant stylistic feature which accounts for the corruption, alongside the difficulty of recognizing asyndeta, and the tendency to assign whole lines to each sentence.

560 genitumque credit Venere, Vulcano satum Only a handful of ancient sources attest Vulcanus' paternity of Eros: the present passage is absent in Roscher, *Lexikon*, s.v. *Hephaistos*, I.2, col. 2065, where only Serv. *ad Aen.* 1.664 and Nonn. *Dion.* 29.334 are mentioned (more dubious instances are given in Chrétien's note ad Nonn. *Dion.* 10.202).

561–562 uis magna mentis blandus atque animi calor | amor est According to the Stoics, the gods were mere allegories, projections of natural and psychological forces: cf. *SVF* (Arnim) II, p. 315, fr. 1076; III, p. 217, fr. 33. Love is equated with a rise in the temperature of the soul in Plut. *Amat.* 764b αὐγὴ δὲ καὶ θερμότης γλυκεῖα, although this is not in the context of a materialistic interpretation of passion.

562–563 iuuenta gignitur, luxu otio | nutritur inter laeta Fortunae bona That Love proliferates among the ease and profligacy of the upper classes was maintained by Phaedra's Nurse in *Phae.* 204–5 (whose polemical target was the insane and illicit love plaguing her mistress) *quisquis secundis rebus exultat nimis | fluitque luxu semper insolita appetit. . . .* This passage is the likeliest source of Seneca's argument, but the idea is commonplace: cf. Eur. 322 N² Ἔρως γὰρ ἀργὸν κἀπὶ τοῖς ἀργοῖς ἔφυ, Plat. *Resp.* 573A; Plut. *Amat.* 757a; Ter. *Heaut.* 109; Ov. *Rem.* 139 *otia si tollas, periere Cupidinis arcus*.

564 quem si fouere atque alere desistas, cadit *cadere* 'to subside', 'to fade away' is often said of passions, like *ira* (cf. *OLD* 12b; *TLL* iii. s.v. coll. 26–7): with reference to love, it also occurs in Lygd. 6.4 *saepe tuo cecidit munere uictus amor*; Sil. *Pun.* 17.361 *et cecidit iam primus amor*. Although not frequently found, it is a rather obvious metaphor (cf. Verg. *Buc.* 10.54 *crescent illae,* *crescetis, amores*); the *uerbum proprium* is *residere*: cf. Ov. *Her.* 17.190 *flamma recens parua sparsa resedit aqua.*

alere presupposes the description of Love as a secret wound which derives nourishment from the lover's own passion, bent on itself: cf. Verg. *Aen.* 4.2 *uulnus alit uenis*; Lucr. *D.R.N.* 4.1068 *ulcus . . . uiuescit et inueterascit alendo*; Sen. *Phae.* 101 *alitur et crescit malum.* The same dittology also in Liv. 42.11.5 (*Persea . . . bellum*) *alere ac fouere omnibus consiliis.*

Strzelecki (1938), 61, suggested writing *et* in place of *atque*, with the argument that synaloephe after the third thesis with a resolved fourth arsis is unparalleled in Seneca. There are, however, exact parallels in the archaic tragedians, leaving scant ground for emendation: cf. Enn. *Scaen.* 14 R² *sileteque et tacete atque animum aduortite*; Acc. *Scaen.* 508 R² *uos ite actutum atque opere magno edicite.*

566 hanc esse uitae maximam causam reor Nero cuts in on Seneca to defend love as a cosmic force ensuring the preservation of life through pleasure. The beginning of his counter-argument, however, is not clearly marked, and the older MSS omitted indication of change of speaker at *hanc esse* . . . (with *Nero* only stepping in at 570), leading Trevet to the false belief that Seneca 'aliqualiter ad commendacionem amoris condescendere'. There is, however, no doubt that 566 is Nero's reply to Seneca. Zwierlein rightly compared Phaedra's parallel defence in *Phae.* 218, *Amoris in me maximum regnum puto*, likewise the first words she pronounces to counter the Nutrix' appeal. 566 *hanc esse* is picked up by the conclusion of Nero's argument at 570, *hic mihi iugales praeferat taedas deus*, exhibiting a similar emphatic demonstrative at the beginning of the line.

The arrangement of words in the line, with a verb of opinion in the present tense at the end and a demonstrative at the beginning, has parallels in *Agam.* 271 *id esse regni maximum pignus putant* and *Phae.* 218. This sententiousness about the nature and the supreme divinity of love has parallels in ancient drama in Caec. *Inc.* 259–60 R² (*Amorem*) *deum qui non summum putet, | aut stultum aut rerum esse imperitum existumem*, perhaps translating Eur. *Auge*, fr. 269 N².

567–569 per quam uoluptas oritur, interitu caret, | cum procreetur semper, humanum genus, | Amore grato, qui truces mulcet feras Once again, Nero's philosophizing tones, asserting nature's rights, remind one of the Nurse at Sen. *Phae.* 466–70. Notice the interwoven arrangement of the cola, with *humanum genus* separated from its verb, *caret. procreetur* is reflexive.

interitu caret: 'is exempt from extinction', that is, never experiences extinction. Normally one is said to be deprived of things necessary or convenient; *careo* can, however, be used for being deprived of unwelcome qualities (*rebus incommodis*, cf. *TLL* iii., s.v. *careo*, 449.35–79), such as cares, fears (cf. Sen. *Vit. beat.* 5.1 *saxa timore et tristitia carent*; *Ira* 3.6.1 (*pars superior mundi*) *omni tumultu caret*; *Phae.* 483 *uitio carens*), guilt (cf. in Greek πόνων ἄπειροι, of the gods in Pind. fr. 147 Turyn;

likewise of the gods in Lucr.) and more generally, of transient conditions. The expression has a Lucretian ring: cf. Lucr. *D.R.N.* 2.19 *cura semota metuque*; 5.317 *priuata fragore. interitus* of humankind also in Porph. ad Hor. *Carm.* 1.2.6; Lucr. *D.R.N.* 5.877 *donec ad interitum genus id natura redegit.*

For parallels in which Amor/Venus is allegorized as the mere biological drive to reproduction, and love is praised as the instrument of the preservation of humankind cf. Lucr. *D.R.N.* 2.173–4 (*uoluptas*) *res per Veneris blanditur saecla propagent, | ne genus occidat humanum*, imitated in Ov. *Fast.* 4.99 *quid genus omne creat uolucrum nisi blanda uoluptas?* and in Sen. *Phae.* 470 (*Venus*) *quae supplet et restituit exhaustum genus. humanum genus* is the subject of both *caret* and *procreetur*, the latter virtually a synonym of *renascatur*. Cf. Cic. *De fin.* 3.62, where the same zeugma occurs, *neque uero haec inter se congruere possent, ut natura et procreari uellet* (sc. *homines*) *et diligi procreatos non curaret. per quam uoluptas oritur, interitu caret* should be understood as two co-ordinated clauses, linked by asyndeton.

570–571 hic mihi iugales praeferat taedas deus | iungatque nostris igne Poppaeam toris The bare *igne* has rightly seemed problematic to some interpreters, and Bothe[2] suggested *ipse. igne* is also difficult to translate, because the 'flame' of the ceremonial torch (unless a distinction is implied, with *igne* designating the flame burning on the altar) has only an accompanying function in the ritual and cannot be said to be the instrument (*igne*) whereby the union is accomplished. We miss an adjective giving *igne* a syntactically more plausible, descriptive function: one normally encounters such phrases as 'under (in-)auspicious torches' (*Oct.* 141–2 *genitamque fratris coniugem . . . toris nefandis flebili iunxit face*) or 'at the light of the royal (happy, solemn) torches' (cf. *Hf.* 346–7 *iuncta regali face | thalamisque*; Ov. *Met.* 7.49 *te face sollemni iunget sibi*). The simple *igne* has an apparent parallel only in Ov. *Her.* 14.9 *igne . . . quem non uiolauimus urat*, where the relative clause provides the equivalent of an adjective.

For the phrase *iungat . . . toris* (presumably a dative) cf. Ov. *Fast.* 3.511 *iuncta toro*; Luc. *Bell. Ciu.* 2.329 *toris melioris iuncta mariti.* The expression *taeda iugalis* (also in 694–5 *Caesari iuncta es tuo | taeda iugali*) does not occur in Senecan tragedy, but is well attested in classical Latin: with *taeda* cf. Cat. *Carm.* 64.302 *nec Thetidis taedas uoluit celebrare iugales* (a list of parallels in Junge (1999), 246 n. 740, esp. Ov. *Met.* 1.483; *Her.* 4.121; *Trist.* 4.5.33; *Pont.* 3.2.55; Val. Fl. *Arg.* 5.443; Sil. *Pun.* 17.73); with *fax* cf. Sen. *H.O.* 339 *meo iugales sanguine extinguam faces*; Stat. *Silu.* 1. 2. 183 *quas ego non gentes, quae non face corda iugali* (sc. *iunxi*).

572–573 uix sustinere possit hos thalamos dolor | uidere populi, sancta nec pietas sinat *sustineo* is often construed with an infinitive, but the sequence of two infinitives *sustinere . . . uidere*, the latter of which could have been dispensed with without detriment to the sense, makes the construction unwieldy. Finding fault with the two dependent infinitives, Heinsius conjectured *fidesque* (also found in some *recc.* according to Giardina's apparatus) to replace the MS *uidere*. The dittology *fides pietasque* in either sequence is often encountered: cf. Verg. *Aen.* 6.878 *heu pietas heu prisca fides*; *supra*, 51 *fides pietasque*. However, the poet of *Oct.* is no stranger to such inelegancies as *sustinere possit . . . videre*; cf. 892 *trahi . . . uidere possunt*, and there are examples of *sustinere* or other verb in the infinitive followed by a further infinitive: cf. Ov. *Trist.* 3.14.31–2 *carmen mirabitur ullum | ducere me tristi sustinuisse manu*; 5.12.9 *an studio uideor debere teneri*; Sen. *Med.* 544 *parere precibus cupere me fateor tuis*.

The construction of *non, uix* etc. *sustineo* with an infinitive is not found in prose before Liv. 23.9.7.

574 prohibebor unus facere quod cunctis licet? By way of answer, Nero flings back a sarcastic question: will he alone be prevented from doing what all and sundry do in Rome? Marriages in upper-class Roman society were mainly arranged affairs between teenagers, and divorce was common practice. Nero's riposte, containing an allusion to the supposed immorality of his fellow-citizens, resembles the negative view of this phenomenon expressed by satirists and moralists who in general blamed women's wantonness (cf. Friedländer, 1.286; Marquardt, *Privatleben* 72–80).

575 maiora populus semper a summo exigit The emperor set the moral standard of the age: cf. Liv. 1.21.2; Plin. *Pan.* 45.6 *nam uita principis censura . . . est: ad hanc dirigimur, ad hanc conuertimur*; 46.5 *manifestum, principum disciplinam capere etiam uulgus*; Cass. Dio *Hist. Rom.* 52.5.2 τὸν δ' ἐκείνου τις τρόπον κανόνα τοῦ βίου ποιησάμενος, Herodian. *Hist.* 1.2.4 φιλεῖ γάρ πως ἀεὶ τὸ ὑπήκοον ζήλωι τῆς τοῦ ἄρχοντος γνώμης βιοῦν. In poetry cf. Ov. *Met.* 15.834 *exemploque suo mores reget* (of Augustus); Claud. *IV cons. Hon.* 299–300 *componitur orbis | regis ad exemplum*.

summus is 'the one who occupies the highest place': in a metaphorical sense with reference to rulers cf. *OLD* s.v., 12, e.g. Luc. *Bell. Ciu.* 1.70 *summisque negatum stare diu*.

576–577 libet experiri uiribus fractus meis | an cedat animis temere conceptus fauor This line may echo *Hf.* 363 *nec coeptus umquam cedat ex animis furor*, but it is open to doubt whether Avantius' *furor* (also adopted by Zwierlein) should be preferred to the transmitted *fauor*. The words 'rashly conceived' (*temere conceptus*) suit *fauor* better, since *furor* already implies an act of unreasonable choice.

For *cedo* 'to depart', with reference to feelings and desires cf. *OLD* s.v. *cedo*, 4c; with *animo/animis* cf. Stat. *Theb.* 5.358 *tum primum ex animis praeceps amentia cessit*; 8.531 *aegra animo uis ac fiducia cessit. concipere furorem* 'to be smitten with madness' or 'to conceive a criminal, irrational plan' is a well attested idiom (cf. Verg. *Aen.* 4.501–2 *nec tantos mente furores | concipit*, where however *concipere* has a different sense; Ov. *Met.* 2.640 *ubi uaticinos concepit mente furores*; *ibid.* 7.9; *Ciris* 164; similarly *infra*, 784 *concepta rabies temere* might also be taken to support *furor*), but *c. amorem* is also frequent (cf. Ov. *Met.* 10.249 *operisque sui concepit amorem*) and sets a good precedent for *fauor*. It is clear from the following line (*obsequere potius* . . .) and from the passage as a whole that Nero has in mind popular support for Octavia: the latter has produced so far no manifestations which could be labelled as *furores*. Nero's subjects entreat the prince not to divorce his loyal and legitimate wife, whom they love.

There are no parallels in the Senecan corpus or in Vergil and Horace for this postponement of *an* after the third word. In Seneca postponement of *an* occurs only after one word, but in this instance the syntactical anomaly is partially excused by the consideration that *uiribus fractus meis* forms an independent participial colon. Cf. perhaps Luc. *Bell. Ciu.* 3.113–14 *uiribus an possint obsistere iura, per unum* | *Libertas experta uirum*, with the same combination *experiri an*.

578–579 SE. **obsequere potius ciuibus placidus tuis.** | NE. **male imperatur, cum regit uulgus duces** This cut and thrust has a precedent in Soph. *Ant.* 733–4, with Creon's indignation at the city's refusal to bow to his will: HAE. οὔ φησι Θήβης τῆσδ' ὁμόπτολις λέως. (sc. that Antigone is a transgressor) KR. πόλις γὰρ ἡμῖν ἁμὲ χρὴ τάσσειν ἐρεῖ;

579–580 NE. **male imperatur** . . . SE. **nihil impetrare cum valet, iuste dolet** *Parechesis* (Lausberg, *HLR*, 277–9), that is the echoing of words pronounced by successive speakers (*imperatur* . . . *impetrare*), is a feature of animated dialogue, comparable to the device whereby a speaker repeats a word already used by his antagonist: on *parechesis*/assonance in Greek and early Latin tragedy cf. Enn. *Scaen.* 41 R^2 (= 34 Joc., with Jocelyn's note for more parallels); in Seneca cf. *Hf.* 399–400 *sceptra uictrici geram* | *dextra regamque cuncta*; 440 *partes meae sunt reddere Alcidae patrem*; Seidensticker, (1969), 43, 87, with Greek precedents. This procedure is related to *paronomasia*, whereby a semantic antithesis is highlighted by phonetic resemblance: e.g. Publ. *Sent.* 55 R^2 *bene perdis gaudium ubi dolor pariter perit.* Cf. ad 433–4.

582 principem cogi nefas Cf. Plin. *Pan.* 6.1 *illud in principatu beatissimum, quod nihil cogitur.*

583–584 NE. **fama sed uictum feret.** | SE. **leuis atque uana.** NE. **sit licet, multos notat** Nero is concerned with the bad name that will accrue to him if he goes back on his decision to divorce Octavia. For the phrasing cf. Sen. *Thy.* 204–5 *fama te populi nihil* | *aduersa terret?*; *Hf.* 352 *inuidia factum ac sermo popularis premet.* In Greek tragedy cf. Aesch. *Agam.* 938 φήμη γε μέντοι δημόθρους μέγα σθένει, adduced by La Penna (1991), 61.

586 merita te diui patris Seneca does not expatiate on what he intends to present as meritorious achievements of Claudius, but emperors are naturally, unless publicly condemned, the benefactors of humankind: cf. Sil. *Pun.* 17.651–2 (*explicit*) *salue inuicte parens, non concessure Quirino* | *laudibus ac meritis*; Plin. *Pan.* 55.10.

587 aetasque frangat coniugis, probitas pudor This use of *frango* for 'to sway, induce to compassion' (*TLL* s.v., 1250.3–33: most notably *infra*, 901 *sic . . . fracta remittit*; Ov. *Met.* 8.508 *animum pietas maternaque nomina frangunt*; *Her.* 1.85, with Palmer; Stat. *Theb.* 7.527; 11.375) is absent from Senecan tragedy (only *H.O.* 913 is close). The plural *frangant* of some *recc.* is a *lectio facilior.* The common predicate of two or more subjects in the singular is also singular if the verb precedes or follows the first subject (*LHS* 2.433).

588–589 desiste tandem, iam grauis nimium mihi, | instare Nero offers a neat example of tyrannical behaviour in his display of impatience at Seneca's persistent opposition to his plans: cf. Soph. *Ant.* 280 παῦσαι πρὶν ὀργῆς καί με μεστῶσαι λέγων (Creon to the chorus). *desiste* is often construed with an infinitive: cf. Acc. *Scaen.* 172–3 R^2 *desiste exercitum | morari*; Verg. *Aen.* 12.60; Luc. *Bell. Ciu.* 5.744 *desiste preces temptare*; *CE* 963.12 *desiste lamenteis me exciere*; Sen. *Ben.* 7.14.5 *desine tibi molestus instare. mihi* is *apo koinou.*

589 liceat facere quod Seneca improbat 'Not even a Seneca, for all his wisdom, could stop me marrying Poppaea.' A more problematic occurrence of the philosopher's name is discussed *infra*, 696. Seneca is set off against Nero as a paragon of morality in Juv. 8.212.

Proper names are sometimes used to encapsulate a character's story and often convey definite allusions to a literary precedent: cf. *Med.* 496 *Medea amores obicit?*

590 et ipse populi uota iam pridem moror *en* for *et* is found in some *recc.* (in Giardina's apparatus), but *et* seems to me acceptable. *et* must be understood as a minor adversative, closely linked to *ipse*: 'and, in any case (or 'furthermore'), I am much too slow in carrying into effect the desires of the people'. For *en*, a deictic particle common in vivid narrative and when a speaker wishes to direct attention towards something, almost making it stand out as a visible object ('lo', 'there', 'see') see ad 827.

morari occurs in this sense ('id est differo', Trevet) with the accusative *iussa* in 439; *uota* (nom.) *morari* is found in Ovid: cf. Ov. *Her.* 7.21 *nec te tua uota morentur*; 18.5 *nam cur mea uota morentur* (with Rosati); for *populi uota* cf. *Pont.* 2.5.76 *quod mecum populi uota precantur idem*; with *desiderium* cf. Stat. *Silu.* 3. *pr.* 19 *desiderium eius moratus* (*sum*). Santoro suggested interpreting *moror* as 'I pay no heed to', 'I don't care for', but only the idiom *nil moror* occurs in this sense cf. *TLL*, s.v., 1499.78; *OLD* s.v., 4.

591 cum portet utero pignus et partem mei Poppaea, expecting a child, is clearly the subject of *portet*, but it is odd not to have her name expressed anywhere after 571. This objection is met by Buecheler's tentative rewriting of 590 *iam pridem et ipse uota Poppaeae moror* (*RhM* 27 (1872), 474), which provides a subject for the subsequent *portet* (along the same lines *nuptae*, proposed by Liberman in place of *populi*). On this interpretation, *uota* refers to Poppaea's wish to become Nero's wife. Buecheler's conjecture is, however, unsatisfactory, and entails too extensive a modification of the transmitted text to be acceptable. By appearing to interpret and obey the wishes of the people

Nero presents the divorce as a far-sighted political necessity, whereas his open admission of yielding to Poppaea's ambitions would be open to censure.

There can be little doubt that the *uota* here referred to by Nero are those of the Roman people, actually or supposedly enthusiastic about the prospect of a new heir who will guarantee peace. There is also no need to attribute to Nero a distorted view of the people's wishes (they were said to favour Octavia throughout the play: cf. 183, 572–3), if *populi vota* is a metonymic designation of any heir, who can be said to realize popular hopes for peace and continuity of government. The people care little for which wife will actually produce such offspring for Nero. In imperial propaganda, stability is seen in the presence of heirs (cf. *supra* 280–1). Birt (1921), 334, acknowledging the want of a reference, alters instead the following line, writing *cui destinamus proximum thalami diem.* Most editors resort to marking a lacuna after 590 (Zwierlein) or 591 (Baehrens, Richter), which is the solution I prefer. Zwierlein's supplement for the proposed lacuna (after 590) was <*cum uacua prole torpeat regis domus, | quam faustus auctet subole Poppaeae sinus*>, where the two-line omission was caused by the occurrence of the same word *cum* here and at 591.

Nero's description of Poppaea's state is couched in almost melodramatic language, with a crescendo of emotion in sharp contrast with his previous display of crude political realism. The bare *pignus* without a genitive, in reference to a child yet to be born, occurs also in Sen. *Med.* 1012 *in matre si quod pignus etiamnunc latet.* The concept that a child is a 'part' of its father, however natural it may appear, is not usually so phrased in Latin, and I can only adduce Curt. Ruf. *Hist. Alex.* 4.14.22 (Darius referring to the captivity of his mother and two daughters) *ipse ego maiore mei parte captiuus sum*; Quint. *Decl. min.* 338.19 (in the words of a mother) *filium . . . partem uiscerum auellis.* Cf. Ov. *Met.* 8.490 *uteri . . . pignora nostri*, with Bömer ad loc.; 10.481 *uix . . . uteri portabat onus*; 10.470 *semina fert utero conceptaque crimina portat. pars* is more commonly used of friends and lovers than of children: cf. Ov. *Trist.* 4.10.32 *coepi parte carere mei* (i.e. *fratre*); *Her.* 10.58 *pars nostri, lectule, maior ubi est? Met.* 11.473; *AL* 445.4 Riese (p. 334) *nunc pars optima me mei reliquit* (of a friend); *CE* 1431.3 *heu iacet hic pars magna mei* (of a wife). Note, however, that *sua uiscera* is a common metonymy used in reference to one's offspring in Ovid: cf. *Met.* 10.465 *accipit . . . sua uiscera lecto* (further parallels given by Bömer ad *Met.* 6.651); 8.478 *rogus iste cremet mea uiscera.*

Notice the alliteration *portet . . . pignus et partem*; such alliterating structures are favoured in early tragedy, especially at line-end: cf. Jocelyn, ad Enn. *Trag.* 4; compare the parody of the grand style in Plaut. *Poen.* 1285 *pro maiore parte prandi pignus cepi.*

592 quin destinamus proximum thalamis diem? The scene is brought to an abrupt conclusion with Nero's seemingly unpremeditated resolve to hasten the marriage (before the divorce has been finalized, or even explicitly announced). Compression of actual events is a feature of the play, as noted several times in this commentary. The inclusion of a marriage ceremony is part of the stock repertory of dramatic plots in comedy: cf. Plaut. *Trin.* 1188 *numquid causaest quin uxorem cras domum ducam* (Santoro); *Aul.* 261–2 *sed nuptias | num quae causa est hodie quin faciamus?*; Ter. *An.* 971 *nec mora ullast quin eam uxorem ducam* (the first and last parallels at the end of their respective plays); Ter. *Ad.* 712 *sed cesso ire intro, ne morae meis nuptiis egomet siem?* (at scene-end); Men. *Sam.* 725. Marriages and preparations for marriage feature less prominently in tragedy, and such as occur are often fated to go badly: cf. Sen. *Med.* 299–300, where Creon, at the end of his altercation scene with Medea, exits to make preparations for the imminent marriage between his daughter and Jason: *sacra me thalami uocant, | uocat precari festus Hymenaeo dies.* Cf. also ad 762.

Nero's declaration about proceeding to the marriage takes the form of an interrogative clause, introduced by the particle *quin*, often found in illocutionary questions equivalent to commands or exhortations: 'Why don't we appoint the next day for the marriage?' Some editors (Zwierlein, Vürtheim) print the sentence without a question mark at the end. Others, who do, translate otherwise: 'eh bien, demain est le jour que je fixe pour notre mariage' (Liberman); 'mieux encore, fixons demain comme jour de nos noces' (Chaumartin). These translations betray a certain reluctance to attribute to Nero the conciliatory tone implied by such a question. Admittedly, the interrogative nuance runs somewhat counter to the behaviour expected from Nero at this point, when he is at his most tyrannical.

LHS 2.676–7 distinguishes two main usages of *quin* in independent clauses: (1) an interrogative *quin* evolving from an original 'why not', in which the interrogative force fades out and which becomes virtually equivalent to a command, often in colloquial contexts; (2) an asseverative, augmentative *quin* meaning 'on the contrary, indeed, in fact'. In this second, emphatic sense, *quin* is mainly followed by a third-person verb in the indicative (e.g. Verg. *Aen.* 10.470–1 *tot gnati cecidere deum; quin occidit una | Sarpedon*). Affirmative adverbial *quin* occurs otherwise at the end of an enumeration (as in Prop. 2.10.15), introducing the final term of a climactic sequence.

When *quin* is followed by a first-person verb in the indicative or in the subjunctive, it tends to introduce an exhortation or an order, often impatiently uttered. In early drama cf. Plaut. *Cas.* 854 *quin imus ergo?*; *Merc.* 582; *Pseud.* 1048 *quin hinc metimur gradibus militariis?* Ter. *Eun.* 811 *quin redeamus*; Cic. *Fam.* 7.8.2 *quin tu urges . . . !* Cf. also O. Kienitz, 'De quin particulae apud priscos scriptores latinos usu' (Progr. Karlsruhe, 1878). In later, more formal use, the composition (*qui* + *non*) appears to be felt more, and the tone of such phrases is less decisively imperative: cf. Liv. 1.5.57 *quin . . . in equos conscendimus?*; Luc. *Bell. Ciu.* 2.319–20 *quin publica signa ducemque | Pompeium sequimur?*; Verg. *Aen.* 4.99–100 *quin potius . . . pactos . . . hymenaeos | exercemus?*, clearly not straightforward orders.

In Senecan tragedy *quin* + indicative is always clearly in sense (1), interrogative or imperative: cf. *Phae.* 866 *quin ense uiduas dexteram . . . ? Med.* 506 *quin potius . . . pectus doma.*

If sense (2) is preferred, *destinamus* acquires the force of a performative (almost 'to sum up: I hereby proclaim that the marriage will be held tomorrow'). Yet, this form of *pluralis maiestatis* occurs in official imperial decrees, but not until late antiquity. For the early empire, the verb-form used throughout in the imperial edicts is the first singular. In addition, *destinare* does not belong to the vocabulary of imperial pronouncements. Imperial edicts before Justinian are collected in Bruns, *FIRA*; for the terminology of later ages cf. Å. J. Fridh, *Terminologie et formules dans les Variae de Cassiodore* (Stockholm, 1956), 95–111, whence it appears that the verbs in most frequent use are *iubemus, sancimus, decernimus, praecipimus*: cf. Iust. *Inst. pr. specialiter mandauimus ut nostra auctoritate nostrisque suasionibus componant Institutiones.*

In Senecan drama, more commonly, tyrants and kings phrase their resolutions in the form of jussive subjunctives, or use gerundive periphrases: *destinemus* or *destinandum*. Cf. e.g. *Thy.* 202 *petatur ultro*; *Hf.* 354 *temptemus igitur*. If *quin* stands for *immo*, a perfect tense form *destinaui* would have been expected: cf. e.g. Ter. *Ad.* 734–5 *quin iam uirginem | despondi.*[16]

I favour (1), perhaps with the additional note that the *ignotus* is reviving the more archaic use of *quin* (= *cur non*) + indicative: cf. Liv. *Trag.* 13–4 R^2 (where Aegisthus presumably orders his underlings to drag Electra away) *quin . . . toleratis temploque hanc deducitis?* 'why don't you take her out of my sight?' Such illocutionary questions are also common in Greek. For a discussion of examples in Greek tragedy see M. Lloyd, *CQ* 49 (1999), 25, 34–5 (orders); cf. Soph. *Ant.* 885 (Creon) οὐκ ἄξεθ' ὡς τάχιστα; Eur. *Hec.* 1284–5 (Agamemnon) οὐχ ὅσον τάχος | νήσων ἐρήμων αὐτὸν ἐκβαλεῖτέ ποι; *Hipp.* 1290 πῶς οὐκ . . . κρύπτεις; on τί οὐ and related expressions cf. Barrett ad Eur. *Hipp.* 1060; K-G 1.165.

For *destino* followed by a dative of the occasion cf. Suet. *Claud.* 26 *ipso die qui erat nuptiis destinatus* (sc. *occidit*); Tac. *Hist.* 4.10.1 *proximus dies causae destinatur*; Apul. *Met.* 10.29; 11.23.

593 *Octavia* does not follow the conventional Greek sequence of *epeisodia* and *stasima*, to which Seneca generally adheres, and the beginning of the new 'act', day two of the action, is not demarcated by a choral ode. Choral odes were often not transcribed in many Hellenistic editions of classical and post-classical tragedy, either because the sung parts were no longer performed or because they were replaced by *embolima*; in many Egyptian papyri of tragedy, the formula *chorou* or a marginal *coronis* marks the action-break, which often involves a lapse of time (cf. O. P. Taplin, *LCM* 1 (1976), 47–50). The structure of

[16] The contracted form *destinamus* for *destinauimus* would have no parallels in Senecan tragedy, and seems confined to early Latin.

post-classical tragedy, or even mime (as argued by Sutton, (1983), 27–31) may have influenced the structure of *Octavia* in this respect.

The second day of the action is only briefly sketched and comprises Agrippina's appearance (early hours of day 2) and Octavia's departure from the palace (representing the divorce). There is some uncertainty whether 669 ff. (see ad loc.) should be assigned to day 2 or to day 3. Octavia speaks at 646 of the present day of festivity, presumably because the marriage will either take place soon or is in fact taking place as she speaks. Later Poppaea's Nurse (at 746–7) makes a reference to lamentations for Octavia performed on the day of the wedding (which in the play's reconstruction of events is contemporary with the divorce), *before* the first night of Poppaea's marriage, a circumstance which in the Nurse's view accounts for the ominous dream related by Poppaea. We may suppose that it is these lamentations Octavia is referring to in 646 with the words *parcite lacrimis*.

Agrippina's ghost is imagined as appearing (593) in the early morning, as ghosts do in tragedy (in Senecan drama cf. *Agam.* 53–6; *Thy.* 120–1). In extant Greek tragedy, ghosts appear both at the beginning and in the middle of a play: cf. Darius in Aesch. *Pers.* 681 and Clytaemnestra in Aesch. *Eum.* 103. In Senecan tragedy, ghost scenes are found only in prologues. This may also be the case for the unassigned fragment quoted by Cicero (*TRF inc.* 73–7 R^2) *adsum atque aduenio Acherunte vix via alta atque ardua* . . .

The appearance of a ghost in the middle of the play has been the cause of some concern among scholars. Leo (*Monolog*, 93; *RhM* 52 (1897), 513) saw the Agrippina-scene as an *Intermezzo* ('ein richtiger Zwischenakt') intended to represent the night intervening between the two days of the action (Leo overlooked the beginning of the third day after 690, and was trying to force the play into the traditional five-act structure). The succession of a narrative prologue (pronounced by a ghost or by a divine agent), a monody of a distressed heroine and, finally, a choral song is a typical tragic beginning (especially in Euripides; cf. Eur. *Hec.* 1–152, where the prologue pronounced by Polydorus is followed by Hecuba's anapaests and then by the parodos), but the analogy should not be pressed any further. The short choral ode of 668 ff., although responding to the heroine's song in so far as it describes the effects of Octavia's dismissal on the Roman people, does not so much represent a *parodos* as an exit in preparation of off-stage action (the mounting of the rebellion). Moreover, Octavia's monody and the ensuing choral ode probably belong to different days of the action.

Act-division in this play (see Introd. pp. 65–9) should probably not be pursued rigidly. The 'law of five acts', largely a construction of Hellenistic literary critics, is generally respected by Seneca, but is unknown to Plautus and Terence and, for all we know, may not have been felt as a binding principle for all dramatic genres.

593 Tellure rupta Tartaro gressum extuli Agrippina does not name herself (although 595–6 make it sufficiently clear that the ghost is Nero's mother): cf. by way of contrast Eur. *Hec.* 1–3 Ἥκω . . . Πολύδωρος. In Senecan tragedy cf. *Thy.* 3–4 *quis male deorum Tantalo uisas domos | ostendit iterum?*; *Agam.* 4 *fugio Thyestes inferos.* In Aesch. *Eum.* 116 the mention of Clytaemnestra's name is used climactically and elicits the first reaction from the sleeping Erinyes: ὄναρ γὰρ ὑμᾶς νῦν Κλυταιμήστρα καλῶ. In Greek tragedy, and occasionally in Seneca, spectres are prone to mention the place from which their journey began: cf. Sen. *Agam.* 1 *opaca linquens Ditis inferni loca*; Eur. *Hec.* 1 Ἥκω . . . λιπών. For *gressum extuli* cf. Verg. *Aen.* 2.753 *qua gressum extuleram*; 6.677 *tulit gressum*; *Georg.* 4.360 *gressus inferret*, both with parallels in *Octavia*.

The fact that Poppaea recounts her vision of Agrippina in a nightmare in ll. 712–39 led Staehlin (1912), 167 to suppose that the two scenes should be considered close in time: this would be important for obtaining a closer understanding of the play's division into days, but on this interpretation the Poppaea-Nutrix scene at 690 ff. takes place on day 2, which is impossible on account of the marriage, which must precede it. A close link between a ghost's appearance on the stage and a character's dream is found in several passages in ancient drama. Cf. Eur. *Hec.* 1 ff., where Polydorus, while delivering the prologue to the tragedy, manifests himself to his mother in the form of repeated visions (54 φάντασμα δειμαίνουσ' ἐμόν, and perhaps also 30–1 νῦν δ' ὑπὲρ μητρὸς φίλης | Ἑκάβης ἀίσσω . . .), whereupon Hecuba in a lament prays Zeus that the sense of these be disclosed to her (69–70 τί ποτ' αἴρομαι ἔννυχος οὕτω | δείμασι φάσμασιν, 72–5 ὄψιν ἣν | . . . δι' ὀνείρων εἶδον); Aesch. *Eum.* 94 ff. (cf. 116, quoted above); Pac. *Scaen.* 197–202 R[2]. As the text stands, this hypothesis could only be maintained if Agrippina's lines were transposed after 668 (or even after 689), since lines 646 to 668 (Octavia's departure from the palace) evidently take place on day 2, but there is no MS support for such a hypothesis. As things stand, 593–645 and 646–68 are set in the early hours of the wedding day (unless we assume that Octavia leaves literally at the moment when the marriage is being celebrated). Agrippina's ghost is introduced to cast a curse over the imminent marriage of Nero. She assumes the (reversed) role of the mother raising the nuptial torch (the present subjunctive *nubat* at 595 also suggests that the marriage has not yet taken place) and describes in the language of prophecy Nero's end, which is near.

594 Stygiam cruenta praeferens dextra facem 'Holding a Stygian (i.e. funereal) torch in my blood-stained hand' because Agrippina has been assassinated. The shades of the victims of murder continue to be disfigured in the Underworld: cf. Verg. *Aen.* 2.286 *cur haec uulnera cerno?*; Aesch. *Eum.* 103 ὅρα δὲ πληγὰς τάσδε, Sen. *Oed.* 624 (of Laius) *stetit per artus sanguine effuso horridus*; cf. F. Cumont, *After life in Roman Paganism* (New York, 1923), 165. When they emerge to haunt the living they exhibit their wounds as marks of their horrific deaths. Alternatively, her blood-stained appearance might be interpreted as the usual attribute of Furies (Santoro): cf. Ov. *Her.* 6.46 *praetulit infaustas sanguinolenta faces*; Sen. *Med.* 960–1 *at cui cruentas agmen infernum faces | intentat?*; Stat. *Theb.* 10.854; Enn. *Scaen.* 48 R^2 *fax obuoluta sanguine*; *TLL* s.v. *fax*, 402.5–15.

595–596 nubat his flammis meo | Poppaea nato iuncta This line alludes to the Greek custom according to which mothers were supposed to carry a torch at their children's weddings (references in Gow-Page, *HE* 2.79, ad 550 f.). In the Roman marriage ceremony, however, while mothers had a prominent function, their presence was not linked to the torch ritual (cf. Daremberg-Saglio, s.v. *matrimonium*, 1656, n. 10; Marquardt, *Privatleben*, 55; *OCD*[3] s.v. 'marriage'). In Greek tragedy, ominous marriages are a recurrent feature: cf. Iphigenia's vengeful words before her sacrifice (as Agamemnon imagines them) at Eur. *I.A.* 463–4 τοιούτους γάμους | γήμειας. Cf. also the falsely exultant entrance of Cassandra rejoicing at her 'marriage' with Agamemnon, which will in fact bring ruin upon him, in Eur. *Troad.* (cf. esp. 322, invocation to Hecate, and 404–5 τοὺς γὰρ ἐχθίστους ἐμοὶ | καὶ σοὶ γάμοισι τοῖς ἐμοῖς διαφθερῶ). For the same reversal of function (funereal flames for nuptial) see *supra* ad 25–6. The closest parallel is Sen. *Troad.* 1134 *tali nubat Hermione modo*, where the silent thoughts of the Trojan captives are reported; cf. also Verg. *Aen.* 7.555–6 *talia coniugia et talis celebrent hymenaeos | egregium Veneris genus et rex ipse Latinus*.

596–597 quas uindex manus | dolorque matris uertet ad tristes rogos Agrippina, like a latter-day Clytemnestra, has cursed her murderous son: it is her curse that will bring about his and Poppaea's ruin. I interpret *uindex manus dolorque matris* as equivalent to 'ego dolens ob iniuriam et uindictam appetens': 'I shall gladly kindle the pyre which will burn your accursed selves.' *dolor* is often [caused by] indignation seeking revenge: cf. *TLL* s.v. 1841.53 ff.

There are no parallels supporting Ballaira's understanding of *uertet ad . . . rogos* as an equivalent to '*mutabit in*', which in Latin is *uertere in* (cf. Leo, *Obs.* 63). The confusion *in/ad* occurs in the corpus in *H.O.* 1760, but there is no reason to suspect *ad* here, and *uertet* must be interpreted in its literal sense ('to turn – to a different purpose' rather than 'transform'). The marriage torches are not actually changed into funereal flames, but will serve to kindle the funereal pyre. Cf. Sen. *Contr.* 6.6 *uersae sunt in exequias nuptiae, mutatusque genialis lectus in funebrem, subiectae rogo felices faces*. The topos 'the same torches used twice' is often found in funerary epigrams: cf. *AP* 7. 712, 5–6 τὰν παῖδ', Ὑμέναιος ἐφ' αἷς ἀείδετο πεύκαις, | ταῖσδ' ἐπὶ καδεστὰς ἔφλεγε πυρκαϊᾶι, 7.182.7–8 (with a variation) αἱ δ' αὐταὶ καὶ φέγγος ἐδαιδούχουν περὶ παστῶι | πεῦκαι καὶ φθιμέναι νέρθεν ἔφαινον ὁδόν, also 7.185–8. In Latin cf. Ov. *Her.* 6.42 *faxque sub arsuros dignior ire rogos*; 14.10; 20(21).172 *face pro thalami fax mihi mortis adest*, with Kenney's note for parallels; see H. Blümner, *Römische Privataltertümer* (München, 1911), 492 n. 3.

More generally see R. Rehm, *Marriage to death: the conflation of wedding and funeral rituals in Greek tragedy* (Princeton, 1994); R. Seaford, *JHS* 107 (1987), 106–30. According to Tac. *Ann.* 16.6 Poppaea was not cremated (*corpus non igni abolitum*), but Agrippina's words need not be interpreted literally.

In addition, Agrippina's words conjure up the pathetic image of a mother holding her torch under a child's funereal pyre ('my grief shall put his nuptial flames under the pyre'), for which other verbs usually employed are as *subdere, subicere faces* (cf. Lucr. *D.R.N.* 6.1285; Verg. *Aen.* 6.223–4 *subiectam more parentum . . . tenuere facem*). The iconography of *Erotes* with inverted torches as a sign of grief is also common; see F. Cumont, *Recherches sur le symbolisme funéraire des Romains* (Paris, 1942), 409; add *CE* 1997.5 *Lucina facis demerso lumine fleuit* (with the notes of Courtney, *Musa Lapidaria* (Atlanta, 1995), ad 190. 5). In one of the reliefs of the tomb of Caluentius Quietus at Pompeii, the figure of a woman holds out a torch, while averting her gaze. J. Overbeck (*Pompeji* (Leipzig, 1875[3]), 363, fig. 211) interpreted this as a family member about to ignite the pyre, but this interpretation has been disputed in more recent studies: cf. V. Kockel, *Die Grabbauten vor dem Herkulaner Tor in Pompeji* (Mainz, 1983), 93, who sees the relief as a Demeter-figure. Some ancient sources state that the task of lighting the pyre was not assigned to female relatives (cf. Serv. ad Verg. *Aen.* 6.223: the pyre itself was kindled by the male relatives, *propinquioribus uirilis sexus*).

vindex is a noun, but is commonly found as an adjective in Augustan poetry: cf. N-W 2[3].31. *vindex manus* has a precedent in Sen. *Phae.* 261 *proin castitatis uindicem armemus manum*. For examples of nouns used as adjectives in Greek cf. Mastronarde ad Eur. *Phoe.* 1569.

598–600 manet inter umbras impiae caedis mihi | semper memoria, manibus nostris grauis | adhuc inultis More fastidious poets would have avoided the succession of the three datives *manibus nostris . . . adhuc inultis* by using, for example, a dicolon, such as *manibus nostris grauis / animaeque inultae*: cf. Ov. *Met.* 8.488 *fraterni manes animaeque recentes*. Notice the paronomasia in *manet . . . mānibus*.

For *manibus . . . grauis* cf. Flor. *Epit.* 2.16(4.6).2 *Caesarem inultus pater et manibus eius graues Cassius et Brutus agitabant*; *ibid.* 2.13(4.2).55 *ultionem clarissimi uiri manibus quaerente Fortuna*; *supra* ad 295; Luc. *Bell. Ciu.* 9.64 *obtulit officium graue manibus*.

In Senecan tragedy *memoria* often occupies the last position in the line; in this position cf. *Oed.* 768 *redit memoria tenue per uestigium*.

600–602 reddita et meritis meis | funesta merces puppis et pretium imperi | nox illa qua naufragia defleui mea In imitation perhaps of *Oed.* 104–5 *laudis hoc pretium tibi | sceptrum et peremptae Sphingis haec merces datur* (= *laudis hoc pretium datur, sceptrum, et haec merces peremptae Sphingis*), but the dyad *pretium . . . merces* is also found in Luc. *Bell. Ciu.* 2.330; for *merces* used ironically to indicate ingratitude cf. Ov. *Her.* 16.9 *esset ut officii merces iniuria tanti*; *Met.* 5.14–15 *meritisne haec gratia tantis | redditur?*; *Pont.* 3.3.39 *pro quibus exilium* *misero est mihi reddita merces*; and μισθός is similarly employed in Greek ironically (cf. [Eur.] *Rhes.* 948–9 καὶ τῶνδε μισθὸν παῖδ' ἔχουσ' ἐν ἀγκάλαις | θρηνῶ).

The phrasing *manet ... caedis semper memoria, et reddita meritis meis funesta merces puppis, et pretium imperi nox illa ...* is grammatically unobjectionable, because the ellipsis of the auxiliary in perfect passive verb forms, especially when these belong to the second element in a dicolon, is frequent: cf. e.g. Ov. *Met.* 11.743–4 *tunc quoque mansit amor nec coniugiale solutum | foedus* (*solutum est v.l.*; much material on ellipsis in Leo, *Obs.* 1.184 ff.; see also ad 536–7). On the other hand, the omission of an abbreviated *est* (= *e* with supralineate bar) is easy to account for, and Buecheler suggested writing *reddita est* for *r. et*, which is also feeble on stylistic grounds if *reddita* etc. is interpreted as the start of a new sentence with ellipse of the auxiliary ('the memory of my death still aggrieves me, and a fated ship was the reward granted to my merits'). I believe, however, that *reddita ... puppis ... et nox* should be interpreted as two further objects of Agrippina's painful remembrance, loosely attached to *memoria*, of which they are two specifications (e.g. *manet memoria caedis. . . puppis et nox illa* = *manet memoria caedis, manet memoria puppis et noctis illius*). The resulting inconcinnity of construction is more effective, almost an outcome of the speaker's emotional distress. The transition *manet memoria caedis ... et ... puppis ... et nox* should be regarded as an example of syntactical zeugma: cf. Ov. *Ars* 1.551 *et color et Theseus* (i.e. *memoria Thesei*) *et uox abiere puellae*; Sil. *Pun.* 7.495–6 *iam monita et Fabium ... exuerat*; Val. Fl. *Arg.* 3.688 *sat lacrimis comitique datum*; more examples given by Leo, *Obs.* 197.

604 deflere uotum fuerat: haud tempus datum est 'I would have wanted to give vent to my affliction and weep': this use of the impersonal periphrasis *uotum esse (alicui)* followed by an infinitive is not very common, but cf. Petr. *Sat.* 73.1 *lauari coeperat uotum esse.*

A similar line-ending occurs in *H.O.* 1806 *nunc datum est tempus, datum est ...*

606–607 sacros | intra penates spiritum effudi grauem *grauis* either because she barely had any breath left at the approach of death or because she was indignant (cf. *supra*, 375–6 *animam ... tristem ... reddit*; Santoro interprets as 'dolente' for her son's treason and the wounds inflicted on her). The epithet is apparently without parallels with *spiritum* (closest parallel in Ov. *Met.* 4.498 *inspirantque graues animas*). *effundere spiritum, uitam, animam*: cf. *TLL* v s.v. *effundo*, 233.29 ff. The line, with its emphasis on sacrilege (*sacros intra penates*), may echo the description of Priam's death before the altar in Verg. *Aen.* 2.550–1 *altaria ad ipsa trementem | traxit*, and also 2.515–7 *Hecuba et natae nequiquam altaria circum ... diuom amplexae simulacra tenebant.*

608–609 erepta pelago sanguine extinxi meo | nec odia nati The participial coda *erepta pelago* is at this stage a pointless complication of the argument. It is probably intended to highlight the unexpectedness of a death which came when she felt she had escaped it, but the contrast *penates/pelagus* is under-developed. Bothe, who was reluctant to accept a postponed *nec*, suggested transposing a hemistich, writing *spiritum effudi grauem. | nec odia nati sanguine extinxi meo, | erepta pelago. saeuit in nomen ferus*, but hyperbaton of co-ordinating particles is common in this play (cf. Introd. pp. 32–3).

610 obrui meritum cupit *obruo* can be used for 'to delete', 'to oblit-erate' (*TLL* ix.2 s.v. *obruo*, 154.54–69): cf. Sen. *Contr.* 1.6.3 *auitas . . . flagitiis obruerunt imagines*; Vell. 2.3.3 *ius ui obrutum*; Liv. 25.38.10 *populi uis atque uirtus non obruta . . . clade Cannensi.*

611 simulacra titulos destruit The only evidence of the *damnatio* of Agrippina in the extant literary sources is Cassius Dio, *Hist. Rom.* 61.16.2[a] Boiss. (= Petr. Patr. *Exc. Vat.* 50) ὅτι εἰσιόντος Νέρωνος εἰς τὴν Ῥώμην τοὺς τῆς Ἀγριππίνης ἀνδριάντας καθεῖλον: cf. Nordmeyer (1892), 259. In Tacitus' chapter relating the Senate's reaction to the news of Agrippina's end, the Senate only decides to include Agrippina's birthday among the 'dies nefasti' (*Ann.* 14.12.1), a form of *damnatio* probably inclusive of the erasure of honorary in-scriptions and other measures commonly taken against disgraced personages: cf. Suet. *Dom.* 23 *eradendos ubique titulos abolendamque omnem memoriam* (*senatus de-creuit*); Mommsen, *RS* III.2.1190–1. The name of Agrippina is assumed to be the one erased in *CIL* X 1574 (although it should be remembered that after Nero's fall, even the names of Poppaea and Statilia Messalina were erased). Mes-salina's name met with the same fate in inscriptions; cf. Furneaux ad Tac. *Ann.* 11.38.4, with epigraphical references; see also G. Alföldi ad *CIL* VI.8.2 (1996), n. 40452.

611–612 mortis metu | totum per orbem 'Under threat of death', or 'sous la menace de la mort' [Chaumartin], but *mortis metu* is am-biguous in the absence of a verbal form explaining whose death (presumably the transgressors', but cf. by contrast Tac. *Ann.* 1.39.4 *intento mortis metu*; Sen. *Phae.* 727 *mortis intentat metum*), especially since *destruit* does not contain the idea of inducing fear. Baden, quoted by Zwierlein, adduced in defence Flor. 2.2.17 *destricta securi imperator metu mortis nauigandi fecit audaciam* where Regulus persuades his reluctant sailors to overcome their terror of the Punic sea and carry on with their expedition. Similarly, Flor. 3.14.5 *praesenti metu mortis* (*eum*) *exterruit ut . . .*; Tac. *Ann.* 13.48.3 *data cohorte praetoria, cuius terrore* (i.e. through the terror inspired by them) *et paucorum supplicio rediit oppidanis concordia.* Zwierlein is right to reject Löfstedt's interpretation (*Late Latin*, 146–7 n. 2) *metu mortuae*, supposedly supported by Prop. *Carm.* 2.13.22 *nec sit in Attalico mors mea nixa toro*, where *mors* stands for *cadauer, funus*, 'corpse' by an easily understandable metonymic substitution. The text can hardly stand as it is, yet an entirely satisfactory proposal has so far not been advanced. Buecheler's *matris metu* is probably the best emendation proposed (cf. Suet. *Nero*, 34.4, where Nero is hounded by his mother's furies); ***nostri metu*** could also be in place. On this interpretation, Nero is terrified by the memory of his crime and attempts to obliterate his deed by effacing all honours previously granted to Agrippina. Other conjectures include *memores mei* (Grotius), *more improbo* (Bothe).

612–613 quem dedit poenam in meam | puero regendum noster infelix amor Notice the usual variation in number, from singular to plural (*meam . . . noster*), already observed *supra*, ad 21. The line-ending *infelix amor*, however common, has a parallel in *Med.* 136 *suasit* (*Peiper*; saeuit *MSS*) *infelix amor*, where the adjective designates an affection which is unhappy not because unreciprocated but because ill-fated, *infaustus*, doomed, or sprung from bloodshed.

614–615 extinctus . . . agitat infestus . . . coniunx Two attributes for one noun are a rarity in classical Latin poetry: see ad 259, with Cortius on Lucan, *Bell. Ciu.* 2.207 *intrepidus . . . sedit securus*; Sen. *H.O.* 19–20 *notos Hebro | cruore pingues hospitum fregi greges*; *Oed.* 20–1 *thalamos parentis Phoebus et diros toros | gnato minatur impia incestos face.* Perhaps this case can be excused if *extinctus* is understood as a participial predicative clause: 'dead, my husband, full of hatred, brandishes his blazing torches in my face'. The verb *agito* is commonly used in the context of the persecution of the living by furies and ghosts: cf. e.g. Verg. *Aen.* 3.331 *scelerum furiis agitatus Orestes.*

614 umbras . . . meas The dead describe their own ghosts as 'shades' in the plural. Haupt ad Ov. *Met.* 1.387 explains it as a case of interference, a combination of the Greek usage of *eidolon*, for 'spirit', and of the Latin plural *manes.* Cf. also Prop. 2.8.19 *exagitet nostros manes, sectetur et umbras*; Liv. 40.56.9 *cum . . . umbrae insontis interempti filii* (sc. *eum*) *agitarent*; Luc. *Bell. Ciu.* 8.434 *nudae sperauimus umbrae.* Although the poet of *Octavia* constantly refers to Claudius as *diuus* and makes Seneca allude to his deification in several passages (cf. Introd. p. 72; see also 534, 586), Claudius is nevertheless depicted in Hades both here and in 967.

615 uultus noxios . . . petit Cf. ad 119 *oculosque et ora fratris infestus petit*; see also *Phoe.* 42–3 *en ecce inanes manibus infestis petit | foditque uultus*, where the wandering Oedipus is assailed by visions of his dead father Laius; the sense of *uultus* is different in the two contexts, but that scene is certainly imitated here. *noxius* may mean either 'guilty' (Agrippina seems conscience-stricken in the Underworld) or 'hateful' (from Claudius' point of view).

616–617 imputat fatum mihi | tumulumque nati Claudius torments Agrippina in the Underworld imputing to her both his own murder and that of his son. The dead can occasionally torment one another. For example, the avenging spirit of Agrippina is said to be tormenting the ghost of Nero in Tartarus in Stat. *Silu.* 2.7.118–19 *pallidumque uisa | matris lampade . . . Neronem*; and in Plut. *De sera num. uind.* 32 (*Mor.* 567). More generally cf. Verg. *Aen.* 4.386 *omnibus umbra locis adero*; Ov. *Ibis* 140 *saeua sed in Manis Manibus arma dabit*; 143–4 *tum quoque factorum ueniam memor umbra tuorum, | insequar et uultus ossea forma tuos*; Stat. *Theb.* 4.565–7, where Pentheus runs away from Agaue, who has returned to her senses (*Penthea . . . insequitur planctu, fugit ille per auia Lethes . . .*). In Greek tragedy cf. Aesch. *Eum.* 96–9, where Clytaemestra describes how the other spirits blame her for the murder of Agamemnon: ὧν μὲν ἔκτανον | ὄνειδος ἐν φθιτοῖσιν οὐκ ἐλλείπεται . . . ἔχω μεγίστην αἰτίαν κείνων ὕπο.

Some early editors found fault with *tumulus* (*imputat . . . tumulumque nati*), with the argument that Claudius is not pointing to the burial mound (the literal sense of the word) of his son. Hence Grotius's *suum atque nati* which, on metrical grounds amongst others, does not seem a good suggestion (synaloephe of the first arsis is without examples in the corpus). The same is true of Heinsius' *imputat tumulum suum | simulque nati* (*Adversaria* 509). Zwierlein's defence (adducing Ov. *Met.* 7.483 *tumulo* [i.e. *Manibus nati*] *solacia posco*) is slightly off target, because the Ovidian passage only illustrates the metonymic use of *tumulus* for 'the soul' of Androgeus, for the satisfaction of whom Minos wages war against Athens. In 617 *tumulus* is a synonym of *fatum* and means 'Britannicus' violent death'. The word emphasizes the notion of death already expressed by *fatum*, in more emotional terms. Synonymic dicola are of course common. With *fatum* cf. Sil. *Pun.* 17.228–9 *genti . . . superbae | Iliacum exitium et proauorum fata dedissem.* The author's propensity for accumulation of synonymous pairs (almost to compensate for his lack of skill in creating elaborate syntactical units) was observed ad 141, with regard to the sequence *prolis suae . . . nato suo . . . sanguine alieno satum. . . . genitamque fratre*; but the image is graphically effective, with Claudius seeming to point Agrippina towards the unfortunate boy's burial mound (in fact, Agrippina was only indirectly responsible for Britannicus' death: see my note ad 170).

imputo occurs in a similar context in Ov. *Met.* 2.399–400 *Phoebus . . . natum* (i.e. *mortem nati*) *. . . obiectat et imputat illis* (i.e. *equis*), which the author may have had in mind when writing this line.

617–618 poscit auctorem necis; | iam parce: dabitur The line closely imitates *Phoe.* 39–40, with which it shares the transition from third person narrative to direct address to an absent interlocutor, in both cases a spectre: *genitor uocat: | sequor sequor, iam parce,* the words of Oedipus, who, haunted by a vision of Laius' shade, turns to address him; cf. also *H.O.* 1005–6 (***E***) *quid me flagranti dira persequeris face, | Megaera? poenas poscis Alcidae? dabo* (where Deianeira is struck by remorse for the murder she has committed) (***A*** has *p. poscit Alcides,* which parallels *poscit auctorem necis* more exactly). Medea is similarly haunted by the brother she has slain in *Med.* 958–67, esp. 964–5 *frater est, poenas petit. | dabimus, sed omnes*; cf. also Ov. *Met.* 2.101–2 *ne dubita, dabitur . . . quodcumque optaris.*

618 tempus haud longum peto Cf. Ov. *Her.* 7.178 *tempora parua peto* (Hosius); Verg. *Aen.* 4.433 *tempus inane peto.*

619–621 ultrix Erinys impio dignum parat | letum tyranno, uerbera et turpem fugam | poenasque quis et Tantali uincat sitim The present passage has traditionally been recognized (as early as Petrarch and Salutati; see Introd. p. 6, n. 15) as the most immediate indication of non-Senecan authorship. Agrippina foretells Nero's end in words so true, if we make allowance for the allusive mode in which this prophecy is expressed, that this passage must have been composed after AD 68. For instance, *uerbera* might be linked to Suet. *Nero* 49.2, containing the death sentence, by flogging, decreed by the Senate, *corpus uirgis ad necem caedi*; *fuga* has been related to Nero's flight to Phaon's *uilla suburbana* (*Nero* 48); for *sitim* cf. *ibid.* 48. 4 *fameque et iterum siti interpellante panem quidem sordidum oblatum aspernatus est* . . . 630 *iugulum hostibus* corresponds to Suet. *Nero* 49.3 *ferrum iugulo adegit.* The somewhat vague phrasing of such allusions is easily explained by the prophetic mode adopted in Agrippina's scene. The mention of a thirsty Nero, which has an exact equivalent in the account of Suetonius, triggers a rather uninventive catalogue of traditional punishments. The same list, as already pointed out by Siegmund (1911, 20), can be found in the invective against an unidentified enemy of the poet in Ov. *Ibis* 157 ff. (157 *uerbera saeua dabunt sonitum nexaeque colubrae*; 159 *his uiuus Furiis agitabere*; 187 *in te transcribet ueterum tormenta uirorum*, that is, Sisyphus (189), Ixion (190), Tantalus (191), Tityos (192). *verbera* are the blows inflicted by the Furies: cf. Sen. *Thy.* 96–7 *quid ora terres uerbere et tortos ferox | minaris angues?* also in *Hf.* 86; *Oed.* 644; *Agam.* 760; *H.O.* 1002, 1013.

On *quis* cf. ad 728.

To an ancient audience, a death on stage, albeit the death of a tyrant, had some redeeming features (compare the final grief and bereavement of Oedipus in Soph. *O.T.* or of Creon in Soph. *Ant.*). *Octavia* could not have represented Nero's end if Nero was consistently to be the villain of the play. Agrippina's prophecy has been included in the play to ensure that justice will triumph in the end, without arousing compassion for the evil tyrant (and without straining the chronology of events). Similarly Poppaea's prophetic dream announces the end of the villainous *princeps* (at 733) without focusing on his final agony and on his feelings in the face of death. On reading the final chapters of Suetonius' biography, it is impossible not to feel sorry for Nero when everybody deserts him except the compassionate Phaon.

624–5 licet exstruat marmoribus atque auro tegat | superbus aulam The term *aula* (originally a yard, an entrance hall) is used in poetry with the meaning 'residence, palace', especially with reference to kings and personages of high standing. It designates here the vast complex of enclosures, baths and sumptuous buildings erected by Nero after the great fire of 64 and extending over part of the Palatine and across to the Esquiline and the Caelian hills. Modern detailed descriptions of these buildings can be found in A. Claridge, *Rome. An Oxford Archaeological Guide* (Oxford, 1998), 268, 290–1, 430; F. Coarelli, *Roma* (Bari, 1997^{2}), 205–11; ancient sources describing these include Tac. *Ann.* 15.42; Suet. *Nero* 31; Plin. *Nat.* 33.54 (*Nero Pompei theatrum operuit auro in unum diem ut Tiridati Armeniae regi ostenderet. et quota pars ei fuit aureae* *domus ambientis urbem*). Some parts of the palace, according to Suet. *Nero* 31, were overlaid with gold (*auro tegat*) and precious marbles were used for the floors and the decoration of the walls. *exstruo* (like *instruo*) means 'to erect' and, by metonymy, 'to adorn' an edifice: cf. Enn. *Scaen.* 85 R² *auro ebore instructam* (*domum*); Verg. *Aen.* 1.637–8 *domus interior regali splendida luxu* | *instruitur.* A part of the buildings of the *Domus* apparently survived Nero (they may have been in use as late as Titus' reign), until they were finally destroyed by fire in AD 104, after which the lower level of the *Domus* became an underground service area of the new Baths of Trajan.

627–628 supplices dextram petant | Parthi cruentam, regna diuitias ferant Cf. the similar wording in Aug. *Res Gest.* 5.29 *Parthos . . . supplices . . . amicitiam pop. R. petere coegi*; Hor. *C.S.* 53–6 *iam . . . manus potentis* | *Medus Albanasque timet securis,* | *iam Scythae responsa petunt, superbi* | *nuper et Indi.* Agrippina alludes to events which took place in 66 (well after Seneca's death!), when Tiridates, a member of the Parthian ruling dynasty, came to Rome to receive the diadem of Armenia from Nero's hands (Tac. *Ann.* 15.29; Suet. *Nero* 13.2). *petere, amplecti dextram* is a common gesture of submission performed by suppliants and by defeated fighters (cf. Sen. *Med.* 247–8 *cum genua attigi* | *fidemque supplex praesidis dextrae peti*; other parallels are quoted in Kragelund (2000), 507 n. 73, also good for the historical background). The phrase *cruenta dextra* occurs also in 594; elsewhere apparently only in Sen. *Oed.* 642 and Sil. *Pun.* 9.210.

Giancotti and Ballaira believe, following Birt (1923) 742, that *regna* should be interpreted as an accusative and linked to *diuitias*: 'no matter how many kingdoms, how many riches the Parthians offer to you'. Giancotti quotes Verg. *Aen.* 1.605 (*di tibi*) *praemia digna ferant* to illustrate this sense of *ferre.* On this interpretation, *regna* should be taken as a poetic plural or, with less likelihood, as a reference to the confederation which formed the Parthian state. A more natural interpretation is to read *regna* as the subject of the sentence, as a collective noun incorporating all the (Eastern) vassal states of the Roman Empire. This antonomastic use of *regna* (just as of *terrae* and *reges*) for 'foreign, barbaric kingdoms' creates no difficulty: Sall. *Iug.* 14.17 *nationesne an reges* (sc. *adpellem*)?; Ov. *Fast.* 5.562 *armaque terrarum milite uicta suo*; 6.178 *nec tellus captas miserat ante feras*; Tac. *Hist.* 4.39 *Kalendis Ianuariis in senatu . . . legatis exercitibusque regibus laudes gratesque decretae,* whereby the kings of the small Eastern vassal kingdoms, allied to Vespasian, are meant; also *Ann.* 1.11.6.

629 ueniet dies tempusque Cf. Sen. *Troad.* 470 *eritne tempus illud ac felix dies*; Verg. *Aen.* 2.324 *uenit summa dies et ineluctabile tempus.*

629–630 reddat suis | animam nocentem sceleribus, iugulum hostibus The usual idiom in Senecan tragedy for 'to have one's throat cut' is *dare iugulum*, but there are several variations on the theme of 'death by throat-cutting', which has sacral connotations (it also implies, as in this case, the unheroic death of the captive, without resistance): cf. Sen. *Agam.* 43 *daturus coniugi iugulum suae*; 972–3; *Oed.* 1037; *Thy.* 723; *Troad.* 50; *H.O.* 991.

The parallelism between the two cola seems to suggest that *suis sceleribus* should be interpreted as a dative: Nero is to 'hand over his soul to [the tribunal] of his crimes', personified as crying out for punishment on the culprit. Cf. *infra* 829 *dolori spiritum reddat meo* and, with *do*, Sen. *Phae.* 937 *sceleribus poenas dabis*; Tac. *Ann.* 1.10 *Cassi et Brutorum exitus paternis inimicitiis datos*; 16.20 *Minucium Thermum . . . Tigellini simultatibus dedit*; *CIL* III.3335 (from Pannonia) *quadragesimo fatis animam reddidit.* On a less effective interpretation, *suis sceleribus* is an ablative governed by *nocentem*: cf. *Phoe.* 538 *scelere . . . nullo nocens*; *Med.* 499. The semantic shift from figurative to literal sense in *reddat animam* to [*reddat*] *iugulum* is a specific type of zeugma, called *syllepsis*, exemplified for instance in Ov. *Met.* 3.46–7 *siue illi tela parabant | siue fugam*; cf. Lausberg, *HLR*, 351–2, § 708; E. J. Kenney, in J. Binns, *Ovid* (London, 1973), 125; id. *CR* 22 (1972), 39; Canter, 162. In Sen. cf. *Phae.* 1101; *Agam.* 987. See also *infra*, ad 802–3.

On *anima nocens for* 'a soul defiled by sin' cf. Ov. *Met.* 4.110 *nostra nocens anima est;* Stat. *Theb.* 12.96–7 *caeloque animas Ereboque nocentes | pellere fas.*

631 desertus ac destructus et cunctis egens Cf. Verg. *Aen.* 4.330 *non equidem omnino capta ac deserta uiderer. ac*, originally a variant of *atque* before a consonant (*LHS* 2.477), is wholly equivalent in sense, though more colloquial: it seems to have been avoided before a velar consonant in classical authors (cf. *TLL* ii, s.v., 1048.74ff.; Axelson *UW* 82–3), although a rule is nowhere clearly stated, for instance by the grammarians. At any rate, it is probably better to adopt the sequence *ac . . . et* of *recc.* in the place of *destructus ac cunctis* found in ***A***. Zwierlein rightly compares *Hf.* 317–18 *demersus ac defossus et toto insuper | oppressus orbe* and *Troad.* 449 *sed fessus ac deiectus et fletu grauis*, exhibiting the same succession *ac . . . et.* Sluiter also compared Suet. *Nero* 32.1 *destitutus atque ita iam exhaustus et egens* (*ut stipendia quoque militum . . . differri necesse esset*, referring to Nero's financial strictures in 64). It has been suggested that the passage echoes *Oct.* 631: cf. Coffey (1958), 174.

632 quo labor, quo uota ceciderunt mea? *cadere* for 'to sink' ('where have my efforts sunk to?') also in Sen. *Phae.* 1270 *huc cecidit decor?*; Tac. *Hist.* 3.53 *in irritum cecidisse labores*; Flor. *Epit.* 2.4.5 *aliorsum uota ceciderunt*; Tib. 2.2.17 *uota cadunt.* The use of *quo* in rhetorical interrogatives is normal: cf. Prop. 4.3.51–2. A related kind of exclamation is found in *Hf.* 269 (*Cadmea proles atque Ophionium genus*) *quo reccidistis?*

633–635 quo te furor prouexit attonitum tuus | et fata, nate, cedat ut tantis malis | genetricis ira, quae tuo scelere occidit? 'To what height of madness has your folly and your fate driven you, son, that even the anger of your mother, whom you murdered, is assuaged by the sight of so many ills?' For the singular predicate *prouexit* in grammatical agreement with the first of a sequence of subjects cf. *supra*, ad 587. A similarly extended construction, comprising a rhetorical interrogative clause and a consecutive, the antecedent of which is implicit in the first clause (i.e. *furor adusque miseriarum te prouexit ut cedat* . . .), occurs at 378–9 (with the parallels given there). In earlier dramatic poetry, poets may have preferred more intricate sense-construction. In classical poetry shorter, more effective sentences are preferred, in blocks of co-ordinated clauses, especially in highly emotional speeches: Ov. *Met.* 8.491–2 *ei mihi, quo rapior?* . . . *deficiunt ad coepta manus*; Verg. *Aen.* 3.480–1 *quid ultra* | *prouehor et fando surgentis demoror Austros?* (as opposed to, e.g. *prouehor ut* . . . *demorer*). One might propose *at* for *ut*, (*quo te furor prouexit* . . . *? cedat at malis tantis genetricis ira*), introducing an objection as in Cat. *Carm.* 64.178 *Idaeosne petam montes? at gurgite lato* . . . , or *cedit en* (cf. Verg. *Georg.* 4.495–6 *quis tantus furor? en iterum crudelia retro* | *fata uocant*), but I think the conclusion *quae tuo scelere occidit* disproves this, making clear that *genetricis ira* must be understood as 'even your mother's anger is overcome by your misery'. The indicative in *q. t. s. occidit* is not abnormal: modal attraction is far from being the rule (*LHS* 2.547–8).

Agrippina is torn between hatred for the man who caused her death and love for the cherished child to whom she gave birth. For such divided-self monologues cf. Tarrant, ad Sen. *Agam.* 126. An important precedent is Ovid's Althaea, equally torn between maternal love and revenge for her brothers (*Met.* 8.445–514).

636–638 utinam, antequam te paruulum in lucem edidi | aluique, saeuae nostra lacerassent ferae | uiscera! A wish that her child had died in infancy is expressed in Althaea's lament, Ov. *Met.* 8.501–2 *o utinam primis arsisses ignibus infans,* | *idque ego passa forem*: cf. Ov. *Her.* 4.125–6 *o utinam* . . . *in medio nisu uiscera rupta forent*; [Sen.] *H.O.* 1805–6 *utinam meis uisceribus Alcides foret* | *exsectus infans*; Stat. *Ach.* 1.132–3 (Thetis, relating a dream in which she saw) *in ubera saeuas* | *ire feras*. In Agrippina's 'modern' world, the wish that wild animals had torn her womb apart seems more exaggerated, and remote from reality, than in her (mythological) counterparts, living in a time of monsters – which suggests imitation (esp. relevant with regard to the question of priority between *H.O.* and *Oct.*).

The diminutive *paruulus*, specifically used as a noun with reference to children, is superfluous here (one only gives birth to infants), but effectively conveys Agrippina's tenderness for her lost child.

638–639 sine sensu, innocens, | meus occidisses The closest Senecan parallel is *Troad.* 417 *torpens malis rigensque sine sensu fero*; for other instances of pyrrhic words in this position cf. Zwierlein *KK* ad *Phoe.* 117. Children who die prematurely are innocent by definition: cf. *Hf.* 1131 *umbrae* . . . *ite innocuae.*

meus, used predicatively with *occidisses*, caused disquiet in earlier scholars: Gronovius proposed *mecum*, but *meus*, as Bothe was right to argue, is 'tenerius'.

This emphatic use of the possessive without a substantive is paralleled in Stat. *Theb.* 11.611 *crudeles, nimiumque mei.*

639–641 iunctus atque haerens mihi | semper quieta cerneres sede inferum | proauos patremque, nominis magni uiros *quieta . . . sede* is a correction of Heinsius (*Adversaria*, 509) for MS *quietam . . . sedem.* The accusative is awkward here, because the 'silent dwelling' of the dead, where Agrippina wishes she and her son could peacefully have found a resting place, and Nero's 'father and ancestors' are not objects of contemplation on equal terms. If *quieta* is restrictive, setting up an implicit opposition between the 'silent' and the more turbulent regions where sinners undergo punishment (cf. Val. Max. 2.6.8 *ut se . . . in meliorem sedis infernae partem deduceret*; Verg. *Aen.* 6.638–9), Agrippina has the Elysian fields in mind. This is indeed where one's illustrious ancestors are expected to reside. On the other hand, the Underworld as a whole is normally designated as *silentum regnum*, except when the speaker wants to stress retribution and punishment; cf. Luc. *Bell. Ciu.* 6.781 *infernam ruperunt arma quietem*; *CE* 1109 *sedes . . . silentum*; 1551 *Ditisque silentia maesti.*

On the pleasure felt in reviewing one's lineage in the Underworld cf. Verg. *Aen.* 6.679 ff. *at pater Anchises . . . conualle uirenti . . . omnem . . . suorum . . . recensebat numerum carosque nepotes.* A new soul descending to the Underworld is saluted by old friends and, above all, by his ancestors: *Cons. Liu.* 330 *inter honoratos excipietur auos* (with the parallels given by Schoonhoven ad loc.). *nominis magni uiros* may echo the earlier *magni . . . nominis umbra* (71), though the genitive performs a different function.

Like Agrippina here, Juturna, in Verg. *Aen.* 12.881 *possem misero fratri comes ire per umbras*, wishes she could die and follow her loved one to the Underworld. In *Phae.* 1179–80, Phaedra similarly promises that she will follow Hippolytus everywhere in Hades, *et te per undas . . . per amnes igneos amens sequar.*

nomen has the sense of '[glorious] family-name': cf. Vell. 2.100.5 *Gracchus et Scipio aliique minoris nominis*; Verg. *Aen.* 12.529–30 *Murranum . . . atauos et auorum antiqua sonantem | nomina*; Mart. 5.17.1 *dum proauos atauosque refers et nomina magna.*

642 quos nunc pudor luctusque perpetuus manet The boast that a deceased person has added glory to his ancestors is common in sepulchral inscriptions: cf. *CE* 654. 1–2 *inter auos proauosque tuos sanctumque parentem | uirtutum meritis . . . emicuisti.* Liberman suspects *manet* (with the argument, faulty in my view, that Nero's crimes have been a disgrace for his and his ancestors' name from the very moment when they were committed) and rather pointlessly conjectures *tenet. perpetuus*, however, projects the ancestors' grief into the future, and fits in well with *manet.* In defence of this high-flown and formulaic use of *maneo*, see ad 530; add Sen. *Phae.* 1228 *quae poena memet maneat et sedes scio*; Tib. 1.8.77. For the transitive use of *maneo*, to indicate a destiny in store for a given person, cf. *TLL* viii, s.v., 291.77 ff.; *OLD* s.v. 4.

644 quid tegere cesso Tartaro uultus meos? *quid . . . cesso* is formulaic in Latin drama in self-address; it often has the function of an implicit stage-direction indicating the exit of a given character: cf. Plaut. *Rud.* 454 *sed quid ego cesso fugere in fanum . . .* ; Plaut. *Pers.* 742–3 *quid ego igitur cesso infelix lamentarier | minas sexaginta.* Other parallels from early Roman drama are given by Tarrant (1978), 255 and n. 171.

Spirits, as well as gods, must depart from the stage after delivering their lines, but this is so far the only instance I have found in which a psychological reason is given for their leaving: Agrippina's ghost, overcome by grief, wishes to hide her face in hell. In Sen. *Agam.* 56 Thyestes must return underground because his presence prevents the rising of the sun: *Phoebum moramur.*

caput uelare, contegere and *tegere, abscondere uultus* frequently occur to mark a display of mourning, affliction, anger, shame (parallels in A. Barchiesi, *MD* 1 (1978), 121 n. 31; K. Sittl, *Gebärden der Griechen und Römer* (Leipzig, 1890), 275): cf. Ov. *Met.* 4.800; 10.450. The conclusion of Agrippina's monologue is modelled on Juturna's lament in Verg. *Aen.* 12 (as already noted ad 639–41), at the point where Juturna, despairing of bringing help to her brother, veils her head and disappears in the waters of the river: cf. 885–6 *caput glauco contexit amictu . . . et se fluuio dea condidit alto.* In Greek cf. the words of Artemis to Theseus in Eur. *Hipp.* 1290–1 πῶς οὐχ ὑπὸ γῆς τάρταρα κρύπτεις | δέμας αἰσχυνθείς;

645 nouerca coniunx mater infelix meis The conclusion of Agrippina's speech echoes in its clausula such epigraphic endings found in sepulchral inscriptions: cf. *CE* 504.1–2 *genetrix duo corpora natos | condidit infelix.* The sense of *infelix* however is an active one (= *exitiosa*): Agrippina has attracted ruin on all she has come in contact with: cf. Ov. *Met.* 4.490 *infelix . . . Erinys*; Verg. *Aen.* 2.245 *monstrum infelix sacrata sistimus arce,* and, with the dative of disadvantage indicating the victim, Pers. *Sat.* 6.12–13 *auster | infelix pecori.* Cf. also Tac. *Ann.* 1.10.5 *Liuia grauis in rem publicam mater, grauis domui Caesarum nouerca* [RJT].

646 The playwright has compressed into one day of action events which took place over at least a period of weeks (as already observed ad 437; see also Introd. p. 4). The divorce, represented at 646 ff. by Octavia's departure from the palace, its immediate aftermath, must obviously have preceded the marriage. The chronological overlapping of the two events, though unrealistic, is intended to enhance the dramatic poignancy of Octavia's fate: her sorrow is set off against a background of public rejoicing. The marriage takes place off-stage, as in Euripides' and Seneca's *Medea* (cf. Sen. *Med.* 116, where the epithalamium is first overheard by Medea, then sung by the chorus on stage as part of the celebrations). In early Roman drama, a marriage ceremony is imminent in Pac. *Scaen.* 113–4 R^2 *hymenaeum fremunt | aequales, aula resonat crepitu musico*; 115 R^2 *gnatam despondit, nuptiis hanc dat diem* (perhaps from a prologue, the announced marriage being that of Electra and Oeax).

The playwright gives a demonstration of remarkable compositional skills, as he represents the marriage from the points of view, in succession, of several characters involved: Agrippina, Octavia, her followers, Poppaea's Nurse and, lastly, the revellers, who celebrate Poppaea's beauty at 762 ff. (see ad loc.). The alternative would have been to introduce a messenger speech in order to give a description of the marriage ceremony. This task is later assigned to Poppaea's Nurse, somewhat to the detriment of dramatic tension there. Here, the *ignotus*, usually inferior to Seneca, has actually delivered a far better result than we might have expected from his main model. A marriage off-stage was presumably celebrated in Ovid's *Medea*, as reconstructed from *Her.* 12.137 ff., and the author of *Octavia* may owe something to the talents of that master of multiple perspectives. In Greek tragedy the convention whereby actions take place off-stage occasions multiple descriptions of the same fact, often bringing in conflicting viewpoints. On the resulting ambiguity and multiplicity of voices as a characteristic of tragic 'discourse' cf. Easterling, *Companion*, 154–5.

After the extended first act, Octavia is depicted only in extreme foreshortening, always as she leaves the 'stage' and addresses mute characters. At 646 Octavia addresses a group of unnamed companions, supposedly lamenting her fate (*parcite lacrimis*). Despite the metrical identity of 646 ff. and 669 ff., which would seem to suggest that the former addresses the latter, I believe with Schmidt (1985), 1447 that *parcite lacrimis* is not addressing the chorus of 669 ff. (which undoubtedly represents a group of men, initiating the revolt against Nero) but a group of female mourners in the house (perhaps the same later mentioned by Poppaea's *Nutrix*, 746–7 *Octauiae discidia planxerunt sacros* | *intra penates fratris*, with no subject expressed). A female audience provides a more appropriate backdrop for Octavia leaving her own house, and weeping is a gendered activity on the tragic stage, more becoming to women than to men. The strong similarity between this scene and Iole's anapaestic lament in *H.O.* 173–232[17] also suggests that a secondary chorus of female extras commiserating with Octavia is more appropriate here.

This abrupt scene beginning, involving two previously unintroduced groups, is without parallels in Greek tragedy, except, of course, in prologues (cf. Aesch. *Septem*, 1; Soph. *O.T.* 1). Discontinuity of the action is less anomalous in comedy, where a character may address someone in the house from which s/he has just come out at the beginning of a new scene. In Men. *Aspis*, 164, *Sam.* 440 a character leaving the house addresses a group of women weeping inside, exhorting them to restraint. In *Epitr.* 430 Sand., Habrotonon comes out of the house imploring some young men to leave her alone: ἐᾶτε μ' ἱκετεύω σε . . . These young men are commonly identified with the revellers referred to at

[17] In both *Agam.* 659 and *H.O.* 173 the words pronounced by Cassandra and Iole are very abrupt (Iole is not even known to be present before she actually speaks).

413, who have presumably performed the interlude signalled by χοροῦ before 419. In Roman comedy cf. Duckworth, *NRC* 125 (e.g. Ter. *Hec.* 76–80; *An.* 481–5); C. Harms, *De introitu personarum in Euripidis et novae comoediae fabulis . . .* (diss. Göttingen, 1914), 31 n. 1. There is no reason to treat condescendingly this compositional shorthand, and in fact the succession of separate *tableaux* which we find deployed in the second half of the play is dramatically more effective than the excessive verbosity of, say, the Octavia-Nutrix scene, and I take it as a sign of the *ignotus*' comparative ease when it comes to dramatic 'direction'. The rapid 'cutting' and discontinuous action of the second half of the play, alien to the style of Greek tragedy, has been interestingly related to the influence of mime: cf. Sutton (1983), 75.

The initial *parcite lacrimis* does not evolve into an exchange with a chorus, and in fact Octavia becomes increasingly absorbed in her own thoughts, which take the form of an anapaestic monody. In Greek tragedy non-initial monodies occur in Aesch. *Prom.* 561; Soph. *Ai.* 394–427; Eur. *Alc.* 393–415; *Andr.* 1173–96; *Suppl.* 990–1030; *Hec.* 1056–1106. Typically, mid-play monodies follow a choral ode, and mark the beginning of a new 'act': in Eur. *Suppl.*, for instance, Euadne sings her monody after the brief third stasimon. This does not mean that a choral ode should be assumed to have been lost here, since its presence would have made the brief second 'act' even more unbalanced. With the exception of the pre-parodic monody, where address to the chorus leads to the *amoibaion*, monodies are normally soliloquies, aiming at conveying isolation and frenzy; mute attendants are nevertheless addressed in Soph. *Trach.* 1004; Eur. *Hipp.* 1358–9; *Hec.* 59: cf. Jens, *Bauformen*, 299; Pac. *Scaen.* 263 R². The peculiar feature of this *Octavia* passage, however, is that Octavia (with *parcite lacrimis*) is addressing some lamenting companions, whereas in all passages listed above (except in Pac.) the monodizing character calls upon mute attendants to refrain from an action or to perform one. The only parallel I can give in tragedy for a character trying to curb the lamentation of a group (as distinct from the situation where a character tries to restrain another individual) is Sen. *Agam.* 659 *cohibete lacrimas*, which is in fact different, because the chorus of Trojan captives has spoken before. Elsewhere in Senecan tragedy, where mute characters on stage are addressed, they are normally named, for instance as *famuli* (*Hf.* 1053; *Phae.* 725; 901), and they are urged to do something, rather than to refrain from speaking. However, the coming and going of choruses is often abrupt in Senecan tragedy: cf. *Troad.* 63, where the monologue of Hecuba develops into an *amoibaion* when Hecuba suddenly turns to address a chorus who had given no signs of being present. Similarly, in *H.O.* 173–232 (a scene which the author of *Oct.* clearly had in mind here; cf. ad 665–6), the song of Iole interrupts the previous choral ode in an unexpected manner.

The scene elaborates on the theme of the girl leaving her house, presumably to meet an early death, a theme common in Greek tragedy. Possibly there are some reminiscences of Eur. *Alc.* 184, 255–6 and the song of Alcestis at 244–72, which follows a song by the chorus, but does not engage in exchange with it.

646 parcite lacrimis The succession of dactyl and anapaest is rarely admitted in Greek tragedy (only in threnodic, i.e. sung, anapaests). Cf. A. M. Dale, *Lyric Metres* (Cambridge, 1948), 49; J. Diggle, *Studies on the Text of Euripides* (Oxford, 1981), 45, ad *El.* 1319–20 on the rarity of this sequence in the non-lyric anapaests of Greek fifth-century tragedy; West, *GM*, 121; Eitrem-Amundsen (1955), 1–87, with post-classical examples. In Senecan tragedy, dactyl and anapaest are found also in *Oct.* 908, *Hf.* 1064; *H.O.* 185, 196, 1883, 1887; cf. Schmidt (1860), 54–5, 67.

646–647 urbis festo | laetoque die *dies festus* may also designate festivals spanning several days in succession cf. e.g. Petr. *Sat.* 45 *in triduo die festa*, from which one might conclude that Octavia leaves the palace during one of the days of celebration for the marriage. In fact, the departure of Octavia can only take place prior to the marriage of Nero and Poppaea. Historically, the divorce must have preceded the marriage of Poppaea by several days, but the poet of *Octavia* needed to telescope these events into one day, even at the expense of dramatic unity.

648–650 ne tantus amor nostrique fauor | principis acres suscitet iras | uobisque ego sim causa malorum Octavia's concern over the retaliation such popular displays of affection and sympathy may trigger has a parallel in Eur. *Herc.* 277–8, where Megara entreats the chorus of old men to moderate their anger, lest they should suffer unjustly on her account, ἡμῶν δ' ἕκατι δεσπόταις θυμούμενοι | πάθητε μηδέν.

The construction with the dative *uobis . . . ego causa malorum* is paralleled in various authors, most notably Luc. *Bell. Ciu.* 5.481 *mundo tantorum causa laborum.* On the sequence of connectives *ne . . . -que* (in place of the expected *ne . . . ue, uobisue*) cf. *supra* ad 297. There may be a verbal echo from Ov. *Met.* 1.509 *et sim tibi causa doloris* [RJT].

On the jingle *amor/fauor* cf. ad 11 (on the frequency of homoeoteleuta in anapaestic sequences).

651–653· non hoc primum pectora uulnus | mea senserunt: grauiora tuli. | dabit hic nostris finem curis | uel morte dies The language of Octavia is too weak for her dramatic situation – that of a dispossessed princess who is about to be executed – and her referring to the wrongs she has suffered as 'wounds' (*uulnera*) almost casts her in the pose of an elegiac heroine. For *uulnus sentire* of the wounds inflicted by love cf. Ov. *Her.* 16.239 *sentis mea uulnera, sentis*; *Met.* 14.771 *mutua uulnera sensit.* There is also a clear reminiscence of Aeneas' address to his companions in Verg. *Aen.* 1.199 *o passi grauiora, dabit deus his quoque finem*; cf. also Ov. *Trist.* 5.11.7–8 *multo grauiora tulisti, | eripuit cum me principis ira tibi.* This confirms a pattern already observed, according to which imitation of hexameter verse becomes predominant in anapaestic sequences, either through the metrical congruence of the two systems or to enhance the 'lyrical' quality of such parts by emphasizing their derivation from high poetic precedents.

653–653ᵃ dabit hic nostris finem curis | uel morte dies: cf. *Phae.* 670 *finem hic dolori faciet aut uitae dies* (Segurado). *dies* must not be taken literally, since Octauia will not be led away by her executioners until the third day of dramatic action (by contrast, the action of Sen. *Phae.* is contained within the span of one day). Acc. *Scaen.* 37 R² *scibam hanc mihi supremam lucem et seruiti finem dari*, supposedly pronounced by Cassandra. *vel morte* ('no matter if by bringing death upon me') was wrongly suspected by Baehrens (who proposed *sine morte*) and after him by Liberman, on account of its supposed inconsistency with the heroine's wish to be spared (659–60 *absint . . . letique metus*). Octavia's display of irresolution is itself a poetic cliché of female monologues, in which the speaker is torn between conflicting emotions and fears (cf. Tarrant, ad *Agam.* 132). The same moving timidity in the face of death is recorded by Tacitus in his narrative of Octavia's last moments: cf. *Ann.* 14.64 *praesagio malorum iam uitae exempta, nondum tamen morte acquiescebat*, the exact interpretation of which is uncertain: either 'she had not yet found peace in death', or 'she could not reconcile herself to the idea of having to die'; on this passage and its possible dependence on *Oct.* cf. Ferri (1998), 353.

654–657 non ego saeui cernere cogar | coniugis ora, | non inuisos intrare mihi | thalamos famulae *non ego* carries no contrastive emphasis (i.e. does not imply a comparison with anyone else). The subject pronoun is often found at line-beginning in hexameter verse: cf. Ov. *Fast.* 3.55 *non ego te*; *Her.* 1.7; *Pont.* 2.2.9; Pease ad Verg. *Aen.* 4.425; Bömer ad Ov. *Met.* 3.568. On this feature cf. J. N. Adams, *ALLP* 97–133, who argues that non-contrastive subject pronouns highlight the emphatic term to which they are attached. The MS *seue* (for *saeuae*), corrected by Avantius, was caused by the wrong interpretation of *coniugis* as a reference to Poppaea.

For *intrare . . . thalamos* cf. *Carm. Bell. Act.* 22 Courtn. *Alexandro thalamos intrare dearum*.

658 soror Augusti, non uxor ero Octavia became Nero's sister after the adoption of the latter into the Claudian family. Cass. Dio-Xiph. *Hist. Rom.* 60.33.2 Boiss. relates, however, that, when she became Nero's wife, Octavia had been nominally adopted by another, unknown, family, to avoid the rumour of incest. Tac. *Ann.* 14.64 may have imitated this passage with his *cum se uiduam et sororem tantum testaretur*, pronounced by an imploring Octavia vainly trying to escape death. These words amount to a public renunciation of Octavia's royal prerogatives, and, especially in Tacitus, to a desperate appeal for her life to be spared. While the dittology 'sister and wife' may have been played up already by one of the Flavian historiographers (this would explain its recurrence in Plut. *Galb.* 19 (*Nero*) τὴν γυναῖκα καὶ ἀδελφὴν ἀποκτείνας . . .), the *Oct.* poet combined the formula of court etiquette (cf. ad 220) with literary reminiscences of Ov. *Met.* 3.265–6 *si sum regina Iouisque | et soror et coniunx, certe soror* and Sen. *Hf.* 1–3; Tarrant's note ad *Agam.* 340 *o magni soror et coniunx.* In Greek, the expression γυνὴ καὶ ἀδελφή occurs various times, in reference to Eastern queens (e.g. Artemisia, Arsinoe, Dareius' wife), and Agrippina is wrongly so identified in Cass. Dio *Hist. Rom.* 61.35 (= Joann. Antioch. fr. 89 M.).

659–662 absint tantum tristes poenae | letique metus – | scelerum diri, miseranda, uiri | potes hoc demens sperare memor? Octavia does not regret the loss of her exalted position: she only wishes that her future life may be free from the fears of persecution (*poenae*, perhaps torture or imprisonment) and death, a natural course of events, given the danger her existence posed for Nero and in light of the precedents set by other members of the imperial family who fell from favour. Zwierlein's note in the apparatus ('660 metus] *i.q.* metuenda scelera; *cf. 380, 107*') is unclear, but probably refers to Octavia's fear of being unjustly accused (cf. 106–7 *non mortis metu, | sed sceleris*), as in fact happened in the end, or of defiling her hands with Nero's blood (cf. 174–5). Either way, his suggestion is only weakly supported by the bare *leti metus.*

The combination *poena metusque* also in Ov. *Met.* 1.91 *poena metusque aberant*, the description of the state of happy innocence of the Golden Age, when punishment and the fear attendant upon it were unknown; Tac. *Ann.* 3.55.18 *poena ex legibus et metus. poena*, however, has a different sense in 659, rather more like 'torture', 'physical suffering', not as a consequence of any crime committed; *infra* 967 *dignum tali morte et poena.*

The contradiction between 653• *uel morte* and 659 has been the cause of some critical concern; Baehrens assigned 661–8 *scelerum . . . gradum* to the chorus (also in some *recc.* according to Giardina and Richter). This may find some support in comparison with *H.O.* 225 ff. (see ad 665–6). On the whole, the suggested allocation of these words to a chorus accompanying Octavia's exit with wise advice is not absurd: these words would provide a very effective commentary *ex persona poetae* (along the lines of 356–60, see ad loc.). *demens*, however, is too abusive a word to be anything other than a form of self-address. In addition, 669 *en illuxit* decidedly sounds like a beginning, and seems to require a change of speaker.

The bleak truth dawns on Octavia immediately after she has expressed her naïve wish to live: it was foolish even to hope that someone who bathed his hands in the blood of his kin could act differently with her. The dash printed in the more modern editions (Zwierlein, Liberman) indicates a pause, or change of intonation, which marks Octavia's sudden awakening to the absurdity of the idea. Self-corrections of this kind in monologues are normal in the corpus cf. e.g. *H.O.* 1406–8; *Troad.* 642 ff.; *Hf.* 295 with Fitch for more parallels. Cf. *Oed.*

103 *quid sera mortis uota nunc demens facis?* which, significantly, ***A*** gave to Jocasta, whereas the present lines are part of a continuous monologue. In *Med.* 174 *parce iam, demens, minis, 'demens'* is said by the *Nutrix*. The long disjunction *scelerum . . . memor* must have been confusing to scribes, and the oldest MSS have *socerum*, which makes little sense; other *recc.* read *soror o*, which is more interesting, but leaves *memor* in a vacuum.

For *scelerum diri . . . uiri . . . memor* cf. Ov. *Met.* 13.570 *veterumque diu memor illa malorum*. Cf. also Sen. *Troad.* 474–5 *sed mei fati memor | tam magna timeo uota*, for a similar monologic 'correction'.

663 hos ad thalamos seruata diu Cf. Verg. *Aen.* 7.60; 11.159 *neque in hunc seruata dolorem*; cf. also *supra* 70; 145. It is not clear if *hos ad thalamos* should be tied to *uictima cades*, as if they were described as an altar, or to *seruata*. *seruata diu*: note the recurrent pattern, in anapaests, *cruciata diu* (940*); *lacerata diu* (956).

664 uictima tandem funesta cades For *cado* with a predicative *uictima* cf. Luc. *Bell. Ciu.* 9.132 *cecidit donati uictima regni*; Sen. *Agam.* 353–4 *ad tua coniunx candida tauri | delubra cadet*; *Med.* 37–9 (Leo, *Obs.* 166); *H.O.* 348 *me nuptiali uictimam feriat die.*

665–666 sed quid patrios saepe penates | respicis udis confusa genis? Octavia, leaving her ancestral abode, looks back one last time, as if unable to wrench herself away, a highly emotional scene which looks back to Alcestis' farewell to her bed-chamber in Eur. *Alc.* 185–95, esp. 187 καὶ πολλὰ θαλάμων ἐξιοῦσ' ἐπεστράφη. In Latin poetry, the motif was exploited in Ov. *Met.* 11.546–7 *patrias quoque uellet ad oras | respicere inque domum supremos uertere uultus*; *Trist.* 3.10.61–2 *pars agitur uinctis post tergum capta lacertis | respiciens frustra rura laremque suum*; Sen. *H.O.* 225–6 *(an) quid regna tui clara parentis | proauosque tuos respicis amens?*, to which I would give chronological priority (cf. Introd. p. 53). *respicere* is frequently employed both in its literal and in its figurative sense.

The expression *udis . . . genis* is found in Ov. *Fast.* 2.406 *hi redeunt udis in sua tecta genis*; *Am.* 1.8.84 *et faciant udas illa uel ille genas* (cf. Junge 1999, 262), where however *genae* indicates the cheeks.

For *sed quid . . . refero / memoro* followed by a verb of speech in self-address cf. Skutsch ad Enn. *Ann.* vi. fr. xvi, giving many parallels; in Greek cf. Lyc. *Alex.* 1451; Verg. *Aen.* 2.101; Cat. *Carm.* 64.116.

667 propera tectis efferre gradus Sutton (1983), 25, interprets *tectis* literally as a sign that Octavia is speaking 'from atop the stage building'. However, *tectis* is a common metonymy for 'palace' and there is no sign that Octavia is speaking from the *fastigium* here. In fact, the address to the unnamed attendants suggests the contrary assumption. Moreover, heroines appear on a roof only when the dramatic circumstances compel them to do so (e.g. Medea, Orestes in Eur. and Sen.; Phaedra in Sen. *Phae.* 1154), either because they are fleeing from their enemies, or because they need to be unreachable by the other characters on stage. Significantly, the language of their movements is then very explicit: cf. Sen. *Med.* 973, 992; *Phae.* 1154 *ab altis . . . tectis*, and Zwierlein (1996), 14–15. Finally, a character about to leave the stage, as Octavia is imagined to be doing here, is not likely to be on a balcony. This would render the implications of *propera tectis efferre gradus* comical, as if suggesting that Octavia was about to jump off the roof.

669–670 en illuxit suspecta diu | fama totiens iactata dies First tidings of revolt, brought about by news of the divorce. *suspecta diu fama totiens iactata dies* picks up 274–5 *utinam falso credita perdat | (fama) frustra totiens iactata fidem*, where the chorus wished that the rumours of the impending divorce might prove false. The role of *fama* in creating public opinion at Rome, and often bringing about important events, is constantly stressed in Tacitus' historical works: cf. e.g. Tac. *Ann.* 12.5 *pactum inter Claudium et Agrippinam matrimonium iam fama . . . firmabatur.*

The immediate succession of a monody and a choral ode is without parallels in fifth-century tragedy, except in *parodoi.* When, in the middle of a play, a monody ushers in a song by the chorus, the latter does not immediately follow (Eur. *Alc.* 393; *Suppl.* 990). A monody in the middle of a play is typically followed by a few trimeters uttered by the chorus or by another character, as in Eur. *Alc.* 416; *Suppl.* 1030; *Hec.* 1085; 1007, and often a new entrance is expected. In fact this monody of Octavia and the brief choral ode which follows belong to different days of the action. 669 *en illuxit suspecta diu . . .* marks the beginning of a new day. The identity of the metre (some have spoken of a 'responsion-like' construction on the basis of the identical ending *principis aulam* at 668 and 689 which I interpret as coincidental) and the fact that the insurrection is presented as a reaction to the first news of the divorce have led some to suppose that the chorus and the 'mourners' addressed by Octavia are the same group and that the revolt itself is imagined to start on day two. The first assumption is almost certainly wrong, though the second is perhaps more plausible.

It would be possible to place Octavia's departure from the palace in the very early hours of day two, and to have the chorus sing at the dawn of day two. Beginning with Aeschylus' *Agam.* the pattern according to which a tragic action develops through the day, starting at dawn, is common in Greek tragedy. Lapse of time is not emphasized by the dramatic structure, which is designed to suggest continuity between the monody of *Octavia* and the anapaests of the chorus. On the other hand, the fact that Poppaea appears already to be Nero's wife in 673 and 683 is irreconcilable with this view, and seems to indicate that day three has already begun. There is nothing to prove incontrovertibly that Octavia's departure is not taking place on the day *after* the marriage ceremony (still a day of festivity, one could imagine). The issue has possibly been blurred intentionally by the dramatist, who intended to emphasize the link between revolt and divorce (contrary to the witness of Tac. *Ann.* 14.60; see *infra*). This feature would be in keeping with a tendency observed at 437 and 877.

In classical Greek tragedy choruses exit only when a special task has been assigned to them to perform: cf. Aesch. *Eum.* 231; Soph. *Ai.* 813; Eur. *Alc.* 741; *Hel.* 585; [*Rhes.*] 564. Entrances and exits of the chorus were presumably a regular feature of early Roman drama.

The verb *illucesco* occurs in Vergil (cf. *Georg.* 2.336–7 *non alios prima crescentis origine mundi | inluxisse dies*), Ov. *Met.*, and [Sen.] *H.O.* 60 *nec ulla nobis segnis illuxit dies*; *en illuxit* to signal the beginning of a new day is paralleled in Ter. *Heaut.* 410 *luciscit hoc iam*, also at the beginning of a new scene. This is the only parallel in extant Roman drama for a play whose action extends over more than one day. The supposed 'rule' prescribing that the action should be contained within one day was transgressed at least as early as Aesch. *Eum.*, and in Arist. *Lys.* and *Plut.* Other cases are discussed by Gomme-Sandbach ad Men. *Epitr.* Act. III (pp. 325–6). The passage from Ter. *Heaut.* baffled Eugraphius (*Don.* Wessn. vol. III), who remarks *notandum . . . , quod in nulla alia comoedia licet reperire, ut biduum tempus in comedia sit.* His reaction, however, need not include tragedy, let alone historical drama, where the task of compressing the action into a single day may understandably have proved more difficult.

674–675 cessat pietas dum nostra graui | compressa metu Cf. Ov. *Met.* 13.663 *uicta metu pietas. pietas* was also a standard item in the vocabulary of devotion to the Roman emperors from the time of Caesar Augustus: cf. Galasso ad Ov. *Pont.* 2.2.21.

676 The chorus' song evokes the virtues of their Republican ancestors, who brought illustrious generals to their knees, passed the laws which made Rome invincible, and assigned the task of leading the state to citizens worthy of it. This passage is crucial for Kragelund's interpretation of 'populism' in *Octavia* (1982, 38–52). Kragelund drew attention to the prominence assigned to the legend P.R. in Galba's coinage (e.g. VICTORIA P.R.). This emphasis on the authority and support of the people of Rome would find a parallel in the prominence assigned to popular initiative in this play. Important as this is, it provides in itself insufficient evidence for assigning the play to the brief reign of Galba. Emphasis on *libertas* is commonplace in the coinage and documentary evidence relating to several successive new emperors, especially after a civil war or any other violent assumption of power (cf. Introd. pp. 6–7; Kragelund (pp. 48–9) admits that the period of Vespasian's rise to power would be equally suitable for *Octavia*). In my view, no clear-cut political programme can be identified in the Republican nostalgia displayed by the choruses of *Octavia*. Throughout the early imperial age, 'the people' are often referred to as the nominal holders of legitimate political power, and many historical personages of the first century are recorded as having appealed to the authority of the 'Roman people', which need mean no more than the Roman Senate. In Cass. Dio *Hist.Rom.* 63.25.2–3, Verginius Rufus, diverting *imperium* from himself, claims its return to the Roman Senate and to the People; the people figure again in the proclamations issued by the aristocrats involved in the assassination of Gaius, who intended to restore full powers to the people (Cass. Dio *Hist. Rom.* 60.1). Outside the formulaic *Senatus populusque*, a distinction is often made between the 'people' and the rabble, which, for example in Cass. Dio *Hist. Rom.* 59.28.10, is pleased with the autocrat's follies.

A related problem regards the imagined social status of this chorus (Kragelund's definition of them as 'the voice of the people of Rome' (1982, 38) sidesteps the question). The alternatives are (1) to consider them a genuine specimen of homespun Romans, who summon themselves to revolt against a wicked tyrant, or (2) to regard them as courtiers supporting Octavia, who rally the people to her defence. It is risky to draw any conclusions about the author's political stance from the confidence that the people may be won over by a just cause, a trust contradicted by the complaint about the unreliability of popular support expressed in 877 ff., which is more in keeping with the mistrustful attitude generally exhibited by Roman writers (see ad loc.). Rousing the people to an insurrection has no parallels in extant Roman imperial history. Conspirators consider whether to go and harangue the praetorians, but rarely the people. Tac. *Ann.* 15.59 relates Piso's failure to appeal to the people, but the general tone of the passage suggests that this would hardly have produced any effect.

The only source mentioning an uprising subsequent to Octavia's divorce is Tacitus (in *Ann.* 14.60.5), who connects it with the rumour of Octavia's return from Campania and therefore presents the reaction of the people as a joyous and welcome event, which is suppressed by the praetorians lest it should degenerate into riots. Schmidt (1985, 1438) is right to observe that the dramatist of *Octavia* conflated what Tacitus describes as two distinct collective reactions: first, repressed disapproval (*inde crebri per uulgus questus*), then, rejoicing, which follows the false news of Octavia's recall to Rome.

Popular support for a member of the imperial house, disgraced, or otherwise thought to have been unfairly treated by the ruling *princeps*, is recorded by Tacitus at *Ann.* 5.4, where the people sit outside the Curia while the Senate deliberates whether to proceed against the elder Agrippina and Nero. Similarly, the people disapprove of Gaius' divorce from Lollia Paulina in Cass. Dio *Hist. Rom.* 59.23.7–8. This nostalgic celebration of Republican Rome does not lead to an open condemnation of the Principate as such. While attempts to restore the traditional Republican liberties are a recurrent feature of the early imperial period, notably after Augustus' and Gaius' death, during the last days of Nero and perhaps even after Domitian, they are regularly ascribed to the initiative of members of the senatorial aristocracy. There are no precise parallels at this date for a spontaneous general insurrection aimed at deposing or overturning a ruling emperor. The eruption of popular violence in Julio-Claudian Rome is constantly linked to food shortages and other day-to-day concerns, and the *plebs* of the imperial age predictably shows no great preoccupation with wider political issues on a large scale. The only exception appears to be Tac. *Ann.* 2.82, who relates a rumour according to which the reason accounting for the deep affection felt by the people for Drusus and Germanicus was their intention to return to the people the freedom they enjoyed under the Republic: this alleged desire to see Republican liberties restored is never elsewhere said to have led to insurrection. On the various occasions giving rise to riots in early imperial Rome cf. Z. Yavetz, *Plebs and Princeps* (Oxford, 1969), 14, emphasizing the absence of political motivation in the various episodes of popular unrest during this period. When riots erupt, they are limited to food shortages; or, typically, the people protest against the defective or unsatisfactory organization of circus games (cf. Tac. *Ann.* 1.77.1 *at theatri licentia . . . grauius tum erupit, occisis non modo e plebe set militibus et centurione, uulnerato tribuno praetoriae cohortis, dum probra in magistratus et dissensionem uulgi prohibent*). In Cass. Dio *Hist. Rom.* 74.13 the people behave more nobly than the Senate in preserving their allegiance to the deceased Pertinax and in refusing to be bribed by Didius Julianus. In later imperial history, there are popular insurrections which end up posing a serious threat to the monarch (cf. ad 780).

There was no precedent, in Roman imperial history, for the removal of a ruler following a popular insurrection. Caligula and Domitian were each eliminated by a plot set up by members of their entourage. The only acceptable precedents for tragedy must have come from the Roman Republican tradition, or legend: Amulius, the Tarquins, or the decemvirs. How much the *ignotus* was inspired by Roman drama is bound to remain an unanswered question, given the extant evidence. It is highly likely that historical tragedies existed which had dramatized the legends relating to the establishment of the Roman Republic (see *infra*). The historiographical tradition alone, and primarily Livius' *Annales*, provided abundant material to feed the imagination of the *ignotus*: he clearly has in mind (as in 291 ff.) the legendary deeds of Republican Rome, and in particular the revolts against Tarquin and against the Decemviri. This may give us a clue to understanding his alleged 'populism', which is an antiquarian's revivalistic celebration of primitive Rome and of its values. Liv. 3.48–58, where the people's anger against Appius reaches its climax after his arrogance has induced Verginius to kill his own daughter, depicts the only spontaneous popular insurrection leading to an overthrow of tyrannical rule. The gallantry of the Romans of *Octavia*, whose emotions are stirred by the sight of the wronged Octavia leaving the palace, may recall the wave of popular emotion excited by Brutus' harangue from a rostrum on which the corpse of Lucretia was exposed in full view (Liv. 1.59). The daggers of Brutus (i.e. the blood-stained daggers that he held aloft to arouse popular indignation) figure on a famous anonymous coin of AD 68, *BMCRE* I, p. cxci (Kragelund n. 213).

In Greek tragedy, the old men in the chorus in Eur. *Herc.* 252 exhort themselves (or, according to others, the people of Thebes) to revolt against Lycos: ὦ γῆς λοχεύματα . . . οὐ σκῆπτρα . . . ἀρεῖτε . . . . Cf. also Aesch. *Agam.* 1348–50 (one of the old men exhorts the others to break in sword in hand); 1650. In the Greek instances the chorus threaten the tyrant in his presence. Perhaps a parody of these tragic scenes can be found in the *parodos* of Ar. *Lys.* 254–386, where the home guard, the old men left to defend the city, march against the Acropolis, which has been occupied by the women. The old men summon their courage by evoking various feats of war in which they displayed their valour (cf. 273, 285). They plan to build a pyre and smoke the women out of the Acropolis (269). Antityrannical insurrections may have figured in Republican drama, though the evidence for this is very insecure. Cf. Ribbeck, *RT* 455 on the hypothesis that a revolt ended Accius' *Atreus*. Naeuius' *Romulus* also apparently depicted a 'popular' insurrection against Amulius (Ribbeck, *RT* 70), and the same must have been true of Accius' *praetexta Brutus*.

676 ubi Romani uis est populi The chorus confess to their shame at not defending Octavia against Nero (cf. 286 ff.). The rhetorical *ubi sunt* acquires, according to the context, different shades of meaning, but usually conveys a reproach (*OLD* 2). As an exhortation to prove true to one's name cf. Liv. 4.42.5; 5.43.7 *indignando mirandoque ubi illi uiri essent qui secum Veios . . . cepissent*; Cic. *Phil.* 8.23 *ubi est ille mos uirtusque maiorum?* Tac. *Ann.* 2.2. *ubi illam gloriam trucidantium Crassum?* In poetry cf. Barchiesi ad Ov. *Her.* 2.31 (with Greek parallels); Val. Fl. *Arg.* 4.469 *o ubi nunc regni generisque ubi gloria?*

Memory of the past glories of Republican Rome elicited many a sigh from later historians who thought they were living in a less heroic age: cf. Tac. *Ann.* 4.32.2, where it is said that previous annalists had a much more desirable field of inquiry, *ingentia illi bella, expugnationes urbium, fusos captosque reges*.

677 fregit claros quae saepe duces Zwierlein accepts Müller's *diros* (1911), 36, which would provide a precedent for the just removal of Nero, but MSS *claros* is above suspicion: the Roman people's bravery is enhanced by the valour of the opponents they defeated. Pyrrhus and Hannibal are the likely objects of this allusion. Cf. Sall. *Cat.* 10, celebrating Rome's achievements before the end of *metus hostilis*: *reges magni bello domiti, nationes ferae et populi ingentes ui subacti*.

678 dedit inuictae leges patriae Rome's greatness in military and social achievements was indebted to the excellence of its institutions as well as moral customs.

679 fasces dignis ciuibus olim By the time of Nero, the electoral and legislative prerogatives of the *comitia* had lapsed, though the last enactment of a law voted by the *comitia* is on record in AD 98 (the elections of the magistrates were transferred to the Senate in AD 14: Mommsen, *RS* 5.198–206). This would suggest referring *olim* to the whole sentence, rather than to *dignis* alone, which in this case is non-restrictive (they happened to deserve the honours bestowed on them). The *comitia* were easily manipulated into electing dishonest candidates, and laments about their corruptibility are commonplace: cf. Hor. *Serm.* 1.6.15–16 *populo, qui stultus honores | saepe dat indignis*; *Epist.* 1.16.33–4 *ut si | detulerit fasces indigno*; Sen. *Phae.* 983–4 *tradere turpi fasces populus | gaudet* (a blatant anachronism for the age of Seneca); Juv. *Sat.* 10.78–9 (*populus*) *qui dabat olim | imperium fasces legiones omnia.*

681 captos reges carcere clausit The most famous foreign king captured and eventually executed after imprisonment is Jugurtha (Sall. *Iug.* 104). The same fate befell Vercingetorix. Cf. Sen. *Hf.* 737 *uidi cruentos carcere includi duces*; Tac. *Agr.* 13.5 *domitae gentes, capti reges*; *Ann.* 4.32.5 (given ad 676). Notice the alliterating sequence *captos . . . carcere clausit*, possibly intentional.

683–684 iam Poppaeae fulget imago | iuncta Neroni The final *-o* in *imago* is scanned short in the corpus: see Fitch (1987), 35–6. No extant statuary groups represent the couple Nero-Poppaea in the posture described by the rebels (*iuncta Neroni*), but several inscribed bases show that such groups had been erected between 62 and 65 in the various provinces of the Empire (evidence collected in C. B. Rose, *Dynastic Commemoration and Imperial Portraiture in the Julio-Claudian period* (Cambridge, 1997), cat. 21, 22, 98, 109; R. R. R. Smith, 'The imperial reliefs from the Sebasteion at Aphrodisias', *JRS* 77 (1987), 88–138). Such honorific statues were normally built as separate blocks, with the two figures standing rigidly next to one another. An exception to this pattern of stiff juxtaposition is provided by a bas-relief excavated at Aphrodisias, representing Claudius and Agrippina hand in hand (Rose, plate 204). Joint portraits of Nero and Poppaea appear in a series of *denarii* struck shortly before Poppaea's death (as can be gathered from the legend *Augusta*). Such statuary groups would hardly have survived destruction in 68, but, given the frequency of the pattern, the *Octavia* poet need not have in mind any particular monument.

685 affligat humo uiolenta manus Smashing of statues is often on record for uprisings: cf. Tac. *Ann.* 3.14.6; Juv. *Sat.* 10.58; Plin. *Pan.* 52.4 *iuuabat illidere solo superbissimos uultus*; Suet. *Dom.* 23 *senatus . . . imagines eius . . . solo adfligi* (*iubebat*), which confirms (alongside 796 *afflicta uulgi manibus*) the reading *affligat* against *affigat*. The pulling down of Poppaea's statues is historical (cf. Tac. *Hist.* 14.61). They were successively reinstalled, then pulled down again after Nero's downfall. Otho had them reinstated at his accession (Tac. *Hist.* 1.78).

violenta manus might mean 'a rioting troop', rather than 'our violent hand', as Ballaira takes it; cf. Stat. *Theb.* 1.191–2 *nos, uilis in omnis | prompta manus casus.*

686 similes nimium uultus dominae The exclamatory and emotional 'resembling, alas, too much' appears to imitate Ovid: cf. *Her.* 12.189 *et nimium similes tibi sunt et imagine tangor*; *Met.* 6.621–2 *a! quam | es similis patri!*, which was already echoed in Sen. *Troad.* 464 *nimiumque patri similis*. For *similis* of artistic products cf. *OLD* s.v. 8. For the pathetic *nimium* with other adjectives cf. Ov. *Her.* 5.123 *a nimium miserae uates mihi uera fuisti*; *Fast.* 1.437; 1.477 *uera nimium cum matre*. This motif normally expresses compassion. In the context, however, the lifelike resemblance of Poppaea's statues to the original naturally fires popular resentment against the loathed schemer who has replaced Octavia. It is odd that statues of Poppaea are in place already on the day of the marriage.

uultus is used with reference to statues in Ov. *Trist.* 1.7.1 *si quis habes nostri similes in imagine uultus*, which also shows *dominae* to be a genitive.

687 ipsamque toris detrahat altis 'The lofty couch' from which Poppaea is to be pulled down, undergoing the same fate as her wretched effigies (*detrahat*), is a reminiscence of Verg. *Aen.* 2.2 *toro . . . ab alto*, where Aeneas begins to tell his story while reclining on a high banquet couch. The *torus* is properly a pillow and, by extension, the bed (*OLD* s.v. 5): the word indicates here, by metonymy, Poppaea's newly-attained status, and it is virtually a synonym for *thalamus*.

688–689 petat infestis mox et flammis | telisque feri principis aulam I interpret *et* as a connective linking *petat* to the preceding clause, although, as MDR has pointed out to me, the author could have written *mox et flammis petat infestis*. For other instances of postponed *et* in this play cf. Introd. p. 32. The alternative would be to regard the sequence *et flammis telisque* as an instance of polysyndeton. Polysyndeton with these two connectives is rare but possible: cf. Liv. 4.2.3 *id et singulis uniuersisque semper honori fuisse*; Cic. *Fam.* 11.13.5 *ut quam paratissimi et ab exercitu reliquisque rebus confligamus*, different from [Verg.] *Cir.* 79 *piscibus et canibusque malis uallata repente*; C. O. Brink, *JRS* 41 (1951), 47–8.

The rebels propose to set the imperial residence on fire (cf. *Phoe.* 565–6 *haec telis petes | flammisque tecta?* also *infra*, 851); stones and firebrands are the usual weapons available to the populace during riots: cf. Tac. *Ann.* 14.45 *conglobata multitudine et saxa ac faces minante*.

The *β*-branch of ***A*** reads *feris*, which is certainly corrupt, because it would leave *principis* without an adjective; *ferus tyrannus* occurs also at 87, 609, 959.

690 Poppaea's dream has no immediately clear dramatic relevance, since the vision related does not anticipate events which will be enacted in the course of the play. Compare, by contrast, the dreams, more carefully embedded in the texture of their respective plots, in Soph. *El.* 417–27; Men. *Dysk.* 410–17; Plaut. *Merc.* 225–54; *Rud.* 593–612 (with Fraenkel, *EP* 190), which adumbrate successive turns of the story. The four main characters involved in the narrative, Agrippina, Poppaea, Crispinus, and Nero, stage a play within the play of a fascinatingly enigmatic type (a lightly hinted love scene between Poppaea and her former husband, then Nero performing a silent, slow-motion hara-kiri), which foreshadows the future developments of their story, but has little to do with Octavia. This centrifugal tendency, signalled by the presence of unacted-upon motifs, is a constant feature of *Octavia*: the same can be said of

Agrippina's prophecy. It may have been a characteristic of historical drama generally, where myth and history were constantly intertwined and the need to praise and celebrate sometimes gained the upper hand over the story. One possible theatrical precedent for this scene is Acc. *Brutus* (*infra* ad 740), where Tarquinius' dream foreshadows the king's downfall and the establishment of the Republic, the latter probably dramatized at the end of the play (but the seer is reticent about the meaning of the dream, inauspicious for the king, and simply declares it to announce great fame for Rome). In an analogous way, Dido's curse on Aeneas in Verg. *Aen.* 4.618–20 alludes to Aeneas' death, not narrated by the poet, but known from the mythical context. As Kragelund rightly observes (1982, 22), the dream operates on two levels, psychological and oracular, both revealing the hopes and fears of the dreamer and at the same time alluding to her approaching end.

690–691 quo trepida gressum coniugis thalamis tui | effers, alumna? Poppaea comes out of her apartments, frightened (*trepida*), but her terror is only 'seen' through the words of her *Nutrix*. Quickly putting aside her initial curiosity about Poppaea's visibly terrified state (690–2), the old woman launches into a description of the marriage which, while psychologically understandable as an attempt to console the anguish-stricken Poppaea, slows down the pace of the action (693–709). In fact this scene could be viewed as a significant indication that the poet of *Octavia* did not try to visualize his play in dramatic terms.

Poppaea appears on stage in a state of panic and distress, but does not speak until 712. Surprise entrances of frightened or agitated female characters are not uncommon in Greek tragedy (cf. e.g. Eur. *Andr.* 823–4, pronounced by the chorus: δωμάτων γὰρ ἐκπερᾶι | φεύγουσα χεῖρας προσπόλων πόθωι θανεῖν), and, in paratragic contexts, in comedy (cf. Plaut. *Cas.* 621). When unannounced, however, these hurrying, frightened characters are expected to speak first, addressing the chorus present on stage (cf. e.g. Eur. *I.T.* 1157; O. P. Taplin, *Stagecraft*, index s.v. 'preparation, lack of'): Deianira, in Soph. *Trach.* 663, suddenly appears in a state of terror, and discloses her fears to the women of the chorus after she has seen the wool melting in the light of the sun. By contrast her mute exit (described by the chorus at 879) effectively adumbrates her unspoken determination to die (the same is true of Eurydice in Soph. *Ant.*). On hurried entrances in Greek tragedy see K. Smith, *HSCPh* 16 (1905), 136; Leo, *Obs.* 96 on other unprepared entrances in Seneca (all cases in which a third interlocutor interrupts a dialogue of two). A mute entrance is that of Helen at Eur. *Hel.* 1186–92, where Theoclymenus suddenly catches sight of his prisoner, who he feared had escaped: τί πέπλους μέλανας ἐξήψω χρόος . . . χλωροῖς τε τέγγεις δάκρυσι σὴν παρηίδα; Helen, like Poppaea, appears distressed and in mourning garments, and Theoclymenus asks if she has been visited by a bad dream or received bad news from home: πότερον ἐννύχοις πεπεισμένη |

στένεις ὀνείροις ἢ φάτιν τιν' οἴκοθεν | κλυοῦσα λύπηι σὰς διέφθαρσαι φρένας; Helen speaks only after this; her silent entrance is motivated by the intention to create suspense and make her story credible for Theoclymenus. The passage from Eur. *Hel.* parallels well enough the concern expressed, in *Oct.*, by the Nurse: *quo trepida gressum . . . quidue secretum petis . . . cur genae fletu madent?*, but the lengthy description of the marriage (supposedly familiar to Poppaea) reveals a poet whose interest in dramatic tension is underdeveloped.

The entrance of two characters on an empty stage is a post-classical development, already exploited in Senecan tragedy. The *Nutrix*–Poppaea scene was clearly inspired by Sen. *Med.* 380 ff. *alumna celerem quo rapis tectis pedem? | resiste et iras comprime . . .* ; *Phae.* 583 has a similar description of Phaedra's distress given by the Nurse, who addresses the queen as she rushes out of the palace: *sed Phaedra praeceps graditur, impatiens morae . . .* (586) *attolle uultus* (cf. Zwierlein 1966, 56). The *Medea* scene, though, provides a closer parallel, because, as in *Oct.* 690, the *Nutrix* and Medea introduce a new scene which follows a choral ode. Stage action, in both passages, is difficult to reconstruct. Presumably the *Nutrix* runs after Medea as she walks in her rage out of the palace. But this scene in Seneca's *Medea* is more purposeful than its *Octavia* counterpart, because the silence of *Medea* is an apt introduction to her monologue. Medea is entirely absorbed in her murderous plans and the Nurse's words provide a good description of her state by describing her changing and inflamed gaze and countenance. There is no such justification for the lengthy description of Poppaea's *Nutrix* here. The close parallelism between the two passages suggests that *thalamis* at *Oct.* 690 is little more than a synonym for *tectis*, meant to signify the early hour at which the present scene is thought to take place (immediately after Nero's and Poppaea's first night). There is no need to imagine a precise location of the scene in the vestibule to Poppaea's bedroom suite.

Note also that the name of Poppaea is never given in the present scene. For a theatrical audience, *alumna* would be enough to designate the speaker as a *Nutrix*, but not to identify Poppaea. In a play intended for the stage, a character rushing out of the palace is expected to speak immediately. On the other hand, in a play meant for recitation, how is one to know that a character is rushing unless they are depicted in the words of the other characters supposedly present? In Turpil. fr. 1 Rychlewska, Stephanio addresses his master, who has come out of his house before dawn, because cares and worries allow him no sleep. The loyal Pseudolus addresses his preoccupied and silent master at the beginning of Plaut. *Pseud.* (cf. the comments of Fraenkel, *EP* 390), esp. 9–10 *quid est quod tu exanimatus iam hos multos dies | gestas tabellas tecum, eas lacrumis lauis?*

691 quidue secretum petis The reading of the older MSS, *quodue* (*GPCV* 'to what recess are you fleeing?'; *quod ut SK*), is acceptable, but I prefer reading *quid*, with *recc.* Although both versions convey the sense of the old woman's surprise at Poppaea's unexpected change of mood (even with *quod* the question is not really an inquiry into the proposed hiding place of Poppaea), *quid* is more effective, and we see Poppaea crouching or hiding her face like a scared child afraid of the dark. Confusions between *quid* and *quod*, indistinguishable in many book-hands, and inconsistently abbreviated, are common. Occasionally *quid* is also used as an adjective; cf. [Verg.] *Cat.* 11.4 *quid immeriti crimen habent cyathi?* Here, however, it stands simply for *cur*.

The line-end imitates *H.O.* 478 *quid istud est quod esse secretum petis?*, exhibiting a phraseology typically occurring in early drama, where it often marks the agitated entrance of a new character at a critical turn: cf. Acc. *Scaen.* 299–300 R^2 *quid istuc, gnata unica, est, Demonassa, obsecro, | quod me tanto expetens timidam e tecto excies?*; Plaut. *Cas.* 630 *quid est quod haec huc timida atque exanimata exsiluit?* Plaut. *Most.* 419; W. Koch, *De personarum comicarum introductione* (diss. Breslau, 1914), 56–7; Lindsay ad Plaut. *Capt.* 541. In early drama, a character announced by a present tense enters immediately. In Senecan drama the same periphrasis occurs in *Phoe.* 205–6 *quid est | quod te efferarit*; *Oed.* 332 *quid istud est quod esse prolatum uolunt*; also *Phae.* 777 *quid deserta petis? secretum petit* at the end of an iambic line also in Phaedr. *Fab.* 4.25(26).6; Plin. *Epist.* 1.5.11 (of someone asking to have a word in private).

The *H.O.* passage which is echoed here describes the frightened entrance of Deianira, when the sight of the wool melting in the sun has revealed to her the treacherous nature of Nessus' gift. In Greek tragedy women leaving their *thalamoi* or private apartments are expected to offer an explanation. In Aesch. *Pers.* 159–60 Atossa has come out to seek the chorus' advice and elucidation of her nightmare. Poppaea has no reason to remain confined within her husband's *thalamus*, unless we assume that the scene takes place in the very early hours of the day.

692 cur genae fletu madent? Cf. *Phae.* 1121 *cur madent fletu genae*; Ov. *Met.* 11.418 *lacrimisque genae maduere profusis*.

694–695 Caesari iuncta es tuo | taeda iugali The adjective *iugalis* for 'matrimonial', or more specifically 'nuptial', is well attested in classical Latin: with *taeda* cf. Cat. *Carm.* 64.302 *nec Thetidis taedas uoluit celebrare iugales* (a list of parallels in Junge 1999, 246 n. 740); Sen. *H.O.* 339 *meo iugales sanguine extinguam faces*. The sequence containing the figura etymologica *iuncta/iugali* is apparently found only here. There might be an echo of Stat. *Silu.* 1.2.183 *quae non face corda iugali* (sc. *iunxi*)? For *Caesar* with a possessive, for 'your beloved Caesar' cf. Ov. *Pont.* 2.8.4 *Caesaribus Liuia iuncta suis*; *infra* ad 716 *Neronis . . . mei*.

695 quem tuus cepit decor For *capio* in the metaphorical sense of 'to conquer' cf. *TLL* iii s.v. 337–8 (cf. e.g. Prop. *Carm.* 1.1 *me cepit ocellis*).

696 et culta sancte tradidit uinctum tibi | genetrix Amoris, maximum numen, Venus *vinctum* is the reading of *recc.*, for *uictum* in ***A***. Both versions yield good sense (for *uictum* cf. Stat. *Silu.* 1.2.77 *edomui uictum*, where Cupid speaks of Stella's *seruitium amoris*), but the image of a fettered

Nero handed over to Poppaea is more vividly effective (cf. *OLD* s.v. 5b, esp. Plaut. *Trin.* 658 *ui Veneris uinctus*; *Bacch.* 180, with Barsby; Ov. *Her.* 20.85, with Kenney, quoting, among others, Tib. 1.1.55 *me retinent uinctum formosae uincla puellae*; 3.19.23 *Veneris sanctae considam uinctus ad aras*; Hor. *Carm.* 4.11.23–4 *tenetque . . . uinctum*).

The transmitted reading *et culpa Senece* ('quo enim magis culpauit te Seneca, eo magis amore tuo captus fuit', Trevet, who must have interpreted *culpa* as an ablative) has been rejected by all modern editors since Gronovius (who proposed *et culpa nuptae*). The tribrach in the second foot (*-pa Sene-*) is acceptable (cf. e.g. *Phae.* 220 *conuexa tetigit*; Strzelecki (1938), 66–7), but there are a number of problems of sense. Supposedly, as Trevet saw, the philosopher's fault resides in his firm opposition to Nero's marriage, which has fired Nero's passion for Poppaea. Yet very little is made of it in the supposedly relevant episode at 435 ff., where Nero is already determined to marry Poppaea. Moreover, the syntactical connection of 696 with the preceding relative clause is defective. On this interpretation, *genetrix amoris . . . Venus* would have to be a vocative (unless *culpa Senecae* is followed by a full stop, as in Trevet: but how could 'Seneca's fault' have 'conquered' Nero?). Yet a sudden address to Venus is very surprising at this point, and comes across as an unmotivated affectation by the *Nutrix*. In the context, the referent of *tibi* can only be Poppaea.

Seneca had been opposed to Nero's liaison with Acte, and Annaeus Serenus, one of Seneca's *familiares*, had offered his services as a cover (Tac. *Ann.* 13.13). Nothing, however, is on record in the ancient sources with regard to any hostility between Seneca and Poppaea: Gasparino Barzizza's *Vita Senecae* 4 (pp. 343–4 Panizza; see Introd.) must be based on this passage and on Tac. *Ann.* 15.61, where Poppaea is present when Nero sends Seneca an injunction to end his life: 'creditum est ab hac muliere conspiratum in mortem Senece, siue quia Neronem sepe conatus erat ab amore huius mulieris retrahere . . . siue quia sciebat non placere Senece que cum Nerone et diceret et faceret.'

Emendation seems unavoidable, and Birt's *culta sancte* is by far the best solution. Of the alternative proposals, the most ingenious is Bothe's *nec culta Senecae*, referring to Seneca's refusal to worship love as a god in *Oct.* 557–65; *culpata Senecae* Leo; *contempta Senecae* Peiper. Helm (1934, 345) convincingly supported Birt's emendation with Stat. *Silu.* 5.1.154–5 *quid probitas aut casta fides, quid numina prosunt | culta deum?*

The prominence assigned by *culta sancte* to Venus' intervention in Poppaea's love-suit could be traced back to Statius. In the Roman, contemporary setting of the *praetexta*, the actions and motives of the characters are not determined by divine intervention (although Messalina's guilt is excused by her daughter Octavia as a love-frenzy induced by Venus at 258), and the special place assigned to Venus and Amor in the winning over of Nero's affection is a motif not developed in the play. It gives us a glimpse of a background of prayers and supplications addressed to the goddess by a nervous Poppaea which has no textual support in *Octavia*. I believe this to be possibly a projection of Stella's long love-suit in Stat. *Silu.* 1.2, where Amor, won over by Stella's prayers, intercedes with Venus on his behalf (compare *Silu.* 1.2.67–8 *at quondam lacrimis et supplice dextra | et uotis precibusque uirum concede moueri* = *Oct.* 693–4 *certe petitus precibus et uotis dies | nostris refulsit*). In a symmetrically analogous way, the devotional acts of Acte at 196 are designed to help maintain the freedwoman's grip on Nero.

698 o qualis altos, quanta pressisti toros Pedroli wrongly links *quanta* to *in aula*, which is metrically unacceptable. For this *apo koinou* pattern of word-order, with exclamatory pronouns, to convey a sense of amazed admiration cf. Cat. *Carm.* 64.336 *qualis adest Thetidi qualis concordia Peleo*, with Kroll ad loc.; Leo, *KS* 1.88; Zwierlein, *KK* 457. A close parallel is provided by Verg. *Aen.* 2.591–2 *qualisque uideri | caelicolis et quanta solet* (where Venus appearing to Aeneas: *quanta* refers to the superhuman size of the goddess: cf. Conington ad loc.); Ov. *Met.* 3.284–5 *quantusque et qualis ab alta | Iunone excipitur* (cf. Bömer ad loc.); Tib. 3.6.23; Val. Fl. *Arg.* 4.604–5 *sed qualis, sed quanta uiris insultat Enyo*; Ov. *Am.* 1.5.19–22 *quos umeros, quales vidi tetigique lacertos . . . quantum et quale latus*; Sen. *H.O.* 56–7 *quanta non fregi mala, | quot scelera nudus!*, always expressing vehement indignation or emphasis; *Cons. Helu.* 12.3; Verg. *Aen.* 9.269.

Poppaea's staggering beauty is enhanced by a majestically abandoned posture, as she reclines on the couch at the banquet following the ceremony, while a procession of notables pays tribute to the newly-married couple: cf. Ov. *Am.* 1.4.15 *cum premet ille torum*; Petr. *Sat.* 131.9 *premebat illa resoluta marmoreis ceruicibus aureum torum.*

699 residens in aula Punctuation in some *recc.* (***M***) ties *residens* to *senatus* in the following line, not impossibly, but somewhat anticlimactically. The senators' astonished and admiring reaction is the aptest commentary on the statuesque beauty displayed by Poppaea at the marriage. The most salient phases of the solemn marriage ceremony are sketched in these lines, but the sequence is not always clear. 698–9 appear to describe the banquet offered by the new couple in the bridegroom's house (*aula*), and indeed *pressisti toros* and *residens in aula* (from *resideo*, not *resido*) point to a scene held indoors. This is not inconsistent with the presence of selected representatives of the Senate, but *residens* is at odds with the subsequent mention of a sacrifice (700–2), which would require the celebrants to stand. In our main sources, the sacrifice precedes the banquet. 703–9 describe the solemn *deductio*, the culminating moment of the ceremony, when the bride was escorted to the bridegroom's house, a popular topic of the literary and iconographic evidence. The *deductio* should precede the sacrifice performed by Poppaea at ll. 699–702 in her new residence (the *aula*). Possibly this is an instance of *hysteron-proteron*. Nero walks by Poppaea's side, whereas elsewhere the bridegroom precedes the bride to his house. The relevant evidence is collected and examined in Blümner, *Römische*

Privataltertümer 357; J. P. V. D. Balsdon, *Roman Women* (London, 1962), 180; Treggiari, *Roman Marriage* (Oxford, 1991), 169; *OCD*[3] (1996), 928.

699–700 uidit attonitus tuam | formam senatus It is not known where royal marriages would take place. Marriages were generally private ceremonies, and therefore expected to take place in private houses, in the presence of appointed friends and relatives. We may suppose, however, that an imperial wedding duly occasioned a public display of pomp. Marquardt (*Römisches Privatleben* 35–6; 52) maintains that marriage ceremonies involving *confarreatio* took place in public buildings, perhaps even in the Curia (where women were not normally admitted), but his opinion is largely founded on his interpretation of this passage. The word *senatus* need not imply more than that all or most senators attended the ceremony. On describing a similar, though admittedly less grandiose, wedding ceremony, Statius hyperbolically mentions the presence of all the highest social orders in the house of the groom: cf. *Silu.* 1.2.233 *omnis honos, cuncti ueniunt ad limina fasces*; Tac. *Ann.* 11.30 *matrimonium Silii uidit populus et senatus* (clearly hyperbolic for 'everybody in Rome').

The stupor of the bystanders and the senators contemplating Poppaea's stunning beauty is clearly hyperbolic. In Augustan poetry and Senecan tragedy, as well as in *Oct.* (35, 436, 633, 785), *attonitus* is used in the context of madness, fear, and divine epiphany. Its increasingly popular use in Silver Latin leads to a weakening of sense, which had, however, a precedent in Ov. *Ars* 2.295–6 *te . . . attonitum forma fac putet esse sua.* Cf. Val. Fl. *Arg.* 6.589–90 *nam te quoque tali | attonitam uirtute reor*; Sil. *Pun.* 12.252; Mart. 5.3.3. For the amazement of the senators, Viansino quoted Hom. *Il.* 3.154–158 (the reaction of the Trojan elders to Helen's beauty). A better parallel is perhaps provided by the intentionally exaggerated description of Stella's reactions in Statius' epithalamium, dumbfounded at the magnitude of the boon received (31–2); later Cupid uses the adjective to describe his astonishment at Stella's previous long-suffering love suit. On the various shades of meaning taken up by *attonitus* in the Senecan corpus cf. Hillen, *Dichtersprache*, 13–18.

700–701 tura cum superis dares | sacrasque grato spargeres aras mero The bride was expected to discharge certain religious duties both before and after the *deductio*, among them a sacrifice to the household gods of the bridegroom at the end of the *deductio* (Macr. *Saturn.* 1.15.22), and the present line might well be alluding to sacrifices offered in the emperor's residence. Messalina performs the required offering in Tac. *Ann.* 11.27 *illam* (sc. *Messalinam*) *. . . sacrificasse apud deos.* In Apul. *Met.* 4.26 it is the husband who performs the ritual sacrifices: *ad nuptias officio frequenti cognatorum et adfinium stipatus templis et aedibus publicis uictimas immolabat.* For incense burned at weddings cf. Val. Fl. *Arg.* 8.248.

702 flammeo tenui *flammeum* was the name of the ritual veil worn by brides in the marriage ceremony.

703–706 et ipse lateri iunctus atque haerens tuo | sublimis inter ciuium laeta omina | incessit habitu atque ore laetitiam gerens | princeps superbo Imitated from Verg. *Aen.* 1.315 *uirginis os habitumque gerens*, but *gero* is used slightly differently: cf. Sen. *Hf.* 329 *minas uultu gerens*; *Med.* 386.

Tac. *Ann.* 12.7 describes the (pretended) exultation of the Roman people on the occasion of Claudius' marriage to his niece Agrippina: *Claudius . . . obuius apud forum praebet se gratantibus.*

The long hyperbaton *et ipse . . . incessit . . . princeps*, separating *ipse* from the noun it is referred to by two entire lines, is remarkable (in this play cf. also 311–13 *Tyrrhenum . . . in aequor*, where the actual number of words is lower, because anapaests are shorter lines, and 827–8 *at illa cui me ciuium subicit furor | suspecta coniunx et soror semper mihi*, where the words from *suspecta* to *mihi* are properly speaking an appositional phrase, and a comma should be printed after *furor*). Such long hyperbata are not rare in Roman poetry of the classical age, and many examples in Horace are collected by Nisbet (in *ALLP*, 140–1). With *ipse* cf. *TLL* vii.2 312.39 ff. (in particular Sen. *Oed.* 940–1 *ipsi, quae tuum magna luit | scelus ruina, flebili patriae*; *Med.* 664–6 *ipse qui praedam spoliumque iussit | aureum prima reuehi carina | ustus accenso Pelias aeno | arsit*; *Phae.* 1112–14; Verg. *Aen.* 12.701–3). On this interpretation *et* is loosely connected to the preceding *uidit*, introducing an entirely new topic: 'and, lo, Nero himself . . .'. Cf. also my note ad 262–3. *sublimis* means 'with head erect'.

706–708 talis emersam freto | spumante Peleus coniugem accepit Thetin | quorum toros celebrasse caelestes ferunt The arrival of Thetis from the sea on the occasion of her marriage is not frequently described in the literary tradition. The iconographic material, by contrast, yields several instances of this type: cf. *LIMC* VII.1–2 s.v. *Peleus*, pp. 265–6, esp. nn. 199–200 (mosaics: Thetis on the back of a Triton). The arrival of Thetis on a dolphin is described in Tib. *Carm.* 1.5.45–6 *talis ad Haemonium Nereis Pelea quondam | uecta est frenato caerula pisce Thetis*, where Thetis provides a comparison for the poet's reluctant mistress, and in Ov. *Met.* 11.236–7 *quo saepe uenire | frenato delphine sedens, Theti, nuda solebas.* The description of the cortège of seagods escorting Thetis to her wedding is then found in Val. Fl. *Arg.* 1.130–5 (an *ecphrasis* of scenes painted on the keel of the Argo) *Tyrrheni tergore piscis | Peleos in thalamos uehitur Thetis: aequora delphin | corripit . . . hanc Panope Dotoque soror . . . prosequitur.* An important model may have been Stat. *Silu.* 1.2.215–17 *nec talem uiderunt Pelea Tempe | cum Thetin Haemoniis Chiron accedere terris . . . prospexit*, where Statius uses the mythological comparison to describe the excitement and joy of Stella on receiving his promised bride. While references to the marriage of Peleus and Thetis were no doubt common in epithalamia, it is significant that both passages concentrate on the same detail of the mythical precedent, the moment when the groom moves forward to meet the approaching bride. The focus is in particular on Nero's exultation (*talis emersam . . . Peleus accepit Thetin; nec talem . . . Pelea*). Although some of the analogies between Stat. *Silu.* 2.1 and *Octavia* may be explained as common topoi (cf. my notes ad 217; 773–4), the similarity of the occasion (description of a wedding ceremony) suggests that the author of *Octavia* was directly inspired by Statius (cf. Introd., pp. 17–27).

For *emersam freto* cf. Cat. *Carm.* 64.14 *emersere freti candenti e gurgite uultus* (*Nereides*), describing the amazement of the Nereides contemplating the progress of the Argo just launched.

For *toros celebrare* cf. Val. Max. 6.1 *pr. tu* (sc. *Pudicitia*) . . . *Iuliae genialem torum assidua statione celebras.* For weddings attended by the Olympian gods cf. Pind. *Pyth.* 3.93; *Nem.* 4.67; R. Reitzenstein, *Hermes* 35 (1900), 73–105, esp. 100 ff.; D. Page, *Sappho and Alcaeus* (Oxford, 1955), 124.

On the Greek accusative ending cf. N-W 1^3.478, where *Thetin* is said to occur only here and in Statius (several instances). Of major poets, only Vergil has the Latin accusative form, *Thetim* (*Buc.* 4.32).

709 consensu pari The same line-ending occurs at Sen. *Thy.* 970.

712–713 confusa tristi proximae noctis metu | uisuque Cf. Stat. *Theb.* 9.570 *tristibus interea somnum turbata figuris.* Poppaea's dream is analysed by Carbone and, above all, by Kragelund (1982), 9–36, to whom the following notes are greatly indebted. *proximus* can be used both for 'next' and 'last'.

714–715 dies | sideribus atris cessit et nocti polus *cessit* bears slightly different senses in the two cola ('gave way', 'yielded', *OLD* 8e; cf. Juv. 4.56–7 *cedente pruinis | autumno*, and 'fell to' *OLD* 15: Luc. *Bell. Ciu.* 2.459 *polus cum cesserit Euro* (Hosius)), because *polus* is not a synonym of *dies.* Whereas day withdraws to make room for the dark stars of night, the sky must occur together with the night (as it normally does: cf. Verg. *Aen.* 5.721 *nox atra polum . . . tenebat*), but the semantic zeugma is hardly noticeable: 'day yielded to the dark stars and the sky to night'.

Bothe observed that *atra* can hardly be said of the stars (he proposed *actis*), and similarly Peiper wrote *atrae*, which is attractive (cf. Hor. *Epod.* 10.9 *nec sidus atra nocte amicum appareat*, and *Aen.* 5.721) and would neatly account for the corruption, produced by a failure to understand postponement of *et.* Yet, even in the absence of exact parallels for *ater* with reference to stars, the largely emotive use of this adjective in poetry may justify its occurrence here: cf. the oxymoronic Sen. *Phae.* 1217 *donator atrae lucis, Alcide*, 'the gift of a life which turned out to be a curse'. Its occurrence fits the mournful tone of Poppaea's narrative. It stands for *sideribus atrae noctis* (as rightly observed in *TLL* ii, s.v. *ater*, 1020.55–60, adducing *Thy.* 699 *atrum cucurrit limitem sidus trahens*, of an ominous comet tinging the sky with dark reflections).

716–717 inter Neronis uincta complexus mei | somno resoluor Prop. 4.7.96 *inter complexus excidit umbra meos*; Apul. *Met.* 5.6 *inter amplexus coniugales.* The occurrence of the possessive with a proper name, *Neronis . . . mei*, is affectionate, and slightly surprising in the diction of tragic characters; it is common in the 'lower' genres: cf. Cat. *Carm.* 5.1 *mea Lesbia*; 10.1; 13.1 (always in addresses), and in comedy, where Donatus (ad *Eun.* 656 *mea Pythias*) describes it as a 'gendered' usage, characteristic of the language of women; see also Plaut. *Cas.* 230 *mea Iuno, non decet esse te tam tristem tuo Ioui.* In Augustan poetry cf. Ov. *Met.* 2.473 *Iouisque mei.* On possessives in amatory poetry (not however with proper names) cf. N-H ad Hor. *Carm.* 1.25.7 *me tuo longas pereunte noctes*, for '*me, qui tuus sum*'.

For *somno resolui* cf. Ov. *Met.* 9.469 *placida resoluta quiete.*

718–719 uisa nam thalamos meos | celebrare turba est maesta As Kragelund pointed out (1982, 9; 33), the dream is a perverted celebration of the wedding held on the previous day: 718–19 calls to mind 708 *quorum toros celebrasse caelestes ferunt*; 728 *in quis* (sc. *toris*) *resedi fessa* echoes 698–9 *pressisti toros | residens in aula. celebro* occurs both in connection with marriage ceremonies (cf. *TLL* iii s.v. 743.64–71) and with funerals (744.54–64).

Cf. Ov. *Met.* 9.687–8 (Telethusa's dream) *Inachis ante torum pompa comitata sacrorum | aut stetit aut uisa est*; Apul. *Met.* 4.27 *nam uisa sum mihi de domo, de thalamo, de cubiculo, de toro denique ipso uiolenter extracta per solitudines auias infortunatissimi mariti nomen inuocare . . .* (a character who has been kidnapped on the day of her wedding; in the same dream, the husband is stabbed to death).

719–720 resolutis comis | matres Latinae flebiles planctus dabant Cf. Verg. *Aen.* 7.400, where Amata roams the hills in a frenzy, calling upon the 'Latin mothers' for help.

721 inter tubarum saepe terribilem sonum The terrifying trumpet blasts provide the apt background for the equally intimidating countenance of Agrippina, who waves a blood-spattered torch. The sense requires the line to mean 'midst oft-repeated and fearful trumpet blasts' (Miller), but this use of the adverb *saepe* in the place of an adjective ('frequent', 'repeated') is peculiar. It looks like a filler, as often in this play: cf. 500–1 *Ioui, | aequatus altos saepe per honorum gradus*, see ad loc. This prompted Heinsius (*Adversaria*, 509) to emend the line to *inter tubarum saepta terribili sono*, with tmesis, which is unconvincing, especially because tmesis is a device unparalleled in Senecan tragedy. The cases of *inter* adverbial (Liberman, to salvage Heinsius' emendation) are rare, mostly epic pseudo-archaisms or Homerisms, and have a locative sense which is not applicable here. Moreover, *saepio*, when used metaphorically, suggests protection (in phrases like *pudore saepta, armis saeptus* cf. *OLD* s.v. *saepio*, 5c; 6).

The other problem connected with this line is the singular *inter sonum*, where a plural would have been expected to suggest a sequence of distinct blasts (cf. Verg. *Aen.* 12.318 *has inter uoces, media inter talia uerba*; Hor. *Epist.* 2.2.79 *inter strepitus nocturnos*). *inter* alone already suggests repetition, especially with the plural *tubarum*: cf. Sen. *Epist.* 94.59 *in tanto fremitu tumultuque falsorum.* The alliterating *tubarum . . . terribilem sonum* echoes Verg. *Aen.* 9.503–4 *at tuba terribilem sonitum . . . increpuit*; cf. Tac. *Ann.* 14.10 *et erant qui crederent sonitum tubae collibus circum editis planctusque tumulo matris audiri*; Ps.-Quint. *Decl.* 9.6 *sonabant clangore ferali tubae.*

722–723 sparsam cruore coniugis genetrix mei | . . . saeua quatiebat facem Agrippina, who appears in the guise of an avenging fury, fulfils the threat uttered at 593 ff., to 'turn the marriage torches into funereal ones'. Indeed, the whole scene unfolding before Poppaea's *thalamus* is a prefiguration of a funeral lamentation for the empress's death. Verg. *Aen.* 5.636–7 *per somnum . . . ardentis dare uisa faces.* On torches as an ominous sign in dreams cf. Kragelund (1982), 71 n. 9.

724–726 quam dum sequor coacta praesenti metu | diducta subito patuit ingenti mihi | tellus hiatu Cf. *Oed.* 582–3 *subito dehiscit terra et immenso sinu | laxata patuit*, suggesting that *subito* is adverbial. Poppaea is dragged along by Agrippina as if she were in a hypnotic trance (*coacta praesenti metu*); Kragelund (1982, 72, n. 21) aptly quotes Verg. *Aen.* 4.465–6 *agit ipse furentem . . . Aeneas*, and Suet. *Nero*, 46 *uidit* (sc. *Nero*) *per quietem . . . trahi . . . se ab Octauia uxore in artissimas tenebras.* Then the ground opens before her feet and she plunges headlong. This fall is clearly meant to foreshadow Poppaea's death. On the night before his assassination, Domitian had a dream in which the statue of Athena fell into an abyss (Cass. Dio *Hist. Rom.* 67.16.1 καὶ αὐτὸς ἐν τῶι ὕπνωι.. τὴν Ἀθηνᾶν.. τὰ ὅπλα ἀποβεβληκέναι καὶ ἐπὶ ἅρματος ἵππων μελάνων ἐς χάσμα ἐσπίπτειν ἔδοξεν).

728 in quis resedi fessa. uenientem intuor In pointed antithesis to her triumphant reclining upon her couch next to Nero, as described at 698–9, Poppaea sinks down on her nuptial couch, both exhausted and terrified by her vision. I interpret *resedi* as a perfect from *resido* rather than *resideo*, which is commonly understood to express a static position (its construction with *in* followed by the ablative or by a bare ablative is idiomatic: see examples given *infra*). The line may be reminiscent of Ov. *Met.* 6.301–2 *orba resedit | exanimes inter natos* (where interpretations of *resedit* vary); cf. also Ov. *Fast.* 3.15 *fessa resedit humo*; Verg. *Aen.* 2.739 *seu lapsa* (*v.l. lassa*) *resedit.*

On *quis* for *quibus* cf. N-W 2.469; Leo, *PF* 316, n. 1. There are five instances of *quis* in the play (621, 728, 809, 961, 963) against only one of *quibus* at 197. In the corpus the ratio is five (*Agam.* 197, *H.O.* 1750, *Med.* 711, *Oed.* 680, *Phae.* 443) to fourteen. Occurrences of *quis* multiply in Augustan literature, especially in epic poetry. Leo considers this one of the numerous archaic and obsolete forms revived by the Augustan poets. In four of the five occurrences in *Octavia*, *quis* and *quibus* are metrical equivalents (728 *in quis resedi* could have been replaced by the simple *quibus*: for the non-prepositional construction of *resido* cf. Verg. *Aen.* 1.506 *solio . . . alte subnixa resedit*; *Aen.* 5.180 *siccaque in rupe resedit*). With *quis* cf. Ov. *Met.* 7.671 *cum quis simul ipse resedit.*

intuor is the only form occurring in Seneca (cf. *Agam.* 917; *H.O.* 1357; 1755; *Phae.* 424; 898; 1168). The third-conjugation form is found in early dramatic literature (Plaut. *Capt.* 557; Ter. *Heaut.* 403; Acc. *Scaen.* 614 R[2]; Pomp. *CRF* 69 R[2]).

729–730 comitante turba coniugem quondam meum | natumque The great cortège of shades surrounding Crispinus must be the crowd of Nero's victims, just as a crowd of people executed by Claudius goes to meet him as he descends to the underworld in Sen. *Apocol.* 13.4–5 (esp. *medius erat in hac cantantium turba . . .*). Giancotti (1954, 31) compares Tac. *Ann.* 16.17 *eodem agmine*, said of the mass condemnations ordered by Nero. I suspect there is a direct echo of the *Apocolocyntosis.* The motif of the great crowd of souls meeting a new arrival (be it Christ coming to release the saved or a mortal, like Aeneas in Verg. *Aen.* 6.479) is universal in eschatological and visionary literature: cf. J. Kroll, *Gott und Hölle* (Leipzig, 1932), 383. Related to that is *Hf.* 835–7 *ducit ad manes uia qua remotos . . . frequens magna comitante turba*; Ov. *Met.* 6.594 *turba comitante*; in epic poetry the idiom is *magna comitante caterua.*

A similar dream is found in Stat. *Theb.* 8.626–8, *conubia uidi | nocte, soror; sponsum unde mihi sopor attulit amens, | uix notum uisu?* The appearance of her legitimate husband, Agamemnon, is one further parallel between the present episode and the dream of Clytemnestra in Soph. *El.* 417–23 (on which see *infra*, ad 756–60).

The line-ending *quondam meum* imitates Sen. *Med.* 924 *liberi quondam mei* (cf. also *Med.* 16 *adeste, thalamis horridae quondam meis*), but the emotional use of the adverb *quondam* with an adjective, especially a possessive, has Augustan precedents: cf. Ov. *Met.* 2.490 *quondamque suis errauit in agris*; Verg. *Aen.* 2.678 *coniunx quondam tua dicta*; *Buc.* 1.74 *felix quondam pecus.* On the syntactical sequence of substantive + possessive at line-end, separated by the insertion of one word in early drama, cf. the list given in E. Fraenkel, *Iktus und Akzent im lateinischen Sprechvers* (Berlin, 1928), 41, e.g. Plaut. *Trin.* 1074 *liberi quid agunt mei; Persa* 338 *filiam uendas tuam.*

730–731 properat petere complexus meos | Crispinus, intermissa libare oscula The name of Poppaea's previous husband had been lost in the MSS (exhibiting the corrupt *pristinus*) and was first proposed by Aegidius Maserius in 1511. Rufrius Crispinus, *PIR*[1] iii.141 (R 121), was forced to commit suicide in 66, in the aftermath of the Pisonian conspiracy. Their son was drowned by order of Nero (Suet. *Nero* 35.5). Their deaths, therefore, follow Poppaea's, which is in contrast with their welcoming her in the underworld, as if they had died earlier (cf. Carbone, 1977, 62).

The absence of caesura after the fifth element (in 731) is paralleled at *Phoe.* 76 *si moreris antecedo* (caesura obscured by a prefix, *ante-*), but this anomaly is enhanced here by the presence of a final cretic coalescing with the preceding word. *libare oscula* is from Verg. *Aen.* 1.256 *oscula libauit natae.* The word *intermissa* is rarely found in poetry: it may be reminiscent of Ov. *Met.* 1.746 *timide uerba intermissa retemptat* (of Io, turning back to her human form); also in Hor. *Carm.* 4.1.1–2 *intermissa diu . . . bella*. As Carbone convincingly argued, Poppaea, by the time she embraces Crispinus, has entered the realm of the dead. Raphelengius' *libans*, while an obvious stylistic improvement, would entail the rare metrical sequence of a final vowel-initial cretic not in synaloephe with the preceding word, only found once in this play (see at 173 for a more extensive discussion of final cretics in the Senecan corpus).

732 irrupit intra tecta cum trepidus mea The adjective *trepidus* suggests the fear of somebody running away from danger (cf. 120 *modo trepidus idem refugit in thalamos meos*, 690–1 *quo trepida gressum . . . effers?*), rather than the determination of a wronged husband demanding satisfaction from his rival. This is a vision of Nero's final moments, as narrated for instance in Suet. *Nero* 49.3 *trepidanter effatus* ἵππων . . . *ferrum iugulo adegit. irrupit*, although stemmatically inferior, is better than *irrumpit* in view of the perfect tense of the co-ordinated second colon, *condidit*.

Postponement of *cum* after the third word occurs in the Senecan corpus only in *Med.* 940 *ut saeua rapidi bella cum uenti gerunt*; *Troad.* 1040 *et nihil praeter mare cum uiderent*; *H.O.* 551–2 *fulmine abiecto deus | cum fronte subita tumuit*; 713–14 *semel profecto premere felices deus | cum coepit*; 1062; 1102. Postponement after the second word occurs in *Troad.* 46, 49; *Phae.* 766; *Oed.* 50; *H.O.* 168, 894, 1629; *Oct.* 539, 580. As noted in the Introd., postponement of conjunctions and *-que* is the most conspicuous aid to metrical composition in *Octavia*. Buecheler (1872, 474) conjectured *intro*, presumably out of a preference for the construction using the simple accusative *irrupit . . . tecta. intra tecta* is, however, well paralleled: cf. Verg. *Aen.* 6.525–8 *intra tecta uocat Menelaum . . . inrumpunt thalamo*; 7.168.

733 ensemque iugulo condidit saeuum Nero I follow Carbone (1977, 57) in understanding that the throat thus gashed open is Nero's, rather than Crispinus' or Poppaea's. True, the sudden irruption of Nero, as if intent on catching the two lovers kissing, prepares for a stabbing inflicted by the jealous husband, but 732 *trepidus* is at odds with this; moreover, *quem cruorem coniugis*, at 739, can only be referred to Nero, and this is the only interpretation which makes sense of the feebly optimistic reading proposed by the *Nutrix*, surely the one intended by the poet. Poppaea's death has been announced already by sufficient signs, and Crispinus is only a marginal character in this scene, included to signal Poppaea's arrival among the dead. On this interpretation, Nero does not interact with the other protagonists of the dream, and performs a suicidal dumb show. This is because the dead couple, Crispinus and Poppaea, foresee future events from which they are removed, both having died before Nero. Kragelund (1982) argues (13, 34) that the ambiguity of *iugulo* is intentional, partly because of the oracular nature of dreams, and also because the end of Crispinus also entails that of Nero.

Dreams are a recurrent way of announcing a monarch's violent death. Cf. the dream of Domitian in Cass. Dio *Hist. Rom.* 67.16.1 (cf. ad 724–5) καὶ αὐτὸς ἐν τῶι ὕπνωι τόν Ῥούστικον ξίφει προσιέναι οἱ . . . ἔδοξεν. In Plut. *Caes.* 63.9, Calpurnia seemed to Caesar to be crying in her sleep while she dreamt of holding the body of her dead husband (. . . κλαίειν, ἐκεῖνον ἐπὶ ταῖς ἀγκάλαις ἔχουσα κατεσφαγμένον).

735 quatit ora et artus horridus nostros tremor Zwierlein printed Buecheler's *ossa*, in view of the recurrence of the idiom *quatere ossa* with reference to fear (cf. *Oed.* 659 *et ossa et artus gelidus inuasit tremor*; Ov. *Her.* 5.37–8 *cucurrit . . . dira per ossa tremor*; *Met.* 10.423–4 *gelidus nutricis in artus | ossaque . . . penetrat tremor*). The transmitted *ora* does not seem indefensible: cf. Ov. *Am.* 3.5.45–6 *gelido mihi sanguis ab ore | fugit*, depicting Ovid's reaction to the seer's interpretation of a dream. Verg. *Aen.* 5.199–200 *creber anhelitus artus | aridaque ora quatit* refers to running; in Sen *Phae.* 1034 *os quassat tremor, os* seems to be from *os, oris*; Stat. *Theb.* 9.857–8 *tremor ora repens ac uiscera torsit | Arcados.*

736 continet uocem timor On *uocem continere* cf. Cic. *Rab. perd.* 18 *quin continetis uocem . . .?* Plin. *Nat.* 14.141 *alii . . . uoces non continent.* Ovid has *uocem tenere* (*Met.* 4.168; 10.421 *saepe tenet uocem*). Leo conjectured *diu*, to avoid repetition with the line-ending of the two immediately contiguous lines.

739 aut quem cruorem coniugis uidi mei The interrogative *quis* (in *quem cruorem*) means 'what is the sense of?' i.e. 'what does the blood I have seen on my husband mean?' Cf. Stat. *Theb.* 3.537–8 *quae saeua repente | uictores agitat leto Iouis ira sinistri?*; 8.633 *quaenam haec dubiae praesagia cladis?* (Ismene, speaking of the dream in which she saw her prospective husband: see *supra* ad 728); Sen. *Hf.* 1194–5 *quid illa . . . harundo?* (uncertain); Ov. *Met.* 9.474–5 *quid uult sibi noctis imago . . . cur haec ego somnia uidi?* Dreamers are often perplexed about the meaning of the signs and features displayed by the persons who have appeared to them: cf. Kragelund (1982), 73 n. 44.

740 The misleading interpretation of the dream is in keeping with the conventionally optimistic character of *trophoi* in Senecan and Euripidean drama, protective but simple-minded old women who ultimately do more harm than good. Tyrants typically receive misguided reassurances after dreaming of their death or comparable mishaps happening to them. In Herod. *Hist.* 6.107, before the battle of Marathon, Hippias dreamt he slept with his mother, which he interpreted as a good omen (cf. also Soph. *O.T.* 981–2). In Curt. Ruf. *Hist. Alex.* 3.3.3 an ominous dream receives diverse explanations from the seers in the Persian camp: *castra Alexandri magno ignis fulgore conlucere ei uisa sunt . . . alii laetum id regi somnium . . . quod castra hostium arsissent.* The *Nutrix* reverses the sense of the vision to comfort Poppaea. This has a parallel in the assumption, common in ancient *Traumdeutung*, that dreams mean the opposite of what they ostensibly represent (cf. Plin. *Epist.* 1.18.2; Artemid. *Oneirocrit.* 2.60; *sch. ad* Luc.

Bell. Ciu. (Endt) 7.21–2). In Apul. *Met.* 4.27 this is the argument of the old woman keeping a benevolent watch over the young bride who has seen her husband's death in a nightmare: *nocturnae uisiones contrarios euentus nonnunquam pronuntiant.* Cf. also Shakespeare, *Jul. Caes.* II.2.83 'This dream is all amiss interpreted' (where however Decimus Brutus is insincere). On dreams in Roman poetry cf. F. Fürbringer, *De somniis in Romanorum poetarum carminibus narratis* (diss. Jena, 1912).

Poppaea's dream is ultimately drawn from Clytemnestra's in Soph. *El.* 417 (also Clytemnestra is said to have seen her lawful husband sitting by her, on the selfsame throne where Aegisthus now sits); cf. also Aesch. *Pers.* 184 ff. (esp. 225, where the chorus give an optimistic interpretation of Atossa's dream); *Choe.* 525 ff.

740 quaecumque mentis agitat intentus uigor The *Nutrix* starts with some generalizing considerations about the nature of dreams, like the seer in Ov. *Am.* 3.5.1. The Nurse elaborates on the widespread notion that dreams are based on the activities in which one's waking thoughts are most occupied: cf. Lucr. *D.R.N.* 4.962 ff. *et quo quisque fere studio deuinctus adhaeret . . . atque in ea ratione fuit contenta magis mens, | in somnis eadem plerumque uidemur obire*; Cic. *Diu.* 2.140 *reliquiae earum rerum mouentur in animis et agitantur, de quibus uigilantes aut cogitauimus aut egimus.* Bailey's note on 4.962 quotes these imitations of Lucretius: Petr. *Sat.* fr. 30; Fronto, *De Feriis Alsiensibus* 3; Claud. *Cons. Hon.* vi. pr. 1–2. The assertion that the day's activities return to populate one's dreams occurs in Stat. *Theb.* 8.623–4 *curam inuigilare quieti, | claraque per somnos animi simulacra reuerti?*, where Ismene endeavours to explain to herself why she should have seen her future husband Atys in a dream; Ov. *Met.* 9.469–70 *placida resoluta quiete | saepe uidet quod amat.*

The transmitted *infestus uigor* does not yield an acceptable sense. I follow Zwierlein in writing Gronovius' *intentus*, which involves a very slight palaeographical modification in most book-hands. *mentis . . . uigor* requires some specification to indicate the waking state, in which such activities are conceived, so as to balance *per quietem* in the following line; *intentus* seems adequate, and corresponds to *deuinctus* in Lucretius' famous passage. I have not found parallels for *intentus* used absolutely (cf. by contrast Ov. *Trist.* 4.1.4 *mens intenta malis ne foret usque suis*; Sen. *Ira* 3.41.1 *intenta mens ad . . .*), but the verb *intendo* commonly occurs in combination with *mentem, animum*; likewise its derivatives indicate alertness, a wakeful state of mind: cf. Sen. *Epist.* 69.5 *adsidua uigilia et intentio*; 71.28 *remittet aliquid ex intentione mentis. uigor mentis* may already have conveyed this sense, because of its etymological connection to *uigeo, uigil* (cf. Cic. *Diu.* 1.63 *iacet enim corpus dormientis ut mortui, uiget autem et uiuit animus*), and *intentus* drives home the idea effectively.

The *Octavia* passage probably echoes, directly or through some dramatic intermediary, Acc. *Praet.* 29–31 R² *rex, | quae in uita usurpant homines, cogitant curant uident, | quaeque agunt uigilantes agitantque, ea si cui in somno accidunt | minus mirum est, sed di rem tantam haut temere improuiso offerunt*, also notable for the occurrence of *quae . . . ea*: see following note. Notice though that the seer in Accius did not try to conceal the truth.

741–742 ea per quietem sacer et arcanus refert | ueloxque sensus While the psychological explanation of dreams advanced at 740 presupposes a rationalistic model, and may ultimately go back to Lucr. *D.R.N.* 4.962 ff., *sacer et arcanus ueloxque sensus* have a mystical ring and presuppose a wholly different intellectual background. 741–2 is possibly an imitation of Verg. *Aen.* 4.422 *arcanos etiam tibi credere sensus*. In Vergil, however, *sensus* indicates Aeneas' most intimate thoughts, with no specific reference to a psychological function. In 742, *sensus* is employed in the less common sense 'an indistinct faculty' (cf. *OLD* 6d), almost a sixth sense, different from the five on which our perception of reality depends. *uelox, uelocitas* are common attributes of psychological processes, but the first two attributes shift the reference to the realm of the supernatural.

Notice the three adjectives modifying *sensus*. Possibly in *uelox . . . sensus* we glimpse a reminiscence of Lucretius' psychology (*D.R.N.* 3.183; 3.202–3 on the quickness and nimbleness of *animus*; 4.722–99 on the reasons for the mind's quickness in forming images of things), but Lucretian terminology is different, and the two adjectives *sacer* and *arcanus* lead in a different direction. The emphasis on the sacredness of the soul or mind points to Stoic psychology: cf. Sen. *Cons. Helu.* 11.7 *animus . . . sacer et aeternus est*; *Epist.* 41.2–5 *sacer intra nos spiritus sedet . . . sic animus, magnus ac sacer . . . conuersatur quidem nobiscum, sed haeret origini suae.*

All forms of the demonstrative *is* tend to be avoided in poetry (cf. Axelson, *UW* 71) and this is the only occurrence of a plural *ea* in the whole corpus of Senecan tragedy. The presence of the anaphoric *is* after a relative pronoun is very rare in classical Latin, and commonest in early drama (*TLL* vii.2 s.v. *is*, 465.50–80, e.g. Plaut. *Truc.* 158 *male quae in nos ais ea omnia tibi dicis*; in Ov. *Met.* only one instance, 15.63–4 *quae natura negabat . . . oculis ea pectoris hausit*; elsewhere cf. *Her.* 17.217–18 *quicumque . . . intrauerit aduena portus, | is tibi . . . causa timoris erit*; Sen. *Med.* 500–1 *cui prodest scelus, | is fecit*).

742 coniugem thalamos toros Asyndetic sequences of three or more nouns, or adjectives, are an archaic feature, revived in Senecan tragedy: cf. Tarrant, *HSCPh* 94 (1992), 339. While often used interchangeably, *thalami* and *tori* bear distinct meanings here ('bed-chamber' and 'bed'). The combination of both terms is found in Sen. *Med.* 285 *per . . . auspicatos regii thalami toros; Oed.* 20 *thalamos parentis . . . et diros toros.*

743–744 amplexu noui | haerens mariti Cf. Val. Fl. *Arg.* 1.316 *longis flentes amplexibus haerent*; Ov. *Pont.* 1.9.19 *haesit in amplexu*; *Met.* 7.143 *auidis . . . amplexibus haerent*; Sil. *Pun.* 13.297.

744–745 sed mouent laeto die | pulsata palmis pectora et fusae comae? *sed* marks a turn in the speech of the Nurse. Small wonder if Poppaea saw her bed-chamber in her dream: was she not lying in her husband's fond embrace (742–4)? Still, does the memory of lamentation and mourning worry her (744–5)? This use of *sed*, anticipating an interlocutor's objection, is wholly idiomatic in Latin: cf. *OLD*, s.v. *sed* 2c, 4c.

The interpretation of this part of Poppaea's vision is even more perverse. The *Traumdeutungen* imparted by Poppaea's *Nutrix* to her terror-stricken pupil in order to dispel her fears follow a well-established rationalistic trend, mainly pleading that all visions are the product of subconscious associations with the objects which most occupy one's waking thoughts, or with things seen or experienced during the last few hours. If Poppaea was frightened by a chorus of lamenting *matres Latinae*, this must surely have been because the maids of Octavia cried for their mistress all night.

The choice of the masculine *laeto* (*die*) in preference to the variant *laeta* is justified by Senecan usage. The more formal masculine is constantly used, even in *Octavia*, except when the word means 'passing of time' or when metrical considerations required a short nominative (vocalic) ending (cf. 714 *laeta nam postquam dies*). In this, Senecan tragedy follows an established linguistic convention of hexameter poetry, where the masculine is used by preference (except in certain fixed constructions and in the nominative), contrary to what appears to have been the dominant trend in contemporary spoken Latin: cf. Fraenkel, *KB* 1.63–72. In *Oct.* 646–7, *festo* | *laetoque die*, masculine and feminine were prosodically equivalent but the poet chose the masculine.

For *pulsata palmis pectora* cf. Sen. *Troad.* 64 *ferite palmis pectora et planctus date*; *Hf.* 1100–1 *percussa sonent* | *pectora palmis*.

For *mouere*, 'to frighten', cf. Ov. *Met.* 1.55 *humanas motura tonitrua mentes*; 11.719 *omine mota est*; *TLL* s.v. 1542.44–54.

746–747 Octauiae discidia planxerunt sacros | intra penates fratris et patrium larem The interior of the house provides an appropriate setting for female mourners: cf. Hom. *Il.* 24.166; Soph. *Ant.* 1248–9, where Eurydice entering her house is said ὑπὸ στέγης ἔσω | δμωαῖς προθήσειν πένθος οἰκεῖον στένειν for the death of Haemon.

As often in this play, reference to previous actions is made in a vague manner which makes it difficult to decide whether the allusion to mourning in the palace should be related to events specifically represented. Here lamentation raised in the palace for Octavia could refer to 646, which was even there only mirrored in the restraining words of the protagonist. Reference to off-stage action is predictably much more frequent in this play than in any other play of the corpus, because the *Octavia* has to accommodate to drama the greatest number of facts.

But *inter* yields an incongruous sense. The view that Octavia's attendants shed tears 'between the house-gods of Britannicus and the *Lar* of Claudius' is debatable ('amidst . . .' Miller, Loeb). Are we to visualize the *kommos*, as it were, for Octavia's dismissal as held between two *aediculae*, opposite to one another? Furthermore, why should the late Britannicus and *diuus Claudius* have worshipped distinct house-gods? In fact, in historical times no distinction was made or understood between the *lares* and *penates* in the domestic cult. *lares* and *penates* shared a little *aedicula* in the hall, filled with several statues of protective deities (Roscher, *Lexicon*, s.v. 'penates', 1881). This is one of the many instances in Latin poetry in which *penates* and *lares* occur as pure synonyms (cf. Verg. *Aen.* 8.543–4 *hesternumque larem paruosque penates* | *laetus adit*; 9. 258–9; Prop. 2.30.21–2 *spargere et alterna communes caede penates* | *et ferre ad patrios praemia dira lares!*; for more parallels cf. Ferri (1999), 636–7).

The metonymic, high-flown sense of both *penates* and *lar* for 'house, palace' is recurrent in *Octavia* (cf. *infra* 789 *reddere penates Claudiae Diui parant*; 277–8 *teneatque suos* | *nupta penates Claudia proles*; between the metonymic and the literal sense 148–9 *cruore foedauit suo* | *patrios penates*; 162–3 *polluit Stygia face* | *sacros penates*) and well-established in Latin (cf. Gross (1911), 390–392; S. Weinstock, in *RE* XIX.1 (1937), s.v. *penates*, 423), and this seems the meaning required here. Yet the transmitted *inter* still poses a problem, because we must conclude that Octavia's maids moved about lamenting 'between' two separate places, the apartments of Britannicus and those of Claudius. What Poppaea's *Nutrix* means, in fact, must be that 'there was mourning last night in the royal apartments'; *penates fratris et patrium larem* refer to only one building, the royal residence, Octavia's rightful abode of which she has been dispossessed. *inter penates* must be corrected, in fact, to ***intra*** *penates*.

It is easy to see how the corruption occurred, with the dyadic expression *penates fratris et patrium larem* (and especially the plural *penates*) encouraging the slip. A similar dittology designed to increase pathos occurs at 892–3 *patriam reddere ciues* | *aulam et fratris uoluere toros*. This correction establishes the right Latin idiom for 'in the palace'. Cf. Vell. Pat. 2.95 *quem intra Caesaris penates enixa erat Liuia*; Sen. *Contr. exc.* 5.5.1 *intra istorum penates*; Sen. *Cons. Marc.* 16.4 *intra penates interemptum suos*; Luc. *Bell. Ciu.* 10.453–4 *intra penates* | *obruitur telis*. Cf. the similar idiom *opperiri intra Palatium* (*iubet*) in Tac. *Ann.* 12.5.2. In addition, scribes might have been misled by the concentration of lines beginning with the word *inter* in this passage: cf. 716 *inter Neronis uincta complexus mei*; 721 *inter tubarum saepe terribilem sonum*; 732 *intra tecta*, for which most MSS have *inter*. A slightly more problematic case is *Oct.* 606–7, where Zwierlein rightly reads *sacros* | *intra penates spiritum effudi grauem* but the tradition is divided between *inter* (abbreviated as *int'*) and *intra* (*intr* with a supralineate serpentine). On first impression, a pathetic *inter* would yield a good sense, 'I breathed my last amidst the protective deities of the house.' Slaughter in a sacred place is a highly sacrilegious act (cf. the death of Priam in Verg. *Aen.* 2.2.550–1 *altaria ad ipsa trementem | traxit*; and also 2.515–17 *Hecuba et natae nequiquam altaria circum . . . diuom amplexae simulacra tenebant*), but *inter* is not the same as *ad*, and I still prefer the reading *intra*.

The confusion *inter/intra* is common in all authors, and at times doubt remains: cf. Hor. *Ep.* 2.2,114 *inter penetralia Vestae*, where early editors printed *intra*, and Verg. *Aen.* 11.882 *inter* (*intra* ***MR***) *tuta domorum*. In the Horace passage, however, the verb *uersentur* (*et uersentur adhuc inter penetralia Vestae*) renders *inter* preferable (contrast *planxerunt* in *Oct.* 746); similarly in [Quint.] *Decl.* 255.8 (p. 46, 17 Ritt.) *uersantur inter domos nostras, inter templa, inter muros*. The only other instances of *inter penates* known to me are cases in which the inclusion of a new god is mentioned: cf. Ov. *Met.* 15.864 *inter sacrata penates*; Suet. *Aug.* 7.1; *Vit.* 2.7 *inter Lares colere*.

Despite the current unanimity, the MS reading *inter* only entered the text in 1867 through Peiper-Richter, but it has remained there ever since. *intra* was printed in the text by Avantius. While this was no doubt a conjectural emendation (though Avantius made no boast of it), it remained in place until the nineteenth century without discussion or mention of the 'true' MS reading *inter*. Renaissance editors, as is well known, did not always regard MS evidence very highly concerning matters of Latinity. However, in this particular case more accurate examination of MS evidence actually led to error rather than improvement, since editors relied on the *paradosis* at the expense of idiomatic Latin and better sense.

Octauiae discidia: Sen. *Agam.* 283 has *repudia*: the two words are not prosodically equivalent, but they can both occupy the initial position in iambic trimeters.

748–750 fax illa, quam secuta es, Augustae manu | praelata, clarum nomen inuidia tibi | partum ominatur Translations betray some confusion as to the meaning of *inuidia . . . partum* (Herrmann: 'une lumineuse gloire que t'aura acquise l'envie même'; Viansino 'presagisce rinomanza luminosa come fonte d'invidia verso di te'; Miller 'the name . . . illumined by envy'). The sense is that a good offshoot, fame, will bloom from its opposite, envy (cf. Chaumartin 'née de l'envie').

The interpretation of the vision here is relatively clear: Agrippina was a powerful enemy for Poppaea, but from her hatred Poppaea's present glory gushed forth. For *pario* with the bare instrumental ablative cf. Cic. *Prou. cons.* 29 *laurea . . . periculis parta*; Sil. *Pun.* 15.497–8 *argenti pondera . . . parta . . . longo discrimine*.

For the metaphorical use of *pario* 'to acquire' cf. Verg. *Aen.* 3.495 *uobis parta quies*; 11.24–5 *sanguine . . . nobis hanc patriam peperere suo*; Cic. *Rep.* 6.11 *cognomen . . . tibi per te partum*.

750–751 inferum sedes toros | stabiles futuros spondet aeternae domus cf. Acc. *Praet.* 38 R[2] *auguratum . . . fore*; *sedes* designates the Underworld, not the state of being seated (*in quis resedi fessa*): cf. Sen. *Thy.* 1 *quis inferorum sede ab infausta trahit?*; *Phoe.* 207–8; Hor. *Carm.* 1.34.10; Arnob. *Nat.* 7.19 *sedes . . . inferas.*

The words of the *Nutrix* are unwittingly ambiguous. The affectionate servant makes the most of the nightmare, and reads it as a prophecy of Poppaea's unchallenged tenure of the imperial throne next to Nero: her words in fact contain a prophecy of Poppaea's approaching end. *domus aeterna* is a common honorific designation for the ruling house (some parallels in Liberman, p. 116). At the same time, the words indicate the eternal dwelling of the dead, either in the Underworld or in the sepulchre (cf. Sen. *Phae.* 1241 *recipe me aeterna domo*; e.g. *CE* 71.4; 72.3). The same ambiguity could be extended to *torus*, which can be said of palliasses placed under the dead body before cremation.

752–753 iugulo quod ensem condidit princeps tuus, | bella haud mouebit, pace sed ferrum teget The scene of murder in the bed-chamber is a traditional ground for scholarly disagreement, with many interpreters insisting that the vision forecasts Poppaea's own death. Kragelund (1982), 72 n. 31 gives information on MS glosses (some presumably prompted by Salutati's letter of 1371) indicating that the throat in question is Nero's. Trevet concurs in this view, which is in my judgement the more reasonable. Lipsius suggested changing *iugulo . . . princeps tuus* to *iugulo . . . princeps tuo*, but cf. *supra*, 716 *Neroni . . . meo*: on the flounderings of older scholars on this point, as well as on *mea* in 732, a useful survey in Kragelund (1982), 18–19. As Ballaira is right to observe, the *Nutrix* exploits the ambiguity of *condo*, which means both 'plunge' and 'hide'. Nero will 'hide' the sword in his own body, an act which represents the universal peace proclaimed by the emperor in 66, when the gates of Janus' temples were closed, following Augustan precedent (cf. Suet. *Nero*, 13; Cass. Dio *Hist. Rom.* 67.5). Thus even the *Nutrix* is in a sense a true prophet. A somewhat similar device (anticipation of events by a speaker who is unaware of their full meaning) is discussed ad 807–8.

The resumptive *quod* ('as to the fact that') occurs in early Latin drama and then in prose, and is probably a colloquial feature (cf. C. E. Bennett, *Syntax of Early Latin* (Boston, 1910), 1.125–6; K-S *Satzlehre* 2.277–8, e.g. Plaut. *Capt.* 586 *filium tuum quod redimere se ait, id ne utiquam mihi placet*, with anaphoric *id* in the main clause). The occurrence of the same syntactic pattern in Acc. *Praet.* 33–8 R^2 *quod de sole ostentum est tibi . . . quod dexterum | cepit cursum . . . pulcherrume | auguratum est rem Romanam publicam summam fore* seems to enhance the plausibility of the suggestion that the poet has in mind the Accian *praetexta* in this episode (see *supra*, ad 740).

754 recollige animum Cf. Ov. *Met.* 9.745 *quin animum firmas teque ipsa recolligis?*

755 redde te thalamis tuis This use of *reddo* for 'to bring oneself back' to a given place is not well identified in *OLD* (the closest parallels under

1b: Liv. 23.9.13 *se ipse conuiuio reddidit*; Apul. *Met.* 2.30 *nec . . . Lari me patrio reddere potui*; also in Sil. *Pun.* 11.366–7 *tum reddere sese* | *festinant epulis*; Hor. *Sat.* 2.7.71).

756–759 delubra et aras petere constitui sacras, | caesis litare uictimis numen deum, | ut expientur noctis et somni minae | terrorque in hostes redeat attonitus meos Reference is often made to Jos. *Ant.* 20.195, where Poppaea briefly features as 'a pious woman' (θεοσεβής), and presumably a proselyte to Judaism. More than by the inclinations of the real-life Poppaea, the scene is inspired, as Ladek (1909), 189 first suggested, by Clytemnestra in Soph. *El.* 647 εἰ δ' ἐχθρά, τοῖς ἐχθροῖσιν ἔμπαλιν μέθες,[18] where the queen addresses Apollo entreating him to turn the omens, if bad, against her enemies. This prayer is probably reproduced in 759 *terrorque in hostes redeat. redeo* can be used as 'recoil', but the implication seems to be that the bad dream is a spell cast on her by her enemies. Poppaea has made no mention of enemies so far (Octavia would be a prime candidate), though she does in the episode sketched in *Ann.* 14.60: the scheming and shrewd Poppaea of Tacitus' characterization begins to emerge here. As often remarked by critics of the play, the play's protagonists receive chameleon-like characterizations, which is, in my view, a by-product of the multi-layered and often diverging traditions combined by the playwright.

For the combination of *delubra* and *aras* cf. Verg. *Aen.* 4.56–7 *principio delubra adeunt, pacemque per aras* | *exquirunt, mactant lectas de more bidentis*; Sen. *Agam.* 392–4 *delubra et aras caelitum . . . supplex adoro*; Drac. *Rom.* 7.488 *delubra petens intrauit ad aras.*

Sacrifices and supplications are a natural expedient to turn to in order to dispel the fears aroused by an ominous vision: for literary parallels cf. Jocelyn ad Enn. *Trag.* 54 Joc.; Palmer ad Ov. *Her.* 13.111–12 *excutior somno . . . nulla caret fumo Thessalis ara meo* (spoken by Laodamia, to whom Protesilaus' pale shade has appeared in her sleep); Aesch. *Pers.* 200 ff. (esp. 215–25, where the chorus gives advice to Atossa on how to supplicate the dead and the spirit of her husband to intervene and change bad omens to good ones).

Zwierlein, followed by Chaumartin, is the first recent editor to print a comma after *sacras*, thus making *petere* and *litare* two co-ordinated infinitives dependent on *constitui*. This seems the most acceptable solution. The resulting asyndeton would be normal in *Oct.* (cf. 730–1 *properat petere complexus meos* | *Crispinus, intermissa libare oscula*).

757 caesis litare uictimis numen deum This construction of *litare* ('to propitiate') with the accusative of the gods receiving the honour and the ablative of the sacrificed animals occurs also *infra*, 980–1 *hospitis illic caede*

[18] Where the exact interpretation of ἔμπαλιν has been an object of controversy, although Jebb's *retro* ('let it recoil upon my foes', rather than 'on the contrary') may find confirmation in *redeat* in our passage (at least this is how our poet understood it).

litatur | *numen superum.* Flinck (1919), 51 is wrong to suppose that the construction of *litare* with the object of the person to whom the supplication is made is a colloquialism (in accordance with his entire theory that colloquialism is a marked feature of *Oct.* as a *praetexta*). *litare* in literary Latin admits three different constructions: *litare sacra* (as an accusative of internal object, as in Verg. *Aen.* 4.50 *tu modo posce ueniam, sacrisque litatis . . .*), *litare hostias, litare deos.* It is worth noting that Seneca always has *litare aliquid alicui*; cf. e.g. *Agam.* 577 *postquam litatum est Ilio*, but the construction found in *Oct.* is also found in Luc. *Bell. Ciu.* 7.169–71 *quae numina . . . litasti? caedo* is also commonly used like *immolo* (cf. *TLL* iii, s.v. 63.60–5, of human victims: Sen. *Troad.* 140 *magnoque Ioui uictima caesus*; Mart. *Epigr.* 10.73.6 *non quacumque manu uictima caesa litat*).

760–1 tu uota pro me suscipe et precibus piis | superos adora, †maneat ut praesens metus† The two lines are marred by a textual corruption in 761. While the transmitted *et uota pro me suscipe et precibus piis* | *superos adora, maneat ut praesens metus* is obviously at fault, a certain solution is difficult to find. Helm's *iam abeat ut p. metus* (1934, 323, n. 1) would yield good sense and has palaeographical plausibility. It is perhaps supported by the parallel use of *abire* for the dispelling of *omina* in a false funeral in Stat. *Theb.* 5.318–19 *cassumque parenti* | *omen et hac dubios leti precor ire timores*, with *timores* paralleling *abeat . . . metus*; also Verg. *Aen.* 3.36 *rite secundarent uisus, omenque leuarent*; Ov. *Her.* 13.92 *fac meus in uentos hic timor omnis eat*; Liv. 5.18.12, with the Roman matrons praying *ut . . .* (*Veios*) *eum auerterent* (sc. *di*) *terrorem*. For *abeat* cf. also Hor. *Ars* 200–1 *deosque precetur et oret* | *ut redeat miseris, abeat Fortuna superbis*. The same metonymical extension is found with Greek φόβος: cf. Soph. *El.* 427 πέμπει μ' ἐκείνη τοῦδε τοῦ φόβου χάριν, where Chrysothemis speaks of her mother's dream; *Hymn. Orph.* 3.12 φόβους ἀπόπεμπε νυχαυγεῖς, Men. *Dysk.* 417–18 ἀλλὰ θύομεν | διὰ τοῦθ', ἵν 'εἰς βέλτιον ἀποβῆι τὸ φοβερόν. Against the conjecture *iam abeat*, one should mention that synaloephe in the first element of a resolved third arsis has only one certain parallel in the Senecan corpus (although it is acceptable in early drama), *Oct.* 564 *quem si fouere atque alere desistas, cadit* (cf. Zwierlein, *Prolegomena* 217). Other Senecan parallels are textually dubious (*Thy.* 1021 <*iam*> *accipe hos potius libens* (Schmidt); *Agam.* 795 *ubi Helena est*, where synaloephe occurs in the second element of the resolved arsis).

status, conjectured by Buecheler, is also attractive (cf. Sen. *Cons. Helu.* 18.6, in a prayer: *deos oro . . . floreat reliqua in suo statu turba*, sc. *nepotum*), but the context, in my judgement, requires *metus*. Whitman supports *status* adducing Soph. *El.* 648–52, where Clytemnestra goes on to ask Apollo that she may be allowed to retain her present *state* (ὧδέ μ' αἰεὶ ζῶσαν ἀβλαβεῖ βίωι | δόμους Ἀτρειδῶν σκηπτρά τ' ἀμφέπειν τάδε, | φίλοισί τε ξυνοῦσαν οἷς ξύνειμι νῦν). Linguistic usage in the play (as well as the various parallels given above) makes it less likely that *metus* should be the corrupt word: cf. *supra* 724 *coacta praesenti metu*, at line-end; 712 *turbata metu* (= a nightmare). *metus* is preferable because to react against the bad omen a stronger expression is needed. Gronovius conjectured *monuit*, which is equally reasonable as the Latin goes.

In Greek tragedy sacrifice often provides an excuse for the exit of a character (in Senecan drama cf. Tarrant ad Sen. *Agam.* 802 for parallels; *Hf.* 515). Here Poppaea sets off to sacrifice to the gods, while additional prayers are entrusted to her subordinate. Cf. Soph. *Ai.* 684–6 σὺ δὲ | ἔσω θεοῖς ἐλθοῦσα διὰ τέλους, γύναι, | εὔχου τελεῖσθαι τοὐμὸν ὧν ἐρᾶι κέαρ, where Ajax bids Tecmessa go inside and pray to the gods on his behalf. In Aesch. *Cho.* 22ff. the chorus of maidens and Electra are dispatched to make libations for the anguished queen. Even in the passage from *Electra* mentioned above, the actual sacrificial procedure is discharged by Clytemnestra's attendant maidens (634 ff.), while the prayer itself is pronounced by the queen. Cf. also Jocasta's prayer in *O.T.* 911–23.

A minor problem is posed by the occurrence of the double *et*, emended by Gronovius, who altered the first to *tu*. The change of subject and verbal mood from the previous line (*terrorque . . . redeat . . . uota pro me suscipe*) makes the correction unavoidable: cf. Verg. *Aen.* 4. 50–1 *tu modo posce deos ueniam, sacrisque litatis | indulge hospitio*, said by Dido to Anna, a passage which the poet may be recalling here. The emphatic use of pronoun subject marks the transition from general statement to precept or order, as in Verg. *Georg.* 2.241–2 *tale dabit specimen: tu spisso uimine qualos . . . deripe*; 3.163; 4.106–7 *nec magnus prohibere labor: tu regibus alas | eripe*; Sen. *Thy.* 333 *nostra tu coepta occule.* There would be no parallels for a double *et* + imperative, with the conjunction in the initial position: the only sort of comparable case would be, e.g., Ov. *Pont.* 2.5.19–20 *tu tamen hic structos . . . uersus | et legis et lectos . . . probas*, which makes the difference clear.

762 A new chorus comes on stage singing the charms of Poppaea: they may be imagined as revellers returning from the wedding celebrations, perhaps soldiers of the guard stationed at the royal palace (cf. 780 *quicumque . . . excubat miles ducis*). Although various elements of this choral ode call to mind a long-established tradition of lyrics composed to celebrate marriages, this is not, by any Greek standards, a wedding song proper (*hymenaeus* or *epithalamium*), since it neither accompanies a nuptial procession nor is it performed at the couple's *thalami* to herald the actual wedding night, this having already passed (by contrast: a chorus singing for the marriage of Phaethon is introduced in Eur. *Phaeth.* 227–44; a mock-marriage scene is preceded by the singing of a *hymenaeus* in Plaut. *Cas.* 799–814). The only other *epithalamium* in the Senecan corpus occurs at *Med.* 56 ff., imitated perhaps here (cf. 775 = *Med.* 80). There were, however, in Roman marriage several sympotic and convivial moments as well as drinking parties giving rise to hilarity and rumbustious behaviour. Even marriages more ordinary than the marriage of Poppaea would have been followed, on the day after the nuptials, by the so-called *repotia*, a name suggesting libations (cf. Hor. *Serm.* 2.2.59–60: Gell. *Noct. Att.* 2.24.14, S. Treggiari, *Roman Marriage*, 169). There were also songs to be performed on the morning following the first night (διεγερτικά, in P.Oxy. 3966 (Menander): cf. F. Perusino–A. Giacomoni, in *Studi Corbato* (Pisa, 1999), 101–7) but this would imply some more precise element in the ode referring to the imagined situation, nor are the married couple thought of as within earshot.

Pedroli ad loc. argues that this chorus is sung by women, on the assumption that the praises of the bride were generally sung by young women in the Roman marriage ceremony, but there is no evidence of this. Choruses of παρθένοι are indeed predominant in the Greek tradition relating to nuptial songs, though by no means exclusively so (a useful review of the Greek evidence in M. Lyghounis, *MD* 27 (1991), 159–98; M. L. West, *Ancient Greek Music* (Oxford, 1992), 22 and nn. 36–7). Roman custom need not have been the same, and there are no obvious gender identifiers in the ode itself. The chorus is no more characterized than the singers of Jason's nuptial song are in Sen. *Med.* 56 ff., where bride and groom are jointly celebrated (*ibid.* 75–92; esp. 91–2 *uincat femina coniuges, | uir longe superet uiros*). No more is said to explain the setting and to justify the presence of the singers here. The theme of the song is the extraordinary beauty of Poppaea, fit for arousing the desire of a god. This theme is indeed expected in wedding celebrations (cf. *supra*, ad 218; in Cat. *Carm.* 61.85 there is only a brief appraisal of the bride's beauty, traditionally said to equal that of Venus) and in love poetry (*supra*, ad 545).

The chorus' euphoria is interrupted by the news of the revolt that has erupted in the meantime. Having no link (at least extrinsic) to the action of the preceding scene, this chorus of previously unknown partisans of Poppaea has been seen as an ideal candidate for act-division, on the analogy of Greek *embolima*-songs (to be compared, in extant texts, with the arrival of revellers and singers in comedy whose *melē* – not written by the author – provide the commonest form of *entr'acte* or choral interlude: cf. e.g. Handley, ad Men. *Dysk.* 230–2; Leo, *PF*, 227 n. 3). Unlike the comic *embolima*, this choral song is fully integrated into the dramatic action of *Octauia*, providing an example of that long-established pattern known as 'tragic irony'. The dramatic impact of this rashly optimistic song resides in its lack of actuality and in the contrast with the dire news brought by the messenger. An effect of peripeteia is achieved in depicting the reduction of the singers from confidence to perplexity and fear. Illusory joy is a recurrent pattern in Greek, notably Sophoclean, tragedy (cf. Soph. *Ai.* 693–718; *Trach.* 633–62; *Ant.* 1115–54; *O.T.* 1086–1109; Eur. *Herc.* 763–814), and occurs also in Seneca (*Hf.* 875–94; *Thy.* 546 ff.). Donatus (ad Ter. *Ad.* c. 200) calls this pattern of optimistic elation followed by a reversal of fortune (and vice versa) *tragica parectasis.* The view that this song should be considered an act-dividing ode, favoured by Münscher (1922), is impugned by Schmidt (1985), 1453, with the argument that the succeeding act would be too short. But a choral ode with no intrinsic link to the action and sung on an empty stage is bound to have been felt as a break in the dramatic action.

762–763 si uera loquax fama Tonantis | furta et gratos narrat amores *loquar* in ***A***, corrected by some *recc.*, is obviously at fault. The language of these lines is unmistakably Ovidian: cf. Ov. *Met.* 9.137–8 *cum fama loquax praecessit ad aures, | Deianira, tuas* (also in *Pont.* 2.9.3 and Luc. *Bell. Ciu.* 8.782). The epithet *loquax* is purely ornamental in this context, because the chorus is not deprecating the stories of amorous dallyings that rumour has told, nor has rumour been the cause of some mishap befalling the lovers. *furta Iouis* for 'furtive escapades' also in Cat. *Carm.* 68.140 *plurima furta Iouis* (where the text is conjectural, for *facta*); Prop. 2.2.4 *Iuppiter ignoro pristina furta tua*; 2.30.28 *dulcia furta Iouis*; *CE* 887.1 *lustrat Amor – taurus latet Ioque – furta Tonantis*; also in Ov. *Met.* 1.606; Germ. *Arat.* 277; Stat. *Theb.* 10.64. On the use of *Tonans* alone for *Iuppiter* cf. Haupt's note ad Ov. *Met.* 11.196.

Expressions of apparent disbelief with regard to the stories of myth are comparatively frequent in classical poetry (cf. Stinton, 'Si credere dignum est', in *Collected Papers on Greek Tragedy* (Oxford, 1990), esp. 256–7, on a similar doubt concerning Helen's birth from the encounter of Leda and the divine swan in Eur. *I.A.*). Yet the passage in *Octavia* lacks all ironical or plaintive undertones usually associated with such formulae in Greek tragedy; the chorus has no theological pronouncements to make and the expression serves only the courtly purpose of paying a compliment to Poppaea's beauty: 'indeed, now is the time for Jove to prove all the stories true and descend from the heavens, so beautiful is the bride'. Parallels for the use of this topos of amatory poetry in Hellenistic times are given ad 217–18. A comparable appeal to the veracity of *fama* in similar narratives of divine passion as a means of strengthening one's argument can be found in Orpheus' plea for the release of Eurydice in Ov. *Met.* 10.28 *famaque si ueteris non est mentita rapinae* (of Persephone's abduction, which asserts the sway of Love even among the gods of the Underworld).

764 pressisse sinum No precise parallels can be found for this sequence, virtually a euphemistic substitute for *Ledam compressisse*: *premo* is often used in erotic contexts to describe the contact of two lovers' bodies: cf. *TLL* x.2, s.v., 1170.26–39 (*premere aliquem, papillas, pectora*): cf. Ov. *Am.* 1.4.35 *nec premat impositis sinito tua colla lacertis*; 1.5.20; 1.5.24 *nudam* (sc. *Corinnam*) *pressi corpus ad usque meum*.

The allusion is to the legend according to which Jupiter, having fallen in love with Leda, took the shape of a swan and pretended to seek shelter in her bosom to escape from a pursuing eagle. The myth, in this form, is post-classical (the earliest literary attestations are in Eur. *Hel.* 16–22; 1145–6 πτανὸς γὰρ ἐν κόλποις σε Λή- | δας ἐτέκνωσε πατήρ, *I.A.* 794–800; *Or.* 1385: cf. *RE* xii.1 (1924), 1116–25, esp. 1119). The scene became very popular in Hellenistic and Roman art, where the encounter of Leda and the swan is often figured in very suggestive postures (cf. *LIMC* VI.1.239–46, esp. nn. 109–35, where a reclining Leda is covered by a swan of quasi-human size, which presses himself against her body).

764–768 (quem modo Ledae pressisse sinum | . . . ferunt, | modo per fluctus . . . Europen | taurum tergo portasse trucem), | quae regit et nunc deseret astra Gods often descend from heaven in order to woo a woman whom they have had a chance to admire from above. This use of *modo . . . modo*, to introduce a list of events that have happened only once, would appear anomalous, because the two correlatives normally designate repeated action, not, as here, 'once . . . another time' (cf. also my note at 205–7): cf. Ov. *Her.* 16.257–8 *et modo cantabam . . . et modo . . . signa. . . . dabam.*

Cf. also, for 765 *tectum plumis pennisque*, Ov. *Her.* 17.46 *pluma tectus adulter erat*; *Am.* 1.10.3 *plumis abditus albis.*

The particular selection of examples of women loved by Jove may derive from Ov. *Am.* 1.10.1 ff., where the poet praises the beauty of his beloved, likening her appearance on a particular occasion to that of the women pursued by the king of the gods: *qualis ab Eurota Phrygiis auecta carinis . . . , qualis erat Lede quam plumis abditus albis | callidus in falsa lusit adulter aue . . . talis eras aquilamque in te taurumque timebam, | et quidquid magno de Ioue fecit amor.* For similar compliments, compare Prop. 1.13.29–32 *nec mirum cum sit Ioue digna et proxima Ledae, | et Ledae partu gratior . . . illa suis uerbis cogat amare Iouem*; 2.2.13–4.

768 quae regit et nunc deseret astra This enclosing word-order (with the relative pronoun preceding its antecedent) occurs with particular frequency with interrogative and relative pronouns and is especially common in poetry: cf. e.g. Ov. *Met.* 1.731 *quos potuit solos, tollens ad sidera uultus*; 2.149 *quae tutus spectes sine me dare lumina terris* (other examples in E. B. Stevens, *CW* 46 (1953), 204). It seems preferable to take *et nunc* with *deseret*, since the point is not that Jupiter is still supreme ruler of the universe, but that he will want to descend on earth 'even now', so high soars the glamour of Poppaea. Cf. Ps.-Quint. *Decl.* 15.8 = 283.22 (*furor*) *qui, si credimus, numina quoque detracta sideribus misit in terram.*

769 petet amplexus, Poppaea, tuos Cf. Ov. *Her.* 16.268 *dum petit amplexus, Deianira, tuos.* This pattern of poetic word order, comprising a plural noun, a vocative, and a possessive according with the earlier noun, usually at line-end, is particularly common in Ovid: cf. also *Am.* 2.8.22; 3.2.16; *Her.* 9.50; *Rem.* 100; *Met.* 10.85; 15.731; *Fasti* 2.598; 2.794; 3.90. In the Senecan corpus cf. *H.O.* 583 (*an.*) *flemus casus, Oenei, tuos*; *Med.* 814; *Phae.* 72. See also Introd, p. 48.

770 quos et Ledae praeferre potest Cf., for a similar elliptical construction, Ov. *Met.* 11.155 *ausus Apollineos prae se contemnere cantus.* The sense of the line is 'Poppaea, whose embrace well may Jove, too, prefer to Leda's'. For *praefero* used to describe women engaged in a contest of beauty cf. Ov.

Met. 7.42 *si facere hoc aliamue potest praeponere nobis*; 7.801 *nec Iouis illa meo thalamos praeferret amori*; 11.321–2 *quae se praeferre Dianae* | *sustinuit*; 11.581. The occurrence of *possum* in the present indicative in 771 is in imitation of a typically Ovidian mannerism, slightly out of context here. In Ovid *potest* for 'may well' occurs when a boy's or girl's beauty is being referred to with an innuendo, by a suitor paying it an apparently shy compliment (attempting the first steps of courtship): cf. Ov. *Her.* 16(17).93–4 *est quoque confiteor facies tibi rara, potestque* | *uelle sub amplexus ire puella tuos*; 15.86 (*ES*) *anni, quos uir amare potest*; *Met.* 7.27 *quem non . . . ore mouere potest?*: 10.614 *nec forma tangor (poteram tamen hac quoque tangi)*; 10.621–2 *tibi nubere nulla* | *nolet et optari potes a sapiente puella*; Stat. *Silu.* 3.4.42–3 *te caerula Nais* | *mallet.*

771–772 et tibi, quondam cui miranti . . . Danae The apostrophe is a common stylistic device for varying a catalogue. The amazement of Danae at the sight of golden rain falling into her womb must also have been a topos. Stupor and amazement are a common reaction when a process of metamorphosis takes place: Ov. *Met.* 2.858 *miratur Agenore nata*; *Ciris* 81 *mirata nouos expalluit artus.* The passage is perhaps reminiscent of Stat. *Silu.* 1.2.207–8 *miratur dulcia Nais* | *oscula nec credit pelago uenisse maritum*, where the metamorphosis is that of a lover, Alpheus, reaching his beloved in the shape of a water current.

772 fuluo . . . fluxit in auro *fuluus* is a common, if somewhat predictable, epithet in descriptions of gold, although here it aptly signifies Danae's amazement at the sight of the golden sheen. Comparison with Ov. *Met.* 4.611 *pluuio Danae conceperat auro* might suggest the metrically and palaeographically convenient *pluuio fluxit in auro*, providing the information, otherwise missing from this context, that Iuppiter descended into Danae's womb in the shape of golden rain. Observe, however, that this notion is in part conveyed by *fluxit.*

The use of *in* (*in auro*) for *tectus, uestitus* is illustrated in *TLL* vii.1 s.v. *in*, 770.9–27, e.g. Cic. *Catil.* 2.4 *quem amare in praetexta (= praetextatus) coeperat*; Verg. *Aen.* 11.779 *captiuo siue ut se ferret in auro*: cf. also note ad 207 *aureus idem fluxit in imbri.* Other passages where reference to the myth of Danae can be found in similar terms in Latin are Ter. *Eun.* 585 *quo pacto Danaae misisse aiunt quondam in gremium imbrem aureum*; [Verg.] *Lydia*, 25–6 *si fabula non uana est, tauro Ioue digna uel auro* (as a compliment addressed to the poet's *puella*, which seems to echo Prop. 1.13 quoted *supra*, ad 764–8); Stat. *Silu.* 1.2.136 *in hanc uero cecidisset Iuppiter auro*, where *uero* is suspected by some editors; Tiberian. 2.7 (cf. E. Baehrens, *Poetae Latini Minores* (Lipsiae, 1879–83), iii, 265) *in gremium Danaes . . . auro fluxit adulter*; Sid. Apoll. *Carm.* 15.178 *hic alio stillabat Iuppiter auro.*

773–774 formam Sparte iactet alumnae | licet, et Phrygius praemia pastor The omission of names when allusion is being made to exceedingly famous mythological characters is a feature of learned poetry, and Paris is *pastor*, with or without *Phrygius*, by virtue of the figure antonomasia, in several passages of Latin poetry: for *pastor* alone cf. N-H ad Hor. *Carm.* 1.15.1;

also Verg. *Aen.* 7.363 *an non sic Phrygius penetrat Lacedaemona pastor?*; Stat. *Silu.* 1.2.43–4 *nec si Dardania pastor temerarius Ida | sedisses, haec dona forent*; 1.2.213–14 *Amyclaeis minus exultauit harenis | pastor ad Idaeas Helena ueniente carinas.*

For *iactet* of a country being much acclaimed for a given mythical episode or character issuing from there that gave glory to it cf. Stat. *Silu.* 1.3.27–8 *Sestiacos nunc fama sinus . . . iactet*; Curt. Ruf. *Hist. Alex.* 4.7.8 *haec Aegyptii uero maiora iactabant*; Claud. *Carm.* 8.134; 26.331 (*Rhaetia silua*) *se Danuuii iactat Rhenique parentem.* In combination with *alumnus*, the child of a given country that has brought glory to it, cf. Verg. *Aen.* 6.876–7 *nec Romula quondam | ullo se tantum tellus iactabit alumno* (more parallels in *TLL* i. s.v. *alumnus*, 1796.52–83; 1798.17–26, esp. Stat. *Silu.* 1.2.263 *pulchra tumeat Sebethos alumna*, also in the epithalamium of Violentilla; *Silu.* 4.3.13–16 *illa licet sacrae placeat sibi nube rapinae . . . at tu grata deis pulchroque insignis alumno*; *Ach.* 1.402 *progeniem caeli Spartaeque potentis alumnam*).

For the use of metaphorical *praemia* in an erotic context, meaning the reward one wins after amatory labours or for passing a trial, and usually with reference to a girl or woman, cf. Ov. *Met.* 4.757–8 *tanti praemia facti | indotata rapit* (of Perseus); 8.850–1 *qui raptae praemia . . . uirginitatis habes*; more specifically with reference to Paris cf. Ov. *Ars* 1.683 *iam dea laudatae dederat mala praemia formae*; Stat. *Ach.* 2.58–9 *petit exitialia iudex | praemia.*

775 uincet uultus haec Tyndaridos Cf. Prop. 2.2.13 *cedite iam diuae quas pastor uiderat olim*; Sen. *Med.* 82–4 *si forma uelit aspici | cedet Aesonio duci | proles fulminis improbi* . . . But comparison with gods may be a stock theme in wedding songs. Cf. also the praises of Violentilla in Stat. *Silu.* 1.2; Sid. Apoll. *Carm.* 11.79–80 (Venus speaking) (*si iudicio*) *forsan mihi quarta fuisset, me quoque . . . damnasset pastor in Ida.*

For the Greek genitive *Tyndaridos* cf. N-W, 1[3]. 452.

778–779 sed quis gressu ruit attonito | aut quid portat pectore anhelo All editors since Peiper–Richter have adopted L. Mueller's emendation of the transmitted *aut quid pectore portat anhelo* (*DRM* 104, already proposed by Ascensius): dactyls are not found in the corpus at the end of an anapaestic metron. On this line and the questions of anapaestic colometry in this play, cf. Introd. pp. 45–64.

The synaloephe which enters the text if Mueller's correction is accepted can be paralleled by *Oct.* 916 *reddere aedon*; *Phae.* 32·, 1147; *Agam.* 366 *nescia aratri*; *H.O.* 671. B. Schmidt's *aut pectore quid portat anhelo* (1860, 66) should perhaps be preferred to Mueller's solution, since it gives a better explanation for the scribal error (normalization of word-order) and makes it possible to retain the hyperbaton *pectore . . . anhelo.*

Choral announcements of a new character's arrival (not implying actual dialogic engagement with the character) were identified by J. G. Fitch (*AJPh* 102 (1981), 306: cf. Introd. p. 39) as a compositional element characteristically found in the (in his view) earliest plays of the corpus, namely at *Agam.* 778; *Phae.*

358, 829, 989; *Oed.* 911, 995, 1004) (one more instance in *Hf.* 202, which Fitch assigns to group 2). It was perhaps meant to provide the plays with a unifying element countering the tendency towards greater isolation of individual scenes, as well as to imitate choral entrance announcements in Greek tragedy. This is, at any rate, the only case of an entrance announcement by the chorus in this play. The closest parallels in the Senecan corpus for an exchange between the chorus and a Messenger (with no entrance announcement of the latter) are *Thy.* 623; *Med.* 879; at *Oed.* 911 the chorus only announces the Messenger without engaging him in an exchange of questions and answers. Cf. also *Phae.* 989–90 *sed quid citato nuntius portat gradu | rigatque maestis lugubrem uultum genis?*

Richter's *ecquid* for *aut quid*, though attractive, is unnecessary (cf. *supra*, ad 544). The sequence of the two interrogative parallel cola linked by a disjunctive particle *sed quis . . . aut quid* is psychologically plausible, expressing a progressive sharpening of focus as the speaker moves towards the more crucial point: '. . . or, more importantly, what terrible news is going to be announced?' In Senecan tragedy, even characters impatient to receive an answer cannot help giving their question the rhetorical shape of dicolon or tricolon: cf. *Med.* 959–61 *quem quaerit* (sc. *turba Furiarum*) *aut quo flammeos ictus parat | aut cui cruentas agmen infernum faces | intentat?*

780 A messenger enters, calling the guard to arms. He is running to Nero, to announce the sedition of the Roman people in support of Octavia and the measures taken by the prefect to contain and suppress the riots. On his way to Nero, the messenger comes across the chorus of Poppaea's partisans, to whom he delivers his news before leaving to complete his mission to Nero. Scenes involving messenger-speeches are often highly artificial in tragedy: the author of *Octavia* attempts to create more natural circumstances for the dialogue between the messenger and the chorus by imagining the *Nuntius* to have been sent to Nero by the commanders of the pretorian guard. Even in this form, the device is a typical feature of the stylization of Greek tragedy, where messengers and heralds often stop on their way to inform a chorus even when they have been charged with bringing an announcement to their ruler. The function of this is to create an atmosphere of expectation and fear, and to justify the chorus' (and audience's) cognizance of the new developments of the plot. Cf. Eur. *Hipp.* 1153–5, where the messenger enters running and asks the chorus about Theseus, who then appears. In Eur. *Ion* 1106, the *therapōn* comes in running in search of Creusa. He comes to warn his mistress that her plot has been foiled and that she must run for safety, but this is only an excuse to introduce a lengthy narrative of the attempted poisoning of Ion. The *therapōn* presumably leaves to complete his mission during the following astrophic song by the chorus. Cf. also Eur. *I.T.* 1284–1306, where the Messenger has come to inform Thoas of the Greeks' flight, and the chorus tries to convince him that Thoas is not inside (in fact Thoas appears soon afterwards, 1307). In Soph.

Ant. 376–87, the guard bringing on Antigone is addressed by the chorus before Creon comes out of the palace. In Soph. *Ai.* 719–83 the messenger has been dispatched by Teucros to warn Ajax that he should confine himself to his tent, but he encounters his sailors first. Seneca, however, in his dramas containing *Botenberichte*, is not noticeably concerned with artificiality or finding plausible motivations. In *Thy.* 623 and *Oed.* 911 no pragmatic and situational context is invented for the announcement of the messenger to the chorus.

Outside tragedy, a comparable scene can be adduced from the *Acta Appiani*, where an *euocatus*, an officer of the imperial guard, runs to announce to the emperor (presumably Commodus) the impending uprising of the Roman people in support of Appianus, who is being led to his place of execution: cf. P.Oxy. 33, col. iii. ll. 11–14, col. iv. ll. 1–2 (= *The Acts of the Pagan Martyrs*, ed. by H. A. Musurillo (Oxford, 1954), 67) ὁ ἠβοκᾶτος εὐθὺς δραμὼν παρέθετο τῶι κυρίωι λέγων· κύριε, κάθηι; ʽΡωμαῖοι γονγύζουσι. αὐτοκράτωρ· περὶ τίνος; ὁ ὕπατος· περὶ τῆς ἀπάξεως τοῦ Ἀλεξανδρέως· αὐτοκράτωρ· μεταπεμφθήτω. The dialogue, in dramatic form, has been shown to have originated from the activities of anti-Roman opposition circles in Alexandria. There are overall similarities with *Octavia* in inspiration, in that both the *Acta* and the play (both in dramatic/dialogic form, though the *praetexta* is more evidently couched in the tradition of theatrical writing) depict their characters as the victims of impious and despicable emperors. Another similar story-pattern can be identified in Prud. *Peristeph.* 10, in iambics, where Romanus, who has been defended in vain by his fellow Christians against the soldiery of Galerius, is brought before a villainous prefect, who tortures him. At ll. 61–3 a military man runs to announce to his commander that the Christians are essaying a fierce resistance: *refert repulsus miles ad subsellia | plebis rebellis esse Romanum ducem, | flagrare cunctos peruicaci audacia.*

In both Greek and Senecan tragedy elaborate messenger-speeches are typically inserted between choral odes. In the present passage, however, the comparative brevity and compression of the messenger's announcement deviates from normal Senecan practice.

780–781 quicumque tectis excubat miles ducis | defendat aulam, cui furor populi imminet The messenger's 'alarum' recalls the words of Jason summoning the people of Corinth at *Med.* 978–9 *quicumque regum cladibus fidus doles, | concurre.* The transmitted reading *miles exultat* was questioned by several editors (the only exception of note being Giardina), and Raphelengius' *excubat* has attracted a very large consent. The verb is a technical term, designating the manning of a position by soldiers, but gives an idiom not foreign to the language of the poets: cf. Verg. *Aen.* 9.174–5 *omnis per muros legio, sortita periclum, | excubat*; in prose, cf. Tac. *Hist.* 1.29 *cohortis quae in Palatio stationem agebat*; *Ann.* 12.69 *(cohors), quae more militiae excubiis adest.* The actual text as established by Raphelengius read *miles excubat*, which was altered by Bothe, since it entailed a short element in the fifth thesis, in defiance of both norms regulating the final elements of an iambic trimeter or senarius, the 'law' of Bentley-Luchs (prescribing that the two elements preceding a final word of iambic quantity cannot be realized by an iambic sequence) and that of Lange-Strzelecki (according to which Seneca allows an iamb in the fifth foot only with words of biiambic quantity e.g. *nepotibus*; cf. Strzelecki 27, Mueller, *DRM* 161). *excubat* is palaeographically convincing, as well as satisfactory in sense: it provides a good complement for the local ablative *tectis* ('those who mount the guard at the palace') and may yield a clue to the imagined hour of the dramatic action ('the night watch', though *excubiae* is often used of day watches as well). There is something to be said for *exultat*, which would refer to the soldiers' celebrations (especially if they are the singers of the epithalamium song at 762) following the royal marriage, highlighting the contrast with the impending threat (so Gruterus: 'tacite taxat satellitum naturam'). It may thus serve to identify the second chorus of the play. It is true, however, that the verb *exulto* is often used to suggest excess and lack of restraint (cf. *infra* ad 834–5 *exultat . . . corrupta turba*), and a speaker summoning a band of inebriated soldiers to face the impending peril might be expected to moralize a little more on the inopportuneness of revels at this time. Also, the generalizing *quicumque* speaks in favour of *excubat*.

782–783 trepidi cohortes ecce praefecti trahunt | praesidia ad urbis Cf. Tarrant ad Sen. *Agam.* 917 *amici . . . praesidia*. The word *praefectus* designated various military and civil positions during the Empire. In the city of Rome, military units commanded by *praefecti* included the pretorians (which had two *praefecti praetorio* jointly in charge at this time), the urban cohorts (under the *praefectus urbi*), and the *uigiles* (cf. also Kragelund, *CQ* 38 (1998), 500). The word *cohortes* might in fact indicate all these units (pretorians and urban cohorts especially, all lodged in the *castra praetoria*), although *praefecti* is more likely to refer to the pretorian commanders.

785 quis iste mentes agitat attonitus furor? Cf. *Phae.* 1156 *quis te dolore percitam instigat furor?*; *Agam.* 913 *quis iste celeres concitus currus agit?*; Verg. *Aen.* 5.670 *quis furor iste nouus . . .*

786–787 Octauiae fauore percussa agmina | et efferata The MSS have *Octauiae furore percussa* ('overcome by a madness inspired by their support for Octavia'), but the reading *furore* was rightly questioned by Grotius, who proposed *fauore*. The idiom *furor* with an objective genitive is awkward in this context, where it is not a question of immoderate desires or sexual appetites (cf. Sen. *Phae.* 540 *impius lucri furor*; Hor. *Serm.* 2.3.325 *mille puellarum, puerorum mille furores*). In addition, the repetition of *furor/furore* at 785 and 786 is also undesirable, whereas the sequence *fauor/furor* occurs at 792–3 (as observed by Zwierlein) *hinc urit animos pertinax nimium fauor, | et in furorem temere praecipites agit*. *Octauiae fauore*, though not impeccable in conjunction with *percussa . . . et* *efferata* (the second participle especially suggesting a more violent emotion than *fauor*: cf. Liv. 5.27.10 *efferati odio iraque*; Petr. *Sat.* 94.9 *ex dolore in rabiem efferatus*), is certainly an improvement, and is confirmed by *Oct.* 467 *absentium cum maneat etiam ingens fauor*. The word designates political allegiance, as in Luc. *Bell. Ciu.* 9.228–9 *partesque fauore* (sc. *Pompei*, 227) | *fecimus*; Tac. *Hist.* 2.85 (*legiones*) *imbutae fauore Othonis*. *fauore percussa* may reflect the idiom commonly found as *amore p.*: cf. Hor. *Epod.* 11.2 *amore percussum graui* (with Mankin ad loc.); Verg. *Georg.* 2.476 *ingenti percussus amore*; Stat. *Theb.* 4.260 *Martis percussus amore*. Avantius' *perculsa* was intended to match the stronger *furore*. On confusion between *percussus* and *perculsus* cf. Housman's note ad Luc. *Bell. Ciu.* 6.595 (596 in his numeration) *mens dubiis percussa pauet* (*percuss-* is better with *amor*/*terror*). Bothe suggested a more extensive rewriting of the whole sequence:

Octauiae furore perculsae agmina
nunc efferata per nefas ingens ruunt

('the populace, seized by fury on behalf of the repudiated Octavia . . .'), which is ingenious, and an improvement in some ways, but entails too many changes. Moreover, there are no parallels in *TLL* x.1, s.v. *percello* in support of this use of *perculsa* for *repulsa*, with reference to marriage. The parallels given above make it clear that *percussa* must be linked to the sentiment from which the upheaval is said to be originating.

The rhythm is made very lame by the proper name *Octauiae* occupying two entire feet, and entailing an unidiomatic caesura after the fourth element. For *agmina* of a crowd of people (as opposed to a military formation) cf. also e.g. Verg. *Aen.* 2.68 *Phrygia agmina circumspexit*; Stat. *Theb.* 6.254 *fremuerunt agmina circo*; Juv. 3.244 *magno populus premit agmine lumbos*.

787 per nefas ingens ruunt *fas* appears never to be used with reference to a specific incident or action, and simply designates 'what is holy'; it is therefore found in prepositional constructions or with an adjective (expressions like *contra*, *ultra fas* meaning 'against all that is holy'). *nefas*, however, can be used with reference to a specific action or incident, and amounts to a synonym of *scelus*, *facinus* (cf. Verg. *Aen.* 6.624 *ausi omnes immane nefas*; Ov. *Met.* 7.425–8 *at genitor . . . attonitus . . . est ingens discrimine paruo* | *committi potuisse nefas*). Accordingly, it is found after a preposition, even with this individualizing meaning (cf. Ov. *Met.* 6.613 *in omne nefas ego me, germana, paraui*).

For *per . . . nefas ruere* cf. Hor. *Carm.* 1.3.25–6 *audax omnia perpeti* | *gens humana ruit per uetitum nefas*; Luc. *Bell. Ciu.* 5.312–13 *per omne* | *fasque nefasque rues?* Prud. *Peristeph.* 10.515 *carnis uoluptas omne per nefas ruit*; id. *Cathem.* 11.93 *quid prona per scelus ruis?* Similar also is Liv. 6.14.10 *ut per omne fas ac nefas secuturi uindicem . . . uiderentur*.

788 quid ausa facere quoue consilio doce There are no parallels in Senecan tragedy for this use of the imperative of *doceo* when a chorus or a speaking character interrogates a messenger (*Hf.* 657 *fare casus horridos*; 760 *ede*; *Thy.* 633 *effare*, 639 *ede*). This mode of expression has parallels, however, in epic poetry: cf. Luc. *Bell. Ciu.* 1.681–2 (a matron prophesying the horror of the civil wars) *quis furor hic, o Phoebe, doce, quo tela manusque | Romanae miscent acies*; also in Stat. *Theb.* 4.659–65; Verg. *Aen.* 1.332; Val. Fl. *Arg.* 2.469.

The pattern of question and answer in messenger-scenes is always very abrupt in Senecan drama, especially when the chorus is involved, and questions only provide the excuse for lengthy descriptive sections, as often also in Greek tragedy.

789–790 reddere penates Claudiae Diui parant | torosque fratris, debitam partem imperi Ritter's *diri* is preferred by Zwierlein to the transmitted *diui*. Similarly Peiper (1863, 40) wanted to emend *diui* to *ciues*. The interlaced word-pattern *penates Claudiae Diui* is paralleled by 941 *thalamis Liuia Drusi*. The absence of a subject is not sufficient ground for emending, since the line is unambiguous and a subject can easily be supplied from 788. In much the same way, the verb *parant* is without a subject at 801 *saepire flammis principis sedem parant*. *diui* occurs without an accompanying noun in fixed (formulaic) phrasal contexts, such as *diui f.*, and patronymic expressions: cf. *Oct.* 534 *generata Diuo*; Verg. *Aen.* 6.792 *diui genus*. In a different context cf. *Acta fratrum Arualium* (AD 145) Henzen, p. clxxii. 5 *in Palatio in (aede) diuorum*. *penates*, on the other hand, must be clarified by an adjective or a noun in the genitive (cf. *infra*, 803 *reddat penates Claudiae uictus suos*): here we expect to find a reference to Octavia's own heritage, her father's house; cf. *supra* 665 *patrios . . . penates*; 803 *reddat penates Claudiae . . . suos*; Tac. *Hist.* 3.86 *paternos penates*. Note also, against *diri*, that a masculine subject is not, strictly speaking, correct, since at 788 the chorus still thinks of *agmina* as the subject (*quid ausa facere*). If emendation is deemed inevitable, it would perhaps be preferable to emend *parant* to *patris* (cf. *supra* 586 *merita . . . diui patris*).

The line presents an initial dactyl, a pattern relatively infrequent in Senecan trimeters (cf. Strzelecki 1938, 71).

790 debitam partem imperi This asyndetic addition to *penates . . . diui . . . torosque fratris* has the function of an explanatory apposition. Burrus once retorted to Nero that, if he wanted to repudiate his wife, he should return also 'her dowry' (Cass. Dio *Hist. Rom.* 62.13), by which he meant the imperial dignity. The words *pars imperi* (the usual form of the genitive up to Cicero, here preferred for metrical reasons) show that in *Octavia* a patrimonial conception of power at Rome has established itself (in the words of Tacitus, *unius familiae possessio*). Octavia, being the legitimate daughter of the previous ruler, is entitled to have a share of her father's 'estate'.

791 quos iam tenet Poppaea concordi fide? Liberman (p. 118) assigns this line to the *Nuntius*, because in his view the chorus is already acquainted with this piece of information (he quotes 673, which in fact was pronounced by a different chorus). It is preferable to give the line to the chorus, with the MSS and the consensus of all previous editors. The question of the chorus is, of course, rhetorical and indignant; moreover, 792 would lose point if it were not conceived as an emphatic answer.

For *(thalamos) tenere* cf. Ov. *Met.* 9.146 (Deianira speaking) *dum licet et nondum thalamos tenet altera nostros.*

792 hinc urit animos pertinax nimium fauor M. Müller's correction (1911, 138) of the transmitted *hic* is certainly right. For this use of *hinc*, even without a verb, to indicate the origin, often psychological or emotional, of a given state, cf. *TLL*, vi, s.v., 2798.7–44; *ibid.* 2799.34–54, e.g. Tib. 2.3.38 *hinc cruor, hinc caedes . . . uenit;* Cic. *Flacc.* 54 *hinc totum odium, hinc omnis offensio*; Stat. *Theb.* 1.302 *hinc causae irarum*; other parallels are adduced by Zwierlein, *KK* ad 837 *inquieta rapitur hinc audacia* (*H.O.* 1886; *Thy.* 236; *Oct.* 143).

A certain choice between the two competing readings *fauor/furor* remains difficult. However, the presence of *furorem* in the following line seems a pretty strong argument against *furor*: the author would be saying that the people are incensed by madness driving them to rush headlong into madness – a tautological thought certainly not acceptable in this form here. *Oct.* 465–6 *pertinax quorum furor*, referring to the madness, in Nero's view, of his opponents, is not a decisive parallel supporting *furor. pertinax* goes equally well with either reading, but *nimium* seems to support *fauor*, the reading of ***A***: sympathy for Octavia is not altogether blameworthy in the eyes of the messenger, but he must concede that popular attachment has ultimately degenerated into an obstinate opposition. For *pertinax* with nouns indicating a passion not negative in itself, but taken to excess, cf. Sen. *Cons. Marc.* 8.2 *tristitia . . . pertinax et obstinata; H.O.* 1854–5 *pertinax si quas* (sc. *matres*) *dolor | adhuc iubet lugere.* With reference to the allegiance of a subject to a former ruler cf. Tac. *Hist.* 1.51 *pertinaci pro Nerone fide.*

794–797 quaecumque claro marmore effigies stetit | aut aere fulgens, ora Poppaeae gerens, | afflicta uulgi manibus et saeuo iacet | euersa ferro Notice the homoeoteleuton *fulgens . . . gerens*: this phenomenon is more frequent in anapaests, where Seneca also allows it more often.

In 796–800 five initial participles with the same ending follow one another: *afflicta . . . euersa . . . diducta . . . calcata . . . immixta*, a sign of the author's limited rhetorical inventiveness.

797–798 membra per partes trahunt | diducta laqueis 'The dismembered (*diducta*) limbs they drag away in different directions (*per partes*) with ropes': this is how in my view the passage should be interpreted, accepting the reading of the older MSS, against *deducta*, printed in the text by Leo, which he must have taken to mean 'pulled down'. *deduco* is not a verb commonly found in the numerous passages describing the overturning of statues and honorific insignia (cf. by contrast Plin. *Pan.* 52.4 *iuuabat illidere solo superbissimos uultus*; Tac. *Ann.* 3.14 *effigiesque Pisonis traxerant in Gemonias ac diuellebant*; Suet. *Iul.* 75 *statuas . . . disiectas reposuit*; id. *Nero* 24 *subuerti et unco trahi abicique in latrinas omnium statuas et imagines imperauit*; *Dom.* 23 (*senatus iussit*) *clipeos . . . et imagines eius coram detrahi et ibidem solo affligi*) and the examples collected in the lexica seem to indicate a sense closer to 'lower' than 'to topple, smash to the ground'. This comes perhaps as an anticlimax after *afflicta uulgi manibus et saeuo iacet* | *euersa ferro. diduco* seems to satisfy the requirements of sense better (Flinck 1919, 73 quotes Arnob. *Nat.* 6.16 *utinam liceret . . . Capitolinos Ioues diducere in membra resolutos*, which is, however, conjectural for the transmitted *deducere*). *per partes* is probably directional ('in all directions'), and defines the meaning of *trahunt* rather than that of *diducta* ('pull to pieces'), where *in partes* would have been expected as the more idiomatic prepositional construct: so regularly with *discido, caedo, findo, diuido, seco*: cf. *TLL* x.1 s.v. *pars*, 450.4–30, the only exception being Hier. *Epist.* 61.4.3 *praecidendam linguam ac per partes et frusta lacerandam* (in *OLD* 8b Man. *Astr.* 3.405 *per tris id diuide partes*, where *per* is in my view distributive, 'by three'). Ropes (*laquei*, to be linked with *trahunt*) are the means used to pull down the statue as well as drag the dismembered limbs once on the ground (as in Juvenal's sarcastic *descendunt statuae restemque secuntur*, 10.58). A reminiscence is called up of *Thy.* 60–1 *membra per partes eant* | *discerpta* (visualizing the dismemberment of the bodies of Thyestes' sons), where *per partes* is an expressionistic detail to be explained by the occurrence of a verb of movement. On the literary evidence for the various forms of *damnatio*, ranging from the overturning of statues, to the destruction of images and the erasure of honorary *tituli*, cf. Friedländer, III.243, 253; Mayor ad Juv. 10.58; Yavetz (1969), 27. Kragelund (1998), 152 n. 3 is especially good on the archaeological evidence.

799–800 uerba conueniunt feris | immixta factis Unspeakable taunts and words of abuse worsen the citizens' crime: cf. Ov. *Met.* 6.210–11 *diro conuicia facto* | *Tantalis adiecit*; 14.522 *addidit obscenis conuicia rustica dictis*; 14.714–15 *factisque immitibus addit* | *uerba superba ferox*; in Seneca cf. *Med.* 737–8 *addit uenenis uerba non illis minus* | *metuenda* (Segurado). Cf. also *infra*, ad 855.

800 quae timor reticet meus The transmitted *recipit* yields no sense, despite Gruterus' attempt to read it as a juridical term (he adduced Gell. *Noct. Att.* 5.10.7 *causas tamen non reciperet*: 'he kept refusing to take up any cases in court', as an advocate, and Plaut. *Trin.* 194 *posticulum hoc recepit quom aedis uendidit* 'to except from the sale', *OLD* s.v. 15), meaning *silere*. A similar error in ***A*** occurred at *Hf.* 571 *Eurydicen dum recipit suam*, for ***E***'s *repetit*. Lipsius ingeniously suggested interpreting these words as a horrified comment expressed by the chorus: *quae timor recipit meus?* but Delrius' *reticet* is very convincing. A similar comment in Liv. 9.34.19 *quod ominari etiam reformidat animus*. RJT has suggested *pudor* in place of *timor*: '[the Nuntius'] fear might be understandable if he were reporting to Nero, but the chorus is hardly likely to punish him for speaking'.

802–803 populi nisi irae coniugem reddat nouam, | reddat penates Claudiae uictus suos The repetition of *reddo* in two different senses (Octavia is to be reinstated in her legitimate rank, while Poppaea is to be 'handed over' to the people's anger), as well as the comparative rarity of *reddo* for 'to hand over', has appeared corrupt to many scholars: amongst the many proposed solutions are *dedat* (Grotius); *cedat* (Baehrens); *tradat* (Gruterus). All of these proposals replace *reddo* with verbs apparently more idiomatic in descriptions of an angry mob demanding an execution (cf. Luke 13.25 *Iesum uero tradidit uoluntati eorum*; Ps.-Quint. *Decl. min.* 253. pr. (p. 35.30 Ritt.) (*tyrannus*) *bellum minatus est nisi darent. fert ipse* (*sc. tyrannicida*) *rogationem ut dedatur.* In fact there is no ground for emendation, and repetition of *reddo* can be defended as an instance of the figure *syllepsis*, particularly frequent in Ovid and in the Senecan corpus: cf. Sen. *Agam.* 987 *fratrem reddat aut animam statim.* Since the basic meaning of *reddo* is 'to return', the sense 'to hand over, to deliver [to a just punishment]' must originate from the idea that the culprit, in receiving his well-deserved punishment, is being returned to what was his due from the instant when the crime was committed. In *OLD*, this sense of *reddo* is insufficiently illustrated (only of the false Nero in Suet. *Nero*, 57): add Plin. *Epist.* 10.31.3 *reddere poenae post longum tempus . . . nimis seuerum arbitrabar* (where however *reddo* is more acceptable, because Pliny has in mind people whose sentences were never carried out); Apul. *Met.* 7.26 *deductus ad magistratus . . . ut poenae redderetur.*

The rebels demand that the emperor surrender his new bride to their wrath, which implies their intention to dispose of her in a violent way. There are few or no examples of such popular insurrections against a member of the imperial family in the historical period covered by Tacitus' works, but in Tac. *Ann.* 3.14.4, on the occasion of the Piso trial, the people surround the Curia, with the intention of lynching Piso if he is acquitted: *simul populi ante curiam uoces audiebantur: non temperaturos manibus si patrum sententias euasisset. effigiesque Pisonis traxerant in Gemonias ac diuellebant, ni iussu principis protectae repositaeque forent.* This practice has parallels in later rather than in earlier imperial history. In Herodian 1. 12.6 riots erupt with the aim of having Cleander, Commodus' favourite and all-powerful freedman, put to death, on account of food-shortages for which his greed is held responsible: (the Roman people rush to Commodus' suburban residence) ἐπελθόντες πανδημεὶ ἐβόων καὶ τὸν Κλέανδρον ἐς θάνατον ᾔτουν . . .

806 In Greek tragedy, an astrophic song by the chorus often follows a messenger speech. Such choral odes convey surprise, astonishment and despair at the news that has been delivered, and at the same time create the necessary interval before the next entrance of a major character.

Although this ode is delivered by the same chorus who sang the praises of Poppaea at 762 ff., now, in addressing the rebellious supporters of Octavia, their words are neither fractious nor partisan. The chorus utters conventional expressions of restraint and deprecation of excess, and conveys no animosity towards the opposing faction. Their main theme is the anger of the offended god, Love, who always brought ruin on those who opposed him. The ode envisions the anticipated course of events in a mythological light: Cupid holds sway over Nero and will drive him to obtain bloody satisfaction over his enemies. The ode then expatiates on the ruinous powers of Love. This, though a commonplace, may derive from the choral song at Soph. *Ant.* 780–800, where Love is seen as the cause of the feud between two of the same kin. Along the same lines, Eur. *Hipp.* 525–64 and the fourth stasimon at 1268–81, similarly short. Other parallels can be found in Livrea's note ad Ap. Rhod. *Argon.* 4.445 (see also *infra*, ad 816–17).

806 quid fera frustra bella mouetis? *bella mouere* is common in epic poetry: Verg. *Aen.* 6.820; Enn. *Ann.* 410 V. and cf. Ov. *Am.* 2.6.25 *non tu fera bella mouebas*. Apostrophe to characters absent from the stage is a feature of Senecan choruses, both in abstractly moralizing contexts and in those where reference is made to a precise action. The chorus' typical line is that of advising restraint and submissive behaviour. Cf. *Thy.* 339–40 *quis uos exagitat furor | alternis dare sanguinem?* addressed to a generic set of brother-rivals, who are being contrasted with the pair Atreus-Thyestes on their supposed reconciliation. In Greek tragedy, apostrophes pronounced by the chorus tend to be more integrated in the dramatic action: cf. for instance Eur. *Med.* 1265–7, addressing Medea, who is now inside the house, and attempting to restrain her from killing her children.

808–809 flammis uestros obruet ignes | quis extinxit fulmina saepe 'Cupid (as the inspirer of Nero's fierce passion for Poppaea) will extinguish your fires with his flames, the selfsame flames with which he quashed the thunderbolts [sc. of Jupiter].' This is an instance of the figure *anticlasis* or *antanaclasis* (the same word occurs twice in the same sentence in two different senses, one metaphorical: cf. e.g. Ov. *Her.* 16.232–3 *ebrietas ignis in igne fuit*; *Met.* 11.523 *ardescunt ignibus ignes*: on this figure cf. Rosati, *Narciso e Pigmalione* (Firenze, 1983), 165–7 and n. 132). The words *flammis . . . extinxit fulmina* (an allusion to the many occasions on which Jove was vanquished by the power of Cupido) may owe something to Ov. *Met.* 2.313 *saeuos compescuit ignibus ignes*, where Phaethon is struck by the thunderbolt of Jove; add *Met.* 4.194–5 *nempe tuis omnes qui terras ignibus uris, | ureris igne nouo*, with the same type of word-play *ignibus/igne*. Extensive use of paradoxical metaphors was characteristic of the declamatory rhetoric which held sway in Silver Latin: cf. Sen. *Contr.* 10. *pr.* 9 *mortibus uiuimus*; *Suas.* 1.13 *Charybdis ipsius maris naufragium*; Stat. *Theb.* 1.422–3 *uirum sudoribus ardet | puluis*. More generally on *cacozelia* and on the frequency of conflicting metaphors in Latin poetry cf. Kroll, *Studien*, 264–6.

The sense of *obruo* for 'to smother, to put out (a fire)' (the more normal sense is 'to cover up', 'to inundate') is illustrated in *OLD* s.v. 3c. In most passages where *obruo* occurs in this sense, it seems to imply a less than perfect exstinction of the fire: cf. Lucr. *D.R.N.* 4.926–8 *cinere ut multa latet obrutus ignis . . . ut ex igni caeco consurgere flamma*; and esp. Liv. 10.24.13 *quem ille obrutum ignem reliquerit ita ut totiens nouum ex inprouiso incendium daret, eum se exstincturum.* The flames are, however, put out for good in Sen. *Clem.* 1.25.5 *incendium uastum . . . parte urbis obruitur* and Prud. *Peristeph.* 10.858 *nimbus . . . aquarum flumine ignes obruit.*

The repression of the riots will not involve the use of fire, but the line contains an allusion to the future Fire of Rome in 64 (cf. 831 *mox tecta flammis concidant urbis meis*, where Nero makes plans to take his revenge on the rebels). One may wonder in passing how the chorus knows about it two years in advance. In fact the chorus is unaware of the prophetic sense of these words, and *flammis* is for them only a vague way of describing the inevitable dire consequences. This is an instance of tragic ambiguity (another case can be observed at 752–3), whereby the chorus, or a character, 'speaks in words more truly than they know' (cf. Soph. *O.T.*, where almost all characters are given words pointing to the truth which will be revealed at the end). For other examples of this in Greek tragedy cf. P. E. Easterling, in Easterling, *Companion*, 164.

810 captumque Iouem caelo traxit See note ad 554–6.

811–812 laeso tristes dabitis poenas | sanguine uestro The transmitted reading *laesi*, defended by Carlsson (1926), 65, as a nominative plural, and accepted by Zwierlein, is too weak to describe the punishment awaiting the rebels when Nero's rage is unleashed. This observation is confirmed by the very parallels Carlsson adduces in support of his view, *Phae.* 330–0' *sacer est ignis – credite laesis – | nimiumque potens*; *ibid.* 186–7 *hic uolucer . . . laesum . . . flammis torret indomitis Iouem*, where *laedo* indicates the 'sting' inflicted by the god upon his victims, and implies moral and emotional rather than physical damage. Bothe's *laeso* (in his second edition) is certainly preferable, highlighting the god's own participation in the pursuit of the rebels and his desire for revenge. *laedo* is commonly found in reference to gods who have been offended or disregarded by humans: cf. Ov. *Ars* 2.397 *laesa Venus iusta arma mouet*; Verg. *Aen.* 1.8 *quo numine laeso*; Hor. *Epod.* 15.3; Ov. *Her.* 20.99–100 *nihil est uiolentius illa, | cum sua . . . numina laesa uidet*; *Trist.* 1.5.84 *ni fuerit laesi mollior ira dei*; *Pont.* 1.4.44 *perstiterit laesi si grauis ira dei*; Luc. *Bell. Ciu.* 7.847–8 *quo tanto crimine, tellus, | laesisti superos?*

A less attractive alternative would be to take *laesi* as a genitive indicating the crime committed by the rebels, *laesi* sc. *Amoris*; cf. Cic. *Att.* 11.8.1 *maximas poenas pendo temeritatis meae*; *De orat.* 3.11 *poena temeritatis non sine magno rei publicae malo constituta*; Ov. *Met.* 4.190 *exigit indicii memorem Cythereia poenam.* For the genitive of crime with the set phrase *dare poenas* cf. *TLL* s.v. *do*, 1665.17–22.

813–813ᶜ non est patiens, feruidus, irae | facilisque regi The question which of the two adjectives governs *irae* is perhaps immaterial, and an *apo koinou* construction could be invoked. I prefer, however, to punctuate *non e. patiens, feruidus, irae*, whereby *feruidus* is almost uttered as a parenthetic apposition ('hot-blooded as he is'). *feruidus* means 'impetuous' 'hot-blooded' (often with reference to Cupid: cf. Hor. *Carm.* 1.30.5). *feruidus* with a genitive, indicating the cause of one's impetuosity, is attested (cf. Sil. *Pun.* 17.413 *feruidus ingenii Masinissa et feruidus aeui*) but such genitives represent an internal quality possessed by the subject, rather than a temporary passion. *patiens/impatiens irae* are much more common, even in the corpus. *feruidus*, unlike *patiens*, can stand alone without qualification, and indicates the cause (juvenile impetuosity) whereby Cupid cannot contain his anger: cf. Verg. *Aen.* 12.950–1 *hoc dicens ferrum aduerso sub pectore condit | feruidus*, with the adjective thrown into relief by its position at line-beginning. On such genitives (especially after *felix, miser, audax*) cf. Lejay on Hor. *Serm.* 1.9.11.

facilisque regi: the enclitic *-ue* would have been expected, but *-que* can be found co-ordinating even two negative cola (= *non est patiens nec facilis regi*), although especially in longer enumerative sequences: cf. *TLL* ii, s.v. *aut*, 1571.21–50; *LHS* 2.500, e.g. Luc. *Bell. Ciu.* 2.360–4 *non . . . uelarunt flammea uultus . . . umerisque haerentia primis | suppara.*

814–815 ille ferocem iussit Achillem | pulsare lyram These lines contain a reference to Achilles' self-imposed withdrawal to his tent consequent upon Briseis' abduction; cf. Hom. *Il.* 9.186–9. In Homer, however, Achilles sings out of boredom rather than to console himself for his lost love, and the theme of his songs is brave feats of war. The romanticization of Achilles' character is a post-Homeric feature, of which we have evidence in Ov. *Trist.* 4.1.15–16 *fertur et abducta Lyrneside tristis Achilles | Haemonia curas attenuasse lyra*; Stat. *Silu.* 4.4.35–6 *cantata Briseide uenit Achilles | acrior*, where Briseis is the actual subject of Achilles' song (cf. also Barchiesi's note ad Ov. *Her.* 3.117–18). Sen. *Troad.* 320–1 *segnis iacebat belli et armorum immemor, | leui canoram uerberans plectro chelyn* presupposes the same view, which makes Achilles into an elegiac lover *ante litteram*. Indeed the occurrence of *iussit* in 814 seems to confirm this. The god has not literally 'ordered' Achilles to play the lyre: the hero's musical activities are a way of giving voice to his torment for the abduction of his beloved, and *iussit* echoes the exhortation to compose sentimental poetry which the elegiac poet claims to have heard from the love god: cf. e.g. Prop. 2.13.2–4 *hic* (sc. *Amor*) *me . . . iussit . . . Ascraeum . . . habitare nemus*; Ov. *Am.* 2.1.3 *hoc quoque iussit Amor*; in Seneca cf. *Phae.* 294–5 (*Cupido*) *iubet caelo superos relicto | uultibus falsis habitare terras.*

816–817ᶜ fregit Danaos, fregit Atriden, | regna euertit Priami, claras | diruit urbes The asyndetic style is more acceptable, and more typical, in anapaests (cf. e.g. *supra*, 676–81). Love has already brought ruin to innumerable kingdoms: Soph. *Ant.* 782 ὃς ἐν κτήμασι πίπτεις, Eur. *Hipp.* 542–4; Cat. *Carm.* 51.15–16 *otium et reges prius et beatas | perdidit urbes*, already picked up in Sen. *Phae.* 561 (*stupris*) *fumant tot urbes, bella tot gentes gerunt.* Here *fregit Atriden* refers to Agamemnon's fateful passion for Briseis, which led to so many calamities befalling the Greeks. The plurals in *claras diruit urbes* are rhetorical, since all that is here referred to is Troy's fall (but Oechalia was another stock subject). In a different context cf. Eur. *Or.* 525 ὃ καὶ γῆν καὶ πόλεις ὄλλυσ' ἀεί (not of love).

The Greek form *Atriden* was restored by Housman, *CP* 2.818.

818–819 et nunc animus quid ferat horret | uis immitis uiolenta dei Older editors wondered whether to take *et nunc* with *animus horret* or with *quid ferat* (cf. Daniel Caietanus 'horresco referens'; Ascensius 'scilicet meminisse'). The latter solution is preferable, since the chorus were not present at the mythological events narrated above. The intertwined word-order (*et nunc, animus, quid ferat, horret, uis . . .*) with the interposition of elements from the subordinate clause in the main clause, is one commonly found in Latin poetry. In Luc. cf. *Bell. Ciu.* 5.387–8 *qua* (sc. *aetate*) *sibi ne ferri ius ullum, Caesar, abesset, | Ausonias uoluit gladiis miscere secures.* Nisbet (*ALLP*, 150) has a list of examples: cf. Hor. *Carm.* 3.27.18–19 *ego quis sit ater | Hadriae noui sinus* (main clause and indirect interrogative); in Greek cf. Soph. *O.T.* 1251 χὤπως μὲν ἐκ τῶνδ' οὐκέτ' οἶδ' ἀπόλλυται. In more colloquial forms of written Latin, such as early drama, the order may be different from that expected when a focused word occupies an emphatic position, as in Ter. *Ad.* 619 *rogito Pamphila quid agat* (cf. H. Pinkster, *Latin Syntax and Semantics* (London, 1990), 170; Hofmann, *LU*, 113–14).

et nunc echoes perhaps the commonly found aetiological *nunc quoque*, to explain present circumstances on the basis of a mythological precedent (on which see Kenney, ad Ov. *Her.* 20.106).

820 The chorus is not expected to remain on stage after delivering its song in Senecan tragedy, and Nero must be imagined alone until the prefect enters at 844–5. Nero's soliloquy is paralleled by Sen. *Thy.* 176–204, where Atreus deliberates how to have his revenge on Thyestes; cf. also *Hf.* 332–53. In Greek tragedy, the thoughts of a tyrant rarely find expression in monologues, and are more commonly expressed in animated *agōnes*. One important exception, however, is Pentheus' entrance monologue in Eur. *Ba.* 215–47, which is also significant in terms of dramatic technique: cf. Tarrant, *HSCPh* 82 (1978), 235; D. Bain, *Actors and Audience* (Oxford, 1987), 64; Zwierlein (1966), 69. In this monologue, Pentheus, like Nero in the present lines, expresses his anger at the lack of discipline shown by his subjects, in allowing the new cult of Bacchus to gain ground in Thebes and in becoming followers of the new god. Pentheus' words are threatening, but he does not reach the zenith of vengefulness attained by Nero. Perhaps Nero's angry monologue, seen as a response to the popular insurrection, can be compared to Sejanus' words, related in the customary indirect style, in Tac. *Ann.* 5.4, when the senators delay proceedings against the elder Agrippina and Nero, and the people peacefully demonstrate outside the Curia: *simul populus effigies Agrippinae ac Neronis gerens circumsistit curiam faustisque in Caesarem ominibus falsas litteras et principe inuito exitium domui eius intendi clamitat. ita nihil triste illo die patratum . . . unde illi* (sc. *Seiano*) *ira uiolentior et materies criminandi: spretum dolorem principis ab senatu, desciuisse populum; audiri iam et legi novas contiones, noua patrum consulta: quid reliquum nisi ut caperent ferrum et, quorum imagines pro uexillis secuti forent, duces imperatoresque deligerent?*

Following convention, the choral ode covers an indefinite length of time. Nero has been reached by the messenger with the news of the sedition, and impatiently waits for the announcement that it has been suppressed in blood.

820–821 o lenta nimium militis nostri manus | et ira patiens post nefas tantum mea Entrance monologues of unannounced characters often begin with some exclamatory remark introduced by *o*. In the Senecan corpus cf. *Med.* 431 *o dura fata semper et sortem asperam*, introducing Jason's predicament; *Troad.* 164 *o longa Danais semper in portu mora*; 1056 *o dura fata saeua miseranda horrida* (followed by a clearly interrogative *quod*-sentence; see following note), all marking a new entrance.

The whole passage, as first noticed by Bruckner (1976, 129), who also analyzes the typology of Senecan revenge-monologues from which the present passage ultimately derives, is modelled on Atreus' entrance monologue, in *Thy.* 176–204 (cf. esp. the self-reproaching *Thy.* 176 *ignaue, iners, eneruis . . .* = *Oct.* 820–1 *o . . . ira patiens . . . mea*; *Thy.* 182–3 *iam flammis agros | lucere et urbes decuit*, in pursuit of the fugitive Thyestes = *Oct.* 822–4 *quod non cruor ciuilis . . . caede nec populi madet | funerea Roma*, 831 *mox tecta flammis concidant urbis meis*; *Thy.* 192–3 *fac quod nulla posteritas probet | sed nulla taceat* = *Oct.* 857 *constituet* (sc. *poenam*) *aetas nulla quam famae eximat*).

Nero's words have an Ovidian flair: cf. *Trist.* 4.1.86 *heu nimium fati tempora lenta mei*; *Am.* 2.19.51 *lentus es et pateris nulli patienda marito.*

822–823 quod non cruor ciuilis accensas faces | extinguit in nos Giardina printed the reading *quid*, thus interpreting the sentence as an interrogative. The two competing readings *quid/quod* are equivalent in sense, but *quod* is perhaps slightly more difficult, and should be preferred. For cases of explicative *quod* following an exclamatory or vocative clause, cf. Cic. *Phil.* 2.110 *o detestabilem hominem, siue quod Caesaris sacerdos es siue quod mortui*; Prop. 4.1.58 *ei mihi, quod nostro est paruus in ore sonus*; Ov. *Met.* 1.523; *Trist.* 1.1.2 *ei mihi quod domino non licet ire tuo* (all with *ei mihi*).

Oct. 822 *cruor ciuilis* is recorded in *TLL* iii, s.v. *ciuilis* 1215, 83–4 under the heading 'ad bellum et pacem ciuium inter se' (and in *OLD* s.v. *ciuilis* 2b, 'of, connected with, or resulting from, civil war'). Indeed, the most common occurrences of the word are in reference to civil wars: cf. Luc. *Bell. Ciu.* 1.14 *hoc quem ciuiles hauserunt sanguine dextrae*, for 'the hands of men engaged in civil war'; or 2.713 *rubuit ciuili sanguine Nereus*; or 4.187 *ciuilis Erinys*. In the present passage, however, *cruor ciuilis* stands for *cruor ciuium*: not 'blood shed in a civil war', but 'blood of one's own fellow-citizens', caused to be shed by some other reason than civil war. This is an instance of the known literary stylistic mannerism whereby an adjective is used instead of a possessive genitive (cf. Löfstedt, *Syntactica*, 1², 109, 115, with discussion of *patrius* = *patris* in Ov. *Met.* 8.211 *patriae tremuere manus*; Maurach, *EP* § 153, quoting Ov. *Met.* 3.128 *fraternaeque fidem pacis petiitque deditque*; *Met.* 7.675 *studiosus . . . caedis . . . ferinae*; Luc. *Bell. Ciu.* 3.679 *hostilem cum torserit . . . hastam . . .* where *hostilis* is the spear thrown by the enemy). For *ciuilis* (= *ciuium*) a parallel can be found in Sall. *Cat.* 14.3 *quos manus atque lingua periurio aut sanguine ciuili alebat*; Sen. *Clem.* 1.11.2 *numquam ciuilem sanguinem fudisse*.

The word-order is rather artificial (for *cruor ciuium non extinguit faces accensas in nos*, 'the blood of my subjects does not smother the firebrands lit against us') as regards the position both of the negative adverb and of the appositive *accensas in nos*. Such displacements of a more logical word-order, especially involving prepositional constructions, are common in the style of Lucan's poem: cf. Luc. *Bell. Ciu.* 1.262–3 *faces belli dubiaeque in proelia menti | urguentes addunt stimulos* (sc. *fata*), where *in proelia* depends on *urguentes*, and 1.311–12 *ueniat longa dux pace solutus | milite cum subito partesque in bella togatae*, where *in bella* is separated from its verb, *ueniat*.

The position of the negative adverb *non* is subject to fewer restrictions in poetry: cf. Luc. *Bell. Ciu.* 1.145 *non uincere bello*, with the parallels given by Housman in his apparatus; Acc. *Scaen.* 458–9 R² *quis erit qui non me spernens, incilans probris | sermone indecorans turpi fama differet*, where *non* should be linked with *differet* ('will not subject me to ill repute'); in Senecan tragedy cf. *Oed.* 1028–30 *non si ipse mundum . . . iaculetur . . . umquam rependam sceleribus poenas pares*; several examples of *non* placed in the initial position and at some remove from its verb are collected in K-S 2.1.819.

823–824 caede nec populi madet | funerea Roma, quae uiros tales tulit The line is ended by a clause occurring in identical form in 372 *monstrum qui tale tulit* in anapaests. The use of *fero* for 'to produce', 'to give rise to' is common both in poetic and prose usage (cf. *OLD* s.v. *fero* 25b, e.g. Verg. *Aen.* 3.94–5 *quae uos a stirpe parentum | prima tulit tellus*; Sen. *Epist.* 97.10 *omne tempus Clodios, non omne Catones feret*); in Senecan tragedy cf. *Hf.* 31 *quidquid pontus aut aer tulit*. For *caede madere* cf. Ov. *Met.* 1.149 *caede madentes* (sc. *terras*); 13.389; 14.199.

825 admissa sed iam morte puniri parum est *admissa* for 'deeds committed' is common in poetry: cf. e.g. Ov. *Met.* 1.210; 11.380; also in Sen. *Agam.* 266, and elsewhere. *commissa* is a frequent alternative.

In words similar to Nero's, Atreus had proclaimed death too mild a punishment for his hated brother (cf. *Thy.* 247–8 *in regno meo, | mors impetratur*). On the commonplace that *mors* should not be seen as a deliverance from suffering under a tyrant's despotic rule cf. Tarrant ad Sen. *Agam.* 995; cf. also *Thy.* 256–7 *nullum est satis:: | ferrum?:: parum est:: quid ignis?:: etiamnunc parum est.*

827 at illa, cui me ciuium subicit furor After a threat of more severe punishment than death for the rebels (*grauiora meruit impium plebis scelus*), Nero's thoughts turn to Octavia: 'But first of all, Octavia shall die . . . at last, then (*mox*, 831) Rome itself shall burn.' I have adopted Bothe's *at* ('populum morte se puniturum negat sed ea solam Octaviam affecturum'), in preference to the transmitted *et.* A mild antithesis is required here, because a distinction is made between the punishment that will be meted out to the people and what awaits Octavia: 'as to her, the woman to whom I am second in the popular esteem' (Nero never utters her name: on the *damnatio nominis* see note ad 361). Cf. the similar gradation in Eur. *I.T.* 1431, where Thoas sends his men in pursuit of the fugitives, while threatening the women of the chorus for their connivance: ὑμᾶς δὲ . . . αὖθις . . . ποινασόμεσθα; cf. also Eur. *Hel.* 1624–5 νῦν δὲ τὴν προδοῦσαν ἡμᾶς τεισόμεσθα σύγγονον, | ἥτις ἐν δόμοις ὁρῶσα Μενέλεων οὐκ εἶπέ μοι.

The examples given in *TLL* v, s.v. *et*, 890 for *et* = '*deinde*' marking a new turn in the argument, such as Verg. *Aen.* 9.781 *et Mnestheus 'quo deinde fugam, quo tenditis?' inquit*: 'and then Mnestheus . . .'. do not fit the present case; Lucr. *D.R.N.* 5.925–6 *et genus humanum multo fuit illud in aruis | durius*, where modern editors print a paragraph, was emended by Lachmann to *at*. The sense *etiam* must be ruled out in this context, since Octavia is not undergoing a similar fate to the rebels'.

Zwierlein's *en* is unconvincing. This particle occurs when the speaker points to an object or person actually seen or imagined as present, or when the thought of this suddenly springs to the speaker's mind. In other cases, *en* is used when the speaker directs attention to himself. A. Kershaw, *HSCPh* 96 (1994), 241–50, defends (250) Zwierlein's text adducing Sall. *Cat.* 20.14.1 *en illa, illa . . . libertas . . . in oculis sita* and Liv. 2.6.7 *ille est uir qui nos extorres expulit patria . . . ipse en ille . . . magnifice incedit . . .* Kershaw finds the occurrence of the nexus *en ille/illa* significant. But in both these passages it is the function of *en* as a deictic particle (= Gk. *idou*) that is important, not the presence of *ille/ipse*. This function is absent here. Zwierlein's own parallels (*en ipse* in *Med.* 995; *Phaed.* 834; *Thy.* 120) are precisely cases when a speaker points his listeners towards a character he is seeing: cf. *Med.* 995 *en ipsa tecti parte praecipiti imminet. et ipse* has the force of 'and I too, for my part . . .' in *Oct.* 592, but there the sequence of tenses (a continuous series of indicatives, stating facts shown to be true) reinforces *et*. In our instance, the shift from the two indicatives at 825–6 (*parum est, meruit*) to the subjunctive *reddat* shows that a stronger break is required.

Previous editors were sceptical about *at* because it figures in *Octavia* only at 457, a line which Leo excised. A parallel quite strongly in support of Bothe's proposal can be found in *Agam.* 1001–3, spoken by Clytemnestra: *at ista* (sc. Cassandra, whereas earlier the doom of Electra had been discussed) *poenas capite persoluet suo, | captiua coniunx, regii paelex tori: | trahite ut sequatur coniugem ereptum mihi*, which is clearly echoed here, with *illa*, because Octavia is not present. Cf. also Don. ad *Ter. An.* 666 *at principium increpationi aptum, ut Vergilius 'at tibi pro scelere'*. Clytemnestra's abusive address to Cassandra as a regal concubine is also closely imitated by the appositive clause *suspecta coniunx et soror semper mihi*. This form of address followed by an appositive clause often couched in abusive tones has parallels in Greek tragedy: cf. Creon's words in Eur. *Med.* 271–2 σὲ τὴν σκυθρωπὸν καὶ πόσει θυμουμένην | Μήδειαν, Soph. *El.* 1445–6 σέ τοι, σὲ κρίνω, ναὶ σέ, τὴν ἐν τῶι πάρος | χρόνωι θρασεῖαν, *Ant.* 441 σὲ δή, σὲ τὴν νεύουσαν ἐς πέδον κάρα. A further reminiscence of *Agam.* 1003 can be identified in *Oct.* 470–1 *inuisa coniunx pereat et carum sibi | fratrem sequatur*. The presence of the future *persoluet* (*persoluat* in *recc.*) in *Agam.* may suggest that *reddet* was the original reading in 829 (but various subjunctives follow).

The verb *subicio* occurs in this sense ('whose authority they place above mine') *supra*, 104–5 *meae | subiecta famulae*, and at 950 (see note there). Nero's resentment at the people's support for Octavia may recall the words of Creon in Soph. *Ant.* 680, who will not endure being defeated by a woman, κοὐκ ἂν γυναικῶν ἥσσονες καλοίμεθ' ἄν. See also note ad 183.

829 tandem dolori spiritum reddat meo Since the emperor, at least this tragic one, is placed on a pedestal as a superhuman being, causing him *dolor* is a capital offence. Cf. Tac. *Ann.* 5.4 (quoted ad 820, *spretum dolorem principis*); Ov. *Trist.* 4.9.8 *induet infelix arma coacta dolor* (= 'I shall have my revenge'). *reddere spiritum, sanguinem* are expressions quite frequently used in Senecan drama: cf. Sen. *Agam.* 987 *fratrem reddat aut animam statim*.

831 mox tecta flammis concidant urbis meis On *mox* 'subsequently', 'next', a meaning alternating with 'soon' at this date, cf. ad 166. In fact, the fire of Rome took place two years later. No other source makes such a link between the rebellion in favour of Octavia and the fire. The rumour that the fire was caused by Nero is related by Tacitus (*Ann.* 15.38) with a guarded attitude, whereas Suetonius (*Nero*, 38.1) and Cassius Dio (*Hist. Rom.* 62.16.2) are more inclined to believe it. For Suetonius, Nero's main motive would have been that of building a better Rome. Only according to Dio did Nero order the fire for the pure pleasure of seeing the city burn.

In Eur. *Herc.* 565–73 an enraged Hercules plans bloody revenge against the citizens of Thebes who lent support to Lycos despite all of Hercules' merits: cf. esp. 568–73 Καδμείων δ' ὅσους | κακοὺς ἐφηῦρον εὖ παθόντας ἐξ ἐμοῦ . . . (cf. *infra* 834–5 *saeculi nostri bonis | corrupta turba*) νεκρῶν ἅπαντ' Ἰσμηνὸν ἐμπλήσω φόνου, | Δίρκης τε νᾶμα λευκὸν αἱμαχθήσεται. Similarly, according to Suetonius (*Cal.* 31), Caligula complained that his rule had not yet been visited by such evils as fire, famine and plague, and wished for some such disaster to occur (*queri etiam palam de condicione temporum suorum solebat, quod nullis calamitatibus publicis insigniretur . . . atque identidem exercituum caedes, famem, pestilentiam, incendia, hiatum aliquem terrae optabat*). The archetype of this lust for a general conflagration is that arch-villain, Sallust's Catiline: cf. *Cat.* 31.9 *incendium meum ruina restinguam* (words uttered on leaving the Roman Senate: note also the coincidence between *flammis . . . meis* and *incendium meum*, although the possessive in 831 indicates not possession but a deed performed).

832–833 ignes ruinae noxium populum premant | turpisque egestas, saeua cum luctu fames This disorderly-seeming sequence comprising two nouns in asyndeton, followed by a third noun linked by *–que*, then by a further noun group in asyndeton expanded by a prepositional construction (*cum luctu*), is peculiar (but cf. *supra*, 547–8 *probitas fidesque coniugis, mores pudor | placeant marito*). By comparison, poetry of the Augustan age seems to prefer more regular patterns of syntactical links: cf. the list of boons bestowed upon the new Golden Age in Hor. *C.S.* 57–60 *iam fides et pax et honos pudorque | priscus et neglecta redire uirtus | audet apparetque beata pleno | copia cornu* (with the last element expanded by the ablative *pleno . . . cornu* = *saeua cum luctu fames*). The initial *dicolon asyndeticum, ignes ruinae*, is an archaic feature well established in Senecan drama, where, more generally, asyndetic lists of nouns (as well as of adjectives) are a feature of archaic style, revived by Seneca (cf. R. J. Tarrant, *HSCPh* 94 (1992), 339 with parallels, e.g. *Agam.* 45–7 *enses secures tela, diuisum graui ictu | bipennis regium uideo caput: | iam scelera prope sunt, iam dolus caedes cruor*).

In Augustan poetry, seemingly chaotic enumerations are found at times for expressive reasons, for instance in Verg. *Aen.* 4.131–2 *retia rara, plagae, lato venabula ferro, | Massylique ruunt equites et odora canum vis* (where however different verbs would be required to provide adequate predicates for each successive element). In 833 Nero's sentence is really concluded by *premant*, and all following elements come as unforeseen codas, thus giving the rest of the sentence a desultory rhythm. Although the construction of the two lines is asymmetrical, a balancing principle of some kind can be detected, inasmuch as the poet has an asyndetic sequence of two bare nouns, in the solemn archaizing fashion, followed by two gradually expanding cola: first a noun-adjective group linked to what precedes it by *–que*, then a last group of nouns, again in asyndeton, consisting of a noun specified by an adjective and expanded by *cum luctu*, to mark off period-end with a longer colon.

Complements introduced by *cum* are in some cases interpreted as the Latin equivalent of a compound epithet in Greek (as e.g. in Enn. *Ann.* 26 Sk. *pater Tiberine tuo cum flumine sancto*, which is seen as an equivalent of the Homeric ἐυρρεής or βραδυδινής: cf. M. Leumann, K-S, 138 n. 3). Instances of enumerative sequences in prose with *cola bimembria* and variation of connectives are given in K-S, *Satzlehre*, 2.154, from which I choose Liv. 9.14.11 *caedunt pariter resistentes fusosque inermes atque armatos seruos liberos puberes impuberes homines iumentaque.* In the less fastidious Latin of Plautus we find enumerations in which the main components are linked without particles, but some more closely related groups of nouns are linked by a conjunction: cf. Plaut. *Merc.* 25–30 (*amori accedunt etiam haec:*) *insomnia, aerumna, error, terror et fuga: | ineptia, stultitiaque adeo et temeritas, | incogitantia excors, | inmodestia, petulantia et cupiditas, maleuolentia, | inerit etiam auiditas, desidia, iniuria, | inopia, contumelia et dispendium . . .*

The succession of the evils which the angry and vengeful Nero now threatens to inflict (831–3) is reminiscent of those always found assembled in an infernal deity's lair in such passages as Verg. *Aen.* 6.274–81 (the *vestibulum* of Avernus) and Ov. *Met.* esp. 12.59–61 (Fama); 4.484–5 (Furia); 8.790–1 (Fames); Sen. *Oed.* 590–4; 652–3 (also in the form of a prophecy pronounced by Laius against his son) *letum luesque, mors labor tabes dolor, | comitatus illo dignus, excedent simul,* where only the first two items of the list are linked by a conjunction; *ibid.* 1059–60; Petr. *Sat.* 123.215–16 *arma cruor caedes incendia totaque bella | ante oculos uolitant*; Soph. *O.C.* 1234–5 φθόνος, στάσεις, ἔρις, μάχαι | καὶ φόνοι. The Vergilian passage at *Aen.* 6.274ff. seems particularly relevant: *luctus et ultrices posuere cubilia curae | pallentesque habitant morbi tristisque senectus | et metus et malesuada fames ac turpis egestas, | terribiles uisu formae, letumque labosque, | tum consanguineus leti sopor*; Val. Fl. *Arg.* 2.204–6 *accelerat pauor et Geticis discordia demens | e stabulis atraeque genis pallentibus irae | et dolus et rabies et leti maior imago.*

833 saeua cum luctu fames Heinsius' *cumuletur* is typical of a correction that improves too much. In addition, *cum* is perfectly defensible: it does not imply a closer association between 'mourning' and 'famine' but is used to vary the syntactical connection of the two last-named calamities of the short catalogue, being in short an equivalent for *et*: cf. e.g. Ov. *Am.* 3.8.37 *aeraque et argentum cumque auro pondera ferri,* where no specific association of gold and iron is envisaged, but Ovid feels a need to vary the syntactical sequence in the second half-line.

On *cum* as an alternative for *et*, parallels, mainly from Ovid, in Bömer, ad Ov. *Met.* 2.212; 7.744 *malo cum coniuge limina fugit.*

There was some shortage of food after the fire. According to Cass. Dio *Hist. Rom.* 62.18.5 Nero discontinued the corn dole in the immediate aftermath of the fire, presumably for a very short while and solely in order to keep prices low (cf. Tac. *Ann.* 15.39 *pretium . . . frumenti minutum usque ad ternos nummos*). Suet. *Nero* 45 blames Nero for the shortages of corn that occurred at the very end of his reign, at the time of the rising of Vindex.

834–835 exultat ingens saeculi nostri bonis | corrupta turba Santoro and Ballaira understand *ingens* as an adverb modifying *exultat,* but cite no linguistic parallels to support this, which is linguistically and stylistically anomalous (*ingens* occurs as an adverb modifying adjectives, e.g. *ingens magnus,* in very late texts). Adjectives can be used predicatively in poetry and poetical prose, in conjunction with verbs, where the adjective is said to stand for an adverb (a mannerism analyzed in Löfstedt, *Syntactica*, 2.368): cf. e.g. Prop. *Carm.* 4.8.49 *rauci sonuerunt . . . postes*, i.e. 'the door-valves creaked producing a rasping sound'; Tac. *Ann.* 4.12 *occulti laetabantur. exultat ingens* finds no support in this, because *ingens* does not describe the manner or circumstances in which the populace is said to exceed its due. The more natural interpretation of *ingens turba* is 'the great crowd' or 'a great crowd' (as in Liv. 26.35.7 *haec . . . ingens turba circumfusi fremebant*, where however *ingens turba* is adverbial: 'the populace, in great numbers'), 'or simply 'la foule' [Chaumartin]. Nero is thinking of his subjects as a whole, not of the specific group of citizens gathering in threatening stance around his palace. It is his subjects as a whole who have proved unworthy of the benefits and the peace Nero has lavished on them: they will incur his anger and his punishment. This makes *ingens* somewhat vacuous in the context, and one would have expected a more significant adjective in this place, e.g. ***audax*** as in Luc. *Bell. Ciu.* 5.259–60 *ipsa metus exsoluerat audax | turba suos.*

The word *exultat* implies excessive and unrestrained behaviour: cf. Verg. *Aen.* 5.397–8 (*inventa*) *qua . . . improbus iste | exultat fidens*; *TRF inc.* 125 R²; Cat. *Carm.* 51.14; Sen. *Phae.* 204; Cic. *Rep.* 1.62 *mira quadam exultasse populum insolentia libertatis*; *Pan. Lat.* 4.35.3 *populi . . . Romani uis illa et magnitudo uenerabilis . . . non licentia effrenis exultat.*

saeculi nostri bonis refers primarily to peace (for which each new ruler tends to be praised, but it was a theme particularly conspicuous in Nero's propaganda) and material welfare, which in Nero's view have produced corruption. That material hardship strengthens the moral values of a nation is a commonplace established early on in Roman culture (for the prominence of this theme in Roman historiography cf. La Penna, *Sallustio e la 'rivoluzione' romana* (Milan, 1968) 232–3; Sall. *Bell. Iug.* 41 *mos partium . . . ortus est otio atque abundantia*; *Cat.* 10.2 *iis otium diuitiae . . . oneri miseriaeque fuere*; *Cat.* 53.5 *postquam luxu atque desidia ciuitas corrupta est.* A different view is expressed by the author of the (Neronian?) *Laus Pis.* 169–70 *dum pace serena | publica securis exsultent otia terris*; cf. also *Buc. Einsiedl.* 1.46–88). Sallust's interpretation was endorsed with no modifications by the historians of the imperial age, who share the same attitude towards the material welfare of the populace (cf. Tac. *Hist.* 3.83.10; *Ann.* 1.16). See A. J. Woodman, '*Otium* in Catullus', *Latomus* 25 (1966), 297 n. 2. For the expression *saeculi nostri bonis* cf. Tac. *Dial.* 41.11 *bono saeculi sui quisque . . . utatur* (i.e. peace restored by the Flavians); Plin. *Pan.* 36.4 *bona saeculi parum intellegit* (i.e. freedom of speech under Trajan); Plin. *Epist.* 10.58.7 *felicitas temporum*, in a passage transcribing an edict issued by Nerva. These parallels suggest that there is a hint of officialese in the words of Nero (and of the *Octavia* poet). There is much material on the language of the imperial chanceries in M. Benner, *The Emperor Says. Studies in the Rhetorical Style in Edicts of the Early Empire* (Göteborg, 1975),

130, adducing the edict of Tiberius Julius Alexander, prefect of Egypt, saying of Galba's rule τῆι μεγίστηι τῶν νῦν καιρῶν εὐδαιμονίαι (*OGIS* 2.669). Also in the *Senatusconsultum Hosidianum* (Bruns 54.1, AD 44–46) *felicitati saeculi instantis.*

837–838 sed inquieta rapitur hinc audacia, | hinc temeritate fertur in praeceps sua The interpretation of *hinc . . . hinc* poses a problem. Some early editors punctuate after *rapitur*, separating *inquieta* (a nominative on this interpretation, which the metre permits) from *audacia.* This, though not impossible, has in my view the disadvantage of leaving *rapitur* in a vacuum ('is carried away' by what?); likewise *audacia* should not be left without an adjective. The expression *inquieta . . . audacia* also seems worth preserving (see note *infra*). Comparison with Stat. *Silu.* 2.1.38–9 *hinc anni stantes in limine uitae, | hinc me forma rapit, rapit inde modestia praecox* and *Laus Pis.* 2–5 *hinc tua . . . nobilitas . . . hinc tua me uirtus rapit* suggests that *rapio* goes well with *hinc . . . hinc*, which stand for 'on one side . . . on the other' rather than for 'consequently' (a sense which is also well established: cf. Verg. *Georg.* 4.532–4 *haec omnis morbi causa, hinc . . . nymphae . . . exitium misere apibus*; in anaphora, cf. *Aen.* 2.97–8 *hinc mihi prima mali labes, hinc semper Ulixes. . .*; Stat. *Theb.* 3.564–5 *hinc pallor et irae, | hinc scelus insidiaeque*).

For *sed* after a string of negative sentences, meaning 'not only that but' or 'on the contrary', cf. *supra*, 753 *bella haud mouebit, pace sed ferrum teget.* The same sequence of conjunctions is found e.g. in Sen. *Oed.* 52–3 *nec ulla pars immunis exitio uacat | sed omnis aetas pariter et sexus ruit*; Luc. *Bell. Ciu.* 1.144–5 *sed non in Caesare tantum nomen erat, nec . . . sed nescia uirtus stare loco*, where the two instances of *sed* have a different value.

Tac. *Ann.* 1.42 relates how Germanicus harangues his rebellious troops. His taunts include blame for the ingratitude shown to their benefactor, Tiberius: *tot praemiis aucta, hanc tam egregiam duci uestro gratiam refertis.*

837 inquieta . . . audacia While *audacia* is common in reference to political agitators (for example Catiline in Sallust), *inquieta* adds philosophical overtones (enhanced by the use of *rapitur*), and the sentence has a decidedly Senecan ring (cf. Sen. *Tranq.* 12.4 (*formicis*) *plerique similem uitam agunt quorum non immerito quis inquietam inertiam dixerit*; *Cons. Helu.* 12.6.6; *Breu.* 12.2 *desidiosa occupatio*; 12.4 *iners negotium*). The rebels' motives are presented as an inner restlessness, which makes them impatient of orderly government. *inquietus* is also the proper term for political disquiet (cf. Sen. *Oed.* 684 *ab inquieto saepe simulatur quies*; Aug. *Ciu. Dei* 5.12, p. 216 Dombart *grauis metus coepit urguere* (sc. *Romanos*) *atque . . . alia maiore cura cohibere animos inquietos.*

839–840 malis domanda est et graui semper iugo | premenda *malum* can have the specific meaning of 'punishment': cf. Liv. 2.54.10 *malo domandam tribuniciam potestatem*; Sen. *Agam.* 959 *agere domita feminam disces malo*; Acc. *Scaen.* 683–4 R² *nullum est ingenium . . . quod non . . . mitescat malo*: cf. *TLL* viii s.v., 209.44–67.

840 ne quid simile temptare audeat 'In order that they never dare the like again'; *ne quid simile* is a colourless expression which is outside the expressive palette of Senecan tragedy, where indeed there are no instances of *(ali)quid simile* in non-interrogative contexts. On the other hand, this vagueness is rather in keeping with the less strict stylistic instincts of the *Octavia* poet. In Ovid I was able to identify only one instance, *Met.* 7.13 *aut aliquid certe simile huic quod amare uocatur*, where the vagueness of *aliquid . . . simile* suits the depiction of Medea's hesitant and reluctant discovery of passion. Elsewhere, cf. Verg. *Aen.* 4.415 *ne quid inexpertum . . . relinquat*; 8.205–6 *ne quid inausum | aut intractatum . . .*; 12.152 *si quid praesentius audes*, but none of these partitive constructions really parallels 840. Significant parallels can only be found in the more colloquial style of early drama and satire: cf. Plaut. *Capt.* 752–3 *ego illis captiuis aliis documentum dabo | ne tale quisquam facinus incipere audeat*; Hor. *Serm.* 1.4.136–7 *numquid ego illi | imprudens olim faciam simile?*

841–842 contraque sanctos coniugis uultus meae | attollere oculos This is an obvious reminiscence of Lucr. *D.R.N.* 1.66–7 *mortalis tollere contra | est oculos ausus*. The rebels have done in fact much more than simply 'raise their eyes' towards Poppaea's effigies, but Nero's words imply that this alone would have been criminal enough to warrant persecution, and also that they will learn to fear even just raising their eyes against their rulers. There is also an element of euphemism, as if merely repeating the words and deeds of the rebellious populace were sacrilegious, and the epithet *sancta* in reference to Poppaea reinforces this impression. Legitimate wives are called *sanctae*, because marriage itself is an institution protected by religion and custom. *sancta* indicates chastity and legitimacy, a quality which Nero is obviously keen to assert for Poppaea. Tac. *Ann.* 14.60 has *sanctitatem dominae* of Octavia; cf. also Verg. *Aen.* 11.158 *sanctissima coniunx*; Ov. *Met.* 15.836 *prolem sancta de coniuge natam*; Sen. *Troad.* 698 *coniugis sanctae torus.*

842–843 fracta per poenas, metu | parere discet principis nutu sui Punctuation is problematic in 842. The populace will learn, through the experience of terror, to obey the very nod of their emperor, let alone his orders. For 'to learn from one's mistakes' and from the unpleasant consequences they have produced cf. perhaps Verg. *Buc.* 10.60–1 *tamquam . . . deus ille malis hominum mitescere discat*; Plin. *Nat.* 29.18 *discunt periculis nostris* (of doctors learning at the expense of their patients); Tac. *Ann.* 1.11. *metu*, however, appears somewhat bare ('in an atmosphere of terror'), and the prepositional phrase *per* + acc. has also been suspected. Various conjectural emendations have been proposed, e.g. Heinsius' *post poenae metu* (in *Adversaria*, 514) and, along the same lines, Liberman's *per poenae metum*. In addition, Nero is not likely to stop at the mere threat of punishment, which would give his monologue a rather lame ending after the harsh words spoken in 831–3. In support of his conjecture Liberman adduces Ovid's portrayal of the good *princeps*, Augustus (*Pont.* 1.2.121–6, esp. 125 *multa metu poenae, poena qui pauca coercet*), depicting a model of behaviour which is very different from Nero's. The text should probably stand as it is, with a punctuation mark after *poenas*. The prepositional nexus *per* with the accusative with the function of an instrumental or agentive complement is very common: cf. Plaut. *Bacch.* 1070 *urbe capta per dolum*; Ov. *Pont.* 1.7.48 *si sua per uestras uicta sit ira preces*; Sen. *Cons. Marc.* 18.8 *per poenam cruciatumque.*

The dative *nutu* (for this form cf. 484 *nutuque . . . subiecit tuo*) is emphatic (that is, stronger than the expected *parere discet principis iussis sui*). *metus* is a state of wariness and caution induced in all by the sight of punishment inflicted on a chosen few.

844–845 sed adesse cerno rara quem pietas uirum | fidesque castris nota praeposuit meis There are insufficient textual clues in the play to identify this *praefectus* with absolute certainty, but I favour Faenius Rufus. If this were Tigellinus (as argued by Thomann ad loc., and, at some length, by Kragelund, *CQ* 38 (1988), 498–503), this presentation of his character would be sarcastic, in retrospect, for those who knew that Tigellinus had defected from Nero in 68 (Tac. *Ann.* 14.57; *Hist.* 1.72). I suspect that no irony is lurking here; the prefect shrinks at first from the prospect of having to put Octavia to death, an unlikely reaction if this is Tigellinus. It is more for dramatic effect that the prefect is made to hesitate to carry out Nero's orders than for the purpose of making the prefect identifiable as a specific historical figure (i.e. Faenius Rufus as opposed to Tigellinus). Similarly, in Seneca's *Thyestes*, the *satelles* first attempts to moderate his master's furious anger. On the other hand, a prefect surpassing Nero in ferocity was unappealing, because it would have robbed Nero of the villain's role. The cruel and despotic ways of a tyrant stand out more clearly if they are opposed by an innocent, reluctant subordinate: a case in point is the dialogue between Kreon and Haemon in Soph. *Ant.* 635–780; cf. also Aesch. *Prom.* 1–87, with the conflicting attitudes exhibited by Hephaistos and Kratos; Eur. *Herc.* 843–61 (exchange between Lyssa and Iris). [I owe these two parallels to MDR.] The only comparable instance in extant Greek tragedy in which a soldier tries the patience of his lord is the *phylax* in *Ant.* 223–331, who is a partly comic figure and does not possess the dignified and honourable manner of this *praefectus.*

All in all, Faenius Rufus is a more suitable candidate than Tigellinus (cf. above all Tac. *Ann.* 15.50, where, on the eve of Piso's conspiracy, it is said of the former *summum robur in Faenio Rufo praefecto uidebatur, quem uita famaque laudatum per saeuitiam impudicitiamque Tigellinus in animo principis anteibat*). Nero's praise of the prefect's *fides* and *pietas* is an intrusion from the ethical world of the *Octavia* poet: tyrants, at least those active in Senecan tragedy, are at best indifferent to these qualities in their subordinates. Probably the poet, in giving *pietas* and *fides* such prominence in the presentation of this character, meant to make him recognizable as the good, but weak, commander of the pretorians ultimately unable to bring down Nero. Characteristically, his words of assent, after Nero has pronounced his final condemnation of Octavia, are not on record in the play, as if to diminish the prefect's guilt (compare, by way of contrast, the brief formula of obeisance pronounced by the other *Praefectus* in 439, indubitably not the same historical personage).

The positive presentation of subordinate characters who end up displeasing their ruler because they refuse to accede to his ferocious demands is also a widespread dramatic feature: cf. in Senecan tragedy the gradual transformation of Oedipus' attitude towards Creon (*Oed.* 210 ff.); in the corresponding episode in Sophocles' *Ant.* 164–9 the chorus have been summoned on account of their faith and constancy shown toward the rulers of the city. Cf. also the words of the tribune Subrius Flavus, involved in the Pisonian conspiracy in Tac. *Ann.* 15.67 *'oderam te,' inquit 'nec quisquam tibi fidelior militum fuit, dum amari meruisti: odisse coepi, postquam parricida matris et uxoris, auriga et histrio et incendiarius extitisti.'*

As noted in Introd. p. 63, the author of *Octavia* deviates from Seneca's practice of making characters suddenly emerge from the shadows and address the soliloquizing character (cf. the Atreus-*Satelles* scene, which is the closest parallel in the corpus, in *Thy.* 204 ff.). The announcement has a point here, however, because the *praefectus* brings news from outside and announces that the rioters have been suppressed. The form of the entrance announcement (*cerno* + an infinitive) has no parallels in Senecan tragedy (except *H.O.* 740–1 *natum pauentem cerno et ardenti pede | gressus ferentem*, in a passage marred by textual corruption) but is attested in early drama: cf Acc. *Scaen.* 289 R[2] *sed iam Amphilocum huc uadere cerno.*

quem pietas uirum | fidesque castris nota praeposuit meis For the practice of introducing entering characters with a descriptive periphrasis without disclosing their names (only for attendants and subordinates), cf. *H.O.* 535 *tu quam meis admittit arcanis fides* (address to a character already present on stage). The word-order is remarkable, with the antecedent *uirum* placed inside the relative clause *quem . . . praeposuit*, but see note ad 818–19. As Tarrant observes ad *Agam.* 391 *fidusque regi semper Eurybates adest*, the faithfulness of retainers is a cliché; all parallels he gives to illustrate the entrance of the herald Eurybates (*H.O.* 569–70 *o quod superbae non habent umquam domus, | fidele semper regibus nomen Licha*) are accompanied by an explicit mention of the faithful servant's name. In early drama cf. Ter. *Ad.* 438–46, where Demea, at the sight of Hegio approaching, stresses his *antiqua uirtus* and *fides*, rare birds in the corruption of their times (*sed quis illic est procul quem uideo? estne Hegio | tribuli' noster? . . . homo antiqua uirtute ac fide!*). *pietas* is the bond between a soldier and his commander (*OLD* s.v. 4b). In Greek, εὐσέβεια is so used in *IG* 7.2713, an edict in which Nero bestows liberty on the Greek people as a reward for loyalty and benevolence demonstrated toward his person.

846–847 populi furorem caede paucorum, diu | qui restiterunt temere, compressum affero Tac. *Ann.* 14.61 states that the revolt was suppressed only *uerberibus et intento ferro. affero* has the function of a deictic element in the speeches pronounced by messengers: cf. Plaut. *Most.* 786 *quod me miseras, affero omne impetratum*; *Stich.* 295 *tam gaudium grande affero.* The method used to repress the riot, the elimination of the ring-leaders, has parallels in the accounts of rebellious behaviour (of military units) in Tac. *Ann.* 1.29 *sublatis seditionis auctoribus*; 1.44 *puniret noxios.*

Parallels for the syntactical break before the final iambus (*paucorum, diu*) are given by Zwierlein, *KK* ad *Troad.* 49: this phenomenon occurs more freely in *Octauia* (406, 420, 473, 500, 505, 846) than in the other plays of the corpus. Outside Senecan tragedy, in iambics, cf. Petr. *Sat.* 89 (*Tr. Hal.*) 24–5 *fremit | captiua pubes intus.*

For *comprimere* of uprisings: Vell. 2.126.2 *compressa theatralis seditio. temere* means 'recklessly, blindly' and designates the mad rage of the rebels (*restiterunt temere*). It can also have the meaning (*OLD* s.v., 4) of 'easily', 'without having to overcome obstacles', but this meaning seems to occur only in negative phrases (*non . . . temere*).

848 et hoc sat est? sic miles audisti ducem? The initial sequence of monosyllables imitates Sen. *Phoe.* 356 *nec hoc sat est.* For the indignant interrogative *hoc sat(satis) est?* cf. *Med.* 126 *hoc meis satis est malis?*; *Oed.* 954 *et flere satis est?*; 938 (at line-end) *hoc patri sat est*; *Thy.* 890 *sed cur satis sit?*; Ov. *Met.* 4.427 *idque mihi satis est? haec una potentia nostra?*. *et* can be used at the beginning of a new sentence to introduce exclamatory-interrogative clauses, expressing indignation or surprise: instances in *TLL* vi, s.v., 890.51 ff. (e.g. Verg. *Aen.* 1.48–9 *et quisquam numen Iunonis adorat | praeterea?* Sen. *Suas.* 5.2 *et hoc agitur, an uicerimus?*).

sic . . . audisti is used in a loaded and compressed sense ('so feebly did you put into execution your commander's orders?').

849 compescis? Nero answers the prefect's triumphant announcement with a contemptuous remark, *haec uindicta debetur mihi*, expressing his vexation at the inadequate punishment meted out to the rebels, who dared to oppose his will. The MS reading *compescis*, however, which modern editors print with an exclamation or question mark, raises a problem. To repeat a statement made by a previous speaker, or what the interlocutor takes to be the most significant part of it, and then to sneer at it, is a common feature of animated dialogue in drama: cf. Sen. *Agam.* 961–2 CL. *et esse demens te parem nobis putas?* | EL. *uobis? quis iste est alter Agamemnon tuus?* where Electra, like Nero, picks up sarcastically a word used by her mother and sneers at it; *Phoe.* 650–2 IOC. *iam numeres licet | fratrem inter istos* – ET. *numeret, est tanti mihi | cum regibus iacere* (on this mannerism of dramatic stichomythia, cf. Don. ad Ter. *Ad.* 742 *corrector! nempe*] *corrector. moris est iratis ab ultimo uerbo contra dicentis incipere*). In this stichomythia, the two speakers pick up each other's words at 855–6 *poena / poenam*;

856–7 *constituet*; 858–9 *ira*. All the more surprising that Nero is here not using the verb used by the prefect, *comprimo*. Accordingly, Peiper took the step of correcting the transmitted *compescis* to *compressit*, not impossibly, the difference in writing between the two words being small in some book-hands. Leo assumed that a line must have gone missing before 849, along the lines of <*cruore paruo tot scelestorum nefas*> (in Düring, *Materialien* IV, 368). In Senecan tragedy, characters sometimes begin a line with a sentence of only one pointed verb, which gives rise to a climax of indignant comments, as in *Med.* 560 *discessit. itane est?*; 565 *timemur. hac aggredere*. One way of defending the transmitted reading is to assume that Nero finds the measures adopted by his guard too weak a response to the humiliation his pride has suffered from the rebellious populace. His *compescis* therefore deliberately misrepresents the reprisal as a mere 'hushing up' of the matter. *compesco* often has the meaning 'to stifle lament, repress tears': cf. Hor. *Carm.* 2.20.23 *compesce clamorem* (at the poet's funeral); Lucr. *D.R.N.* 3.955 *compesce querellas*; Sen. *H.O.* 1427 *compesce uoces*. The verb is appropriate to a non-violent cessation of the riots (cf. Tac. *Ann.* 1.42 *seditionem . . . uerbo uno compescuit*), and does not rule out recourse to arms: cf. Vell. 2.12.6 *furorem* (sc. *Glauciae Saturninique*) *rem publicam lacerantium . . . consul armis compescuit*; Suet. *Tib.* 37 *hostiles motus . . . per legatos compescuit* where the verb sounds like an understatement. Nero's anger is especially incensed by the prefect's *caede paucorum*. Some blood has been shed, but hardly enough to satisfy Nero's vengefulness. Buecheler's *compressus*, therefore, may well hit the mark, thereby also doing away with the need to postulate a lacuna to make up for a supposedly missing line pronounced by the prefect and answered by Nero's *compescis*. Zwierlein printed a *lacuna* after 848, to explain the lack of a pointed antecedent for Nero's *compescis*.

Liberman has suggested that *compressum* and *compescis* are felt as parts of the same verbal paradigm (*compesco* has no supine), but I can find no evidence to support this argument.

849 haec uindicta debetur mihi Cf. Ov. *Met.* 6.538 *hostis mihi debita poena*.

850 cecidere motus impii ferro duces The prefect's timid attempt to appease Nero with the reminder that the ringleaders at least paid with their lives was corrupt in the MSS (*c. metus impio f. d.*). The emendation *motus* was suggested by Bernardino Marmita; the correction *impii* appears already in many *recc.*

851 quid illa turba The passage is reminiscent of Oedipus' reported monologue in *Oed.* 936 ff., which resembles Nero's tirade in the indignant questioning and in the assertion that his self-inflicted punishment fails to satisfy the souls of the dead which he has wronged: *itane? tam magnis breues | poenas sceleribus soluis, atque uno omnia | pensabis ictu? moreris. hoc patri sat est; | quid deinde matri, quid male in lucem editis | natis, quid ipsi . . . patriae dabis?*

Some early editors (Gronovius, Schroederus) and, lastly, Chaumartin add a punctuation mark after *quid*, taken as exclamatory or interrogative: *quid? illa turba . . . debita poena uacat?* I adopt Zwierlein's punctuation (already in Bothe). The same ellipsis (*passa est*) is found at *Agam.* 701 *quid illa felix turba fraterni gregis?*; *Phae.* 149–50 *quid ille . . . pater?* (sc. *faciet*); *Oed.* 307 *quid flamma? largas iamne comprendit dapes?* and also *OLD* s.v. 12b. The exclamatory use (as distinct from the elliptical) of *quid* 'what?' is usually styled a colloquialism (cf. Hofmann, *LU*, 66–8), and accordingly avoided in the more refined poetical genres. This need not be a rule, as even allegedly 'colloquial' features may occasionally make their way into more fastidious genres for reasons of emphasis or to express indignation. In Senecan tragedy, however, the only certain case of exclamatory *quid* is found in *Hf.* 459–60 *quid, qui gubernat astra . . . non latuit infans?* Zwierlein's punctuation in *Oed.* 751 *quid? Cadmei fata nepotis . . .* is not acceptable, and should be replaced with *quid* (sc. *dicam*) *Cadmei fata nepotis, cum. . . .* , as in *Med.* 350 *quid cum . . .* and 355. The last three instances provide an illustration of a different use of *quid*, with ellipse of a verb, in enumerative sequences. *quid?* is linguistically acceptable, yet, while Nero's response to the prefect's report of the ringleaders' death is to demand punishment also for their followers, comparison with *Agam.* 701 suggests that ellipsis should be preferred.

853 abstrahere nostris coniugem caram toris Leo printed *coniugem tantam* (also found in ***M***) in place of *c. caram*, adducing in support 953 *parens tanta Neronis* and Ov. *Her.* 16.373–4 *nec tamen indigner pro tanta sumere ferrum | coniuge.*

854–855 uiolare quantum licuit incesta manu | et uoce dira? There is some uncertainty over whether *quantum licuit* should be read as an adverbial clause, or as the object of *uiolare*, which is how translators normally interpret it. An exception is provided by Chaumartin, 'la souiller, autant qu'elle l'a pu, de sa main impudique et de ses cris sinistres'. Of the earlier editors, Ascensius, whose note ad loc. reads 'quod ei permissum est', places *quantum licuit* in parenthesis; likewise, Gronovius and Ritter between commas, which suggests they took it as a self-contained, limitative clause ('in so far as they were allowed to'). In this case, the object of *uiolare* must be supplied from the preceding clause, *coniugem* (any such insult to the imperial spouse must count as a profanation). In Ovid, for instance, *quantum licuit* is found only in parenthetic adverbial clauses: e.g. Ov. *Am.* 2.19.13 *quantum . . . licebat* (to the extent to which) *insonti, speciem praebuit esse nocens*; *Pont.* 1.7.65 *quantumque licet meminisse, solebas. . .* On the other hand, this interpretation would give the colon a rhetorical imbalance, with *uiolare* lacking a specific object. On consideration, it is perhaps preferable to see *q. l.* as the object of *uiolare*: '*violate* all they were able to', which is more indignant, and which was for a Roman reader the most natural interpretation of this sequence. The violence exerted by the rebels on the statues and insignia of Poppaea is represented as a sacrilegious act: cf. *Dig.*

xlviii.4.7.4 *crimine maiestatis facto uel uiolatis statuis uel imaginibus maxime exacerbatur in milites.*

An additional problem is presented by *licet*, the more commonly attested meaning of which is 'what one has been given permission to do', 'what is licit' according to tradition and conforming to divine precept, or human and natural law (cf. *TLL* vii.2, s.v., 1358.60–5, e.g. Cic. *Phil.* 13.14 *quod legibus, quod more maiorum institutisque conceditur*). The sense required here, however, seems to be that the rebels did 'all they were able to', an extensional sense which is also common ('to be permitted by circumstances': cf. some of the examples given in *OLD* s.v. 3), emphasizing popular guilt, which Nero is here keen to assert in order to justify his retaliation. If *licuit* implies instead that they were 'permitted' to desecrate Poppaea's statues without fear of punishment, his words carry a sting, amounting to an impeachment of the loyalty of his commanders, who through negligence or connivance allowed this to happen. It is strange, however, for the prefect not to exculpate himself from this charge in the exchange which follows. The closest parallel in *TLL* is Liv. 8.31.7 *quidquid licuerit in magistro equitum, in militibus ausurum*, where *licuerit* is in place, because the words of the speaker carry a criticism for his audience, 'what he has been allowed to do by our inertia'.

Various solutions are possible, for instance a change in punctuation, with question mark after *quid illa turba . . . toris?* and after *dira?* i.e. *uiolare quantum licuit incesta manu et uoce dira?* 'how far have they been permitted to go in their trampling on all that is most sacred?' This correction, however, would leave *debita poena uacat* somewhat suspended and without a proper antecedent. A better option is perhaps to retain the longer sentence as it is and write instead ***libuit*** (the confusion is very common; cf. Sen. *Beat.* 4.2, with *licet* ς: *libet* ω; other instances are listed in *TLL* vii.2, s.v. *liceo*, 1358.79–80), 'they violated all they fancied'. For *quantum* as a relative-indefinite pronoun (= *quidquid*) cf. *OLD*, s.v. *quantum*[1], B4, e.g. Cic. *Ad Att.* 14.17.5 *Ciceroni meo . . . suppeditabis quantum uidebitur.*

Nero's anger flares up at the insulting words (855, *uoce dira*) levelled against Poppaea and himself by the rebelling populace (cf. also 799–800). In Aesch. *Agam.* 1662–3 Aegisthus counters Clytaemnestra's pacificatory proposals by adducing the outrageous behaviour of the old men against him: ἀλλὰ τούσδ' ἐμοὶ ματαίαν γλῶσσαν ὧδ' ἀπανθίσαι | κἀκβαλεῖν ἔπη τοιαῦτα . . .

In the various historical episodes of popular disapproval towards a *princeps* whenever a member of the royal family falls out of favour, the people make a point of protesting their attachment to the ruling prince: cf. Tac. *Ann.* 5.4 (given in full ad 820) *faustis . . . in Caesarem ominibus.*

855 debita poena uacat? For the set phrase *poena uacare* cf. Ov. *Trist.* 5.3.40 *impia nec poena Pentheos umbra uacet*; similar is also Tac. *Ann.* 4.70 *quem enim diem uacuum poena? uaco* ('to be idle', 'to be unoccupied') is a favourite verb with Seneca: cf. ad 382–3; cf. also Sen. *Oed.* 976 *debitas poenas tuli*, in the same metrical position.

856 poenam dolor constituet in ciues tuos? Pedroli ad loc. adduced Cic. *De Off.* 1.89 *prohibenda . . . maxime est ira in puniendo*; for other parallels on the thought that a good judge should not let himself be ruled by anger see Dyck's note ad loc. Cf. also Sen. *Ira* 1.15.3 *nil minus quam irasci punientem decet*. In *Thy.* 259 *maius hoc ira est malum* the *satelles* voices a timid criticism of the excessive punishment planned by Atreus as his revenge.

The line has no explicit interrogative element, but this is quite common in Senecan drama (cf. e.g. *Hf.* 352), and in Latin poetry in general. The interrogative character has to be inferred from the general tone of the passage.

ciuis is used of the subjects of an emperor in Nerva's edict quoted ad 834 (*ciuium meorum persuasio*: see Benner, *The Emperor Says*, 156; Sherwin-White, *The Letters of Pliny* (Oxford, 1966) 644). Also in Plin. *Epist.* 10.12.2.

857 constituet, aetas nulla quam famae eximat Nero alludes to the Great Fire of 64, with a megalomaniac reminiscence from Verg. *Aen.* 9.447 *nulla dies umquam memori uos eximet aeuo*.

858 tua temperet nos ira, non noster timor 'Let your wrath rule us, not our fear.' I accept Buecheler's emendation, *tua*, for the impossible MS *qua*. The prefect bows to Nero's will, declaring that he intends to implement his lord's orders, in spite of all misgivings he may have. His words have a formulaic ring, like a slogan learned by heart, and mark the subordinate's absolute acceptance of his master's will in place of his own, surrendering himself to Nero's superior authority. Earlier attempts to make sense of the transmitted version put a strain on the Latin: '*qua* id est in qua poena inroganda *non temperet* i.e. regat et moderetur *ira, non timor noster*, sed illis contrariae uirtutes, longanimitas et modestia' (Ascensius). On this interpretation of the passage, which also implies acceptance of the reading *non ira*, found in some *recc.*, the prefect makes a plea for caution and restraint; *noster*, however, clearly sets up a contrast between *timor* (the prefect's, because of his loyalty to all the members of the imperial house) and *ira* (Nero's). In addition, *qua* is too distant from *poena* to be intelligible, and the prominence of *ira* in Nero's answer in 859 suggests that *ira* is the important word in 858.

An alternative interpretation has been proposed by Alenius and Kragelund (in Kragelund 1988, 494), who suggested writing a question mark at the end of the sentence, *tua temperet nos ira, non noster timor?* On their interpretation, as I understand it, the prefect is made to react with rhetorical indignation at the prospect that Nero's faithful subjects need anger (i.e. punitive measures) to restrain them, and that their *timor* (presumably 'respect' or 'allegiance', generating fear of offending their ruler) is not deemed by Nero to be enough to ensure their obedience. But the wording of 858 is too compressed and elliptical to express this notion of *fear*: one would have expected the idea to receive more detailed treatment in the subsequent argument; Nero's answer at 859 picks up only *ira*, and no comment is made on *timor* alone having proved insufficient to prevent the deeds of violence and abuse against the emperor described at 851–5.

Metrical parallels for the word-end after the first thesis in *Octavia* are 37 *modo*, 101 *nisi*, 139 *manet*, 176 *dolor*, 383 *ubi*, 482 *tibi*, 562 *amor*, and elsewhere.

temperare, literally 'to moderate', 'to restrain' or 'curb', is used metaphorically to describe the power of the emperors in superhuman terms: the verb is normally applied to a god's rule over the universe: cf. Sen. *Epist.* 95.50 (*di*) *uniuersa ui sua temperant*; 65.23 *deus ista temperat*; 74.28 *modo latius uirtus funditur, regna urbes, prouincias temperat*. In relation to human rule cf. Mart. *Epigr.* 7.80.1-2 *quatenus Odrysios iam pax Romana triones | temperat*; Stat. *Silu.* 3.3.138 *qui nutu superas nunc temperat arces* (of the deified Vespasian). The metaphor implies that Nero's subjects are fundamentally an unruly and irrational mass, who need to be restrained by a normally benevolent, yet, if need be, implacable ruler. This view of the people is typical of Roman imperial writers, and repeatedly emerges in Seneca's writings: cf. *N.Q.* 2.43.2 *nociturum temperent* (sc. *quicumque magnam inter homines adepti sunt potentiam*); *infra*, 877 ff.

In this passage *temperet* carries the implication that the rule of the emperor has beneficial effects and restrains the negative impulses of the people. This representation of an emperor as a superhuman being whose will and judgement are infinitely superior to those of his subjects has precedents in the literature of the early imperial age and is not far from Seneca's own representation of the relation between the emperor and the world he rules, envisaged as a mass of irrational beings whose instincts are restrained by the *princeps*, the embodiment of natural reason on earth. Ovid, in his exilic poetry, stresses the point that the emperor's anger was just, indeed less vehement than the poet's mistake might have deserved (cf. e.g. *Trist.* 5.2.60 *tua peccato lenior ira meo est*). Sen. *Cons. Pol.* describes the lightning hurled by the emperor against him as a just punishment (13.4 *scias licet ea demum fulmina esse iustissima quae etiam percussi colunt*). A good example of the indirect, conceited style used in talking not of what a ruler wants, but what his virtues imply, can be found in the style of Pliny's addresses in Bk. 10: cf. 1.1 *tua quidem pietas, imperator sanctissime, optauerat ut quam tardissime succederes patri.*

859 iram expiabit prima quae meruit meam The (unmetrical) MS reading *expectabit*, or *explicabit*, was emended by Erasmus (in Ascensius' 1514 edition) to *expiabit*, 'atone'. To atone is to make up for the sins one has committed; here the sense is that Octavia's guilt has produced Nero's anger, and this is in itself a sin crying out for expiation. The idiom *expiare iram*, with reference normally to the gods' anger, is well established: cf. Liv. 9.1.3 *expiatum est quidquid . . . irarum in nos caelestium fuit*; Claud. *Carm.* 18.19–20 *quae tantas expiet* *iras uictima?* For *merere iram* cf. Ov. *Pont.* 1.1.49; *Trist.* 2.29 *ira . . . quidem iusta est nec me meruisse negabo*. Nero carries on the linguistic assumption, initiated by the prefect, that turns him into a demi-god, whose anger, once it has been aroused, can only be placated by the offer of appropriate sacrifice, in this case the head of Octavia.

860 quam poscat ede, nostra ne parcat manus Cf. Sen. *Oed.* 222 *quem memoret ede Phoebus, ut poenas luat.*

861 caedem sororis poscit et dirum caput *caput* is used metonymically for 'life' (cf. ad 133), which makes the sequence a dicolon of two synonymous expressions.

862 horrore uinctum trepidus astrinxit rigor *rigor* used metaphorically of fear has no parallels in the Senecan corpus (where however, as in Ovid, *rigeo* is commonly so used: cf. Ov. *Met.* 3.100 *gelido . . . comae terrore rigebant*; Sen. *Oed.* 659 *et ossa et artus gelidus inuasit tremor*); Val. Fl. *Arg.* 3.263 *tenet exsangues rigor horridus artus.*

863–864 NE. **parere dubitas?** PR. **cur meam damnas fidem?** | NE. **quod parcis hosti** The line bears a striking resemblance to *H.O.* 909 *cur tuas damnas manus?* On the relationship between *Oct.* and *H.O.* and on their relative chronology see Introd. pp. 50–4. In Greek tragedy socially subordinate characters are always treated condescendingly and are not expected to display honour and courage. For example the *phylax* in Soph. *Ant.* 436–40, who fears for his life until the flouter of the edict is found, may sympathize with Antigone, but admits that nothing is better than one's own safety. The horrified, implicitly critical, reaction of the prefect is elsewhere attributed to choruses, who are often free citizens and therefore allowed to retain a sense of dignity and independence, or at least attempt to restrain their ruler when he is carried away by fury: cf. the exchange between Oedipus and the chorus in Soph. *O.T.* 656–67, where the chorus entreats Oedipus to acquit Creon and the king's response is to accuse the chorus of wanting his own death; see also Soph. *Ant.* 770. It must be noted, however, that the social status of the *praefectus praetorio* was not comparable to that of attendants and soldiers in Greek tragedy, since he was of equestrian rank.

864–865 PR. **femina hoc nomen capit?** | NE. **si scelera cepit** This is an example of the figure *anaclasis*, common in animated dialogue (cf. Lausberg, *HLR*, par. 292), whereby the same word is used by two speakers in two different senses. The phraseology *nomen capere* is common; the use of *capio* for 'to embrace' 'to launch into' is more pointed. It is sometimes interpreted as an instance of *simplex pro composito* (= *concepi*): cf. *Agam.* 31 *cepi nefas* (perhaps corrupt; cf. Zwierlein (1977), 165); *H.O.* 1124 *quis tantum capiet nefas*. Some examples of this usage are collected in *TLL* iii s.v. 321.51 ff., for instance Luc. *Bell. Ciu.* 1.184–5 (*Caesar*) *ingentes . . . animo motus bellumque futurum | ceperat.*

865–866 PR. **estne qui sontem arguat?** | NE. **populi furor.** PR. **quis regere dementes ualet?** There are only five occurrences of *est* with the enclitic interrogative particle *-ne* in Seneca, all in the tragedies. The pair *sons/insons* is the high-flown synonym of *nocens/innocens*. Seneca avoids *sons* in his prose works, and its occurrence is restricted to the tragedies. In the imperial age, it is only found in the historians (cf. J. N. Adams, *CQ* n.s. 22 (1972), 357).

Liberman defends Baehrens' *fauor*, but *dementes* in the prefect's reply supports the transmitted version.

In Prud. *Peristeph.* 10.78–85 Romanus is accused by the imperial magistrate of having fomented the popular unrest: *tu uentilator urbis et uulgi leuis | procella mentes inquietas mobiles, | ne se imperita turba dedat legibus* . . . (84) *ut se per aeuum consecrandos autument | si bella diuis ceu gigantes inferant | uictique flammis obruantur montium* (observe that the description of the people as a fickle multitude, which is commonplace, is similar to that used *infra* in 877–81; 85 seems reminiscent of *Oct.* 808 *flammis uestros obruet ignes*). An edict issued by the prefect of Egypt Rutilius Lupus on the occasion of riots in the city of Alexandria (*c.* AD 115) has come down to us (cf. *Corpus Pap. Iud.* (Cambridge, Mass., 1960), vol. II, 231, n. 435, col. II, ll. 23–4, col. III, ll. 1–11). The Roman magistrate engages in a dialogue with a fictive antagonist, to exculpate himself pre-emptively against the objection that the prefect's measures are too harsh, and that only a few are guilty of the events that have shaken the city: ἐπειτά τις ἐρεῖ ὀλίγους εἶναι τοὺς ταῦτα τολμῶντας . . . οἶδα ὅτι εἰσίν ὀλίγοι· ἀλλ' ἐγφέρουσιν αὐτοὺς οἱ πλείονες καὶ τρέφουσιν οἱ κρείσσονες . . . τὸ ἐν ὀλίγοις μεισούμενον οὐκ ἀδίκως ὅλης πόλεώς ἐστιν ἔγκλημα . . . μὴ πιστευέτωσαν μου τῆι εὐπετίαι: the notables of the Greek community are apparently accused of fomenting the revolt, even if the number of people involved is small; let them not trust too far the prefect's clemency lest they taste his punishment.

866–867 PR. **quis regere dementes ualet?** | NE. **qui concitare potuit** *A* reads *quis* in 867, by wrong assimilation to the preceding interrogative form: Nero gives pointed and sharp replies, and does not fling back questions to the *praefectus*. The masculine *qui* has a generalizing value: 'the person who'.

867–868 PR. **haud quemquam reor.** | NE. **mulier . . .** I prefer to retain the allocation of the speeches found in the MSS, with *mulier* as the initial word of Nero's response to the prefect. The most significant alteration to the MS version has been proposed by Zwierlein (1978), 158–9, and in his edition, who gives *mulier* to the prefect (an emendation first proposed by Lipsius):

PR. quis regere dementes ualet?
NE. qui concitare potuit. PR. haud quemquam, reor,
mulier- NE. dedit natura cui pronum malo
animum

This emendation yields very effective sense; *mulier* picks up the prefect's *femina hoc nomen capit* at 864. The new text is also attractive because it makes the speakers' exchange syntactically more animated and less constrained by excessive adherence to the metrical units, in a manner which vividly conjures up the tense mood of the debate. There are eight instances in the Senecan corpus in which a change of speaker occurs after the first arsis (including cases in which the sentence is carried across from the previous line): *Thy.* 257, 321, 745, 747, 1102; *Med.* 882; *Phae.* 240, 241. In early drama, compare Naev. *Trag.* 40–1 R[2] *egone an ille iniurie | facimus* (after the first thesis). By way of parallels for a pointed answer beginning with a relative pronoun, adding a polemical correction to the topic introduced by the previous speaker (*dedit natura cui . . . ?*), Zwierlein gives *Troad.* 663–4 *funditus busta eruam*:: | *quae uendidistis?*; *Hf.* 453; other instances in Seidensticker (1969), 38 n. 85b. Some edd. prefer *haudquaquam*, which is an 'archaic' negative adverb.

For all the merits of Zwierlein's solution, I have preferred to maintain the traditional MS speech allocation, together with the majority of previous editors: *haud quemquam reor* (sc. *ualuisse regere dementes*). NE. *mulier* . . . The word *mulier* is often abusive in classical Latin, and especially so in Augustan or post-Augustan poetry, where *femina* is the preferential, neutral term for 'woman' (cf. J. N. Adams, 'Latin words for "woman" and "wife"' *Glotta* 50 (1980), 234–9). Accordingly, *femina* occurs 25 times in Senecan tragedy, against only two instances of *mulier* in the corpus. On the fluctuations in the use of the two words cf. Axelson, *UW* 53–6. Significantly, the prefect has used *femina* at 864 ('woman', but also 'lady') in his attempt to exculpate Octavia, whom he still refers to as a princess of royal blood, and it would be strange for him to have recourse now to the cruder, more realistic expression for the sake of variation. Although both words can be used in abusive contexts (for *femina* cf. *infra*, ad 869), *mulier* has more immediate pejorative connotations ('female'): cf. *TLL* viii, s.v. *mulier*, 1573.3–30. *mulier* is used as a sneer in the only other example in the Senecan corpus, Sen. *Med.* 193 *quae causa pellat, innocens mulier rogat* (an oxymoronic pair in Creon's sarcastic reply to Medea); *Const.* 14.1 *mulier . . . imprudens animal est . . . ferum, cupiditatium incontinens*. The word has the wrong connotations in a context in which supposedly the speaker, if we follow Zwierlein, is to stress Octavia's innocence: *uirgo* would have been a more felicitous choice.

On the interpretation proposed by Zwierlein, *reor*, a formal and comparatively rare term in Latin, is used parenthetically (cf. Zwierlein (1978), 158–9; *LHS* 2.528–9; K-S 2.2.161–2; Hofmann, *LU*, 114–16). Parentheses with verbs of opinion (e.g. *opinor, credo, puto*) are common in colloquial Latin, where, as generally in the spoken registers, parataxis is preferred to hypotaxis. Even in the more formal genres, such expressions are used in speeches when a speaker intends to moderate his statement: cf. e.g. Verg. *Aen.* 5.56–7 *haud equidem sine mente, reor, sine numine diuum | adsumus*; 1.387–8 *haud, credo, inuisus caelestibus auras* | *uitalis carpis*. In Senecan tragedy, only imperative expressions are used as parenthetic interruptions, and *reor* only occurs, usually at line-end, governing an infinitival clause (in *Oct.* cf. 447 *aetate in hac satis esse consilii reor*; 566 *hanc esse uitae maximam causam reor*). The accusative pronoun *haud quemquam* creates the expectation that an infinitival construction will follow: a parenthetic insertion *reor* would make the syntax ambiguous. Instead, *reor* governs an infinitival clause elliptical of the verb: 'I don't believe anybody (sc. could have roused such an ungovernable mob)'. The ellipsis of a dependent infinitive is infrequent, and restricted to contexts of rapid, informal dialogue, where the sense suffers no diminution because the speech situation is clear to all speakers involved: cf. Plaut. *Bacch.* 208 *immo ut eam (pendere) credis?*; *Persa* 834; *Vid.* 44–5 *non edepol equidem credo mercennarium* | *te esse:: an non credis?*; Cic. *Ad Att.* 12.6a.2 *Atticam doleo tam diu* (sc. *febri laborare*); cf. Hofmann, *LU* 171–2. The extraction (also known as prolepsis or left-dislocation) of the subject in the acc. + inf. construction is extremely common (cf. Rosén, *Latine loqui*, 154–5): cf. Acc. *Scaen.* 312–13 R² *neque quemquam arbitror* | *tuae paeniturum laudis*. Zwierlein's speech attribution is also inadequate from a rhetorical standpoint. In the context (PR. Who could possibly have directed an irrational, madness-driven crowd? NE. The very person who first suborned them), the expected rejoinder was 'I don't think anybody (needs to be supposed to have aroused the populace)', *haud quemquam reor* (sc. *concitare ualuisse*), in answer to Nero's *qui concitare potuit*. The discussion turns not on whom or how many a woman could ever have rallied against the emperor, but on the necessity of the supposition that anybody masterminded the revolt.

868–869 dedit natura cui pronum malo | animum, ad nocendum pectus instruxit dolis Nero is quick in his rejoinder that women are by nature prone to evil. The misogyny of his suspicious and angry words, though traditional (cf. Verg. *Aen.* 4.569–70 *uarium et mutabile semper* | *femina*, with the emphatic *femina* thrown into prominence by the position at line-beginning; Ov. *Met.* 10.244–5 *quae* (sc. *uitia*) *plurima menti* | *femineae natura dedit*), seems influenced by Sen. *Med.* 266–8 *tu tu malorum machinatrix facinorum* | *cui feminae nequitia, ad audendum omnia* | *robur uirile*, which is here imitated even in the asyndetic link; cf. also *Phae.* 559 *sed dux malorum femina*. Vürtheim quoted Eur. *Med.* 266–7 ὅταν δ' ἐς εὐνὴν ἠδικημένη κυρῆι, | οὐκ ἔστιν ἄλλη φρὴν μιαιφονωτέρα.

For *pectus instruxit dolis* cf. Verg. *Aen.* 2.152 *dolis instructus et arte Pelasga*.

870–871 PR. **sed uim negauit.** NE. **ut ne inexpugnabilis | esset** It is impossible to retain the allocation of 868–876 to Nero as they are transmitted in the MSS. Kragelund (1988), 495–7 has revived Ritter's proposal to attribute both 870 and 871 to the prefect, but the argument on the strength of which this emendation is supported, namely that the author of *Oct.* never allows a speech to begin in mid-verse in *antilabai*, has little force, given the limited extension of this play. *Octavia* brims with dramatic *hapax legomena* of all kinds which it would be unwise to emend on the grounds of the *usus auctoris*, when they are elsewhere amply attested in the tradition from which this poet derives his craftsmanship. I follow Zwierlein's speech allocation (1978, 158–60). Peiper was the first to break the line in two halves and to attribute 870a only, *sed uim negauit*, to the prefect. The brief objection reflects the character's increasingly resigned attempts to oppose Nero.

The sequence *ut ne* does not occur in the corpus elsewhere, but is frequent in early dramatic poetry and in prose up to Cicero (cf. J. André, *REL* 35 (1957), 165; K-S 2.2.209): cf. Enn. *Scaen.* 353 R² *ut ne res temere tractent turbidas*; Pacuv. *Scaen.* 72 R² *semper sat agere ut ne in amore animum occupes*. *sed* introducing a positive alternative seems unobjectionable.

The metrical layout of this line, exhibiting synaloephe in the seventh element and a single word spanning the three final feet, has numerous precedents in Latin drama (for the long final adjective in *-bilis* cf. Pacuv. *Scaen.* 122–3 R² *ni me inexorabilem | faxis*; see Lindsay ad Plaut. *Capt.* 56) and in Seneca, where it is strongly expressive, as well as a marker of the tragic genre: cf. *Phoe.* 133 *quid simile posuit, quid tam inextricabile* (imitating in turn Acc. *Scaen.* 75 R² *quid tam obscuridicum est tamue inenodabile*); *Phoe.* 165 *hac extrahe animam duram inexpugnabilem* (but the *Oct.* poet ignores the dicolon asyndeticum with a pair of adjectives); *Phae.* 229 *quis huius animum flectet intractabilem?*; 271 *temptemus animum tristem et intractabilem*; 580); Prud. *Peristeph.* 5.171 *inuictum inexsuperabilem*. On this topic, cf. Soubiran (1964), 429–69.

The adjective *inexpugnabilis* occurs in poetry only after Ovid (*Met.* 11.767–8 *nec inexpugnabile amori | pectus*; *Trist.* 4.10.65–6 *molle Cupidineis nec inexpugnabile telis | cor mihi*). The occurrence of long words at line-end is also an expressive device common in Augustan poets, notably Ovid, who exhibits many *hapax legomena* at such junctures. These long adjectives often convey a sense of sadness or accompany the expression of reflections concerning human life (cf. Verg. *Aen.* 6.27 *et inextricabilis error*; 10.467 *breue et inreparabile tempus*; Hor. *Carm.* 2.14.6–7 (*non si*) *places inlacrimabilem | Plutona tauris*).

871 sed aegras frangeret uires timor Buecheler proposed to emend *aegras* to *acres*, but *aegras* seems in place, either with proleptic value or denoting a lack of stability innate in women: cf. *TLL* i, s.v. *aeger*, 942.5–10, e.g. Stat. *Theb.* 8.531 *aegra animo uis ac fiducia cessit*.

872–873 uel poena, quae iam sera damnatam premet | diu nocentem *nocens* is a poetical substitute for *reus* (cf. Ov. *Met.* 4.110 *nocens anima*; Stat. *Theb.* 3.368 *uitae . . . nocens*); other synonyms occurring in poetic language are *sons, noxius*. The MSS read *iam* (*v.l.* tam *GTβ*) *sera damnatam premit*, which was corrected by Bothe².

873 tolle consilium ac preces This use of *tollo* as a negative periphrastic imperative is poetical (cf. *supra* ad 270): cf. Hor. *Carm.* 2.5.9 *tolle cupidinem*; Ov. *Met.* 11.685 *solantia tollite uerba*.

874–875 deuectam rate | procul in remotum litus interimi iube Cf. Soph. *Ant.* 773–4 ἄγων ἐρῆμος ἔνθ' ἂν ᾖι βροτῶν στίβος | κρύψω, Eur. *Hec.* 1284–5 οὐχ ὅσον τάχος | νήσων ἐρήμων αὐτὸν ἐκβαλεῖτέ ποι; Sen. *Agam.* 997–8 *abripite . . . auectam procul . . . ultimo in regni angulo | uincite.* In Eur. 472e Kann. (= P.Berl. 13217) ll. 45–8 Minos orders that Pasiphae be imprisoned in a sequestered dungeon (Pasiphae appears to be present).

On *litus, litora* to indicate islands in poetry cf. ad 971.

876 tandem ut residat pectoris nostri tumor *tumor* is certainly preferable to the competing reading *timor*, and is a synonym for *ira*, which demands blood vengeance (cf. *OLD* s.v. 3a; Junge 1999, 218): cf. *Thy.* 519–20 *ponatur omnis ira et ex animo tumor | erasus abeat* (Ballaira).

877 The protracted finale of *Octavia* is a long *amoibaion* shared by a sympathetic chorus and the heroine, who, however, answers the chorus only once (958). In structure, the final act resembles the so-called *Ecceschlüsse*, or 'demonstrative' endings, of Greek tragedy (on which see Kremer, in Jens, *Bauformen*, 116–41) often with a strong choral element, or with a song in responsion: cf. Aesch. *Pers.*, *Sept.*, *Suppl.*; Eur. *Troad.*; see also Mastronarde ad Eur. *Phoe.* 1710. In contrast with this closural pattern of Greek tragedy, which primarily looks back at what has been enacted in the previous scenes and has a threnodic character, the scene brings the drama's action to its culminating point, with the final exit of Octavia, attended upon by Nero's guards, silent, and by a chorus expressing compassion for the protagonist, and endeavouring to console her. The principal model, however, Soph. *Ant.* 806–82 (see *infra* ad 924), is not closural.

There is some disagreement about the identity of the present chorus, with some interpreters viewing this as the chorus of Octavia's supporters, who sang at 273 and 669 (so Ballaira ad loc., Zwierlein (1966), 86; Kragelund (1982), 79; La Penna (1991), 42). Considerations of dramatic continuity suggest, however, that this chorus is identical with that of Poppaea's partisans present in 762 ff., as suggested by Herington (1961), 22 n. 5; see also Manuwald, 292–331. The chorus of citizens loyal to Octavia left in 689, and their unannounced reappearance now would be surprising, in view of the fact that they have been dispersed by Nero's guards after taking part in the rebellion to which they summon themselves in 669 ff.

The sympathy shown to Octavia's plight is not at odds with their devotion to Poppaea, since tragic choruses commiserate with former enemies on many occasions. In Soph. *Ant.* (especially relevant if this is the main dramatic precedent for the final exit scene; see *infra*), the chorus is loyal to Creon and seeks to distance itself from Antigone: nevertheless they express sympathy for the doomed heroine. The way in which this chorus describes the inconstancy of popular support, and the frustration of the *ciues* who can now see Octavia being led away to meet her fate, suggest the estrangement of a third party somewhat distant from the events (894–5 *nunc ad poenam trahi . . . miseram cernere possunt*).

The presence of two choruses is not without parallels in ancient drama (cf. Tarrant ad Sen. *Agam.* 586 on secondary choruses; in Greek tragedy cf. Aesch. *Suppl.*, *Eum.*; Eur. *Hipp.*, *Suppl.*), but in all instances the chorus which makes its appearance after the parodos has a more limited function, usually that of providing a retinue for a new character of high social standing (for instance Cassandra or Iole), and exits or fails to reappear prominently in the subsequent scenes. Different in nature are the two semichoruses at the end of Aesch. *Septem*, 1070 ff., where it is more a case of a single chorus dividing to perform the ritual mourning over the bodies of the two rival brothers. *Octavia* seems to be unique in having two choruses of equal importance acting in two successive sections of the play. On the other instances in which, in Greek tragedy, a chorus divides into semichoruses cf. Di Marco, *Tragedia*, 175–6.

Historically Octavia was deported to Pandataria from the place of her preliminary banishment in Campania, and not directly from Rome (cf. Tac. *Ann.* 14.63–4), but the tragedy shows no awareness of this, or at least overlooks it as an irrelevance for dramatic purposes. When Octavia claims to see 'her brother's ship', this can be regarded as no more than a prophetic anticipation of death, expressed in the visionary language of Verg. *Aen.* 6.86–7 *bella, horrida bella | et Thybrim multo spumantem sanguine cerno.* Perhaps more explicitly relating to a seashore setting are 969 ff., where Octavia prepares to embark.

A further possibility is that the chorus speaking at 877 ff. and the consolers of Octavia are not the same group of people. On this interpretation the ode at 877 ff. unobtrusively introduces a ('mental') scene change from Rome to Campania, an unprepared scene change on the pattern of Sen. *Phoe.* 427 ff., where the scene on the battlefield overlaps to an extent with the scene described by the messenger on the battlements: cf. R. J. Tarrant, *HSCPh* 82 (1978), 229. The montage of the tragedy, with its melodramatic, highly emotional finale centered on the heroine's departure, has parallels in Eur. *Troad.*, *Hec.*; Sen. *Troad.*, *Agam.*

877–881 O funestus multis populi | dirusque fauor, | qui cum flatu uela secundo | ratis impleuit uexitque procul, | languidus idem deserit alto | saeuoque mari The 'ship' whose sails are filled and released in quick succession by the breezes of popular infatuation is the demagogue who foolhardily commits himself to his untrustworthy supporters. Popular support is implicitly likened to a wind driving the vessels (the leaders who embrace the popular cause) out into the open sea and then suddenly giving way to a calm (*languidus*), leaving the ship motionless in mid-sea. The choral ode, however, is not consistently elaborated as an allegory, nor is it a fully fledged simile, since it lacks syntactical markers of comparison. Among the most significant precedents for this metaphoric field cf. Sen. *Hf.* 169–71 *illum populi fauor attonitum | fluctuque magis mobile uulgus | aura tumidum tollit inani* (where the boundaries between the two terms of the comparison are similarly blurred); Hor. *Carm.* 1.1.7 *mobilium turba Quiritium* (with N–H's note, quoting Dem. 19.136 ὁ μὲν δῆμός ἐστιν . . . ὥσπερ ἐν θαλάττηι κῦμ' ἀκατάστατον, ὡς ἂν τύχηι κινούμενον); 3.2.20 *arbitrio popularis aurae*; *Epist.* 1.19.37 *uentosae plebis suffragia*; Verg. *Aen.* 6.816; Cic. *Mur.* 35 with less notable condescension, *quod enim fretum . . . tam uarias habere putatis agitationes . . . fluctuum quantas perturbationes et quantos aestus habet ratio comitiorum?* In Greek tragedy, the people's anger is likened to fire and the fury of a storm at sea, whereas the ruler must prove a helmsman, able to wait for a calm, in Eur. *Or.* 696–701; along the same lines Soph. *Ant.* 715. These two Greek passages, however, refer to rebellion, rather than to favour with ruinous consequences. In Eur. *Heracl.* 427–32 Iolaus likens the suppliants (when the people of Athens exert pressure on Demophon to hand them back to the Argives) to a ship approaching a safe harbour, but suddenly driven back by a strong wind towards the open sea. More parallels for this frequent imagery in F. Cairns, *Generic Composition* (Edinburgh, 1987), 218–20; Hutchinson, ad Aesch. *Septem*, 62–3. Since the ode is delivered by a chorus of courtiers and Roman aristocrats (cf. *supra*, ad 877), the complaint of the unreliability of the *uulgus* is in character with their putative social status.

For the occurrence of the same metaphorical field in different contexts cf. Quint. *Inst.* 12 *pr.* 2–4 *uelut aura sollicitante prouecti longius . . . postea . . . quam in altum simus ablati sentire coepimus*; Ov. *Ars* 1.373 *ne uela cadant auraeque residant.*

The unreliability of the *uulgus* is a topos in Latin (cf. *supra*, ad 834), especially in the historiographical tradition, on which cf. Z. Yavetz, *Plebs and Princeps* (Oxford, 1969), 5 n.1. Santoro quoted Tac. *Ann.* 2.41 *breues et infaustos populi Romani amores*, which does not, however, refer to political favour, but to bad fortune; Liv. 6.17 *audiebantur itaque propalam uoces exprobrantium multitudini, quod defensores suos semper in praecipitem locum fauore tollat, deinde in ipso discrimine periculi destituat . . . saginare plebem populares suos ut iugulentur*; Cass. Dio *Rom. Hist.* fr. 19 (book 5) Boiss. Κάσσιος τοὺς 'Ρωμαίους εὐεργετήσας ὑπ' αὐτῶν ἐκείνων ἐθανατώθη· ὥστε καὶ ἐκ τούτου διαδειχθῆναι ὅτι πιστὸν οὐδὲν ἐν τοῖς πλήθεσιν ἐστίν. In the corpus cf. Sen. *Phae.* 488; *Thy.* 351. The chorus illustrates a general sense with the use of examples, as *infra* at 929 ff. where, however, the tone is consolatory because the chorus is addressing Octavia in a 'lyrical' dialogue. The examples of illustrious individuals brought down by their incautious reliance on the populace have no consolatory function. In technique, this resembles the use of mythical paradigms in Greek tragedy, for instance Eur. *Hipp.* 545–64, where Semele and Iole are chosen to illustrate the destructive powers of Eros.

882 fleuit Gracchos miseranda parens The parallelism established between Octavia and the Gracchi and Livius Drusus is somewhat strained, because Octavia played no prominent role in political agitation, and she was only, according at least to the version of the events adopted by this playwright, a passive recipient of popular favour. The shift to Cornelia's point of view suggests that the prime inspiration for this catalogue of demagogues brought down by their incautious reliance on the populace came from Sen. *Cons. Marc.* 16.3–4, where Seneca, while consoling Marcia, invites her to follow the example of other famous women who faced their grief bravely (16.3 *quod tibi si uis exempla referri feminarum quae suos fortiter desiderauerint*): Cornelia, the mother of the Gracchi (also in *Cons. Helu.* 16.6; *Ben.* 6.34.2), and Cornelia, the mother of Livius Drusus. This is not the first time that the presence of Seneca's *Consolationes* can be observed in this play (see *supra* ad 382, 385). The same list of demagogues, with the addition of Saturninus, is found in Tac. *Ann.* 3.27.3.

Vell. 2.7.1, representing a negative tradition about the Gracchi, blames the brothers' ambition as the cause that brought ruin on them. Plutarch (a favourable source) relates that the main incitement to embrace political action came to Tiberius from the people, who exhorted him wherever he went to restore the common land to the poor (*Tib.* 8.4). In Plutarch, however, Tiberius and Gaius were not abandoned by the people, who, in fact, retained a loyal attachment to their memory (*Tib.* 21; *Gaius* 18).

883–883ᐧ perdidit ingens quos plebis amor | nimiusque fauor Cf. Ov. *Met.* 4.148–9 *tua te manus . . . amorque | perdidit.*

884–886 genere illustres, pietate, fide, | lingua claros, pectore fortes, | legibus acres Hosius adduced as a parallel Luc. *Bell. Ciu.* 6.796 *legibus immodicos ausosque ingentia Gracchos* (where however *l. i.* refers to the Drusi, mentioned in the previous line). Viansino translates 'attivi nel proporre leggi'. *pectore fortes* alludes to the brothers' courage, with a periphrasis which has a vaguely epic ring: cf. Verg. *Aen.* 2.348–9 *iuuenes, fortissima frustra | pectora*; 4.11 *forti pectore et armis. pietate fide* refers to the brothers' reciprocal bond of loyalty and affection, also proverbial: cf. Cic. *Brut.* 126 *utinam non tam fratri pietatem quam patriae praestare uoluisset!* (Pedroli). Cf. also Flor. *Epit.* 2.2 *Ti. Gracchus . . . genere, forma, eloquentia facile princeps.*

887–888 te quoque, Liui, simili leto | fortuna dedit *leto dare* in Verg. *Aen.* 5.806; 11.172; 12.348.

889–890 quem neque fasces texere sui | nec tecta domus Zwierlein writes *suae* in place of the MS *sui* at 889, a correction suggested by Wilamowitz to Leo, who was the first to print it in his edition. Wilamowitz raised an objection against the previously unquestioned reading *sui* for reasons of historical accuracy, the *tribuni plebis* not being known for having had *lictores* (although Cass. Dio *Hist. Rom.* 60.12.2 suggests that the tribunes could use their *apparitores* for coercive purposes) and, in fact, being the only Roman magistracy for which our sources explicitly state the absence of lictors and *fasces.* In fact, the transmitted *sui* must be read: the passage is modelled on Verg. *Aen.*

12.540–1 *nec di texere Cupencum . . . sui*; and also *Aen.* 2.426 ff., esp. *nec te tua plurima, Panthu, | labentem pietas nec Apollinis infula texit.*

tui of some *recc.* is an adjustment aimed at eliminating the odd change of person, admittedly difficult: cf. perhaps Verg. *Aen.* 10.390–2 *uos etiam, gemini, Rutulis cecidistis in aruis . . . simillima proles | indiscreta suis*; Ov. *Met.* 3.432–7 (poet's apostrophe followed by a description in third person) *credule, quid frustra . . . non illum . . .* ; Sen. *Phoe.* 493–4 *quotiens necesse fallere aut falli a suis, | patiare potius ipse quam facias scelus*; Sil. *Pun.* 3.611–13 *nam te* (sc. *Domitianum*) *longa manent nostri consortia mundi. | huic* (sc. *Domitiano*) *laxos arcus olim Gangetica pubes | summittet*; 4.235–6 *occidis et tristi, pugnax Lepontice, fato. | nam dum frena ferox obiecto corpore prensat . . .* On the other hand, the relative pronoun seems to encourage the transition from direct address to third person narrative: cf. Ov. *Met.* 5.111–16 *tu quoque Lampetide* (sc. *cecidisti*) *. . . quem procul adstantem . . . Paetalus inridens . . . dixit . . . et laeuo mucronem tempore fixit*; Luc. *Bell. Ciu.* 5.58–61 (dubious). Cf. Ferri (1996), 311–14. Other instances of 'commutatio secundae et tertiae personae' in Housman ad Man. *Astr.* 1.697.

As Ballaira is right to maintain, *fasces* is said generically for *honores*, as in 679 and in Sen. *Phae.* 983–4 *tradere turpi fasces populus gaudet* (but Farnaby already had a note 'magistratus dignitas; nulli enim tribunis lictores'); in a similar way Horace employs *secures* in *Carm.* 3.2.19–20 *nec sumit aut ponit . . . securis | arbitrio popularis aurae.*

neque fasces . . . . nec tecta is the only instance of polysyndeton in *Octavia.* The same sequence also at *Oed.* 381–2 *neque ista . . . armenti . . . uox est nec usquam territi resonant greges.* These are the two sole instances of *neque* in the corpus of Senecan tragedy, against some two hundred occurrences of *nec.* Löfstedt, *Syntactica* 1.338, discusses the fluctuations of *neque* in classical Latin, where the word is progressively ousted by the more common *nec.* Cf. also Axelson, *UW* 116, for its relative rarity in Augustan poetry.

The expression *fasces . . . sui* is related to the idiom *dii sui*, 'to have the gods on one's side', as in Ov. *Met.* 4.373 *uota suos habuere deos*; Hor. *Epod.* 9.30 *uentis iturus non suis. tego* is used in both a metaphorical and a literal sense: for other instances of the same shift from literal to metaphorical and vice versa in the same sentence see ad 807–8. For this use of *texere*, in addition to the Vergil passage given above, cf. also Luc. *Bell. Ciu.* 2.71–2 *stagna auidi texere soli . . . depositum, Fortuna, tuum* (of Gaius Marius).

890–891 plura referre | prohibet praesens exempla dolor This manner of suddenly breaking off reference to exempla echoes Ovidian language: cf. Ov. *Met.* 11.708 *plura dolor prohibet*; 9.328–9 *quamquam lacrimaeque dolorque | impediunt prohibentque loqui*; *CE* 670.1 *prohibet dolor ipse fateri.* Cf. Ov. *Fast.* 1.491–2 *passus idem Tydeus et idem Pagasaeus Iason | et quos praeterea longa referre mora est.* Greek tragic choruses tend to express sympathy or compassion for the main character (cf. Soph. *Ai.* 200 ἐμοὶ δ' ἄχος ἔστακεν, *Ant.* 801–5, cited *infra*, ad 892–5). In Greek tragedy, however, grief or tears choking up one's voice are not presented as the reason for breaking off a list, whereas reticence can be caused by either fear of a ruler (cf. Aesch. *Agam.* 56) or fear of blasphemy. In Sen. *Phae.* 356–7 *quid plura canam? uincit saeuas* | *cura nouercas* the rhetorical interrogative clause serves to introduce the final *pointe*.

Since the third syllable of *referre* is short, 890 would provide one more instance of *breuis in longo* in *Octavia*. This assumption seems better than Zwierlein's tentative correction *referri*, attempting to solve the prosodic problem posed by the sequence *–re pro* if *plura* begins a new line. Indeed, lengthening of a final open syllable before initial *pr-* (in *referre prohibet*) is without parallels in the Senecan corpus, where 'irrational' lengthening only occurs before *sp-* in *Hf.* 950 and *sc-* in *Phae.* 1026 (cf. Leo, *Obs.* 203, n. 4). Outside the Senecan corpus, irrational lengthening before *tr- fr- br-* is found in Catullus (cf. Fordyce, ad Cat. *Carm.* 4.9), but rarely elsewhere. Early Latin poetry is even more restrictive on this point; cf. Lindsay, Plaut. *Capt.*, Introd. 43; Acc. *Scaen.* 534 R[2] *dictus Prometheus* (from an anapaestic *canticum*). In Greek tragedy, lengthening before an initial consonant cluster of this type is rare, and mainly restricted to lyrics, although the phenomenon is on the increase in fourth-century drama and later (cf. West, *GM* 17 n. 32, 160 n. 74; Hutchinson, ad Aesch. *Septem* 1056; Eitrem-Amundsen (1955), 8). It is a mark of the more artificial enunciation of tragedy.

The chorus' list of pitiful exempla comes to a sudden end, in an outburst of emotion which is graphically expressed by the sense-break after the first metron. There are parallels for such sudden changes even in Zwierlein's colometry (cf. 962 *testor superos – quid agis demens?*). Strict adherence to the so-called *Kongruenzgesetz* often proves difficult to maintain, and Zwierlein too occasionally prints monometers also at the beginning of a new clause (cf. *Troad.* 79; 130; *Med.* 361). Fitch (1987), 25, 37–8 makes a very strong case for alternative arrangements of cola in anapaestic sequences. He shows that Zwierlein's own treatment is often inconsistent, influenced by Leo's idea that final monometers are a frequent feature in imitation of paroemiacs in Greek tragedy, and indeed Fitch's analysis strongly corroborates the presence of initial monometers. Fitch favours monometer here, with *br. in longo* marking line-end: | *plura referre* | *prohibet praesens exempla dolor.*

The parallels given above seem further to suggest that Zwierlein's *referri* is also unidiomatic. The construction of *prohibeo* with an active infinitive and no subject expressed, even when this is different from the subject of the main clause, is idiomatic in Latin (*LHS* 2.346, 356; *OLD* s.v. 4b) and frequently found in poetry (cf. e.g. Ov. *Met.* 7.717 *prohibebant credere mores*; 8.652 *et sentire moram prohibent*; 9.59; Luc. *Bell. Ciu.* 8.70 *prohibetque* (sc. *Corneliam*) *succumbere fatis*). The acc. + inf. construction is mainly found when the infinitive is passive.

892–895 modo cui patriam reddere ciues | aulam . . . nunc ad poenam letumque trahi | flentem miseram cernere possunt Cf. Soph. *Ant.* 801–5 νῦν δ' ἤδη 'γὼ καὐτὸς θεσμῶν | ἔξω φέρομαι τάδ' ὁρῶν, ἴσχειν δ' | οὐκέτι πηγὰς δύναμαι δακρύων, | τὸν παγκοίταν ὅθ' ὁρῶ θάλαμον | τήνδ' Ἀντιγόνην ἀνύτουσαν, Sen. Rh. *Suas.* 6.17 *uix attollentes prae lacrimis oculos intueri truncata membra ciues poterant*; Luc. *Bell. Ciu.* 8.152–3 *quam . . . discedere cernens | ingemuit populus.*

The reading of ***A***, *possit*, yielding impossible sense, was emended in more recent manuscripts to *possunt* (Σ), or *possis*. The choice between competing readings opens up a number of problems relating to the identity of the speakers in this section. *possis* removes the oddity of having the chorus refer to the Roman citizens watching Octavia's exit as an alien body. This is perhaps slightly anomalous if the lines are spoken, as I believe, by the same chorus which will engage in lyrical dialogue with Octavia in the following scene. The impersonal potential subjunctive, however, seems out of place, because the scene they describe is in fact taking place more or less in synchrony with their words. If *possunt* is right, we perceive the chorus' intention, for all their sympathy for Octavia, to distance themselves from the rebels. In this, the author imitates Soph. *Antigone*, where the chorus of Theban elders hold a middle course between compassion for the rebellious daughter of Oedipus and allegiance to their ruler. The partisans of Octavia, here referred to as *ciues*, have been dispersed by Nero's guards. Against the consideration that *ciues* seems too positive an epithet for what the speakers are expected to regard as their enemy, one could argue perhaps that the playwright does not always succeed in maintaining characterization strictly; moreover, the singers of choral odes have wavering identities – this happens even in Senecan tragedy – and oscillate between the voice of impersonal observers and that of involved participants.

A jesting hostile chorus would have been out of place. Nero's monstrous nature was thrown into relief by the presence of a foil, weakly opposing his will (Seneca, the prefect). Similarly the pitiful sight of Octavia being taken away is reflected in the chorus' emotional outburst. Her miseries are so great that even Poppaea's partisans cannot restrain their tears.

The spatial setting of the scene is undecipherable, and the allusion to ships and a seashore evokes a sudden scene change, comparable to Sen. *Phoe.* 427–77, where Jocasta's swift flight to the battlefield is described as seen by the messenger on the walls of Thebes, and then, shortly afterwards, Jocasta herself speaks, while kneeling between the two hostile brothers, on the battlefield.

892–893 patriam reddere . . . | aulam et fratris . . . toros The 'brother' here being referred to is certainly Nero, because Britannicus died an adolescent and still unmarried: *toros* is here used metonymically for 'marriage'. Octavia was to be restored to her legitimate place next to her brother-husband Nero.

896–898 bene paupertas humili tecto | contenta latet; | quatiunt altas saepe procellae | aut euertit Fortuna domos The sentiment that the humble life of simple folk is less exposed to danger than the pride of kings is commonplace in tragedy, and is the traditional wisdom of the chorus. In Senecan tragedy this topos occurs in *Hf.* 197–201; *Phae.* 1123–40; *Agam.* 57–107; *Oed.* 882–910; *H.O.* 604–99. N-H, ad Hor. *Carm.* 2.10.9–11, *saepius uentis agitatur ingens | pinus et celsae grauiore casu | decidunt turres*, observe that *saepe* and similar adverbs are common in gnomic statements.

899–900 quo me trahitis quodue tyrannus | aut exilium regina iubet? Much is made of the contrast between a scheming Poppaea and a virginal Octavia in Tac. *Ann.* 14, where, however, the two women are never made to meet. This is the only time in *Octavia* where the same characterization of Poppaea as the architect of Octavia's end seems to emerge.

The interlaced word-order, *quodue tyrannus aut exilium regina iubet*, with one constituent spread over what are in effect two consecutive cola, seems more common in anapaests: see ad 81–2; 698; 818–19. *regina* is slightly awkward in a Roman context, but is here meant as a feminine equivalent of *tyrannus*. It is, besides, the usual poetical form for 'princess' (cf. Serv. ad Verg. *Aen.* 1.273). On *rex* and its derivatives in reference to emperors cf. Mommsen, *RS* 2.764–5 n. 4. Before the *Historia Augusta*, *regina* of an emperor's wife is found only here and in Plin. *Nat.* 29.21 *item Valentis* (sc. *adulterium*) *in qua dictum est regina* (sc. *Messalina*); *regnum*, however, is said (with obvious hostility) of the rule of Caesar and of his successors in Luc. *Bell. Ciu.* 4.692; 6.301–2; 7.444; 9.210; Mart. *Spect.* 2.3 *inuidiosa feri radiabant atria regis* (sc. *Neronis*).

901–902 sic mihi uitam fracta remittit, | tot iam nostris euicta malis? MSS have *si*, which Ballaira accepts, but the logic of the sentence is faulty with 'if they grant me life, why am I being sent into exile?'. For a political enemy who risked death (as happened to Seneca) exile was the commonest form of mercy. Gronovius suggested emending *euicta* to *et uicta*, but *euicta* is blameless: cf. Verg. *Aen.* 4.548 *tu lacrimis euicta meis*; Ov. *Fast.* 3.688 *euictas precibus uix dedit illa manus*; *Trist.* 3.1.76 *euictus longo tempore Caesar erit* and especially Sen. *Med.* 491 *lacrimis meis euictus exilium dabit. fracta* and *euicta* are synonyms.

903–904 sin caede mea cumulare parat | luctus nostros *cumulare* means 'to crown', 'to complete'; cf. Verg. *Aen.* 4.436 *cumulatam morte remittam*; Ov. *Her.* 2.57 *turpiter hospitium lecto cumulasse iugali*, with Barchiesi's note; Drac. *Orest.* 901 *crimen adulterii cumulat . . . morte mariti*. The sequence *si . . . sin . . . cur* is often found in poetry: cf. Verg. *Aen.* 11.411–24.

904–905 inuidet etiam | cur in patria mihi saeua mori? On the sequence dactyl–anapaest see ad 646. The use of *inuideo* for 'refuse, deny' is poetic: cf. *TLL* s.v. *inuideo*, 194–5, either with an infinitive (cf. Hor. *Carm.* 1.37.30–1 *scilicet inuidens | priuata deduci triumpho*; Ov. *Met.* 4.157 *componi tumulo* *non inuideatis eodem*) or with *ut/ne* (cf. Verg. *Aen.* 11.269–70 *inuidisse deos patriis ut redditus aris | coniugium optatum et pulchram Calydona uiderem?*).

907 fratris cerno miseranda ratem Octavia's reference to a ship, and later to sails and a helmsman (969–70) has suggested to some that the scene takes place in a harbour, perhaps Ostia. In my judgement, these references should not be pressed too far; the playwright seems to have intentionally blurred the issue of location, and *cerno* is compatible with an interpretation of these words as a prophetic anticipation of what is to happen: cf. Eur. *Alc.* 252 ὁρῶ δίκωπον, ὁρῶ σκάφος, Verg. *Aen.* 6.86–7 *bella, horrida bella | et Thybrim multo spumantem sanguine cerno.* See also *supra*, ad 877. For a discussion of earlier views concerning the location of this scene cf. Ferri (1998), 347 n. 11; S. Grazzini, 'La visione di Ottavia: nota ad *Octavia* 906 ss.' *Maia*, 50 (1998), 89–94; Kragelund (1999), 245–7; Manuwald (2001), 269–72; Kragelund (2002), 46–8 nn. 119 and 125.

908–910 haec est cuius uecta carina | quondam est genetrix; nunc et thalamis | expulsa soror miseranda uehar MSS read *hac est*, which I believe to be corrupt. Octavia seems to lay stress on how she is to undergo the same fate as Nero's mother, a link being provided by 'the same ship' which she now believes herself to see, the 'black ship of death' which Alcestis purports to see in her agony (see previous note). Miller's translation attempts to stress this parallelism by linking grammatically the two successive clauses, *cuius . . . carina* and *nunc et . . . uehar*: 'on that vessel on which his mother once was borne, now, driven from his chamber, his wretched sister too shall sail away'. This is not, however, the Latin we have in 908–10, where there is one anaphoric pronoun too many, for one clause, and *hac* and *cuius* seem to me to conflict ('whose mother was carried on this ship, now I, his divorced sister, alike, will be borne'). One possibility is to think, with Zwierlein, *KK*, that the poet simply put too much in one sentence (cf. ad 557), and reference could be made to the poet's habit of joining successive co-ordinated clauses by an initial relative pronoun: cf. 45–7 *cuius* (sc. *Neronis*) *exstinctus iacet | frater uenenis, maeret infelix soror | eademque coniunx* (cf. Introd. p. 37), yet 908–9 seems to me to go beyond the limits of the acceptable even in *Octavia*.

Emendation is probably required. After 907, *ratem*, we expect the emphasis to be placed on *hac carina*, not on *cuius genetrix*, and I think *haec est* (in Trevet and *recc.*) is on the whole a good solution, with a separate sentence starting after *genetrix*: 'this is (or, better: *there it is*) the ship on board which (Nero's) mother was borne: now I too, a divorced sister, will be borne (away)'. Agrippina was not Octavia's mother, but *genetrix* can be accepted even without a clarifying genitive, just like the following *soror* with no further specification: they are both defined in relation to their kinship to Nero. Other emendations are aimed at linking more closely *cuius . . .* and *nunc et*: Damsté's ***hac est eius*** (1919), 271, makes the syntax smoother, but oblique cases of *is* are avoided in poetry (*eius* has only one occurrence in Senecan tragedy, *Thy.* 300). I had thought of ***cuius*** (i.e. *Neronis*) ***<ut> hac*** *est uecta carina quondam genetrix* . . . (the typical position for a relative connective is just before a subordinating conjunction: cf. e.g. Ov. *Met.* 8.761 *cuius ut in trunco*), but the process of corruption is too complicated. On my interpretation, it is necessary to supplement ***est***, preferably after *quondam* in 909.

For *nunc et thalamis expulsa uehar* cf. Ov. *Met.* 13.510 *nunc trahor exsul*; *H.O.* 757 *nunc uidua nunc expulsa nunc ferar obruta*.

911–913 nullum Pietas nunc numen habet | nec sunt superi: | regnat mundo tristis Erinys The cry that gods no longer exist and all values are overturned is a typically tragic (especially Euripidean) recrimination, pronounced by characters suffering abuse and injustice: cf. Eur. *I.A.* 1092–5 τὸ μὲν ἄσεπτον ἔχει | δύνασιν, ἁ δ' Ἀρετὰ κατόπι- | σθεν θνατοῖς ἀμελεῖται, | Ἀνομία δὲ νόμων κρατεῖ, *Phoe.* 1726–7 οὐκ ὁρᾶι Δίκα κακοὺς | οὐδ' ἀμείβεται βροτῶν ἀσυνεσίας, *Med.* 412; fr. 286.2 N²; fr. adesp. 465.1 N². In Latin cf. Ov. *Fast.* 6.366; Sen. Rh. *Contr.* 1.2.8; Sen. *Med.* 1027; Luc. *Bell. Ciu.* 7.445–6; Stat. *Theb.* 7.494. From the fragments of Republican tragedy cf. Acc. *Scaen.* 142–3 R² (from *Antigone*) *iam iam neque di regunt* | *neque profecto deum supremus rex <res> curat hominibus*.

Parallels for this use of *Erinys* as an abstract force, the personification of evil: Ov. *Met.* 1.241 *qua terra patet fera regnat Erinys*; 11.14 *insanaque regnat Erinys*.

914–915˙ quis mea digne deflere potest | mala? quae lacrimis nostris questus | reddere aedon? Cf. Sen. *Agam.* 670–7: *non quae uerno mobile carmen* | *ramo cantat tristis aedon . . . lugere tuam poterit digne* | *conquesta domum*; *Hf.* 1227–8 *quis uos . . . deflere digne poterit?* The reading of ***A***, *redderet*, was probably produced by the erroneous simplification of the disyllabic *ae(don)* to *e–*, which made the metre faulty, and perhaps also assimilation to the following *fugerem* (918) played a part. *Recc.* emended the word to *reddat*, but *reddere* is closer to the reading of the older MSS and the ellipse / *apo koinou*-construction of *potest* is preferable. *digne* 'in a manner equal to my sufferings' (cf. *Agam.* 676) must be understood *apo koinou* as governing *lacrimis nostris* in the second colon, as also implied by the use of *reddere* ('answer with equal laments', 'utter in reply', *OLD*, s.v. vii.).

The passage is one of numerous variations on the commonplace of Senecan mourners, that their grief is not to be compared to anybody's (*Thy.* 1036–7 *quas miser uoces dabo* | *questusque quos? quae uerba sufficient mihi?*); their desire for lament is not to be satisfied by even the most proverbial mourners of mythology (cf. *Agam.* 670 ff. with Tarrant's note; *H.O.* 185–206, where Iole prays that the gods change her into the bird from Daulis: (190 ff.) *qualis natum Daulias ales* | *solet Ismaria flere sub umbra,* | *formam lacrimis aptate meis . . . patrioque sedens ales in agro* | *referam querulo murmure casus*). The inherited theme is given an original twist, in that the nightingale is engaged in a kind of amoebaean lament with

Octavia. When *reddo* means 'produce' a sound, the idea is suggested that this sound comes as a reflected sound or echo (as in Verg. *Aen.* 3.40 *uox reddita fertur ad auris*; 1.409; 7.95). The nightingale echoing Octavia's 'tears' (for this metonymy, cf. *supra*, ad 75; 270) was perhaps suggested by Ov. *Met.* 3.498, where Echo, moved to compassion for Narcissus, can only reproduce his laments: (496–8) *haec resonis iterabat uocibus 'eheu' | cumque suos manibus percusserat ille lacertos, | haec quoque reddebat sonitum plangoris eundem*; also Sen. *Troad.* 111 *totos reddat Troiae gemitus* (sc. *Echo*). Liberman finds fault with the line, proposing to emend to *lacrimas nostras questu:* 'quel rossignol (pourrait) rendre mes larmes en sa lament?', where *reddo* is taken to mean 'to reproduce', not impossibly, but this correction misses the point that the bird must *echo* Octavia's lament. Octavia wishes to find a compassionate being in nature responding to her, and the transmitted reading is beyond reproach. In Greek tragedy, cf. Eur. *Hel.* 169–76, where the heroine calls upon the Sirens to come and accompany with musical instruments the song of her miseries (Σειρῆνες, εἴθ' ἐμοῖς | γόοις μόλοιτ' ἔχουσαι Λίβυν | λωτὸν ἢ σύριγγας ἢ | φόρμιγγας, αἰλίνοις κακοῖς | τοῖς ἐμοῖσι σύνοχα δάκρυα). In Soph. *Ai.* 629–30, the dirge which Ajax' elderly mother will raise will not be comparable to the nightingale's plaintive and querulous song. Cf. also Eur. *Phoe.* 1515–18. In 7–8, Octavia exhorted herself to surpass with her laments the songs of halcyons and nightingales.

The Latin word for 'nightingale' is *luscinia*, but its poetic equivalent is the mythological substitute, *Philomela*. The Greek word ἀηδών (*aedon* and its derivative *aedonius*) has very few occurrences in Latin (*Laus Pisonis* 79; Petr. *Sat.* 131.8.6; Calp. Sic. *Buc.* 6.8; Sen. *Agam.* 676).

916–917 cuius pennas utinam miserae | mihi fata darent! Two different topoi are conflated here, that of Procne's lament and the Greek tragic motif of escape on wings, for which cf. Soph. *O.C.* 1081; Eur. *Hel.* 1418 (for a positive purpose, flight to a given place); Soph. fr. 476 N[2]; Eur. *Ion*, 746; *Andr.* 861–5 (to escape an intolerable situation). Cf. esp. Sen. *H.O.* 201. In early Roman drama cf. *Trag. inc.* 119 R[2] (*euolare*) *ubi nec Pelopidarum nomen nec facta aut famam audiam*. In Greek tragedy, however, only the wish to flee from an intolerable impasse is found, without any association with a metamorphosis (originally seen as a form of punishment) into any of those morally dubious mythical figures. The conflation of the two motifs is not Greek, but belongs to post-classical Latin.

918–919 fugerem luctus ablata meos | penna uolucri procul Verg. *Aen.* 3.258 *in siluas pinnis ablata refugit* supports the MS reading *ablata*, rejected by Leo, who wrote Buecheler's *sublata*.

The spelling *pe-* reflects the normal phonetic evolution of short Latin *i*, but the two forms *penna/pinna* coexist in classical Latin, and it is impossible to decide which should be preferred in *Octavia*. In the corpus, *pinna/penna* in the sense of 'feather, wing' occur 14 times, with ***E*** consistently writing *pi-*, whereas *pe-* is the spelling of ***A*** MSS throughout, except at *Phae.* 46, where *pi-* is transmitted by both branches (cf. Zwierlein, *OCT.*, Orthographica, 459).

919–920 et coetus | hominum tristes caedemque feram Octavia's wish to fly away from the cruelty of humankind echoes the description of Astraea's final departure from earth at 422–3, *terras fugit et mores feros | hominum, cruenta caede pollutas manus*. The word *coetus* sometimes denotes a primitive society, in opposition to *populus*, or *ciuitas*. Cf. also Cat. *Carm.* 64.407 *nec tales dignantur uisere coetus*, where the gods no longer dwell among humans. *tristis* is used here with the extensional sense of 'grim', 'savage': cf. *OLD* s.v. 7.

921–923 sola in uacuo nemore et tenui | ramo pendens | querulo possem gutture maestum | fundere murmur The accumulation *sola in uacuo nemore* is certainly expressive, and tinged with the protagonist's melancholy, even if slightly counterintuitive (why should the nightingale's song be set in a deserted forest?). For similar cases of expressive pleonasm in preceding literature (*sola* + a noun phrase with *uacuus, uiduus, relictus, desertus*), cf. Verg. *Aen.* 4.82 *sola domo maeret uacua*; Stat. *Theb.* 1.166 *uacua . . . solus in aula*; also close Cat. *Carm.* 64.57 *desertam in sola miseram se cernat harena*; Tib. 3.6.40 *fleuisti ignoto sola relicta mari.*

tenui ramo pendens imitates Sen. *Hf.* 146 (description of the song of birds at sunrise) *pendet summo stridula ramo . . . Thracia paelex*; Billerbeck, ad loc., observes that *pendeo*, 'hang in suspension', is not the verb most commonly used to describe the position of birds perched on a tree-branch (in *TLL* x.1, s.v. *pendeo*, 1036.15–16; the only other parallel is Curt. *Hist. Alex.* 8.9.25 *ramis aues pendent quas cantu . . . obstrepere docuerunt*). *sedeo* has the same meaning elsewhere (cf. e.g. Verg. *Georg.* 4.514).

The double synaloephe in 921 is paralleled at 7 and at 9 (see ad loc., for the avoidance of the phenomenon in Senecan anapaests).

924 The scene of Octavia's exit is probably an adaptation of the *kommos* in Soph. *Ant.* 806–82 and of the fourth *stasimon*, *Ant.* 944–87. Also relevant are the final *kommoi* in Aesch. *Pers.*; Eur. *Suppl.*, *Troad.* Significantly, Octavia has already invoked Electra as her precursor in the *exordium* of the tragedy.

The parallelism between *Antigone* and *Octavia* is apparent in the dramatic structure, the grand theatricality of which had an obvious appeal for the anonymous dramatist. Octavia, like Antigone, the victim of an angry tyrant, is brought in under guard on her way to the place of her death (892–4). She laments in a song her pitiful lot (899–923). As the heroine is leaving the 'stage', a chorus of compassionate citizens endeavours to console her, perhaps to stifle the guilty feelings aroused in their hearts by the sight of the unfortunate victim. This is done by listing a catalogue of previous heroines of her family line, similarly doomed, justly or unjustly (924–57: Agrippina I, Livia, Julia, Messalina, Agrippina II).

In Soph. *Ant.* 801 ff. Antigone is brought in under guard from within the palace. The chorus of Theban elders announces her arrival (804–5); then Antigone opens her *kommos* (806 ff.); the heroine bewails her bitter fate; the chorus of Theban elders attempts, if clumsily, to console her. Then, as Antigone is finally led away by the guards to be enclosed in her death chamber, the chorus, still addressing her as *pais*, sings of famous paradigms of ill-fortune, mythical heroes and heroines implicitly comparable to Antigone (944–87).

The selection of exempla in this stasimon (and therefore the exact extent of the comparison with the heroine) has puzzled ancient and modern commentators alike. Notice (in the Greek stasimon) the simultaneous presence of positive and negative models (Danae, Lycurgus, Cleopatra). In a similar way, positive and negative heroines succeed each other in the Latin anapaests. Next to Agrippina comes the disgraced Livia, the accomplice of Sejanus in the poisoning of Drusus her husband. The parallelism between Agrippina and Danae seems the most sustained. Agrippina, like Danae, was of eminent lineage, but suffered imprisonment and torture, though she had given birth to a royal progeny; cf. 934 ff.

A catalogue in a consolatory context is found in Eur. *Hyps.* fr. 1.iii 18 ff. Bond (Europa, Io). On the motif of *non tibi soli* in consolatory *parodoi* of Greek tragedy cf. Di Benedetto-Medda, 259–260; M. G. Ciani, *Boll. Ist. Filol. Gr. Padova* 2 (1975), 89–129; consolatory technique is also mentioned by Giancotti, 76–7. See also *supra* ad 201.

The scene is, however, recorded in Tac. *Ann.* 14.63.2 as well, with details of arresting similarity: cf. esp. *non alia exul uisentium oculos maiore misericordia adfecit. meminerant adhuc Agrippinae a Tiberio, recentior Iuliae memoria obuersabatur a Claudio pulsae* (a typical scene in Tacitus: cf. *Ann.* 1.40–1): the technique of sketching popular reaction to highlight a pathetic incident is a favourite bravura piece of ancient historians, but in this case the resemblance of the two passages is, I believe, beyond coincidence, and possibly Tacitus knew *Octavia* (I discuss this fully in *HSCPh* 98 (1998), 339–56). For examples of mass scenes in imperial historiography featuring choral reaction to a particularly touching or scandalous event cf. Tac. *Ann.* 3.1–6 (Agrippina's return and the citizens' disapproval of Tiberius' demeanour); *Hist.* 3.68 *nec quisquam adeo rerum humanarum immemor quem non commoueret illa facies, Romanum principem et generis humani paulo ante dominum relicta fortunae suae sede per populum, per urbem exire de imperio. nihil tale uiderant, nihil audierant. repentina uis dictatorem Caesarem oppresserat, occultae Gaium insidiae, nox et ignotum rus fugam Neronis absconderat, Piso et Galba tamquam in acie cecidere: in sua contione Vitellius, inter suos milites, prospectantibus etiam feminis, pauca et praesenti maestitiae congruentia locutus . . . pugionem . . . reddebat*; Cass. Dio *Hist. Rom.* 56.43; 61.17.4–5; 61.19.

On the reasons why dependence on Tacitus seems to be ruled out (the author of *Octavia* has a more detailed knowledge of the facts) cf. Introd. p. 30 and n. 72.

924–928 *A* reads:

regitur fatis mortale genus
nec sibi quisquam spondere potest
firmum et stabile per quem casus
uoluit uarios semper nobis
metuenda dies

The MS colometry is untenable, because *stabile* is a tribrach and cannot fill the second foot of an anapaestic metron, except if we write *firmum et stabile* at line end, or as a monometer, interpreting *-le* at line-end as *breuis in longo* (*sp+an*). The metrical objection raised by Fitch against this proposed arrangement (1987, 66, observing that this would be the only instance in the corpus of a *br. in l.* in a proparoxytone tribrach) need not be decisive, but *firmum et stabile* alone does not provide an object for *spondere*, and *quicquam* of some *recentiores* seems inescapable. Yet the combination of a metrical and a textual flaw has seemed suspicious to many, and most editors write, or attempt to supplement, a lacuna after *stabile*, for instance Richter's <*m uitae cursum*>. Other conjectural proposals include Leo's *firmum et stabilem per cuncta deum tempora uitae* and Bothe's *firmam et stabilem Parcam* for *per quam* of *recc.* The latter is interpreted by Giardina and Ballaira as one word, the archaizing intensive adverb *perquam*, but the word is absent from poetry after Lucretius, and the resulting word-order, with the modifier removed from the word it modifies, is unsatisfactory. The same objection can be raised against Düring's *pro! quam* (*Materialien*, 4.346)

pro! quam casus uoluit uarios
semper nobis metuenda dies

close to *Phae.* 1123–27 *quanti casus humana rotant!* | *minor in paruis Fortuna furit . . . non capit umquam magnos motus* | *humilis tecti plebeia domus* (cf. *Oct.* 896–9).

Following Zwierlein, I have adopted Herington's ingenious *quem per* (1977, 277), which yields very good sense with very little change, and may well be right. My only objection to this is the resulting clash of pronominal expressions, with the transition from a neutral generalizing collective *mortale genus* to an impersonal masculine *(ille) quem* and, lastly, to a first person plural (*nobis*) *semper nobis metuenda dies*. Cf. however *Agam.* 665 for *quos* as a generalizing, unprepared masculine, although the chorus is made up of women.

For *per casus uoluit uarios* cf. Verg. *Aen.* 1.9–10 (*impulerit Aenean*) *tot uoluere casus . . . tot adire labores*; 10.352 *per uarios sternit casus*; Sil. *Pun.* 6.121 *per uarios praeceps casus rota uoluitur aeui* (Zwierlein); similar also are Sen. *H.O.* 703–4 *quae te . . . fortuna rotat, miseranda, refer*; 715 *quis . . . miseranda te casus rotat?*

On *dies* as 'the course of time', a sense in which the word is usually feminine (cf. *OLD* s.v., 10), cf. Verg. *Aen.* 11.425–6 *multa dies uariique labor mutabilis aeui* | *rettulit in melius*. *semper nobis metuenda dies* is explained by the concurrent topos 'the space of one day may bring the most extraordinary changes', cf. Skutsch, ad Enn. *Ann.* VIII. iv (pp. 440–1), adducing several occurrences in Greek tragedy: for all cf. Soph. *Ai.* 131–2 ὡς ἡμέρα κλίνει τε κἀνάγει πάλιν | ἅπαντα τἀνθρώπεια (related to the topos 'no man can call himself happy till his last day has elapsed': Jebb ad Soph. *O.T.* 1528 with parallels; also Men. *Aspis* 419; Ov. *Met.* 3.135–6 *sed scilicet ultima semper* | *exspectanda dies homini*). Other parallels, from Seneca and elsewhere, are given by Zwierlein, *KK*, ad loc.: cf. especially *Thy.* 613–14 *quem dies uidit ueniens superbum,* | *hunc dies uidit fugiens iacentem.* I would rule out a more specific sense of *dies*, referring to the day of the tragic action, as in Sen. *Med.* 877 *mergat diem timendum . . . Hesperus*, where the chorus expresses the vow that the fearful day may soon expire.

genus mortale for mankind occurs in Sen. *Oed.* 983 *quicquid patimur mortale genus*; Tac. *Ann.* 13.55.5 *generi mortalium*; *CIL* 11.6753.

The lament on the unreliability of fortune is a typical topic for the *embolima* of post-Euripidean tragedy: cf. the anapaestic sequence from Acc. *Scaen.* 422–3 R^2 (probably choral) *fors dominatur neque quicquam ulli* | *proprium in uita est*; in Greek cf. Eur. *Hipp.* 1109–10 ἄλλα γὰρ ἄλλοθεν ἀμείβεται, μετὰ δ' ἵσταται ἀνδράσιν αἰών | πολυπλάνητος αἰεί. The chorus' reflections move from the general to the particular, following a well-established pattern of lament and consolation in tragedy (cf. W. Kranz, *Stasimon* (Berlin, 1933), 206, 217).

930–931 iam multa domus quae uestra tulit. | quid saeuior est fortuna tibi? Ov. *Met.* 13.525 *non haec est Fortuna domus.* This consolatory argument is probably inspired by Sen. *Cons. Pol.* 14 ff. (Claudius' prosopopoeia); cf. 14.2 *non te solum fortuna desumpsit sibi quem tam graui adficeret iniuria*; 15.2 *contentus nostrae domus exemplis ero*; 16.3 *sed ut omnia alia exempla praeteream, ut in me quoque ipso alia taceam funera, bis me fraterno luctu adgressa fortuna est.*

932–933 tu mihi primum tot natorum | memoranda parens, nata Agrippae *tu mihi primum . . . memoranda* elaborates an epic formula: cf. Verg. *Aen.* 10.793 *non equidem nec te, iuuenis memorande, silebo*; *Georg.* 3.1–2 *et te, memorande, canemus,* | *pastor ab Amphryso*; Ov. *Trist.* 1.5.1 *o mihi post nullos umquam memorande sodales*; *Pont.* 4.13.1.

934 nurus Augusti, Caesaris uxor The epithet *Caesar* pertains to both Tiberius and Germanicus, but here a distinction is made for convenience of reference. *Augustus* is elsewhere not found alone as a name designating Tiberius in our literary evidence: Tiberius, it is said, refused the title offered to him by the Senate, and restricted it to relations with foreign kings: Suet. *Tib.* 26; Cass. Dio *Hist. Rom.* 57.8. Nevertheless *Augustus* is common in the epigraphic evidence with reference to Tiberius, though usually alongside *Tiberius Caesar* (cf. ad 284). An anachronism might be identified in the use of *Caesar* for Germanicus, which here obviously indicates the heir apparent, a practice which became common only in the Hadrianic age (Augustus had in fact forced Tiberius to adopt Germanicus with the prospect of the latter succeeding him in turn). But, while the limitation of the title *Caesar* to the heir apparent can only be dated to the Hadrianic or Trajanic age, its unofficial use probably goes back earlier: Nero, at his adoption, was given the name *Caesar*. So were Piso (Tac. *Hist.* 1.29 *Caesar adscitus sum*) and Domitian (*ibid.* 3.86 *Domitianum . . . Caesarem consalutatum*), though Tacitus might be anachronistic; cf. also Cass. Dio *Hist. Rom.* 66.1; 68.3.4; Mommsen, *RS*[3] II.770–1. In fact, the pair Tiberius-Germanicus occur together in at least one official designation, the inscription of the first two consuls for the year 18 in the *Fasti Antiates Minores* (cf. Degrassi, *Inscr. Ital.* xiii.1 n. 26 (fast. ant. min.), p. 303), *Ti. Caesar August(us) III Germanic(us) Caes(ar) II.*

940˙ cruciata The participle has a passive meaning despite the diathesis of *crucior*: cf. Ov. *Met.* 9.292 *totidem cruciata diebus*.

941–942 felix thalamis Liuia Drusi | natisque The mention of Livia is somewhat surprising, occurring as it does between Agrippina and the unfortunate Iulia, two personages of undisputed virtuosity. Livia was seduced by Sejanus and involved in Drusus' poisoning. The account of her end is given by Cass. *Hist. Rom.* Dio, 58.11.7; our sources call her both Livia and Livilla. For *felix thalamis . . . natisque* cf. Verg. *Aen.* 6.783 *felix prole uirum*, of Rome; Ov. *Met.* 4.420–1 *aspicit hanc natis thalamoque Athamantis habentem | sublimes animos*; 11.266 *felix et nato, felix et coniuge Peleus*. *Drusi* is governed by *thalamis*. A possessive genitive, indicating the husband, is often found after a woman's name, especially in inscriptions (cf. *CIL* VIII.4193; Sen. *Cons. Marc.* 16.4 *Cornelia Liui Drusi*; Flinck (1919), 50, n. 4); *Liuia Drusi Caesaris* occurs in *CIL* VI.4349; 5226; 8899 (Pedroli). It is however a colloquialism (*LHS* 2.823); the solemn tone of the passage suggests tying *Drusi* to *thalamis*.

944–946 Iulia matris fata secuta est: | post longa tamen tempora ferro | caesa est, quamuis crimine nullo There is some uncertainty as to the identity of this Iulia. One character of that name was the daughter of Livia and Drusus (cf. Cass. Dio *Hist. Rom.* 60.18.4 (ἀπέσφαξε); Sen. *Apocol.* 10.4 *duas Iulias proneptes meas occidit, alteram ferro, alteram fame*). A second Iulia, daughter of Agrippina I, and sister to Caligula, was banished under Claudius (cf. Cass. Dio, *Hist. Rom.* 60.8.5). In the short catalogue found in Tac. *Ann.* 14.63.2 (see ad 924 ff.), *Iulia* must be the daughter of Agrippina I: *recentior Iuliae memoria obuersabatur a Claudio pulsae*. However priority is decided between Tacitus and the poet of *Octavia*, the *Iulia* in the tragedy must be Livia's daughter. This conclusion is prompted (1) by the order in which the characters are listed (2) *quamuis crimine nullo* only makes sense in reference to Iulia Drusi, the innocent daughter of a corrupt and scheming mother. The other Iulia was a notoriously ambitious and allegedly adulterous character. *matris fata secuta est* is a high-flown periphrasis for 'she also died'. Hosius compared Verg. *Aen.* 9.204 *magnanimum Aenean et fata extrema secutus*, where, however, the idea of motion is more prominent; Ov. *Trist.* 3.7.27–8 *forsitan exemplo . . . tu quoque sis poenae* *fata secuta meae*; Man. *Astr.* 2.585; Luc. *Bell. Ciu.* 3.303 *ausa est . . . causas non fata* (sc. *belli fortunas*) *sequi*; Mart. *Epigr.* 7.44.4 *ausus es et profugi, non tua fata, sequi* (sc. *comitari*); *CIL* IX.5140 *duo . . . una fata secuti*, where the movement is simply metaphorical. *matris fata secuta* might also conceal a more specific reference to the actual charge brought up against Iulia by Claudius in 43 (not on record elsewhere: cf. Tac. *Ann.* 13.32 *dolo Messalinae interfectam*), suggesting that Iulia was somehow accused of being involved in the plot set up by Sejanus and Livia her mother against Iulia's husband, Nero (cf. Tac. *Ann.* 4.60: Tacitus actually implies that Iulia was manipulated by her mother into betraying Nero without her knowledge). This interpretation has the advantage of giving more point to *post longa tamen tempora*. For *post longa tamen tempora* cf. Verg. *Buc.* 1.27–9 *libertas quae, sera, tamen respexit inertem . . . respexit tamen et longo post tempore uenit*; [Verg.] *Cir.* 74 *ast tamen exegit longo post tempore poenas*.

949 cara marito partuque potens For this use of *potens* to indicate the strengthening of a woman's position in a household consequent upon marriage or upon a successful pregnancy, cf. *supra*, 146 *hymenaeis potens*; Tac. *Ann.* 14.60 *mariti potens*. The phrase (*-que*) *potens* with an ablative indicating the quality whereby one is conspicuous is common in poetry: cf. Acc. *Scaen.* 521–2 R² *claroque potens | pectore*; Verg. *Aen.* 7.56 *Turnus auis atauisque potens*; Ov. *Met.* 6.426 *opibusque uirisque potentem*; 13.509 *tot generis natisque potens nuribusque uiroque*.

950 eadem famulo subiecta suo The identification of the *famulus* in this line has been questioned. Silius (Ballaira) could hardly be called a *famulus*; perhaps Mnester is meant, although he was not responsible for Messalina's ultimate disgrace: on Mnester cf. Cass. Dio *Hist. Rom.* 60.22. *subiecta* in this case would designate sexual submission: cf. Suet. *Iul.* 7.2 *mater quam subiectam sibi uidisset*. Vürtheim's explanation, that we should recognize Narcissus under the label of *famulus*, is more plausible on grounds of sense: Messalina was overthrown by a freedman's initiative ('she succumbed to one of her servants'). This also succeeds in establishing a logical link with the following *cecidit diri militis ense* and corresponds to the *usus* of the poet: cf. 104–5 *meae | subiecta famulae* (where either Acte or Poppaea is meant); 827 *at illa, cui me ciuium subicit furor*. The line contains a compressed reference to the frantic activities of Narcissus to bring down Messalina after her marriage to Silius; cf. Tac. *Ann.* 11.28–38. This dwelling on the details and personalia of Julio-Claudian Rome presupposes an 'audience' well acquainted with the stories of court intrigue of the period, as perhaps made popular by Flavian historians. This poet's allusions are equally obscure, for us at least, whether he speaks of characters who lived under Tiberius and Claudius or under Nero.

952–953 quid, cui licuit regnum in caelum | sperare The transmitted reading *in caelum* is discarded by Zwierlein, who proposed instead *regnum caeli* in *KK* ad loc., and later printed in his *OCT* Watt's *et caelum*. The metonymic *caelum* = *caelestes honores* is in itself acceptable (cf. Tac. *Ann.* 1.73.3

non ideo decretum patri suo caelum, with Goodyear's note; Ov. *Ars* 2.218 *qui meruit caelum quod prior ipse tulit*), but I prefer to retain the paradosis. Against *licuit regnum et caelum sperare*, Agrippina cannot be said to have had only a prospect of *regnum*: she did indeed enjoy 'regal' prerogatives in full, as since 49 she was legitimately the wife of the emperor, and then (after 54) the all-powerful mother of the young ruler. *regnum in caelum*, to designate in general terms a prince's apotheosis, is a perfectly apt, if indeed hyperbolic, expression, both grammatically and conceptually. The main objection against the paradosis is perhaps the presence of the accusative *in caelum* (*regnum* seems to exclude the idea of motion), but the construction with the accusative can be paralleled, especially indicating the domain over which a given rule extends: with *regno*, cf. Tac. *Ann.* 11.24 *aduenae in nos regnauerunt;* Man. *Astr.* 4.239 *regnat in illas;* with *regnum*, cf. Prop. 3.10.18 *in . . . meum semper stent tua regna caput;* Sen. *Phae.* 218 *amoris in me maximum regnum puto.*

regnum in caelum need not carry the somewhat hubristic implication that Agrippina will become the supreme ruler of the universe: allowance must be made for a measure of expressive compression, especially in anapaests; deification itself is a form of kingship. Cf. the apotheosis of Nero as prophesied in Luc. *Bell. Ciu.* 1.51–2 *iurisque tui natura relinquet | quis deus esse uelis, ubi regnum ponere mundi*; cf. also Plaut. *Mil.* 1083 *si hic pridie natus foret quam illest, hic haberet regnum in caelo*; Val. Max. 8.15. pr. *cui* (sc. *domui Augustae*) *ascensus in caelum patet.*

Whatever the text, the sense is that Agrippina was in a position to hope for deification after death. Note, however, that amongst women of imperial rank apotheosis was exceptional in 62, when only Livia (Iulia Augusta) in 42 and Caligula's sister, Drusilla, in 38 had been deified. Although Nero had both Claudia Augusta and Poppaea consecrated, and several princes appear to have received the same honours under the Flavians, deification of emperors' wives becomes an established practice only in the age of the Adoptive Emperors (with Plotina, Sabina, and both Faustinae: cf. G. Wissowa, *Religion und Kultus der Römer* (Munich, 1912[2]), 344, n. 4).

953 parens tanta Neronis Cf. Verg. *Aen.* 1.606 *qui tanti talem genuere parentes?*; Nep. *Hann.* 13.2 *hic tantus uir.* After *quid* supply perhaps *passa est*, or *non potuit*, as at 947. Alternatively, *parens* may be tied to *non . . . iacuit:* 'And more (a usual emphatic sense of *quid*), was Nero's mother not slain, she to whom . . .'

954–955 funesta uiolata manu | remigis ante The account of even minor details of this historical event corresponds closely to Tacitus and, when available, the other historians. Some of the ship's sailors were involved in the murder plot, and attempted to finish off the survivors from the wreck, but Agrippina managed to keep her cool and swim to safety in the dark: cf. Tac. *Ann.* 14.5 *Acerronia . . . contis et remis et quae fors obtulerat naualibus telis* *conficitur. Agrippina silens eoque minus agnita (unum tamen uulnus umero excepit)* . . . Cass. Dio-Xiph. *Hist. Rom.* 61.13.3 τῶν τε ναυτῶν ταῖς κώπαις ἐπ' αὐτὴν χρωμένων.

uiolata has religious undertones: either because the queen mother is regarded as a sacred person or because murder of one's mother is in itself a sacrilegious act. For *uiolare* in connection with offences committed against members of the imperial family cf. Tac. *Ann.* 2.34 *quamquam Augusta se uiolari et imminui quereretur*; Suet. *Iul.* 89 *nonnulli semet eodem illo pugione, quo Caesarem uiolauerant, interemerunt.*

956 lacerata diu The combination of *diu*, expressing duration, with *lacerata* captures the savage cruelty of the soldiers charged with the killing, bent on wreaking havoc on Agrippina's body with their weapons, a detail of which we catch a glimpse also in the narrative of Tac. *Ann.* 14.8: *circumsistunt lectum percussores et prior trierarchus fusti caput eius adflixit . . . multisque vulneribus confecta est.* The same tendency to dwell with some exaggeration on the gory details of disfigurement and killing has been observed in the description of Messalina's corpse: see *supra* ad 17.

958 me quoque tristes mittit ad umbras Cf. Eur. *Andr.* 503 πέμπομαι κατὰ γαίας. This line provides the only instance in which Octavia acknowledges the presence of this chorus on stage: they address her explicitly throughout. Lack of contact between a chorus or other consoling actor and a distressed character is common in Greek tragedy: cf. e.g. Eur. *Alc.* 903 ff., where the chorus seeks to console Admetus upon his loss, while he follows his own thoughts of despair without responding; Aesch. *Agam.* 1072–1177 (Cassandra's visions on entering the palace of Agamemnon). In the Senecan corpus, *Phae.* 358–60 *altrix, profare* is the only instance of a character answering a question put by the chorus (with the exception of messenger scenes).

For *mittit ad umbras* at line-end in hexametric poetry see ad 79.

960 quid iam frustra miseranda moror cf. Verg. *Aen.* 2.101–3 *sed quid ego haec autem nequiquam ingrata reuoluo | quidue moror? . . . iamdudum sumite poenas*; Ov. *Met.* 13.516–7 *quo ferrea resto | quidue moror? quo me seruas, annosa senectus?*

961–961ᵃ rapite ad letum quis ius in nos | Fortuna dedit Octavia addresses now Nero's guards who lead her away. In the tragedies of doomed heroines and unjustly sacrificed virgins, the victims often show bravery and courage when facing death: cf. Eur. *I.A.* 1475 ἄγετέ με . . . ; Cassandra in Sen. *Agam.* 1004 *trahite*; *Troad.* 1147 (of Polyxena on her way to the sacrifice).

962–963 testor superos – quid agis demens? | parce precari quis inuisa es Cf. Soph. *Ant.* 922–3 (Antigone addressing herself): τί χρή με τὴν δύστηνον ἐς θεοὺς ἔτι | βλέπειν; Sen. *Hf.* 518–19 *impiam . . . compesce dextram – quid deos frustra precor?*; *Troad.* 28 *testor deorum numen aduersum mihi*; Val. Fl. *Arg.* 7.311–13; Stat. *Theb.* 5.622 *quos arguo diuos?* Also *Med.* 174 *parce iam, demens, minis*, said by the *Nutrix* to Medea.

964–967 Tartara testor | Erebique deas scelerum ultrices | et te, genitor, | dignum tali morte et poena Like Turnus as he sees his end certain and his cause rejected by the gods (Verg. *Aen.* 12.646–9 *uos o mihi, Manes, | este boni, quoniam superis auersa uoluntas. | sancta ad uos anima, atque istius inscia culpae | descendam, magnorum haud umquam indignus auorum*), Octavia now turns to address the infernal deities. Cf. also Sen. *Troad.* 28 *testor deorum numen aduersum mihi.* The virulent invective of Octavia against her dead father may strike one on first impression as an oddity, after the lament on Claudius' death which had opened the play. This has attracted suspicion against the line. Leo proposed to supply *et te genitor: <perde tyrannum>*. But Courtney (*RFIC* 111 (1985), 302) has rightly rejected Leo's conjecture with the argument that *testor superos* (962) must be followed by a statement, not by an imperative (cf. Ov. *Met.* 6.608–9 *testarique deos per uim sibi dedecus illud | inlatum*). Courtney did not propose an emendation of his own, but suggested that a line must be missing of this import *<facibus saeuis qui regem ipsum mox agitabis>* (*regem*, however, is out of place as an epithet designating Nero). Tacitus, curiously, while describing Octavia's final moments in *Ann.* 14.64, has her invoke Agrippina: *cum iam uiduam se et tantum sororem testaretur communisque Germanicos et postremo Agrippinae nomen cieret, qua incolumi infelix quidem matrimonium sed sine exitio pertulisset.* An emendation ***genetrix, dignam*** is however out of the question, especially since Agrippina is never so addressed in the play (though Messalina is so designated in 10 *semper genetrix deflenda mihi*). An address to Agrippina would occur more naturally than one to Claudius in a list of Furies and infernal deities, but the parallelism with Tacitus is not a cogent reason to alter the paradosis, and should not in any case be pressed too far, since Octavia faces death in Tacitus' account so much less resolutely than here, where she is playing the 'tragic' heroine (cf. the parallels adduced ad 961). Zwierlein, *KK*, puts forward tentatively the suggestion that Octavia is here wishing her father had died a death similar to hers, rather than the shameful poisoning he fell victim to, but this is unconvincing. More acceptable is his conjecture *genitor, digna haut tali morte ac poena*, where *digna* is, presumably, a nominative referring to Octavia, and a new sentence begins in the following line. This is, in my view, the most persuasive solution advanced hitherto. In defence of the paradosis, one could argue that an element of excess may have been felt to convey more adequately the desperation of the doomed heroine, who has been abandoned even by her closest kin. From the parody of Euripides' Andromeda in Aristophanes, *Thesm.* 1038–9 (which yields, however, no clear fragment of the original), we gather that Andromeda, while tied to the rock and waiting for the sea-monster to devour her, voiced her resentment against her parents who had delivered her to such death. On the whole, therefore, I am inclined to retain the text as transmitted. It has been mentioned before that the characterization of Octavia is notable for seemingly conflicting features, whereby a conflict of literary stereotypes and details inherited from historical accounts comes to the surface. Animosity against Claudius' alleged mistreatment of his family had previously been expressed by the *Nutrix* alone (cf. *supra*, ad 138), but Octavia is now being led to her execution, for which she can indirectly blame her father's ruinous union to Agrippina: hence, perhaps, her anger.

morte et poena are virtually a synonymous pair: cf. Sil. *Pun.* 2.301 *sic propria luat hoc poena* (that is, by dying); Luc. *Bell. Ciu.* 8.395 *mors ultima poena.*

968 non inuisa est mors ista mihi Cf. *supra* 108 *mori iuuabit*; Eur. *Hec.* 548 ἑκοῦσα θνῄσκω, *I.A.* 1503 θανοῦσα . . . οὐκ ἀναίνομαι. *mors ista* strikes an inelegant note after *tali morte*.

969–970 armate ratem, date uela fretis | uentisque Perhaps reminiscent of Dido's angry *ferte citi flammas, date tela, impellite remos* (*Aen.* 4.594), where *date uela* was the commonly accepted reading before Wagner (an ancient variant, of which this would be very early testimony). Cf. also *Trag. inc.* 251–2 R[2] (possibly anapaestic) *agite, o pelagi cursores, | cupidam in patriam portate* (Iphigenia?). The punctuation adopted by Zwierlein, with comma after *uentisque*, in preference to *date uela fretis, uentisque petat* . . . is certainly right. Departure by sea and deportation of captive women famously concludes all 'Trojan Women' plays, even Sen. *Troades.*

971 Pandatariae litora terrae The transmitted reading *tandem Pharie*, although ingenious (*Pharius* for 'Egyptian' is common especially in Augustan and Silver Latin poetry), is untenable, against the agreement with which the rest of our tradition designates Pandateria (modern Ventotene) as a place of relegation (not to mention Tacitus' explicit reference to *Pandateria* as Octavia's final destination; see *infra*). Among modern editors, the MS reading is still preferred by Giardina, Ballaira and Barbera, who refer to a passage in *Dig.* 48.22.7.5 (first adduced by Pedroli), from Ulpian's *De off. procons.*, where, in a survey of the local administrators' penal prerogatives, their right is asserted to designate within their jurisdiction specific places of confinement (so the prefect of Egypt, for lack of islands adjacent to Egypt, will be entitled to relegate culprits *in oasin*): *est quoddam genus quasi in insulam relegationis in provincia Aegypto in oasin relegare.* The passage has little bearing on Octavia's case, and, as Zwierlein rightly observed, Nero himself in 875 had commanded that Octavia be sent to a remote island, where death is in store for her.

The line probably imitates Verg. *Aen.* 7.10 *proxima Circaeae raduntur litora terrae*, a parallel which shows that *terra* is unobjectionable for an island (like χθών in Greek: cf. e.g. Soph. *Phil.* 1–2 ἀκτὴ μὲν ἥδε τῆς περιρρύτου χθονὸς | Λήμνου); similar also Prop. 3.21.23 *Piraei . . . litora portus. Pandatariae* is here used as an adjective, a poetical usage on which cf. Heinsius' note ad Ov. *Fast.* 4.362 (where, however, *Gallia humus* is a *varia lectio*); see also Sall. *Hist.* fr. 40.23 *Galliae mulieres*; Ov. *Fast.* 4.419–20 *terra . . . Trinacris*; Gell. *Noct. Att.* 3.7 *terra Sicilia*; 9.4 *terra India.* The mannerism is quite common in Greek poetry: cf. Eur. *Hec.* 102–3 πόλεως . . . τῆς Ἰλιάδος. This development occurs alongside the fashion, introduced by the Augustan poets, of favouring the corresponding Greek adjectival form in *-is* (for instance *Persis*, *Parthis*, with or without *terra*): cf. *Italis ora* in *AL* 425.5 R *illa . . . Britannis*, 425.6: cf. Tandoi, *SIFC* 34.2 (1963), 165 (= *Scritti*, 505).

The name of the island is attested in different forms (*RE.* xviii.3, col. 507): Ptol. 3.1 and Mart. Cap. 6.644 have Πανδατωρία. Πανδαταρία/*Pandataria*, the form re-established by Lipsius, occurs only in Suet. *Tib.* 53.2, but is likely to have been the original form in Strab. 2.123; 5.233, in place of the corrupt MS Πανδαρία. The island's name is Πανδατερία / *Pandateria* in all the other sources (Var. *Rust.* 1.8.5; Plin. *Nat.* 3.82; Tac. *Ann.* 1.53; 14.63; Suet. *Cal.* 15.1; Cass. Dio *Hist. Rom.* 55.10.14; Mela, *Chorog.* 2.121). A variant form occurs in one verse inscription ('nequioris aeui'), *CIL* x.6785 (= *CE* 1189.5) *praefuit hic longum tibi, Pandotira, per aeuum*, a transcription of Πανδώτειρα, which Herington (*Gnomon*, 1977, 277) proposed to consider the correct spelling. In the inscription, however, *Pandoteira*, an epithet with strong cultic associations, especially in connection with Demeter, should probably be regarded as a speaking name, rather than the real name of the island.

Nothing certain can be asserted about the prosody of *Pandataria*, but, whatever quantity is assigned to the vowel, Zwierlein is right to dismiss the prosodic question as irrelevant, by referring to the rather free treatment of the prosody of Greek nouns in poetry, especially as regards geographic expressions and proper names: in the Senecan corpus see Sen. *Troad.* 932, where *Sigeon* with short *e* stands for Greek Σίγειον (with Fantham's note; for Ovidian usage cf. also Kenney, *Style* 127, especially the treatment of *o* in *Sidonius/Sidonis*).

It is slightly pedantic to have Octavia spell out the name of her final destination, but this is in line with the playwright's tendency to fill in all gaps. Octavia seems not to know where she is being led at 899 ff. *quo me trahitis . . .?*, but there ignorance of her lot is intended to enhance the sense of the heroine's frailty and wronged innocence.

972 In a brief concluding ode, the chorus delivers a prayer to the winds: may they come to bring Octavia away, just as Iphigenia, they say, was hidden away by an ethereal cloud.

In the Senecan corpus, only *Octavia* and *H.O.* end with a choral ode, as is usual in Euripides (see Barrett on Eur. *Hipp.* 1462–6), but this instance is more elaborate and specific than the Euripidean moralizing tailpieces. Seneca more often concludes his dramas with some pointed *sententia*, or in pointing onwards to further dramatic implementation of the mythical plot. In Greek tragedy, actors sometimes deliver conclusive short odes in anapaests, often a prayer, as in Soph. *Phil.*, *Ai.*, *Trach.*

972 lenes aurae Zephyrique leues The dicolon is Senecan: cf. *Oed.* 37–8 *non aura . . . lenis . . . non Zephyri leues*; *Agam.* 431; a prayer to the winds occurs in Eur. *Hec.* 444–8 αὔρα, ποντιὰς αὔρα . . . ποῖ με τὰν μελέαν πορεύ - | σεις; (imitated by Seneca in *Troad.* 814 ff.). There is an address to the winds also in Ov. *Trist.* 4.4.87–8, alluding to the myth of Iphigenia in Tauris *o utinam uenti quibus est ablatus Orestes | placato referant et mea uela deo!*

973–975 tectam quondam nube aetheria | qui uexistis raptam saeuae | uirginis aris Iphigeniam The participial clause *tectam . . . nube aetheria* seems to derive from Ov. *Pont.* 3.2.61 ff., which contains a narrative of the meeting between Iphigenia and Orestes, *liquidas fecisse per auras | nescioquam dicunt Iphigenian iter, | quam leuibus uentis sub nube per aera uectam . . .*

The spelling variants found in the MSS, *aetherius* and *aethereus*, are common alternatives for derivatives from Greek -ιος forms (compare *aerius, aereus*), but the former spelling appears to be more acceptable in a classical text (the change from short Latin *i* to *e* being a common phenomenon in the transition to the Romance languages). *aetherius* is accordingly preferred by Zwierlein throughout the corpus, and this form generally prevails in ***E***: cf. *OCT*, Orthographica, p. 458. As a general rule, in Latin, *-ius* suffixes indicate belonging ('placed in', or 'descending from'), while *-eus* is sometimes specialized to designate the substance of which something is made (*LHS* 1.263): 'the ethereal cloud' of 973, however, is both 'made of' and 'descended from' the ether, and therefore no decision can be reached on considerations of meaning (cf. Man. *Astr.* 1.726–7 *orbis | aeriam in nebulam . . . uersus* where a similar problem seems to arise). The same variants appear at 215–16 *aetherio . . . toro*, where unquestionably the adjective indicates position ('in the heavens'), not material.

Position at line-end, where hiatus is relatively common in *Oct.* (cf. Introd. p. 43), makes it impossible to alter the transmitted spelling *Iphigeniam.* The Latin ending is just as common as the Greek.

12, 217, 974 are the only anapaests entirely made of spondees in *Octavia* (and in the Senecan corpus); spondaic anapaests, in Greek tragedy, are a feature of dirges, in the form of both acatalectic and catalectic lines, in which case they mark the end of a system (the passages are listed by Kaibel, ad Soph. *El.* 86–120: cf. esp. Eur. *Hec.* 156 ff.; *I.T.* 143 ff.). In *Oct.*, however, spondaic anapaests neither signal a clear expressive intention nor mark the end of a section.

977 precor The chorus has already spoken in the singular at 932–3, *tu mihi primum . . . memoranda*, while a plural form occurs at 288, *nos quoque nostri sumus immemores*. Greek choruses can use both singular and plural forms: cf. Kaimio, *The Chorus of Greek Drama within the Light of the Person and Number Used* (Helsinki, 1970), with examples. Conversely, Octavia uses plural forms of address at 646 *parcite*, and 650 *uobis*, but it is unclear to whom those words are addressed.

978–979 urbe est nostra mitior Aulis | et Taurorum barbara tellus A comparison perhaps suggested by Ov. *Pont.* 3.2.101–2 *quid facere Ausonia geniti debetis in urbe, cum tangant duros talia facta Getas?* (Bruckner 1976, 205, n. 418).

980–982 hospitis illic caede litatur | numen superum; | ciuis gaudet Roma cruore Cf. Ov. *Trist.* 4.4.51 *illi quos audis hominum gaudere cruore*. Symmetry with 980, *hospitis*, suggests that *ciuis* might be taken as a collective singular, as suggested by the author of *TLL* s.v. 1227.80, intended to evoke the horrors of persecution during the civil wars; it is also intended to attract sympathy for Octavia, who is viewed as one of many innocent subjects oppressed by Nero. For the use of *ciuis* in reference to members of the imperial house cf. e.g. Tac. *Ann.* 12.5.2 *ille unum se ciuium . . . respondit.* For *ciuis* of women cf. Verg. *Aen.* 5.671 *heu miserae ciues*; Luc. *Bell. Ciu.* 8.151–2 *quam . . . tot tempore belli | ut ciuem uidere suam* (of Cornelia at Lesbos).

APPENDIXES

APPENDIX A
IMITATIONS OF SENECAN TRAGEDY

OCTAVIA	SENECAN TRAGEDY
1–2 *iam uaga caelo sidera fulgens | Aurora fugat*	*Hf.* 125–6 *iam rara micant sidera prono | languida mundo*
17 *sparsa cruore*; 722 *sparsam cruore*	*Hf.* 445 *sparsam cruore*; *Med.* 709; *Agam.* 448
45, 166 *extinctus iacet | iaces*	*Hf.* 1160 *confecti iacent*; *Troad.* 603 *inter extinctos iacet*; *Oed.* 789 *defunctus iacet*; *Thy.* 197 *abiectus iacet*
53 *nec regi mentis potest*	*Troad.* 279 *sed regi frenis nequit*
76 *testis nostri fida doloris*	*Troad.* 83 *fidae casus nostri comites*
119 *ora fratris infestus petit*	*Phoe.* 42–3 *manibus infestis petit | foditque uultus*
125 *adice his*	*Med.* 471 *adice*; 527 *his adice*; 783
134 *emergere umbris*	*Hf.* 279 *emerge coniunx*
147 *pro facinus ingens!*	*Thy.* 234 *hunc facinus ingens*
151 *principis factus gener*	*Phoe.* 510 *hostium es factus gener*
169 *Britannice, heu me*	*Phae.* 997 *Hippolytus, heu me*
177 *immitem uirum*	*Phae.* 273 *immitis uiri*
195 *nempe praelatam sibi*	*H.O.* 304 *capta praelata est mihi*
227 *principis dirum caput*	*Thy.* 244 *profare dirum qua caput mactem uia*
233–4 *plaustra tardus . . . regit Bootes*	*Med.* 314–15 *flectitque . . . Arctica tardus plaustra Bootes*
233 *noctis alterna uice*; 388 *sortis alternae uices*	*Phae.* 410–11 *noctis decus | cuius relucet mundus alterna uice*; *Agam.* 561 *fervetque semper fluctus alterna uice*; *Thy.* 25 *certetur omni scelere et alterna uice*
234 *frigore Arctoo rigens*	*Med.* 683 *frigore Arctoo rigens*; *Oed.* 546 *frigore aeterno rigens*
242 *spiritum fratri abstulit*	*Troad.* 328 *cur dextra regi spiritum eripuit tua?*
245 *pro! summe genitor*	*H.O.* 290 *summe pro rector deum*; *ibid.* 1275
259 *furore miserae dura genetricis meae*	*Phae.* 113 *fatale miserae matris agnosco malum*
264 *raptasque thalamis sanguine extinxit faces*	*H.O.* 339 *meo iugales sanguine extinguam faces*
309–10 *haec quoque nati uidere nefas | saecula magnum*	*Oed.* 444 *uelut ignotum uidere nefas*
396 *tenente regna Saturno poli*	*H.O.* 1940 *quid me tenentem regna siderei poli*
397 *tunc illa uirgo*	*Phae.* 206 *tunc illa magnae dira fortunae comes*
401–2 *cingere assuerant suas | muris nec urbes*	*Phae.* 531–2 *non uasto aggere | crebraque turre cinxerant urbes latus*
402 *peruium cunctis iter*	*Troad.* 179 *peruium ad superos iter*, *ibid.* 433
409–10 *quod sequi cursu feras | auderet acres*	*Phae.* 110 *consequi cursu feras*

OCTAVIA	SENECAN TRAGEDY
418 *mox et armauit manus*	*Phae.* 261 *uindicem armemus manum*
421 *aut petit praedae imminens*	*Oed.* 95 *iam praedae imminens*
431 *impietas furens*	*Hf.* 97 *impietas ferox*
436 *mente horreo*	*Agam.* 226 *mente horrui*
442 *magnum timoris remedium clementia est*	*Oed.* 515 *iners malorum remedium ignorantia est*
471 *quicquid excelsum est cadat*	*Oed.* 702 *omne quod dubium est cadat*
476 *petitur hac caelum uia*	*Phae.* 1213 *patuit ad caelum uia*
501 *saepe per honorum gradus*; 429 *per tot aetates diu*	*Hf.* 291 *tot per annorum gradus*
534 *Claudiae gentis decus*	*Phae.* 900 *gentis Actaeae decus*; *Troad.* 876 *Pelasgae maximum gentis decus*
544 *dignamque thalamis coniugem inueni meis*	*Oed.* 977 *inuenta thalamis digna nox tandem meis*
548 *sola perpetuo manent*	*Med.* 196 *iniqua numquam regna perpetuo manent*
557–8 *uolucrem esse Amorem fingit immitem deum* | *mortalis error*	*Phae.* 195–6 *deum esse Amorem turpis et uitio fauens* | *finxit libido*
577 *an cedat animis temere conceptus fauor*	*Hf.* 363 *nec coeptus umquam cedat ex animis furor*
591 *et partem mei*	*Phoe.* 45 *fortis in partem tui*
600–2 *reddita et meritis meis* | *funesta merces puppis et pretium imperi* | *nox illa qua naufragia defleui mea*	*Oed.* 104–5 *laudis hoc pretium tibi* | *sceptrum et peremptae Sphingis haec merces datur*
613 *noster infelix amor*	*Med.* 136 *suasit infelix amor*
617–18 *poscit auctorem necis*; | *iam parce: dabitur*	*H.O.* 1006 *poenas poscis Alcidae? dabo*
631 *desertus ac destructus et cunctis egens*	*Hf.* 317–18 *demersus ac defossus et toto insuper* | *oppressus orbe*; *Troad.* 449 *sed fessus ac deiectus et fletu grauis*
688–9 *petat infestis mox et flammis* | *telisque . . . aulam*	*Phoe.* 565 *haec telis petes flammisque tecta?*
691 *quidue secretum petis*	*H.O.* 478 *quid istud est quod esse secretum petis?*
692 *cur genae fletu madent?*	*Phae.* 1121 *cur madent fletu genae?*
693–4 *certe petitus precibus et uotis dies* | *nostris refulsit*	*Oed.* 205 *adest petitus omnibus uotis Creo*
729 *comitante turba*	*Hf.* 837 *comitante turba*
729 *coniugem quondam meum*	*Med.* 924 *liberi quondam mei*
751 *(toros) stabiles futuros spondet aeternae domus*	*Phae.* 1241 *recipe me aeterna domo*
785 *quis iste mentes agitat attonitus furor?*	*Phae.* 1156 *quis te dolore percitam instigat furor?*; *Thy.* 339 *quis uos exagitat furor?*; *Phoe.* 557
793 *et in furorem temere praecipites agit*	*Phoe.* 299 *ira praecipites agit*
797–8 *membra per partes trahunt* | *diducta laqueis*	*Thy.* 60–1 *membra per partes eant* | *discerpta*

OCTAVIA	SENECAN TRAGEDY
848 *et hoc sat est? sic miles audisti ducem?*	*Phoe.* 356 *nec hoc sat est; Med.* 126 *hoc meis satis est malis?*; *Oed.* 954 *et flere satis est?*: *ibid.* 938 (at line-end) *hoc patri sat est?*; *Thy.* 890 *sed cur satis sit?*
855 *debita poena uacat?*	*Hf.* 643 *debitas poenas dabit*; 729 *debitas poenas dare*; *Oed.* 976 *debitas poenas tuli*
863 *cur meam damnas fidem?*	*H.O.* 909 *cur tuas damnas manus?*
870–1 *ut ne inexpugnabilis* | *esset*	*Phoe.* 165 *hac extrahe animam duram, inexpugnabilem*
972 *lenes aurae Zephyrique leues*	*Oed.* 37–9 *non aura gelido lenis afflatu fouet . . . non Zephyri leues* | *spirant*

APPENDIX B
IMITATIONS OF AUGUSTAN POETS

OCTAVIA	AUGUSTAN POETS
11 *prima meorum causa malorum*; 650	Verg. *Aen.* 11.361 *o Latio caput horum et causa malorum?*; Luc. *Bell. Ciu.* 1.84
21–2 *tulimus saeuae iussa nouercae, | hostilem animum uultusque truces*	Verg. *Aen.* 3.326–7 *stirpis Achilleae fastus iuuenemque superbum . . . tulimus*
23–4 *illa, illa meis tristis Erinys | thalamis Stygios praetulit ignis*	Ov. *Her.* 6.45 *tristis Erinys | praetulit infaustas sanguinolenta faces*
26 *modo cui totus paruit orbis*	Ov. *Pont.* 4.3.43 *cuique uiro totus terrarum paruit orbis*
70 *in luctus seruata meos*	Verg. *Aen.* 11.159 *in hunc seruata dolorem*
79 *qui me Stygias mittet ad umbras*; 958	Ov. *Met.* 6.676 *dolor Tartareas Pandiona misit ad umbras; ibid.* 12.257 *uulnere Tartareas geminato mittit ad umbras*; Hom. Lat. 431 *et Strophio genitum Stygias demittit ad umbras.*
119 *oculosque et ora fratris infestus petit*	Ov. *Met.* 10.350 *facibus saeuis oculos atque ora petentes*
132–3 *pretium stupri | iustae maritum coniugis captat caput*	Ov. *Her.* 5.143 *nec pretium stupri gemmas aurumue poposci*
157 *quis tot referre facinorum formas potest*	Verg. *Aen.* 6.626 *omnis scelerum comprendere formas*
203 *cum se formas uertit in omnes*	Verg. *Georg.* 4.411 *formas se uertet in omnes*
208 *fulgent caelo sidera Ledae*	Ov. *Am.* 2.11.29 *tum generosa uoces fecundae sidera Ledae*
212 *cuius gener est qui fuit hostis*	Ov. *Trist.* 3.5.42 *Iunonis gener qui prius hostis erat*
311–12* *Tyrrhenum . . . misit in aequor*	Ov. *Met.* 4.23–4 *Tyrrhenaque mittis in aequor | corpora*
319–20 *tollitur ingens clamor ad astra | cum femineo mixtus planctu*	Verg. *Aen.* 11.877–8 *matres | femineum clamorem ad caeli sidera tollunt*
447 *aetate in hac satis esse consilii reor*	Ov. *Met.* 6.40 *consilii satis est in me mihi*
618 *tempus haud longum peto*	Ov. *Her.* 7.178 *tempora parua peto*; Verg. *Aen.* 4.433 *tempus inane peto*
652–3* *grauiora tuli. | dabit hic nostris finem curis . . . dies*	Verg. *Aen.* 1.199 *o passi grauiora, dabit deus his quoque finem*
666 *udis confusa genis*	Verg. *Aen.* 12.64–5 *lacrimis . . . perfusa genis*
694 *Caesari iuncta es tuo*	Ov. *Pont.* 2.8.4 *Caesaribus Liuia iuncta suis*
698 *o qualis altos, quanta pressisti toros*	Verg. *Aen.* 2.591–2 *qualisque uideri | caelicolis et quanta solet*

OCTAVIA	AUGUSTAN POETS
705 *habitu atque ore laetitiam gerens*	Verg. *Aen.* 1.315 *uirginis os habitumque gerens*
718–19 *uisa . . . thalamos meos | celebrare turba est maesta*	Ov. *Met.* 9.687–8 *Inachis ante torum pompa comitata sacrorum | aut stetit aut uisa est*
769 *petet amplexus, Poppaea, tuos*	Ov. *Her.* 16.268 *dum petit amplexus, Deianira, tuos*
889 *quem neque fasces texere sui*	Verg. *Aen.* 12.539–40 *nec di texere Cupencum . . . sui*
913 *regnat mundo tristis Erinys*	Ov. *Met.* 1.241 *qua terra patet fera regnat Erinys*
918–19 *fugerem luctus ablata meos | penna uolucri procul*	Verg. *Aen.* 3.258 *in siluam pinnis ablata refugit*
927 *quem per casus uoluit uarios*	Verg. *Aen.* 1.9–10 *tot uoluere casus . . . tot adire labores*
969–70 *armate ratem, date uela fretis | uentisque*	Verg. *Aen.* 4.594 *ferte citi flammas, date tela, impellite remos*
970–1 *petat puppis rector | Pandatariae litora terrae*	Verg. *Aen.* 7.10 *proxima Circaeae raduntur litora terrae*
973–5 *tectam quondam nube aetheria | qui uexistis raptam saeuae | uirginis aris Iphigeniam*	Ov. *Pont.* 3.2.61–3 *liquidas fecisse per auras | nescioquam dicunt Iphigenian iter, | quam leuibus uentis sub nube per aethera uectam . . .*
982 *ciuis gaudet Roma cruore*	Ov. *Trist.* 4.4.61 *illi quos audis hominum gaudere cruore*

APPENDIX C
DISJUNCTIONS OF DEMONSTRATIVES IN AUGUSTAN POETRY

I have collected in this appendix a series of cases of disjunction involving demonstratives, from a representative corpus of Latin poetical texts (Lucretius, Catullus, Horace, Vergil, Ovid, Lucan, Manilius, Senecan tragedy, Valerius Flaccus, Statius, Silius, Martial, Juvenal), through database-assisted word-searching (using PHI 5.3). The examples are intended to test the linguistic plausibility of the conjecture proposed by Zwierlein at *Oct.* 262–3, *illos soluto crine, succincta anguibus, | ultrix Erinys uenit ad Stygios toros*, where *illos* replaces the MS *illo*.

I shall start with a list of all occurrences of prepositional constructions of the types *ill- . . . ad, ill- . . . in* and *ill- . . . a(b)* in this or in the reverse order, with or without intervening words, out of a total of over 5,500 cases of *ille* in the corpus of texts searched.

ill[o/a/u]- . . . ad (= *illos . . . ad, illa . . . ad, illas ad*, etc.), 1 case:

Ov. *Fast.* 2.323 *armillas non illa ad bracchia factas*

ad . . . ill[o/a/u]- 4 cases:

Ov. *Pont.* 4.9.3 *missaque* (sc. *salus*) *di faciant Auroram occurrat ad illam*

Sen. *H.O.* 1706–7 *sed ire ad illos umbra quos uici deos, | pater, erubesco,*

Juv. 8.167–9 *Lateranus ad illos | thermarum calices inscriptaque lintea uadit | maturus bello*

Juv. 14.84–5 *progenies festinat ad illam | quam primum praedam rupto gustauerat ouo*

ill[o/a/i]- . . . in (= *illo . . . in, illis . . . in, illas . . . in*, etc.), 6 cases:

Verg. *Aen.* 1.140 *illa se iactet in aula*

Ov. *Rem.* 789–90 *illo Lotophagos, illo Sirenas in antro | esse puta*

Ov. *Met.* 14.176 *aut tumulo aut certe non illa condar in aluo*

Sen. *H.O.* 128 *illo Thessalicus pastor in oppido . . .*

Stat. *Silu.* 1.3.74 *illa recubat Tiburnus in umbra*

Juv. 4.93 *his armis illa quoque tutus in aula*

in . . . ill[o/a/u/i]- (= *in . . . illo, in . . . illam, in . . . illis* etc.), 54 cases (excluding here cases of *ill-* used pronominally), of which I give a selection:

Ov. *Her.* 18.197 *optabo tamen ut partis expellar in illas*

Ars 1.175 *quis non inuenit turba quod amaret in illa*

Met. 2.332 *aliquisque malo fuit usus in illo*

Met. 5.428–9 *quarum fuerat magnum modo numen, in illas | extenuatur aquas*

Met. 9.109–10 *'officio'que 'meo ripa sistetur in illa | haec' ait 'Alcide. tu uiribus utere nando'*

Met. 9.297–8 *subsedit in illa | ante fores ara*

Met. 14.233–4 *inde Lami ueterem Laestrygonis' inquit 'in urbem | uenimus. Antiphates terra regnabat in illa'*

Fasti 6.297 *ignis inextinctus templo celatur in illo*

Pont. 3.2.41–2 *forte senex quidam, coetu cum staret in illo, | reddidit ad nostros talia uerba sonos*

Sen. *Oed.* 809–10 OED. *in illa temet nemora quis casus tulit?* SEN. *illo sequebar monte cornigeros greges*

Luc. *Bell. Ciu.* 7.328–9 *uallo tendetis in illo | unde acies peritura uenit*

ill[a/o/i]- . . . a (*ab*), 2 cases;

Ov. *Trist.* 1.1.72 *uenit in hoc illa fulmen ab arce caput*

Sen. *H.O.* 88–9 *illa licebit fulmen a parte auferas | ego quam tuebor*

The search for hyperbata of prepositional syntagms could be extended to include other pronominals, for instance *hic* and *ipse*:

h[o/a]- . . . ad (= *hos, has, haec, hanc . . . ad*), 11 cases:

Lucr. *D.R.N.* 6.939 *(quamquam multas hoc pertinet ad res | noscere) cum primis hanc ad rem protinus ipsam*

Verg. *Georg.* 4.40 *collectumque haec ipsa ad munera gluten*

Aen. 3.643 *centum alii curua haec habitant ad litora uulgo*

Ov. *Met.* 5.111 *tu quoque, Lampetide, non hos adhibendus ad usus*

[Sen.] *Oct.* 663 *hos ad thalamos seruata diu*

Stat. *Theb.* 1.456 *haec ad limina*

Theb. 7.544 *haec trahis ad commercia natum*

Theb. 8.384 *(Bellipotens) iamque hos clipeum iam uertit ad illos*

Theb. 10.211 *haec ad limina*

Theb. 11.207 *nec pater aetherius diuumque has ullus ad aras*

Val. Fl. *Arg.* 6.406 *miserat infelix non haec ad proelia Thybris*

ips[o/u/a]- . . . ad, 5 cases:

Verg. *Georg.* 4.40 *collectumque haec ipsa ad munera gluten*

Georg. 4.75–6 *ipsa ad praetoria densae | miscentur*

Sen. *Troad.* 45 *ipsasque ad aras maius admissum scelus*

H.O. 1942–3 *iam uirtus mihi | in astra et ipsos fecit ad superos iter*

Sil. *Pun.* 10.187–8 *Tyrius quos fallere doctos | hanc ipsam pugnae rector formarat ad artem*

Longer disjunctions (always within the space of one line) occur with possessives, a class of pronominals which can be thought of as related to demonstratives. The longest disjunctions occur in Ovid's pentameters.

me[o/u/a]- . . . ad, tu[o/u/a]- . . . ad, su[o/u/a]- . . . ad

Stat. *Theb.* 9.722–3 *et nunc illa meas ingentem plangit ad aras | inuidiam*

Stat. *Silu.* 5.2.161 *et mea Romulei uenient ad carmina patres*

Val. *Arg.* 4.586 *aut mea iam saeuae redeunt ad pabula Dirae*

Verg. *Aen.* 2.81 *fando aliquod si forte tuas peruenit ad auris . . .*

Aen. 3.155 *. . . et tua nos en ultro ad limina mittit*

Aen. 7.221 *Troius Aeneas tua nos ad limina misit*

Ov. *Pont.* 2.4.13 *saepe tuas uenit factum modo carmen ad auris*

Stat. *Theb.* 12.266 *tu mihi pande uias tuaque ipse ad funera deduc*

Achill. 1.728–9 *magna, reor, pridemque tuas peruenit ad aures | fama*

Lucr. *D.R.N.* 6.1238 *nam quicumque suos fugitabant uisere ad aegros*

Ov. *Her.* 13.129 *ipse suam non praebet iter Neptunus ad urbem*

Her. 19.169 *atque ita quisque suas iterum redeamus ad urbes*

Met. 4.269–70 *illa suum, quamuis radice tenetur, | uertitur ad Solem*

Stat. *Theb.* 3.116 *quisque suas auidi ad lacrimas miserabile currunt*
Val. Fl. *Arg.* 3.343 . . . *ille suam uultus conuersus ad urbem*

Some of these disjunctions have clearly acquired quasi-formulaic status in poetry (notably *tuas peruenit ad aures*), a factor which makes them easier to decipher in reading and listening. Two cases exhibit disjunctions in which the pronominal is extracted from the clause in which it grammatically belongs (Ov. *Pont.* 2.4.13 *saepe tuas uenit factum modo carmen ad auris* and Ov. *Met.* 4.269–70 *illa suum, quamuis radice tenetur, | uertitur ad Solem*).

Longer disjunctions can be found (with *ille*) in non-prepositional constructions. The search is limited to Senecan tragedy; only a selection is presented.

Most hyperbata involve a different semantic class of the demonstrative, namely when *ille* is cataphoric, i.e. followed by a relative clause. Some restriction seems to operate against a non-prepositional indirect construction (dative, ablative *illis*), for which I can present no examples of long dislocated constructions in Seneca.

Hf. 296–7 *unde illum mihi | quo te tuamque dexteram amplectar diem?*
Hf. 1210–11 *illa quae pontum Scythen | Symplegas artat*
Hf. 1243–4 *illa te Alcides uocat | facere innocentes terra quae superos solet*
Med. 695–6 *huc ille uasti more torrentis iacens | descendat anguis*

In some cases the postponed noun can be considered an apposition:

Agam. 22 *sed ille nostrae pars quota est culpae senex?* ('but him, the old man, what little part was he of our guilt?')
Agam. 165–6 *quos ille dignos Pelopia fecit domo | cum stetit ad aras ore sacrifico pater*
Agam. 812–13 *tuus ille bis seno meruit labore | adlegi caelo magnus Alcides*

In Ovid cf.

Ov. *Her.* 3.147–8 *me petat ille tuus, qui si dea passa fuisset, | ensis in Atridae pectus iturus erat*
Her. 4.31–2 *si tamen ille prior quo me sine crimine gessi candor* . . .
Her. 10.145–6 *has tibi plangendo lugubria pectora lassas | infelix tendo trans freta longa manus.*
Met. 1.185–6 *tamen illud ab uno | corpore et ex una pendebat origine bellum*

A difference seems to emerge between hyperbata with pronominals in direct and indirect (mainly prepositional) cases. The restriction concerning prepositional constructions is perhaps related to the greater difficulty of disambiguating these hyperbata in a recitational/aural context.

The finds suggest that disjunctions involving *ille, hic, ipse* in prepositional syntagms (in the presence or absence of anastrophe) are limited as to the number of words interposed between the adjective and its nominal referent. The most commonly interposed constituent is typically the verb. The limited domain of these trajections may be due to the nature of these pronominals, which are less independent of their nominal referents than qualifying adjectives. This is in itself enough to place a strong doubt on the linguistic plausibility of Zwierlein's conjecture *illos . . . ad Stygios toros*, across two inserted relative (i.e. participial) clauses *soluta crine, succincta anguibus*. The insertion of self-contained subordinate clauses between the disjoined elements is found only with possessives.

BIBLIOGRAPHY AND ABBREVIATIONS

EDITIONS, COMMENTARIES, ADVERSARIA, TRANSLATIONS

Belfortis — Andreas Belfortis, *Lucii Annaei Senecae Tragoediae* (Ferrariae, 1484, *princeps*).

Marmita — Gellius Bernardinus Marmita, *Lucii Annaei Senecae Tragoediae cum commentario G. B. M.* (Lugduni, per Antonium Lambillon et Marinum Sarazin, 1491); . . . *cum commentariis G. B. M. et Danielis Caietani* (Venetiis, per Matheum Capcasam Parmensem, 1493).

Philologus — Benedictus Philologus [Benedetto Riccardini, *dictus* Philologus] (Florentiae, apud Philippum de Giunta, 1506; 1513).

Avantius[1] — Hieronymus, Avantius, *Emendationes Tragoediarum Senecae* (Venetiis, 1507).

Ascensius — Iodocus Badius Ascensius, *Lucii Annaei Senecae tragoediae pristinae integritati restitutae per exactissimi iudicii uiros post Auantium et Philologum D(esiderium) Erasmum Roterodamum, Gerardum Vercellanum, Aegidium Maserium . . . explanatae diligentissime tribus commentariis Gellio Bernardino Marmita Parmensi, Daniele Gaietano Cremonensi, Iodoco Badio Ascensio* (Parisiis, 1514).

Avantius[2] — Hieronymus Avantius (Venetiis, in aedibus Aldi et Andreae soceri, 1517). Same text in Bernardinus Marmita; Daniel Caietanus, *Lucii Annaei Senecae Clarissimi Stoici Philosophi Nec non poetae acutissimi Opus Tragoediarum* . . . (Venetiis, per Bernardinum de Vianis de Lexona Vercellensem, 1522).

Delrius — Martinus Antonius Delrius, *Syntagma tragoediae Latinae*. iii. *Syntagmatis tragici Pars ultima, seu nouus Commentarius in decem Tragoedias quae vulgo Senecae ascribuntur* (Antverpiae, ex officina Plantiniana, 1576, 1594[2]).

Lipsius	Justus Lipsius, *Animaduersiones in tragoedias quae L. Annaeo Senecae tribuuntur* (Lugduni Batauorum, 1588).
Raphelengius	Franciscus Raphelengius, *Decem tragoediae quae Lucio Annaeo Senecae tribuuntur: operâ Francisci Raphelengii fr. f. Plantiniani ope u. cl. Iusti Lipsi emendatiores* (Antverpiae, apud Martinum Nutium, 1601).
Gruterus	Ianus Gruterus, *Lucii Annaei Senecae Cordubensis Tragoediae* (Heidelbergae, 1604).
Scriverius	Petrus Scriverius, *Lucius Annaeus Seneca, tragicus, ex recensione et museo Petri Scriverii* (Lugduni Batauorum, 1621).
Farnabius	Thomas Farnabius, *L. & M. Annaei Senecae tragoediae, cum notis Th. Farnabii* (Lugduni Batauorum, 1623).
Gronovius	Joannes Fredericus Gronovius (Lugduni Batauorum, 1661; Amstelodamii, 1682).
Schroederus	Joannes Casparus Schroederus, *Lucii Annaei Senecae Tragoediae cum notis integris J. F. Gronovii et selectis Justi Lipsii, M. Antonii Delrii, Jani Gruteri, H. Commelini, Josephi Scaligeri, Danielis et Nicolai Heinsiorum, Thomae Farnabii, aliorumque; itemque observationibus nonnullis Hugonis Grotii* (Delphis, 1728).
Heinsius	N. Heinsius, *Aduersariorum libri IV* (Harlingae, 1742), pp. 467–73; 498–514.
Withof	J. H. Withof, *Praemetium crucium criticarum praecipue ex Seneca tragico* (Lugduni Batavorum, 1749).
Baden	T. Baden, *L. Annaei Senecae Tragoediqe* (Havniae; Lipsiae, 1821).
Bothe	F. H. Bothe, *L. A. Senecae, tragoediarum volumen tertium* (Lipsiae, 1819; 1834²).
Ritter	F. Ritter, *Octauia praetexta. Curiatio Materno uindicatam . . . edidit Franciscus Ritter* (Bonnae, 1843).
Peiper, Richter	R. Peiper, G. Richter, *L. Annaei Senecae tragoediae* (Lipsiae, 1867, 1906²).
Leo	F. Leo, *L. Annaei Senecae Tragoediae. accedit Octavia praetexta*, 2 vols. (Berolini, 1878–9 (rist. 1963)).

Vürtheim	I. Vürtheim, *Octavia praetexta cum prolegomenis, annotatione critica, notis exegeticis* (Lugduni Batavorum, 1909).
Miller	F. J. Miller, *Seneca's Tragedies. vol.* II (London-Cambridge, Mass., Loeb, 1917).
Santoro	A. Santoro, *Incerti poetae Octavia* (Bologna, 1917, 1955[2]).
Ageno	F. Ageno, *Ottavia, tragedia latina d'incerto autore recata in versi italiani* (Firenze, 1920).
Hosius	C. Hosius, *Octavia praetexta, cum elementis commentarii* (Bonnae, 1922).
Herrmann	L. Herrmann, *Sénèque. Tragédies, tome* II. *Pseudo-Sénèque. Octavie* (Paris, 1924).
Sluiter	T. H. Sluiter, *Octavia fabula praetexta toegeschreven aan L. Annaeus Seneca* (Leiden, 1949).
Pedroli	L. Pedroli, *Fabularum praetextarum quae extant* (Genova, 1954).
Thomann	T. Thomann, *Seneca. Sämtliche Tragödien* (Zürich–Stuttgart, 1961), Bd. I.
Viansino, I.	I. Viansino, *L. Annaei Senecae . . . incerti poetae Octavia* (Augustae Taurinorum, 1965).
Giardina	G. C. Giardina, *L. Annaei Senecae Tragoediae*, vols. 2 (Bononiae, 1966).
Rizza	P. Rizza, *La pretesta Octavia* (Firenze, 1970).
Segurado e Campos	J. A. Segurado e Campos, *A tragédia Octávia, a obra e a época,* I*: Estudo histórico-literário.* II*: Octavia praetexta. Texto, tradução, commentario e indices* (Lisboa, 1972).
Ballaira	G. Ballaira, *Seneca. Ottavia* (Torino, 1974).
Whitman	L. Y. Whitman, *Octavia. Introduction, Text and Commentary* (Bern–Stuttgart, 1978).
Zwierlein	O. Zwierlein, *Lucii Annaei Senecae tragoediae. Incertorum auctorum Hercules [Oetaeus], Octauia* (Oxford, 1986; 1989[2]; 1991[3]; 1994[5]).
Viansino, G.	G. Viansino, *Lucio Anneo Seneca. Teatro* (Milano, 1993).
Chaumartin	F. R. Chaumartin, *Sénèque. Tragédies* (Paris, 1998).
Liberman	G. Liberman, *Pseudo-Sénèque Octavie* (Paris, 1998).
Barbera	E. Barbera, *Lucio Anneo Seneca, Ottavia* (Lecce, 2000).

WORKS CITED IN ABBREVIATED FORM

AL	*Anthologia Latina, siue poesis Latinae supplementum. Ediderunt Franciscus Buecheler et Alexander Riese. Pars prior. Carmina in codicibus scripta* (Lipsiae, 1894).
ALLP	*Aspects of the Language of Latin Poetry* (ed. J. N. Adams–R. G. Mayer) 'Proceedings of the British Academy' 93 (1999).
Axelson, *NSS*	B. Axelson, *Neue Seneca-studien* (Lund, 1939).
Axelson, *UW*	B. Axelson, *Unpoetische Wörter* (Lund, 1945).
Barrett, *Eur. Hipp.*	W. S. Barrett, *Euripides: Hippolytus* (Oxford, 1964).
Beaujeu, *Rel. rom.*	P. Beaujeu, *La religion romaine à l'apogée de l'Empire*, I–II (Paris, 1955).
Bers, *Enallage*	V. Bers, *Enallage in Greek Style* (Leiden, 1974).
Blümner	H. Blümner, *Die römischen Privataltertümer* (München, 1911[3]).
BMCRE	*Coins of the Roman Empire in the British Museum*, vols. 1–6 (London, 1923–62).
Bömer	P. Ovidius Naso, *Metamorphosen*. Kommentar von Franz Bömer (Heidelberg, 1969–86).
Bruns, *FIRA*	C. G. Bruns–O. Gradenwitz, *Fontes iuris Romani antiqui* (Tübingen, 1909[7]).
CAH[1–2]	*The Cambridge Ancient History*. 1st and 2nd edn., vols. x–xi (1936), x (1996), xi (2000).
Calcante	C. M. Calcante, *Genera dicendi e retorica del sublime* (Pisa, 2000).
Canter	H. V. Canter, *Rhetorical Elements in the Tragedies of Seneca*, University of Illinois Studies in Language and Literature 10.1 (Urbana, 1925).
CE	*Carmina Latina Epigraphica*, ediderunt F. Buecheler (1–2: Leipzig, 1895–7), E. Lommatzsch (3: Leipzig, 1926).
CHCL	*The Cambridge History of Classical Literature*, eds. P. E. Easterling, E. J. Kenney, 2 vols. (Cambridge, 1982, 1985).
CIL	*Corpus Inscriptionum Latinarum* (Berlin, 1863–).
Coleman	Statius. *Siluae IV*. Edited with an English translation and commentary by K. M. Coleman (Oxford, 1988).

Conington	*The Works of Virgil*, with a Commentary by J. Conington and H. Nettleship, I–III (London, 1898[5]).
Conte	G. B. Conte, *La guerra civile di Lucano* (Urbino, 1988) [includes a commentary on *Bell. Ciu.* 6.118–260, previously published separately as *Saggio di commento a Lucano* (Pisa, 1974)].
Cortius	*M. Annaei Lucani Pharsalia. Cum notis G. Cortii aliorumque*, I–II (Lipsiae 1828–9).
Courtney	E. Courtney, *The Fragmentary Latin Poets* (Oxford, 1993).
CRF	*Comicorum Romanorum praeter Plautum et Terentium Fragmenta*, in *Scaenicae Romanorum Poesis Fragmenta, ed. O. Ribbeck* (Leipzig, 1852–5, 1871[2], 1897–8[3]).
Daremberg–Saglio	C. Daremberg–E. Saglio, *Dictionnaire des antiquités grecques et romaines d'après les textes et les monuments* (Paris, 1877–1919).
De Rossi	G. B. De Rossi (ed.), *Inscriptiones Christianae urbis Romae sept. saec. Antiquiores* (Rome, 1857–61).
Devine–Stephens, *DS*	A. M. Devine–L. D. Stephens, *Discontinuous Syntax* (Oxford–New York, 1999).
Devine–Stephens, *PGS*	A. M. Devine–L. D. Stephens, *The Prosody of Greek Speech* (Oxford–New York, 1994).
Di Benedetto–Medda	V. Di Benedetto–E. Medda, *La tragedia sulla scena. La tragedia greca in quanto spettacolo teatrale* (Torino, 1997).
Di Marco, *Tragedia*	M. Di Marco, *La tragedia greca. Forma, gioco scenico, tecniche drammatiche* (Roma, 2000).
DMLBS	*Dictionary of Medieval Latin from British Sources. A-L* (Oxford, 1997).
Duckworth, *NRC*	G. E. Duckworth, *The Nature of Roman Comedy* (Princeton, 1952, 2nd edn. Bristol, 1994).
Düring, *Materialien*	T. Düring–W. Hoffa, *Materialien für eine Neuausgabe von Senecas Tragödien* (unpublished) 4 vols., Niedersächsische Staats- und Universitätsbibliothek, Göttingen, Cod. ms. philol. 142[n] [*non uidi*: cf. Zwierlein, *KK*].
Easterling, *Companion*	P. E. Easterling (ed.), *The Cambridge Companion to Greek Tragedy* (Cambridge, 1997).
EO	S. Mariotti (ed.), *Enciclopedia oraziana* vols. I–III, (Roma, 1996–8).

EV — F. Della Corte (ed.), *Enciclopedia virgiliana*, vols. I–V (Roma, 1984–1990).

FGE — D. L. Page (ed.), *Further Greek Epigrams* (Cambridge, 1981).

Fitch — *Seneca's Hercules furens*. A critical text with introduction and commentary by J. G. Fitch (Ithaca and London, 1987).

Fraenkel, *EP* — E. Fraenkel, *Elementi plautini in Plauto* (Florence, 1960).

Fraenkel, *Horace* — E. Fraenkel, *Horace* (Oxford, 1957).

Fraenkel, *KB* — E. Fraenkel, *Kleine Beiträge zur klassischen Philologie*, 2 vols. (Rome, 1964).

Friedländer — L. Friedländer, *Darstellungen aus der Sittengeschichte Roms* (Leipzig, 1922[10]).

Frost, *Menander* — K. B. Frost, *Exits and Entrances in Menander* (Oxford, 1988).

GLK — *Grammatici Latini, ediderunt H. Keil et al.*, 7 vols. and suppl. vol. (Leipzig, 1855–1880).

Gomme–Sandbach — A. W. Gomme–F. H. Sandbach, *Menander. A commentary* (Oxford, 1973).

Goodyear — *The Annals of Tacitus. Books 1–6*, edited with a commentary by F. R. D. Goodyear (Cambridge, 1972).

Gow-Page, *HE* — A. S. F. Gow-D. L. Page, *The Greek Anthology. Hellenistic Epigrams*, 2 vols. (Cambridge, 1965).

Griffin, *Nero* — M. T. Griffin, *Nero. The End of a Dynasty* (London, 1984).

Griffin, *Seneca* — M. T. Griffin, *Seneca. A Philosopher in Politics* (Oxford, 1976, 1992[2]).

Hand, *Tursellinus* — F. Hand, *Tursellinus, seu de particulis Latinis commentarii* (Leipzig, 1829–45).

Harrison — *Vergil. Aeneid 10*. With introduction, translation and commentary by S. J. Harrison (Oxford, 1991).

Henzen, *Acta* — W. Henzen, *Acta fratrum Arvalium quae supersunt* (Berlin, 1874).

Hillen — M. Hillen, *Studien zur Dichtersprache Senecas. Abundanz. Explikatives Ablativ. Hypallage* (Berlin-New York, 1989).

HLSM — P. Stotz, *Handbuch zur lateinischen Sprache des Mittelalters. Vierter Band. Formenlehre, Syntax und Stilistik* (München, 1998).

Hofmann, *LU* — J. B. Hofmann, *Lateinische Umgangssprache* (Heidelberg, 1926; augmented Ital. translation by L. Ricottilli, Bologna, 1985).

Housman, *CP* — A. E. Housman, *The Classical Papers* (Cambridge, 1972), I–III.

Housman, *ad* Man. *Astr.* — Marci Manilii *Astronomicon*, recensuit et enarravit Alfred Edward Housman (London, 1903–16).

IG — *Inscriptiones Graecae* (Berlin, 1873–).

IGRR — *Inscriptiones Graecae ad res Romanas pertinentes*, ed. R. Cagnat, J. Toutain, et al., vols. 1, 3, 4 (Paris, 1901–27).

ILS — *Inscriptiones Latinae Selectae*, 5 vols., ed. H. Dessau (Berlin, 1892–1916).

Jens, *Bauformen* — W. Jens, *Die Bauformen der griechischen Tragödie* (München, 1971).

Jocelyn, *Ennius* — H. D. Jocelyn, *The Tragedies of Ennius. The Fragments edited with an Introduction and Commentary* (Cambridge, 1967).

Kaibel, *EG* — G. Kaibel, *Epigrammata Graeca ex lapidibus conlecta* (Berlin, 1878).

Kalb, *Juristenlatein* — W. Kalb, *Das Juristenlatein. Versuch einer Charakteristik auf Grundlage der Digesten* (Nürnberg, 1888).

Kenney, *Style* — E. J. Kenney, *The Style of the* Metamorphoses, in J. W. Binns, ed., *Ovid* (London, 1973).

K-G — R. Kühner–B. Gerth, *Ausführliche Grammatik der griechischen Sprache*, vols. 1–2 (München, 1963).

Klotz — A. Klotz, *Scaenicorum Romanorum Fragmenta, volumen prius. tragicorum fragmenta* (München, 1953).

Kroll, *Studien* — W. Kroll, *Studien zum Verständnis der römischen Literatur* (Stuttgart, 1924).

K-S — R. Kühner–C. Stegmann, *Ausführliche Grammatik der lateinischen Sprache*, vols. 1–2 (Hannover, 1912–14²).

Langen — *Valerius Flaccus. Argonauticon libri octo. Enarravit P. Langen* (Berlin, 1896–7).

Lausberg, *HLR* — H. Lausberg, *Handbuch der literarischen Rhetorik*, 2 vols. (München, 1960; 1973²; 1990³).

Leeman — A. D. Leeman, *Orationis ratio. The Stylistic Theories and Practice of the Roman Orators, Historians and Philosophers* (Amsterdam, 1963).

Leo, *KS* — F. Leo, *Kleine Schriften* (Rome, 1960).

Leo, *Monolog* — F. Leo, 'Der Monolog im Drama. Ein Beitrag zur griechisch-römischen Poetik', *Abhandlungen der königlichen Gesellschaft der Wissenschaften zu Göttingen. philologisch-historische Klasse*, N.F. 10.5 (Berlin, 1908).

Leo, *Obs.* — F. Leo, *De Senecae tragoediis observationes criticae* (Berlin, 1878).

Leo, *PF* — F. Leo, *Plautinische Forschungen zur Kritik und Geschichte der Komödie* (Berlin, 1912²).

Leonhardt, *DS* — J. Leonhardt, *Dimensio syllabarum. Studien zur lateinischen Prosodie- und Verslehre von der Spätantike bis zur frühen Renaissance* (Göttingen, 1989).

Leumann, *KS* — M. Leumann, *Kleine Schriften* (Zürich-Stuttgart, 1959).

LHS — M. Leumann-J. B. Hofmann-A. Szantyr, *Lateinische Grammatik*. Vol. I *Laut- und Formenlehre*; vol. II *Syntax und Stilistik* (München, 1965–77).

LIMC — *Lexicon Iconographicum Mythologiae Classicae* (1981–).

Lindsay, *ELV* — W. M. Lindsay, *Early Latin Verse* (Oxford, 1922).

Lindsay, *LL* — *The Latin Language* (Oxford, 1894).

Löfstedt, *Coniectanea* — E. Löfstedt, *Coniectanea. Untersuchungen auf dem Gebiete der antiken und mittelalterlichen Latinität* (Stockholm, 1950).

Löfstedt, *Late Latin* — E. Löfstedt, *Late Latin* (Oslo, 1959).

Löfstedt, *Syntactica* — E. Löfstedt, *Syntactica. Studien und Beiträge zur historischen Syntax des Lateins.* I–II (Lund, 1942; 1956).

Löfstedt, *VS* — E. Löfstedt, *Vermischte Studien zur lateinischen Sprachkunde und Syntax* (Lund, 1936).

LSJ — H. G. Liddell–R. Scott–H. S. Jones, *Greek-English Lexicon* (Oxford, 1940⁹).

Lunelli, *LP* — A. Lunelli (ed.), *La lingua poetica latina* (Bologna, 1988³).

Maas, *KS* — P. Maas, *Kleine Schriften* (München, 1973).

Malaspina — *Lucii Annaei Senecae de clementia libri duo*, edited by E. Malaspina (Alessandria, 2001).

Manuwald — G. Manuwald, *Fabulae praetextae. Spuren einer literarischen Gattung* (München, 2001).

Marouzeau, *Ordre* — J. Marouzeau, *L'ordre des mots dans la phrase latine* (Paris, 1949).

Marouzeau, *Styl.*	J. Marouzeau, *Traité de stylistique latine* (Paris, 1970[5]).
Marquardt, *Privatleben*	J. Marquardt, *Das Privatleben der Römer* (Leipzig, 1886[2]).
Mastandrea	P. Mastandrea, *De fine versus. Repertorio di clausole ricorrenti nella poesia dattilica Latina* (Hildesheim–Zürich–New York, 1993).
Mastronarde, *CD*	D. Mastronarde, *Contact and Discontinuity* (Berkeley, 1980).
Maurach, *EP*	G. Maurach, *Enchiridion poeticum. Hilfsbuch zur lateinischen Dichtersprache* (Darmstadt, 1983).
McKeown	J. C. McKeown (ed.), *Ovid. Amores. Text, Prolegomena and Commentary in four volumes* (Leeds, 1987–98).
MGH	*Monumenta Germaniae Historica*, 15 vols. (1877–1919).
MLW	*Mittellateinisches Wörterbuch*, I–II- (München, 1999–).
Momigliano	A. D. Momigliano, *Contributi alla storia degli studi classici*, I–IX (Roma, 1954–99).
Mommsen, *Ephem. Epigr.*	*Ephemeris Epigraphica, Corporis Inscr. Latinarum Supplementum*, 9 vols. (Berlin, 1872–1913).
Mommsen, *RS*	T. Mommsen, *Römisches Staatsrecht*, vols. 1[3], 2[3] (Leipzig, 1887–8).
Mueller, *DRM*	L. Mueller, *De re metrica poetarum latinorum praeter Plautum et Terentium* (St. Petersburg, 1894[2]).
N-H	Horace. *Odes, Book* I, comm. by R. G. M. Nisbet and M. Hubbard (Oxford, 1970); *Book* II (Oxford, 1978).
Nock, *Essays*	A. D. Nock. *Essays on Religion and the Ancient World* (Oxford, 1972).
Norden, *Agn. Th.*	E. Norden, *Agnostos Theos. Untersuchungen zur Formengeschichte religiöser Rede* (Stuttgart, 1912, 1923[2]).
Norden, *AK*	E. Norden, *Die antike Kunstprosa vom VI Jahrhundert v. Chr. bis in die Zeit der Renaissance* (Leipzig, 1915[3]).
Norden, *Kommentar*	E. Norden, *Vergil. Aeneis Buch* VI (Leipzig, 1927[3]).
N-W	F. Neue-C. Wagener, *Formenlehre der lateinischen Sprache* (Leipzig, 1892–1905[3]).
OCD[3]	*Oxford Classical Dictionary.* Third edition, edited by S. Hornblower and A. Spawforth (Oxford–New York, 1996).

OGIS — *Orientis Graeci Inscriptiones Selectae*, ed. W. Dittenberger, 2 vols. (Leipzig, 1903–5).

Otto — A. Otto, *Die Sprichwörter und sprichwörtlichen Redensarten der Römer* (Lepzig, 1890).

Page, *GLP* — D. L. Page, *Greek Literary Papyri*, 2 vols. (London–Cambridge, Mass., 1942)

PCG — *Poetae Comici Graeci* ediderunt R. Kassel, C. Austin (Berlin, 1989–).

Peek, *GV* — *Griechische Vers-Inschriften* (herausgegeben von W. Peek) (Berlin, 1955).

PHI — Packard Humanities Institute CD-ROM#5.3 (Latin Texts), 1997.

Pickard-Cambridge — A. Pickard-Cambridge, *The Dramatic Festivals of Athens* (Oxford, 1968[1–2]).

PIR[1–2] — *Prosopographia Imperii Romani saec. I.II.III*, edd. K. Klebs, H. Dessau, P. von Rohden, 3 vols. (Berlin, 1897–8); *Prosopographia Imperii Romani saec. I.II.III*, edd. E. Groag, A. Stein, L. Petersen, 5 vols. (Berlin-Leipzig, 1933–70[2]).

Platnauer — M. Platnauer, *Latin elegiac verse. A study of the metrical usages of Tibullus, Propertius and Ovid* (Cambridge, 1951).

Preller–Robert, *GM* — L. Preller–L. Robert, *Griechische Mythologie*, I–III (Leipzig, 1897[4]).

RE — *Paulys Realencyclopädie der classischen Altertumswissenschaft*[2], ed. G. Wissowa et al. (Stuttgart-Munich, 1894–).

Ribbeck, *RT* — O. Ribbeck, *Die römische Tragödie im Zeitalter der Republik* (Leipzig, 1875).

RIC[2] — C. H. V. Sutherland–R. A. G. Carson, *The Roman Imperial Coinage* I (London, 1984[2]).

Roscher, *Lexicon* — W. H. Roscher (ed.), *Ausführliches Lexicon der griechischen und römischen Mythologie* (Leipzig, 1886–90), I–VI; VII *Supplement* (Leipzig, 1893).

Rosén, *Latine loqui* — H. Rosén, *Latine loqui. Trends and Directions in the Crystallization of Classical Latin* (München, 1999).

RPC — *Roman Provincial Coinage*, ed. A. Burnett, M. Amandry, P. P. Ripollès, 2 vols. (London-Paris, 1998[2]

Solin, *Personennamen* — H. Solin, *Die griechischen Personennamen in Rom. Ein Namenbuch* (Berlin, 1982).

Sommer — F. Sommer, *Handbuch der Lateinischen Laut- und Formenlehre* (Heidelberg, 1902)

Soubiran, *Essai* — J. Soubiran, *Essai sur la versification dramatique des Romains* (Paris, 1988).

Strack, *Untersuchungen* — P. Strack, *Untersuchungen zur römischen Reichsprägung des zweiten Jahrhunderts* (Stuttgart, 1931).

SVF — *Stoicorum Veterum Fragmenta*, edidit H. v. Arnim (Leipzig, 1903).

Syme, *RR* — R. Syme, *The Roman Revolution* (Oxford, 1939)

Syme, *Tacitus* — R. Syme, *Tacitus*, 2 vols. (Oxford, 1958)

Tandoi (*Scritti*) — V. Tandoi, *Scritti di filologia e di storia della cultura classica*, 2 vols. (Pisa, 1992).

Taplin, *Stagecraft* — O. Taplin, *The Stagecraft of Aeschylus. The dramatic use of exits and entrances in Greek tragedy* (Oxford, 1977).

Tarrant, *Agam.* — *Seneca*: *Agamemnon*. Edited with a commentary by R. J. Tarrant (Cambridge, 1976).

Timpanaro, *NC* — S. Timpanaro, *Nuovi contributi di filologia e storia della lingua Latina* (Bologna, 1994).

TLL — *Thesaurus Linguae Latinae* (Munich, 1990).

Treggiari, *Roman Marriage* — S. Treggiari, *Roman Marriage* (Oxford, 1991).

Trevet — *see* Junge (1999).

TRF — *Tragicorum Romanorum Fragmenta*, in *Scaenicae Romanorum Poesis Fragmenta*, ed. O. Ribbeck (Leipzig, 1852–5, 1871–3^{2}, 1897–8^{3}).

TrGF — *Tragicorum Graecorum Fragmenta* ed. B. Snell, R. Kannicht, S. Radt, 4 vols. (Göttingen, 1971–85).

Trillitzsch, *Seneca* — W. Trillitzsch, *Seneca im literarischen Urteil der Antike* I–II (Amsterdam, 1971).

Vahlen, *GPhS* — J. Vahlen, *Gesammelte philologische Schriften* (Leipzig–Berlin, 1911).

Vahlen, *Opuscula* — J. Vahlen, *Opuscula academica*, 2 vols. (Leipzig, 1907–8)

Vollmer — Publius Papinius Statius. *Silvarum libri.* Herausgegeben und erklärt von F. Vollmer (Leipzig, 1898).

Weinstock, *Diuus Iulius* — S. Weinstock, *Diuus Iulius* (Oxford, 1971).

Weissenborn-Müller — *Titi Livi ab Vrbe condita libri.* Bearbeitet von W. Weissenborn und H. J. Müller (Berlin, 1908[9]).

West, *GM* — M. L. West, *Greek Metre* (Oxford, 1982).

Wills, *Repetition* — J. Wills, *Repetition in Latin poetry* (Oxford, 1996).

Zwierlein, *KK* — O. Zwierlein, *Kritischer Kommentar zu den Tragödien Senecas*, Akademie der Wissenschaften und der Literatur. Mainz. Abhandlungen der Geistes- und Sozialwissenschaftlichen Klasse 6 (Mainz, 1986).

Zwierlein, *Prolegomena* — O. Zwierlein, *Prolegomena zu einer kritischen Ausgabe der Tragödien Senecas*, Akademie der Wissenschaften und der Literatur. Mainz. Abhandlungen der Geistes- und Sozialwissenschaftlichen Klasse 3 (Mainz, 1983).

WORKS CITED BY AUTHOR AND DATE

Baehrens (1878) — E. Baehrens, *Miscellanea Critica* (Groningae, 1878), 114–122.

Baehrens (1923) — W. Baehrens, 'Die Octavia praetexta und Seneca', *PhW* 43 (1923), 668–71.

Barnes (1982) — T. D. Barnes, 'The date of the *Octavia*', *MH* 39 (1982), 215–17.

Bellandi (1997) — F. Bellandi, 'Tra Seneca e Sofocle: sulla scena d'apertura di *Octavia* di Ps.-Seneca', *Paideia* 52 (1997), 31–56.

Billerbeck (1988) — M. Billerbeck, 'Senecas Tragödien. Sprachliche und stilistische Untersuchungen', *Mnem.* Suppl. 105 (Leiden, 1988), 172–3.

Birt (1921) — T. Birt, 'Zur Octavia des vermeintlichen Seneca', *PhW* 41 (1921), 333–6.

Birt (1923) — T. Birt, 'Nochmals die Octavia des sogenannten Seneca', *PhW* 43 (1923), 740–4.

Bragington (1933) — M. V. Bragington, *The Supernatural in Seneca's Tragedies* (diss. Yale, New Haven, 1933), 93–8.

Braun (1863) — W. Braun, *Die Tragödie Octavia und die Zeit ihrer Entstehung* (Kiel, 1863).

Bruckner (1976) — F. Bruckner, *Interpretationen zur Pseudo-Seneca Tragödie Octavia* (diss. Erlangen, 1976).

Buecheler (1872) F. Buecheler, 'Coniectanea', *RhM* 27 (1872), 474–5 (= *Kleine Schriften* (Leipzig, 1915–30), 2.30–1).

Carbone (1977) M. E. Carbone, '*Octavia*: Structure, date, and authenticity', *Phoenix* 31 (1977), 48–67.

Carlsson (1926) G. Carlsson, *Die Überlieferung der Seneca-Tragödien*. Lunds Universitets Årsskrift, N.F. Avd 1. Bd. 21. Nr. 5 (Lund, 1926).

Coffey (1957) M. Coffey, 'Seneca Tragicus 1922–55', *Lustrum* 2 (1957), 174–84.

Courtney (1985) E. Courtney, 'Emendations in Seneca's tragedies', *RFIC* 111 (1985), 297–302.

Damsté (1919) P. H. Damsté 'Ad Octaviam praetextam', *Mnemosyne* 47 (1919), 271–81.

Dingel (1974) J. Dingel, *Seneca und die Dichtung* (Heidelberg, 1974).

Düring (1907) T. Düring, 'Die Überlieferung des Interpolirten Textes von Senecas Tragödien', *Hermes* 42 (1907), 113–26.

Düring (1912) T. Düring, 'Zur Überlieferung von Senecas Tragödien', *Hermes* 47 (1912), 182–98.

Düring (1913) T. Düring, *Zur Überlieferung von Senekas Tragödien* (Leipzig, 1913).

Eitrem-Amundsen (1955) S. Eitrem–L. Amundsen, 'Fragments of unknown Greek tragic texts with musical notation', *SO* 31 (1955), 1–87.

Enk (1926) P. J. Enk, 'De Octavia praetexta', *Mnemosyne* 54 (1926), 390–415.

Ferri (1996) R. Ferri, 'Ps.-Sen. *Octavia* 887 ff. and Verg. *Aen.* 539 ff.', *CQ* n.s. 46.1 (1996), 311–14.

Ferri (1998) R. Ferri, 'Octavia's heroines. Tac. *Ann.* 14.63–4 and the *Praetexta Octavia*', *HSCPh* 98 (1998), 339–56.

Ferri (1999) R. Ferri, 'Two textual notes on Ps.-Sen. Octavia (458, 747)', *CQ* n.s. 49.2 (1999), 634–7.

Fitch (1981) J. G. Fitch, 'Sense-pauses and relative dating in Seneca, Sophocles and Shakespeare', *AJPH* 102 (1981), 289–307.

Fitch (1987) J. G. Fitch, *Seneca's anapaests. Metre, colometry, text and artistry in the anapaests of Seneca's tragedies* (Atlanta, 1987).

Flinck (1919) E. Flinck, 'De *Octauiae* praetextae auctore', *Suomalaisen Tiedeakatemian Toimituksia*, sarja B, tom. 11, n. 12 (Helsingforsiae, 1919).

Flower, H. I. (1995) — '*Fabulae praetextae* in context: when were plays on contemporary subjects performed in Republican Rome?', *CQ* 45.1 (1995), 170–90.

Frassinetti (1973) — P. Frassinetti, 'Problemi testuali nell'*Octavia*', *Rendiconti dell'Istituto lombardo. Lettere* 107 (1973), 1097–1118.

Fuchs (1977) — H. Fuchs, 'Textgestaltungen in der Tragödie Octavia' in *Latinität und alte Kirche. Festschrift für R. Hanslik zum 70. Geburtstag. Wien. Stud.* Beih. 8 (1977), 71–7.

Galimberti-Ramelli (2001) — A. Galimberti-I. Ramelli, 'L'*Octavia* e il suo autore: P. Pomponio Secondo?', *Aevum* 75 (2001), 79–99.

Gercke (1896) — A. Gercke, 'Plinius in der Octavia', in 'Seneca-Studien' *Jahrbücher f. class. Philol.* Supplb., N.F. 22 (Leipzig, 1896), 195–200.

Giancotti (1954) — F. Giancotti, *L'Octavia attribuita a Seneca* (Torino, 1954).

Giardina (1965) — G. C. Giardina, 'La tradizione manoscritta di Seneca tragico', *Vichiana*, 2 (1965), 31–74.

Griffin (1983) — M. T. Griffin, rev. of Kragelund, *Prophecy, populism and propaganda in the 'Octavia'*, in *CR*, n.s. 33 (1983), 321–2.

Gross (1911) — O. Gross, 'De metonymiis sermonis Latini a deorum nominibus petitis', *Diss. Phil. Hal.* 19.4 (1911), 297–410.

Hahlbrock (1968) — P. Hahlbrock, 'Beobachtungen zum jambischen Trimeter in den Tragödien des L. Annaeus Seneca', *WS* N.F. 2 (1968), 171–192.

Harrison (2000) — G. W. Harrison (ed.), *Seneca in Performance* (London, 2000).

Helm (1934) — R. Helm, 'Die Praetexta *Octavia*', *SBDA* (*Sitzungsberichte der Preussischen Akademie der Wissenschaften*) philologisch-historische Klasse 16 (1934), 283–347.

Herington (1958) — C. J. Herington, 'A thirteenth-century manuscript of the Octavia praetexta in Exeter', *RhM* 101 (1958), 353–77.

Herington (1961) — C. J. Herington, 'Octavia Praetexta: a survey', *CQ* n.s. 11 (1961), 18–30.

Herington (1977) C. J. Herington, rev. of Ballaira, *Gnomon* 49 (1977), 275–9.

Herington (1980) C. J. Herington, rev. of Whitman, *AJPh* 101 (1980), 504–8.

Herrmann (1924) L. Herrmann, *Octavia prétexte. Texte et traduction* (Paris, 1924).

Herrmann (1958) L. Herrmann, *Le second Lucilius*, Coll. Latomus, 34 (1958).

Herzog-Hauser (1932) G. Herzog-Hauser, 'Zur Textgestaltung und Erklärung der Praetexta Octavia', *WS* 50 (1932), 114–21.

Herzog-Hauser (1936) G. Herzog-Hauser, 'Reim und Stabreim in der Praetexta Octavia', *Glotta* 25 (1936), 109–16.

Junge (1999) R. Junge, *Nicholas Trevet und die Octavia praetexta. Editio princeps des mittelalterlichen Kommentars und Untersuchungen zum pseudo-senecanischen Drama* (Paderborn, 1999).

Kragelund (1982) P. Kragelund, 'Prophecy, populism and propaganda in the *Octavia*', *Mus. Tusc. Suppl.* 25 (Copenhagen, 1982).

Kragelund (1987) P. Kragelund, 'Vatinius, Nero and Curiatius Maternus', *CQ* n.s. 37 (1987), 197–202.

Kragelund (1988) P. Kragelund, 'The Prefect's dilemma and the date of *Octavia*', *CQ* n.s. 38 (1988), 492–508.

Kragelund (1998) P. Kragelund, 'Galba's *pietas*, Nero's victims and the Mausoleum of Augustus', *Historia* 47. 2 (1998), 152–73.

Kragelund (1999) P. Kragelund, 'Senecan tragedy: back on stage?', *CM* 50 (1999), 235–47.

Kragelund (2000) P. Kragelund, 'Nero's *luxuria*, in Tacitus and in *Octauia*', *CQ* n.s. 50.2 (2000), 494–515.

Kragelund (2002) P. Kragelund, 'Historical drama in ancient Rome. Republican flourishing and Imperial decline?', *SO* 73 (2002), 1–51; 88–105.

Kurfess (1927) A. Kurfess, 'Zu Senecas Octavia', *PhW* 47 (1927), 569–71.

La Penna (1991) A. La Penna, 'Palazzo, coro e popolo nella tragedia antica e nella tragedia umanistica', in *Tersite censurato* (Pisa, 1991), 37–67.

Ladek (1891) F. Ladek, 'De Octavia praetexta', *Dissertationes Philologae Vindobonenses* 3.4 (Vindobonae, 1891), 3–107.

Ladek (1909) F. Ladek, 'Die römische Tragödie *Octavia* und die *Elektra* des Sophokles', *Wiener Eranos* (Wien, 1909), 189–99.

Leo (1897) F. Leo, 'Die Composition der Chorlieder Senecas', *RhM* N.F. 52 (1897), 509–18.

MacGregor (1971) A. P. MacGregor, 'The MS tradition of Seneca's tragedies: ante renatas in Italia litteras', *TAPA* 102 (1971), 327–56.

MacGregor (1978) A. P. MacGregor, 'Parisinus 8031: Cod. Opt. for the A-MSS of Seneca's tragedies', *Philologus* 122 (1978), 88–110.

MacGregor (1985) A. P. MacGregor, 'The manuscripts of Seneca's tragedies: A handlist', *ANRW* 32.2 (Berlin–New York, 1985), 1135–1241.

Mantke (1957–8) I. Mantke, 'De Senecae tragici anapaestis', *Eos* 49 (1957–8), 101–22.

Marchitelli (1999) S. Marchitelli, 'Nicholas Trevet und die Renaissance der Seneca-Tragödien', *MH* 56 (1999) 36–63 (I); 87–104 (II).

Martellotti (1972) G. Martellotti, 'La questione dei due Seneca da Petrarca a Benvenuto', *IMU* 15 (1972), 149–69.

Meise (1969) E. Meise, 'Untersuchungen zur Geschichte der Julisch-Claudischen Dynastie', *Vestigia*, 10 (München, 1969).

Mette (1964) H. J. Mette, 'Die Römische Tragödie und die Neufunde zur Griechischen Tragödie', *Lustrum* 9 (1964), 5–213.

Müller (1911) M. Müller, *Beiträge zur Textkritik* (Posen, 1911), 125–40.

Müller (1912) M. Müller, 'Beiträge zur Textkritik. I. Zur praetexta Octavia', *Beilage zum Jahresbericht des königlichen Gymnasiums in Patschkau* (Posen, 1912).

Münscher (1922) K. Münscher, 'Senecas Werke. Untersuchungen zur Abfassungszeit und Echtheit', *Philol. Supplb.* 16 (Leipzig, 1922), 126–42.

Nisbet (1995) R. G. M. Nisbet, *Collected Papers on Latin Literature*, ed. S. J. Harrison (Oxford, 1995).

Nordmeyer (1892) G. Nordmeyer, 'De Octaviae fabula', *Jahrbuch für classiche Philologie* Supplb. 19 (Leipzig, 1892), 257–317.

Pantzerhielm Thomas (1945) — S. Pantzerhielm Thomas, 'De Octavia praetexta', *SO* 24 (1945) 48–87.

Peiper (1863) — R. Peiper, *Observatorum in Senecae tragoediis libellus* (Vratislaviae, 1863), 38–40.

Peiper (1870) — R. Peiper, *Praefationis in Senecae tragoedias nuper editas supplementum* (Vratislaviae, 1870).

Poe (1989) — J. P. Poe, '*Octavia praetexta* and its Senecan model', *AJPh* 110 (1989), 434–59.

Premerstein (1937) — A. V. Premerstein, *Vom Werden und Wesen des Prinzipats* (Munich, 1937).

Ribbeck (1892) — O. Ribbeck, *Geschichte d. röm. Dichtung*, III (Stuttgart, 1892), 84–8.

Richter (1862) — G. Richter, *De Seneca tragoediarum auctore* (diss., Bonn, 1862).

Rouse (1971) — R. H. Rouse, 'The A text of Seneca's tragedies in the thirteenth century', *Revue d'Histoire des Textes* 1 (1971), 93–121.

Runchina (1964) — G. Runchina, 'Sulla pretesta *Ottavia* e le tragedie di Seneca', *RCCM* 6 (1964), 47–63.

Runchina (1977–8) — G. Runchina, 'Il prologo della pretesta *Octavia*', *Ann. Fac. Magist. Cagliari* n.s. 2 (1977–8), 65–86.

Schmidt (1860) — B. Schmidt, *De emendandarum Senecae tragoediarum rationibus prosodiacis et metricis* (Berolini, 1860).

Schmidt (1865) — B. Schmidt, *Obseruationes criticae in L. Annaei Senecae tragoedias* (Ienae, 1865).

Schmidt (1978) — P. L. Schmidt 'Rezeption und Überlieferung der Tragödien Senecas bis zum Ausgang des Mittelalters' , in E. Lefèvre, (ed.) *Der Einfluss Senecas auf das europäische Drama* (Darmstadt, 1978), 12–73.

Schmidt (1985) — P. L. Schmidt, 'Die Poetisierung und Mythisierung der Geschichte in der Tragödie Octavia', *ANRW* 32. 2 (1985), 1421–1453.

Seidensticker (1969) — B. Seidensticker, *Die Gesprächsverdichtung in den Tragödien Senecas* (Heidelberg, 1969).

Siegmund (1911) — A. Siegmund, *Zur Texteskritik der Tragödie Octavia* (Leipzig und Wien, 1907) = *Jahresberichte des Staatsgymnasiums in Böhm-Leipa für das Schuljahr 1910–11*, Böhm-Leipa 1911, I, 1–21; II, 1–31.

Soubiran (1964) J. Soubiran, 'Recherches sur la clausule du sénaire (trimètre) latin: les mots longs finaux', *REL* 42 (1964), 429–69.

Soubiran (1966) J. Soubiran, *L'élision dans la poésie latine* (Paris, 1966).

Soubiran (1984a) J. Soubiran, 'Le sénaire tragique de Cicéron', *Ciceroniana* 5 (1984), 69–80.

Soubiran (1984b) J. Soubiran, 'Les débuts du trimètre tragique à Rome. I. Le fragment de l'*Athamas* D'Ennius', *Pallas* 31, (1984), 83–96.

Soubiran (1987) J. Soubiran, 'Les débuts du trimètre tragique à Rome. II. Varius et Gracchus', in *Studi offerti a Francesco Della Corte* (Urbino, 1987), 3.109–24.

Staehlin (1912) R. Staehlin, 'Das Motiv der Mantik im antiken Drama', *Religionsgeschichtliche Versuche und Vorarbeiten* 12.2 (Giessen, 1912).

Strzelecki (1938) L. Strzelecki, *De Senecae trimetro iambico quaestiones selectae* (Krakow, 1938).

Stuart (1911) C. E. Stuart, 'Notes and Emendations on the Tragedies of Seneca', *CQ* 5 (1911), 32–41.

Stuart (1912) C. E. Stuart, 'The MSS of the interpolated (A) tradition of the tragedies of Seneca', *CQ* 6 (1912), 1–20.

Sutton (1983) D. F. Sutton, *The Dramaturgy of Octauia* (Königstein, 1983).

Tarrant (1978) R. J. Tarrant, 'Senecan Drama and its Antecedents', *HSCPh* 82 (1978), 213–63.

Torrini (1934) M. Torrini, *L'Octavia* (Pisa, 1934).

Trillitzsch W. Trillitzsch, 'Seneca tragicus. Nachleben und Beurteilung im lateinischen Mittelalter von der Spätantike bis zum Renaissancehumanismus', *Philologus* 122 (1978), 120–36.

Vitale (1991) M. T. Vitale, 'Sul testo dell'*Ottavia* nell'edizione Zwierlein', *SRIC* 8 (1991), 177–95.

Watt (1989) W. S. Watt, 'Notes on Seneca's Tragedies', *HSCPh* 92 (1989), 329–47.

Watt (1996) W. S. Watt, 'Notes on Seneca's Tragedies and the Octavia', *MH* 53 (1996), 248–55.

Westman (1961) R. Westman, *Das Futurprinzip als Ausdrucksmittel in Seneca* (Helsinki, 1961).

Williams (1994) G. D. Williams, 'Nero, Seneca and Stoicism in the *Octavia*', in *Reflections of Nero*, ed. J. Elsner-J. Masters (London, 1994), 178–95.

Woesler (1965) W. Woesler, *Senecas Tragödien. Die Überlieferung der α-Klasse dargestellt am Beispiel der Phaedra*, Diss. Münster, 1965.

Yavetz (1969) Z. Yavetz, *Plebs and Princeps* (Oxford, 1969).

Zwierlein (1966) O. Zwierlein, *Die Rezitationsdramen Senecas* (Meisenheim am Glan, 1966).

Zwierlein (1976) O. Zwierlein, 'Versinterpolationen und Korruptelen in den Tragödien Senecas', *WJA* N.F. 2 (1976), 181–217.

Zwierlein (1977) O. Zwierlein, 'Weiteres zum Seneca Tragicus (I)', *WJA* N.F. 3 (1977), 149–77.

Zwierlein (1978) O. Zwierlein, 'Weiteres zum Seneca Tragicus (II)', *WJA* N.F. 4 (1978), 143–60.

Zwierlein (1979) O. Zwierlein, 'Weiteres zum Seneca Tragicus (III)', *WJA* N.F. 5 (1979), 163–87.

Zwierlein (1980) O. Zwierlein, 'Weiteres zum Seneca Tragicus (IV)', *WJA* N.F. 6a (1980), 181–95.

Zwierlein (1984) O. Zwierlein, *Senecas Hercules im Lichte kaiserzeitlicher und spätantiker Deutung. Mit einem Anhang über 'tragische Schuld' sowie Seneca-Imitationen bei Claudian und Boethius*, Akademie der Wissenschaften und der Literatur. Mainz. Abhandlungen der Geistes- und Sozialwissenschaftlichen Klasse 6 (Mainz, 1984).

Zwierlein (1992) O. Zwierlein, rev. of Billerbeck, *Gnomon* 64 (1992), 502–6.

INDEXES

PASSAGES DISCUSSED

PASSAGES DISCUSSED

MODERN AUTHORS

SUBJECTS